Beating the
ADOPTION
ODDS

Beating the ADOPTION ODDS

USING YOUR HEAD *AND* YOUR HEART TO ADOPT

CYNTHIA MARTIN, PH.D.

DRU MARTIN GROVES, M.A.

A Harvest Original
Harcourt Brace & Company
San Diego   New York   London

This book is designed to educate and inform you about various
aspects of adoption. No single book can address all the legal and
other issues you may be faced with, and the counsel of an
appropriate professional may be advisable in a given situation.

All the incidents used as examples throughout this book are true.
The people cited are real, but their names and identifying data
have been changed.

Library of Congress Cataloging-in-Publication Data
Martin, Cynthia D.
Beating the adoption odds: using your head and your heart to
adopt/Cynthia Martin, Dru Martin Groves.—1st Harvest ed.
p.   cm.
"A Harvest original."
Rev. ed. of: Beating the adoption game. 1st Harvest/HBJ ed.,
Rev. ed. 1988.
Includes bibliographical references and index.
ISBN 0-15-600522-0
1. Adoption—United States.   I. Groves, Dru Martin.   II. Martin,
Cynthia D. Beating the adoption game.   III. Title.
HV875.M369   1998
362.73'4—dc21   97-41249

Text set in Minion
Designed by Lydia D'moch

Printed in the United States of America
First Harvest edition 1998
A C E D B

CONTENTS

ACKNOWLEDGMENTS

As with any book, there are many people we wish to thank:

- Certainly our thanks go to our husbands, David and David, who read the material, heard the stories, made their own dinners, and helped far more than usual.
- Our thanks to Leona—mother, grandmother, great-grandmother, ex-English teacher, and current proofreader—who helped over and over again.
- Our thanks to Shaine and Nohl (daughters and sisters), who helped with research for the book and patience for their mother and sister.
- Our thanks to Anthony (son and brother) and Ryan (son-in-law and brother-in-law), who helped with the problems that plague those of us who are less computer-literate.
- Our thanks to Elizabeth, who was eager to help both as a birth mother in our family and also, fortunately, as a librarian; her contact on the Internet with other librarians across the United States was exceedingly helpful.
- Our thanks to the book distributors from Adoptive Families and Tapestry Press.
- Our thanks to our publisher, Harcourt Brace, who has supported our efforts for many years and who continues to believe in the need to supply information on the field of adoption to readers.

- Our special thanks to Christa Malone, our editor, whose efforts and perseverance helped us over some very difficult spots.
- Our thanks to the many people in adoption whose lives have enabled us to learn about adoption and whose stories appear in the many vignettes that you will read.
- And our very special thanks to the many agencies, attorneys, and others involved in the field of adoption who thoughtfully filled out questionnaires on current problems in adoption, significant changes taking place, and needed changes to improve the process. Their help set the tone for much of what has been included in the book. The level of concern and caring of the many people who work in this field is really quite impressive.

INTRODUCTION

THIS BOOK IS YOUR GUIDE to understanding the lifetime implications of adoption both for you and for your child. It will also tell you about the options available for finding a child. You alone, however, will make the decision about which options are right for you.

We encourage you to look into each section of the book rather than to skip reading about issues that you think have no relevance to you. Most people start in one place and find their search leads them into areas they didn't think about originally. So while today you may not be thinking about adopting a special-needs child, read about it. You may find yourself involved in an adoption that becomes special-needs, and then you will have some understanding of the issues. Or you may find yourself more willing to think about special-needs adoptions once you read about them.

By presenting the many aspects of adoption, this book will prepare you for the commitment that adoption demands. You may think it strange that we discuss talking with your child about adoption when you don't even have a child. Or you may find it odd that we discuss the birth families' long-term response to adoption when you haven't found a birth mother yet. But if you see that all these can be part of adoption, it will help you decide if you are really willing to be involved in the total commitment adoption requires. We also believe that by looking at these issues ahead of time you will be prepared for the questions that will be asked you by agencies or birth families. This is a process that you need to prepare well for, before you meet each of the issues.

Adoption is a very different scene today than it was twenty years ago or even ten years ago. The changes have been exciting, dramatic, scary, and filled with compassion for each of the participants in the adoption process. Certainly some areas still need improvement, but the changes that have occurred are special because few institutions respond to people as much as adoption has.

It is important as you proceed in adoption that you make your imprint on this field, as others have. As you find yourself a child to adopt, add to the institution in a positive way. Once you find a child, continue your involvement in adoption. Help change the problems you discovered and talk about the positives you encountered along the way. You are now part of the Institution of Adoption.

Adoption is a personal issue, and it certainly has been so for both of us. Part of our commitment to being honest and open with you is letting you know what our experiences with adoption have been and how we feel about them.

FROM CYNTHIA: An Adopting Mother's View

As one who struggled with infertility, I have seen the options increase over the years. Choices I believed were open to me at one time in my life have changed, and others have appeared.

I always knew that being a mother was very important to me and thought it would be easy to achieve. I grew up, got married, but the next step—children—did not happen. Being a product of my time, I had a hard time accepting the infertility that confronted my husband, David, and me. At times, I could minimize the absence of a child from my life; at other times, my insides would not allow this pretense.

We adopted three children in the next eleven years. Our first two, Scott and Dru, were adopted through adoption agencies. Our third child, Nohl, was adopted independently. When Nohl was four, I got pregnant.

Our jokes over the years about how I would get pregnant when I was forty weren't too far off. Our fourth child, Shaine, was born the week before I turned thirty-eight.

Our first two children were easy to adopt. Our third child was adopted at a time when children were becoming hard to find, so we were fortunate to find her. Our fourth child, our surprise, was truly unplanned, but after our initial shock and disbelief, she was a most welcome addition.

Almost as surprising was the addition of our fifth child. We were sure that our family was complete until we heard about Anthony. Because he was older (seven), and from a racially mixed background, and because his birth mother did not want him to spend any time in foster care, finding a home for him was difficult. When we heard about him, we thought he would fit nicely into our family, especially because of his closeness in age to our youngest child. After consulting with the younger children, we decided we wanted to meet him. The next day he came home with us. It has amazed us how well we have adapted to a new family member. He, too, has added immeasurably to our lives and our feelings about adoption.

Our decision to adopt Anthony was somewhat of a shock to our two older children. They were in college, so we felt it had less impact on them than on the younger two. We probably could have done a better job of introducing them to Anthony. But they were resilient and got over our ignoring their position.

This same shock awaited all of our children when we decided to add three more children to our family this last year. The concerns of the older children were clear. Their opinions came from concern for us and also concern for themselves. They were each allowed to voice their opinions. However, David and I felt that the decision was up to the two of us. We were the ones who had decided to raise three more children. We were the ones who had decided that our lives would be enriched by adopting older children again and that we were up to that responsibility even at our ages. (We were the ones who would look at the shocked, and at times envious, expressions on our friends' and acquaintances' faces.)

While each of our older children had his or her special concerns about the adoption, there was also some excitement. Anthony was especially pleased because he had joined our family under circumstances similar to those of our new arrivals. And as before, all the children rallied behind us and welcomed Katrina (twelve), Travis (thirteen), and Amy (fourteen) into the family.

Adoption for our family is something very special. It is not important for us to have the children look like us. Our blond, blue-eyed daughter is a sharp contrast to our dark-skinned, curly-haired son. Each one of our children looks different and acts differently from the others. Our looks and numbers alone make us stand out. Our family has been exciting to raise: each of our eight children does some dumb things and gets into trouble from time to time, but each is also funny, lovable, and beautiful. We are just like any normal wonderful family—except that six of our children are first-born!

Adoption is not the same as having children biologically. It is neither more nor less satisfying, but it is different—and definitely special.

It has always been easy for me to talk with our children about their adoptions. The background information we had on them was freely shared as they grew. We read stories about adoption, discussed my own involvement in adoption, and attempted to answer questions as they came up. Adoption has been a part of their lives, even the life of our child who was not adopted, but I don't think it has been the focus of their lives. It is an issue that has always been there but only comes to the forefront from time to time. Growing up has been the focus and that has been remarkably normal.

Sometimes I want to be the only mother for my children. But these are the times I remind myself about the evolution of my personal feelings about adoption. These are the times I think back to the pain of infertility and my wishing that life were the ideal I believed in as I grew up. My views on adoption have changed radically since we first adopted, but then so have my views on life. One thing remains the same: I know, no matter how hard it might be to adopt a child, I would find a child to adopt.

FROM DRU: An Adoptive Daughter's View

For me, being adopted and growing up in a family created primarily through adoption has been a lifelong journey of experience, emotion, and self-discovery. And now that I'm older, I understand how fortunate I've been to have such great parents and such a diverse group of siblings with whom to share that experience. My family is a source of great comfort, strength, and pride to me. I have been blessed to have such wonderful people in my life.

My adoptive parents provided more than just a loving environment in which to grow; they provided a sense of stability and normalcy in what many would consider a very unusual family. Although we all look different, have different interests and talents, we truly are a family.

Sure, I can remember times when we would question our parents' sanity as the family would grow with sudden irregularity. In fact, our family is still growing with our most recent adoptions of Amy, Katrina, and Travis.

Because my adoption was a closed agency adoption, I grew up knowing very little about my birth family. From the time I was fully aware I was adopted and what that meant, I can remember wondering what my birth family was like. At different times in my life, this curiosity would heighten. When I became a teenager, and closer to the age when my birth mother became pregnant with me and placed me for adoption, it became of more interest to me. I became more intrigued with families who were not created by adoption. Spending time with my good friends at their homes and seeing how so many of them looked like their siblings and their parents and shared so many of the same talents and interests seemed to amplify how different my family was.

During that time, as I gradually became an adult, I think I was struggling with identity issues, many of which were developmentally appropriate and some of which were adoption related, long before I understood what identity issues were. The long-denied realization that I probably would never know who my biological family was left me feeling as if I was missing something from my core. Without this information I felt that I would not be able to answer that universal question, Who am I?

Then as an adult, I learned my birth mother's identity and over time created a wonderful relationship with her and her extended family. Although the outcome of the reunion has been great, it has been the process which has been profound. Once the denial of wanting to know about my biological family was lifted and I had met them, I felt empowered and had a greater sense of feeling connected to others. My confidence and self-esteem increased. Ultimately, it was a part of a healing journey which continues to progress.

Part of this journey is related to growing, being a mother, being a wife, and just being older. Certainly, my life hasn't focused only on adoption. It has focused on what has been important at particular periods in my life; at times that has been adoption. Yes, I am adopted but I am mostly just Dru. Would I change my life and not be adopted? Definitely not. I love my adoptive family and can't imagine having been raised by anyone else. They are my parents and my siblings. But is it normal to have these other kinds of feelings when you have been adopted? Again, definitely. Adoption has issues for each of us.

So what does this have to do with the adoption process? I feel I bring a unique perspective to this book. My own adoption is one piece, but another is my daily work in the area of adoption. As my mother and I operate an adoption agency, I am regularly reminded of the issues and challenges faced by each person involved in the adoption process, not only as he or she gets started, but also as he or she looks ahead to the future. The constant exposure I have to the joys and challenges of adoption has become an important part of my own journey. I also see that some adoptive parents, birth parents, and even adoptees do a better job in adoption than others. I want to help make the process a healthy one. I firmly believe that adoption is a beautiful way to create a family and a wonderful way for me to be a part of two families.

Adoption isn't something you jump into. You need to think about it, dream about it, study it, imagine it. In reality, adoption is something that you do with both your heart and your head.

As you enter the adoption process, you need to believe you can succeed. If you don't believe it, why should you even try? Adoption *is* a beautiful way to have a family. It is beautiful, however, only if it works. And the important thing to remember is, almost all adoptions work. They work for the adopting parents, the birth parents, and the adoptee. Adoption has worked for us, and it can work for you, too. In this book, we will show you how.

Cynthia Martin
Dru Martin Groves

1

CONSIDERING ADOPTION:

What to Know Before You Begin

CHAPTER 1

Adoption Works

ADOPTING IS A MARVELOUS WAY to have a family. It is filled with excitement and surprises. It contains wonderful stories and great adventures. It teaches about love, joy, sharing, individuality, and compassion. Unfortunately, it also has some downs that go with the ups—but then again, so does life. The important point you need to remember is *you can adopt!*

Adoption stories have been plentiful in recent years. Headlines about babies being taken back by birth mothers or birth fathers have generated angry responses, not only among those who are involved directly in adoption but also among bystanders who agonize over the legal wranglings. Across the nation, such stories spark lengthy discussions over coffee and in beauty shops about what should or should not have taken place.

Welfare benefits for single mothers are debated. Political accusations are prevalent about burgeoning welfare rolls and whether single mothers are actually *encouraged* to have children.[1] The controversies of same-sex marriage and same-sex partners adopting is debated state by state.[2] Senators debate the merits of interracial adoptions.[3] Adopting parents listen.

Adoptees and adoptive parents object to the way adopted people are labeled in the media.[4] The overuse of the "adopted child defense" to justify any antisocial behavior[5] seems to overshadow the fact that Bill

Clinton, Greg Louganis, Moses, Marilyn Monroe, James Michener, Gerald Ford, and even Superman were adopted.

Determining the degree of problems in adoption is impossible.[6] Though most adoptions work just fine, these seldom make the headlines; the stories of failures and scams are more interesting, so they are told and retold. Those people considering adoption become frightened.

In addition to the headlines, the paranoia of potential adopters is increased by the personal stories of lengthy waiting lists, astronomical costs, adoption failures, and the problems of adoption, so they wonder and worry. They hear of the hundreds of thousands of people waiting for the few babies who are available, and they give up before they begin. They want a baby, but what if they get pregnant right after they adopt? They want a baby but hear of the fantastic advances in infertility treatment and wait for the cure for their problems. They hear of scams and subsequently approach adoption with skepticism or paranoia. They hear about the loud and angry protests of birth parents who have felt ignored or coerced in the adoption process, and they become alarmed. Even stories about adoptees' responses to adoption tend to dwell on the vocal minority who have negative experiences. TV talk shows spotlight interracial families' inability to adjust, but seldom do you find shows about the majority of interracial adoptees who do well in their adoptive homes.

The truth behind the stories is hard to find. People trying to adopt are counted in statistics over and over again as they go to agencies, attorneys, facilitators, and physicians. In reality, we just aren't sure how many people are actively seeking a baby. Similarly, women who become pregnant after adopting are told that this happens all the time; people think it happens frequently because they hear the same stories repeated time and again. In reality, the number of women who conceive after they adopt is relatively small. And while stories of international adoptions leaving children without a cultural identity receive top billing, articles about the everyday successes of these adoptions are seldom published. Yet at the same time we know that most adoptions are successful in the eyes of the adoptees. Almost all studies show overwhelmingly that adoptees are satisfied with their adoptions.

Learning about Adoption

You need to become an expert on adoption. If you adopt, you probably will become an expert through experience. First you need to understand the extreme stories, the screaming headlines, the inflated figures, the doomsday scenarios, and the negative approaches to adoption—and not be deterred by them. You need to understand that adoptions are individual arrangements among people from all kinds of backgrounds, with different levels of knowledge and understanding of the process, with unique levels of ability and emotional resources: Each adoption is a unique case. Your adoption will be defined in part by who you are and what you bring to the process. Your adoption will be different from every other adoption in many ways.

As you begin to learn more about adoption, the process may seem overwhelming. Keep in mind that lots of people have done this, and so can you. There is just a lot to learn. You need to learn about different ways and places to search, different kinds of agencies, different kinds of helpers, the kinds of children available, how to make the process healthy, the importance of how you respond to a birth family, what is legal and what isn't, and ultimately, the uniqueness of raising an adopted child. The more you know about the process, the fewer mistakes you will make and the faster the process is likely to go.

One of the important lessons of adoption is that you are in charge. There are many points at which you will make a decision one way or the other as you proceed. Those decisions, which no one else but you can make, will determine how your adoption evolves. No one can tell you whether you should consider adoption, when is the right time, how fast you should move, or how you should do it.

Being in charge in your life has some marked advantages. You can decide how far you will go or won't go, who will help you and who won't, and how you will set up the adoption you pick. Certainly you will not make all of these decisions alone. You probably have a partner or someone with whom you can discuss the process. That will help. You will find great numbers of people who will be happy to advise you on what you should or shouldn't do. Some will charge you for this information and others will simply give it to you; some of the information will be worth a great deal to you and some will be worth nothing. How you evaluate the information is up to you.

If you were going to have a biological child, not many choices would be available to you. Adoption is a time in your life when you can be expansive. Check out your limits. See in what ways you can expand those limits. How open can you be? How willing are you to take a child who might look different from one who might have born to you? Could you take a child who has a significant problem?

There are many kinds of adoptions available to you today. The system is more open than ever before. There are children of all ages, colors, and cultural backgrounds, with more individual differences than you may have imagined. There are more ways to find these children than in the past and more ways to adopt them.

But the joys of parenting a child through adoption remain the same. Adopting a child allows you to become a parent in the fullest sense. It is not a second-rate way to have a family; it is a different way.

Probably the most important thing you can learn about adoption before you begin is to believe in yourself. That doesn't mean you should enter the adoption process naively; you certainly need to be realistic. But in your realistic approach it is important to remember that most adoptions work. With a thorough understanding of the system and the options you have, you can try approaches that you may never have imagined possible. In some arrangements you need to rely on other people, and in others you must rely on yourself. Ideally, your new approaches will lead you to the child you want.

It is difficult to compare the way you go about adopting with the experiences of others. You don't know how others approach the issues of parenting or their relationship with a birth family, their energy as they search for a child, the personal resources they bring to the search for a child, their integrity in working with others, and their basic beliefs about the institutions of adoption. The outcomes of their search for a child and their degree of success with adoption could be totally different from yours. You are the only person who can vouch for how you will proceed with your adoption; the rest is speculation.

The stories in this book are about people who have succeeded in adoption and about some who have failed. They are based upon actual cases but the identities have been changed. Reading these stories will help you consider new approaches to adoption and even rehearse what you might do in similar circumstances. They will prepare you for the many different situations that you might confront as you begin this process. They are meant to help you learn what you are capable of doing.

Most people simply need information and courage to find a baby or child. If you really want a baby, go out and find one. *Be positive, be creative, be flexible, and be assertive.* If you really want to find a child to become a part of your family—you can.

Does Adoption Really Work?

How can you be sure that adoption really works? If you open yourself up to adoption and you find a baby, will your new family be happy? Will your child love you? Will your child turn out to be what you expect?

The overwhelming response to these questions by those who have experienced adoption is yes![7] Whether a child was adopted at birth or later, and whether contact with the birth family was maintained or not, adoption *has* worked. Even in difficult situations with special-needs children, the responses remain mostly positive. In cases where adoptees probably have greater psychological problems than their nonadopted counterparts, most are still satisfied with the outcome of their adoption. Even when the adoptee is significantly different from the adoptive parents and the family struggles with the differences, the parents and the adoptee tend to voice positive feelings about adoption.

Certainly some adoptions haven't worked out; but similar situations occur in nonadoptive families. You need to understand why adoptions succeed or fail so you can modify your behavior accordingly. Your understanding of adoption can make a difference in your level of satisfaction with adoption as well as your adopted child's satisfaction.

The issue of genetics versus environment has raged for decades. At no time in our history has it been any clearer than the genetic component of who a person is shows significantly not only in appearance, but also in personality, and in predisposition toward physical and mental health. Genes make a tremendous difference.[8] But even if your child doesn't look like you or think like you, or has few personality characteristics like yours, that doesn't mean you can't succeed in helping him develop into the person he was meant to be.

Most adoptive parents want to believe that environment is the major influencing factor in how a child will turn out in life. But that probably isn't true. Of course, you do make a difference in how your child turns out. But just as you can't change the color of her hair or the build of his body, you can't change many other things about the child you will adopt. If your child is artistically talented (just like her birth mother, for example) and you don't know how to draw, you can still help your child develop her talent. If your child turns out to be a slow starter (just like, say, his birth father), you may have to help him begin tasks and show him the value of that help; you'll need to accept that he may never be a self-starter like you are, but some minor modifications are possible. If your child is slow developing physically (and you don't know why), you can provide opportunities for him to improve his skills. If your child has a genetic predisposition to hyperactivity, depression, antisocial behavior, breast cancer, or drug addiction, you may never know exactly where these came from, but you must accept that such predispositions will influence your child's behavior and health.[9]

But even with these basic differences that can exist, adoption still works. We don't need to have our children be clones of us for our adoptions to succeed. In fact, our differences may help each of us grow in ways that otherwise would not be possible. Maybe what we are learning is that accepting our child's biological heritage will help us be accepting of our child.

Your part as the adoptive parent is important, and so is the part the birth parents play. The merging of genes and environment will produce a child who is uniquely himself. But you will be in the fortunate position to have helped raise a special person. With this in mind, you are ready to begin your search for a child.

A Philosophical and Practical Approach

With many people trying to find a child to adopt, and with the decreasing number of babies available, can you still find a baby? We believe that anyone who is willing to do the work, open to unusual methods of searching, creative, receptive to new ideas, and willing to consider the many types of children who are available for adoption, can find a child.

There are many different kinds of people searching for a baby to adopt. Some are easier to help than others. The success of your search depends on your willingness to try different options and your openness to different situations.

- If you are forty-five years old and your partner is fifty and you want to find a blond, blue-eyed baby girl whose mother has some college in her background and has had no involvement with drugs or alcohol, a child whose birth father will sign relinquishment papers immediately and is very supportive of the birth mother's decision—you are in a tough situation. Not impossible, but it could take a long time.
- If you are a single mother who wants the same perfect baby as most adopting couples and will consider nothing else, your search may take longer.
- If you are a couple with absolutely no money to spend on the adoption—to help the birth mother with medical expenses, to pay an attorney, to travel to meet the birth mother, or to help with other expenses of any kind—you are at a distinct disadvantage.
- If you are a gay couple who want to adopt the same child as a straight couple, you will probably come in second.
- If you are a couple who has decided you will not pursue any adoption in which money might be given to the birth mother, for fear that it will seem like you are buying a baby, most birth mothers will likely place you somewhere low down the list of desirable parents.
- If you are a couple with advanced degrees and will only accept a child whose birth mother and father have demonstrated their intellectual abilities in some way, you may be slow in finding a match.

- If you are a couple totally unwilling to meet with a potential birth mother, you will find yourselves eliminated from many possible situations.
- If you are a couple or a single parent who will not go ahead with an adoption if the birth mother has any history of smoking, drugs, or alcohol, it may take a while for you to find a situation.
- If you are a couple in your thirties who are open to adopting a child of mixed racial background and are fairly willing to consider a variety of situations, you will be a lot easier to help.

Remember: The speed of your adoption and your potential for success in finding a child depend greatly on you. When you know you have a condition that decreases your chances of success in finding a child, try to be more open in other areas. If you are gay or are very limited financially, try to be receptive to more situations so that your chances are increased. If you are completely against any contact with the birth family, could you do something, read something, or meet someone who might help you to be a bit more open? By expanding your limits and using your head, you can significantly increase your odds of finding a child.

Most people wanting to adopt will probably be able to find a child at some time, if they put effort into the process. So in addition to your preferences in adoption, another factor in your speed and success is what you are willing to do to find a child. Some people are willing to become very involved in searching; others want the baby to arrive immediately after they have decorated the nursery. Your involvement, or your willingness to find people whose involvement will substitute for yours, is essential to your success. Keep in mind that all the people who can help find children—whether they be agencies, attorneys, mediators/facilitators, or counselors—are not equal. The people you hire represent you—so hire carefully.

Other factors in your success are your personality and your appearance. What kind of a person are you? How do you come across to other people? Are you friendly? Are you open? What do you look like? Do you have some obvious problems that might make it difficult for you to be chosen? Do you have an easy time talking to others? Are you interesting? Are you sincere? Are you honest? Your personality makes a difference in how likely you are to be chosen by a birth mother or a birth father and in how likely you are to find the resources and the people to help you in your adoption.

Adoption Etiquette

We are amazed by the different ways people approach adoption. Some people become their own worst enemies as they seek a child. It is easy with infertility and adoption to begin to feel sorry for yourself—*Why me? Why do I have to do all of this to find a baby when someone else just becomes pregnant at the drop of a hat?* Sure, you can feel sorry for yourself if you want to, but you can get stuck in this mode and really cause problems for yourself. No one said life would be fair. Just ask anyone else who faces tough things in their life. Some might even think infertility is a pretty minor problem in the grand scheme of things.

It is OK to feel sorry for yourself for a while. But then it is important to move forward, leave your negative feelings behind, and get to a place where you eagerly, positively, and openly enter this process. If you are angry, you will convey your anger to those you work with. If you feel as if everyone is out to get you and is trying to take your money, you will find yourself turning away people who really want to help you. Then if you renege on your agreements, you will find people learning to distrust what you say and what you do.

Not every failure in adoption is caused by the people helping. Adoption failures have many causes. Sometimes the birth mother just changes her mind and everyone is surprised. If this happens, don't pull back from trying again with a different birth mother on a different child. Some adoptions were not meant to be, and no one can prevent problems from developing in them. Sometimes *you* might be the problem. You may not even know that you have inadvertently antagonized the birth mother and she has pulled out because of what you said.

We are always surprised by the number of angry people we find who are trying to adopt. Perhaps the anger comes from unresolved feelings of hurt over not being able to have a biological child. Maybe it's from the media, which publicizes the scams and failures in adoption. Maybe it is due to the fact that they are being asked to pay someone to help them to find a baby. Whatever the cause of their hostility and suspicion, people who think everyone is out to take them for all they are worth will inevitably have problems adopting. No matter what we do as adoption helpers, we will "fail" them. And at some point, we may be unwilling to help. It is difficult to help people who maintain this feeling.

Keep in mind, most people are honest; they want to help you. Certainly you need to be cautious, but you don't need to be paranoid. Most birth mothers are not scam artists. Most agencies and attorneys are not exploiters. Most counselors and therapists are not trying to rip you off. Don't treat people poorly because they are asking you to pay for their services. It's true that adoption can be expensive. While you need to be realistic about the money involved, think how much you paid for your new car or couch or even how much you may have put into infertility treatment. Give people a chance before you start to believe they are after you.

Remember, you do need people to help you, and one of the greatest motivations for people in this field is the pleasure of helping others. Helpers get rewards for the work they do that go beyond the money they receive. The people who will help you most are the ones who like you and who approve of how you are proceeding in the adoption process. You want them to continue to help you because they may be the key to finding a child.

Developing a Personal Honesty about Your Adoption

Be honest as you begin your adoption process. Such simple advice—*be honest*—and yet it is so complex. Maybe biological parents *should* consider some of the philosophical issues surrounding honesty also, but there are additional reasons for adopting parents to examine their approach to adoption. The "differentness" of adopting causes new problems for families and compounds the usual ones. When we say we should be honest in order to avoid unnecessary conflicts in the adoption, most people readily agree. But to put this concept into practice is the real test. We want the birth parents to be honest with us as they give us personal information about their lives. We want the adoption helpers to be honest with the information they give us, their recommendations, and their help. As you become a potential adoptive parent, this same honesty is expected of you.

As an adoptive parent you must first be honest with yourself about your substitute method of parenting. In order to be honest and loving with your child, you must learn to first be honest with yourself. Without this personal honesty, which precedes sureness and confidence, adoptive parents cannot fully understand or empathize with their adopted child and his or her pain. Love is a critical ingredient in all families, but the adoptive family also needs understanding and empathy.

The adoptive family is built on loss. It is based on loss for the adopting parents, the adopted child, and the birth parents. We gloss over this as we talk of "chosen babies" and "how lucky we are to have found you" and how "your first mother gave you away because she loved you." But in truth, that is not what happened. These phrases pretend that pain and loss are not there—they describe specialness by omission. Adoptive families *are* special; we have no doubt about it. But the specialness comes out mostly with honesty, not with omissions, illusions, fantasies, and pretenses.

It is make believe if you pretend that your adopted family is like a "regular" family. It isn't. It is different. If you try to live with the illusions, then comments about "other" parents or "real" parents become especially painful. These comments plunge you back into reality. You leave yourself open to hurt when you fool yourself about yourself. If you acknowledge that your family is different, you don't have to have your defenses up when someone tells you your family is different. You have a foundation that is based on reality.

If you are infertile, the importance of coming to grips with your infertility is essential. If you have pretended that it was not important that you failed to become pregnant when in fact it *was* important, this lie stays with you for a long time—perhaps forever. Rather than pretend, if you can tell your spouse or some other significant person how truly important infertility was, you are laying the foundation of honesty with yourself.

Honesty once you begin the adoption process is also essential. You are going to make an agreement with a birth mother, a birth family, or perhaps an adoption agency. You will promise to do certain things. If you say you will do them, do them. If you don't believe you can do them, don't agree to them.

We will give you many potential situations to imagine being involved in; it is for you to rehearse how you would respond. Most people would not be comfortable in all of them. This is a time to check your own limits. No matter how much you want a baby, don't agree to anything unless you will be able to carry through on your agreement. It isn't the end of the world or of your adoption hopes if you give up on a situation with which you are uncomfortable. It is a major ethical problem to agree to something you will be unable to do, just to get someone to give you her baby.

If you are clear in your own mind about adoption and how your family will fit into society, the questions from your child about his or her adoption will be easy to answer at any time. Feeling secure yourself about adoption lets your child also feel secure. If you hide your feelings about or other aspects of your child's adoption, you imply that something about it must be bad.

When your three-year-old adopted daughter asks about her birth, tell her the truth. Never lie to her. You are beginning a long process that tests your trustworthiness and your self-confidence. Even if it is easy to handle the three-year-old's questions with fibs or fabrications, the three-year-old will soon be a thirteen-year-old, and she needs to be able to trust you.

One school of thought on adoption says never to tell the child that he or she is adopted or to wait until the child is of school age. The psychological issues that are involved here are clear. In all theories of child development, the importance of a trusting relationship with the parents is stressed. The child uses the parent as a sounding board to the larger world. The child who feels betrayed because his parents lied to him has great difficulty developing the ability to trust others. The child thinks, "If these people who love me lie to me, then, of course, other people who don't love me will lie to me, too." There simply is no need to lie about adoption.

The messages and questions of the older child are subtle. The eight-year-old adopted boy whose friend's parents have divorced and each re-married can talk about how hard it is for his friend to have two sets of parents. Now you should ask yourself, What is he really saying? Is he talking about himself? Why not ask? Why not draw the unspoken parallel for him—why not use this as an opportunity for openness and honesty about his adoption? If you present adoption as only beautiful and rosy, he feels there must be something wrong with him when the emotion he feels is confusion or hurt.

Honesty carries over to areas that you might not like—for example, how relatives respond to your child's adoption. When relatives ask about your adopted child's background, it is important to be up-front with them. There is no need to reveal everything if you don't want to, but whatever you do choose to tell them should be true. The stories you tell these people will ultimately be stories told to your adopted children. You will want the stories they hear from Auntie and Grandma to be the same ones they hear from you.

One adopted child's grandmother consistently introduced her grandson as her *adopted* grandson. She was proud of him—she even liked the specialness that came from his adoption. The adoptive mother finally told her mother that she didn't like her son being introduced this way. They discussed together that this was not intended to be negative and that the grandmother was indeed proud of this little boy and loved him deeply. This discussion, held openly and honestly, enabled them both to deal with their feelings about adoption and how being told you're special sometimes doesn't feel good. That discussion hurt a little bit because grandmothers, like most people, don't like to be criticized. But ultimately it helped because it was truthful and solved a problem openly.

Sometimes it's OK to hurt when you are being honest also. One mother had a neighbor who continually pried into the background of her newly adopted child. It started out fairly innocuously—How old was the birth mother? Was she from this area? Then the questions became more specific. The adoptive mother finally said to the woman, "I am uncomfortable with your questions about Tony's background. We feel this is a very personal thing and we don't want to talk about it." The neighbor was indignant. She said she hadn't wanted to pry. A rift developed between the neighbor and this family, and that's sad. It didn't need to end that way. You do not need to supply all the details about your child's adoption in order to be honest. There are definite distinctions between honesty, secrecy, and privacy.[10]

This adoption will be your process. From the beginning to the end (if there really can ever be said to be one since adoption is for life) it is yours. How you search for a child to adopt can be something that you are proud of and that makes you feel good. How you deal with the people who seek to help you should be conducted with a sense of personal etiquette. How you relate to the birth family is something that you can proudly share with your child. How you raise your child will be influenced by your beliefs about adoption and your child's uniqueness. How you discuss adoption should be filled with truth and understanding. How you handle your child's questions should be with honesty and forthrightness. How you help your child if he seeks to find his heritage should be with love and support.

While we know you only want a child and that doesn't sound so complex, it is. Many people are involved in your adoption process; each party affects the others. You only have control over your part of the process, but it impacts the others. Do it well.

Summary

Adoption is a wonderful institution. It is imperfect and needs many changes to make it more responsive to the needs of those involved in adoption, but despite its flaws, it remains remarkably successful. It is a system that gives people who want a child a means of becoming a family; it allows those who find themselves pregnant and unprepared to parent a way to act responsibly in finding homes for their children; it allows children who might otherwise be raised in homes reluctant to accept them to live in a family with people who are committed to being parents.

Despite the media's tendency to focus on the negative, adoption works. People have made significant changes in the adoption process in the last twenty years. The changes in adoption involve a newfound openness in the process, which has changed the institution to its very core. This openness has forced a new level of honesty, not only from agencies but also from the individuals involved in adoption. In order to help people achieve more healthy adoptions, these changes toward openness and honesty need to continue.

How you approach adoption is your personal issue. That is true for each of us involved in adoption. There is no wrong choice or direction, but there is a right way for you.

Adoption meets an incredible need in our society. It is filled with positives that should give each of us a sense of joy to be a part of the process. Begin with the determination to do your adoption right. Open your life to another human being by being truly proud of how you go about adopting and raising your child. Raising a child to become a healthy adult can only be done with honesty and openness. Learn about adoption and its long-term implications. Conduct your adoption as if the entire institution were at stake. By how you adopt, you are setting a standard of how adoption should be.

The question is not, Can you find a baby to adopt? You can. The question is, Can you do your adoption right?

CHAPTER 2

Before You Begin

YOU CAN ADOPT A BABY. You can have a child even if you cannot become pregnant and even if you are turned down by an adoption agency. You don't need a lot of money or a fancy house. You can adopt a baby if you are overweight, old, disabled, or single. There is a baby somewhere for you—if you are willing to try some new ways to obtain one.

Babies are available. Certainly there are not as many potential babies to adopt as there were at other times in our history. But there are babies for the people who are really willing to do what it takes to find one.

Actually it is quite a simple matter. The people who want babies and cannot make them need to meet either people who are able to make babies or medical people who are able to fix reproductive problems. These are the only options. But the many ways to pursue these options present a variety of choices.

If you want a baby, you must look at the choices and then look at yourself. You need to understand the options that are out there for you, the impact of your infertility on your potential adoption, sources for finding babies, and how you fit into this process. There is no right or wrong choice or direction, but there is a right way for you.

Where Do You Begin?

You have decided you are ready to adopt . . . now what? The next step isn't as obvious. Merely looking in the Yellow Pages under "Adoption" can be overwhelming. In years past, one or two listings would be found; today there are dozens of names, boxed ads, and pictures. It is difficult to know where to even begin.

Adoption today is big business. You have the choice of dozens of different adoption agencies. Some have cute names and others indicate a religious affiliation. Attorneys galore advertise adoption services in the Yellow Pages. Counselors or facilitators, seeking to appeal to the birth mother, claim that they offer the right choice for you and for your baby, and in the next line they advertise closed or open adoption services and legal advice. At times even groups advocating abortion or keeping the baby will have listings under adoption services. You can tell as you look that you have a lot to learn about adoption. This isn't an easy process for you, nor is it easy for a birth mother, who has equal difficulty sorting out the vast numbers of "helpers" who are out there.

We will discuss the differences among adoption agencies in Chapter 5 and independent non-agency options in Chapter 6. But before you begin deciding who to approach to help you with this process, you need to learn more about how adoption works and where you fit.

There are many ways that you can go; you just need to understand what they are. First of all, become aware of the people you know who have adopted; people who have gone through the system are a valuable source of help. Try looking into your local chapter of RESOLVE, Inc., an infertility group with chapters throughout the United States (see Appendix F). Many of their members have adopted, and in a variety of ways. Other adoption support groups are found throughout the country. Adoptive Families of America and the National Adoption Information Clearinghouse (see Appendix F) will send you lists of adoptive parent support groups in your state. These groups will be quick to lend you a helping hand and share their stories of success and failure, and you can learn from both. These people have approached adoption from many different directions and talking with them will allow you to see where you might feel most comfortable as you begin your adoption process. No one's experience will be just like yours, but you can learn from the experiences of others. No one has the right way for you to do this; you are merely gathering information.

Take the time to sort things out before you begin. Understanding the different options you have at this point will save you time, money, frustration, and stress in the long run.

Many Kinds of Adoption

Not long ago, the most common way to adopt a baby was through an agency. The adoption picture is no longer that simple. Today the direction you proceed on your adoption is based on your openness and your ability to be comfortable with different kinds of situations and also on your knowledge of the various kinds of adoptions available to you.

You need to explore which ways of seeking a baby are comfortable for you. At first glance, some of the methods discussed in this book may seem inappropriate for you, but think about them. You might try familiar approaches first; but later, if you have had no luck with the familiar ways, you may become more comfortable with some of the newer or "riskier" ways. Keep in mind that what may have seemed risky ten years ago has now become commonplace. (If you talk to people who adopted a generation ago, they would express amazement at what is regularly done today.) Even now, you need to assess which alternatives are acceptable to you. Part of making your choice is understanding your limits and how far you can stretch them.

For some people, the traditional modes of obtaining a baby are the only ones they have ever considered and the only ones with which they would be comfortable. If you have discovered that you have an infertility problem and if the problem cannot be corrected, you will reach some level of acceptance of your infertility. After that, "traditional" takes on new meaning. Assuming that you are accepted by a traditional adoption agency, you follow the set process until the exciting day you are called about your baby or child.

This procedure has been followed by thousands of people. For many people today, however, this method will not lead to success.

The traditional approach contrasts sharply with the risk taken by a couple who had the same goal—a baby. After the initial medical exams, John and Debbie learned that she could not get pregnant. While thoroughly and openly discussing their feelings about Debbie's infertility, the couple discovered it was important for them to have a child who was genetically theirs, even if only partly. They decided to find a surrogate mother to carry John's child, and they placed an ad in a national magazine. Risky? Of course. However, sixteen months later they had their baby.

For others, the need to explore all the medical possibilities for having a biological child is a critical factor. England's Baby Louise, the first so-called test-tube baby, was one couple's way. This procedure, in vitro fertilization, has become more commonplace, and new methods are continually being developed to help infertile couples have a biological (at least to some extent) child.

These couples may consider adoption, but only after trying every reasonable medical remedy for their infertility, which is usually very costly. Some would say these people are poor risks for adoption because they have been unable to resolve their feelings about their infertility. (Perhaps the best resolution for infertility *is* a baby). Others would admire these people's perseverance and willingness to pursue advances that seemed improbable a short time ago.

The desperation of some couples drives them to utilize a source currently considered illegal—the black market. People are willing to pay $40,000 or more to get a baby. Most people are shocked that a couple would elect to *buy* a baby. (These same people need to look at the costs of treating infertility, which may far exceed the $40,000 hypothetical cost of buying a baby.) However, if you really wanted a baby and had been thwarted in every way, and someone told you that for $40,000 you could have a baby about to be born, what would you do? Patty and Jim, a couple in their early forties who had been turned down by two adoption agencies, had that chance and took it. To them, it was a bargain!

The desperation of this couple caused them to break the law. In actuality, they could have found a baby without resorting to anything illegal. Trudi and Bryan did exactly that.

Like most people, Trudi and Bryan weren't willing to buy a baby, but they were willing to help a birth mother. They had no objection to the financial side of black market adoptions but they didn't want to do anything illegal. They went to an attorney who required a retainer of $5,000. He promised to call them about leads. He did about six months later. Marlo was twenty-two, divorced, and the mother of two children. She was five-months pregnant and was having difficulties getting to her job, which was in a warehouse where she was paid $11 per hour plus benefits. She needed help. She liked Trudi and Bryan and they were willing to pay her the same amount she was getting at work until she had recuperated from the delivery. She also needed to move to another apartment, since her roommate had just moved out; the couple felt it was beneficial to them to help her with her moving expenses. Of course, Marlo also needed them to pay her doctor as well as the hospital and delivery costs. She knew she would need to have a cesarean delivery since her two other children had been delivered that way; Trudi and Bryan decided it was most appropriate to continue to pay her insurance premium so that some medical costs would be partially covered. They rented her a car since she had no transportation and she would not have been able to get to her prenatal care appointments. They wanted to make sure that Marlo knew what she was doing, so they agreed to pay for her to have counseling until two months after the baby was born.

No one anticipated that the baby would have problems when he was born, but he did; his care for an additional six days in the hospital added significantly to the medical bills. In all, Trudi and Bryan paid $42,000 for the adoption of their son, Alan. They also thought they got a bargain. Everything they had done was completely legal.

Melanie and Tim wanted a baby, but money was an issue. They did not have the funds to continue long, expensive, and frequently futile attempts at infertility treatments. They decided to find a child through a small agency they had heard good things about from a neighbor who had adopted a child the previous year. They were open to meeting a birth mother but wanted to keep the cost down as much as possible because Melanie wanted to stay home with the baby. The race of the child was not important to them.

They didn't spend very long waiting before they heard about a woman who was carrying a child who would be part African American, part Hispanic, and part Caucasian. That sounded great to them. After being told a number of details about the birth mother by the social worker, they set up the telephone interview. Each of them, Melanie, Tim, and the birth mother, felt positive about the contact. They didn't worry about all the problems that might come up, they acted. Melanie and Tim had a baby within five months of deciding to adopt and the cost was within their range. It included $500 for the birth mother's clothing, $2,400 for time the social worker worked with them and on their behalf with the hospital and the birth mother, $850 for a home study, $1,800 for the attorney, and $800 to advertise for the birth father whose whereabouts were unknown. The hospital cost was covered by the state since the birth mother was on medical assistance. Melanie and Tim send pictures to the birth mother twice a year and agreed to telephone contact with her for the first few months after the birth. They were open, eager, and ready to go. They found a way that gave them a baby with relative ease.

Other couples will not find a child as fast or will want only a child of their race. Some will be unwilling to have contact with the birth mother. Some will want assurances that the birth mother will not or cannot change her mind. Some will make the situation so difficult for themselves they will be unable to find a child to adopt.

Who are the people willing to seek babies in nontraditional ways? Are they different from "normal" couples who get pregnant or who adopt by traditional means? Yes, definitely. They want a baby and aren't willing to wait indefinitely. Their choices are to be creative and perhaps take risks or to remain childless.

Some will find it hard to identify with these people and their search. Others may tell them to find fulfillment in their lives in alternate meaningful ways, like taking in foster children, raising some nice pets, or becoming teachers. While these substitutes may be enough for some people, they do not provide a baby to love. There is no substitute for your own baby.

We strongly support and encourage those willing to take risks. Children are available to adopt. Open up to new ways to find a baby. Create new ways to find one. Think, explore, search, try. You *can* find a baby!

Openness in Adoption

For anyone considering adoption, it is crucial to understand open adoption; the opening up of adoption is one of the most significant changes that has occurred in adoption in this generation. Adoptions in the past were filled with secrecy and pretense. These closed adoptions are almost, but not quite completely, things of the past. It is refreshing to look at the creative approaches that are being used in today's adoptions.

People who hear about open adoptions can become alarmed at first. But "openness" is a relative term as regards adoption. In actuality, open adoptions have become custom-made adoptions with variations based on the desires of the primary people involved: the birth family and the adoptive parents. There are as many definitions of openness as there are different situations. Open adoption basically means there is some contact between the principals involved; the amount of contact varies. All independent adoptions (adoptions arranged directly between the birth parents and the people adopting the baby) are to some extent open.

Some degree of openness is beginning to emerge among many of the adoption agencies as they compete with the advantages offered by more open independent arrangements. Controversy within the ranks of social workers over the long-term effects of open adoptions is causing change to be slow. Research will necessarily be slow because the children being raised in open adoptions are still young and the consequences are not yet clear.

There are many reasons for this change in the amount of openness. Probably the biggest single reason is the birth mother's increasing power in the process. The second reason would be the difficulties many adopted adolescents experience due to identity issues and their desire for more information about their birth parents. The third would be the general belief that secrecy has serious drawbacks in that it conveys something negative to the adopted person about his or her background. The fourth reason would be the expanding role of independent adoptions throughout the United States; independent adoptions have been increasing, and with them, openness.

Potential adopters like you who enter the process with little background are at first likely to pull back from this concept. Your friends and relatives will caution you about openness and tell you negative stories they have heard. You may fear the birth mother who in open adoption knows your identity or perhaps even where you live. As you become more involved, you are likely to begin to see the advantages of some degree of openness. How far you will go into having an open adoption is a matter of choice. Some people may even feel forced into openness but that should be avoided.[1] As adopters become comfortable with the idea, most agree that openness is more positive than negative. Some great publications on open adoption are now available; they are well worth taking the time to read so that you can understand this concept more fully.[2]

Openness even becomes an issue for little children. Most adoption books for children fail to consider that an adoption can be open. They usually refer to someone who is a go-between and barely mention how an adoption is arranged and what happens to the birth mother. Parents involved in open adoptions have searched for books that reflect the way adoption has changed. Books addressing openness are becoming more common to meet the needs of growing numbers of people involved in these kinds of adoptions.[3]

Some adoptions begin at one level of openness and change to another. While this shift may pose some significant problems, it is a possibility you need to be aware of as you enter the process. Everyone generally agrees that it is important to have a clear perception of your views on openness before you begin an adoption and to plan from the beginning for some degree of openness in your adoption. It is not unusual for the amount of openness to be put in writing to help clarify the guidelines for all of the parties involved. (These legal agreements will be discussed later.) Sometimes the openness extends to other family members such as grandparents, aunts, and uncles.

Some degree of openness in adoption has now become the norm. Before you can begin the process, you need to understand what your views are on this subject, because they will influence how you go about every other step we will discuss in this book.

Different Degrees of Openness

To illustrate the tremendous variety of options in open adoption, it is worthwhile to describe some examples. *Minimal, moderate,* and *maximum contact* adoptions are the terms used to describe the varying degrees of openness. As a means of classifying material together (even though examples seldom fit this neatly), we have chosen to define *minimal contact* as contact between birth parents and adoptive parents only up until the birth of the child and no further. *Moderate contact* is used to describe adoptions where there is some continuing contact (phone calls, letters, photographs), but no face-to-face contact. The maximum degree of openness comes in where visitations (face-to-face contact) continue between the child, birth parents, and adoptive parents while the adopted child lives with the adoptive parents.

MINIMAL CONTACT

Probably most independent adoptions would fit into the category of minimal contact. At a minimum, names of birth parents and adoptive parents are exchanged. At times a pre-adoption meeting is arranged and contact in the hospital occurs, but both sides agree to not continue contact after the baby is relinquished.

Many times this minimal contact between birth parents and adoptive parents is the most feared part of independent adoptions. In open adoptions it is an accepted part of the process and is viewed as a planning and exchange session between two sets of caring parents.

Hank and Teresa had a chance to participate in an open adoption twenty-five years ago. (They didn't realize how far ahead of their time they were.) Hank and Teresa could not make babies, even though they had tried every fertility specialist in their area. They were planning to apply for adoption with an agency when they heard from a neighbor about her sixteen-year-old niece, Mary Beth, who was pregnant and wanted to place the child for adoption. The neighbor arranged for Hank and Teresa to meet Mary Beth; it just seemed the right thing to do at the time. After a couple of hours of discussing adoption issues and observing each other, the three people agreed that Hank and Teresa would raise Mary Beth's baby after it was born. The couple agreed to pay for Mary Beth's prenatal care.

Just before the baby was born, Mary Beth's parents also wanted to meet Hank and Teresa. This time the five of them sat down together and talked about the baby. This would be the first grandchild for Mary Beth's parents, and they were concerned about the welfare of the child. The meeting lasted three hours and included a friendly dinner together. Everyone wanted what was best for the child, and they all wanted to feel good about their role in the adoption. As Mary Beth and her parents talked to Hank and Teresa, they found out a great deal about the home in which this child would be raised. In turn, they felt they had a chance to let Hank and Teresa know about each of them and their beliefs and interests. When the meeting was over, everyone left with an extremely positive feeling.

Three weeks later a baby girl was born. Hank and Teresa visited Mary Beth in the hospital. They wanted to bring their new daughter home immediately, but it was also important to them to see Mary Beth, who had become a very special person to them. At that time, Mary Beth said she didn't want to maintain contact with them. She said the contact would be too painful for her and would prevent her from moving ahead with her life. She also told them she didn't need contact because she knew how well Hank and Teresa would raise her baby. Mary Beth never again made contact with Hank and Teresa. However, the couple felt they could always talk positively to their daughter about the caring, involved people who had been part of her life before they adopted her.

This example of a minimal contact adoption went especially well for all the people involved who didn't see anything particularly unusual in their open adoption. What they did seemed natural to them, and the limits arose naturally.

Today this kind of minimal contact in adoption is routine. Frequently a birth mother will choose to write a letter and give it to the adoptive couple to pass on to the child when the time seems appropriate. Some adopting parents give a birth mother a book that she can write in to give to the adopted child.[4]

Very few people have problems with this kind of openness in adoption. But even with this minimal level of contact, you will have an opportunity to obtain important information to pass on to your child because you have met the birth mother and come to know her personally. This is far different from the kind of adoption in which facts and statistics about the birth mother and birth father are recited to you by an impersonal third party, and you don't get to know the biological parents as people.

MODERATE CONTACT

Moderate contact involves more extensive contact between the people involved but not ongoing personal contact afterwards. It is easy to identify with the examples that involve no hesitation between the people involved, but sometimes there are problems.

The case involving Gloria and Don's adoption of a baby boy was filled with problems. They heard about a baby boy who had been left with a neighbor by a young woman, Julie. The neighbor knew Julie's sister. Julie had been involved in drugs and sex since she was twelve. She was a high school dropout at fourteen and her parents had no control over her. She was slightly retarded from an injury at birth that had also caused her to develop epilepsy. She had been in and out of foster homes and juvenile hall. At eighteen, she had gotten pregnant by a man she barely knew. His history of violent behavior and a short term in jail for armed robbery didn't deter Julie from having her baby. After she delivered the baby boy, the father said he didn't want it, but she could come with him if she left the baby. Julie left the boy with Gloria and Don's neighbor and took off.

When Don and Gloria heard about the child, they were very interested in adopting him. They wanted to know more about him and contacted the physician who delivered him, who openly said to them that this child was a "mess." He warned them about the mother's lack of prenatal care and the potential for long-term physical and mental damage. He advised them to pass up this adoption.

Then they met the grandmother of the boy. It was reassuring to see that she seemed normal and without evidence of mental retardation.

Somehow, the boy's father heard that Don and Gloria were interested in the baby. When he talked to them on the phone, they became alarmed. He sounded so rough and coarse. They worried that he would try to get money for the boy by making threats to take the child away. They became fearful and said they didn't want the child. They were willing to pass on any information, good and bad to anyone else who was interested in adopting the baby.

The next couple, Susan and Joel, learned all of the details from Don and Gloria. Susan and Joel made some additional contacts with the family members, had some testing done on the boy, who was then seven weeks old, and consulted an attorney. Everything seemed acceptable to them—not good, but acceptable. Their attorney said he would handle the case as long as the couple did not go along with any of the birth father's demands if he made any. They agreed.

The one stipulation the birth family made was that Susan and Joel maintain contact with the child's biological grandparents. Joel and Susan felt that this was reasonable. They agreed to write to the grandparents regularly, to send pictures of the boy as he grew, and to meet with the grandmother at least once a year.

Joel and Susan hoped to get the birth mother and the birth father to sign relinquishment papers. Since the birth parents' whereabouts were unknown, this possibility was uncertain. If they were not found, the plan was to begin to prove the boy had been abandoned. The boy's extended biological family completely supported Joel and Susan's adoption. They knew that if this boy, with all the negative factors in his background, entered into the adoption agency system, he would be viewed as a "special-needs" child; his adoption could be delayed by months, maybe years. They knew they needed to find an accepting couple who would be able to handle the negative as well as the positive information about this boy. Joel and Susan were that couple.

The exceptional part of this story is that nothing was hidden. Everything was out in the open, and the adoptive parents felt the information could be handled. Their son, Del, finally became theirs after lengthy abandonment procedures were filed. The birth parents never came forward. Del has some developmental issues that continue to make school difficult for him, but he is doing fine outside of school. He is nice looking, an excellent goalie in soccer, a wonderful brother to his six-year-old adopted sister, and a delightful nine-year-old son.

Most moderate contact adoptions are not as complex as this one. In fact, the case of the Kennersons is probably much more typical. The Kennersons found their child by sending a letter to a physician in Missouri. When Merideth, a bright twenty-one-year-old woman said she could not keep the baby she'd learned she was carrying, the physician passed on the information about the Kennersons to her. Merideth knew she was not ready to raise a child, but she was also not willing to lose total contact when she placed her child for adoption. The Kennersons sounded like warm, giving people who might consider having contact with her throughout her child's growing years. She was right. All three discussed what Merideth expected from the Kennersons and what they in turn expected from her. Everyone seemed satisfied, so when Merideth delivered an eight-pound baby girl, the Kennersons became the delighted parents. Merideth's desire to keep in contact with them has always been honored. In the seven years since the birth, letters and pictures have gone back and forth between the two households. No one's position is threatened because everyone wants what is best for the daughter they share and they all trust each other.

Adoptions are sometimes very simple and other times very complex. The desire to adopt a child is strong enough for most people to weather the complexities that may face them. The protective screening of information, even negative information, implies that people are not able to handle it or work the situation through. This simply is not the case. Adults, like children, are resilient. You just need to find the right people to handle each situation.

Most moderate contact adoptions involve yearly pictures and letters to update the birth mother, the adopting parents, and, eventually, the child. Not only are these letters a way to keep in touch, but they also keep everyone up to date on address changes. This is the most important part, a way to maintain contact with the birth parents, who will be available for your child as the years go by.

MAXIMUM CONTACT

The greatest amount of contact between the birth parents and the adoptive parents occurs when a birth parent remains involved in the child's life even after the adoption. It is clear that there is a huge difference between the minimal and maximum level of contact. These varying degrees of openness make research on open adoptions very difficult, because the levels of, and the issues involved in, openness can be vastly different. Historically we have seen maximum contact adoptions within families where a grandmother raises a child and the birth mother takes on the role of sister to a child. In most maximum contact adoptions, the child knows the identity of the birth mother from the very beginning. There are no surprises. The child is raised knowing her birth mother.

In most maximum contact cases, the role of the birth mother is agreed upon before the birth of the child. The birth mother may attend celebrations, be a regular guest, may know friends of the adoptive couple, and even be known to the child as her birth mother. The potential ways that the birth mother can be involved are endless.

Some newer adoption agencies will work only with people who agree to open adoptions at the maximum level of openness. Agencies will let you know this before you begin the process.

Kent and Adrianne had never considered adoption. In the five years they had been married, they'd had two children and were quite content with their family. They were shocked when their very good friend Tricia called in a state of panic to tell them she was pregnant. Adrianne and Tricia had been roommates before Adrianne married Kent. Tricia had never married; she remained a close friend to Adrianne and Kent and their children. Adrianne encouraged her to come over and talk about the situation.

Tricia was extremely agitated as she told Adrianne about her pregnancy. She had never dreamed she would become pregnant. She had been sexually involved with a man with whom she had broken up two months ago. When her periods seemed a bit irregular, she'd thought little about it until the previous month, when she didn't have one at all. Thinking it was related to stress over being out of work, she did nothing. Then, as she didn't feel quite like herself, she decided to go to her doctor for a checkup. She was amazed to learn that she was pregnant and very pregnant at that—more than three months along. There was no way Tricia, who was Roman Catholic, would consider having an abortion, especially that far into her pregnancy.

As Tricia talked more and more with Adrianne about the situation, she calmed down considerably. She discussed adoption and how hard it would be to give her baby away to strangers. She discussed keeping the child, which she felt was impossible in her circumstances. She kept coming back to adoption but felt it would simply be too much for her to handle. Then she surprised Adrianne by suggesting that Adrianne and Kent adopt her baby. At that time Adrianne didn't know what to say.

Adrianne and Kent talked the situation over. They finally decided that if certain issues could be agreed upon with Tricia, they would seriously consider the possibility. The three of them talked about the situation numerous times over the next five months. They all agreed that if the adoption took place, Kent and Adrianne would be parents—totally. Tricia would not be able to interfere in the way they chose to raise the baby. They felt that it was difficult enough for two people to agree on raising children without adding a third point of view. Tricia completely agreed. Tricia was also very approving of Kent and Adrianne's approach with their one- and three-year-olds; her knowledge of how they were as parents made her confident about how they would raise her child.

They all agreed that they would not tell the child that Tricia was the birth mother unless the child asked if she was or if she had a strong desire later in life to know the identity of her birth mother. They were determined to be honest with the child. They felt that if the child discovered that Tricia was his or her mother, the knowledge would not destroy Kent and Adrianne's relationship with the child; at the same time, they all agreed that it was easiest for the child to relate to Kent and Adrianne in the growing-up years as his or her only parents.

The adoption happened. These days Adrianne and Kent are delighted with their three children. Their youngest daughter, Carrie, is a joy. Tricia is a regular visitor to the home and enjoys seeing Carrie and the other children grow. She would never dream of interfering. She is grateful to Kent and Adrianne, who agreed to this unusual open adoption. Kent and Adrianne are also grateful to her.

This is not a typical maximum contact adoption; but maybe there is no typical situation. Adoption with maximum contact will not appeal to everyone, but it doesn't need to. The world is full of many types of people—there should be room for many types of adoptions. This is one kind of adoption you need to give a lot of thought to before you begin the adoption process. That doesn't mean you should agree to this kind of adoption unless you can be comfortable with it.

Open Adoption Historically and Cross-Culturally

Open adoption was more prevalent in our society in earlier times. In the 1920s and 1930s, especially in rural areas, informal contact between adoptive parents and birth parents was more common. As the adoption agency system expanded and became more powerful, these open adoptions decreased. But some of the lessons from the past and some from other cultures are valuable today.

In the past, open adoption contacts often included the adopted child's full knowledge that this other woman was his or her birth mother. Open adoptions have even included temporary visits with the birth mother, which appear to have been beneficial to each of the people involved. There is no evidence to prove that any damage resulted to the child from these open adoptions.

In some parts of the world, adoption has remained open despite certain changes within the system over time. In the Hawaiian and Eskimo cultures, for example, forms of open adoption have been successfully practiced for years. Any problems with adoption in these cultures seem to arise not because of the openness, but when the modern American form of secret adoption is imposed.

Before effective birth control, people often practiced informal adoption within their extended families. While this form of adoption is used far less today, some ethnic groups who do not trust agencies to work on their behalf, still use more informal adoption procedures within their own family networks—a woman raises her sister's child or a grandmother raises one additional child.

Cynthia notes: *Our own family adopted a daughter twenty-six years ago, in an open adoption involving some physical contact with the birth parents after she had been relinquished to us. In this situation, we found many advantages over the more secretive types of adoption that character-ized the adoptions of our first two children. We could tell our daughter more about her birth parents than we could tell our other children. We could ob-tain birth parents' medical records as they grew older. Knowing that we could, at some time in the future, help her to make contact was also an ad-vantage. Occasional calls and contact from the birth parents, while not our favorite activities, in the long run were positive events in our lives.*

Adoption Agencies and Open Adoption

Open adoptions significantly change the role of adoption agencies. When a birth mother and adopting parents make a personal adoption agreement, the role of the agency becomes very different and the focus of control changes. Many agencies, steeped in traditional practice, are reluctant to move ahead on anything but minimal contact adoptions. Some of their reasons are valid; others are self-protective.

The best single reason for being cautious about some kinds of open adoption is the lack of research on how it affects the child, the birth parents, and the adoptive parents in our own culture. It seems fairly clear that less secrecy is a benefit in most adoptions; however, there is a big difference between minimal secrecy and having the birth mother come to your home as a regular guest. Agencies are incorporating open-ness into their adoptions in order to compete with independent adop-tions. But beyond letting the birth mother have a chance to read background information or personal letters written by people seeking to adopt, there are still only a few traditional adoption agencies advocating open adoptions. The trend toward openness is clear, but its progress within agencies is slow.

One of the first dissenting voices from the traditional stance advocating no contact between adoptive parents and birth parents came from the adoption agency that began advocating the opening of sealed birth records, Vista Del Mar Child and Family Services, in California (see Appendix F). The writings of Annette Baran and Reuben Pannor on this subject have been significant in opening adoption to a greater level of honesty. Their current work emphasizes having adopting parents and birth parents working in partnerships to provide for the child as he or she grows.[5] In fact, they now look at this as the only acceptable approach. But most people would agree it is important not to go to extremes in advocating totally open or totally closed adoptions. There is room for many kinds of adoption in our society and not all of them need to be open.

One nontraditional adoption agency gives both sets of parents the option to exchange names, grant visitation rights, and share personal histories. Their social workers require all the people involved to keep the agency up-to-date so that the birth parents know about the child they have placed for adoption. The agency believes this more open approach will make "more children available for adoption while making adoption healthier for the child and all other parties involved."[6] The agency believes that open adoption provides a way to decrease the adopted child's sense of rejection by having the birth parents continue to be involved in his or her life. They feel that meetings between the birth parents and the adoptive parents lessen the birth parents' sense of guilt over leaving the child. As part of this approach, the agency opens their adoption records to the child when she or he becomes an adult.

Obviously this agency's approach and that of other progressive agencies which have accepted open adoption have set examples for other agencies. Their courage to be different in this regard deserves applause and support. There is now a national association of agencies committed to open adoptions, the American Association of Open Adoption Agencies (see Appendix F). While this group does not represent all agencies involved in open adoptions, it is a helpful resource for people seeking some help in finding agencies for this kind of adoption.

There remains a significant role for adoption agencies to play, even as openness becomes more common. In many ways there is an increasing need for help, because of the complexities of these adoptions and the families' need for lifelong support. Potential conflicts and disagreements among the parties may need help to be resolved.[7] An agency providing assistance for this complex, ongoing process is a valuable asset to everyone involved.

Risks, Dangers, and Disadvantages

No choice you can make in adoption comes without risks. If there were one alternative that had all of the advantages and none of the disadvantages, dangers, or risks, everyone would advocate that as the only way to adopt.

Of course there are risks in open adoption. The ultimate risk is *"Can I lose my adopted child?"* Yes, you can. *But you can lose any child.* Remember, no one owns his or her children, adopted or biological. In our experience, the risk of losing a child to the birth parent in an open adoption is not significantly greater than the risk of losing your child in a traditional adoption. When you know and can identify the other parent, the risk is simply more apparent.

This is true in divorce cases also. In divorce cases, however, there is generally more overt competition for the child; in open adoption, the basic underlying agreement is that there will be no competition for the child. We believe you probably have far less risk of losing your child in an open adoption than you might have of losing your child in a divorce. If there is competition, however, remember that in many ways it is easier to know who your "rival" is. To compete with a child's fantasy of his or her birth parent can be much more difficult than when the parent's identity is clearly out in the open.

The risks involved in open adoption often depend on the degree of contact you choose. Most problems center on adoptions in which there is face-to-face contact after the adoption. Risks are increased when the child knows the birth parents yet even these risks are seldom major. And fewer risks are likely if you just exchange names and identifying information, or even pass letters and gifts from birth parents on to your child.

The biggest concern in open adoptions, especially those involving physical contact after the adoption, is that the child will become confused (not understand who his parents really are). Since research is lacking at this time, the best way to assess this risk is by watching what happens with the individual child, so if you find that confusion is a problem with yours, the arrangement might need to be modified. In this day and age of many different kinds of families, confusion is not as likely to be a problem. It isn't unusual for a child to have multiple parents because of a divorce, and this is a similar situation. If the adopting parents are clear about this issue, it is unlikely to trouble the child.

Another risk involved is what happens when the child becomes a teenager and becomes less inclined to follow the adoptive parents' rules. Will he or she choose to go to live with this other set of parents, as frequently happens in divorce situations? We don't have the answers to this question and only long-term studies can assess the extent of the problem. We do know that potential adolescent rebellions should be thoroughly discussed when making plans about contact—and remember, each child is different, just as each adoption is different. Some may never feel the need to rebel.

There are some who feel that openness in adoption prevents the adopting parents from bonding with the child because they become insecure about their roles in relation to those of the birth parents. Who will the child really love? Issues of bonding can arise in any adoption, whether open or closed, and in parenting any child, adopted or biological. If problems present themselves, they need to be brought out in the open and discussed. While failure to bond is a common fear, the research that is available does not indicate that this is a bigger problem in open adoptions than in confidential ones. (It may be that the people who enter into open adoptions are more confident of their parenting skills than those who choose not to be involved.) And a child has the ability to love many people.

One of the most frequently asked questions about open adoption is whether a young birth mother understands the long-term implications of openness. Contact may help her initially with the grief and loss she will experience, but it may also prolong that grief if she becomes overly dependent on the adopting parents, or if she is unable to separate herself from the baby she is relinquishing. Most young mothers have many distracting things in life that are likely to help them separate from the baby and from the adopting parents. If fact, if we wanted the birth mother to remain intensely involved, we would probably have more difficulty having that happen.

But as you struggle with understanding how open you are to contact, there are some distinct advantages to remember and consider.[8]

Advantages of Open Adoption for the Adopting Parents

- More situations are available if you are willing to be involved in open adoptions.
- You are likely to feel a greater sense of control over the process.
- You can decide for yourself which child you will adopt and if this situation is right for you.
- By meeting the birth parents, you will obtain more information and be aware of possible special needs that might require early intervention.
- You will learn a lot about the birth mother (father) and that will lessen your fantasies about her (them).
- You will also be in a much better position to answer your child's questions about his or her birth family.
- You will be sure that the birth mother has freely chosen adoption and that will relieve fears of her reappearing to reclaim the child at a later time.

Advantages of Open Adoption for the Adopted Child

- Information about birth parents' lives is readily available to the child.
- The child has more information about his or her biological heritage.
- The sense of being abandoned is lessened.
- If the child decides to search, he or she can find the birth family.
- If biological siblings arrive, this open contact would minimize the shock to the adopted child.
- Some parents feel that the more people who love their children, the better for the children.

- Open adoption provides answers to the child from the birth mother (and hopefully birth father) about why she or he was relinquished for adoption.

Advantages of Open Adoption for the Birth Parents

- Most people feel the process is more humane and compassionate when the birth parents choose the child's new family.
- The additional control she has in an open adoption is empowering for the birth mother and lessens her pain of loss and possible guilt.
- The birth mother's anxiety may be decreased through updates about where and how her baby is.
- Ongoing contact can decrease the guilt birth parents may feel at "abandoning the child."

Summary

You are about to begin an exciting process. You will be confronted with new ideas, new lessons, and new people. How you enter this process determines your success.

The process may seem daunting as you begin but don't feel too overwhelmed. Millions of people have completed the process before you; there is no reason you can't succeed, too. Don't become discouraged; people are there to help. You have choices about the direction and the process; you are in charge.

With an understanding of the general picture of openness that exists today in adoption, you can make an informed decision about the degree of openness you are willing to consider. Remember that most people who have become involved in open adoptions are satisfied with the experience.[9] And for many people, openness is almost a given in adoption. If you are unwilling to have any contact whatsoever with a birth family, you will be passing up large numbers of potential adoption situations. Remember the more willing you are to be flexible and open, the easier it is for you to find a situation that will meet your needs. So before you begin remind yourself, you are only looking for one baby.

CHAPTER 3

An Underlying Issue

THIS IS NOT A BOOK about infertility. Yet the issue of infertility can permeate adoption. Not all people come to adoption because they are infertile; perhaps they come because they are single or gay or maybe they simply believe there are already enough children in the world and they choose to raise one that has already arrived. But most people adopt because they cannot biologically have a child.

No matter where you begin in this process, you need to look at your motivation for adopting. If you have issues about your infertility that create problems for you, read about it, join groups to help resolve those issues, and don't let them interfere with your ability to adopt a child. If you have issues about people having too many babies, work them out; if you are hostile toward the women who are placing children for adoption it will interfere with your ability to adopt a child. Some women become pregnant too easily, and others not at all. These underlying differences can cause problems throughout the process. Understand the differences and prevent them from affecting your adoption.

Adopting couples have difficulty understanding how a birth mother could possibly give up her child. Wanting so much to have a child prevents the infertile couple from being able to place themselves in the position of the birth mother, and it can even create some alienation. It increases their fears that the birth mother will change her mind, and it may even cause them to look down on her.

So try to understand your infertility if that is how you come to adoption, but then try to understand the birth mother's fertility. All adopting couples need to view the dilemma of an unwanted pregnancy from the birth mother's perspective—a perspective which may have grown foreign to them especially if they have struggled with their own infertility. Your understanding of your issues will result in your being more understanding of her issues.

If You're Infertile

Infertility is always an emotionally painful and frequently private matter. But considering adoption changes the private side of infertility. In adoption, you must be open about the fact that you are infertile. And in order to be open about your infertility, you need to understand it. You need to understand it not only for yourself but also for others involved in the adoption decision; they need to understand the place of infertility in your life.

Few people can empathize with your inability to have a baby. The emotional issues of infertility can dominate your life and your partner's and put strains on you as individuals and as a couple. At times the strains show to the world; they underscore your struggle and may complicate your ability to find a child.

In some ways, not having a child displays to the world an individual's "deficiency." If we are poor, financial inadequacy may or may not show to the world. If we are insecure, the world may not necessarily know. But sexuality still remains so blurred and confusing to most people that fertility is one of our primary means of demonstrating it. If we are childless, our reproductive deficiency is exhibited for all the world to view. To understand the emotional consequences of infertility is to understand the plight of feeling inadequate.

The fragility of our sexual identities is clear. Early sexual activity may be an attempt to "prove" adequacy. Having frequent sex is another way of proving sexuality. Often men seek to improve their sense of sexuality by the number of climaxes they can achieve or the number of women with whom they have had sex or their frequency of intercourse. Bragging about conquests to bolster personal feelings about sexuality is still part of our culture, and some people pride themselves on the number of children they have created for the same reason. Contraceptive clinics in low-income areas have failed at times because too often the positive identity of parents is based on how many children they have. They may be poor, but they are "good" parents because they have many children. The same unwed father who says no to abortion and offers no support for his unborn child may brag to his friends about his girlfriend being pregnant.

The couple experiencing infertility must first come to grips with how this factor affects each of them individually. Each must search for new ways to establish a firm sexual identity. The person who is sure of his or her sexuality will be less affected than the person who is less sure. If you are confident in your sexuality, demonstrating it to yourself or your friends or the world becomes less important. Basically, the more "together" the person, the easier a time he or she may have accepting his or her infertility—easier, but still not too easy.

Your relationship with your partner may become strained with your infertility struggle. This is one of the major problem areas—such as a new job, a new home, being fired, a relative coming to live with you, the death of a relative, an injury to one of the partners—that can cause shifts and changes in the marital relationship. Sometimes the changes are for the better and sometimes for the worse; in any case, these are vulnerable periods. Infertility may be one of the most significant experiences you will ever have, and it may change your life. But that change doesn't have to be bad.

Communicating openly in your relationship is critical at this time. Blaming yourself or harboring feelings of blame toward your sterile spouse can cause long-term, irreparable damage to the relationship. Doctor-recommended scheduled sexual relations and the stress of medical tests put severe strains on any relationship. If this stress is paired with hidden hostility and unspoken blame, the couple will have difficulty overcoming the strain of infertility. They may end up not only without a child, but also without each other.

Attitudes of relatives, friends, and coworkers may also be a significant problem for the infertile couple. Relationships with others may be filled with references to the couple's infertility. Perhaps the potential grandmother has her advice to give. The potential aunts and uncles, going through their own period of child rearing, may be quick to offer tips concerning your childlessness. Baby showers where people say "You're next" can become ordeals and alter your relationships with your friends.

With no knowledge of your pain or your inability to conceive, our society may view you with confusion and skepticism. You are likely to be pictured as selfish for not wanting children—which is ever so far from the truth. Even if your childlessness is known to be not by your choice, society is likely to offer little sympathy; people with children have difficulty identifying with the pain of infertility. People openly sympathize with mourning couples whose child has been lost through death, but they fail to comprehend the mourning of the couple whose potential child is lost through infertility. In this time of overpopulation, your problems will be viewed as less significant and perhaps lacking in substance. At times, outsiders may view you in your childlessness as neurotic or immature. Newspapers and magazines you read may relate your childlessness to selfishness, frigidity, or sexual immaturity.

If the desire for pregnancy supersedes most things in your life, you need to find acceptable ways to handle your feelings about your infertility. The primary way to deal with these feelings is to talk with people—especially your partner. Express your emotions to sympathetic listeners, if you have feelings of guilt or deficiency. But pick your listeners carefully—all listeners are not equal. If you have difficulty finding someone to talk with, seek professional help from a counselor, psychologist, or psychiatrist. And look for support from others who have faced the same issues; support groups can be valuable assets at this time of isolation.

Redirecting your energies is another means of coping with your feelings. For months you may have been engrossed with fertility tests, temperature charting, medical appointments, and scheduled sexual activities.

Infertility may have dominated your existence. At some point you have to accept the fact that there may be no solution to your infertility or that you are not willing to wait any longer to find one. So now what are you going to do? You need to change direction. One new path may lie in trying to find a child to adopt, or you may redirect yourself toward a different kind of creativity. A change in direction, however, *is* critical.

But you need to accept that you'll have a period of mourning. Don't expect the feelings you have to go away immediately. You are mourning for the child you couldn't have. Expect this period to last at least six months. You will find your feelings of depression, anger, and anxiety decreasing with time, with redirection of your energies, with reading, and by talking openly about your problem.[1]

The emotional consequences of infertility are surmountable. The individual dealing openly, honestly, and thoroughly with his or her feelings of inadequacy and anger is much more likely to overcome these emotions than the person who pretends everything is fine when, in fact, it isn't. The scarcity of babies available for adoption makes it even more critical that your feelings about infertility are resolved and not simply denied. People who enter this process with anger over unresolved feelings about not being able to have a biological child may even sabotage their own efforts to find a baby. You need to be ready to pursue other courses for your life. Your options, now that you are certain of your infertility, take strength to pursue. If you remain handicapped by the discovery of your infertility, you will be less likely to effectively pursue the options you still have to obtain a baby.

Pathways to Parenthood: Special Issues for the Infertile Couple

The growing number of people confronted with infertility means increasing demand for new ways to become a parent. Close to 20 percent of the couples in the United States are currently experiencing infertility.[2] The 4 percent increase seen in the last twenty years has been dramatic.[3]

While more options to infertility exist today than ever before, each option has some disadvantages. Some are ways to find a child, and others emphasize a redirection away from parenting. As in many areas we are discussing, there is no right or wrong way to resolve your desire to parent; there is, however, a way with which you are likely to feel most comfortable. You may pursue several options before you find the one that best suits you. You may eliminate an option now that later might suit you better. Meet your needs in your own way.

CHILDLESSNESS

One of the options to infertility is to remain childless—an option that is and has been chosen far more frequently than is generally believed. In the past, people who were not up to the rigors of adoption may have decided to remain childless. Today, childlessness may in part result from fear about the risks of adopting a child who might be taken back by the birth parents. Recent media attention to sensational adoption cases has undoubtedly increased the number of people who fear adoption risks and thus remain childless. We don't know how many people today fit in the fear category and how many are Generation X'ers who have decided to remain childless by choice. The Census Bureau estimates that up to 24 percent of women now between eighteen and twenty-four will never have children, some because of the circumstances of their lives and others because of the choice to remain childless.[4]

Childlessness has only recently been studied. We know that during certain periods of our history, such as the Depression, proportionally greater numbers of couples have not had children; perhaps this decrease is the result of fear of the future, lack of money, or merely depression over current life circumstances. Explanations for the decreased fertility rates are purely speculative. A resurgence of childlessness was seen in the seventies and is beginning to be more prevalent at the turn of the century. Advocates for childlessness have undoubtedly increased the acceptability of nonparenting as a viable alternative for couples; support groups are sometimes available.

Studies have assessed why people are childless and how this affects their lives, and they've found that childless couples are just as satisfied with their lives as those who have children.[5] The common assumption that childless couples will be lonely in later life and that life will hold less meaning for them thus appears invalid. Another group of studies, published in the fifties, focused on the failed marriages of childless couples. The results were presented to the childless as a reason to have children: If you don't have a baby, your marriage is more likely to fail. In recent years, these same studies have been shown to be invalid. Marriages that end in divorce early on are frequently childless because they are brief. So assessing the effect of childlessness on the failure of the marriage becomes impossible.

Where does this leave people who remain childless but not by choice? Does their childlessness have a negative effect on their marriages or on their lives in general? What can people do to minimize any negative effect that remaining childless might have on them?

Babies don't hold marriages together for long. The quality of a marriage is most directly related to the commitment and work of the two people involved, not to their children. Open communication can help any couple surmount a specific difficulty. The *primary* means of making sure your life is fulfilling is in yourself, not in whether you have children.

EXPERIMENTAL METHODS OF REPRODUCTION

Some people are willing to go further than others to correct their infertility problems. More extraordinary help is available as a result of fertility studies than ever before. Many times the solution to infertility is achieved rather easily.[6] Some people are very fortunate and succeed in becoming pregnant, but for every one couple who succeeds, three others will not succeed.[7] With these kinds of odds and with the staggering costs of high tech intervention, it is important for the couple to thoroughly explore the chances of success before beginning any high tech means of reproduction. In reality, we are still in the infancy stages of understanding how to succeed with experimental methods of reproduction.[8]

There are some additional problems with pursuing this option. You may have already spent several years trying to become pregnant. Your life can be thoroughly dominated by this primary goal. It is likely that the strain of your pursuit shows in your relationships with your spouse, family, and friends. At the rapid rate of medical advances, there will always be another new method to try to become pregnant. If you wait to try everything available, you may find yourself too old to adopt easily or even to want a child.

Carefully evaluate your potential ways of medically overcoming your infertility. Read about infertility issues and understand the complexity of the new procedures before you begin.[9] Find out from your physician what your chance of success is before you decide to proceed with any new medical procedures. Even procedures receiving great attention have a very small chance of success. Look at the costs; they, too, can be extraordinary. For sure get a second opinion and a second estimate for these financially and emotionally costly medical procedures. Even look into alternative methods such as nutrition, relaxation, and imagery.[10] Be an aware consumer.

ADOPTION

If you choose not to pursue the more elaborate or experimental techniques of reproduction, or if you have pursued them as far as you want to, adoption may be the option you choose to attain parenthood. Many avenues to finding children will be discussed in this book; find the one that best meets your needs.

In order to seek a child through the process of adoption, you should first feel comfortable with how far you have gone in the quest to end your infertility. Occasionally infertility can actually *help* you in the adoption process. Some adoption agencies will only work with you if you cannot become pregnant. Even in independent adoptions, many birth mothers may want to know your infertility status; some, but not all, birth mothers look more favorably on couples who cannot biologically have a child.

Adoption is probably not an infertile couple's first choice. That doesn't make adoption an inferior way of producing a family, it merely makes it a different way.

FOSTER PARENTING

At times people confuse foster parents with adoptive parents. There are very few similarities. Foster parents are usually temporary parents who do not have legal custody of the child. The child can be taken from the foster home at any time. Foster parents are paid for the care of the child. Adoptive parents, on the contrary, provide permanent homes; the parents have permanent legal custody of the child. Becoming foster parents can be a rewarding opportunity to participate in the raising of a child or many children.

The foster care system in this country has come under considerable attack in recent years. There may be as many as 500,000 children in foster care.[11] Agencies running foster care programs also often help with adoptions. Not all, but many, of these agencies have been accused of deliberately keeping potentially adoptable children in foster care because the state pays the agency for each child in the foster care system; if these children are placed in adoptive homes, the agency will no longer receive funds from the state. This is an obvious conflict of interest. Critics of the system point out that the agencies have no incentive to place these children in adoptive homes. Others say that state legislatures force agencies to make superhuman efforts to reunite biological families, and that causes delays in placements.

None of these criticisms negate the great good being done by foster parents who willingly offer temporary homes to children in need. The ideal foster parent is one with an ability to love without having to feel the relationship will go on forever. This is not an easy kind of love for many people to offer, so there is often a lack of good foster parents. Much is expected of foster parents, and there aren't enough good foster homes to keep up with the need.

Children in the foster care system come from three groups. The first group is children who are waiting to be placed in adoptive homes. Babies and young children usually spend the shortest time in foster homes. Older children waiting to be adopted are frequently kept in foster homes for a longer period of time, to make certain the correct type of home is found for them. The second group are children whose parents are temporarily unable to care for them, but who do not want to place them for adoption. This is a situation that allows the parent to maintain contact with the child while the parent stabilizes his or her life. Some of these children are voluntarily placed in foster care by their parents; at other times the court system has intervened because the parent has not cared adequately for the child. Children in the third group are the ones whose parents have little contact with them; these children remain in foster care far longer than the others and longer than should be necessary. As with the previous groups, these children are placed in foster care both voluntarily and by the courts. The longer the child is in foster care, the less likely it is that the child will be adopted.

Foster parents who adopt the children in their care have become more common in recent years. This is especially true in cases involving special-needs children. For older children in the foster system, one of the best predictors of a successful adoption is adoption by their foster parent.[12] In any situation where a child has been in foster care for an extended period of time, this home should be considered the first-choice situation for adoption.

With the exception of situations involving special needs, adoption of babies by foster parents seldom occurs. Babies are in demand by many people and foster parents are not the ones likely to be given these children.

Although more foster care adoptions are occurring now, this is not a very sure way to find a child to adopt. In the past, any kind of adoption by foster parents was strictly forbidden by the adoption agencies. Agencies did not want to lose their foster parents by having them adopt the babies, nor did they want this to be a way to avoid going through the usual adoption process. Again, the agency had a conflict of interest.

Agencies have recently tried another type of adoption. It is called fost-adopt. The theory is that parents seeking to adopt can have a child before he or she has been fully released from the custody of the birth parent. In most cases the relinquishment is fairly firm, so this is a way of beginning the adoption process early. Obviously there are risks that a birth parent will not complete the relinquishment of the child and may choose to take the child back; these risks are made clear to the adoptive parents considering fost-adopt. This is especially important since the parents being considered are clearly people seeking to adopt, and are not foster parents who understand the temporary nature of the placement.

SUBSTITUTE PARENTING

Some people may choose to remain childless but become intimately involved in parenting vicariously. There are many means of being a substitute parent.

One of the ways to be a substitute parent is with the children of relatives. Some aunts or uncles are extremely involved with their nieces and nephews. They take them places, spend time with them, travel with them. They are involved in their holidays and in other joyous events. They are able to participate in the children's growing years.

Other childless people wanting to participate in child rearing seek out close relationships with children in the neighborhood or do extensive baby-sitting. Other people become Big Brothers or Big Sisters for children who do not have an adult of their own sex in their lives. These people may find that part-time parenting meets some of their needs for contact with children.

Another way people become substitute parents is by teaching children. Becoming a teacher or helping in a nursery school will sometimes substitute for not having children. The teacher spends four to six hours a day with lots of children. That may be more hours of parenting than many actual parents spend.

The people who choose substitute parenting are saying it is important to them to have children in their lives. They are not actually remaining childless. They simply have children who are slightly more "borrowed" than those who adopt or who have foster children. In truth, all our children—the ones we produce, the ones we adopt, and the ones we merely nurture for a while—are borrowed. No one *owns* a child.

Basically, these are the options infertile couples have. You may elect to try some of the options simultaneously. You may try new, experimental ways to get pregnant while looking for a child to adopt. You may elect to go from one option to another. You may try being very active with children as a substitute parent and decide later that you don't want to continue. Then you may decide to pursue medical remedies further or to pursue adoption.

Abby and Glen's story illustrates the uneven course that many couples experience in dealing with infertility. Abby never questioned whether Glen wanted children before they married; parenthood wasn't a high priority to Glen, but it was OK with him. So it wasn't a major disappointment for Glen when Abby didn't become pregnant after a year of trying. But it was for Abby. At her urging, they went through infertility studies and found Glen had a low sperm count that probably caused their infertility. Abby wanted a baby, but how they would get the baby wasn't important to her. Glen went along, and they rather easily adopted a child from a local private adoption agency.

Everything was going fine until they began to have marital problems. As they came closer and closer to a divorce, they realized that the unexplored and undiscussed areas of Glen's sterility and Abby's desire for a family were significant factors in the hostility Abby was feeling. As this came more to the foreground, they saw that many problems actually revolved around their infertility and had been ignored or denied. With discussion came improvement in the marriage.

What had started out to be a dissolution of the relationship changed into resumption of their fertility tests, to see if they had gone as far as they needed to in trying to produce a child. After some additional tests, they decided to try artificial insemination; it didn't work. As a result, they discovered that Abby, too, was part of the infertility problem. She had some tubal blockage that might be correctable, but success was uncertain. They spoke with their physician, who discussed in vitro fertilization with them.

They did not want to pursue something that expensive with such a small chance of success. They knew that adoption felt good to them and they decided to look for another child while also trying artificial insemination. As they pursued another adoption, they also made a great effort to improve their communication, in order to avoid what had happened to them before. In the end they learned a lot about life—far more than about infertility.

Abby and Glen exemplify the multiple attempts and changes a couple can experience while they seek an acceptable alternative to their infertility. Try what sounds best to you. Don't hesitate to say, after a time, that the option you chose is the wrong one and you want to try another one. Life changes, and so can you.

Many people and other sources are out there to help you to solve and accept the problems you may be experiencing.[13] This very emotional issue is difficult to handle alone. Seeking help is not a sign of weakness—it's a sign of intelligence.

Don't underestimate the pain of sterility. It makes people cry, it makes them angry, it makes them feel incomplete. It's hard to determine and it's hard to accept. It's clinical and it's emotional. It can dominate your life and yet it is hard to know when to stop struggling.

The Flip Side:
Others' Unplanned Pregnancies

A SOURCE OF BABIES FOR THE INFERTILE

Infertility is perplexing. While you suffer its pains, another person suffers from a pregnancy she doesn't want—too much fertility, in fact. Why would a woman who says she doesn't want to be pregnant actually get pregnant? Why would a woman not take the necessary precautions to prevent an unwanted pregnancy? Why does fate treat us this way?

Understanding unplanned pregnancy is important for those considering adoption. This may seem like a digression in a book on adoption, but it really isn't; if you understand unplanned pregnancies you will know where to look for and how to deal with the birth mother of your child. It will help you understand and empathize with her once you have found her, and as you tell your child about her.

Some women get pregnant because of contraceptive failures. Other women believe the risks or the disadvantages of taking the necessary contraceptive precautions are too great, and they would rather take a chance on an unwanted pregnancy. (The age of AIDS has probably reduced the number of women who have this view.) Many who experience unplanned pregnancies may at some deep level want to be pregnant.

CONTRACEPTIVES

In the past, fear of pregnancy prevented women from being sexually active. Most women can now minimize that fear if they or their partners choose to use contraception. Just about everyone today, no matter his or her age or socioeconomic status, knows about contraception. Most large cities offer free contraception upon request. Yet some women become pregnant and don't want to be.

Certainly some women become pregnant who aren't willing participants in the sexual act: rape and incest victims do not have the option of using contraception. But women involved in consensual sex do, yet some of these women still get pregnant despite the knowledge of how to prevent a pregnancy, the availability of contraceptives, and the advantages of being able to control unwanted conceptions. Several explanations account for these pregnancies:

- A contraceptive fails.
- Some contraceptive techniques are not easy to use, which discourages their faithful or effective use.
- A woman may deliberately, although unconsciously, expose herself to an unwanted pregnancy.
- Some women don't care if they get pregnant, because they view abortion as an easy way out. (These women may change their view if they are personally faced with abortion.)
- Some women want to become pregnant and then change their minds because of their personal experiences.

Making contraceptives available sounds like an easy way to prevent unplanned pregnancies. It would be, if people weren't so complex.

THE UNCONSCIOUS DESIRE TO BE PREGNANT

One reason unplanned pregnancies occur is that many women, at some unconscious level, desire to be pregnant. The fact that contraception is available, but not being used, substantiates the probability of this desire. If you *really* don't want to get pregnant, you do something to prevent it. The woman who cannot find any methods of contraception that are acceptable to her may be saying she doesn't want to find any methods to prevent a pregnancy. The woman who is an occasional contraceptive user is one who may be inclined to getting pregnant.

A woman's stated desire not to be pregnant must seriously be questioned if she keeps putting herself in a position to conceive. For example, women who may have some strong underlying reasons for wanting to be pregnant are perhaps the biggest source of babies who might be available for adoption. For that reason, it is useful to understand the factors that cause a woman to expose herself to a pregnancy when she says she doesn't want to be pregnant. These are the women who would consider adoption if they knew about it.

For some women, especially the adolescent woman, pregnancy is a means of establishing identity as an adult. The adolescent's primary psychological task is her search for a firm sense of who she is—her identity. In seeking to find her unique identity, she may use her developing sexual behavior as a form of saying, "Look, I am an adult, too!"

For some adolescent girls, having sexual feelings and the recognition of their developing bodies is enough to establish their sense of sexual identity. For others, further proof of adulthood is needed and is achieved through active sexual behavior. Still others, unsure of who they are, need a pregnancy to prove to themselves that they are women. However, bearing a child and mothering it may not be essential to such a girl in developing her female identity. Some of these very young women with a need to be pregnant are good candidates for placing their babies for adoption.

Another reason a woman might expose herself to an unwanted pregnancy is to maintain a relationship with a man. Often in a deteriorating relationship, the woman seeks pregnancy as a way to maintain it; but babies make poor glue. Historically, this tactic may have prompted many marriages, but this result is no longer as common. In fact, accidental pregnancies are likely to cause the breakup of nonmarital relationships. Again, women in these circumstances are excellent sources of adoptable children.

People help others who are in trouble. At times this well-intentioned help might in itself lead to a pregnancy, as it did with Sharon. She was a lonely nineteen-year-old with few friends. She had difficulty talking to people. In fact, she said that sometimes it was easier to go to bed with a guy than to try to talk to him. Not surprisingly, she got pregnant.

Sharon's life immediately changed. Agencies opened their doors to her. Volunteer counselors spent time with her whenever she needed them. New friends helped her get to and from the agencies. Sharon said it was the best time of her life. Then she had an abortion and was back where she was before her pregnancy. The "friends" were no longer there.

Her next pregnancy was not much of an accident. She needed help, and the second pregnancy gave her the opportunity to get it, even though it consisted of short-term abortion counseling. Sharon actually needed long-term professional counseling to avoid unwanted pregnancies and to help her solve her personal problems. If she had considered carrying her pregnancy to full term and placing the baby for adoption, she would have received more counseling.

At times a pregnancy may result from an attempt to compensate for a previous abortion. The woman, feeling the unresolved loss of the previous pregnancy, may inadvertently expose herself to another "accidental" pregnancy to "undo" the abortion. For this woman, carrying the child to term may be a good choice. She may feel better about herself if she allows herself to complete the pregnancy, and she will provide another child for adoption.

Fears of sterility can also motivate women toward pregnancy. A doctor told Evelyn, who was adopted as an infant, that she was unlikely ever to get pregnant. To prove her womanliness to herself, she became pregnant at an early age. She typifies the woman who gives birth in order to allay her fears of infertility. Evelyn may also have rejected abortion since she owed her existence to her natural mother's choice not to abort.

Some women deliberately keep their lives in a constant negative state; Jennifer was one. Her primary way of relating to people was through the negative events that were "happening to her." She saw herself as a victim. She had a late abortion in a difficult laborlike procedure. The procedure took more than fourteen hours; she left the hospital angry with the staff and with the father of the child. Later, the new man in her life did not treat her as she felt she deserved. She was angry that he did not pay for her birth control pills, so to spite him, she quit taking them. Jennifer paid for her anger with another pregnancy. Unable to take responsibility for her own actions, she *was* a victim in her own unhappy way. At one of the pregnancy crisis points in her life she might have considered placing the baby for adoption as an alternative to abortion.

These examples typify some of the more than one million women each year who have unwanted pregnancies. Most women will elect to abort their unwanted pregnancy, and it will be the right decision for them. Some will debate their decision or have mixed feelings about what they should do. Counseling services seldom attempt to pinpoint the reasons why a woman becomes pregnant. Often, they simply arrange for abortions. Some of these women who are given abortions might be much better off giving up their babies for adoption; many of them may have never even considered adoption as an alternative.

THE DILEMMA OF UNWANTED PREGNANCY

No matter what the reasons for an accidental pregnancy, whether contraceptive failure or an unconscious desire to be pregnant, once the woman is pregnant, she faces a new dilemma. She is no longer involved in risk taking; she is on her way to having a baby. Whether she is single or married, she has only four choices open to her.

1. She can have the baby and raise it.
2. She can have the baby and place it for adoption.
3. She can terminate the pregnancy with an abortion.
4. She can have the baby and place the child in long-term foster care.

If she doesn't want a baby, all the choices are difficult, and she chooses the least offensive.

She is now about to be bombarded by all the people who would like to have input in her decision-making process. She begins with her own view, which involves her feelings about herself and her relationship to others—the father of the child, parents, siblings, and friends. Her personal view of what to do is influenced by her religious and moral feelings. Her view of herself as a woman and as a "maybe" mother enter into the decision. She is often filled with ambivalence and confusion.

There is in each woman a view of herself as a potential mother. The conflict between her thoughts of childlessness and motherhood can cause alarm in a woman who is not sure that she wants to be pregnant. She resents the child's intrusion on her life, while at the same time fantasizing about her new life with a baby. She immediately begins to form a view of herself as a "mother," no matter what decision she will make about the baby she carries.

In this moment of great uncertainty, many others give their opinions about the unplanned pregnancy. Everyone *knows* what the unhappily pregnant woman should do. Everyone tells her what she should do. Parents, siblings, friends—all give her their opinions on the subject. And all she gets is more confused. The woman, confused and hurried by time pressures, needs to look objectively at all available alternatives. There are advocates, not necessarily equally represented, for each of the alternatives.

The father of the child has his say, even though it is quite limited legally; he has no legal right to prevent or to force termination of the pregnancy. Jeff, age fifteen, found this out the hard way. He convinced Sue, age sixteen, that they should "get rid of the baby" the first time she was pregnant. A friend told her that if she took a lot of birth control pills, she would miscarry—and she did. The second pregnancy in the same year found her reluctant to abort. Jeff convinced her again to get an abortion. She delayed as long as possible, then finally terminated twins. Jeff insisted to no avail that she use the pill or some other contraceptive. She never "remembered." Her third pregnancy, at seventeen—which she decided to complete—surprised him. He tried to convince her to abort, but she refused. He was responsible financially for the baby boy she later delivered. He made child support payments for about two years and then disappeared.

The unmarried father seldom has a legal right to prevent the pregnant woman from placing the child for adoption; however, he does have a legal right to be considered as the appropriate home for the child. Well-publicized recent court cases have clearly, and at times painfully, demonstrated this right. Although the birth father's rights are limited, they are increasing.

No one else has a legal say in the mother's decision making about the fate of her unborn child. Grandparents' rights are not considered, but we know that grandparents have tremendous impact on pregnancy decisions.[14] Siblings are not considered. Thus the impact of others is likely to be felt but is not being sustained in the courts.

And if the woman looks for help outside of her family, where does she turn? Today, most young women finding themselves pregnant consider only abortion or keeping the baby; that is what their friends did.

Raising the baby is an option increasingly chosen. At one point, the single mother was viewed with alarm. Now, with unwed single mothers merging with other women who are frequently in and out of marriages, society barely takes a second glance. Celebrities, not just television characters, who have elected to remain single while carrying a child actually glamorize this choice. The romanticism and independence of having a baby and handling it on one's own (although "own" usually means with help from parents or the government) also encourages single parenting. But under the Welfare Reform Act, single parenting is under fire from Congress and beleaguered taxpayers who want welfare rolls decreased. This could have a marked effect on children available for adoption.

"Pregnancy counseling," as it is popularly called, is a deception. The alternatives to a pregnancy are not commonly presented in an unbiased manner. Each group that does "pregnancy counseling" has something to advocate—to sell. Most groups adhere to a philosophy that causes them to champion one specific solution or another. They may believe in zero population growth, or they may believe that abortion is murder. Seldom is this bias made explicit to the woman who seeks help. If you open your newspaper, you are likely to find classified ads for "pregnancy counseling" under the Personals heading. The young woman who turns to the "counselors" for help is trying to make a good decision about her unborn child. Unfortunately, she seldom has a chance to explore equally all the alternatives open to her. The biases of the counselor prevent this exploration.

The sad part is that the unsuspecting woman, usually young, does not even realize she has not explored all her options. She believes she has had pregnancy counseling in order to make the best decision. Women who have truly explored all of the alternatives might consider adoption. Women who have not even considered adoption represent a virtually untapped source of babies for people seeking a child to adopt.

Adoption has only recently begun to have effective advocates. The adoption agencies' workers are not a visible or vocal group advocating adoption. Outreach programs and searches for potential biological parents to place children for adoption are unheard of. But a new group of dedicated individuals is changing this. This group is looking for babies to adopt and they are looking everywhere. You read about them in the newspapers. You see them on the talk shows. You even come across their personal letters seeking babies on the Internet. It is not a group advocacy, and it doesn't usually result in legislation, but it is a ripple that is being felt in adoption that is long overdue.

Summary

Some women become pregnant too easily, and others not at all. This underlying difference can cause problems throughout the adoption process. If you understand the cause of these problems, you can perhaps prevent them from affecting your adoption.

Adoptive couples very often have difficulty understanding how a birth mother could possibly give up her child. Wanting so much to have a child prevents the infertile couple from being able to place themselves in the position of the birth mother and can even create some alienation. It increases their fears that the birth mother will change her mind, and it may even cause them to look down on her. Adopting couples need to view the dilemma of an unwanted pregnancy from the woman's perspective which may have grown foreign to them in their struggle with infertility.

Put yourself in a different place as you begin your search. Attempt to understand how someone who doesn't want to be pregnant might still risk a pregnancy. (You may even have been there at another time in your life, before you discovered that you couldn't get pregnant.) Look at the complexities of pregnancy from the perspective of one who accidentally gets pregnant. (You certainly are able to understand the complexities from the perspective of one who *cannot* get pregnant.) You are doing two things by trying to change your perspective: learning places to explore in your search for a baby and learning to understand and accept the birth mother of your child.

Come to grips with the angry feelings you have about someone who can so easily do that which you cannot. People entering adoption with anger toward birth mothers are likely to have problems in the process. Without understanding and resolving your feelings of anger, you may create problems or cause the failure of the adoption you so much want.

An unhappily pregnant woman might consider adoption if she understood how many people would like to raise the child she is carrying. Even today, a pregnant woman is likely to view her child as unwanted. Women who abandon or "throw away" babies they don't want are unaware of the strong desire of infertile people who search for a child to adopt. The need to change this misconception is evident. In reality, the woman carries within her a valuable person desperately wanted by thousands of people. Perhaps adoption offers a solution for herself, the child, and some potential parents. She needs to feel she can do something beneficial for her baby. Adoption is a viable, healthy alternative to unwanted pregnancy and needs to be promoted as an alternative for pregnant women to consider.

If you, the adopting couple, understand the reasons women use or do not use contraceptives, you will learn the best places to search for women who might place a child for adoption with you. An understanding of some women's unconscious motivation to become pregnant might give you additional clues in your search. Knowing the inadequacies of the counseling system open to the pregnant woman gives you an additional source of potential babies to explore. Understanding your own feelings, even angry feelings, about the ease of fertility the birth mother has and you don't have, will help you relate to her. If you know where the babies have gone, it helps you to understand where they might still be found.

CHAPTER 4

Special Parents
with Special Needs

TODAY'S FAMILIES COME IN ALL different sizes and shapes. In response, our definition of "family" has been forced to change. No longer do adoption agencies dare look only for the ideal family; the increased militancy of various groups has made it more difficult to say no on the basis of undocumented criteria—unless they want a lawsuit. This doesn't mean that traditional agencies are now receptive to any kind of family—it means they are *more* receptive. It also means that losing business to less traditional agencies, independent adoption, and international adoption is forcing them to be more flexible in selecting what is acceptable for a parent or parents.

The newly accepted parents in our society include single and unmarried parents, physically disabled parents, parents with medical problems, parents of large families, older parents, military parents, foster parents, and same-sex-couple parents. A new group that has begun to gain acceptance for adoption is made up of low-income people. All of these groups of people have traditionally run into problems when seeking to adopt a child, even though most professionals wouldn't suggest that children born to parents in these less-than-traditional groups should be taken from their parents. Certain characteristics may be used against these special parents in disputed custody arrangements, but they aren't grounds for the state agency in charge of protecting children to come in and say that they are unfit guardians. Some may not fit the traditional picture of the ideal parents, but they usually find their capacity to parent being questioned only when they seek to adopt. Even if you fit one of these categories, now you *can* adopt a child.

Single Parents

Single people have been adopting children ever since adoption has been part of our society. At times these arrangements were made informally between the birth parent and a friend or relative. Many times arrangements were made through independent adoptions. Earlier in this century, single parents were able to find acceptance within agencies primarily by adopting "special" children. Then, just as single parents were becoming more widely acceptable, the number of babies available declined, leaving fewer children; babies for single parents became a rarity as two-parent families pushed single-parent adoptions aside.

Single parenting is not a new idea. Many families with two parents are, in reality, examples of single parenting, and the rise in divorce rates in recent years has made single parenting commonplace. Even children placed in adoptive homes with couples must contend with the possibility that they, too, will be raised by a single parent for a period of time. Adopting a child is no marital guarantee. Divorce, or even death, is a possibility in all families whether the child is or is not adopted. The emphasis of traditional adoption agencies on two-parent homes can be an exercise in futility. Frequently when a divorced parent raises a child or when a single parent adopts, we are talking more about temporary singleness rather than single parenting. Many single parents are single only for a time.

Studies of single parents who adopt compared with couples find that the children from single-parent homes actually do better emotionally, with fewer failed adoptions occurring.[1] When other factors are controlled, such as the age of the child at placement, the researchers find that little difference exists between a child's adjustment to a single-parent adoption and to adoption by two parents. Studies do find differences in adoptions characterized by the age of adoptive parents, their level of education, their amount of income, and other demographic details, but not on the success of adoption or the adjustment of the child to adoption.

Nonetheless, adoption agencies view single parents who seek to adopt as second-choice parents, to be considered only if two-parent homes are unavailable. They are probably not the last choice, but they are way down the list. And ironically, the adoption agencies give the least desirable, hardest-to-raise children to the parents at the bottom of the list, the ones the agencies think are the least desirable and least equipped to be good parents.

Agencies carefully scrutinize the motives of the single person seeking a child, so be prepared with appropriate answers for their questions. (Actually, some of the same questions will be asked of you by birth parents in an independent adoption.) They really ought to be asked of any parent. Areas of concern include:

- *Support systems:* Who are the supportive people in your family and among your friends? All people considering a family should determine where they will find support as they begin the demanding task of parenting. Support can be found from relatives and friends, churches, clubs, neighborhoods, and from whatever source the person looks to when they are in need of help. Single parents who have strong relationships with friends and relatives are viewed much more favorably than those who don't.
- *Child care plan:* Who will care for the child when you are working? Have a plan; you want to show that you are informed and that you have looked at this thoughtfully and know how to handle it. You also need a plan for when your child is sick and you have to be at work. Again, these issues should be addressed by anyone who is planning a family, but as a single parent, you are more likely to be asked questions about them.
- *People of opposite sex:* A child being raised by a single person needs to be around people of both sexes. Show the social worker or the birth

parents that the child will have both men and women in his or her life.

- *Marriage plans:* It is interesting that people become concerned about the potential marriage of someone who is a single parent. They are worried first that the person will be a single parent raising a child, and then they want to know what will happen if the person gets married. Be prepared for questions about your future and marriage plans— they will undoubtedly be asked.
- *Disaster plan:* Each of us should have a plan about what will happen to our children if something happens to us, but this question is more likely to be raised when you are adopting as a single parent.

Potential single parents should consider these factors as well as all of the ordinary parenting traits adoption agencies and birth parents are looking for.

You, as a single parent, are in a difficult place to compete if you are going through an adoption agency to find a child. Even when you clearly demonstrate that you meet all of the agency's criteria, you will still stand only a minimal chance against a couple who wants the same child. In many ways you are a long shot even in an independent adoption, because one of the main reasons many women elect to place a child for adoption is that they feel they cannot do an adequate job of raising the child as a single mother. You need to be prepared to overcome these negative odds.

A few situations compel the adoption agencies to seek single-parent homes for children they place. A child may have some specific problems that preclude adjustment to two parents at the same time. For example, a child may have been the victim of sexual abuse in a previous home, which may hinder his or her adjustment with a couple. Another child might simply not find an adoptive placement with a couple; most agencies would believe that a permanent placement with a single parent is far better than no placement at all.

Alicia was thirty-two, single, and African American. Her singleness was not in her favor when she went to adopt, but her race was. The fact that she wanted a child who was at least five years old was also a distinct advantage. The adoption agency welcomed her with open arms. They had far more black children than they had black homes. If they could not place an African American child with a couple, their second choice would certainly be an African American single woman. Even though Caucasian couples actively seek black children, such a placement would be a last alternative for many adoption agencies.

While most Caucasian couples would wait a long time to have a child placed with them, Alicia was rapidly processed and approved. Within six months of her initial inquiry, the agency invited her to hear about Alexandra. Alexandra was six years old; she had been relinquished ten months earlier because her birth mother felt unable to care for her. Before her relinquishment, Alexandra had had a series of babysitters as primary caretakers. She seemed exceptionally mature in her ability to handle many situations, but exceptionally immature in dealing with people. Because Alexandra had difficulty in group situations and tended to withdraw from all people in those circumstances, the agency worker felt a single-parent situation had some advantages for her. With this in mind, the adoption agency worker reasoned the home Alicia could provide would be a desirable one. Alexandra would not be as overwhelmed as she might be in a two-parent home. In reality, the primary reason she was placed with Alicia was not because of her tendency to withdraw but because the agency needed a home with an African American parent.

Alicia and Alexandra met and slowly got to know each other. The placement did not occur until Alicia had a vacation from her job as a schoolteacher, so they could spend time together before school began. The first day of Christmas vacation, Alexandra brought one small suitcase as she came to stay permanently in her new home. Only now is she beginning to believe this is a permanent home for her; her adoption has been finalized and she has been with Alicia for over a year. She had never been with any one person for that length of time before.

As a single parent who seeks to adopt, help teach your agency about the role a single parent can have in remedying problems of certain "special" children like Alexandra. Convince the agency of your ability to help with the special-needs child, remembering that your chance of proving to them that you are the best parent for a "normal" infant is small.

Harriet was an exceptionally bright, independent woman who had completed medical school and was in private practice in a small community. She had never been married and did not consider this likely in the near future, but she did want to have a child. She believed she had a great deal to offer. She felt very strongly about the effect of early childhood experiences, and therefore she wanted an infant. When she approached an adoption agency, everyone who met her was impressed with her friendly, intelligent manner. Her financial independence was obviously in her favor, and at thirty-one, she was well within the age limits the agency sought. Yet her single status worked against her. At any other time when babies were more available, the adoption agency would probably have accepted an applicant of Harriet's caliber. But in this time of infants' scarcity the agency would not consider giving her an infant. Harriet's application was denied. The social worker from the agency talked with her about older children or children with other special needs, but Harriet really felt she wanted an infant and was not ready to compromise. She gave up on the agency. Alone, she simply could not compete with a couple in the agency's view of what was needed to be a good parent. She adopted independently.

In reality, the easiest way for most single people to find babies is to adopt independently. If you, as a single parent, expect to find a child through an adoption agency, be prepared for a long, arduous process. Be prepared to prove your parenting skills and motives. Be prepared to be put far down on a waiting list for a child to adopt. Be prepared to accept a special-needs child. The singles who are most likely to adopt a child are those who really go out and find one on their own. You may pursue the agencies, but also pursue a child independently.

Jake was twenty-nine and single. He had been active in Big Brothers for five years, and he decided he wanted to do even more with children. He wanted a son to share his life. He knew he had little chance with an adoption agency. He found it was even more difficult for a single male to be accepted than for a single female—people tend to suspect that a male who wants to adopt is a potential child molester. He had almost given up hope when he met Jason.

Jason was five years old and one of eight children. Both of his parents worked and he and his siblings were pretty much left on their own.

Jason was spending more and more time alone and at Big Brothers groups, where he met Jake. They immediately hit it off. Every day Jason came to Jake's house or to the fire station where Jake worked; because of Jake's work schedule, he was able to spend a lot of time with the boy. Jake had Jason over to dinner most nights of the week. They even traveled together during summer vacation. It wasn't long before Jason was hardly ever at his "real" home.

Jason was outspoken about wanting to live with Jake. He asked Jake if he could stay permanently. Jake agree that he, too, would like this, but he didn't know if Jason's parents would accept the idea. After numerous meetings and lengthy discussions about Jason's best interests, the boy's mother and father agreed to allow Jake to legally adopt Jason. This was an unusual way for anyone to find a son, but it worked. Of course, it's possible that Jake's strong desire for a son led him into a situation where he could find one. Jason still has contact with his birth parents and his brothers and sisters, but he calls Jake "Dad."

Mary had read a great deal about adoption and decided she wanted to be a single parent. She began her quest looking into independent arrangements. She had a lot to offer, but her most important feature was her willingness to take a child of any race. She approached an attorney who specialized in adoption and didn't have to wait very long. When he learned of her willingness to take a child of any race, he put the word out, and within two months she had two leads. Because this was not an agency adoption, her willingness to take a child of a different race enabled her to find a baby and to find not just one but two— quickly. In her case, being single caused little problem in her search.

Find out about the problems of both obtaining and raising a child as a single person. All of the literature on single parenting is as appropriate for adoptive parents as it is for other single parents. Contact the National Council for Single Adoptive Parents (see Appendix F) or find a list of single-parent support groups on the Internet or through Adoptive Families of America, Inc. (see Appendix F). Other organizations to contact are the Adoption Resource Exchange for Single Parents, Inc., or the National Adoption Information Clearinghouse (see Appendix F). Some of these groups will be specifically for adoptive parents. Attend group meetings of parents who have special-needs children, because if you get a child through an adoption agency, that is probably the kind of child who will be placed with you. Also read books on single parenting such as *In Praise of Single Parents: Mothers and Fathers Embracing the Challenge; Single Mothers by Choice: A Guidebook for Single Women Who Are Considering Motherhood;* or *The Handbook for Single Adoptive Parents.*[2] The more informed you are, the better job you will do.

Physically Disabled Parents

Someone who has a physical disability can expect to meet with difficulties when adopting. The chance of an adoption agency placing a child with a parent who has a major physical disability is slight, except in unusual circumstances. Agencies seldom publicize this criterion, because that would invite lawsuits charging them with discrimination. Nevertheless, though neither written nor spoken, discrimination is there.

If there were many babies and few applicants, physically disabled people would have less difficulty adopting through an agency. Since just the reverse is true, those with disabilities are in an extremely difficult position. They simply are too far down the list of acceptable applicants to have much chance for a child.

In certain situations, adoption agencies believe that a child with a physical disability might be best placed in a home where one of the parents also has a physical disability. For instance, the special needs of a child who must use a wheelchair mandate that the home be able to accommodate the wheelchair. To convert a home to accommodate a wheelchair can be quite costly, but a parent with a similar physical disability may provide a home already equipped for the child. Another instance would be when a child's adjustment to his or her disability is not going well; the emotional support of a parent who also has a disability might help the child accept his or her own challenge.

Lauren is one example of a child who did not adjust well to her disability. At twelve years old she had spent most of her life in a wheelchair due to cerebral palsy, and she was withdrawn and depressed. She made two suicide attempts that caused her to be made a ward of the court, because her birth mother felt unable to cope with her depression and her rages. At the time, much negative publicity concerning long-term foster care caused Lauren's social worker to approach the birth mother about relinquishing Lauren for adoption rather than having her remain in her current foster home. Lauren's mother felt that any chance would be worth taking if Lauren could be happier. Lauren had been in psychotherapy for several years; her therapist felt her depression was related to seeing herself as different from everyone else and recommended that, if possible, she be placed with a person who had a similar disability. The adoption agency's psychological evaluation also found evidence that Lauren would be best placed in a home with someone who had a similar problem.

These recommendations gave Ted and Marie their chance to adopt a child. Marie had used a wheelchair since she was paralyzed in an automobile accident at the age of nine. Since that time, she had learned to be relatively self-sufficient. She drove a specially equipped car, and she and Ted had made changes in their house to accommodate her wheelchair. The halls were wider than usual, there was a ramp to the front door, the shower was specially designed, and all of the doors were wide. Ted's help and understanding and Marie's fortitude and perseverance enabled her to function rather independently. The adoption agency felt Marie's example and Ted's help could be extremely beneficial to Lauren.

Lauren met Ted and Marie but she told her social worker that she didn't like them. The social worker encouraged Lauren to give the relationship some time to develop. Lauren stayed overnight with them and watched Marie maneuver about the house expertly in her wheelchair. The young girl could see Marie doing things she had never considered doing for herself. More visits followed; each one brought Lauren closer to Ted and Marie. She finally told the social worker that she wanted to stay with them. Lauren has changed dramatically in her new home; she is happy and feeling good about herself. It doesn't always happen so quickly. Lauren found a new way of life because she found some "special" parents who wanted to adopt a child.

Most disabled people would not be willing to wait for these occasional occurrences. As a result, these special parents generally seek a child independently rather than through an adoption agency. Even if they would prefer to adopt through an agency, they recognize that such a choice is seldom available to them.

Cynthia received a letter from one woman who describes beautifully the plight of the physically disabled person seeking to adopt. We hesitate to include a "fan" letter, but we believe this woman tells the story better than we possibly could. We have never met her, but her letter tells a great deal about her and about the possibilities in independent adoption:

Dear Cynthia:

There are no words to adequately describe what you have done to my life. As I write this my three-month-old son is squealing with delight at the antics of his father. He fills my heart with a joy I would never have known without you and your work. Your book once again gave my husband and me the courage to try to adopt.

Even though I have cerebral palsy and have been in a wheelchair for twelve years, my husband and I were devastated by our rejection by the state Adoption Exchange nine years ago. After allowing us to go through the interviews and screening process for a year we were turned down on the basis of my disability. It was a shock to us, as we felt we had much to offer a child and felt that the agency would see that through the process. Unfortunately, they couldn't see anything past my wheelchair.

During the years afterward, we filled our lives with careers and each other. We were always happy, yet we were truly incomplete. We resolved to forget about a family but never could. Nothing filled the void of what might have been.

One of the ways I tried to compensate for the lack of a child was my involvement in the disability movement. It was this involvement which made me aware of the new laws that prohibit discrimination. Our hope that things had changed was the foundation of our decision last July to try once again to adopt.

The very first step we took was buying your book. I went in to find information on adoption and I found you. I read (I should say devoured) it in two days. My husband took it the next two, and within the week we had appointments with agencies and gynecologists and had the name of a good attorney. We followed your instructions to a T, however we didn't get very far with the agencies. On the second Tuesday of our "project," I made contact with a woman who worked as a clerk in a shop we often went into. We told her (as we decided we would tell as many people as possible) that we wanted to adopt and if she heard of any pregnant women who might be interested in adoption to please let us know. She called four days later, we referred her to the attorney whom we had contacted in the meantime, and four months after that our son was born.

Our attorney is wonderful. The woman in the shop is wonderful and will keep the information about the birth and adoptive parents confidential at the request of all concerned. At this point, the state from which we are adopting him was not discriminatory in any way.

The next step is the final one in court. We hope to get a court date within the next two weeks.

Dearest Cynthia, the next time you get burnt out by the injustices in the world or the frustrations that befall each of us, know that two thousand miles away is a family that is complete because you cared enough to share your heart and soul with the world. If I could wrap you in a rainbow, it wouldn't be enough.

Her letter speaks for the problems many disabled people are forced to face, and for the joys of adopting.

Disabled people are not very well understood in our society. We look at them from afar and generally our response is pity and gratitude about not being in their place. We debate philosophically at what point we would no longer want to survive as a disabled person. This is easy to debate when it isn't reality. Few people understand the richness and the value of living that is open to the physically challenged person. Unless you have personal knowledge of someone who is disabled, it is difficult to comprehend that life. Very few disabled people would consider their lives worthless or unproductive. They anticipate and enjoy life in many ways that people without disabilities do and in some ways that others do not.

In the past, disabled people were not expected to live long or productive lives. With technical and medical advances, the life span and capabilities of even the most seriously disabled people have been significantly improved. However, our society's responses to them are still antiquated. Our primary concessions to the physically disadvantaged population are convenient parking places and special restroom facilities, and some people resent even these accommodations. We are not yet able to view the disabled as people with familiar needs, concerns, and dreams. We are not able to view them as meeting our criteria for becoming adequate parents.

A person with a physical disability who wants to adopt an infant needs to be prepared for a difficult struggle. Do your homework, understand the obstacles you face, and anticipate the questions you will be asked. Don't rule out adoption for yourself. Just know that it is going to be more difficult for you than for someone else. If you give up, you won't have a baby for sure. And if you try, you may find people willing to help. You may find an adoption agency that will help you. You may find a birth parent who will identify with your struggle for some reason and pick you. You may look into another country where attitudes about your disability are different. Who knows who might be looking for adoptive parents just like you.

Parents with Other Medical Problems

People with serious medical problems who want to adopt children through an agency are in an extremely difficult position. Agencies routinely seek a medical checkup before they will consider placing a child with a couple; if this checkup indicates any serious medical conditions, the adoption agency will place this home on the ineligible list.

Although people who are not in the best of health get pregnant and people who already have children may discover at any point that they have a medical problem, this same "luxury" is denied the infertile couple. Excellent health is a prerequisite for parenting—at least if you are adopting through most agencies, which currently have a limited number of babies.

John and Susan sought a child through an agency and were turned down. John is a diabetic and uses insulin to control his disease. The adoption agency denied their application because of his medical problem; the couple felt they had no other choice but to look for a child in another country.

Sarah and Allan wanted to adopt a child through a public adoption agency, but Sarah had a heart problem and the agency would not consider their application. Sarah and Allan knew that she might not live to an old age, but they did believe she was likely to raise a child to adulthood, and despite the uncertainty of their future, they knew they wanted a child in it. Their search took slightly longer than average, but they found a child. They spoke honestly with the birth mother about Sarah's condition. The birth mother is quite satisfied with the home she chose for her son and is confident in Allan's ability to parent if anything ever happens to Sarah.

Margo and Brian had been married for four years when they approached the adoption agency. They knew Margo was unlikely to become pregnant because of severely scarred tubes, but they felt positive about adopting. So they went to the local public adoption agency but received a very cold response. Their application for a child was never accepted. No one told them why they were rejected, but they both believe it was because of Margo's size. Margo weighs 225 pounds. Neither she nor Brian believed her weight would affect her ability to adequately mother a child. The fact that they have subsequently adopted two children who are happy and healthy verifies Margo's belief in herself as a mother. The question for them was not, Will we adopt?, but How will we adopt?

Kelly and Frank presented a different problem. They knew an agency would not consider them because Kelly had cancer. The cancer had been in remission for four years and they felt they didn't want to wait any longer to begin experiencing the joys of parenting, so they decided to pursue independent adoption. Kelly wasn't sure what to say about her health. She agonized over this because she was an honest person who knew she could not hide the problem from the birth mother.

However, to mention cancer in her résumé seemed too much of a red flag. She finally decided not to discuss her health in a letter, but to tell the birth mother after she met her. Her honesty was repaid when Kelly and Frank met Beverly. Beverly really liked Kelly and appreciated Kelly's candor. Kelly's long period of remission convinced Beverly that Kelly was free of cancer, and Beverly's strong positive feelings toward Frank and about the kind of father he would be gave the backup she needed. The quality of parenting was the most important factor to Beverly, she decided these were the people for her child. She gave them Michael, seven pounds and two ounces.

All these couples wanted a child but their medical problems precluded receiving help from traditional adoption agencies, which, seeking the "best" parents, had set standards none of them could meet. This is an understandable problem in today's adoption scene, but it does not make it fair to the many applicants who are eliminated.

Fortunately, many newer agencies will leave the decision on the importance of medical problems to the birth parents. Otherwise, you can always go outside the agency system and look to independent and international adoptions as a way to have a family. If you have a medical problem, don't despair. Babies are available, but they just may take some extra work to find.

Older Parents

People who are older than most biological parents fall into the "special" category—they do not fit into the fixed limits that adoption agencies have set as the "proper" ages for parenting. The greater the number of children available, the greater the age range considered appropriate for an adoptive parent of an infant. So, in this time of scarcity, when older couples seek to adopt at a traditional agency, the only children they are offered are probably special needs. Usually this means disabled or older children.

Nature has set a biological limit on women who want to give birth. Once a woman has reached menopause, usually in her late forties, she can no longer conceive. In our society, women have traditionally had children in their twenties, but this age is increasing because many women are delaying their first pregnancy. The adoption agencies are looking for parents of what they would consider "normal" childbearing age. In general, this means someone who is between twenty-two and thirty years older than the child they wish to adopt. As the woman's age increases, she stands less and less chance of adopting an infant because the agency deems her not within the normal range.

Millie and Lester had led an interesting life during their twelve-year marriage. They first met in their early twenties when they served in the Peace Corps. They both loved to travel, so when they met again years later and married, they set off to see the world. They collaborated on articles that paid their expenses as they lived in one country after another. When they finally decided they were ready to settle down in one place and raise a family, Millie was forty-one and Lester was forty-three. They found no reason that would explain their infertility. After trying to conceive for a year, they approached an agency to adopt a baby. The social worker spoke with them about the scarcity of babies and about the greater availability of older children. But Millie and Lester felt they wanted to experience a baby, so the adoption agency turned them down.

Fortunately, in their world travels Lester and Millie had met many people in different countries and so had a long list of contacts. These connections eventually led them to an infant born in Colombia. They flew there, filled out the numerous necessary papers, received their baby, and came home. Their adventure in baby hunting gave them not only a darling baby daughter, Lina, but also material for an article that they subsequently sold.

Obviously, Millie and Lester didn't fit the agency's criteria for suitable parents for a baby. At the same time, it certainly seems that their interesting lives would enrich the life of any child they would adopt. From the adoption agency's standpoint, they should probably have enriched an older child's life rather than a baby's. But it's hardly as if Millie or Lester were elderly; many parents have successfully raised children they conceived late in life.

Similarly, Sandy and Al wanted a child even though they were in their early forties. When they approached the adoption agencies, they were encouraged to consider adopting an older child. When they heard about this option, it seemed extremely appealing to them. A baby wasn't a necessity for them, so they were able to work within the agency system. This doesn't make them any better parents than Millie or Lester, who couldn't fit into the adoption agency system; it just made them easier to help.

An increasing number of potential couples involve one person who has already raised a family and is now married to another who has never had children. That was the case with Lisa and Donald. It was a third marriage for Donald, who already had three children. He was sixty-three when he met Lisa and he felt he had it all. He was wealthy, distinguished looking, and the CEO of a company he had started. Lisa was forty-two and had been married once but had no children. She had no hesitation about marrying Donald, and for three years she was content. Then she began to talk more and more about adoption.

Donald and Lisa were in a unique position because of the financial status they enjoyed. They went to an attorney who specialized in adoptions, and often expensive ones. The birth mothers who came to this attorney enjoyed the support from couples who could afford to help them generously but legally. Despite the couple's ages, they presented themselves very well to Christy, who was four months along. She decided she would place her baby with them.

Lisa accompanied Christy to all of her medical appointments. She and Donald helped the young woman move into a comfortable apartment near the hospital. They provided a car for her to get to her doctor's appointments. They helped her buy maternity clothes that would have been the envy of many pregnant women. And not only did they provide these material items for Christy, they were also there for her emotionally. They cared for her, spent time with her, and liked her, and she liked them.

Lisa and Donald are now parents to four-year-old Catherine. She is a delight to both of them. Donald's other family has mixed feelings about Catherine but is growing to accept her; Lisa and Donald maintain contact with Christy and send pictures twice a year. There is no question that one of the reasons they have this child is because of their financial resources. But it took more than that. They did the right things financially *and* emotionally for Christy. They also followed through on all of their agreements and treated her with respect. Everyone gained from this adoption.

One couple much like Lisa and Donald asked their regular attorney to find out how they could adopt. He made calls to many agencies and individuals involved in adoption and spent hours researching the process for them; he found many sources including a *Directory for Adoptive Parents over 40,* which identifies approximately two hundred groups and individuals willing to help older people find and adopt a child.[3] He found a surprisingly large number of newer, less traditional agencies that would be willing to take applications for adoption from the couple. But he also found it can be very expensive and complex to sort out all of the potential places anyone can go. Within six months, Lisa and Donald had a lead from one of the agencies working with couples who adopt independently.

In contrast to Lisa and Donald's experience, Cynthia and her husband, David, decided to adopt and it cost them virtually nothing. Cynthia was sixty and David was sixty-three. They read about three available children in the newspaper and pursued it. They succeeded. One of the reasons they succeeded is lack of anyone else who was interested in adopting three children, especially three children who were teenagers.

Older parents definitely fit into the category of special moms and dads. If these special parents want special children, they may be able to adopt through an agency. The quality of parenting from older parents is not the issue, because there is no reason to believe older people make better or worse parents than others. The issue is more that older parents aren't "normal," and the adoption agency system is currently designed primarily for "normal" moms and dads.

Older people need to be resourceful as they approach adoption. They need to be more creative than younger couples. This certainly doesn't mean that adoption is impossible for older couples, though it probably does mean that they stand very little chance of adopting from a traditional agency. A more progressive agency, an independent adoption, or an international adoption are all possible ways for the older couple to adopt.

Parents of Large Families

While motion pictures may glorify large families, our society tends to have mixed feelings about them. Couples who already have two or more children get little chance of adopting through an agency. This may be because of the lack of adoptable children and a desire to give childless couples a first chance, but another cause could be that, once again, these adopters fit into the "different" category. According to agencies, couples with more than two children are termed large families.

The agencies' belief that a large family cannot meet the special needs of an adopted child, especially one who may have some difficulties, usually prevents the placement of children in these homes. While the successes of large adoptive families such as the DeBolts with their thirteen adopted children are well known, it is clear that even they could not have found their children through the traditional agencies.[4] Probably most traditional agencies would have rejected the DeBolts before they adopted any children at all, on the basis that they already had biological children.

A large family, rather than being detrimental or a family of second choice, would be the best home available for some children. Margaret Ward, a Canadian writer, speaks of the kinds of children who might be better placed in a large-family adoptive home:[5]

- Children who cannot relate easily to adults or parental figures
- Children who are emotionally detached, who need to move slowly in forming new relationships
- Children who become stifled by demands for intense parent-child relationships
- Children who need to experience social contact in a small, close situation before being able to handle the demands of society for social contact
- Children who are withdrawn, who may need stimulation
- Children who have language problems because they have not learned to verbalize adequately
- Children who need structure, but structure with flexibility
- Children at high risk

- Children in need of nurturing
- Children lacking a firm sense of identity

The involvement of not only adoptive parents but also multiple siblings provides diverse role models and sources of contact. At the same time, the contacts are not as concentrated or as intense as in small families. Large families are generally quite verbal, which enhances communication. Siblings take on more important roles in large families, which may be especially beneficial to certain adopted children. Having many members in a family gives many sources of love and affection and offers a miniature society in which children can experiment with different behaviors. And large families, while generally imposing structure and demands on each member in order to function, are seldom rigid; they simply don't have the time. This allows the flexibility that many children need.

Occasionally adoption agencies will bend their rules to accommodate a birth mother's request, and this may help a special parent. Molly came from a family of nine children and Tim from a family of five children. When they married, they knew they would also like to have a large family. They had three children by birth and then, unexpectedly, Molly had to have a hysterectomy. Undaunted, they went to an adoption agency intent upon enlarging their family in a different way. They were good parents, acceptable to the agency in every way—except that they already had three children. Despite all their pleas, they were told that their application would not be accepted because there were simply not enough children to go around to all the people who wanted them. Molly and Tim didn't know where else to go. Two months after their rejection, the social worker from the agency called them and asked them to come in for another interview. She had learned of a birth mother who insisted that her child be placed in a home with at least three or four children. The agency now wanted Molly and Tim to complete a home study so that this child could be placed with them. They had a fourth child in their family within two months.

Molly and Tim are a good example of an adoption agency bending rules. They are also a good example of the control the birth mother can have in placing her child through an agency, if she insists on certain requirements. Great pressure may be needed to convince adoption agencies to modify procedures that do not seem relevant or timely. Parents who wish to adopt and who are in this position need to take a more aggressive role in educating the agencies about the quality of life in large families.

The concept of the large family as a desirable choice for some children being placed for adoption has not been well studied. It is difficult to study something that is available so rarely. The obvious and common successes of large families created by birth should indicate the appropriateness of children being placed in this type of family situation. As progressive agencies offer birth parents a more active role in selecting adoptive parents, some birth parents will choose larger families. But for most people looking to have a large family through adoption, independent and international adoption continue to be the best options.

Foster Parents

Foster parents are not like any other kinds of parents. They have children, either through an agency or some other arrangement, but they don't *really* have them. They are supposed to love them and commit to them, but easily give them up when the "temporary" placement is ended. They are supposed to be available to, but not demanding of, the social workers with whom they work. They are supposed to be knowledgeable about raising children, but they are infrequently involved with decisions about a child's welfare. If children in foster care are called children in limbo, foster parents could well be called parents in limbo.

Many children are currently in foster homes; estimates range as high as 500,000.[6] Children in foster homes are those whose birth parents for some reason do not choose to or are unable to care for them. The state may take a child from her parents and place her in foster care, or parents may seek it themselves. Parents who can't cope with their children, for one reason or another, may ask someone to become a substitute parent. Overwhelmed people who have little money may have their children put in foster homes. Overwhelmed people who have enough money to hire a substitute parent use baby-sitters, boarding schools, or nannies. Some people are able to solicit help from relatives. If we could add up the many children who are being raised by people other than birth parents but are not actually in state foster care, the figures would be alarmingly high.

Children in foster homes fall into one of several categories.

- *Children waiting for adoption:* These are children who have been relinquished and for whom no permanent home has yet been found. Many of these children will have no difficulty being placed for adoption.
- *Children whose birth parents are committed to them:* These children's parents, due to temporary problems, are unable to care for them. While they do have contact with their families, these children live temporarily in foster homes.
- *Children whose birth parents are not committed to them:* These children have not been released for adoption, but their original families are not committed to them. Nothing is being done to change the circumstances for the child, nor is anything being done to change the circumstances of the parents. These are the children we read about in the newspapers, lost in the foster care system. They stay and stay and stay.

Foster parents of these different groups of children have different feelings about their situations. Foster parents of the first two groups see their role as temporary, as indeed it usually is. The third group of parents finds themselves providing homes for these children on a more permanent basis. At times they want to adopt a child for whom they have become primary parents; the permanency of the situation can create strong family ties.[7] Previously, adoption agency workers who saw this closeness developing between foster parents and foster children often removed the child immediately.[8] These people had been approved as foster parents, not adoptive parents. To allow them to adopt would drain a valuable source of good foster homes.

The rules for becoming adoptive parents have traditionally been more stringent than for becoming foster parents; many foster parents are older, less educated, and less financially stable than the pool of parents seeking to adopt. Since many times the most difficult to raise children are kept in foster homes, it would seem that the foster parent is the parent who should be most carefully screened.

The term *psychological parent,* which entered the adoption scene with the publication of the book *Beyond the Best Interests of the Child,*[9] has changed the status of foster parents and made a tremendous impact on the overall view of long-term foster care. The amount of time a child can be kept apart from his or her parents before experiencing feelings of abandonment has been reconsidered. Psychological abandonment is now felt to vary on the basis of the child's age; the younger the child, the sooner the child feels abandoned. As a result, long-term foster care is being given careful scrutiny. At times, agencies are aggressively trying to have foster children declared legally abandoned, so they can be more quickly placed in a permanent adoptive home.[10]

The biggest difficulty for children caught in the foster care system is not being able to establish a feeling of permanence or rootedness. Children who learn that all homes are temporary learn to withhold love. When these children are finally released for adoption, the task for the new parents is a difficult one. This is why the current push toward shortening the stay of children in foster homes has occurred; it is also the reason that, in some cases, adoption of children by their foster parents is now being allowed. At least the beginning stage of establishing roots has been started in the foster home.

Resenting the contradictions of their role and the unfairness in past practices regarding their eligibility to adopt, foster parents have become more organized. Groups such as the National Foster Parent Association (see Appendix F) help foster parents gain greater control over the children they raise. National groups like this are a means of finding regional affiliates around the country; they also provide information to foster parents who want to adopt the children they have been raising, and they disseminate information on subsidized adoption programs.

Some states now have laws mandating that in long-term foster placements, if the foster parents want the child, they must be the home first considered. But even in states where this is the case, the rights of the foster parents can be ignored. Lois, for example, was Deek's foster mother for three years. She and her husband, Walter, had grown more attached to Deek than to any of their previous twelve foster children; when they heard that he was to be placed for adoption, they indicated their interest to their supervisor. (His birth mother was in a mental institution and unable to sign the relinquishment papers; the court had finally released him for adoption.) The supervisor made it clear to Lois and Walter that they were not considered an appropriate home because of their ages and that a more suitable home would be found. Lois was crushed.

She sought help and found out that age could not legally be used as a factor against her in the adoption process. She approached the supervisor again, but the reason for rejection was changed. Now she was told that because of Deek's birth mother's problems, he needed to be in a home that could accommodate his potential psychological problems. Lois told the worker that she and Walter were totally familiar with his background and felt sure they could handle the situation. The worker insisted that they read books on mental problems to be sure they knew what they were doing, and she continued to discourage the placement.

Lois and Walter were persistent; they read the books and said they still wanted Deek. The worker still told them they were not qualified to be his adoptive parents. She indicated there were more qualified people to raise Deek. Lois and Walter decided to hire an attorney, who approached the social worker to clarify Lois and Walter's rights. One appointment with the attorney seemed to convince the social worker that this couple would indeed be appropriate. The irony is that the agency would even consider placing this child with potential problems elsewhere before first trying to have him remain where he was secure and loved. Deek's best chance of growing up normally was in the home he had known since he was two days old, and to disrupt his life after more than three years in a secure and loving home would significantly increase his chances of having emotional problems. Deek's adoption took three years to complete; Lois and Walter's determination was the key to their success.

The good news is that foster parents are slowly gaining more control in decisions involving the children in their care. At times, their opinions are solicited before adoption proceedings are formalized or placements are made. They are seeking greater say in the length of time a child will stay with them and the conditions under which the child will be removed. Most important, foster parenting can be a way to *become* an adoptive parent.[11]

Arlene and Howard had been foster parents ever since their biological children entered school. It was a way for Arlene to earn money while she stayed home, but her primary motivation was her real love for children. They already had two foster children when two-year-old Jody came to live with them. It was supposed to be a temporary placement, but the birth mother repeatedly refused to sign the relinquishment papers that would have allowed Jody to be adopted. Her visits became shorter and less frequent, but nothing could be done to persuade her to relinquish. Meanwhile Arlene and Howard became "Mommy" and "Daddy" to Jody, who also heard her foster brother and sister refer to them as such.

Jody had one additional problem—she had only one arm. Arlene and Howard helped her adjust to her disability, enjoyed being with her, loved her, and saw her through two additional years of her life. This was the first foster child they had nurtured for a long period of time; they understandably became very attached to her, and she to them. When Arlene and Howard learned that Jody's birth mother had finally signed the relinquishment papers, they asked the social worker for consideration as Jody's adoptive parents. The social worker was hesitant. Even though Jody was considered a special-needs child, she would be easier to place than many others because she was still under five and a girl. Arlene and Howard persisted in their requests. After a lot of investigation, they were finally approved as a potential adoptive home, but they had to go through the same process as people who were completely unknown to the system. Finally, six months later, Jody became their legal daughter.

Arlene and Howard were fortunate that they had no strikes against them. Anything that could possibly have been used to deny their petition to adopt Jody would have been. Foster parents are not first-choice adoptive applicants.

A different approach to foster parenting is being taken by some adoption agencies. In order to facilitate the early placement of children in permanent homes, children are sometimes being fostered in the home that is expected to adopt them, and they are placed prior to the birth mother's signing the relinquishment. The approach, termed *fost-adopt*, has some risks, such as when the fost-adopt parents become very attached and the birth mother changes her mind. However, it does help the child develop a sense of permanence as early as possible, which is of major importance.

Tricia and Ken were one couple that tried this new system. Both Tricia and Ken were very confident in their ability to parent, even though they had waited until both of them had well-established careers before trying to have a child. When Ken was diagnosed with problems that would prevent them from conceiving, they immediately went to an adoption agency. After hearing about the fost-adopt program, they knew they wanted to try it. They really hoped to have a baby right out of the hospital and this was one way to do that. Knowing the risks in this program did not deter Tricia and Ken from bonding with the two baby girls they brought home, even though the twins were not fully re-linquished by the birth mother for two months. Tricia and Ken maintained contact with the birth mother while she struggled with her decision. Ultimately their bond with Amy and Alisa convinced the mother that this was the best decision for her babies, and Tricia and Ken were able to adopt the twins.

While the role of foster parents remains in flux, positive changes have been made in recent years. The fost-adopt program is one way agencies have devised to create successful adoptions from foster home placements and allow early placements. However, the primary way foster parents are viewed remains as potential permanent homes for special-needs children.

Gay and Lesbian Parents

Few areas of adoption elicit as much emotional response as the topic of same-sex couples adopting. In the past, when same-sex couples wanted to adopt, either one of them adopted as a single parent or they made an independent arrangement. It is only recently that homosexual couples have cautiously approached agencies with the intention of seeking a child to adopt. In fairness to the agencies, they are also responding to the outcries of the public; as many as 65 percent of Americans oppose adoptions by gays and lesbians,[12] and the interest of same-sex couples in adoption has been met with condemnation from anti-gay-rights groups.

Gays and lesbians have begun to legally win the battle against discrimination in our society, but public tolerance is slow in coming, in adoption as well as other areas. As parents, gays and lesbians are as good or as bad as any other group one could evaluate.[13] There is no proof to substantiate fears that children raised by homosexuals become homosexuals themselves. Yet the sexual orientation of gay people can affect court decisions about parenting rights and how adoption agencies view them as potential parents. While few would advocate that the four million children being raised by gay or lesbian parents in the United States should be taken from their homes, the outcome of individual court cases involving adoption is less likely to be sure.[14]

Homosexuals seeking a child through an adoption agency are fighting an uphill battle if they expect to be treated equally. Most agencies will consider same-sex couples for certain special-needs children if they do not have a "regular" couple in mind. Independent adoptions are probably no easier: Most birth parents will pick heterosexual couples over same-sex couples. The easiest way for lesbians to have children is to have them biologically (as most do); many men in a similar situation are likely to have children only through a previous heterosexual relationship.

Despite data that indicate gays and lesbians are like any other parents, agencies do not consider same-sex couples as a first choice in adoption. While same-sex couples argue that they should have the same rights here as any other couple, mainstream tolerance does not go that far.

Discrimination is not a new concept for adoption agencies, who, like any group discriminating against another, has tended to select a small group that is not vocal. They discriminated against would-be African American parents until African Americans gained more power and became vocal; then the outcry of the African American community forced changes. Adoption agency discrimination against gays has shown the same pattern. As gay-rights activists have gained power politically and legally, same-sex couples have begun to come out of hiding. Only recently has it been possible for them to admit their homosexuality and couple status when adopting, as several states have ruled that a couple, whether heterosexual or homosexual, does not have to be married to adopt a child together.[15] While these changes continue and appear inevitable, that does not mean that the struggles are over for gays and lesbians.[16]

Lori and Sally knew discrimination. They had lived together in a lesbian relationship for over six years. They were happy, productive, and otherwise enjoying a "normal" life. Lori was a social worker; Sally reluctantly worked as a grocery store clerk, but her real desire was to be a mother. Sally went to a physician for artificial insemination, but it was unsuccessful. After six months of trying, she gave up on the idea of becoming pregnant. Because Lori's job with the Department of Welfare kept her abreast of adoption agency procedures, she recognized that she and Sally were not going to get a child from an agency. Sally nevertheless went to a traditional agency in an attempt to adopt as a single mother, but she was told there were no children available for single women.

Then Lori heard of a woman on welfare who was unhappily pregnant and too far along for an abortion. Lori talked to her about the child; she was open about her relationship with Sally. She emphasized their stability and how loving Sally was. The birth mother met Sally and liked her. She already liked Lori, so she decided she would give them her child when it was born. Sally adopted the child legally, as a single mother. The agency investigating the home never learned about her relationship with Lori. In many ways Sally and Lori were lucky—the odds really were against their adopting a child, but they did it. While Lori is in a precarious position as a parent if anything were to happen to Sally or to her relationship with Sally, they at least have a child.

An even more difficult battle faces homosexual men who want to adopt. If agencies are hesitant with lesbians, they are far more so with gay men. The state of Washington placed a child with two gay men and found itself involved in a prolonged legal case and a controversy generated by anti-gay sentiment. The story made the front page: Megan

Lucas had relinquished her son for adoption, but when she learned that her son was being adopted by homosexuals, Luis and Ross Lopton, she decided she would file a petition to adopt him herself. The birth mother's case argued that placing a child with a gay couple put the child at heightened risk for abnormal social development, sexual molestation, and a homosexual orientation. Some believe conservative groups eager to advance anti-gay-rights legislation had approached Megan Lucas.[17]

Even though Lucas eventually dropped her petition, it was only after great negative publicity about her background. Few felt she had demonstrated the skills necessary to be a good parent, while the skills of the adopting couple were exemplary. Almost any parents would have appeared better than Lucas, so the victory was hardly a boost for gay adoptions. Fortunately, most adoptions involving gays are quieter.

Same-sex couples who enter the adoption scene need to be better prepared than most people who seek to adopt. Read books that discuss raising a child and the issues of same-sex parents.[18] Know the issues by attending meetings of support groups for gay and lesbian parents. You can find them through the Gay & Lesbian Parents Coalition International or the National Center for Lesbian Rights (see Appendix F). These organizations will also connect you with local groups who can be a great source of information and support. Contact large adoption agencies in metropolitan areas that may offer gay and lesbian parent adoption support groups. The Internet has updated information about the same-sex parents support groups for people considering adoption. One of the best sources of inspiration is the book *Getting Simon: Two Gay Doctors' Journey to Fatherhood*.[19] This book realistically discusses the process of trying to find a baby, including the conflicting legal and medical advice and the prejudice and stumbling blocks that one gay couple encountered in adopting their son.

Despite the widespread discrimination, claims that gays and lesbians are unfit for parenting are unsubstantiated. Though the subject is seldom studied at all, a recent study of a small group of lesbian families showed that children raised by lesbians were just as psychologically healthy as children of heterosexual couples.[20] But one study reported in the *Lesbian Tide* found that children of lesbians *are* different from children raised by nonlesbians: The researcher found that the sons of lesbians were more gentle and concerned with other people's feelings than were other boys. She also found the daughters of lesbians had stronger qualities of leadership and were more outgoing than other girls.[21] Further studies of lesbian mothers are finding that they raise their children in highly traditional ways and that the children show no increase in gender-related problems, sex-role confusion, or differences in general development.[22] (Gay adoption studies are noticeably lacking.) Few same-sex couples wishing to adopt have felt the impact of these studies.

Are we advocating placing children with avowed homosexuals? We advocate placing children with anyone who wants them, unless it can be shown that such a placement would be harmful to the child. If it can be proved that there would be harm in letting a child be raised by a particular homosexual, then a child should not be placed in that home. If that cannot be proved, then why not do it.

Adoption at best isn't easy, and for same-sex adoptive parents it is even harder. The nice part about your situation is that at least you are part of a couple, so you have someone to share the frustrations and difficulties of the process. And the changes in recent years for same-sex couples have been startling and encouraging. Now you can proceed in adoption with an honest approach; in the past, that honesty would have prevented you from adopting.

Low-Income Parents

People who are economically limited have always had difficulty adopting. The process can be expensive, and at times having low income alone would have eliminated you. That has changed.

Adoption subsidies now defray additional costs associated with raising children who have a medical or psychological problem. This gives some people a new opportunity to adopt, and it has been especially helpful in foster care situations.

Another change has been in laws related to discrimination; adoption agencies are not allowed to discriminate against people because of their income. Therefore, even a person on welfare is eligible to adopt a child.

Nan had this experience. She had a medical problem that prevented her from working and allowed her to receive medical help from the state. She had always wanted to adopt but never felt she could, because of the cost. Nan, a single person, was not particularly attractive, and she had some speech problems that caused great difficulty when she met people. But she really wanted a baby, any baby, and she was willing to do whatever it took to find one.

Nan didn't stand much chance through most traditional agencies, but she found another kind of agency that was open to helping her. That agency felt it was not their responsibility to screen people out of the process unless there was evidence that those people were unfit to parent. They didn't find this with Nan and so they set out to help her. They also explained to her that she would have to be willing to meet a birth mother and that the birth mother would be told that she relied on state aid.

Nan's story has a happy ending. The agency found a mother who was going to have a mixed-race child. That was fine with Nan. Faith, the birth mother, already had three children and she was desperate to find a home for this child whom she knew she couldn't raise. Faith and Nan met. At first it was tense, but Nan had a way with people and the barriers began to come down. Faith felt that Nan was the answer to her prayers; Faith was due to deliver soon and no one else had said they were even interested in her baby. They spent the next three weeks together, part of the time even after the baby was born. By the time Nan was ready to take her new daughter and go home, they had become friends.

Faith might not have picked Nan if there had been someone else waiting for her child, but she doesn't feel that she made a wrong choice. Nan and her new daughter are still on cloud nine as her daughter's third birthday approaches. Faith will be there for the birthday party.

Not all stories end happily. Tommy had been in foster care for five of his seven years of life. After repeated attempts to have him released for adoption, the state agency succeeded. His mother signed relinquishment papers and the agency worker promised Tommy they would find him a home—but nothing happened. Tommy needed to be moved from the foster home he had been in for over eighteen months and he wanted a permanent home. Since the agency was not having success in finding a placement for Tommy, one of the workers, a friend of Dru's, approached her.

Finding a home for Tommy really wasn't a problem. Dru probably made only ten phone calls before she found a couple in another state who only wanted an older child. Lyle and Peg had been married for twelve years and had one child; Lyle had been adopted when he was four years old and he especially felt empathetic when he heard of Tommy's plight. They contacted the state agency to see if they could adopt Tommy.

The state agency worker quizzed them about their financial status and was upset to hear that Lyle only had a part-time job, as a janitor. Peg had been the primary breadwinner ever since they were married. It didn't help when the worker learned they lived in a trailer. And when she heard that they would need some financial help for the counseling that Tommy would need, that finished the potential adoption. The agency turned them down. Lyle and Peg decided to give up on trying to adopt another child.

It would be wonderful if changes in the laws always resulted in what they were intended to do. But many times, changes are ignored or overlooked and the same discrimination that existed ten or twenty years ago goes on. Money determines a lot of things in life, but it doesn't have to determine whether someone can adopt. There are ways to adopt that don't cost a lot.

Of course, while the cost of your adoption can be relatively low, the cost of raising a child is significant. But many people raise children on limited incomes. Again, we don't take children away from families because they have a limited income, so why shouldn't low-income people have an opportunity to adopt?

Military Parents

It is rather ironic to have to list families in the military service as "special" families who encounter difficulties adopting, but they are. Because they move so often, military families run into problems completing adoptions before they might be reassigned. For that reason, many agencies avoid beginning the process with these families.

Other prejudicial views exist toward military families; they are believed to be too strict with their children or unstable because of a parent's long absence from home. As a military family seeking to adopt, you need to convince your social worker or a birth parent that these problems are readily solved or nonexistent.

The military family can offer great advantages in some adoptions. Military duty has become more like regular work, with pay being comparable to what's found in the private sector. Certainly these families provide a stable income and available medical care. (Currently, the military even offers reimbursements of up to $2,000 for adoption expenses.) The military environment is culturally diverse and a positive place to have transracial placements. In many cases, wives do not work outside of the home because of frequent transfers, so they may be able to spend a lot of time caring for a child.

At the same time, the military also poses some real barriers to adoption. Large families can be a problem if the parent is assigned to a facility with inadequate housing. Since many children being adopted are special-needs children, military people worry about their superiors' reactions to the added expense. In actuality, the military wants to keep their best people in the service so they are becoming more friendly in helping their personnel adopt.

Bill and Jean learned fairly early in their marriage that Jean would be unable to have biological children. She knew she wanted to adopt and she spoke with friends she had met at the base where Bill was stationed. She met two other military families who had attempted to adopt and who had failed. Both had been caught in the dilemma of starting adoptions and then having been transferred before a child was placed with them. Jean decided to do research to figure out how to solve this problem because she knew she was going to find a baby to adopt.

Jean found an agency in Washington that was a different kind of agency; they worked with people adopting independently and helped with just a part of the adoption as well as helped couples find babies to adopt. The month after completing their home study, they heard about a woman who was going to have a baby. They were excited but deeply worried because Bill was due to be transferred within the next six months. Their concern was whether they could get the baby and complete the process before the transfer took place. The agency assured them there would be no problem because in the state of Washington, there wasn't a long waiting period to finalize adoptions. The worker also told them that even if they transferred, they could continue this adoption as an independent adoption in another state. Bill and Jean felt they had found a valuable resource as well as the baby they had been waiting to adopt.

In order to adopt, couples in the military need to find agencies or individuals who are tuned in to military life. Speed of the home study is essential, and the agency needs to make efforts to see that their records can be transferred if the family is reassigned. Find people who will help you look at adoption creatively, to overcome the barriers your occupation has created for you. Support groups exist in the military for those who have successfully adopted domestically and internationally; they are well worth contacting for help. Check into international adoption if your assignment is overseas. Be encouraged knowing that many people in the military adopt children.

Just because you are more difficult to help if you are in the military, don't let that discourage you from pursuing adoption. You are a valuable asset in the adoption field, so find an agency that will view you in this way. If you can't find the right agency, check your state laws to see if you can adopt independently—you probably can. And if you end up in one of the few states where independent adoption is not legal, you will likely be moving soon, and the chances are in the next state it will be legal. You, like everyone else trying to adopt, have to be hardy and persevere even when people say it will be difficult or it can't be done. Your tenacity will pay off.

Summary

Diversity today is causing changes in the very way we define family and how we help families adopt. One of the positives in the changing picture of adoption has been the increased number of special-needs children who have found homes. But this same positive change does not exist for the "special" parents who are seeking to adopt but who do not fit into the "easy to find a child for" category.

Our society is becoming more accepting of different kinds of families, but when adopting, parents who are "different" remain parents of second choice. Even though large segments of our population can be labeled "special" or "disabled," adoption remains a difficult and, at times, seemingly impossible process for those people. It is hard enough in the United States for anyone to adopt, but for people who are not parents of first choice, it can be very discouraging. The few who succeed are those who really push to prove their parenting ability and those who are just plain lucky.

To find it more difficult to adopt because you are disabled, older, gay, or low-income causes anger. To realize that being a foster parent or in the service—something to be proud of—can cause you to be turned down by some adoption agencies is difficult to accept. It isn't enough to have laws preventing discrimination; we need to enforce these laws. And even with the laws, it is still difficult to realize that you are a parent of second choice for most agencies and birth parents.

No matter what your chances, believe in your ability to be a good parent and in your ability to find a child to adopt. Fight the system if you want a child, but be prepared to lose. Your options may be somewhat limited, but that isn't to say you can't make up for that limitation. Get on the agencies' waiting lists, and be prepared to wait indefinitely. But don't get on just one list—get on as many as possible to increase your chances. And don't rely just on the agencies' lists; check into independent and international adoption. If you really want to be a parent, look around—look harder, look in different ways, look everywhere. You may be a second choice for some people, but you won't be for the child you find.

2

YOUR ADOPTION OPTIONS

CHAPTER 5

Agencies in Transition

YEARS AGO IF YOU WANTED to adopt a baby, you merely gave your name to the agency of your choice, did what they told you to do, and as long as you weren't blatantly inadequate, you obtained the baby you requested. There were too many babies. The agencies needed you.

Today the picture has changed markedly. Few babies are available. Adoption agencies have become more rigorous and choosy.

Agencies are looking for couples who will accept a wide range of children. The sought-after blond, blue-eyed girl is seldom available. Particularly in a public agency, the emphasis is often on how to eliminate applications, not on how to serve couples wishing to adopt a child. To be too specific about your desires as a potential adoptive parent—to say you want an infant or a child without any physical disabilities, or a child who is not from a mixed racial background—may very likely spell your elimination from the waiting list.

Waits of three to six years are now common. Adoption agencies seek ways to trim down the ever-lengthening list of adoptive parent applicants,[1] so by their criteria (often unstated) you may find yourself considered unacceptable. If rejected, you can abandon hope for a child, seek an agency that offers a different kind of service with different criteria, or try on your own—perhaps alternative methods of pregnancy, independent adoption, international adoption, and black market adoption.

These problems aside, adoptions through agencies are potentially the most advantageous kind if performed properly. Agencies have access to the greatest number of babies, children, and adoptive parents, and they have the trained workers and the facilities to get the job done really well. That doesn't mean all agencies are doing a good job, but they could be.

Since agencies (in general) are the first resource potential adopting parents look to for help in adopting, it is critical to understand the vast differences that exist today in adoption agencies, how they work, what they are looking for, and how to work with them.

Sorting Out the Agencies

Adoption agencies are not all the same. There are huge differences from one to another. Some agencies take a very traditional approach and others base themselves on fresh ideas, philosophies, and methods. One major change in recent years is that adoption has become a big business.[2] In some ways this is an advantage for the adoptive parents, because people adopting now have more choices than ever before; in other ways this presents disadvantages: the costs have increased, the competition has increased, and the consumer is often left confused.

No matter what they advertise, agencies must be evaluated individually. It may be difficult to make broad generalizations about the differences between public and private or for-profit and nonprofit adoption agencies, because there is so much overlap and similarity between the public and private sectors.[3] For someone coming into the adoption process, it is difficult to sort through this maze, but we can give you some general guidelines.

PUBLIC ADOPTION AGENCIES

Public adoption agencies are state operated. If we were to describe one set of adoption agencies as "traditional," it would be the public ones. Traditional agencies are adoption agencies that usually have control over the children and the placements of these children, can work at the pace they choose, do not have to answer to their clients, and usually have been in adoptions for many years. While this description fits most public adoption agencies, you will find some public agencies that will *not* fit into this category; they have changed more with the times and have adapted to some of the newer adoption ideas. In general, however, while each public agency has some wonderful workers, the agencies themselves have been slow to change and are often mired down in regulations from days gone by. They are most likely to have rules that limit their ability to change with the times.

Public adoption agencies are also the most likely to have charge of children who have been taken from their biological parents because of neglect or abuse. They often have older children, children with special needs, and children who have been in the system for longer periods of time.

Most people wanting to adopt probably think of going to public agencies first, but these may not be the best choice depending upon your circumstances and the kind of child you are seeking. Their costs are usually lower than at private agencies, but their waits are frequently long.

PRIVATE ADOPTION AGENCIES

Private adoption agencies are licensed by, but not run by, the state. Many might also be considered traditional, especially those that have been in existence for a long time. While longevity may give stability to an agency, it also gives it time to set lots of rules and restrictions. Time also allows agencies to grow in size, and sometimes bigger ones are less adaptable to change.

Private adoption agencies have a wide variation in how they operate. They can be one-person operations or have huge staffs. They can operate in one state or many, domestically, internationally, or both. They can be either for-profit or nonprofit. Remember that "nonprofit" merely means they have passed some screening by their individual states and the Internal Revenue Service. They must be more careful in how they operate, but they, too, make money.

The recent proliferation of private adoption agencies has several causes. One is the need to change and to allow more flexibility within the system; the traditional system was not meeting the needs of the parties involved. Another reason has been the cry for more openness in the adoption process. While most public and many private adoption agencies still maintain secrecy of identify for their clients, newer agencies are attempting to respond to the desire for less secrecy.

Many of these newer agencies were begun by the very people who a decade ago were fighting policies and restrictions of other agencies. They became so good at providing an alternative form of adoption that they became agencies themselves.

Deciding on an Agency

So how does someone make a choice? This is a tough question. People who succeed with an agency think it is great and those who don't succeed see it as a rip-off. Discovering the best agency for you isn't an easy process. You need to find out about each agency to see how it operates.

You can get some answers by just calling and asking questions.

- What types of children do you place? (ages, nationalities, special needs)
- Do you restrict who can adopt through your agency? (age, length of marriage, number of children, religion, income, gays, singles)
- How much is the adoption fee, and what does it cover?
- What support services do you offer before adopting, during the process, and after the adoption?
- If one adoption doesn't work out, where will I stand in terms of waiting time and costs?
- May I speak with people who have adopted from your agency?
- How many children did you place last year?
- How many couples do you have on your waiting list? (If you can't get the answer to this question, the last one has no relevance.)
- How soon after I apply will the process begin?
- How long before the home study will be completed?
- If I am not approved, will I be told the reasons?
- If I don't take a child offered to me, will I be eliminated?

None of the answers to these questions will tell you enough to determine which agency you should work with, but they will identify a few groups you may want to skip. Even the person who answers the phone offers a contact that lets you evaluate the agency.

No one single factor will tell you which agency will best meet your needs. Agencies have failures as well as successes. A specific agency may place three times as many children as another agency, but they may have three or four or five times as many people waiting. A large fee may be a better bargain than a small one, depending on what services it covers.

All of this confusion underscores the need for you to do your homework. Go out and ask questions of others who know about the agencies in your area. Find out from others how each specific agency operates. Go to group meetings at various agencies and listen to people's stories; you will learn a great deal this way. Send for their material and read it very carefully. Then proceed cautiously.

The Agency Process

We will take you through the process at the most traditional kind of an agency to give you some insight into how an agency works. When you begin, you may not be sure exactly which kind of agency you are working with, so we want you to know the inner workings with which you may be confronted.

Begin by calling the agency and conducting the phone interview discussed above. They will probably tell you of a group meeting for prospective parents. Anyone wishing to consider adoption is encouraged to attend; even if it isn't mandatory, you want to be sure to go. The meeting will explain the lack of available children and the general time period couples should expect to wait before a baby or other child might become available. A worker discusses the types of children you might be offered and explains a series of interviews you'll have to go through. The agency's fees and general requirements are outlined.

The meeting sounds fairly innocuous. It isn't. Listen carefully, because the worker at this point is telling you exactly what this particular agency is looking for in each couple it examines. At no other point in the adoption process will the agency provide you with this specific information.

No matter what you hear and how much you enjoy the meeting, visit another agency. You need to have something to compare it with.

If you decide to continue, you will be asked to fill out an application and set up an appointment with a social worker. Remember, the agency has not said that it will accept your application, but that you may submit one.

When the agency officials meet with you for the initial individual interview, your entire case is on the line. Some agencies will screen you in or out on the basis of this one interview and your application. Be careful. A flexible attitude is one of the single most important characteristics that agencies seek in prospective parents. You will be asked what you want in terms of adoption. If your answer is "a Caucasian infant under four months of age with no physical problems," you're in trouble. The reason is clear: The agency has approximately twenty couples for each child. They need to select a couple who will accept just about any of the children they have. If you listened carefully in the first general meeting, you learned what kind of children this particular agency has. So you have a clue as to what you need to say at this point.

If you are meeting with an agency that has primarily older children from foster care or special-needs children, your situation's very different than if you are with an agency that deals primarily with infants. The couple most likely to get on the waiting list of an adoption agency that has primarily special-needs children will say they want a child under eight, the younger the better, and they are willing to take a child with physical or emotional problems. If you don't get on the list now, you have no chance. You may not even get another interview. You can see why it is important to understand the agency with which you are dealing.

Does this mean you should show no preferences? No, not exactly. It means you should be careful not to show *too many* preferences. Does this mean you will get an eight-year-old developmentally disabled child of mixed racial background? Not necessarily. It means you have kept the door open. You can turn down the child you are offered. Will you definitely get a child? Perhaps. You still have a lot of other interviews ahead of you. At times, before you go on to individual sessions, additional group meetings are required. This is especially true if couples are considering special-needs children.

If you "pass" the initial interview, the agency will accept your application and your application fee. At this point you will begin your home study. A home study is a compilation of the material the agency will gather about you. It will contain answers to questions you will be asked at different interviews and information requested from other sources. (See Appendix B.) As part of the home study, you will be asked for medical histories and perhaps doctors' reports dealing with your infertility; many agencies will not place infants with couples who do not have a diagnosed infertility problem. You will also be given financial forms to complete.

Most agencies will also request a biographical statement now. They'll want to know about your life as a child and as an adult. You don't have to be an outstanding writer to complete this, but you should do it right away. Sometimes people become so frightened about their writing abilities that they delay the process by putting off this simple step.

Letters of recommendation are usually expected. It is obvious, as in all letters of recommendation, that you should get the right people to send them. They will have to evaluate your potential as parents. People like ministers who meet lots of other people and can make comparative judgments are usually good references. People who have seen you with children and who can comment on your ability to deal with them are also good. Do not hesitate to tell people what to put in their letters. If you often socialize with a couple who has children, make certain you tell them to write about your good interaction with their little ones.

Some letters will not help you, even if they should. For instance, it is usually unwise to have a therapist send a letter; in fact, you probably shouldn't tell the agency you have had any psychotherapy unless you are certain they would accept this information positively. If you do tell them, and if you ask your therapist for a letter, first make certain he or she will send a positive one.

After your application has been accepted, another interview with you as a couple is usually scheduled. At this point, questions are again geared toward what you will accept in a child, but now the social worker is likely to get into your experience with children, your acceptance of your infertility problem, your marital strengths and weaknesses, and your current support system of friends and relatives. Ideally, you will come across as a couple who loves and accepts children, even those who are not yours. You should seem to be people who wish they could have had biological children, but who have come to accept infertility. Your marriage should appear sound, but not unrealistically perfect. Your friends and relatives should seem important, but not people upon whom you are unduly dependent for your emotional well-being. In general, you want to appear "normal"—whatever that means. You want to present a picture of emotional stability and security.

The next step is an individual interview with each member of the couple. The intent of these sessions is to make certain both partners are in agreement. The worker is checking to see if the less verbal partner believes the same things as the more verbal one.

A final interview is then conducted, usually in the prospective adoptive parents' home. If the social worker comes to your house, he or she will not go into drawers or check for dirt in the corners. The worker will be seeing how you live and what arrangements you have made for a potential child. The house that appears too perfect may be just as suspect as the house that is in shambles.

Some agencies currently involve prospective parents in a self-evaluation. Since this is a relatively recent technique, it is hard to say how these evaluations will be used. Perhaps they help applicants determine which kind of child they could best be paired with. On the other hand, these evaluations may be a way of screening out potential parents who have little hope of ever receiving a child.

After your final interview, you will receive notice that your home study is completed and (hopefully) approved; you now enter the waiting stage. The time varies, but for everyone it seems long. For some, however, it really will be forever—because even though they have been approved, the "right" child never comes along. Some agencies have been known to accept people but never have a child come up for them. After a long wait, most will suggest the couple drop off the list, since no child is available.

One of the reasons couples must wait at this point is that many agencies now allow the biological mother a chance to read several histories or to hear about several potential adoptive families and choose the one for her child. It is possible that no mother will choose you. It is also possible that you will just get "shuffled around" and that after a period of time you will be somewhat forgotten. If you haven't heard from the agency in two or three months, demonstrate your continuing desire to adopt by calling them. Ask them if it would help for you to revise something that is shown to the birth mother or if they have any other suggestions to improve your chances.

If you are finally matched with a child, you are called into the agency to see if you like the background of the child the agency has chosen for you. The worker will tell you about the child and the biological parents. This is your best opportunity to discuss anything you have been told, so ask questions. If you find anything objectionable in the background information you hear, the worker will want to talk it over. Perhaps you are confused about the father, or perhaps you want to know more about the child's physical health. If your questions do not clear up your hesitation at this point, the worker may choose not to go any further in placing this specific child with you. However, if you hear about the child and everything meets with your approval, you will be allowed to see the child. Seldom will the agency let you take the child home at this point. Most frequently they will give you until the next day, to allow time for you to change your mind or to prepare for your new child, now that you know the age and sex.

If you are selected to receive an older child, more emphasis is placed on your reaction to the child and that of the child to you. Several meetings may occur before an actual placement is made. At times, a temporary placement is made to see how readily everyone is able to adjust to the new situation.

The child is not yours until you go to court to finalize the adoption. This can take up to six months or even longer from the time a child is placed. During this period you have visits from the agency social worker, who monitors how you, your spouse, and the child are adjusting. Ideally, these visits should offer a chance to explore any difficulties you have encountered, but the specter of the agency still being the guardian of the child is real. *The child still belongs to the agency, not to you.*

The Wilsons found this out. They were the ideal couple the adoption agency cited in its introductory group interview for prospective parents. They were both professional people who had ample money and two previously adopted children who seemed very happy and adjusted. Dan, the husband, was exceptionally involved with the children, far more so than most fathers. Ellen presented a beautiful combination of the traditional mother and a modern one working part-time outside the home. They luckily had a third child placed with them. Five months into the adoption, they had marital problems and considered divorcing. Because they believed what the agency had said about calling if they ever needed help, they told the agency of their marital difficulties. The worker was understanding and said it was no problem; the agency would give Dan and Ellen time to work out their problems. One month later when all of the problems had not been resolved, they were told the agency wanted the child returned.

All the pleas notwithstanding, the child was taken back. Dan and Ellen had no recourse because they had no legal rights to the child. Seven months later they had reconciled. But there was lasting trauma over the loss of the child they had loved and nurtured for almost six months. The trauma extended, of course, to the two previously adopted children, who had to cope with their own fears of their possible return to the agency. The adoption agency is definitely in control until the child is legally adopted.

After the trial period is over, you retain an attorney and go to court to finalize the adoption. Now the child is yours—unless someone can show that fraud has been committed, no one can take your child back once you have gone to court! This is an event that warrants celebration.

How Honest Should You Be?

There are basically three ways you can approach this process. You can be absolutely truthful and self-revealing, holding back nothing. You can be selective in the amount and quality of the information you provide. Or you can present yourself in the way that is most likely to get you the child you want, whether it's completely honest or not.

The first approach—being honest, open, and forthright—is ideal. The interviews and meetings should be opportunities to explore all your feelings about this potential parenting experience: You should be able to discuss your limits and your potential for extending them. You should be able to explore flaws in your marriage in the hope of gaining insight into dealing with problems. You should be able to reveal your resolved and unresolved feelings about your inability to have a biological child and, in the process, understand and live with them more comfortably. You should feel the agency is one-hundred-percent behind your efforts and is working with you toward your parenting goal.

This is how adopting through an agency should be and could be. Unfortunately, it is unlikely to be the way adopting through an agency *is*.

Your second option, and probably the one most frequently used, is to be selective in what you say to the adoption agency. In this scenario, you are well aware that the agency has what you want, so you do some judicious editing of yourself. You neglect to tell the interviewers of your husband's irritability when he comes home tired. You decide not to tell them about your mother-in-law, who believes that "illegitimate babies come only from lower-class people and are basically inferior." When social workers ask you how you feel about your infertility, you decide it isn't important to tell them you still cry each month when you have your period. You take a basically honest approach, but you remember that these workers are judging you to see if you fit into their preconceived ideals.

If you choose the third option, you try to find out what the agency is looking for and you give it to them. You find out as much as possible about their methods of selection and their reasons for turning people down, and you act in response to this information.

Of course, adoption workers are appalled at the mere suggestion of acting in this way. They would say the first option, honesty and openness, is the only way to approach the process. For them, it is. For you who want a child, we're not sure. If you really want a baby, you have to go about getting a baby in the best way you can. Say you know you will be eliminated if you tell them that you, the wife, love your job and want to work throughout the new child's growing years; what do you do? You might choose to say that you intend to stay home with the child and do so until you go to court and finalize the adoption. After that, the agency has no say in how you lead your life. If you know you will be eliminated if you tell the agency that you really would have great difficulty loving a child of a mixed racial background, what do you do? Again, you might choose to say that you are open to the possibility of accepting a child from a mixed racial background and hope that things never come to the point where you have to say no to a child offered to you. (Remember: *You don't have to take any child they offer.* Obviously, you lessen your chances when you turn down a child, but at least you have a chance as long as you are being considered by the agency.)

What approach do we suggest? We're not sure. The way you approach the agency must be thoroughly, thoughtfully, and individually considered. The more you know about the various agencies, the better equipped you will be to choose the one you can be most comfortable and honest with. Hopefully, with time the direction agencies will go will be toward helping all parents, and honesty will be rewarded. In the meantime, if you understand the different alternative means of obtaining a child, the better equipped you will be to choose between agencies—and among those approaches to adoption that do not use agencies.

What *Are* Agencies Looking For?

Now that you are familiar with the general procedures for adopting a child through an agency, it is important to look at the specific criteria that the adoption agencies say they are looking for in prospective parents. No matter what kind of agency you work with, these are the kinds of traits it will be looking for; it may put more emphasis on certain traits than others, but you should know that these are the areas agencies are checking and that form the basis of what is called a home study. We have enclosed a copy of one example of home study guidelines in Appendix B for you.

DESIRE TO ADOPT

The prospective parents must convey their strong desire for a child; the social worker has to believe that having a child is exceptionally important—a high priority in these people's lives. Without conveying this intense feeling, they won't get a baby. The Brunsons were a good example. Bob and Eileen Brunson were quiet people, not very demonstrative or expressive. They each came from homes where self-sufficiency, not vulnerability, was valued. They had not responded with outward emotion to Eileen's fertility problem, nor did they respond with any intensity when the social worker questioned them about their desire for a child. They knew that they wanted a child; their lack of intensity in expressing this desire did not lessen their wish. Their low-keyed, quiet approach to life was interpreted to mean a child was not very important to them. They were rejected because their inability to fully express their desire to have a child left their adoption worker unconvinced that a child was a high priority in their lives.

FLEXIBILITY

A flexible attitude on the part of parents is a characteristic that entered the selection process only as scarcity replaced abundance and children replaced babies. This is the single most frequently mentioned characteristic agencies cite in looking for prospective parents.

Flexibility primarily concerns what type of child you can accept. Public adoption agencies especially are seeking people who are willing to take older children as well as infants. These agencies are accepting people who will take physically handicapped children and screening out people who want only physically healthy children. They are eliminating people who would not consider an emotionally disturbed child in favor of those people who would. But if you are willing to take a special-needs child, expect additional screening to assess your ability to handle the demands of this kind of child.

OPENNESS

Today's adoption agencies should be looking into how open an adoption you are willing to be involved in. Some agencies will not even bring up this issue because they only have one way of dealing with open adoptions—they don't make them. Other agencies, especially the newer, more progressive ones, are created specifically to facilitate open adoptions.

You need to be sure of your feelings about open adoption in order to answer the questions such an agency will ask. (See Chapter 2.) If you don't know the answers, tell the agency representative that you want to learn about different kinds of openness.

FINANCIAL STATUS

In the war between love and poverty, poverty usually wins. Poverty causes so much anxiety that even the best marriages are severely tested. This is not the home environment agencies want for their adoptive families. The primary factor that an adoption agency looks for when examining potential parents' financial status is stability. All things being equal, the agency would obviously prefer that the adoptive parents be in the best financial situation possible. Your income cannot be a stated criterion, yet there is no question that it is important. Fair or not, the more money and job stability you have, the better are your chances of adopting a baby.

At times the agency will look at your housing as a means of determining financial security. Checking employment records also helps to determine the stability of the family's financial situation. Agencies look for a couple whose income allows one of the parents to remain at home with the child.

Many agencies, especially the public ones offer sliding fees for people of modest incomes. Yet there's a limit to the number of cases in which fees can be lowered.

More and more financial subsidies, especially for children with special needs, are becoming accessible. Adoption by foster parents can be funded through these subsidies, especially if the child is hard to place. As long as a couple remain foster parents, they receive state aid. The moment they adopt that same child, they lose all state support—unless specific criteria are met. Some families would be unable to handle the financial burden this might involve, especially since the medical expenses of some of these children are very high.

AGE

Recent court decisions have significantly changed the agencies' tendency to use age as a criterion for acceptance, but some admit that they still do. Some say you must be over twenty-one, others say over twenty-three, some over twenty-four or twenty-five. Obviously, no one knows which minimum age is the "correct" one.

The primary concern is on the other end of the age spectrum. While most agencies won't say so because it would be a violation of federal civil rights, they tend to choose adoptive parents who would be the "normal" biological age to give birth to the child who is placed with them. Generally, this means less than a forty-year difference between the parent's age and the child's. Be aware that if you are about forty, you have less chance of adopting an infant through an agency than a couple of thirty, even if all your other qualifications are equal. Some agencies believe it is permissible for the father to be older, and older applicants are considered for older children.

Linda and Sam found their age a deterrent to adoption. They married when he was forty-two and she was thirty-nine; Sam had been married and divorced before, and had two children. She had never been married, nor did she have children. When she did not get pregnant after eighteen months, they sought a child through a local agency. They were unsuccessful. The reason the agency rejected them was Linda's age, but even more important was the fact that she had never had any children. The agency was concerned about her adapting to a child, even an older one, at such a late period in her life. Sam and Linda were told they could consider being foster parents, but they were not specifically told that their age had worked against them.

As with many other factors the agencies use to discriminate among potential parents, age will not be specified as a reason for refusing your application. In fact, most agencies insist that age is not a criterion. The truth, however, is revealed in the placements. Agencies are not placing children with people who exceed the "normal" age difference between parents and children. Despite the recent increases in the age difference between biological parents and their children, there is no evidence that agencies have revised their placement procedures.

EDUCATIONAL BACKGROUND

Although educational level is not usually acknowledged as a factor, it is subtly influential. Some agencies state that they want their parents to be able to "provide a stimulating environment" or to "provide a positive cultural environment," but few go further.

However, education is highly valued in our society. Since all social workers have a college background, it is not surprising to find that college would be an asset in your application. The higher the degree, the better, especially if the man is highly educated; a woman's advanced degree (M.D. or Ph.D.) at times causes an agency to question her commitment to children as a high priority.

Martha and Charles found that education was a door opener with the agencies. They had a fairly distant relationship in their marriage, and that was fine with each of them. They were both bright people; Charles was a medical doctor. They tended to be very intimidating to many people they met, but their verbal ability made a good impression on the agency, and Charles's financial ability was also viewed very positively. While the agencies noticed their aloofness, its workers, like many other people, were awed. Charles and Martha received a baby with little difficulty. Their personal qualities were not the kind the agencies say they want in their adoptive parents. In fact, many of their acquaintances were surprised that they even received a child from the agency. The primary factor that set them apart from others was that he was a physician; so they got a baby. Education can make a difference.

MEDICAL HISTORY

A medical history of each potential parent is required in virtually all adoptions. The results are expected to indicate that each person is in good physical health (except that there may be an infertility problem).

Now infertility is an asset—*finally*. In fact, many agencies will not consider your application if you are fertile. The irony is that it has become increasingly difficult to know whether you have exhausted your means of achieving a pregnancy before you look at adoption. Medical advances continue to expand the possibility of a biological child for the infertile couple; the couple who wait until their late twenties or early thirties to try to have a baby may now spend so long pursuing every alternative of infertility treatment that time runs out for them. To be totally sure you have exhausted every possibility of becoming pregnant and to be absolutely sure you have resolved your feelings about your infertility before you consider adoption may be unrealistic today because the possibilities are never-ending. The goal may be to become resolved about the uncertainty of your fertility, rather than the absoluteness of your infertility.

Many couples proceed with an agency adoption without telling the agency they are continuing with fertility work. They are comfortable with the possibility of adopting and perhaps becoming pregnant within a close period of time, but they don't feel the need to say so. The adoption agency wants you to have resolved your feelings about your infertility; pursuing pregnancy does not indicate to the agency that you have resolved these feelings. Saying that you are continuing to attempt a pregnancy will probably cause you to be eliminated.

Health does not fit neatly into categories of good or bad, so how does it work as a qualification for becoming a parent? The answer to the question depends on which agency and which social worker you are asking. In general, the more serious the medical problem, the more it will affect your chances to adopt.

Sometimes the criteria may seem unfair. People who weigh more than average have had difficulty being approved for adoption by the agencies since children became scarcer. With over a third of the population of the United States overweight, this obviously places greater restrictions on the overweight person who also wants to adopt.[4] Most couples will not be told their rejection is because of weight, but they can be denied the opportunity to adopt even if their physicians say they are in good health, and even though an overweight couple can certainly have a child biologically.

Smokers have also felt discriminated against.[5] Maybe this is fair: We know that secondhand smoke can be just as unhealthy for children as smoking is for adults. However, since we have not chosen to take children away from biological parents who smoke, is it fair to prevent smokers from adopting?

People with health issues such as obesity and smoking are easy to eliminate because these problems are visible. Alcohol abuse, frequently hidden, does not always meet with the same ready rejection. However, an applicant who is an alcoholic, even a reformed one, will probably be rejected if the agency learns of the problem.

Serious illnesses mentioned in doctors' reports can affect the agencies' decisions. Kathy felt that her problems with cancer were behind her when she had passed the five-year nonactive time limit. The agency, however, denied her application. Her doctor's protests that Kathy was no more likely than anyone else to develop cancer at this point did not help her.

Physical disabilities such as loss of limbs or mobility are seldom included in the list of criteria used by adoption agencies. Mostly they are ignored, at least verbally and in writing. An adoption agency would have to be quite naive to state that the reason a couple has not been accepted is because one of the parties is disabled. A lawsuit would be immediate. (See Chapter 4.)

RACE AND ETHNICITY

Race and ethnicity cannot legally be identified as a quality used for screening potential adopters. But in the past and still today, they have been used to justify denying a child's placement. Federal legislation deters but never prevents this from happening. But the workers who remember the strong stand taken in 1992 by the National Association of Black Social Workers against black children being placed in white homes will not easily revise their opinions. They believe, as do many blacks, that a white family cannot help a black child identify with his or her cultural heritage.

Cassie decided to place her son for adoption with an agency after struggling for five years to do a good job of parenting and not doing well at it. She set up an appointment to discuss placement and was surprised to learn that the social workers were hesitant to take the boy on since he was African American and they would have difficulties finding a home for him. She said she was Caucasian and it was fine with her if her child went to a Caucasian home, since that was what he was used to.

The worker told her that children with African American blood were only placed in African American homes. This didn't make a great deal of sense to Cassie. She left and found a Caucasian home on her own that welcomed her son with open arms.

Large groups of parents who have adopted children of other races and nationalities believe these adoptions have been successful. But adoption agencies, mindful of the position of the African American social workers, have discouraged couples from adopting children of a different race. Proposed federal penalties are now changing this entrenched pattern.

ETHNIC SENSITIVITY

Your ethnic sensitivity will not come into question unless you are considering adopting a child from a different culture or ethnic group. Then you will be quizzed on this issue. (Perhaps the ethnic sensitivity of those *not* considering adopting a child of a different race should be more in question, but it isn't.) You need to have good answers ready about how you will help your child of a different race or culture deal with these issues throughout his or her life.

RELIGION

Except for private religious agencies, most agencies do not have specific requirements for religious backgrounds of applicants. Catholic and Jewish agencies are the most common private religious agencies. The religious requirement from these agencies is obvious.

At times, the birth mother has specific religious criteria for her child; an adoption agency is likely to honor her request. Her request may be quite general, such as "I want my child to be raised by people who believe in God," or "I want my child to be raised in a home where religion is a significant part of the family's life." Some mothers may want their children specifically raised Catholic or Methodist. Since the biological mother may find out the histories of several families seeking to adopt, her religious preferences may enter into her decision.

Agencies do not specifically prevent people of any faith from adopting children, but under circumstances where religion affects the child's care, the agency will consider the case separately. Religions that prevent a child from receiving medical care are viewed skeptically. Again, since it does not fall into the "normal" range, a less popular religion is likely to be considered a disadvantage in a prospective adopting family.

MARITAL RELATIONSHIP

Length and strength of marriage are criteria used to select most adoptive parents. The length of the marriage is easy to measure; the strength of a marriage is harder to discern.

Some agencies specify how long a couple must be married before they will consider that couple's application for adoption. Most require between one and three years of marriage. This requirement has three purposes. The first is to ascertain the stability of the relationship. The second is to help preserve that stability by not adding the stress of placing a child too early. (This reason has much less validity now that there is such a long wait after the application is accepted.) The third is to determine with certainty that a fertility problem does exist. Sometimes the stress of trying to have a baby will cause fertility problems that can be resolved without treatment. Almost anyone can tell the story of a friend who got pregnant right after adopting a baby. This is not as common as it may seem, but it does happen.

When the agencies attempt to determine strength and stability in the marriage, they work from a precarious position. Who knows what makes a good marriage? Some marriages that people would consider strong and secure are relationships others would not, under any circumstances, consider satisfactory—yet for the couples involved, they work. Our society doesn't have one good kind of marriage; but for some reason, if you are seeking to adopt a child, your marriage has to meet a certain set of criteria.

Characteristics exemplifying marital strength vary with the agencies. They are usually positively influenced if the marriage seems to show "communication between the partners," a "sharing relationship," and "being committed to the marriage." One agency looks for a "growing" marital relationship. While all these characteristics are worthy, they cannot be reliably assessed. Even if an adoption agency could measure whatever criteria it feels creates a good marriage, it is obvious that some marriages can and do work successfully without all these factors present or maybe even without any of them present.

Some adoption agencies have different requirements for the marriage if one of the partners was previously married. Any couple with a previous marriage is given extra scrutiny. Despite the large numbers of people who have been divorced, divorce is still viewed negatively by most agencies. They are unlikely to eliminate you for that factor alone, but it is one more black mark that works against you.

MOTHER'S EMPLOYMENT

Adoption agencies have fluctuated on how critically they view an adopting mother who works. When babies are plentiful, employment of the mother has been acceptable. With the current scarcity of babies, some agencies want one parent to remain home. While more and more people are recognizing that men are quite capable of being the primary parent, it is a rare case where an adoption agency will place a child in a home where the father is to care for the child. Again, this does not fit into the "normal" pattern. Strong questions would be raised about the adoptive mother's ability to mother, which would lessen a couple's chances of having a baby placed with them.

Other agencies require that "acceptable arrangements be made for the care of the child." Marie and John found that this sounded better than it turned out to be in reality. Marie was a doctoral candidate in chemistry and very excited about many areas of her life. She wanted it all and she had the energy and drive to do it all. She was thirty-two and felt she had to go ahead immediately if they wanted to adopt. She also loved her work and had several exciting professional opportunities coming up. To pass them up now was to pass them up forever. John fully agreed. The adoption agency didn't. The couple's application was denied. For the agency, Marie's choice was either baby or work. Despite large numbers of working mothers in the United States, traditional agencies want the family to be the way they *believe it should be*—with a full-time mother. With few exceptions, other arrangements do not qualify.

PARENTING SKILLS

Deciding what constitutes quality parenting is like evaluating what makes a good marriage. No one can say, if you do this or that, your child will turn out well-adjusted. We simply do not know what makes good parents. The best predictor of parenting ability is "successful" parenting, but the agency is usually evaluating people who don't have children. Given these rather serious limitations, the agencies set out to do exactly what no one has shown they can do: evaluate who will make a good parent. While their task is impossible, their intentions are admirable.

Goal in mind, the agencies say they search for potential adoptive parents who can "love and accept a child they did not produce." They want "parents who can be open about the biological parents" and who can be "understanding of their adoption decision"; "respect for the biological roots of the child" and "a willingness to discuss the child's adoption with him or her" are other ingredients. Generally, prospective parents who are open and speak easily with a social worker will be viewed as potentially able to be open and communicate well with a child.

Beyond the adoption issue of parenting, an agency looks for the basic skills used in raising children. They want parents who can allow a child to grow to his or her own potential, who are able to give and receive love from a child, who can meet the needs of a child, who have a realistic approach to parenting, who are accepting, nurturing, supportive, and understanding. Basically the agencies seek parents with good, healthy child-rearing skills.

The adoption agency uses several criteria in evaluating these skills. What the potential parents say, what experience they have had with children, and what their relationships and experiences with their own parents are like are all part of the parenting-skills evaluation.

To evaluate your experience with children, the worker will want to know all the contacts you've had with babies and children—the more, the better. If you have had none, the agency may feel that you lack the skills necessary to parent. Search your background. Remember every baby-sitting experience, the Christmas with your sister's family including her three children, the day at the zoo with the neighbors and their children, your airplane ride and discussion with the four-year-old who ended up in the seat next to you. You need to prove you have parenting skills.

DISCIPLINE

In the past, discipline methods were seldom discussed by agencies evaluating people to adopt. Today that is different. The awareness of child abuse and neglect has caused all agencies dealing with children to give more focus to this topic.

Your potential methods of disciplining your child will be discussed at length. Some agencies will expect you to submit a written statement describing how you plan to discipline your child. It is not OK to say that physical punishment will be a part of it. Learn something about appropriate discipline before you begin the adoption process.

OTHER CHILDREN

Adoption agencies are frequently confronted with couples who already have children but who want to adopt another. When this is the case, the agency worker has a real opportunity to evaluate you as parents.

If you have other children, their reactions to having a new sibling will be an important issue. Be sure to include those children in your planning because they will be directly involved in the adoption; their views will be considered as the worker decides about placing another child with your family.

PERSONAL HISTORY

What kind of a family do you come from? What is your relationship with your siblings and parents? While these questions may seem somewhat irrelevant if, say, you have been married and on your own for ten years, most agencies are looking for people who come from stable family backgrounds.

When Lori and Scott went to adopt, they did not know their childhoods would be evaluated. They were both proud of the fact that Scott had overcome a very difficult childhood. He had been badly neglected and was eventually, at age twelve, sent to live in a boys' home. He really pulled himself up on his own and established a close and loving relationship with Lori, whom he married when he was twenty-five. Lori and Scott were turned down by the adoption agency because Scott lacked the proper parenting model, and it was a great blow to them. After this rejection, they felt they'd made a mistake in telling the agency about Scott's childhood at all.

We know that abused children may become abusive parents. Although this isn't always the case, when agencies see abuse in family backgrounds, it is a red flag and they will check it out very carefully.

Other issues that cause agencies to hesitate about you as a potential parent are a family history of alcoholism, psychological problems, drug addiction, sexual abuse, or depression. If you discuss these as part of your family history, you need to explain them fully to your social worker or they may create problems for you.

ATTITUDE TOWARD ADOPTION

Increasingly, adoption agencies view trying to assess a couple's attitude toward adoption as a lifelong process. This is almost certainly in response to the increased input from adult adoptees and birth parents. Research is showing that adoptive families are not like other families; they have unique issues. If they pretend to be the same as biological families, the child's problems increase in the adolescent and adult years.

Agencies are looking for families who recognize that adoption has some unique issues. They are also looking for couples who will openly discuss adoption with their children.

CRIMINAL BACKGROUND

One criterion that is sure to be considered, and that usually is the easiest to check, is your criminal background. You will be asked to authorize a background check so that your records can be verified. The agency will receive a clearance if you have no criminal history. If you have a drunk-driving arrest, criminal charges, or negative involvement with the state agency which protects abused or neglected children, these will show up on the clearance check.

Be honest, because the agency will find out. Jenny and Ryan thought they didn't have a record; when their older daughter went to the child protection agency after her father hit her, no action was taken. Even though a social worker visited them, the investigation had stopped at that point.

They seemed like a wonderful couple to the worker. Their older daughter was no longer living with them, but their younger son was still at home. The son seemed to love his father and also got along very well with his mother. The agency was indeed surprised when the report came back saying that they had a record of child abuse. The couple was angry and tried to explain. While the agency tried to sort out the disparity in their stories and the story from the child protection agency, Ryan and Jenny became more angry. The agency went to bat for the couple against the state and ultimately was able to gain approval, if the couple took a parenting class and an anger management class.

Jenny and Ryan took the classes but Jenny's resentment grew. She became angry with the agency even though they had continued to try to work with her through this process. She was already angry with the state, and her anger toward her older daughter increased. The anger management class clearly wasn't effective. She finally decided she didn't want to move ahead with the adoption process.

PERSONALITY FACTORS

If you describe an emotionally stable and mature person, you have just included the personality factors the adoption agencies are seeking in their potential adopting parents. The agencies' descriptions of successful applicants include the following:

- emotional maturity
- sense of humor
- ability to deal well with others
- affectionate
- accepting
- problem-solving ability
- good self-image
- stability
- awareness of own dependency needs
- sensitivity and caring

- commitment to whatever he or she undertakes
- security within self
- ability to see small gains
- optimism about life
- honesty and receptivity
- self-integration
- wholesomeness
- empathy
- self-awareness
- common sense
- motivation
- character
- willingness to share
- understanding
- ego strength
- warmth
- stable, meaningful relationships
- success with struggles
- healthy distance and perspective
- ability to cope with stress and change
- flexibility to handle whatever comes along
- acceptance of responsibility
- realistic expectations
- ability to delay gratification
- acknowledgment of own imperfections
- ability to handle frustration and anger
- support of extended family
- ability to relate positively and grow
- ability to turn to others for assistance if needed
- high expectations of life, of self, and of others

What does this lengthy list of characteristics tell us? It means if you have yourself really together, the adoption agency will consider you "normal" and will see whether it has a child for you.

———————

Seeking the best possible homes for their limited number of adoptable children and trying to make the best placements possible, the agencies have an extremely difficult job. They necessarily work in the dark, because no one knows which homes will be the best for the available children. Unfortunately, many fine people are turned down because they do not adequately fit the undocumented criteria for becoming good parents.

Fighting an Agency's Rejection

If you go through part or all of the adoption agency process and are rejected, is that it? Or are there ways to fight the agency's decision? Is there a chance you can be reconsidered?

The way to begin trying to reverse an agency's decision is to find out the cause. This sounds easy but is not. Many times agencies will be vague, saying they simply have too many applicants for the number of children they have to place. Try to get the agency to be specific about why you were eliminated, but be tactful; you are still trying to work within its system.

Annie and Ed decided to fight the rejection they received from one agency. They were a fine young couple who looked like ideal parents, but they made several tactical errors with the agency. They waited until they had been married nine years to seek a child, so the agency felt a child was not too important to them. Annie worked as a teacher and loved it, but the agency felt this could be a problem if she decided to go back to work after adopting. Annie and Ed thought they could ask for a baby, since that was their first choice, but the agency believed the request demonstrated their lack of flexibility. They led a busy, active life, so the agency felt it would be difficult for them to incorporate a child into their lifestyle. So they were rejected. And they were crushed.

They went back to find out the reasons for their rejection and whether the agency would reconsider. Of course, this effort alone indicated to the agency a greater desire for a child than previously believed. So the agency, knowing of Ed's powerful position with a television station in the community, decided to allow them to be evaluated by an agency psychologist for their potential parenting ability. Ed and Annie were bright enough to know that you should not let the person who has rejected you send you to his or her colleague for a second opinion. They asked if they could have an evaluation from another psychologist, and the agency agreed. The psychologist they found gave them a glowing evaluation, which they well deserved. The agency reconsidered their rejection, and within six months they had a darling baby boy. They had fought and won.

Most people's chances of fighting and winning are not good. However, it's better to fight than to do nothing. Or with the increasing number of agencies available, you may simply go to a different agency if you are rejected. If your finances limit your choice to the public adoption agency and they reject you, either fight or figure out a financial solution. You always have options outside of agencies that are worth considering, as well as the option of adopting internationally. Remember, the people who manage to adopt today are those who really know how to work within the system, or as others would say, to work the system. Or they find children through other methods.

Agencies Changing Their Approach

All agencies, and for that matter everyone working in adoption, need to continually evaluate their services to see if they are meeting the needs of their clients. Right now, public and private agencies are changing. They are changing whether they want to or not.

The most fundamental change that agencies need to make in the adoption process is to be more responsive to the individuals who use their services. Whether this means encouraging openness, counseling, eliminating secrecy, providing subsidies, changing the criteria for selection, changing the agency's philosophy, or changing whatever isn't working well, agencies are meant to serve their clients. If they are not doing that, it is time for a change.

AGENCIES AND ADOPTEES

The adoption agency system today is supposedly designed to be in the best interest of the child. In some ways we need to be less concerned about the child, to become equally concerned with all of the other adoption participants.

Even voicing this need to change is considered heresy in the adoption field. For years agencies have gotten away with questionable policies and procedures by hiding behind the all-encompassing concept "the best interest of the child." Saying you are in favor of "the best interest of the child" is like saying you are in favor of apple pie and motherhood. Who can question someone who has this at heart? But we need to question the concept. When we ignore the best interest of each person involved in adoption, we may, in fact, be ignoring the best interest of the child. If birth parents, adoptive parents, and foster parents were all treated with more compassion, we could significantly improve the mental health of everyone involved in adoption, which in turn would enhance the life of the children.

One of the most significant ways to improve the system for children (and others) is to speed up the process. The research on early childhood development is clear about the importance of the early months and years of a child's life. No child should stay in foster care a day longer than is absolutely necessary. Any child who stays in the system beyond what is absolutely necessary represents a failure on the part of the system.

To thoroughly serve the child who has been adopted means to provide service after placement. This can be done only if all parties are equal priorities for the agencies. Today, the primary emphasis is on the child's placement, but the "best interest of the child" after placement is often neglected. The child and/or the adoptive parents who are having difficulty cannot consult with the adoption agency for fear that doing so might indicate weakness and jeopardize the adoption. This is not in anyone's best interest. Similarly, grown-up adoptees who seek information about their biological parents are not served by an agency that tells them there is no way it can help and that they should be grateful for the adoptive parents they have. The teenage child who seeks information about his or her adoption could also benefit from some careful counseling, taking into account the current concerns being expressed. To serve the child also requires updating the medical records so newer medical problems of biological parents can be communicated to adoptive parents on an ongoing basis. In this way the health of the growing child is protected.

AGENCIES AND BIRTH PARENTS

You know that people frequently judge you without saying a word. You also know that when you dislike someone you convey this to them. Adoption agency workers are likely to show in some way their feelings toward the clients they serve. The negative view that adoption workers sometimes have of birth parents is difficult, if not impossible, to hide.

This attitude comes out in many ways. A small-group meeting in one class on adoption brought this point out vividly. The head of an agency who had worked for twenty years with pregnant women planning to give up their babies was addressing the group. She was discussing not adoption, but sex. She felt premarital sex was *absolutely immoral.* There were no circumstances that she could think of that would justify this type of behavior. All sex outside of marriage indicated promiscuous behavior. It would have been impossible for this woman not to convey her feelings to the hundreds of birth mothers and, at times, birth fathers with whom she was working. And it would have been difficult for these birth parents to gain positive feelings about themselves in this stressful time when their own social worker felt so negatively toward them.

The social worker who wants to be effective with her birth parent client must be able to genuinely like, respect, and care for that person. To try to provide help for someone you do not like, respect, or approve of is impossible and dishonest. In order to provide information to someone, a therapeutic relationship isn't necessary. But to counsel someone, to help him or her therapeutically, is impossible if the counselor has negative feelings about that person. When a social worker feels the client is so incompetent that he or she cannot make decisions, there should be no pretense that the client is being counseled. The client may be told what to do, but he or she should not be manipulated under the guise of counseling.

Does this mean social workers have to like every client? *Yes.* If they want to help the client, it's imperative. When workers find that they do not have positive regard for a client, they should be honest with themselves and turn the case over to another social worker. Either the clients should be sent to workers who can feel positively toward them or they should be told that they will be given information only.

In serving any client therapeutically, the social worker must first find out that person's feelings about and wishes for the relationship. *The role of a social worker in an adoption agency is not to provide solutions for people, but to help people find the best solutions for themselves.* The social worker is a facilitator in the client's growth, not the leader. The social worker is a helper toward the client's goal, not the director of his or her fate.

The client who is truly being helped will be given thorough consideration. The social worker should find out the best way for the individual client to relinquish the child and should work to make the relinquishment as healthy and growth producing as possible. To do this may entail modifying agency procedures. If this is impossible within an adoption agency, the adoption agency is wrong.

Birth parents sometimes shy away from public adoption agencies because they want updates on how their child is doing from time to time. This, too, should present no problem to an adaptable agency. As long as adoptive parents know this is part of the arrangement, what is the problem with periodic updates for the birth parents? Birth parents also resist using public adoption agencies because they want to know the adoptive parents. This desire should not be too difficult to comply with, and many adoptive parents would readily agree to meet and talk together with the birth parents. If the primary parties involved aren't against this idea, why should the adoption agency prevent any openness when clients want it?

Birth parents may hesitate to use adoption agencies because they give little or no financial support while parents are pregnant. This should be an issue addressed by each agency. Offering financial help does not mean a baby is being sold. Financial help allows a woman to maintain her dignity and the health of her unborn child, despite the fact that the child will be placed for adoption.

One thing agencies do offer at this stage is counseling. It is a valuable service. Frequently, the biological parents become involved in a group counseling session where they share a common bond with others in the same predicament.

AGENCIES AND ADOPTIVE PARENTS

Adoption agencies should view the fact that they sometimes feel threatening to people who apply to them for a child as a failure on their part, and some do. Certainly the agencies are in a position of power in the adoption process, but their goal should be service, not power.

If the adoption agencies viewed potential adoptive parents as clients to be served, how much more effective and honest everyone could be with each other. If you as an adoptive parent felt that the agency worker were there to help you rather than eliminate you, how much more beneficial this time would be for you.

Adoption agencies do not prevent all potential parents they reject from adopting babies. An agency may say you are not good enough for them, but that doesn't stop you from going elsewhere to adopt. Recognizing this, it seems the agencies should examine why they feel a couple is not ready for a child and help them to prepare, rather than just eliminate them from the system or force them to find a child elsewhere. This is the only place in our entire society where people are screened for parenting. (Some states actually evaluate the quality of the work private agencies are doing by making sure they turn down some people who want to adopt.) Why not use this vehicle as a place to improve parenting skills rather than simply say no? The emphasis in adoption home studies should be on preparing people for parenting.

The adoption agencies, of course, reply that because there are too many parents and not enough children to adopt, they must eliminate applicants. Why? Why don't they instead seek to improve their services to all the people involved? Maybe then the idea of putting a baby up for adoption would appeal to more women and the scarcity of infants would be alleviated.

The agency should be involved in recruiting babies to help serve the people who wish to adopt. Agencies should actively promote adoption to women who contemplate abortion. Who can better be advocates for adoption than those who work in the field and who see the need?

The time potential parents spend with a social worker should be real counseling time. All their feelings of deficiency and inadequacy about infertility should come out here. Their fears about adopting a child should be discussed here. Their disappointments or reservations about this kind of parenting should be dealt with here. These are not insurmountable problems that indicate a couple *should not* adopt a child. Adoption agencies say that counseling does occur, but how can it, when the adoption agency is trying to judge your fitness to parent? Judging and counseling are incompatible. Counseling adoptive parents can be effective only if the system's goal is to help the adoptive parents become the best parents possible. Some people may become better parents than others, but that is not the question. The goal of the adoption agency needs to be changed from judging to helping.

AGENCIES AND FOSTER PARENTS

While foster parents are not usually discussed in adoption books, their role within the agency system could be more effectively used. Unfortunately foster homes often become a place to tuck away children while a social worker decides their fate. Foster parents become isolated and alienated from the child's past and future, which makes it hard for them to be involved in his or her present situation. It also hinders adoptive parents, who need to have as much information as possible in order to help a child make the best transition.

Under the present state-run system, a child is placed with foster parents until an adoptive home is located. In actuality, the foster placement in most adoptions should be eliminated, and when foster placement is absolutely necessary, the stay should be as brief as possible. When there are complications with the child or with the birth parents, the child's stay may be longer but seldom needs to be as long as most foster home placements are. While we strongly believe these stays should be brief, we also believe that foster homes need to be integrated into the adoption process. The increased involvement of foster parents as important participants in adoption can improve the process for the child, the birth parents, the adoptive parents, and the foster parents.

The foster parents who believe their opinion is valued could become more involved with the child's care. The adoption agency should want to know how the foster parents evaluate this particular child. How does this child respond to change? What upsets this child? Is this a demanding or an easygoing child? Is the child socially responsive? The foster parents can make a valuable contribution to the evaluation of a child because they know him or her. Especially in long-term foster care, who knows more about the child than the foster parents? Even in short-term foster care in which one or two months are spent with an infant, there is seldom anyone else who knows as much about the child as the foster parents. As you increase the importance of their position in adoption, you are also likely to attract more qualified people to fostering.

The birth parent who turns the child over to an agency should also turn the child over to the foster parents. What information the birth mother has about her child will be most valuable to the people who will be caring for the child, and the transition will be healthier for everyone involved. The birth mother has a chance to view herself as caring enough to help this transition be smooth.

The foster parents should also be involved in the transition of the child from their home to the adoptive home. There should be an opportunity for the two sets of parents to talk about the child's habits and behavior patterns. To ask the foster parents merely to write down the child's schedule and a few words about him or her minimizes the role they have played in the child's life. Meeting the foster parents, like meeting the birth parents, also makes them more real to the adoptive parents. The adoptive parents can see how the child likes to be cared for— how the diapers are put on, how the bottle is held, how the bath is given. Even as infants, children are creatures of habit. Changes in routine are not easily tolerated. The fewer changes made during major transitions, the better for the child.

The role the foster parents might have as potential adoptive parents is discussed in Chapter 4. The primary area of discussion at this point is the need for foster parents not to become invisible in this transition period. Eliminating the separateness between each of his or her homes should help the child find greater consistency and stability.

———

Many of the things adoption agencies can do to increase honesty and openness in adoption are simple. The changes don't require the system being shaken to the core. The changes need to equally value each of the people involved in the adoption process. The changes require adoption agencies' commitment to the elimination of secrecy and separation, and to the addition of honesty and openness in their place. Many agencies, though certainly not all of them, are beginning to make these changes.

Summary

People who really want babies are going to find them somewhere, somehow. They will find children even if they will be unfit parents or even if they are seriously disturbed. To work with these people and everyone else who really wants a child within the framework of an organized setting would increase their potential for raising happy, healthy children. To force these people out of the system only causes them to look elsewhere and to lose the support and help that could come from the adoption agency and occasionally does.

There are many advantages to utilizing the adoption agency system. The biological parents usually receive more prerelinquishment counseling than in independent adoption. If the birth mother or birth father wishes not to be identified, he or she has the greatest chance of anonymity in the agency system. And counseling is usually very accessible.

Advantages for the adoptive parents include the knowledge that the child they adopt has been fully and legally relinquished before they receive the child. They usually feel confident that the child has been physically screened and that they will be told of any medical problems.

The adopted child also gains some advantages by being adopted through an agency. The child has a good chance of being placed in the home that most fits his or her needs. For instance, a child whose biological mother and father had demonstrated superior intelligence might experience great difficulty being adopted into a home with parents of less than average intelligence. The child with special needs will best fit in a home that can accept his or her limitations. The fact that an agency will probably still be in business in the future means there is someone who is in charge of the child's records.

The best way to increase your chances with adoption agencies is to thoroughly understand their method of operation. It is important that you understand who their primary client is and where you fit in the current adoption picture. With this knowledge of the agencies, you stand the best chance of getting your baby. We wish you luck!

CHAPTER 6

Different Ways
for Different People

INDEPENDENT, OR PRIVATE, ADOPTIONS used to be the kind of adoptions that were hidden, and people felt that they were almost illegal. Today, independent adoptions are the primary way adoptions take place. While alarming stories of adoptions gone wrong continue to circulate, most independent adoptions are just as successful as agency adoptions.

In the United States, there are five ways to adopt:

1. Adoption through an agency
2. International adoption
3. Independent adoptions (also called private, identified, or designated adoptions)
4. Family adoptions (stepparent, grandparent, or other family member adoptions)
5. Black market adoptions (illegal adoptions, baby selling)

Independent adoptions are legal in most states, although some states have specific provisions that must be met for them to be legal (see Appendix A).

Understanding Independent Adoption

Basically an independent adoption is one that is arranged directly between the adopting couple and the birth mother or birth parents. While there may be an intermediary, such as an attorney or an adoption facilitator, there is direct contact between the birth parents and the adopting parents.

At times people confuse independent or private adoption with open adoption. The one has nothing to do with the other. You can have a closed or a very open independent adoption. The confusing part is that open adoptions originated in independent adoptions and many independent adoptions have considerable openness. We discussed openness in Chapter 2 and strongly believe it is a concept that anyone considering adoption should carefully think through before they proceed. If you are willing to have openness as part of your adoption, you significantly increase the number of potential adoptions you can pursue.

Independent or private adoptions have gained in acceptance because of the roadblocks that people who want to adopt have encountered. When the requirements become barriers and the selection process becomes arbitrary, people wanting a child decide to pursue a different way.

Sometimes birth parents deliberately choose independent arrangements so they can be intimately involved in choosing the home into which their child is adopted. At other times, a birth mother might decide how she wants her child placed on the basis of who talks with her first. While some people talk of the disadvantages of meeting the birth parents, this can be a most important advantage. To later be able to tell an adopted child about his or her birth parents can be extremely positive for all concerned. For the birth mother, having personal knowledge about the people who will be raising her child makes letting go easier. You can learn many facts about each other if you go through an agency to get your child. But if you meet, you know each other as responsible adults forever concerned about the child. The biggest single advantage to adopting independently is that this may be the only way you can get a baby.

The immediate placement from birth parents to adoptive parents is another extremely significant advantage in independent adoptions. As one woman stated, "I could never just give my child away to an agency.

I wanted to know exactly where and who she is with or I would be uncomfortable for the rest of my life." Agency adoptions emphasize the conservative approach; placements usually do not occur until all relinquishment papers have been signed. This approach may offer the greatest legal safeguard, but it is definitely not in the best interest of the child or of the adoptive parents. The importance of early bonding between parents and child cannot be overestimated—it is critical. In some independent adoptions, the adoptive parents are allowed to spend time with the newborn within hours after birth. Psychologically this is a distinct advantage to the child and the adoptive parents. It is also to the advantage of a birth mother concerned about the child easily fitting into the new family.

The biggest difficulty in adopting independently is trying to figure out how to do it; the process can become very complex. But before you become overwhelmed with the process, it is important to understand the great number of people who are available to help with your adoption.

Sorting Out the Helpers

One of the most confusing parts about adoption to those just beginning this process is who are the people, the helpers, involved. The Yellow Page listings have many different people to call if you want help, but trying to figure out who to call is not easy. As we have suggested, seek help from others who have been through the process. They know some of the pitfalls that can await you. Check out more than one place. There is great variety among attorneys, consultants, and agencies, and you need to know with whom you will be working. Trying to sort out the people involved is a major undertaking. So understanding what each of the people or groups does is generally a good place to start. Each of the groups we describe may have some role to play in your independent adoption.

PUBLIC ADOPTION AGENCIES

Each state operates a number of public adoption agencies, which are considered the most traditional way to adopt. These public agencies look after many children with special needs, too, and are not as likely to have infants. Applicants may have longer waits before finding a child.

At times these agencies become involved in adoptions that began as independent adoptions and then become what is called designated adoptions. In these adoptions, the agency takes over the adoption once the match has been made.

These public adoption agencies are usually the agencies who are involved in the post-placement study of independent adoptions.

The cost for public agencies' services is generally relatively low because of the number of special-needs adoptions they are involved in. Post-placement reports are usually free to the adopting couple and paid by the state. The cost for being involved in designated adoptions will vary and you need to check into this before beginning.

PRIVATE ADOPTION AGENCIES

Private adoption agencies are more numerous. Some emphasize open adoptions, some have religious orientation, and others are just general-service agencies. It is difficult to tell one agency from another unless you read their literature, go to their meetings, or hear about them from another source. In some states, the only people or organizations, besides attorneys, who can assist in adoptions, are state-licensed agencies.

People may use private adoption agencies to either do their home study or to do their post-placement study in independent adoptions. These agencies may also assist in designated adoptions.

The cost for their services varies, so you want to know ahead of time what the fee is and what services it covers. These agencies generally cost more than public agencies; they are also most likely to have infants.

ATTORNEYS

In most states, attorneys are involved in adoption services. At the very least, attorneys are used in order to finalize the adoption process in court in independent as well as agency adoptions.

While many people would argue that lawyers should be involved only with the legal aspect of adoption, most adoption attorneys are also involved in finding children. Not all lawyers will get involved in adoptions. If you want to work with an attorney, make sure that the one you select knows something about adoptions. There is no one group who handles adoptions, though some specialists have formed an organization called the American Academy of Adoption Attorneys (see Appendix F). Not all adoption attorneys belong to or support some of this group's beliefs.

Costs vary greatly and are something that you should check before you retain any attorney to help you. If you need an attorney only to legalize the process after you have found a child, you have more flexibility in which attorney to use. If you are adopting a child from another state, there are additional laws you need to be familiar with; you may need attorneys in both states, and you certainly need to know the laws in each state.[1] The actual legal process of adopting is not very complex in most normal adoption situations; if the adoption is contested, you need the best and most knowledgeable attorney you can find.

COUNSELORS, PSYCHOLOGISTS, PSYCHIATRISTS, AND OTHER THERAPISTS

In most states, counselors, psychologists, and other licensed therapists can help with adoptions. How involved they can get depends on the laws of each state. In most cases, we strongly believe that some kind of professional counseling should be available to the birth mother who wants it. In independent adoption, that means you need to find and pay for the appropriate counseling for the birth mother you are working with.

When you consult one of these professionals for help finding a child or for counseling about infertility or adoption, make sure the person is well informed about these issues. While therapists must be licensed by the state, their training may not cover the area you need. You can obtain referrals from the American Psychological Association, the American Psychiatric Association, the American Association of Marriage and Family Therapists, and the National Association of Social Workers (see Appendix F). Always ask if they have a specialty in the area of adoption.

Costs for these therapeutic services vary. If you are hiring a professional to counsel a birth mother, clarify ahead of time the number of sessions and/or the fee you will pay for these services.

ADOPTION FACILITATORS

Adoption facilitators, or mediators, became a part of the process as independent adoption became more popular. In fact, the use of adoption facilitators has been one of the most significant changes in adoption in recent years. People, frequently those who were dissatisfied with their own adoption experience, realized that they could help others in adopting; they began to provide services informally and met with an enthusiastic response. From there, they went into business as adoption facilitators.

Some facilitators see their role as one of matching birth mothers and prospective adoptive couples, but they do not give assistance after the process begins. Others merely sell leads about a potential birth mother to someone interested in adopting. Others work more broadly. There is no licensing requirement for facilitators, and therefore, it is impossible to take complaints to a governing board if you are unhappy with the services provided to you. Some untrained facilitators have become outstanding sources of help for people wishing to adopt.

In general, the cost of the services of adoption facilitators is lower than that of many other helpers but not always. Check out the costs ahead of time.

ADOPTION SERVICE PROVIDERS (ASP)

A new legal helper in California is called the Adoption Service Provider, or ASP. This individual provides services to birth mothers or birth parents in independent adoptions. The goal of the state in requiring that this service be offered to birth parents was to make sure that birth parents are not taken advantage of. The way this idea has evolved has solved some problems and created others. Different states may have specialists like this, so learn about your own individual state laws.

When this service is required, it adds an additional cost to the adoption that the adopting parents must pay.

The way to receive the help you need on your adoption is to become informed. Thoroughly investigate the people you may hire to help you. Adoption is a business. The people who are helping you may have strong altruistic feelings about the services that they provide, but they are also earning a living. Even the workers in public agencies or the therapists or the workers in nonprofit corporations have to make a living; you cannot assume agencies or people are there merely to help you.

You also need to be very careful about hiring people because of the cost involved. Sometimes you can go to an attorney who will take a $4,000 retainer—and then nothing happens. You never hear from him again. This same thing can occur if you go to an agency that requires a large retainer. So if you speak with several groups, facilitators, and attorneys, and give each of them a retainer, you can invest a great deal of money in this process and still have no assurance that you will be able to adopt a child. Be careful how you spend your money in the initial phases of your adoption process.

Some states require everyone who provides help in adoption to be licensed. Through licensing, the state monitors groups to protect the public from unscrupulous, unethical, or illegal practices. But while this sounds good, it does not often work. More effort is spent on enforcing rules and regulations than on rooting out unscrupulous, unethical, or illegal practices. The agency that usually oversees the private agencies is the same group that watches over public ones; the result is that some unnecessary rules and regulations that encumber traditional public agencies also weigh down the private ones. At times the people policing the private agencies are from public agencies that are not sure if private agencies should be operating.

Remember that licensing is only a minimal requirement. It doesn't mean the agency will meet your needs or will do things the "right way." Efforts at applying standards from state to state, and even from agency to agency, have been unsuccessful.

Once you have found the people you want to work with, the process becomes clearer. If you go through an attorney who advertises across the United States, he may tell you that he has leads coming in regularly and you don't need to do anything except wait. Another attorney will tell you what to do to find a lead for yourself. These same differences can be found in facilitators or agencies. So the process you will follow will be determined somewhat by who you hire to assist you.

Conflict over Independent Adoption

Independent adoptions are legal in most states (see Appendix A), despite attempts to make them appear shady or somewhat illegal. Most independent adoptions go smoothly, with no problems. For many adopting parents, an independent adoption allows them to begin to feel that they are now taking charge of their own lives by taking charge of their adoption process.

In the past, adoption agencies have attempted to have independent adoptions ruled illegal; only in a few states have they been successful. Some agencies claim that independent adoptions should be outlawed in order to protect the welfare of the child and that somehow making adoption a private business opens the door to abuse and fraud. These agencies say that private-adoptive homes are not thoroughly investigated prior to placement and, therefore, are sometimes inappropriate or unsatisfactory. (Could this argument be carried further, to say the state should investigate married couples before allowing them to conceive and raise children?)

If the adoption agencies could clearly demonstrate a higher quality of parenting in agency-chosen homes, they might have some reason to advocate only their own kind of adoption. But no research has shown that agency adoptions are any more or less "successful" than independent ones. Some workers point out the difficulties in evaluating potential parents and maintain that evaluations ought to be replaced with preparation for parenting.

Another reason some agencies want independent adoptions stopped is that they decrease agency business. Many agencies across the country have closed because the commodity they deal with, namely children, is no longer available in sufficient numbers to support the agencies' expenses. A child placed independently might under other circumstances have been placed through an agency.

Some agencies maintain that independent adoption does not meet the interests of all the people involved. They claim that anyone who has been rejected by an agency as unfit can still go out and adopt independently. They claim that counseling is not always provided to the woman relinquishing her child and that the child is a pawn in the process. At times these criticisms are justified. However, the same criticisms can properly be directed toward some agency adoptions as well.

There are several advantages to using an adoption agency to find a child to adopt. First, agencies may not have many babies, but they have more than any other single place. The second advantage is that most of the legal issues of adoption are taken care of by the agency. If you feel you would be uncomfortable with the exchange of names that usually (but not always) occurs in an independent adoption, this would be another reason to go to an adoption agency. With the possibility of records becoming open to all adult adoptees (see Chapter 15), the emphasis on maintaining anonymity becomes less valid. The fourth reason is that there can be a closer matching of qualities of the child with the adoptive parents because an agency has a greater number of both available.

Despite these advantages, many people still adopt independently—some because they feel they have been unfairly rejected by the agencies, others because they believe that the advantages of independent adoption outweigh the risks. Frequently people adopt this way because they believe it is a faster method to get a child.

Today, a merging of independent adoption with agency adoption has begun. Many people providing services in independent adoptions have started private state-licensed agencies, and some of the advantages of independent adoptions are being incorporated into other private adoption agencies. These agencies are responding to the need for more openness in adoption and more control of the process by the birth and adopting parents.

The existence of independent adoption keeps proper checks and balances on adoption agencies. It puts an appropriate amount of pressure on the agencies so they will examine the relevance of their methods in today's society. It also offers a choice to people who would have difficulty working within the often rigid system in some of the agencies. Research comparing independent and agency adoption results has found that neither is better or worse than the other—they are merely different ways available to you.

Before you go very far in the adoption process, be clear about the difference between independent and agency arrangements. You should know how an independent placement works and the advantages and disadvantages of adopting a child independently. You have a much greater responsibility if you choose to adopt this way. And in these adoptions, more than in most, you really need to understand exactly what you need to do.

How Independent Adoption Works

All independent adoptions are similar, but you can tailor your arrangements to suit your needs.

HOME STUDY

In most states, you are required to have a home study, an interview with a social worker in your home, before you can begin the legal proceedings for an independent adoption. (See Chapter 5). If this is the case, you hire someone who is qualified to do a home study and go through that process. This should be done early because some birth parents want to see a home study before agreeing to an adoption. Another reason for moving ahead on your home study is that you'll definitely need it if your adoption involves more than one state, because of a law called the Interstate Compact on the Placement of Children (ICPC).

FINDING A CHILD

In order to adopt independently, you have to find a birth mother or someone who has or knows about a child available for adoption. This is the main difference between independent adoptions and agency adoptions—you yourself have to find the contact who can provide the child.

The primary contacts for adoptable children outside of agencies have historically been physicians and attorneys. But these professionals, like the agencies, have seen the availability of children decline in recent years.

Many other potential contacts are available for the resourceful person who is trying to find a child. These potential sources are discussed in detail in Chapter 10. You make the only limit on the number of possible contacts you find. If you search long enough and thoroughly enough in the right places, you *will* find a child.

In order to locate a child or birth mother, tell as many people as possible about your situation and how they might help you. Seek leads from everyone you talk to, so that even if they don't personally know of a child for you, they can suggest someone else who might. You will have to contact many people in the hope of finding just one child. The more people who know of your situation, the greater the chance of finding the one child you want.

Above all, prepare. What do you do when someone says, "I heard about this baby I thought you would be interested in knowing about"? Are you prepared? Do you know where to go for the next step? Read Chapter 11 for help with your preparations.

HIRING AN ATTORNEY

Some people hire an attorney before they begin the adoption process. Others wait until they have found a possible child to adopt. Sometimes the easiest arrangements are made through attorneys. They know all the steps (or at least they should know them), so it is a bit easier for you to proceed if an attorney is the one who tells you about a baby. In no way does this mean you should limit your contacts to attorneys. You can and should hire one to handle the legal issues after you have found a child, but you don't necessarily have to have one to find that child.

It is important that you follow the laws of the state in which you live. In some cases it is best to hire a lawyer to merely give you legal advice on how to proceed. But if you hire an attorney to find a child for you and subsequently find, on your own, another adoption situation where an attorney is already involved, you may end up paying double legal costs.

All lawyers are not the same. If you have a legal problem related to a business contract, you want an attorney who has expertise in business contracts. If you are planning to adopt a child, you want an attorney who knows something about independent adoptions. Some attorneys know little or nothing about adoption—you don't want to hire one of those.

To assess the level of knowledge of your potential attorney, you need to interview several, then choose the one who seems best for you. Ask the attorney how many independent and agency adoptions he or she has handled. What have been the outcomes of those adoptions? The legal side of agency adoptions is far simpler than the legal side of independent adoptions. What are the laws under which you will have to operate in your area? In general, you are trying to figure out if the attorney knows what he or she is talking about. If you interview several lawyers, you will see very quickly which ones know most about the subject.

If you don't know where to begin to find the right attorney, call any attorney you know and ask for a suggestion. If you have read about any controversial adoption proceedings in your local area, find out who represented the parents. If someone teaches classes on adoption, ask the instructor for recommendations. If none of these suggestions work, call your local bar association and ask for names of attorneys who do adoptions.

Your attorney must know adoption law, agree with your philosophy about adoption, and represent you positively if the birth mother desires contact with him or her. The Ridgeways learned how important their attorney had been after their potential adoption fell through. They had been searching for about eight months when they heard from a cousin about a woman in Illinois who wanted to place her unborn child for adoption. They immediately wrote to her, sent her a picture, told her about themselves, and asked her to contact them or their attorney. She chose to contact the lawyer. But she and the attorney did not get along. The Ridgeways heard from the cousin that the birth mother did not like the cold, legal tone of the attorney, who made the process seem so much like a business. The Ridgeways had hired someone who did not represent them in a way that helped them.

Matt and Kate's situation was a bit different. They went out to interview attorneys in their area and found huge differences in their philosophies about adoption and in their costs; even legal facts were presented in different manners. They found one attorney who said that if the couple planned to pay anything other than doctors' bills, the adoption was illegal and he would not represent them. They went to another attorney who totally disagreed. He maintained that the state laws allowed them to pay for the birth mother's counseling, maternity clothes, car payments due while she couldn't work, and her dental work. Both of these attorneys, who did adoptions on a regular basis, were ethical and responsible members of their profession. It was important for Matt and Kate to choose the attorney whose philosophy most closely resembled theirs.

After you have settled on an attorney, you need to be positive that you are going about this adoption in a legal way. Your lawyer should be able to tell you exactly what is legal in your state. As the laws pertaining to adoption and their enforcement vary in different states, your attorney should be able to answer any questions you may have.

The law is not known for its consistency of application. Even if this book were longer, it would be difficult to clearly state specific laws from each state so that you could know exactly what you might encounter. Some state laws are not enforced, while other less specific laws may be enforced far more stringently.

No attorney can decide if you should go ahead with a specific adoption or not, but an attorney should be able to tell you exactly what the potential legal risks are. Then you should be able to choose whether or not to proceed with the adoption.

How great a legal risk would you be willing to take in order to have a child? That question is difficult for anyone to answer with certainty, but it is something you may need to decide. If you have had great difficulty finding a child and you are strongly motivated, you might be willing to take a reasonable risk. Most people who really want a child will take some legal chances rather than give up. Only the potential adoptive couple can decide whether and how far they should challenge unclear laws. An ordinary adoption can be handled rather simply. In times of problems, the adopting couple obviously needs the best legal help they can find.

INTERSTATE ADOPTIONS

Before you receive a call, it is difficult to predict in which state the birth mother may reside. Certainly this is true when you put résumés on the

Internet or mail your résumé to other parts of the country. Once you begin to put the word out that you are looking for a baby, you need to be prepared for the possibility that your baby may come from another state or even another country.

The process of adopting from a state in which you do not reside is a bit different than adopting in your own state. Once you have an identified situation, be sure to check with your attorney about how to proceed. There are a few additional steps when you are involved in an Interstate Compact for the Placement of Children.

The Interstate Compact on the Placement of Children is involved if a child is born in one state and the adopting parents live in a different state. The ICPC is an agreement between the states that they will cooperate with each other to be sure certain protections for the child will be followed when a child is being brought across state lines for adoption. It applies in both independent and agency adoptions. You must make contact with the state ICPC coordinator in both states and sometimes that takes extra time. Don't delay on this process or it may delay your adoption.

Some people who are involved in complex adoptions which present problems try to determine if the laws of other states might be more beneficial to them. They shop for a state where what they want to do is legal. While in some cases this "state law shopping" may be possible, it is important to be sure that you obtain legal advice before trying it.

DETERMINING THE AMOUNT OF OPENNESS

One of the primary deterrents for couples seeking a child through independent adoption is the potential contact they might have with the birth mother. Without question, you are more likely to have contact with one or both birth parents in an independent adoption than in an agency adoption. How much contact you might have will vary from situation to situation. It may be as minimal as an exchange of names or it may continue as long as you're raising the child. Examples of different levels of contact are given in Chapter 2.

The amount of contact you might have is difficult to predict. At times, you start out with one level, but the birth mother, who is usually in control, may decide to change that amount, as Wendy and Mickey found. This couple had waited a long time for a child. They were delighted to hear about a pregnant woman who wanted to place her child for adoption independently. They agreed to pay medical and other expenses incurred in her pregnancy. The birth mother was satisfied with the arrangement and chose not to have any direct contact with them at first. She wanted to know a lot of details about the adoptive parents from the intermediary, but she did not want to meet them. That was fine with Wendy and Mickey, who kept their fingers crossed each day of the pregnancy. At last "their" baby boy arrived. Everything was great. The birth mother never wavered in her decision to let them have the child—but after her son arrived, she decided she wanted to meet and talk with Wendy and Mickey.

The demand for this meeting was met with great uncertainty by Wendy and Mickey—they were scared. What if, after they'd finally got this close, she changed her mind? What if she didn't like them? However, the birth mother had what they wanted, "their" baby, so she could make the rules; they arranged to meet her at the hospital.

Wendy and Mickey left the meeting without the anxiety they'd come with. They were thrilled; they really liked the birth mother and felt she liked them. They had a long, meaningful talk and left feeling grateful that they had met her. The birth mother, too, felt that way. She said any previous doubts were gone after meeting the couple. She said that she was doing something that was important and that made her feel really good about herself. She felt her baby was going to have an excellent home, and she was absolutely certain that she had done the right thing after meeting Wendy and Mickey.

While most experiences are good, others cause more anxiety. Books can take you through the process from the viewpoint of both the birth mother and the adoptive parents, which may help to familiarize you with the advantages of this type of adoption.[2]

SETTING UP PRE-ADOPTION CONTACT AGREEMENTS

It is not unusual today for a birth mother to ask you to sign a pre-adoption contact agreement before a baby is relinquished. This doesn't mean she distrusts you; in fact, it is probably a sound practice for both sides.

A pre-adoption contact agreement is a legal document that describes what has been agreed to by the parties involved. It may spell out any visitation agreements, decisions on information sharing, times proposed for meetings between the child and the birth parents, the frequency of letters and picture exchanges, and other contact with the birth family. This agreement should be entered into willingly by each party. If either party is uncomfortable with any parts of the contract, they should discuss it all before proceeding. In years past this kind of agreement was seldom used, but the rights of all of the parties appear to be better served by using it.

COUNSELING

The most frequent criticism of independent adoption is that many times no counseling is available for the birth mother. (It may also need to be available for the birth father.) Anyone involved in an independent adoption should make sure that the birth mother has the option of getting some counseling as part of the process. It is the best insurance you can have for your adoption. You don't want a birth mother who is unsure of her decision to place her child with you; if she has doubts, find out about them early in the process.

If you are providing counseling sessions for your birth mother, be sure the counselor knows about adoption issues. Don't hesitate to ask if she or he knows anything about adoption, grief, loss, or relinquishing a child. If someone doesn't understand adoption, they may assume a birth mother's grief is a sign she doesn't want to move ahead when, in reality, grief is a natural part of a difficult process.

You can also limit the sessions or the amount you will pay for the counseling. Certainly no one expects you to provide counseling indefinitely.

MEDICAL CONSENT FORMS

One of the first things you should do upon receiving a child is have the birth mother sign a medical consent form so you can legally get medical treatment for the child. This is the type of document you don't have to be concerned with in an agency adoption; the agency obtains it for you. In an independent arrangement, you should be cautious about taking the baby until this document is signed.

Usually the hospital will have the birth mother sign this document before they will release the baby to you. If they do not have a standard form, you can ask the birth mother to sign a medical authorization, which you must provide or your attorney can prepare. When possible, it is worthwhile to have the document notarized, although this is not always critical. The most important thing is that the birth mother sign it.

If for some reason the form is not available, should you not take the child? Again, this is your choice. You increase your risks, but you also have the child. it is best to have the medical consent *and* the baby.

WORKING WITH A STATE AGENCY

After a child is placed with you in an independent adoption, you need to begin formal proceedings for adopting him or her. In most states, a court representative or an agency delegated by the state investigates you and your home and makes a report and recommendation. This investigation is usually conducted by a social worker trying to understand your background and see your home. He or she will want to understand who you are, your relationship within your family, how you will discipline the child, how you got the child, what money you paid to the birth mother, what arrangements you have made for future contacts with the birth mother, and how the child is doing now. The worker will go over what papers the state needs to complete the postplacement report.

The emphasis in the state's report is far different from, and generally more superficial than, the home study done before you find a child. In some cases, the state worker assigned to you will have less training than a social worker doing agency adoptions. The state is merely trying to make certain you can provide a fit home instead of trying to decide if you are the best or most appropriate home available. The burden of proof is on them, not on you.

Even though you are in a position of strength, don't underestimate the agency. Two examples illustrate the control that agencies continue to try to exert in independent adoption placements.

Thelma decided to place her racially mixed child for adoption after raising him until he was eight years old. She knew her son was spending too much time on the street. His abilities were going to waste as he performed poorly in school and was becoming increasingly difficult at home. Her attempts to provide guidance were unsuccessful, and she felt her own need to have a life apart from children. After much soul searching, she finally approached an adoption agency. She was shocked to learn that he would be placed in foster care for an indefinite period of time. She delayed her decision until she learned of independent adoption as an alternative. She heard of a potential adoptive couple who sounded perfect for her son: They had two older racially mixed adopted children who seemed to be doing well. The couple, who were Caucasian, and their other children were excited about having another child.

Everything proceeded as the couple had hoped. Hank, their new son, flourished in his new environment. After the usual "testing" period, he responded well to the guidance that came from his new family. His grades in school soared. Everyone was pleased with his pronounced progress.

The social worker, however, was skeptical. When Thelma went in to sign the papers, the worker told her she was sure that Hank must be having a difficult time despite the glowing letters of recommendation she'd received about the couple and Hank. The social worker felt a placement with Caucasian parents was inappropriate and would cause him problems (even though she had never asked the adopting couple one question about the racial issue). She doubted that he would adjust to the adoption because it implied rejection by his birth mother. Thelma was angry. She knew the couple and she knew Hank's progress; she felt certain he was doing well. She was sure she knew more about how he was doing than the social worker did, and she resented the implication that it was wrong to have placed Hank. After expressing her anger toward the worker, she insisted on signing the relinquishment form and stormed out of the office. The adoption did go through, but there were bad feelings for Thelma.

In another case, the Kents learned the hard way about working with the state agency in their independent adoption. They didn't know a lot about the process when they heard about a woman wishing to place her racially mixed child in their racially mixed family. They jumped at the chance, and soon Eliza was a part of their family. They had agreed to certain things with the birth mother before Eliza was given to them: Pictures would be sent yearly through an intermediary, and Eliza would be told about the adoption throughout her life so that it would not come as a shock to her. The couple had mixed feelings about these requests but agreed to them.

In their first meeting, the social worker indicated to the Kents that independent adoption was a poor arrangement and she thoroughly disapproved of it. After hearing that the birth mother had asked for regular pictures of Eliza, the social worker told them that many couples initially agree to provide pictures, but few actually do. The Kents were surprised but thought perhaps they also wouldn't need to send pictures. The social worker sensed their unsureness and continued to question their knowledge of adoption issues. Since Eliza had become theirs so easily, they really hadn't discussed some of these issues. They had spoken with a counselor who told them about Eliza, but now they felt the counselor might have been wrong on how she suggested they proceed. Their confusion showed. After telling the Kents that everything was fine at the end of the interview, the social worker wrote a negative report about them and it was given to the birth mother.

The birth mother was distressed to learn that the agency was recommending against the adoption. She asked the counselor who had assisted her in placing Eliza to intervene and set up a meeting with the Kents to discuss the situation. They reconfirmed their commitment to provide information about Eliza as she grew up and to keep a positive and open relationship between them. Over the objection of the state social worker, the birth mother strongly requested that the adoption proceed. She wrote letters of protest to the social worker's supervisor expressing her displeasure about how her case had been handled. She felt the original agreement with the Kents had been significantly undermined by the social worker's "meddling," that her case had not been handled in a professional manner—not "in the interest of anyone involved in the adoption." The adoption was completed despite the social worker's disapproval.

Social workers who disapprove of independent adoption should not be working with couples who adopt independently; however, such a person might be assigned to your case. Certainly there is a need for some investigation about the suitability of people adopting a child, but the goal of that investigation should be clear. Hostility toward birth parents, adopting parents, and independent adoption should not be a part of the social worker's interview.

In some states, you do not go to court until the post-placement report is finished and discussed with the birth mother, the birth mother's relinquishment has been taken, and a report has been filed with the court. In other states the process goes very quickly, and in a matter of days you are in court to finalize the adoption. Probationary periods are required in a few states, with some as long as six months; the waiting starts at the time your attorney files the petition to adopt.

RELINQUISHMENT PAPERS

The signing of the relinquishment or consent-to-adopt papers is *the* crucial point in the adoption process. In an independent adoption, the relinquishment papers are signed *after* the child has been placed with the new adoptive family. It is not the responsibility of the adoptive parents to obtain the consent to adopt. In an independent adoption, an agency designated by the state or an attorney (usually a public adoption agency) obtains the relinquishment. At times, a state may accept the birth parents' notarized signatures. The consent or relinquishment is the most important legal issue involved in adoption.

Actually, consent of the adoptive parents is also obtained. They give their consent by filing the petition to adopt. It is possible that adoptive parents can be unhappy with the child placed with them or feel that they were not fully informed about the child's background or medical history. They, like anyone unhappy with the adoption, can ask to stop the proceedings before they're finalized or declare the adoption void after finalization if they can prove that fraud occurred.

The consent of the child may also be necessary if he or she is an older child. Usually this consent is given at the court finalization hearing. At this time, the judge will ask if the child agrees to the adoption.

In some states, the consent of a foster parent is also recognized. Foster parents' rights have increased in recent years. Occasionally foster parents are allowed to contest the adoption if they believe it is not in the best interest of the child.

The critical person involved in consenting to the adoption is the birth mother. In the case of unmarried birth parents, the birth mother must consent to the adoption even if she is a minor. The only exceptions would be if (1) the birth mother is legally incompetent and unable to give consent, (2) the birth mother has had her legal rights to the child terminated because of abandonment, or (3) the birth mother has already relinquished the child to someone else or to an adoption agency.

The laws governing the consent of the birth father are unclear and less consistent in cases where the child is illegitimate. A landmark Supreme Court decision in 1972, *Stanley v. Illinois,* has had a significant impact on the rights of the unmarried father. The Court ruled that all parents, legitimate or not, are entitled to a court hearing before their children can be removed from their custody. This decision was based on the case of a man and woman who had lived together out of wedlock for a long period of time. They had several children, but after the woman died, these children were taken from the father on the grounds that he had no rights to his children. The major impact of the Court's decision was that it considered the man's rights as a father and not simply the family unit that had been established.

With this decision, adoption procedures for the relinquishment of the child were changed. Some states established what is called the Uniform Adoption Act. This, in effect, says the father must be notified before the child is adopted. He must then deny paternity, sign consent forms for the adoption, or do nothing and lose his parental rights. The law requires published notices of a pending adoption in the newspaper, stating that the father should claim the child if he wishes to exert his rights. State laws vary on how this may be done. If no one comes forth to acknowledge fatherhood, the father's legal rights are terminated and the adoption can proceed without the father's consent. Reading through the tremendous variety of state legal decisions leaves one convinced that the courts are inconsistent in how they view the rights of the unmarried father and at what point the father has or does not have parental rights. Clearly the best way to ensure the security of the adoption is to have the father's signature, but all issues pertaining to the father's rights are currently being given careful scrutiny.

Obviously the identity of the birth father is important. In most cases, the birth father is considered whoever the birth mother says he is. You have no way of knowing for sure that this is, in fact, the father of the child unless you do DNA testing. To go to this extreme to protect your adoption is probably overzealous. However, if the birth mother has not told you the truth, and if someone maintains and can prove that he is, in fact, the actual father, your adoption can be set aside. This is an extreme rarity.

If the birth mother is married at the time of conception, this legal father is also expected to sign relinquishment papers. In some cases, courts have ruled that, depending on what the birth mother says about their relationship at the time of conception, his signature may not be necessary. Exceptions are made on a case-by-case basis.

It is important to understand exactly how your state operates and to act within the law in obtaining the consent of the birth mother and birth father. Courts can nullify or void an adoption when it can be proven that the consent of the birth parents, especially the birth mother, was obtained fraudulently. Some states will not allow birth mothers to sign relinquishment papers until at least three days after the birth of the baby and then allow her up to six months to change her mind. On the other side of the spectrum are states where adoption relinquishments are immediately obtained from the birth mother and the adoption may be completed within a few days.

Usually, once a consent has been signed, it may not be withdrawn without the approval of the court. If the birth parent can prove that the consent was obtained by fraud, misrepresentation, or coercion, the court may decide to cancel the consent. If the parent has merely change her or his mind, the case will depend on the circumstances. The overriding factor in these decisions is what the judge deems to be in the best interest of the child.

The longer the child has been in the adoptive home, the less likely it is that the child will be removed. More and more, the courts are recognizing the concept of the psychological parent, the one the child has bonded with. This concept is clearly spelled out in legal precedents. At times the circumstances of the birth mother's relinquishment are less important than the length of time the child has been with the adoptive parents. But this tendency can be taken too literally, as in the case of couples deliberately delaying the process in order to increase the chances that the child will remain with them.[3] If the courts see that the delay has been caused with this in mind, they are less likely to rule in favor of the adoptive parents who caused the delays.

Even in cases where fraud was involved in obtaining consent of the birth parents, they must act within a "reasonable" length of time in order to have the adoption rescinded. The same is true if the adoptive parents believe they were not fully informed of pertinent facts at the time of the adoption. The courts expect people to act promptly if they believe a problem exists.

Timely relinquishment is beneficial for all persons in the adoption. Some state laws specify that the relinquishment must be obtained within a certain length of time, for example, forty-five days after the petition to adopt has been filed. This is worthwhile and can minimize the risk of the birth mother's changing her mind. Relinquishments are not always obtained in a timely fashion, so it is important that you have the best legal advice possible. Your attorney should be able to tell you how to best proceed if any question arises.

GOING TO COURT

Adoption court proceedings vary from state to state. Some adoption proceedings are conducted in superior courts, others in circuit courts, surrogate courts, domestic relations courts, county courts, orphan's courts, and so on. Your attorney will know the court in which your adoption should be conducted.

All people involved in consenting to the adoption must be notified of the court hearing. Again, your attorney will know how this notification must be made.

The actual court appearance will probably be in a judge's chambers or in a private session with the judge. The hearing is a legal formality but is usually a friendly informal session. Usually just the adoptive parents and the child, especially if the child is older, will appear for the hearing. Sometimes the attorney must attend. Some states do not require anyone to be there. It is a jubilant time for the adoptive parents, because it means the child is now theirs *legally.*

In some states the court hearing is merely a probationary hearing that declares the home is now open to be investigated. At other times, if there is some question about the fitness of the adoptive parents, the judge may require a further probationary period in which to examine their qualifications.

The state-appointed agency that completed the post-placement report plays an important role in this court hearing. If the agency says the adoptive home is not good for the child, the judge will probably not approve the adoption at this time. The agency's recommendation matters. If the judge has questions about the home, it is common to have a more extensive investigation. Remember, though, the agency must prove your unfitness. Generally, the investigation is cursory and rarely negative.

Following the granting of the final adoption decree, an amended birth certificate is issued for the adopted child. The new birth certificate lists the adoptive parents as the parents of the child, and the child's surname as that of the adoptive parents. In some states, the adoptive parents may request deletion of the birth city and county of the adopted child. These are details you need to be aware of so that you can decide how you want them handled. Your attorney should be able to keep you advised before you face each of these steps.

Adoption Expenses

Questions about the cost of adoption are some of the most frequently asked. People often assume that independent adoption will be too expensive—that isn't always the case. People with very limited finances might have fewer situations available to them, but it doesn't preclude them from finding a baby.

So what can you expect to pay for an adoption? How can you tell if your adoption is becoming an illegal adoption by what you are paying?

How can you pay what is fair and not too much? Is help available to defray adoption expenses as there is if you have a child biologically?

Certain expenses are part of most independent adoptions. Some of these expenses are found in agency adoptions also.

- Home study costs for the adopting couple
- Medical care for the birth mother (includes prenatal vitamins, other tests related to the pregnancy, doctor visits, delivery, care for the birth mother and baby in the hospital)
- Legal costs for the adopting couple
- Legal costs for the birth mother
- Other costs you might be expected to pay include living expenses, counseling, dental care, lost wages, and transportation.

These additional living expenses can add up rather quickly. However, in most adoptions you won't cover all of the possible expenses.

Each adoption is different and independent adoption expenses can vary a great deal; it is not always easy to determine if the fees being charged are legal. Don't hesitate to ask for an itemization of all moneys paid. Inflation quickly dates exact figures, but in general there are some guidelines you can follow: Adoptions that cost over $25,000 are likely to fall into the questionable category. You can expect medical costs of several thousand dollars; in deliveries where there are complications, the doctors' fees and hospital expenses could easily double. Legal costs should usually not be more than $3,000, but may be more if the attorney also makes the placement arrangements.

The main difference between black market adoption and legal independent adoption is the financial arrangement. In a legal adoption, no one is supposed to make a profit from the transfer of a child from the birth parent to the adoptive parent. The medical costs of the pregnancy, other pregnancy-related expenses, and legal costs are the only expenses allowed in a legal, independent adoption. Most states require a full disclosure of funds that the parties have exchanged in the adoption.

No one says, "Do you want to buy a baby?" Adoptive parents must be able to identify the circumstances that would make a black market adoption. The fact that a baby is being sold on the black market will not be disclosed.

Allison, a single woman, wanted a baby, and she wanted it legally. A friend told her about an attorney who knew of a woman about to deliver a child. She had her friend call the attorney to find out some of the details. The friend asked about the costs involved. The attorney said the adoption would be $18,500. The friend gasped and asked why it was so much. He said it was $7,000 for the medical costs, $3,500 for psychotherapy because the woman had been raped, $4,000 for expenses so the woman could "relocate," and $4,000 for the legal fees. The longer they talked, the more uncomfortable the attorney became with Allison's friend's comments and questions. He finally said, "I think you're right. This sounds too sticky and I don't want to be a part of it." They hung up. Allison then had her own attorney call the one with the baby. It was apparent that the attorney with the baby still did want to be involved. The total fee was the same, but the itemization was different from the day before. This lawyer told Allison's attorney to act quickly because several people were considering this child.

As you can see, an attorney can make the fees seem reasonable. Someone could consider this baby even though they didn't want an illegal adoption. It is not as obvious as the situation where a baby is offered for $50,000, an unmistakably illegal proposition.

In one case, an adoption was far less expensive than others but was clearly illegal. A woman calling herself Josephina called a couple she'd heard were looking for a Hispanic child. She told them about an expectant birth mother who wanted to place her baby for $5,000 and who would sign a paper that promised she would never bother them again. According to Josephina, the birth mother didn't want to meet the couple and wanted the money, in cash, to be paid to Josephina. Two days later, the baby was born, and Josephina wanted the money before the baby would be given to them. The couple, unwilling to take the chance of being involved in an illegal adoption, declined the offer.

It is worthwhile to formalize in the early stages exactly what expenses you, the adoptive parents, will pay; it is very difficult to say no to requests for money as the delivery of the child approaches. You also need to have an agreement as to what happens financially if the birth mother changes her mind and does not relinquish the child for adoption. This is a very sensitive area. It is also important to understand that most agreements would not be legally binding. For this reason, few people will be repaid the money they have invested in an adoption that doesn't work out.

While this is an issue usually discussed only in relationship to expenses paid the birth mother, it should also be considered with respect to your attorney or facilitator or even any agency you work with. At times, professionals who have worked with you on a failed adoption will allow you to work with them again on a second situation at no additional cost or with a special arrangement. Because there is no rule about how this is handled, it is worthwhile to be cautious and to ask questions ahead of time.

Some couples are resorting to a special kind of adoption insurance because of the growing costs for adoptions. If the birth mother backs out or changes her mind, the couple can recoup some of their expenses. Only certain agencies and attorneys make this service available to adopting parents.

Individual businesses are also responding to the increased numbers of people involved in adoption by making adoption benefits available to those who decide to adopt. Some employers now offer help and financial reimbursement for some adoption expenses such as:

- Help locating adoption providers (attorneys, facilitators, counselors, agencies)
- Help with legal expenses related to the adoption
- Payment of travel expenses, immunization, and translation services in international adoptions
- Psychological evaluation of the child you are considering adopting
- Medical expenses and examination of the child before the adoption
- Adoption agency (public or private) fees
- Post-adoption counseling for adoptive parents and family counseling
- Assistance on problems related to raising an adopted child
- Counseling on unexpected adoption issues

Companies provide payment for these services in order to offer equity between childbirth and adoption expenses. Usually company benefits range up to about $6,000 per adoption, but the coverage varies considerably from one company to another. Companies can provide this service at a very reasonable cost while providing a social benefit to their employees and helping them feel positively about their employer. Each company has specific guidelines for eligibility, so check with the personnel department or with the employee assistance program if one is available.

John worked for a large company that had benefits for adopting couples. When he and Nayla decided to adopt from Romania, they were delighted with the help they received. His company paid for the fee to their international adoption agency ($5,500), a part of the legal expenses that were necessary in the United States ($2,000), a portion of their travel expenses ($2,800), and expenses for translating documents ($575). In all the company paid for just about half of the costs of their adoption. Without their company's help, John and Nayla believed this adoption might have been beyond their means.

The federal tax credit of $5,000 for adopting families whose income is under $75,000 a year is one more way that you can help keep costs of your adoption down. Banks are also beginning to recognize the financial needs of couples adopting. MBNA America (see Appendix F) and others have available low-interest adoption loans for up to $25,000. You can even apply over the phone or through the mail.

Neither Kurt nor Chris was employed by a company with a reimbursement plan, but they did read and know about the federal tax credit that recently was enacted. Because their income was not over $75,000 they were eligible to write off $5,000 from their tax bill for the year they adopted their daughter, Hanna. Of course, their expenses were that high, but this tax credit helped make their adoption a lot easier on them financially than it otherwise would have been.

Health insurance frequently covers adoptions. As a result of federal legislation, companies with over fifty employees are required to provide up to twelve weeks of unpaid leave within a twelve-month period for new adoptive parents. Health insurance is required to cover most adopted children whose families have group health insurance coverage; this coverage extends from the time of placement with no exclusion for pre-existing conditions. All companies don't offer this, but it is well worth checking out.

It is also worthwhile to check out potential benefits the birth mother may have. In many cases she is eligible for state aid which will cover her birth expenses. Since she cannot legally decide about relinquishing her child until after the child is born, it is usually legal to have these expenses paid by the state. If the child has problems before he or she leaves the hospital, the state will frequently pick up these costs. (You can also check to see if your insurance covers the child from the moment of birth or if it only begins once you take the child home.) Your birth mother may have some other kind of coverage through her parents or her place of employment that will help pay for, or at least defray, some of the expenses you might otherwise incur.

So before you decide how much you can afford to spend on your adoption, see what help is available to you. Explore different options for finding your child. And remember what you may already have spent to try to have a baby; this helps keep adoption costs in perspective.

Family Adoption

The primary focus of this book is not on family adoptions, but they are one of the different types available. Half of all adoptions are made by relatives and present little difficulty. As long as the adoption is agreed upon by all the individuals, it is relatively simple. Usually no home study of suitability for parenting or probationary period is involved. While the same consent forms are necessary, the courts at times waive some restrictions that otherwise might be imposed. However, even in this type of adoption, it is worthwhile to hire an attorney to make certain that you proceed in a legal manner. Adoption is too permanent to let anything be overlooked.

The main concern in family adoptions is the potential for fights over the child. To have an aunt and uncle or grandmother and grandfather raise a child sometimes sounds good to the birth mother until she sees her relatives becoming "parents" to her child. Legalization of the new family arrangement prevents the relatives from moving the child about at whim because of family feuds.

The other form of adoption by relatives is stepparent adoption, and now that divorce has become common, there has been a significant increase in this type. The primary requisite in stepparent adoption is obtaining consent of the parent abdicating his or her parental rights; generally, this is the father. In some states, if the parent who does not have custody of the child fails for one year or more to pay child support or to visit the child, his or her consent to the adoption is no longer required.

As with all kinds of adoptions, you need to know the laws where you live. While these adoptions are different because you've already found the child you want, they still can be complex because of family history and dynamics.

Black Market Adoption

Of the several kinds of adoptions available, none elicits more emotional response from the public than those made on the black market. These are the adoptions where large sums of money are exchanged for a baby and the money is not related to the expenses of the pregnancy. They are not legal. They cause people to question the entire idea of independent adoption.

Cynthia adds: *When I last wrote on this subject, these black market adoptions caused the greatest furor. I have reread these words on many occasions since I first wrote them. Each time I try to understand what upsets people so much. I believe it has to do just with the concept of selling babies and not with what actually occurs. I would urge the reader to try to understand how black market adoptions are not much different from our current adoption practices. I would further urge you to be open to what is being written to see if it can't help you put any adoption into a different perspective. I have chosen to leave this section much as it was originally written. I believe the words are as true today as ever and are important to remember as you approach adoption. I also want you to know that this section of the book contains my personal views on adoption and the black market.*

Black market adoptions are not legal. In every state, laws prohibit people from profiting unduly from the placement of children for adoption. We have no way of really knowing how many babies are placed in this manner. It is estimated that five thousand to ten thousand babies are placed this way each year.[4]

Confusion exists about the difference between black market adoptions and independent arrangements, which are sometimes called gray market adoptions. The primary difference is in the exchange of money that takes place. The expenses that can be legally paid in an independent adoption are sometimes difficult to define. In a regular independent adoption, theoretically, no money is paid to have a child placed. However, the line between black market babies and gray market babies is not at all distinct. The law regarding the exchange of money in adoption cases varies from state to state, and many people circumvent it. Anytime anyone pays expenses that are not strictly necessary and perhaps should not have been paid, you in effect have a black market adoption. (This could include giving a twenty-dollar necklace to the birth mother as a gift.)

Why would any couple pay $40,000 or $50,000 for a baby when they could go to the local adoption agency or find another child independently at a fraction of the cost? Why would anyone risk getting involved in an illegal arrangement to get a baby? The answer to both of these questions is, they wouldn't. Couples would go to an adoption agency if they could or they would find a baby independently. Illegally obtaining a child is never someone's first choice, but it may become their only choice. People turn to the black market when they can't adopt from an agency, not necessarily because they are unfit or wouldn't be good parents, but rather because they don't fit the image of a parent the adoption agencies are seeking.

Black market adoptions thrive under certain conditions. Those conditions exist right now. There is a scarcity of infants available for adoption. There is a need for someone who cares about supplying what these prospective parents dearly want—babies. The traditional agency system does nothing to remedy the scarcity, nor does it do anything about taking care of all of the potential parents' needs for a child. As a consequence, a different group has emerged to handle these unmet needs—people who sell babies.

WHY NOT SELL BABIES?

Why are people upset about baby selling? If it is meeting a need and no one is hurt, why not sell babies? Selling babies would not work if there were no need and demand for the service. People are quick to criticize those involved in selling babies, but the ones who would come to their defense, those who have obtained children this way, are necessarily quiet.

Several concerns may be driving these criticisms. Is it the profit being made by the intermediary? Does baby selling sound like slavery? Will selling babies cause women to become pregnant just for the money? Do babies become more of a commodity this way than at an adoption agency? Are we concerned that the birth mother is being taken advantage of, or do we object to the birth mother making a profit from her nine months of labor? Just exactly what upsets us about black market adoptions?

The profit being made on black market adoptions seems to be the main concern for some people. They argue that intermediaries or baby brokers shouldn't profit from people's miseries. That sounds right, but in reality many people profit from other people's miseries. The surgeon operates on you for a fee, the dentist charges you for the tooth he or she pulls, the mortician profits from the death of your loved ones, the psychotherapist charges you for listening to your problems. Even adoption agencies make enough money in their "nonprofit" organizations to have nice facilities, good salaries, and pleasant working conditions. Our society is set up in such a way that you pay for the things you want, especially when you need them very badly. We seek these services only if we cannot provide them ourselves. Many people in our society profit from the needs of other people; but for some reason, to do this by selling babies really upsets people.

Many people believe it is horrible that an unwed mother became pregnant in the first place, and bad enough that she would consider giving the baby away, but for her to make a profit is, in their view, deplorable. Perhaps the reason people are so against the mother making a profit is that they really want the mother punished. If we pay her for her transgressions, aren't we rewarding evil? But are intercourse and pregnancy really evil? She may not be doing a good thing for society, but she certainly is doing a fantastic thing for the childless couple who have been stopped at each turn from finding the child they so much want.

If profit is what most upsets us in black market adoptions, perhaps the way to solve the problem is to figure out how to decrease the profits. One of the age-old ways to decrease profits is to allow supply and demand to equalize. Currently there is a great demand for babies. If we remove the legal restrictions from people profiting by selling babies and allow the supply to meet the demand, the cost of buying a baby will go down radically, and the profits will be cut drastically. Perhaps all the legal restrictions we put on baby selling are creating the very problem we deplore: large profits.

Perhaps we fear that the birth mother will be exploited. Will the offer of money for her baby keep her from doing the right thing for herself? Maybe she should have an abortion or maybe she should keep the baby. Maybe she needs counseling to decide what is best. If there is any possibility that she is being exploited, it is most likely to occur while this process remains illegal and underground. If a woman feels she is doing something worthwhile in placing her child for adoption, she can freely choose which alternative is best for her. Yet if the prevailing attitude is to punish her for what she has done, even in subtle ways, she is much more vulnerable to being exploited. All businesses, even baby selling, are easiest to regulate if they are not driven underground. Prohibition taught us this most vividly.

The criticism that baby selling is a form of slavery is difficult to substantiate. Perhaps all forms of parenting are types of slavery. (I'm not certain for whom—the parents or the child.) Certainly, any form of adoption could be subject to this same criticism. It would be difficult to say whether more slavery is involved when a child is bought for $40,000 from a baby broker or for $18,000 from a social worker.

Another complaint raised by critics of black market adoptions is that the fitness of the parents who are seeking to adopt has not been verified. Sex perverts and child abusers can obtain children by these unscrupulous means. Why any sex pervert or child abuser would go to all this trouble is beyond me—especially when it might be easier for such persons to have their own children and not have to pay so much for them. No one makes us pass any tests for parenting unless we want to adopt a child. Just about anyone, no matter how unfit for parenting, can have a baby. Only the infertile must offer proof of fitness for parenthood.

Another objection raised about black market babies is that they potentially take available babies from legal adoption sources. A related criticism is raised when some say that young girls are hired to get pregnant so that large profits can be made from the babies they produce. If this second criticism is true, then the first one is not. If it is possible to take potential children from the adoption agencies because of the profit to the mother when she sells her baby, then we should examine how we can learn from this. Should we offer greater incentives, better living conditions, and financial allowance to the birth mother who elects to place her child with an adoption agency? Again, instead of expecting penitence from her, let us demonstrate to the woman that her pregnancy is not such a terrible thing. Someone is going to benefit from her possible mistake and inconvenience.

People will respond that the approach just described would encourage women to have babies for profit. The feelings of remorse that are an inherent part of placing a child for adoption and the length of time it takes to produce a child will ultimately limit and discourage this practice. However, if someone is really good at making babies and can make them for others who are not, then why not?

One of the most poignant arguments against black market babies came from a pregnant woman about to give up her baby for independent adoption. She said she could never sell her baby because she was sure that someday her child would find her. How then could she explain selling her baby? As long as making a profit on giving up a baby for adoption is condemned, as it is today, she is right. Ultimately, the birth parent and the child may realize that, regardless of money, the most worthwhile situation occurred—a loving mother or father raised a loving child. That should be the focus in the debate over selling babies.

Another argument used against high-priced black market adoptions is that they discriminate against poor people who cannot afford to participate. This argument is a strong one only if you believe that black market adoptions are worthwhile. Again, if supply meets demand, the cost of buying a baby will be more affordable to people with less money.

Obviously, the stand I am taking on black market adoptions is not widely accepted. One writer on adoption boldly stated, "Baby selling is abhorrent to all civilized people."[5] I believe we should consider changing current adoption laws to allow the mother and those involved with arranging adoptions to make a profit. I take this stand for several reasons. I have known the pangs of infertility. I have known the intensity of the desire to have a child. I have met couples who desperately wanted a child they could not find. I have known women who loved being pregnant but who did not want to be mothers. I have seen poor women struggle financially with a pregnancy that would eventually become an adoption, fearful of taking any money because it might look like a black market adoption. Somehow there should be a way to accommodate all these people in their times of need.

People will say, "What of the abuses?" But the abuses will always be there. They are there now in parenting by birth and in adoptions through traditional agencies, independent adoptions, stepparent adoptions, grandparent adoptions—and black market adoptions. The abuses are least likely to occur when the system can be scrutinized—and the system can be scrutinized when the system is legalized.

PROBLEMS WITH BLACK MARKET ADOPTION

That said, a person should be very careful about getting involved in a black market adoption. As in all illegal businesses, unscrupulous people can be involved. Illegal business is unfamiliar to most of us, so we don't know our way around the system.

The biggest single risk in black market arrangements is that the adoption decree might be set aside if the illegality is discovered. As a consequence, people adopting in this way live in fear for years, knowing that someone can take their child from them. Of course, this fear diminishes over time. At some point, even if it is found out that you had paid $35,000 for your child, the judge is unlikely to take your child of five years away from the only home he or she has ever known. Living with this secret for years, however, is bound to take a toll on you. It also makes you vulnerable to threats of blackmail.

The financial risk in black market adoption, as it is currently practiced, is significantly greater than that incurred in adoption through an agency. The first figure quoted to a couple may not be the final cost. As with independent adoptions, it is important to have an agreement before you begin and to enforce it. After you have agreed to pay $40,000 and you have paid it, it is difficult to say "Forget it" when the baby seller says he or she needs $5,000 more. You can't say, "That's not fair" or "I am going to report you." Remember, the law does not look upon your baby transaction with favor.

Another problem with obtaining a baby through the black market is that when you go to court to finalize the adoption, you have to commit perjury. When the court requests an accounting of the expenses involved in the adoption, you obviously cannot tell the truth. The lie you tell, if discovered, could cause the adoption to be set aside.

As black market adoptions are currently conducted, the rights of the birth father may be ignored. If the birth mother indicates the father is unknown when he is really known, she is depriving him of his rights to his child. If this is later discovered, once again, the adoption could be set aside. (This could happen in any adoption, not just black market adoptions.)

At times the woman first agrees to place the child for adoption and later changes her mind. In a reputable adoption process, whether through an agency or in an independent adoption, the proceedings should stop at this point. In a black market adoption, the woman might be pressured into continuing. Threats of having to pay back money already spent on prenatal care might intimidate the woman into signing relinquishment papers she would not otherwise have signed. But if it can be proved to the satisfaction of a judge that the woman was coerced into signing consent forms, the finalized adoption can still be nullified and the baby returned to the birth mother.

In some black market adoptions, the birth mother enters the hospital and registers in the name of the adoptive mother. When the birth certificate is filed, the adoptive parents are listed as the birth parents. (In some cases involving international adoptions this same method of supplying false information is used.) Of course, this is illegal, and it, too, is grounds for taking the child from the adoptive parents; the child has not been legally adopted.

As you can see, there are definite risks in black market adoptions. Because of the risks, and mostly because these adoptions are illegal, we do not recommend finding a child in this way. On the other hand, there is much to be learned from the success of some black market adoptions.

Very few differences, other than those already mentioned, exist between independent adoptions and black market adoptions in relationship to the adoptive parents. The primary difference is how you obtain the baby. You need to make contact with someone who knows of a baby available for a sum of money. After that, the investigation and the legal process are usually the same. I believe most black market adoptions go rather smoothly, and most of the children adopted in this manner remain in the home of the adoptive parents, just as in any other adoption.

Summary

Adoptions that involve children being placed independently comprise the majority of adoptions in the United States. Independent adoptions are legal in most states. Some children are adopted through the black market, where money is exchanged not based on expenses but as payment for a child.

An infertile couple seeking a baby would probably choose an agency adoption if that choice were open to them. Agencies can offer many advantages, but many potential adopting parents are eliminated because of the scarcity of babies available. Newer agencies are beginning to offer other alternatives to the more restrictive and uncreative approaches to adoption that have dominated traditional adoption agencies. When agency alternatives are unavailable, the choice of most couples is independent adoption.

Putting together an adoption on your own is a complex process but a rewarding one; you will feel in charge of your own lives. In order for people to explore the concept of adopting independently, it is important that the process be thoroughly understood. Since you are doing this mostly on your own, you need to know all of the steps necessary and where to find the help you may need. While there are risks in all kinds of adoptions, you need to know that most of these adoptions work and are as successful as any other kind. They do take extra work.

Sometimes, searching for a child, you will encounter an opportunity to buy one. If you have been rejected by the agencies and are having difficulties finding a child through regular independent means, you may end up considering a black market adoption. This is not a good way to seek a child, but it is all that is left for the desperate. It is difficult to condemn the people who are driven to this point by our system's inability to allow them the child they so much want.

Independent adoptions, no matter how they occur, offer a choice. The need for this choice is apparent by the number of people who adopt in this way. Independent adoptions and intercountry adoptions are the only opportunities left for the people whom traditional agencies see as less fit for parenting. In no way does this make these people lesser parents; it only forces them to become parents a different way because the adoption agencies choose not to help them.

CHAPTER 7

A Distant Resource

SOMETIMES OUT OF FEAR, sometimes out of empathy or ignorance, sometimes out of feeling a cultural connection, and sometimes out of desire to merely find a baby, people go anywhere and everywhere to find a child. International adoption is not a recent phenomenon; it has long been an alternative means of adopting children. Adoption abroad is on the rise as older couples, single people, and others leave the country to search for a baby. They are often unwilling to deal with the potential problems of adoptions going wrong or being denied an opportunity to adopt in their own country.

Americans have always been eager to adopt from other countries. Following World War II, Americans adopted many European orphans. After both the Korean and the Vietnam Wars, airplanes full of orphans were flown to the United States for adoption. More recently, an outpouring of sympathy following news of political chaos and violence in Romania resulted in many Romanian children being adopted, as adoption agencies were inundated with inquiries from people wanting to know how they could adopt these children. And after earthquakes and other natural disasters, American couples seek ways to bring orphans of these tragedies to this country for adoption.

For people considering adopting from another country, the first question asked is, "Can we do it?" and the second is, "Do international adoptions work?" The answer to both of these questions is yes. Let's look at both of these questions.

Can you do an international adoption? We know that despite the complications that can occur in international adoptions, people get through the paperwork, handle the travel requirements and language barriers, find the help they need, and come home with a baby or a young child. While we spend considerable time in this chapter going over the details of how this is accomplished, it is important to remember that it *is* accomplished. Success is the norm in international and domestic adoptions, but knowledge and expertise are needed to have success in an emotionally satisfying, financially viable, and timely manner.

Do international adoptions work? Just as stories about stealing children from other countries make headlines, so do stories about children who fail to adjust to their adoption because of being uprooted from their home culture. But these stories are misleading. The research is very clear that most adoptees and adopting parents are satisfied with the outcome of international adoptions.[1] But there is little data on the birth parents involved.

Each country responds differently to Americans' desires to adopt. Some countries prefer to have no relations with the United States at all, while other countries in need welcome the people who want to provide homes for children who would otherwise be a burden. This view can change radically if the foreign country becomes better able to provide for its homeless children or if negative publicity tarnishes the country's image; then a government can make adoption by foreigners much more difficult and sometimes impossible. At times, the only children allowed to leave are disabled or in sibling groups, while children who are easier to adopt are assimilated into families within the country.

The increased interest in international adoption sometimes collides with or even produces increased hostility from other countries toward these adoptions. Some countries in Latin America have become embroiled in controversy over these adoptions. Our high-tech society has brought a new dimension to how people respond to what they view as "rich foreigners" taking their children; rumors of children being taken to use for organ transplants have triggered what is considered a dangerous situation for American travelers in some areas.[2] While no cases of adoption for organ transplants have been documented, the large number of missing children in Guatemala, for example, has not been explained. Some travelers in Guatemala have been attacked because they were believed to be there to "harvest" children. Fears of American baby selling, kidnapping, and trafficking in babies are fanned by news reports of some isolated incidents of these abuses. Many times, adopting parents are not aware of these problems when they take their search to these countries, but they should be.

The Latin American problems are an extreme example, but many other countries view adoption of their children in the same way that some African Americans view adoption of black children by Caucasian families. They believe it insults their pride and is, in effect, cultural genocide. Americans pursuing adoption internationally need to be cautious in approaching foreigners to avoid offending them. There is in fact much in common between international adoption and interracial adoption. Some people will criticize these adoptions as breaking a child away from his cultural roots. Others will praise these adoptions as bridging cultural and racial barriers. To consider international adoption, you must certainly belong to the latter group.

It is critical for those considering international adoption to be aware of the many facets of this kind of adoption. They need to know of possible international hostility, of abuses, and of their potential to be exploited. With this knowledge, they can be more positive emissaries of adoption and avoid some of the problems that may otherwise be encountered.

Those who pursue this path must realize that they will be forever different. They will not only be a family through adoption, but also a racially or ethnically mixed family with all the benefits and challenges this implies. Those who choose this alternative to create a family will also find their lives enriched, their understanding of other peoples broadened, and their view of other races and other countries altered. It can be a very exciting adventure.

A Changing Scene

While the number of international adoptions is increasing, it still accounts for only a small portion of the adoptions in this country. It is estimated that 15 percent of all adoptions in the United States are from foreign countries, and there are over 15,000 international adoptions annually throughout the world.[3] We in the United States are beginning to be more aware of international adoptions because available infants are scarce here and some news articles suggest adopting from other counties is safe or fast. (We forget that at times even people from other countries come to the United States to adopt. While it is a small number compared to the 11,340 children brought into the country, estimates are that between 100 and 500 U.S.-born children and perhaps many more were adopted by families from Asia, Europe, and Canada in 1996.)[4]

The international adoption scene is constantly changing. Events affecting adoption in the most recent years include the breakup of the Soviet Union, limiting parents to one child in China, the Baby Richard and Baby Jessica legal cases in America, the fall of the dictator in Romania, and random natural disasters.[5] In 1991 after the political unrest in Romania was publicized, over 2,500 children were adopted from there. The negative publicity that followed, claiming people were "selling babies," reduced the number to 121 in the following year.[6] One writer commenting on the volatility of international adoption said:

> Private and public adoption agencies track wars, famine, overpopulation and economic misery with the market-driven fervor of stock brokers. Countries-of-the-month open and close their borders with ever-changing laws and often questionable adoption practices, while Third World nations try to balance their desire to find homes for their children with their embarrassment—sometimes anger—over their inability to look after their own.[7]

People deciding to pursue this kind of adoption need to be prepared for the rapid changes that may occur.

The rules and regulations of foreign adoption, while difficult to understand, used to be fairly easy to meet. The flexibility of people seeking to adopt internationally was enhanced by the added flexibility in the screening of prospective parents. Even though people considering international adoption have to meet the criteria of not only a domestic agency but also the foreign country or an agency from that country, the criteria are still more flexible than with most domestic adoption agencies.

There is a trend toward tightening the screening of prospective international adoptive parents. Some agencies are looking for couples who meet the same requirements as for a domestic adoption. While this sounds positive, it does have some drawbacks. If we are sure that our criteria are reasonable and proven, then it seems reasonable to impose them here. We certainly want good parents for children adopted from other countries as much as we want good parents for children from this country. No one should be able to fault careful screening. Unfortunately, we just don't know how to do it. If the criteria used to determine who can adopt internationally is based on the current tight standards that result from a baby shortage in this country, then they are unnecessarily restrictive. In the past, people wanting to adopt internationally were not always the most traditional couples. International adoption was the only route open to singles, older people, those who already had children, and those turned down by agencies who sought a more perfect couple. In general, adopting internationally followed many of the same philosophical requirements as adopting a special-needs child.

Neither our own laws nor the adoption laws of foreign countries actively facilitate international adoptions.[8] While recent proposed laws in the United States may help to ease some of the restrictions in effect since "only orphan" adoptions were permitted, they won't solve most problems. In many cases, children whose home country considers them available for adoption cannot be adopted here because they do not fit into our country's definition of orphans. Legal problems exist in many foreign countries also. Few of them will change their laws to accommodate foreigners who wish to adopt. It almost seems that the more accessible and reasonable their adoption policies are, the greater the pressure they are under to decrease adoptions from their country. The issues involved in international adoption are being scrutinized as the countries of the world continue to debate the possibility of more uniform international adoption laws.[9]

The most difficult part of international adoption is that someone planning to adopt can be caught in the middle of a changing situation. The Lambs found out about this firsthand. They had begun to adopt a baby girl through an agency that was helping people adopt from Peru. They had finished their home study, assembled all the necessary documents, obtained their visa, and purchased their airline tickets. They were ready to go when a precarious political situation stopped U.S. adoptions in Peru. Fortunately they were able to wait until the situation changed and then proceed with their adoption. They were also fortunate that the situation was resolved relatively quickly and their plans could move ahead; that isn't always the case.

At times, countries allow children to be adopted because they are unable to care for them. As "have-not" countries gain greater economic stability, they are better able to care for all of their children and there are fewer to be adopted by foreigners. Countries are sensitive about the world's response when they allow their children to be adopted. Recent critical remarks about Chinese adoptions have caused many in the adoption business to fear that adoption of these children might be halted because of the negative publicity.

Other changes are occurring in the United States regarding international adoption. A home study by a state-approved agency is now required. Until this law was passed, international adoptions were largely just an alternative for people rejected by domestic adoption agencies. While that still may be the case, prospective adoptive parents may now have to go to the adoption agencies that have rejected them in order to obtain a home study; in some areas, separate agencies handle home studies for those pursuing international adoption. The formalization of the home study process by a state-approved agency has tightened the process, but still, most international adoption agencies have a tendency not to expect perfection from the individuals with whom they are working.

You are in a position to know what is happening with individual countries on a day-to-day basis. On the Internet, you can monitor the constant changes in politics, law, and availability, and when the State Department lists the requirements specific countries make for adoption, they are readily available on-line.

Those whose international adoptions go smoothly say the process is easy and fast; those who run into complications say it is one big headache. Change can be exciting and frightening. Be ready to feel both responses as you adapt to the changes that will be part of your life as you pursue an international adoption.

Similarities with Domestic Adoptions

International adoptions have more in common with domestic adoptions than one might think. While there are differences, the issues of raising foreign children are similar to those involved in domestic adoptions. (See Chapters 8 and 12.) Let's consider some of the many similarities:

- Honesty is important throughout the adoption process and as you raise your child.
- Those helping with the process have a strong business side as well as altruistic motivations.
- Costs can get higher than you may have anticipated.
- Health concerns are an issue.
- Both can have the same long waiting period.
- Both require a home study.
- All adopters fear that something can go wrong.
- Parents need to continue dealing with adoption issues throughout the child's life.
- You need to accept the differences between you and your child and recognize who your child is.
- You must accept grief and loss as part of adoption.
- You have to acknowledge that you are a family by adoption.
- The child's biological heritage is a fact of life.

- You should discuss adoption with your child honestly and openly.
- You get the joy of raising a child.

There are also some unique aspects to international adoptions:

- You may get a better idea of approximately how long it will take for you to find a child.
- You will be unlikely to have contact with a birth parent. While for some people this is an advantage, others will view it as a disadvantage.
- You will not deal financially with birth parents.
- You will not have to risk birth parents changing their mind, because these are children who have been "abandoned" or are orphans.
- Children are seldom placed at birth.
- A child who is older at the time of the adoption will probably have spent most of his or her life in an orphanage or foster care. Certain bonding issues need to be considered with this background.
- The costs may be even higher than in domestic adoptions.
- The paperwork can be even more overwhelming than in domestic adoptions.
- The potential for undiagnosed or unknown medical problems is higher.
- Rapid changes in rules, requirements, and availability of children are not unusual.

Sara looked at the differences between domestic and international adoption and decided to seek a child outside the United States. Her story is fairly typical of people who choose this option. She was a single mother who had a strong desire to adopt a healthy infant and who wanted only a girl. After pursuing two domestic adoption leads, she came to the conclusion that an open adoption of any kind was not in her comfort zone; she did not want to have contact with birth parents either before or after the baby was born. After realizing this, Sara looked into international adoption.

She did her research and decided that she wanted to adopt a little girl from China. China was accepting single parents as adoptive applicants and she felt that the overall program of an agency specializing in international adoptions met her needs. After completing an international home study and fulfilling all of the requirements from the United States and from China, she arrived home with her beautiful seven-month-old daughter, Marina, eight months after she began the process.

Sara was aware of the importance of having as much information ready for her child as possible. Marina was an orphan and the orphanage provided no information on her medical or social background, but Sara documented her entire trip to China with photographs and video recordings to provide her daughter with a sense of her own cultural and geographic history.

Where to Get Understanding and Help for International Adoption

As more people pursue international adoption, more people have made it their business to help make these situations work. Years ago few resources were available; today there are people to educate and guide you through the complex process. Once you have your child, resources are also available to help you raise him or her.

You can adopt internationally through an agency or independently, or combine these approaches by using a private agency with international contacts to help on parts of the adoption. Some countries will not allow independent adoptions. Others allow only those conducted by nonprofit agencies.

There are groups whose goal is to help people adopt foreign homeless children; other organizations may provide information, if not help. They help people understand how to begin and where to go; they are a great resource because of their personal experience. The International Concerns Committee for Children (see Appendix F) publishes a bimonthly newsletter on all aspects of international adoption and their Report on Foreign Adoption gives bimonthly updates on international adoptions. The U.S. Department of State Bureau on Consular Affairs (see Appendix F) and the Immigration and Naturalization Service (INS) (see local, state, and federal telephone listings in your area) can be helpful sources of information on current regulations and areas of concern. Adoptive Families of America, Inc. (see Appendix F) helps solve problems and provides information on all kinds of adoptions. If you want to adopt internationally, they are worth contacting. Their magazine, *Adoptive Families,* has helpful articles on international adoptions and on raising children from other countries. They also maintain a list of support groups throughout the country. A similar magazine, *Roots & Wings* (see Appendix F) is available, discussing both international and domestic adoptions.

Most support groups are local and too numerous to mention. One national group, Latin American Parents Association (see Appendix F) can put you in touch with local chapters. It is difficult to know which groups will meet your needs or how reliable any specific group might be until you speak to people who have worked with them. Find out about the group you intend to work with before you join or give money to them. As with many support groups, membership regularly changes.

If you want to adopt internationally but through an adoption agency, the agency may provide support services through their own groups. For example, the International Waiting Children Program at Children's Home Society of Minnesota (see Appendix F) has information on available international children. They also provide education and support groups. These groups are a source of valuable information, similar to the support groups available when you pursue domestic adoptions.

As we said before, probably the most detailed and up-to-date source of information on the complexities of international adoption today is the Internet. The specific web sites are too numerous to list and are constantly changing, but they can be easily accessed by looking for "international adoption." Many have links to other similar sites. They offer a wealth of information. If you are not familiar with the Internet, find someone who will help you. This source of information offers current information on where adoptions are taking place, the requirements of each country, agencies that can help you adopt, and agencies that can help even if you are going to adopt independently.

There are also numerous books about international adoptions, and even though they are not as up-to-date as the Internet, they are a valuable source of help.[10] They also give you more detailed information on international adoptions than you will find on-line. Besides describing how to adopt internationally, books also help you evaluate your own readiness to adopt a child from a different culture and the implications of that for your family. They allow you the time to imagine different kinds of adoption by reading about other people's experiences. You'll have a chance to examine your own motivation for adopting, look at the issues of adopting someone of a different culture and/or a different race, and also see how others have handled the experience. We recommend:

M. F. Conroy, *A World of Love*

B. Holtan, *They Became Part of Us: The Experiences of Families Adopting Children Everywhere*

J. Knoll and M. K. Murphy, *International Adoption: Sensitive Advice for Prospective Parents*

F. M. Koh, *Adopted from Asia*

F. M. Koh, *Oriental Children in American Homes: How Do They Adjust?*

M. Miller and N. Ward, *With Eyes Wide Open: A Workbook for Parents Adopting International Children over Age One*

J. Nelson-Erichsen and H. R. Erichsen, *Butterflies in the Wind: Spanish/Indian Children with White Parents*

J. Peterson, *Tapestry: Exploring the World of Trans-Racial Adoption*

C. Pohl and K. Harris, *Transracial Adoption: Children and Parents Speak*

C. Register, *"Are Those Kids Yours?"*

L. Strassberger, *Our Children from Latin America*

H. S. P. Wilkinson, *Birth Is More Than Once: The Inner World of Adopted Korean Children*

Many of the books on transracial adoptions (see Chapter 8) also apply to international adoptions.

Another excellent way to learn about international adoptions is to talk personally and at length with someone who has adopted from the country or with the agency you are using. You are trying to understand international adoption from a personal perspective, to see where you fit.

International Adoption Through Agencies

If you want to adopt from another country, you need to know what you are doing. That isn't easy to figure out. One of the first hurdles is choosing a "good" agency. You cannot assume that because an agency is licensed it is doing a good job; you need to know a lot more to determine whether you should pay its fee. Adopting a child from a foreign country with the help of an agency is similar to any agency adoption. Many of the criteria listed in Chapter 5 apply, and selecting an agency here is as complex as in domestic adoptions.

Talk to people who have adopted internationally to find out which agencies are the best and which you should avoid. You can even ask questions on the Internet to learn if others are satisfied with the agency and what things you should check out. Adoptive parents are always a great resource.

You need to ask questions of any agency you are considering, to help you evaluate if this is the group you want to work with, and read their material carefully. If an agency tells you only good things about international adoption and makes it sound relatively easy, they are leaving out some important information. Ask the agencies not only how many adoptions they are handling but how many disruptions (failures after placement) occur. This tells you much about the placements they are making. You also need to find out how many people are on their waiting lists for a specific country and how long they have been there. You need to attend their intake interviews, which will give you considerable information about the way they operate. You need to gather information and make an informed decision on who will help you best.

Find an agency that is responsive to you. Do they return your phone calls? Are they prompt? Do they answer your questions? Do they follow through on what you ask? Will they give you the names of people they have worked with? Do they accurately tell you of the problems you face? Are they realistic about the problems you might encounter in adopting a child from a foreign country?

Your agency can be a tremendous asset as you proceed. They should be able to keep you on track, tell you what is needed, and look out for your best interests as well as the best interests of the child. Your success and happiness in this process will greatly depend upon your choice of an agency.

PROCEDURES FOR INTERNATIONAL AGENCY ADOPTION

Adopting internationally can be a challenge. Sometimes it's difficult even to know where to begin. As you do your research, learn which agencies in the United States handle foreign adoptions in the country where you want to adopt. You don't necessarily have to work with a local agency, but you do need to work with a reliable one. Some agencies will work with anyone in the United States; they will have you complete your home study in your local area and will walk you through the rest of the process on the telephone.

The agency fee may range from under $1,000 to several times that. These costs may vary from state to state. Agencies may charge only a percentage of their regular fee for low-income adoptive families. Some agency fees will cover everything, but usually what is covered is quite limited.

Other costs will be added to the agency fee. In general, most international adoptions range in price from $8,000 to $20,000. There are foreign program fees (fees associated with the intake agency or program in the other country), expenses for document processing here and abroad, immigration fees, and travel expenses for you and your child. You need to be sure you understand what the agency fee covers, so don't hesitate to ask questions.

After you are satisfied that this is the agency that best meets your needs, and you have arranged to finance the various fees, the process begins. If you are working with a local agency, you will probably have a group intake meeting, followed by an individual meeting with the agency worker, you, and your spouse (where appropriate); then the worker will meet with each of you alone, ending with a meeting in your home. It is worthwhile to familiarize yourself with what the agency social worker is looking for in any adoption; so carefully read the Agency Process section in Chapter 5. Spend some time understanding why you are choosing to adopt a child from another country, because that will surely be covered in your home study.

In international adoptions, people with parenting experience are considered to be the best candidates to handle the special problems of these children. In fact, adoption agencies believe that couples best suited for these children are couples whose lives revolve around their existing children. This fits in with the view that international children have special needs and will take a great deal of time and energy to raise properly. Like most people interested in special-needs children, those adopting from foreign countries are usually optimistic.

During each of the meetings you will have over the next several weeks or months (depending on the agency's requirements, the number of applicants, and your response to obtaining information for your agency), the social worker will attempt to do several things: make certain that you will be appropriate parents, educate you about the adoption of a child from a foreign country, ensure that you can provide a safe and nurturing environment, and assess whether you are ready to parent. If you work with an agency outside of your area, these steps will be covered by whoever is authorized to do your home study. An example of an international home study is in Appendix C; while each country has its own requirements, Appendix C gives a general idea of the issues covered during a home study.

You will also, as part of the home study, be asked to provide certain documents:

- birth certificates
- marriage license
- any divorce decrees
- medical reports from a physician (may be required for each person in household)
- tax returns (and, perhaps, statements of assets and liabilities)
- letter from your bank describing your accounts
- confirmation from your employer of position, salary, and length of employment
- police records, FBI fingerprint clearance, and child abuse clearance

Usually you need multiple notarized copies of each document. Sometimes you will need to have translations made for the child's country, and the cost can run from as low as $60 to as high as $500, depending on how your agency operates. Many times the agency you are working with will do these translations.

Once these documents and the home study are completed the agency will send them to the appropriate state-level agencies, plus the U.S. Department of State (see Appendix F) and the appropriate foreign consulate. Usually at this point some money is sent to the foreign program.

After you have been selected by an agency for a foreign program, you need to file a petition for approval to adopt a foreign orphan (called the I-600A, Application for Advance Processing of an Orphan Petition). Obtain the booklet M-249 from the U.S. Immigration and Naturalization Service (INS), entitled *The Immigration of Adopted and Prospective Adoptive Children;* get it from either your agency or your local INS office (see your local state and federal telephone listings). Usually your agency will file this paper for you, but you will again need to provide your fingerprints, your home study, proof of U.S. citizenship, proof of marriage, and documentation of divorces. INS will send notice of favorable determination after your papers are processed. This notice also needs to be sent to the consulate of the country in which you plan to adopt.

Waiting, at which you have probably become quite good, now begins. First you wait to be approved in the United States; then you wait until a child has been located for you. Next you wait to be approved for that specific child. Then you wait while the legal procedures and arrangements are made. During all of the waiting, be sure you maintain a good relationship with the agency staff, even though they can do very little to hurry the process. Don't give up even if this stage takes a long time. You have done a great deal of work, so keep up your good spirits, and your patience and hard work will pay off.

As with domestic adoptions, the more flexible you are about what kind of child you will take, the faster the process will be. Once a child is offered to you for possible placement, you should request all possible information about the child, especially about his or her health and orphan status. These facts will help you determine whether to move ahead in the process. Don't be pressured to continue without this information. Once you commit to a specific child, some countries will begin charging you for his or her care. This is why it is important to be sure before you proceed.

Foreign courts will also require information about the child's identity, proof that the child is an orphan or available for adoption or guardianship under the laws of that country, and proof that the adopting parent(s) will be suitable for this particular child. Some countries will allow an adoption to proceed without you being there, but others will require the presence of one or both of the adoptive parents. Other countries will grant you guardianship of the child with the understanding that you will subsequently adopt in the United States.

You can see that there are many scenarios in an international adoption. Agencies can be extremely helpful, but ultimately you are the one responsible for your decisions and for the completion of whatever is required; stay informed as you proceed.

Once you have legally adopted or been given guardianship of the child, you need to file INS form I-600, Petition to Classify an Orphan as an Immediate Relative. If you are going to be in the country from which you are adopting your child, you may file the petition with the U.S. embassy or consulate there.

No matter where you file the petition, you must present the following documents with it: proof of the child's identity (birth certificate, passport, national identity card); proof of the child's orphan status (by [1] death certificates or other proof that both parents have died, [2] proof that a court of competent authority declared the child abandoned or severed the biological parents' ties by declaring the child a ward of the state, or [3] proof that the child has been irrevocably relinquished to an orphanage); proof that a court of competent authority has granted you guardianship of the child or that the court finalized your adoption of the child.

The Department of State consular officer (see local state and federal listings) who judges the child's immigrant visa application is trying to determine the orphan status of the child and to ensure the child does not suffer from a medical condition of which adoptive parents are unaware. For this purpose, an approved foreign physician will now examine the child.

After you receive the Approval of Relative Immigrant Visa Petition (form I-171), you need to complete a visa application (Form OF-230) and a passport application for your child. Your child will have one of two types of immigrant visas; one requires readoption and the other does not. Some people adopting would recommend that you readopt no matter what the circumstances.

The last form to complete is the Application for Certificate of Citizenship on Behalf of an Adopted Child (form N-643). Since your child is not automatically a U.S. citizen just because you have an adoption decree, you still have to apply for citizenship for him. If you complete this form, no court hearing is required for him to become a citizen.

This is a long process and no one but you seems anxious to hurry. But the waiting period before your child arrives offers positive benefits. The educational process is extremely valuable, so use this time to read further. Ideally, too, you are using this period to make contacts with other people who have adopted internationally so that you will have resources to get help if any future problems or questions arise.

You should also reflect on your expectations. The social worker should help you to be realistic about what your expectations are for this foreign adoption and its potential problems; helping people be realistic in international adoptions is a major issue. Many adopting parents are unprepared for the frequently undernourished and fearful child who they go to meet and who does not share their language. The child may have defects or health problems that are worse than what may have been described to you.

When the child arrives, he or she undoubtedly will look older than you thought, because time will have passed since the description of the child was made or the photograph was taken. It is hoped that at this point, all the education the adoption agency has given you, your meetings with others who have adopted internationally, and the material you have read about international adoption will have prepared you to relate well with your child. Yet nothing can prepare you completely—this is something only you can experience.

While you still have more work to do to complete your adoption, when your child arrives the difficult part is finished. You still probably have to go through a post-placement period in which you continue to be investigated to make certain the adjustment is going along fine and the child is doing well. Sometimes foreign countries require this of you and sometimes it is merely part of the adoption process once you have brought the child to this country. Actually this period can be very helpful, especially if you are involved in support groups. All of these hurdles seem minor because your child is already here.

ONE INTERNATIONAL AGENCY ADOPTION

The Worths are a good example of a family adopting internationally through an agency. Doug and Janine had two biological children: Marni, eight, and Mike, seven. Adoption had never been a consideration for them until one Sunday evening they went to a church program that discussed the plight of different nations' homeless children, who could be adopted by American couples. The representative from the international adoption who put on the program really impressed the Worth family. They felt they had ample love and money to provide for another child, so they made contact with an agency in their state that handled international adoptions.

They went to a group meeting of nine couples interested in finding out about international adoptions. The woman who gave the presentation sounded extremely discouraging about adopting from another country; in fact, she was more discouraging than encouraging. She seemed to imply that any couple who tried to get a foreign child should be prepared for the very worst. The Worths left the meeting surprised; this wasn't quite what they had heard about international adoptions.

The Worths discussed the matter thoroughly with each other and with their children. They regained their enthusiasm and decided to go ahead despite this agency's presentation. Janine and Doug called the agency to begin the next step.

They met with another worker, who was only slightly more positive than the first. Nonetheless, by now they knew for sure that this was something they definitely wanted to pursue. The worker liked them very much, as they personified just what the agency sought in parents:

They were loving, optimistic, and flexible. They had a stable marriage and sufficient income. They had many friends and their religious background, while not an essential feature, was a plus. Also, they were willing to take any child the agency felt they could help. Their relatives supported the idea of an international adoption. Their neighborhood was primarily Caucasian but was about 25 percent non-Caucasians; it would easily accept a racially mixed child. And the children were as eager about the pending adoption as Doug and Janine. This was just about all any agency could ask for.

Because the Worths so ideally fit the agency's criteria, it was easy for them to work together. The Worths felt everyone went out of their way to make the procedure simple for them, and it did go exceptionally smoothly.

Eight months after they heard the man speak in the church, and after much paperwork, the Worth family learned about the Korean child who would soon be theirs. He was six years old and an orphan. He had been crippled at birth and walked only with the aid of crutches. The orphanage where he lived believed this handicap might be correctable; in Korea, however, there was no chance for him to get the appropriate medical attention. He spoke no English, but everything else seemed fine to Doug and Janine, and they wanted to proceed.

Five months later, their new son arrived. They were delighted, but Yeong, the boy, wasn't so comfortable. It wasn't instant family or instant love. The first months weren't easy with him. Yeong was quiet and moody and seemed unhappy. He didn't eat very much, but he did sneak food when he thought no one was watching him.

Slowly the little boy began to open up. Within three months, Yeong was an active playmate for Marni and Mike, who thought he was great fun. Surgery was delayed for at least a year, so he could adjust to this country and his new home before he was put into another strange situation. The family also did not enroll him in school at first, for the same reason.

Doug and Janine are really glad they heard the man who spoke at their church. They don't plan to adopt any more children, but this additional bonus to their lives was just what they wanted. To them, the adoption was a complete success. They fit perfectly into the system, so it was easy to feel comfortable.

International adoption was an excellent option for this family. Although the Worths had no prior experience with adoption, they eagerly embraced the educational process and learned about international adoption in Korea. They felt prepared for Yeong's arrival, and their preparation made them feel they could handle any potential problems that might arise.

Using an adoption agency can smooth out many of the complexities in adopting internationally. While the agency helps with the procedure, it also prepares for your child's arrival by helping you learn how to handle the cultural differences your new child will experience. This helps make adoption easier for you and for your new child. At times the agency's approach may discourage couples; people must be dedicated to the idea of adopting internationally and committed to moving ahead despite the discouragement they will receive from many people, perhaps even the agency. This discouragement ultimately eliminates people who are not certain of their course of action.

Independent International Adoption

Independent international adoptions are similar to, but more complex than, independent adoptions within the United States. These arrangements are also called *parent-initiated international adoptions.* The difference between these and agency international adoptions is that now you are expected to find the child to adopt and also to know of all the steps you must complete—on your own.

Independent adoptions in another country are not easy, but for some people, especially those with strong ties to specific countries, independent adoption is a good way to go. You need to be resourceful, self-reliant, willing to read, and willing to travel. While some countries prohibit independent adoptions, the definition of what constitutes an independent adoption is unclear. All independent international adoptions actually involve an agency in some way. For instance, the home study for an international adoption must be done by an agency. But a resourceful person can still do much of the other work.

A few years ago, it was easier to arrange an independent international adoption. There were fewer rules and regulations. A person who traveled a great deal and who was not intimidated by the prospect of going through the laws of foreign nations was able to find a child and to make the process work. Partly because of abuses and partly to make order out of the many different regulations in each country, efforts have been made in recent years to tighten the procedure. The tightening has resulted in far fewer people attempting to adopt independently.

Whereas an international adoption agency will take care of many of the details and make sure you take the right steps and complete the right papers, this will be your responsibility in an independent adoption. Anyone considering independent adoption in another country should read the previous section on international agency adoptions; it gives information on the kinds of paperwork that will be needed. You need to be familiar with each of these documents because you will be completing them on your own.

As with independent adoption within the United States, you must make your own contact to find an international baby. You must meet your own state's regulations and those of the country from which you want to adopt; to do this you will probably need legal help in the other country as well as here. And besides legal help, you need a contact who will do the searching for a child in the foreign country.

Support groups for independent international adopters are beginning to emerge. One example is a group called Americans Adopting Orphans (see Appendix F). This group is a licensed agency that specializes in coordinating and facilitating independent international adoptions in China; they provide a program to help you with whatever part of adoption you need assistance with. Their work is similar to that of a facilitator helping in independent domestic adoptions. (This agency can manage the entire process, but then you will be involved in an agency international adoption.) This group is based in Washington, but you are likely to find similar groups in other parts of the country as the demand increases.

STATE AND FOREIGN REGULATIONS

The regulations pertaining to independent international adoptions are different in each state and in each country. It is up to you to know them. Some U.S. states and foreign countries, in fact, do not allow independent international adoptions. Even if you're told independent international adoptions are not allowed in your state or the country you choose, you may be able to handle much of the process yourself. You just need to know what parts of your international adoption you can do and what parts need to be done by an agency.

First, find a domestic attorney who knows about international adoptions. This is a very specialized area, so many attorneys will know little about it. Remember, just because people say they know something about this process, it doesn't mean they do: Find out how many adoptions they have done. Find out what countries they have worked with and see if the list includes the country you are interested in. A good way of finding knowledgeable attorneys in the area of international adoption is to get names from other attorneys or from someone who has adopted a child from another country.

A qualified attorney will be a valuable source of information on all aspects of international adoption; however, hiring an attorney should not be considered a substitute for doing your own homework. When you have a fair understanding of what is involved, you will find that the attorney's input is much more valuable to you. If this sounds as though you need to become an expert first, you are right.

It is very simple to say you should understand as much as possible about independent international adoption; to gain that knowledge isn't quite so simple. Yet there are many sources from which you can learn. You can profit from learning about any kind of international adoption; certainly read the section in this book on agency international adoptions to get an overview of the process. The support groups mentioned earlier in this chapter can also be very helpful. Explore them all!

MAKING INTERNATIONAL CONTACTS

As you continue to gather information on independent international adoptions, you will learn of many ways to contact people in foreign countries who might be able to help you find a child to adopt. Other people who have already adopted internationally are excellent sources of information about potential foreign contacts. If you already have a contact, it is much easier.

Your foreign contact person can be anyone who might put you in touch with someone who has a child to adopt. Americans living or working abroad sometimes become contacts for people in the United States; foreign attorneys and physicians at times also act as contacts, just as they do in the United States. People who work in orphanages or with poor people in foreign countries also become involved in international adoptions. People involved in religious work sometimes know of children who need homes.

You need to be able to trust the person who becomes your foreign contact. It is like being able to trust your attorney—you will depend on the accuracy of the information this person gives you. The best basis for trust is to have someone you know recommend a contact to you. If others have used this person before in the adopting process, you know more about his or her procedures and honesty.

If your intermediary is not someone you know about, check with the United States Bureau of Consular Affairs in the country from which you will be adopting. You may be able to eliminate disreputable people known to prey on others. The consular staff is a good source to keep in close contact with throughout your adoption process.

Many times people pick a specific country because they already have a contact there. This can greatly help in securing a child. Mel and Becky were helped in adopting their daughter by one of Mel's students. Mel taught college and became close to one of his students from Colombia. When Juan came to their home for dinner, Mel and Becky were able to talk with him about one of their dreams—to adopt a child from another country. Juan became actively involved in their dream. His family in Colombia located a four-year-old girl at an orphanage in a small town. They also helped Mel and Becky make contact with a reputable attorney who took care of their legal work. Then they went to their local adoption agency for a home study for this specific little girl. Everything went smoothly, and because of their contact through Juan's family, all they had to do was pay the legal costs and send money for the child to come to this country. They also sent part of the airline fare for someone to accompany their new daughter and two other Colombian children who were also being placed for adoption in this country.

Juan, Mel, and Becky met the tired little girl, Luisa, at the airport. Juan helped bridge the language barrier for her and allay the fears she had at coming to this new country and these new parents. He also helped Mel and Becky understand the culture of Colombia; his knowledge helped Mel and Becky avoid overwhelming their new daughter with new foods, a new language, and new customs. Juan and his family, in effect, took on the role that many agencies perform in international adoptions.

The importance of your contact person cannot be overstated. He or she is selecting a child for you in a country about which you probably know very little. Ideally, this person will be familiar with the laws related to adoption; the legality of what you are doing depends on who is helping you. You need to be able to trust and to depend on this important person.

In sum, adopting a child from another country without an agency is not easy. At some point in all independent adoptions, an agency is involved; you need to understand how much agency involvement is needed and how much you can do on your own. You need to have a contact within the country to help you search for a child, unless you already know of one you are considering adopting. This is a complex adoption and you will need a great deal of information and as much support as you can find.

Health of Children Adopted Internationally

You probably have no way of knowing exactly what has occurred in the background of a child you are planning to adopt. Often the child's birth date is not even known, so how can you expect to know his or her medical and health history? Once again, the adopting couple's flexibility is essential.

Because what you can learn about an adoptable child is not always clear, he or she may have some significant problems. Since the children being placed for adoption are frequently from poverty-stricken parents, many are malnourished. You should assume that the medical care the child has received is minimal. It may have consisted of only a simple examination prior to the adoption.

In an agency international adoption, you may be told ahead of time about known medical problems. That health history is likely to be more complete than in an independent international adoption. The entire process in an independent international adoption is aimed at a specific child whom you may or may not know very much about until you are committed to that adoption. For many people, perhaps for you, that poses no problem at all. Some people have relied on the simple medical examinations given to the child before he left the country. These examinations many times do not discover problems that may be diagnosed once the child comes into the United States; this has increasingly been found with Hepatitis B. Few of these examinations identified children who would ultimately be developmentally delayed.[11]

Although these children may have some health problems, most people who have adopted children internationally are amazed at their resiliency.[12] The malnourished child quickly becomes healthier, the quiet child learns to open up, and the child who seemed less bright learns faster than originally anticipated. Children have a marvelous capacity to heal, to change, and to adapt.

Risks in International Adoption

The risks involved in international adoption are in some respects greater than the risks in domestic adoptions. It is interesting that many people adopt internationally because of fear of complications in domestic adoptions, yet the risks in international adoptions are just as significant.

The risks in international adoption are increased over domestic arrangements by several factors. International rules and regulations add another hurdle to your own state's regulations. Lack of knowledge about your contact person also might increase your risk. Missing information or inaccurate health and background data on the child are certainly an additional risk. The difficulty in exchanging information is greater because of differences in language, the distance, and often because of inaccessibility of telephone service in some rural areas.

The language barrier that must be surmounted in international adoption is significant. All information will need to be translated. When an adoption agency is involved, they help you with this process. In an independent international adoption, this is up to you. Word-by-word translations from a dictionary will not substitute for finding someone who has a working knowledge of the language and who can help you understand the intent of the messages. Try to hire someone who is thoroughly familiar with both the language and the country with which you are working.

Navigating the dual regulations of both your own state and the foreign country involves risks. The risks can be minimized by using an attorney, but these regulations add to the complexity of the adoption process. Before you begin an adoption of this kind, be sure that you are completely familiar with or advised about your own state's regulations. You will save yourself time and frustration if you do this at the beginning of the process. Be sure you are meeting the laws of the country from which you are adopting. Never get involved in adoptions that involve fraudulently listing yourself as the birth parent.

Without any question, the risks are even higher in an independent international adoption than in an agency adoption. Agencies have a track record; if the agency has been successful in the past and with few problems, you can be somewhat sure of success. Agencies know ahead of time what to do to minimize problems. They do a lot of this work for you. The adoption agency is working with many children and many people who want to adopt, so they may have greater flexibility in meeting any specific demands you might have.

However, the agency approach also takes longer, and you have a more passive role in the entire procedure. The agency may not have the contacts within a given country that you have, and that might make the procedure go more slowly than if you searched for yourself. You may also have a specific child in mind whom you have met or whom you know about; only a handful of agencies are able to help in these kinds of situations.

Morena and David decided they wanted an international adoption but without some of the risks. They wanted to avoid some red tape by approaching an international adoption in a different way. David worked frequently in Mexico and therefore knew many people who would be able to help them. They put out the word they were looking for a baby to adopt. One of their sources helped them locate Isabella, who was eight months pregnant. The advantage of knowing the language helped David and Morena speak personally with her. They made arrangements for her to come to the United States for the delivery of her child, which she would then place with them for adoption. They felt the medical care she would receive in this country outweighed the longer delays that an adoption in this country would entail. Danger in the delivery room was not an acceptable risk.

Morena and David made living arrangements for Isabella with a nearby friend who had a room for rent. The three of them spent the next month getting to know each other. Morena was able to take Isabella to all of her medical appointments and also took her sightseeing. After the baby was born and both Isabella and the baby were released from the hospital, Isabella stayed in the United States for a couple of weeks while she regained her strength and recovered from the birth. At the time of Isabella's departure, she stated that even though placing her baby for adoption was extremely difficult, she felt comforted because she knew Morena and David and had the opportunity to spend time with them in the environment in which her child would be raised. The flexibility with which Morena and David approached this adoption allowed them to reduce some of the red tape that is typically involved in an international adoption.

Reliance on others is certainly a risk in international adoptions. In agency or independent adoptions in the United States, if you don't like what is happening, you can fire your contact. But in international adoptions you probably won't even know exactly what your contact person or agency is doing. But *try* to know the people who are working for you; you need to be able to trust them. Check them out. Talk to others who have worked with them. In any independent adoption, unscrupulous and inept people can take advantage of those who very strongly want something.

While a lack of health information remains a risk, research is reassuring about the improvement in health of adopted foreign children after a period of time. Infants and children are fairly resilient. Once they are placed in a stable, healthy environment with plenty of attention, security, good nutrition, and medical care, their physical and mental health can improve dramatically. An agency will attempt to supply some information about the child's health and background, but the amount you receive in an independent adoption will depend on the contact person.

The difficulty of exchanging information about the child you are adopting is another risk that should be taken into account. In independent adoptions in the United States, you may learn a great deal about your child; you may meet birth parents and even grandparents. In international adoptions you are unlikely to be given as much specific information about the child you are adopting. You are likely to know some minimal details about this child's medical background before you agree to the adoption, and that's all. You probably will not be able to learn any of the birth parents' medical history or background.

There are many unknowns in international adoption. People have to maintain a flexible approach to the child they are going to receive, and they also must keep in mind the risks involved in the process they have chosen. No adoption is completely without risk, but knowing the risks allows you to take precautions that can minimize their impact on your family.

Understanding Your Motivations

Each of us needs to understand our own motivation as we approach adoption, and for that matter, as we approach biological parenting. Consider yourself. What are you looking for and why have you chosen this route? Altruism has a place in both domestic and international adoption, but it will not support the long-term demands of parenting.

SAVING A CHILD

If you are expecting gratitude from a child you have "saved" from a difficult life in a poverty-stricken country, you will be disappointed. Few children, saved or not, will express gratitude. Your view of yourself as a parent and what you can do to help raise a healthy and happy person is a better reason to adopt.

ROMANCE OF INTERNATIONAL ADOPTION

There is romance, panache perhaps, in adopting from a foreign country. But that is soon lost in the realities of everyday life. Your child may look different from you and his or her peers, and you need to be prepared for the multitude of questions and even stares your family will elicit.

WANTING A CHILD WHO LOOKS LIKE YOU

Going to another country to find a child who looks like you may present some problems. Many of the parents going to Romania so they would find a light-skinned baby were very surprised when they received a child who was much darker than expected. If you would have a problem accepting a child from a particular country, don't explore adoption possibilities in that country. For example, paying higher costs in Mexico for a light-skinned child may be saying something about your lack of acceptance of children from that country. Be honest with yourself.

RELUCTANCE TO MAKE A SPECIAL-NEEDS ADOPTION

If you are adopting from another country because you have heard that the children available in the United States are only special-needs children with problems, be prepared. Many of those who come from other parts of the world also have special needs. Most of them will have experienced deprivation in their early months of life, many will be malnourished, and others will have significant health problems. Some of these children will be older when they arrive, and others will experience developmental delays. Most of these children will not look like you and will need to understand the racial differences between themselves and their parents and siblings. All of them will need help understanding their cultural heritage.

AVOIDING BIRTH PARENTS

People adopting from another country may be hoping to distance themselves from birth parents. They don't want to have to deal with the question of biological family as the child grows older. While that problem may be avoided, the child will probably still want information about his birth parents and his background. In fact, an increasing number of people who were adopted as infants from other countries are now seeking information about birth parents and hoping for reunions.[13] You need to understand that your child may have a different view than you do about the importance of this information.

Some Questions to Consider

Why adopt? Why adopt a child from a different country? Why have a child biologically? This is the time to question your reasons for adopting and why you are adopting this child. You can also examine to what degree your motivation is based on your needs and how well they will fit with your child's future needs.

Adopting a child from another country obviously has strong implications for the direction of your family. You need to examine your heart and make sure that you are not trying to find a way around issues that will still exist after you adopt a child from another country.

YOUR PERSONAL VIEWS ABOUT RACE

What are your views about race? How important to you is the way your child looks? Would you be comfortable with a child whose skin coloring is distinctly different from yours? What coloring do you think people who come from Romania, Asia, or Latin America have? What if they turn out to be darker or lighter than you expect? What other physical features do people from these countries have—height, hair, facial characteristics? Will you be comfortable seeing a child who looks totally different from you and your other relatives in photos that hang on your wall or fill your albums?

THE PUBLIC'S VIEW OF YOUR ADOPTION

How do you feel about people looking at or staring at your different family? Will this attention pose problems to other members of your family? What if your child continues to have medical problems that cause her to develop at a slow rate? Will you be comfortable with questions about your adoption?

YOUR CHILD'S UNIQUE IDENTITY

How can you help your child have an identity that represents him both in your family and as part of a different ethnic group? What can you do to make him comfortable with his ethnic background? What adaptations will you and your family need to make to be sure this happens? Are you willing to learn more about his country of origin, its traditions, beliefs, and people?

THE PROBLEMS OF PREJUDICE

How will you be able to help a child whose race is different from yours to be comfortable with people of her own race? Can you be comfortable helping her reach out to others of a different race—yours? Can you help your child understand the implications of not being white in a predominantly white society? Are there ways that you can prepare her for the prejudice that she will experience when that has not been part of your own experience? If she has physical problems, will you be able to help her with the prejudice she encounters? What can you do to help the other members of your family who are not of the same race as your child or who do not have her physical limitations understand about the prejudice they, too, may experience?

THE CHANGING PICTURE OF YOUR FAMILY

If it is easy to consider adopting a child of a different race or ethnic background now, will that change as your child grows? Will it bother you if people assume your partner is from a race different from yours when they see you with your child? Will it bother you if your child dates or marries someone of a race different from yours? What if your child seeks people of his own background for friends?

In no way are these questions posed to cause you to change your mind about adopting from another country. They are meant to help you seriously and thoughtfully consider your views and reasons for adopting this way. But these are questions to consider not only if you are adopting a child from a different country but even if you are adopting a child in this country who comes from a background that is different from your own. Many areas of parenting will need to be worked out as you go along, and we don't expect you to anticipate every possible way you will respond when your child is older. But adopting a child from a different race or a different culture is not the same as other adoptions, and knowing of certain issues you will be confronted with allows you to evaluate how you will handle situations before they arise. Take the time in order to be fair to yourself and to your child.

A Cultural Commitment

While you are still trying to decide how to approach adoption, it may be too early to look thoroughly at the issue of raising a child from a different culture in a sensitive way, but it is not too early to understand the importance of this issue. All adoptions come with another family as part of the adoption. To accept a child whose racial or cultural background is different from yours brings some special issues.

Cultural connectedness begins from the earliest days of an adoption and extends throughout a person's life. Once you adopt a child from a different race or culture, your life will forever be different. You are a multinational family that may also be multicultural or multiracial or both.

Learn about the importance of instilling cultural pride. Look, for example, at some of the many ways of understanding cultural pride. Cultural pride is an issue that involves everyone in your family. It means becoming sensitive to the words you use and the subtle ways we and our families may unconsciously reflect prejudice. It includes making those around us equally sensitive to language that reflects prejudice. It involves reading magazines and books with hints about cultural issues, multicultural events, and ideas about holidays, foods, dress, music, and other cultural customs from your child's country of birth. These same magazines and books should be shared with extended family members so they also become sensitive to the child's cultural heritage. It means making a specific plan to help your child develop a cultural identity that reflects who he or she is. It is about establishing cultural connectedness for your child so that he is proud of his culture and his race and therefore has the ability to handle the questions of others as well as his own questions. It also means being prepared for the eventual racial comments and inappropriate responses from others both for yourself and for your child.[14]

Talk to those who have gone through this process for specific ideas for helping a child feel good about her culture. One family keeps a box with items from their son's birth country; they all go through it from time to time. Another family has fabrics and other material from their child's native country; she will be able to share it with classmates when she is in school. Another family helped begin a support group for families who have children from ethnic or cultural backgrounds different from their parents'; they meet once a month for informal picnics, talks, play times, and general support. One mother has been resourceful in finding dolls from the country of her daughter's birth. One family made a point of naming their new son after someone in the family to help them all understand the permanence of the adoption. A father found a beautiful topographical map of his child's birth country to put on the wall of his room; another remembered to bring home a flag. One little boy had furniture from his country of origin in his room. A single mom adopting from China brought back small presents from the area in which her daughter was born; she plans to give her daughter one on each of her next eighteen birthdays.

Certainly you may hear about families who take their teenage children back to their countries of birth as a way to help them reconnect. For some teenagers, this is a very positive experience, but for others, mixed feelings result. These trips certainly show the children the difference between the way they were raised and what might have been, but it may also underscore their sense of being different.

Once your child from another country becomes used to life in the United States, it can be easy to forget the commitment to help the child learn about his cultural and ethnic heritage. Even if your child appears to have adjusted well to the changes in her life, this apparent comfort is not a reason to believe this area is any less important. In fact, it means that your child should go another step in learning about herself.

But it is not merely the things you surround your child with that give him a firm ethnic identity. In an issue of the *Adopted Child,* a newsletter on adoption issues (see Appendix F), Lois Melina helps parents understand the difference between culture, belonging, ethnicity, and ethnic identity. A person's ethnic identity is "a unique mix of biology, group history, and personal experience."[15] She encourages parents to seek help from people of the same ethnic background as their child and to become comfortable discussing the birth family, which is necessary to encourage a child to develop this part of his identity.

Even the American Psychological Association has been struggling with defining *ethnicity.* One of their researchers writes that the term is used to refer to broad groupings of Americans on the basis of both race and culture of origin. It encompasses (1) the cultural values, attitudes, and behavior that distinguish ethnic groups, (2) the subjective sense of ethnic group membership that is held by the members, and (3) the experiences associated with minority status, including powerlessness, discrimination, and prejudice.[16] Parents adopting from another country will become experts on the use of the term *ethnicity.*

When you adopt an older child from another country, the importance of understanding the culture is even greater. Attitudes about smiling, saying no and meaning yes, giving and receiving gifts, and referring to age can cause confusion from one culture to another.[17] Books, magazines, or support groups can help you to learn about many of these differences so that you can help your child adjust to his new environment.

Two books, *The Rainbow Generation: Teaching Your Children to Be Successful in a Multicultural Society* and *Different and Wonderful: Raising Black Children in a Race Conscious Society,*[18] have been written by a couple who understand about the importance of differences in our society. The large number of books for children about being adopted from other countries is one of the most positive additions to adoption literature (see Appendix G). A special new book for families who will be going away to adopt a child from a foreign country is *Seeds of Love: For Brothers and Sisters of International Adoption;* this book is for young children to understand being separated from their parents at this special time.[19] Children also love some of the wonderful books that do not discuss adoption but look at other issues related to being different:

B. J. Kates, *We're Different, We're the Same* (2 to 6 years)
N. Simon, *Why Am I Different?* (3 to 8 years)
N. Pellegrini, *Families Are Different* (4 to 8 years)
Arnold Adoff, *All the Colors of the Race* (7 to adolescent)

Children from different backgrounds, as in all cases of adopted children, are likely to go through a period of rejecting their "differentness." They want *not* to be from a different culture; they want the same color skin and the same kind of hair as their parents, the same traditions and beliefs. It is important to be understanding of these strong feelings when they occur. Then tell your little one how beautiful her hair is or how much you love his skin. You can be accepting of a child's desire to be like her friends while still telling her how good she is the way she is.

With adoption of a child from another country or domestically, you need to be able to discuss ethnicity openly, but you don't want it to be a dominant theme in your home. Your child may be different, but he is your child and he needs to feel that sense of connection with you. Too much pointing out of the ways someone is different from you may cause the differences to dominate. You may be very excited about how you have this special child—but he just wants to be your child. Keep his adoption in perspective (see Chapter 14). Adoption, differentness, race, and ethnicity are issues to touch upon when appropriate, but they should not be in daily discussion.

Remember that this adoption, as with all adoptions, is a lifelong process. But it is also a process that offers rewards not only to your adopted child but to all of your family members whose lives are enriched by this adoption from another culture.

Summary

While some people will seek children from other countries before considering any other kind of adoption, adopting internationally is probably not the first choice for most people. Some people adopt internationally because they have been unsuccessful adopting in the United States, because they are fearful of the potential problems in a domestic adoption, because they think it will take too long or be impossible to adopt in the United States, or because they believe they will help some needy child. Most adoption agencies would say that the desire to "save a child" is not sufficient motivation for a successful adoption. Some people adopt from countries of their family's ethnic origin or because they know someone else who adopted from a specific country.

Because of the added responsibilities of raising a child from a different country, it is important for potential adoptive parents to scrutinize their motivation for adopting this way. As with all adoptions, understanding what you are doing and why you are doing it ahead of time will help you avoid problems.

International adoptions bring with them the responsibility of teaching your child not only about himself but also about his country of origin. Cultural sensitivity is essential for helping children accept who they are. This is a dimension added to the other areas of helping an adopted child form a strong sense of identity. But with continuing parenting education and lots of love and patience, the end results are wonderful.

People adopting these children are those who believe so strongly that they want a child that they will go through a great deal to adopt from another part of the world. Maybe this is a good way for you to proceed. If it leads you to the child you want, it's worth it.

International adoption is a constantly changing scene. Laws differ from country to country, and laws often change within a country. In the United States, the rules change about the specific children who can be brought into this country. Those people considering adoption from other countries need to be aware of the many changes that occur and be prepared for changes to happen while they are in the process. With luck, the changes will be positive, as they are in most international adoptions.

The procedure for adopting internationally is more complex than for adopting domestically. The child adopted in this way, however, is just as cherished as a child adopted in any other way. Those seeking to adopt internationally must be prepared for many requirements. They must meet demands from their own state, the immigration service, the foreign country, the adoption agency, and the demands imposed on them by a special child from a different culture. Adoption from other countries is a wonderful resource, but adopting internationally takes dedication.

CHAPTER 8

An Option
Worth Considering

WHAT IS AN UNADOPTABLE CHILD? We aren't sure such a child exists. Some children are more difficult to place than others; they are known as *special-needs children*. What does *special* mean? It is a euphemism for hard-to-place, at risk, physically disabled, mentally disabled, learning-challenged, emotionally disturbed, or racially mixed children.

You might be tempted to skip this chapter now and say you aren't interested or this isn't relevant to you, but don't. You should consider special-needs children because you may be offered one. You may not seek a child who has a problem, but you may find yourself faced with an adoption that involves a child who may have some kind of a problem.

In the past, these children were shuffled aside so that large numbers of easy-to-handle, easy-to-place children could go through the adoption system. Twenty-five years ago, there wasn't even a category called "special-needs" children. Couples who adopted had a choice, and they wanted "normal" babies and "normal" families; that left the special-needs child languishing indefinitely in the foster care system. Agencies didn't believe there were families who would take these children; they were so sure, they didn't even ask. This same criticism might be made of potential adopting parents. They, too, frequently overlooked these children in favor of easier-to-raise "normal" children. As "normal" children became less numerous, special children began to have a chance to be considered by adopting parents.

Five groups of adoptees constitute special-needs children:

- High-risk children (known to have potential problems, but only because of the known health and mental history of the mother. Includes drug- and alcohol-affected babies and babies whose mothers test positive for HIV)
- Disabled children (includes physically, mentally, and emotionally challenged children)
- Some non-Caucasian children
- Older children (generally over the age of three; may have been in foster care for an extended period of time)
- Sibling groups

It is not unusual for these groups of special-needs children to overlap. You may have a child who falls into more than one category.

One major change in adoption recently has been that children who previously were considered unadoptable are finding homes. The primary reason for this change is the greater demand for children to adopt. Adopting parents are considering special-needs children since the alternative may be to remain childless. The adoption system has become better at "selling" the idea of these children. The use of TV, newspapers, and even the Internet has helped introduce these children to many potential families, and greater numbers of them are finding homes.

Another change in the adoption scene has been the increasing number of "high-risk" infants. We aren't sure why this is happening. Some would say the reason is the drug use that has become prevalent in our society. Others believe it is the increased toxicity of our environment. Still others would say that the rising numbers of learning disabilities and emotional disabilities are the result of a new system of identifying children and giving them labels. But no matter what the cause, all people considering adoption are well advised to learn about all of the children who are available.

Are *all* special-needs children up for adoption now being placed? No. Are all children who may have special needs identified before they are born, and will you definitely know before you decide to adopt one? No. But significantly more hard-to-adopt special-needs children are being placed than ever before, and significantly more children being placed for adoption are being found to have some kind of special problem.

The increasing number of children born with some kind of special need has also increased pressure on birth parents. Giving birth to a child with disabilities is an added strain whether a birth mother is finding an adoptive home or keeping the child. For some mothers, placing a child with a problem is more difficult than placing a child without a problem. Guilt that her behavior may have affected the pregnancy and birth of her child may make this decision even more difficult.[1]

In the past, the unique needs of some of these children sometimes precluded independent adoption. Today, some considering independent adoption are totally open to the idea of taking a child with special needs—it is not a second choice or something they end up doing inadvertently. Others find themselves receptive to the idea when they hear of a situation that might turn out to involve a child with some special needs because they have become tired of waiting for a "perfect" child. Certainly adopting across racial lines has become more prevalent in adoptions made independently or through private agencies.

Sometimes finding the right special-needs child may still be difficult. You'll need your creativity here, too. Kathy and Ed wanted only a hearing-impaired child. Kathy's brother was deaf and she grew up understanding the complexities of raising such a child. She wanted to raise a child who might otherwise not find a home. After approaching agencies to find a deaf child, they realized that this might not be as easy as it sounds. They went another route—to the Internet. There they put out their message to people who had adopted internationally. They found a woman who had adopted a handicapped child from Romania and who told them of two deaf children she met when she went to pick up her daughter. Kathy and Ed made connections with some people dealing with Romanian adoptions and went many miles to find their special-needs child. An independent international adoption was their route to the deaf son they so much wanted.

One of the strengths that all parents of children with special needs must have is the ability to become the child's advocate. Parents need to learn the system and how to make it work for their child. Those who adopt independently will have to be resourceful to find out what programs are available to their child. At no time in our history has there been more support available for specific groups of people with special needs.

The largest group of special-needs children are placed through public agencies. Though both private and public adoption agencies may include special-needs children, today when you go to most public adoption agencies, the children most readily available will be "specials." Note that interracial adoptions through public agencies are still rare. If you are willing to consider one or more of the special kinds of children available, you will be kept on the agency's active list. If not, you may not find a child through a public agency; you may have to look elsewhere.

Even though it benefits you not to eliminate any special-needs children immediately in order to be kept on the agency's list, you should not take a child you do not want! The last thing these special children need is to be placed in a home that is unprepared for or reluctant to have them. Be open about which children you will consider, but at any time you can decline any child you feel is beyond your limits. To go beyond what you really feel comfortable with is a disservice both to you and to the child.

The more severely disabled or psychologically disturbed a child might be, the greater the need for more careful screening and support systems. They also frequently need medical or psychological attention. Too often, unless special children are adopted through public adoption agencies, there is little or no follow-up or support service available; the importance of these services should not be underestimated.[2] Since more parents are not interested in adopting children in these categories, many parents need to be available in order for the adoption agency to find a few who would be suitable for these children. Great emphasis in recent years has been placed on preparation for special-needs adoptions; prospective parents study handbooks and participate in group discussions.[3] As in most areas of adoption, we encourage you to read about the issues to help you understand what the problems are that you might encounter.[4] People are now writing about these issues for other parents; in the past the books were for professionals. Take advantage of the wealth of material available to you to learn more about adopting special-needs children.

Where to Go for Information

One of the advantages of working with agencies is their access to a clearinghouse of information on special-needs children. They share their information with each other, too, communicating about hard-to-place children and about parents seeking them. Organizations that share information also include Children Awaiting Parents (CAP), Adopt a Special Kid, the Adoption Resource Exchange for Single Parents, and the National Adoption Center (see Appendix F); if you ask them for help, they will transmit your name over a broad network. Using these resources and others like them is rather like posting your house on a multiple listing; you significantly increase the exposure of your house by advertising, thereby multiplying the number of prospective buyers who know it's for sale. Basically, that's what happens with hard-to-place children. The adoption agencies advertise them to other agencies in the hope of finding them parents. This listing has been a tremendous benefit in finding homes for special-needs children. Some of these exchange groups are also showing pictures of children and giving brief stories about them on the Internet.

These groups and Adoptive Families of America, the North American Council on Adoptable Children, and the Child Welfare League of America (see Appendix F) disseminate material, publicize special-needs issues, encourage local contacts for people interested in special-needs children, and advocate for many issues related to children. Their reading lists, magazines, and newsletters are helpful.

Reading is one of the best ways to assess your ability to parent a child with special needs. Many times potential adoptive parents have little understanding of the kinds of needs special children have. Reading about different situations might help you to consider the rewards of adopting a different kind of child. Books describing personal experiences can be helpful.[5] *Self-Awareness, Self-Selection and Success: A Parent Preparation Guidebook for Special Needs Adoptions,*[6] published by the North American Council on Adoptable Children (see Appendix F) is another source to help you determine how well you might parent a special child. Articles in magazines such as *Adoptive Families* (published by Adoptive Families of America, Inc.) or *Roots & Wings* (see Appendix F) address adopting children who are considered to have special needs.

The magazine *Adoptive Families* has many hints for parents who are considering adopting and parents who have already adopted; one issue featured an article devoted to "reading between the lines" of a waiting-child description:[7]

Phrase	*Interpretation*
☐ All boy, tomboy or very active, needs attention	☐ May indicate attention deficit hyperactive disorder (ADHD)
☐ Requires structure and supervision, bossy, grieving	☐ May indicate emotional and/or behavioral problems
☐ Victim of neglect	☐ May indicate attachment disorder, sexual abuse, or malnourishment
☐ Difficulty in school	☐ May mean learning disabilities
☐ Moody or sad	☐ May indicate depression
☐ Exposure to drugs/alcohol in womb	☐ May mean fetal alcohol effect or fetal alcohol syndrome
☐ Developmentally delayed	☐ May mean mild to severe mental retardation
☐ An early riser	☐ May mean sleep problems

This author encourages potential adoptive parents to ask questions so it is clear what problems they are dealing with in any potential adoption. She also encourages people to call immediately because these listings change quickly and children who are available at one time are not necessarily available soon after.

A newer trend in this kind of effort is found on the Internet. Through this medium, still in its infancy, a person can find pictures and brief stories previously only available to adoption agencies. Making this information on the Internet available to all people will undoubtedly open up even more adoptions to people who will be touched by the many children waiting for homes.

Screening Potential Parents

While some people would categorically reject the idea of knowingly adopting an older child or a "defective" child, others feel that this situation was meant for them. Some people would say that to adopt a child of a race different from their own would be detrimental to the child, while others view interracial adoption as the ultimate solution to racial prejudice and divisiveness. No group is right or wrong; their views are merely different. Surely our society has room for differing views on a subject as basic as the right of each child to a home and loving parents.

Agencies do a great deal of screening of prospective parents of special-needs children. They seek people who sincerely want special children; they try to weed out those parents who are only settling for "specials" because they can't get what they really want. Agencies think families should not take a special-needs child as a second choice or out of pity. Ideally, we concur completely. However, many times these children are taken because no "normal" ones are available and the adoptive parents don't have much choice. If you don't have much choice, then these children *are* second-choice children. But then, isn't adoption itself a second choice for most people? Actually, many who adopt special-needs children are motivated in part by pity. They feel that taking a child no one else wants is a worthwhile thing to do. Others take a hard-to-place child because they believe this will strengthen and improve our world. These "do-gooders" can make good parents. Altruism has a place among parents, too.

The primary intent in agency screening of potential adoptive parents needs to change; it should focus less on an applicant's motivation for adopting a special-needs child and more on making certain that parents understand the potential problems as well as the potential joys of these children. (Ask any parent of a special-needs child of the joys of parenting a specific child. Most would speak of the same joys and even some extra ones of raising a child who is special.)

Although it would be ideal for all parents of special-needs children to be outstanding parents (this is true for all adopted children and children by birth), this is probably less critical than the parents' willingness to be parents under special circumstances. Certainly the same motivation is not always present in those who biologically produce a special-needs child. *Screening out* potential adoptive parents is inappropriate, but *screening in* is critical. Simply having a family itself can be very healing.[8]

Special-needs children need homes—they need parents, they need families, they need to be part of a community, they need activities, they need stability, and they need love. They need to be adopted. The potential is there for these children to be adopted; the potential is there for them to lead more normal lives. Every effort needs to be made by all of us involved in adoption to secure homes for these special kids.

The Children as Adoptees

HIGH-RISK CHILDREN

Some children are considered higher risk children; they are children who *could* have problems but we aren't sure. Drug and alcohol use, potential genetic diseases that may surface after a child is born, and certainly the potential of AIDS increases the risks in all adoptions; these problems are found across all ethnic and socioeconomic groups and should cause all couples considering adoption to understand the potential risks involved.

You may not set out to have a child who has special needs, but you may find yourself faced with that issue. If your résumé is chosen by a birth mother who has a history of physical problems, you know ahead of time that the baby *might* have a disability of some kind. You may also have to face a problem that surfaces only some time after you have the child, such as discovering that the child is hearing impaired. You may learn of a birth mother who has used "some" drugs or alcohol during the pregnancy; you then have to assess the risk of your child developing problems that may place him in the special-needs category. Independent adoption today involves special-needs children.

Some parents know ahead of time that the birth mother of their child was involved with drugs or alcohol during the pregnancy. No one is sure exactly what that means for the health of the child. We know that it is best if no drugs or alcohol are consumed during the pregnancy and we know that is what we would like for our child. But because of the number of people involved in drugs and alcohol, it is worth your time—however you plan to adopt—to learn about the effects of substance abuse on unborn children. There are many books to help you explore the issues and the potential outcomes from these possible situations.[9]

We fully understand how devastating fetal alcohol syndrome (FAS) can be, but we aren't sure how much or at what stage during the pregnancy the birth mother must drink to cause this to happen. We know that children born to drug-affected mothers have to go through withdrawal before their bodies can react to life normally. There is no direct correlation between a child's passive substance abuse and the child's future prospects. Most studies done on drug-affected babies are on those who remain with the drug-dependent mother. How can we separate the chemical effect of the drugs themselves from the effect of the child being raised by a drug-dependent parent or in a drug-filled environment? This difficult question has been addressed in several studies that have found (1) that drug-exposed children did very well when raised in a healthy adoptive environment, and (2) that parents were as satisfied with their adoptions as any other group of adopting parents.[10]

Other researchers are less certain. Some question the connection between the higher incidence of learning disabilities in adopted children and drug usage by birth mothers.[11] The damaging effect of prenatal alcohol use has been found to cause mental health problems, disrupted education, social trouble, and other problems that cause growing concern for the developing child,[12] but direct studies on these two factors together have not yet been done. Even in the studies that indicate there may be some correlation, the environment in which the child is raised still has a significant impact.

While reports of environmental influence are reassuring, they are not enough to reassure some couples. Some are unwilling to adopt a high-risk child, even if the process was started before the risks were discovered. Many times a couple begins planning to adopt a certain child only to learn down the line of the birth mother's drug or alcohol problem. Sometimes they find out about the drug or alcohol involvement only at the birth of the child. You can put months and years of thought into adoption but then be faced at the last minute with the most important decision: Are you going to take the potentially special-needs child or not?

Missy and Josh were faced with this kind of instant decision. They were at the hospital when their baby boy was born. The birth mother, Emily, was doing fine. Emily had signed papers to allow all information on her health care to be given to the adoptive parents. She had told the hospital that she had used some drugs at other times in her life; the hospital routinely screened any babies whose birth mothers answered yes to that question. Missy and Josh hadn't discussed this issue with Emily, and when the nurse asked them if they knew of Emily's history with drugs, they were stunned.

Their new baby tested positive for drugs. What should they do?

They spoke with Emily and consulted with their physician. Both people reassured them. Emily said she used marijuana occasionally, but she was not a heavy user. The physician told them of studies that had found there was no problem if the adoptive home provided a stable environment. Missy and Josh went ahead with the adoption. Actually, their own occasional use of marijuana made them more comfortable adopting their new son.

Another situation where a last-minute decision comes up is when a child or the birth mother tests positive for HIV in the hospital. This is always a shock to adoptive parents. Without going into detail about HIV, it is important for adopting parents to know that if the birth mother tests positive, it doesn't mean that her baby will.[13] Even if the baby does test positive, he or she won't necessarily develop AIDS; we don't know why, but researchers believe the antibodies of the mother might temporarily show up in the baby and then disappear. Babies who test positive for HIV need to be retested after fifteen to eighteen months of age to be certain. We know that if mothers who test HIV positive have good prenatal care and take AZT during the pregnancy, the risk can be as low as 10 percent that their babies will develop AIDS; where prenatal care is less ideal, the risk is still only 25 percent.[14]

There are many pivotal decisions for adoptive parents to make amid the confusion and lack of information about AIDS and alcohol and drug use. As in many other adoption situations, there is no one right way to proceed. One birth mother who had been asked about her use of drugs and alcohol by a potential adopting mother taught us a lesson. She said that she should be the one who should be most concerned about alcohol and drug use—in the potential adoptive parents with whom she was considering leaving her child. She considered the drug and alcohol use of the adoptive parents to be a far bigger issue for the child they would be raising than her own use history. While this may not be altogether true, she certainly had a point.

DISABLED CHILDREN

The decision to adopt a disabled child also needs to be seriously considered before beginning the adoption process. The variety of disabilities is far too vast for most people to grasp; it includes mental and emotional problems as well as physical ones.

Physically Challenged Children

Physically disabled children come most readily to mind when people think of special-needs children. Perhaps this is because imagination works visually and physical disability can most easily be pictured. Though many kinds of disabilities cannot be seen, we imagine a child in a wheelchair or blind or in leg braces.

Physical difficulties cover a wide variety of situations, and what appears to be severe to one person may not be considered serious by someone else. Some couples would be overwhelmed to have a child who is epileptic; this same physical limitation in another home might be considered only a minor inconvenience.

In the past, the standard question of the adoption worker was,

"Would you consider taking a child with a correctable physical handicap?" Adoptive parents had a choice; in fact, they had three ways to answer the query:

1. No, I want a child who has no known physical problem.
2. Yes, I will take a child with a physical problem, as long as it is correctable.
3. Yes, I will take a child with a minor physical problem, even if it is permanent.

Yet a fourth choice remained: a child with a major problem that is not correctable. It was rarely mentioned to adopting parents in the past. These children were placed for adoption only when a couple actively sought a severely handicapped child. As you can imagine, this was not frequent. Most children with disabilities, especially severe ones, were placed in foster care indefinitely. Today, many of these children have a chance to be adopted.[15]

Before you begin to pursue adopting a child with a physical disability, find out about the kinds of physical challenges. Learn what the different disabilities might mean to your life. Most people have only heard of cerebral palsy; few people could describe what a child with cerebral palsy actually faces. Do you know? What about a child with spina bifida? What about a child who can't hear? What about a child without arms? The list could go on.

While you probably cannot learn about every physical difficulty a prospective adoptee might have, you can know some things in general about how you would feel about a physically disabled child. Is it important to you to have a child who looks normal? Is it important to have a child who can be treated in a rural facility if your current home is not in a city? Is it important to have a child who can travel, because that is a big part of your life? Is it important to have a child who does not use a wheelchair, because your home's bedrooms are all upstairs and you have no extra money to change this or to move? Is it important to have financial help if the child accrues significant medical bills that your family cannot afford? Is it important that the child have the capabilities to live alone as an adult? You also need to think about what kinds of physical disabilities could be integrated into your life without disrupting it. Not every child with a disability will enter a given family with the same ease.

Fortunately, you don't have to know exactly how every different disability might affect you and the child. You can learn gradually about different kinds of problems from an adoption agency worker. The worker will not hastily place a disabled child without giving you time to consider how the child would fit into your family. You will have plenty of time to consider, to read about, and to plan how a specific physically challenged child would fit into your home.

Adopting a child with a physical challenge is a major commitment that exceeds the commitment to raise a normal child. Not all people can do this. The DeBolt family, depicted on television, most vividly demonstrates the commitment it takes to make adoption of a physical challenged child truly successful.[16] Their story probably did more to advertise the joy of adopting a child with a physical disability than any adoption agency promotion ever did. Their love, affection, and caring for one another are apparent; their family experiences the normal aspects of raising children—the trials and tribulations, the joy and love—more than the issues related to disabled children. Their thirteen adopted children, many with severe physical disabilities, cause most of us to look on with sheer admiration at the life they have chosen. But it is important to remember that even they adopted most of their children in small steps, usually one at a time.

One of the significant advances in this area in recent years has been state and federal subsidies for adoption of handicapped children.[17] These subsidies allow people of moderate or low incomes, who would otherwise be unable to afford expensive medical costs, to adopt children who are physically challenged. This also opens the way for the foster parents who have cared for one of these children for long periods of time to adopt him or her without losing the financial support that they need.

Foster parents are, in fact, a valuable part of special-needs adoptions. While most adoptions work, even in special-needs situations, adoptions by foster parents can still minimize a child's problems.[18] Perhaps it is because these parents have adjusted to the children or because they are already willing to take special-needs children, but they can make a difference in successful adoptions.

Maggie was placed in a foster home when she was just three years old. Her birth mother had great difficulty deciding finally to relinquish her, and another eighteen months passed. In the months she had been with them, Maggie's foster parents, June and Jess, grew to love her as they helped her struggle with spina bifida. They were caring and loving and willing to do what Maggie needed. When she didn't feel heat or pain because of her disease, they worked to teach her how to protect herself. Her many infections kept them up numerous nights, caring for her. They were even there when her physician inserted a shunt to drain fluid from her brain. Almost from the beginning they had wanted to adopt her but knew she was not yet available; even if she were, they felt unable to meet her medical costs.

The adoption worker was well aware of the asset these foster parents were to Maggie. Recognizing their financial situation and wanting to avoid other foster homes for Maggie, she approached June and Jess about adopting Maggie with a subsidy to help with medical costs. No one hesitated. Even Maggie's birth mother was happy with the solution. She had seen the love the foster family had for Maggie and was absolutely supportive of the adoption.

In some cases, assistance for the high medical costs of raising a physically disabled child is given by charitable groups like the International Shrine Headquarters (see Appendix F). They will help children at one of their three burn centers or nineteen orthopedic hospitals throughout the United States. While their specialty is burn victims, they are a great resource for help for all disabled children from birth to eighteen years of age. The North American Council on Adoptable Children (see Appendix F) is a wonderful source of information about federal and state adoption assistance and subsidies.

Gary had been crippled with arthritis from birth. His adoptive parents felt totally able to handle the problems Gary's handicap presented. He needed considerable attention, and the exercises he required to prevent extreme pain could also be somewhat painful. Yet these time-consuming and emotionally draining activities presented no problem to the people who adopted Gary. His arthritis was not only painful but visible. As Gary grew older, the loving support of his adoptive parents helped him with the taunts and jeers he received from his not-too-understanding peers. While the family could handle raising Gary and could meet the normal medical costs most of the time, sometimes they needed some extra help, which they received through the Shriners' program.

Undoubtedly, the assimilation of a child with a physical disability into a new family is far more difficult than when a "normal" child is adopted. But none of us know whether any child might develop a disability. More important than being a special child is being merely a child.

Mentally Challenged Children

The range of children who are considered learning challenged is much broader than in the past. We used to group some children under the category "mentally handicapped," which meant a child was mentally "slow"; the degree of slowness could vary from moderate to so severe the child had difficulty functioning. Today, we also place children who have a special problem in learning in the mentally challenged category. These would include children with attention deficit disorder, learning disabilities, and even some children prenatally exposed to drugs and alcohol. The categories the children fall into are not clear, and many overlap with those for physically disabled children.

The point at which a child becomes special-needs due to a learning problem is not clear. For couples who want only a quick-learning and bright child, a child of even average ability could appear mentally disabled. Some adopting parents want a child with at least average intelligence and then discover their child needs special help to learn. And the new category of learning-disabled children includes many children who have difficulty learning but who are not mentally retarded. What level of challenge are you willing to accept?

Choosing to adopt one of these children is similar to choosing a physically disabled child. You need to fully understand what this means to you and to your life situation. If you enter this process with a clear understanding of what adopting a mentally challenged child will mean, you are likely to find the experience rewarding. If you know that a child's history strongly indicates that she could have problems learning, you will know better how to react or whether you want to move ahead. If you enter this process unsure of what you are undertaking, you can end up feeling overwhelmed and disappointed.

Few people have the chance to experience the problems encountered by those who work with or raise children who are mentally limited. If you consider adopting one and have not been with children who are mentally challenged, make the opportunity. Visit schools for mentally challenged youngsters. Learn the difference between a slightly retarded child, a moderately retarded child, and a severely retarded child. These school can tell you about parent groups in your area. Go to the group meetings and learn about the problems and delights of raising a child with this unique and special need. When you hear others speak of raising this special-needs child, you may find yourself amazed how the joys and the problems sound just like those experienced by anyone raising a child. Certainly there are extra issues such as coping with the difficulties of school, setting occupational goals, dealing with dating, or keeping expectations at realistic levels. The problems of these children are slightly different but in many ways the same as those of any child.

The family who adopts a mentally challenged child is relieved of certain burdens. While our society believes a child's physical disability can result through no fault of the parents, less understanding is given to the family that produces a mentally or emotionally challenged child. In some ways the family stigma of these disabilities is removed from the family who adopts the child. They do not have to bear the burden of guilt that might come with giving birth to such a child. This is true even though mental retardation knows no more limits than physical disabilities do; every family is at some risk of having a child who is mentally impaired.

Environment plays a role in changing a particular child's level of functioning, as most researchers agree. If a child is extremely limited in his or her level of mental functioning, a positive, healthy environment can improve this situation, though it will not make a bright child out of one who is considerably below average. Modifying, enhancing, and influencing the disability are all possible through the environment—you will bring the child closer to his or her potential in a stimulating, loving, attention-providing environment. But adopting parents need to understand the limits of environment. A change such as the one in *Flowers for Algernon,* in which a mentally retarded man becomes a brilliant person, is simply not possible.[19]

Some parents are very clear on what can be expected from a child with a mental disadvantage. An attorney once called us about an infant born with Down's syndrome. The birth parents had not considered adoption until the syndrome was discovered, and now there was no way the father would keep the child. After calling several sources who had indicated a willingness to take special-needs children, we came in contact with a group whose members only adopt children with Down's syndrome. A couple had been waiting for just such a little girl and were absolutely delighted. They already had adopted one child with Down's syndrome and were well aware of the issues of raising a child with this problem; not only were they ready, but they also had a built-in support group to provide help and assistance with what to them was a truly special child, in the very best sense.

No one can guarantee that your child will be bright when you give birth or when you adopt a child. You may not always be aware of a child's mental disability until he or she grows older; this is one of the ways in which adopting is like having a child by birth. Many children with no known family history that would indicate disability may develop problems in learning. Fortunately, adopting parents are like most parents and adapt to the problem. They seek what help is needed and do the best they can.

People planning to adopt a child with a known mental disability need especially to be prepared for the response of others. Friends, relatives, neighbors, and even professionals frequently discourage their adoption. For example, Elizabeth and Roger had spent a long time considering adoption to increase the size of their family. Their two boys were nine and eleven, and Elizabeth and Roger wanted a girl. But they also wanted to adopt a child who might have difficulty finding a home. Elizabeth felt she had the time, patience, and energy to consider raising another child—a special one. After spending many hours discussing different kinds of special-needs children with their caseworker from an adoption agency, they finally decided that a mentally challenged girl was what they most wanted. As they sought to share their enthusiasm in this new venture, they found none of the child's future grandparents very eager for this new family addition; in fact, both sets of grandparents repeatedly suggested they not do this "radical" thing. They told Elizabeth and Roger that a mentally impaired child would be a burden and would not fit into the family.

Elizabeth and Roger were upset with their parents' response, but they were determined to succeed. The agency social worker urged them to give the future grandparents time to digest the thought as both Elizabeth and Roger had. Eventually the grandparents came to accept the new baby granddaughter Elizabeth and Roger brought them, but their reluctance had made the process much more difficult. Only absolute confidence in what they were doing gave Elizabeth and Roger the strength to pursue their goal despite family discouragement.

It is much more difficult to predict which children will have learned disabilities than which will be mentally disabled. Usually a learning disorder becomes obvious once the child has entered school. Until then, many parents struggle with children who seem to be more out of control than they had anticipated, but they do not necessarily understand the extent of the problem.

Probably no disorder has received as much publicity as attention deficit disorder (ADD). For some the disorder is called hyperactivity or attention deficit hyperactivity disorder (ADHD). Other terms being used to describe this disorder and similar disorders are *learning differences, learning challenged,* and *learning disabled (LD).* It is estimated that 5 to 10 percent of children have attention deficit disorders and a third also have other learning disabilities.[20] One researcher believes that 20 to 40 percent of adoptees are thought to have ADD, compared to 3 to 5 percent of the nonadopted population.[21] While the existence, the extent, and the treatment of these disorders is debated, we are finding an increasing number of adopted children who experience these kinds of problems.

Trudy and Hal aren't positive if their child has ADD, but they know she has a problem. They adopted Ellie when she was two days old; no one talked with them during the adoption about having a child with ADD. The first years were great and she seemed to progress normally; she was a little wild and had trouble settling down at night, but they figured that was normal. When she entered school, they became concerned about her ability to handle schoolwork and to sit still in a regular class. After many sessions with the teacher and a counselor, they are now becoming experts on ADD. They didn't choose it, but their child seems to have it.

One of the most important things you can do is to help your child accept his own challenges. The fortunate part of adopting children with some kind of disability or potential challenge is that there is lots of help available. Obviously the best way to evaluate the situation is to go through a similar experience ahead of time. But for many situations in life, you aren't given a chance to prepare; instead you have to look for solutions as problems arise. Fortunately, there are many ways to get help, and the resources for children with learning disabilities are extensive.[22]

The growing body of literature for children with learning problems is a great asset to parents who unexpectedly find themselves with a child whose self-esteem is threatened because of the problems he is experiencing in life. Some of the books your child might enjoy and that will help him feel OK about his own problems include:

M. R. Galvin, *Otto Learns about His Medicine* (4 to 8 years)

J. Gehret, *Eagle Eyes: A Child's Guide to Paying Attention* (4 to 10 years)

M. Gordon, *Jumpin' Johnny, Get Back to Work!* (4 to 10 years)

D. Sanford, *Don't Look at Me* (5 to 10 years)

J. Gehret, *The Don't-Give-Up Kid and Learning Differences* (6 to 12 years)

P. O. Quinn and J. M. Stern, *Putting on the Brakes* (8 to adolescent)

R. Cummings and G. Fisher, *The Second Survival Guide for Kids with LD: Ways to Make Learning Easier and More Fun* (8 to adolescent)

L. Clayton and J. Morrison, *Coping with a Learning Disability* (9 to adolescent)

S. K. Welch, *Don't Call Me Marda* (10 to adolescent)

Ask your local librarian for help on finding other titles or more recent ones. Some children's books address specific problems.[23] They can be very helpful in raising any child, because all children at times face issues that need special attention. One of the nice things about having a problem that is widely publicized is that books will continue to be published to keep up with the demand. It is important to remember that having a learning problem isn't easy for children, either.

We don't know why so many children who are adopted seem to have learning disabilities. (It isn't just in children adopted from this country; the same is being found for children adopted internationally.) Maybe some really don't have a problem, but adoptive parents may be more likely to seek help with their children. Maybe professionals are quick to report a learning problem before it is actually diagnosed. The cause of learning problems is equally elusive: There may be some relationship between maternal drug use and learning disabilities. Other people would hypothesize that chemicals in our environment are the cause of an increase in problems. We really don't know for sure, but we know it impacts many children—and not just adoptive children.

In some ways it is easier to prepare yourself to adopt a child with a mental disability than it is one with a physical disability, because a mental disability can be more limited and more specific. You can focus your attention on one area and learn about it. With a physically disabled child, you may have great difficulty anticipating what physical problems your child might have. On the other hand, people are generally more accepting and less cruel to children and adults who have physical limitations than to those who have mental limitations. As learning problems show themselves in disruptive classroom behavior, you may find other parents less accepting of your child. But no matter which type of disability your adopted child has, it is clear that a loving, supportive home can best provide these youngsters with the stability they need to face a world that sometimes stares at and frequently whispers about them.

Emotionally Challenged Children

Of all of the disabilities that children may have when adopted, the most difficult for parents seem to be those that are emotional. This may be because most emotionally challenged children being placed for adoption are also older children. These children are high-risk adoptees. It is estimated that one in eight of these children is returned to an agency before the adoption is finalized.[24]

Emotionally challenged children are more closely related to mentally challenged than physically challenged children in the problems they experience. Again, the problems are less visible and for most people harder to understand than those which accompany a physical disability. However, children with emotional problems are probably less understood, and, consequently, shunned even more than mentally challenged children.

Emotional difficulties present themselves in a variety of ways. Children with compulsive personalities often need order to maintain their aggressive feelings, and this need may present itself in extreme behaviors. Frequently children who have been shifted from home to home can develop mistrustful personalities; they become suspicious and paranoid. At times, children experiencing emotional problems may become isolated; they retreat into a fantasy life. Other children react to their life situations with emotional problems that they act out; they become aggressive and difficult and have problems connecting with others. Many of these behaviors can be the behaviors that children who have been sexually abused exhibit.

These are only some of the kinds of behaviors that can confront parents who consider adopting an emotionally challenged child. Without knowing what particular disorder your child might have, it is difficult to prepare for the unique problems he or she might bring to your home. If you are working with an adoption agency, your social worker will discuss the different children available who are exhibiting symptoms of emotional disturbance. However, in order for you to evaluate how a potential adoptee could fit into your life, you need to understand the specific problems that confront the specific child you might adopt. Your social worker will explore each issue as well as possible.

The way to determine how impaired a given child might be and how likely you are to help him or her is to find out as much as possible about the birth parents and the child's history. You want to understand the genetic basis of the disorder and its potential course. Then either consult someone who specializes in helping emotionally disturbed children or read about this particular kind of disturbance so that you clearly understand what this child might mean in your life.

The belief that love will conquer all leaves families in a weaker position to find solutions than if they had studied the problems and adequately prepared for them. Before you move ahead with an adoption, find out what the chances of success and resolution are for a given disorder. Find out if this disorder is caused by the child's life situation or if it is a hereditary problem that you are unlikely to be able to solve. Gather the information you need to evaluate your ability to handle the situation in the best possible way. Read other parents' accounts of adopting a child with a similar problem.[25] Read everything you can about emotional disorders.[26]

Rob and Diane met in college when they were both training to teach classes for disabled children. Their similar interests drew them together immediately and they married a year later. Soon thereafter, Diane had their first child. They had always wanted to adopt because they felt overpopulation was the most significant problem facing the world, so they decided that they would adopt their second child. They also decided since they had special skills, they could bring those skills to parenting a special-needs child. Diane especially wanted this opportunity, because as a stay-at-home mom she had never had a chance to use her experience and training in teaching.

An adoption agency in Pennsylvania gave Rob and Diane their chance. After a lot of scrutiny about their motives, the social worker from the adoption agency began to speak with them about Tiana. Tiana was four and had recently been relinquished by her birth mother after a long legal battle. Tiana's mother had routinely abused her. Perhaps her mother's divorce at the time of Tiana's birth had caused the woman to focus all her negative feelings on Tiana. Perhaps because Tiana was premature and had spent her first month in a hospital the bonding process was not firmly established. No matter what the cause, Tiana was a frightened, withdrawn child who had asthma, nightmares, and little trust for anyone. The adoption worker felt Tiana might be just the child Rob and Diane wanted, and they might be just who Tiana needed. They took Tiana home.

The process of establishing trust was extremely slow. Diane's patience was critical; her ability to reach out to Tiana, but to not overwhelm her, helped the little girl struggle with her many fears. Both Rob and Diane learned a great deal about child abuse and the effects it has on a child. They are still trying to understand the birth mother, in order to help Tiana understand as she grows older what might have been happening in her early years. Even after many years, Tiana's early years still come back to overwhelm her. Diane and Rob feel that they make progress and then lose ground. They have gone to support groups with parents of other difficult children and note that Tiana's problems seem less severe than many others. And they have never regretted their decision. Obviously their college training has helped them understand special children, but even more important to their success has been their willingness to be open, to seek help when needed, to learn, to read, and to listen.

Children with emotional difficulties are often among the older children placed for adoption. These children may have been in other adoptive placements that have failed, or they may have been removed from home situations that failed them. Studies indicate that 75 percent of school-age children awaiting adoption have been sexually abused.[27] Even with the problems presented, life for these children is significantly improved by adoption. Remaining in their homes of origin, most of these children would have become even more emotionally disturbed. Certainly most adoptees feel that it is better to be in a permanent home than to be raised in foster care.

We aren't totally clear about why some of these children succeed against the kinds of overwhelming odds they face. By looking at children who do go on to be successful despite stressful environments and high risk factors, we may find the answers. Researchers in Hawaii have studied the effects of adverse early rearing conditions on children's development; this longitudinal study has been in existence for three decades.[28] Their findings have much to teach us about who survives difficult prenatal and childhood trauma. They concluded that protective factors help vulnerable children escape the problems through their resiliency. They found that "competence, confidence, and caring can flourish even under adverse circumstances if your children encounter people in their lives who provide them with a secure basis for development of trust, autonomy, and initiative."[29] This is what adoptive parents can give these children.

DIFFERENT-RACE AND RACIALLY MIXED CHILDREN

The area of special needs that has received the most publicity and remains embroiled in the most controversy is when children are of a race different from their adoptive parents. Adoption of a child of a different race seems to polarize all segments of our society, especially adoption professionals. Yet the issues involving races other than African American are somewhat ignored. The complexity of classifying children of more than one race is often solved by allotting them to the race that has been the most verbal in its protests of ethnic genocide.[30] To date, the groups most upset with these adoptions are Native Americans and African Americans.

The primary controversy is about Caucasian parents who adopt racially different children. Native Americans and African Americans have criticized the placement of their children in Caucasian homes. Families attempting adoption where children have any known Native American ancestry are quick to find out the problems facing them.[31] Having some part of the child's background be Native American may not preclude the adoption, but this will depend on the specific tribe. The Native American issue was resolved for a time when tribal leaders succeeded in getting the Indian Child Welfare Act of 1978 passed; the interpretation of this law places adoptions under the jurisdiction of the child's tribe. Federal legislation to loosen the guidelines of this act as they relate to adoption are now being considered. More effort is now being made to assimilate Native American children within the Native American community by using groups such as the Council of Three Rivers and the Three Feathers Associates, National American Indian Adoption Service (see Appendix F) which have listings of children available.

In 1972 the National Association of Black Social Workers spoke out strongly, taking the position that African American children should be placed only in African American homes, whether for foster care or permanent adoption. In response, transracial adoption of African American or partly African American children plummeted. Public agencies have taken the path of least resistance and limited these placements; perhaps the limits came in response to their black social workers' stance, but perhaps they were a part of the agencies' own collective beliefs. The emotional reaction to this decrease from minority groups and from Caucasian neighbors of some adoptive families has been varied.

The stand of the National Association of Black Social Workers brought positive changes in the recruiting of black adopting parents within the African American community.[32] But these efforts did not keep up with the increasing numbers of African American children entering the foster care system. Some African Americans would say that the lack of flexibility in the definition of what constitutes a family, as well as high costs and restrictive criteria for adoptive parents, have caused barriers to these adoptions.[33] No matter what the cause, too many minority children spend most of their growing years in foster care. The emergence of groups such as PACT and the Institute for Black Parenting (see Appendix F), which offer help on issues related to children of color, will, we hope, help reverse this trend.[34]

Meanwhile, independent racially mixed adoptions are occurring in increasing numbers. New federal legislation decrees that adoption should be "color blind" may help change attitudes; however, minority children now represent almost half of the children currently in foster care.[35]

While other-race children have been adopted and continue to be adopted by Caucasian families from other countries, these international adoptions have not caused a furor from ethnic groups. In fact, the most frequent form of transracial adoption in the United States is the adoption of Korean-born children by Caucasian parents.

What does all this furor mean to someone who is considering adopting? For those Caucasians considering adopting a child of color, it certainly means that there are more children available than there are Caucasian infants. And, too, transracial adoptions have been researched for years; there is strong evidence that these adoptions are working well and that the children have self-esteem at least as high as nonadopted children's.[36] Racial identity issues seem to be handled adequately by most adopting parents, who generally make an effort to help their children form a strong sense of self. For interracial families who need assistance in this area, new groups are emerging to help parents give their child a firm identity within his or her racial group.[37] We now know that families committed to helping raise healthy children will probably be just as successful raising a child of a different race as they will be raising a child of the same race.

Megan and Les wanted a large family and knew the only way they would have one would be to adopt. The racial background of the child was not an issue to them. They heard that the process would be easier and faster if they were open to a child of mixed racial background, and they were. They were not big readers on the subject, but they talked a lot about it. They knew what they wanted. Their openness to the child's racial background was just one part of their openness; they were also adaptable to complex situations, situations that needed quick answers, situations that others might stay away from. They were open to meeting birth mothers and birth fathers. They would be supportive during the pregnancies, but they were not interested in ongoing contact, and about that issue, they were very clear. That restriction had to be acceptable to the birth parents of the children they adopted.

They now have six children. It is exciting to watch their family interact. The children are from a variety of backgrounds. One child who was supposed to have an African American father obviously didn't. But that was OK, too. Megan and Les are truly color-blind with their children.

Transracial adoptions are not an issue in this country alone. In Canada and Great Britain, too, even with the increased recruiting of minority parents, the number of adoptive families still lags behind the demand for them. Minority children frequently become special-needs children for reasons other than race alone. Because they are harder to place, they frequently are older before homes are found; their lack of stable homes in their early years increases their emotional difficulties.

If you are willing to take a child of a different race and choose to go through an agency, you need to be strong. As in all areas of adoption, shop around. Not all agencies are open to this kind of adoption and you need to find out which ones are. Find an agency that will provide the service you want.

Adoption agencies have been slow to understand the parents who seek to adopt a child of a race different from their own; as a result, traditional agency workers are frequently skeptical of those seeking "different" children. Until recently, adoption regulations required agencies in the state of Washington to document their efforts to find a same-race placement for all minority children or to risk losing their license. Today, federal legislation prohibits these same agencies from delaying adoptions based on race. This is a volatile period for transracial adoptions. Become an advocate for what you want.

Many transracial adoptions take place in the independent realm. While independent adoption is primarily a Caucasian institution, as is adoption in general, more and more African American couples are considering adopting independently, and more and more women pregnant with children of color are looking to adoption as a means of providing a good home. Their reasons are the same as other birth mothers'. They know they can get some financial help with the pregnancy and have some say in choosing the family who will raise their baby; they know the child will not be in foster care, and they realize that they can probably maintain some contact with the adopting family to see how the child is developing.

Roxanne was nineteen when she discovered she was pregnant. She already had one child and was barely getting by as a single mom. She knew that if she had another baby she would have to go on welfare to survive. She wasn't going to do that. The birth father was eighteen years old and didn't want marriage or a child. Roxanne first met with one adoption agency; there she was alarmed to hear that her racially mixed child would be in foster care until a suitable home was found. Such a delay was totally unacceptable to her. Then she called four attorneys, trying to find out about independent adoption. Three of them told her that they couldn't help. The fourth one explained what she was up against, listed her choices, and helped her find a family for her child. The services of this attorney were free to her, and he even arranged for the Caucasian couple she had chosen to supplement her living costs when she had to quit work in the last two months of the pregnancy. She wrote a letter to her baby to explain why she had placed the little girl for adoption, and she has an agreement with the adoptive parents that they will send yearly pictures and a letter about how she is doing. She feels she has made a good decision for her baby—and for her other child, who remains with her.

We frequently ask adoptive couples how they would feel about adopting a child of another race or a racially mixed child. Their responses vary a great deal. One of the most frequent is that it wouldn't be fair to the child. We don't usually pursue the issue with these couples because this response generally tells us they are not ready for that specific situation, and that is fine. The part these couples don't understand is that, in all fairness to the child, he or she is better off in some home rather than no home. The first choice may be a home that is just like his birth family. However, many times that home isn't available; then we must look to other solutions. Another response we frequently hear is that these children will have problems when raised in a family that isn't the same race they are. Studies have shown the opposite; children in transracial adoptions usually do very well.[38]

Couples involved in independent adoptions across racial lines may or may not be asked questions about their readiness to accept a child of another race. This in no way lessens your need to understand the problems you might encounter in an interracial adoption, so you should be aware of the support systems in your community. Adoptive Families of America and the National Adoption Information Clearinghouse (see

Appendix F) can provide names of support groups in different geographic regions. These groups have meetings at which you can learn about the problems and peculiarities involved in interracial adoptions. The individuals involved in these organizations are also a great source of information about the response you might receive from your local adoption agency when you seek a child of a different race. Adoptive parents who have worked through the system can also give you valuable information on how it works.

Some magazines specifically address the issue of race. *Biracial Child* and *Child of Colors* have now merged into one, *Interrace* (see Appendix F). *Adoptive Families* and *Roots & Wings* (see Appendix F) also regularly feature articles related to interracial adoption.

Several books have been published on the subject of interracial adoption[39] and on helping children of color handle the barriers in life based on race.[40] There are also some excellent books for children in mixed racial families that are worth reading to understand the child's perspective on his unusual family:

K. Kasza, *A Mother for Choco* (2 to 6 years)

R. Dauer, *Bullfrog and Gertrude Go Camping* (4 to 7 years)

H. C. Andersen (retold by L. B. Cauley), *The Ugly Duckling* (4 to 8 years)

J. Cannon, *Stellaluna* (4 to 8 years)

S. D. Lawrence, *We Are Family* (4 to 10 years)

A. Angel, *Real for Sure Sister* (6 to 12 years)

M. B. Rosenberg, *Living in Two Worlds* (6 to 12 years)

M. A. Waybill, *Chinese Eyes* (6 to 12 years)

C. Bunin and S. Bunin, *Is That Your Sister?* (7 to adolescent)

A. Adoff, *All the Colors of the Race* (7 to adult)

D. Dillon, *Many Thousand Gone* (9 to adolescent)

P. S. Buck, *Matthew, Mark, Luke, and John* (10 to adolescent)

P. Gillespie, *Of Many Colors: Portraits of Multiracial Families* (10 to adolescent)

The Black Adoption Consortium (see Appendix F) is publishing a series of children's books that feature adoptive families. Anyone who considers adopting a child of another race should read the story of *Edgar Allan,* which vividly tells of such an adoption that failed.[41]

Another way to understand interracial adoptions is by speaking with people of any age who have been adopted. Cynthia reports: *Anthony, our son, who was adopted when he was seven, added a new dimension to my knowledge of adopting an older, racially mixed child. He teaches all of us daily. One particularly poignant lesson occurred the second week we had him at home. He, his two sisters, and I sat comfortably in the yogurt shop one day after school. He asked nonchalantly if I thought it was strange that he was the only black person in our family. I defensively reminded him that he was not all black, but then asked him what he thought about it. He replied, "I think we owe it all to Martin Luther King." I think he is quite right. Without the steps that have taken place in the last years toward greater understanding across racial lines, an adoption like ours would not have occurred.*

Adopting a child of a different race, like adopting any special-needs child, has some unique problems and some unique joys, and it can offer many rewards. For some people the opportunity to visibly show the world that mixed families work is a source of pride. Adopting a child of a different race forces adopting parents to look at the issues of race and prejudice in a new light with a greater sense of understanding. The expansion of your own personal limits on racial tolerance is a direct result of being the mother or father of a child who looks different than you do. The positive response from people who have expanded the racial mixtures of their families is strong testimonial for transracial adoptions. Don't overlook this option. But remember that, like all adoptions, it is best entered into if you fully understand the process and your feelings before you begin.

OLDER CHILDREN

Older children were the original special-needs adoptions. Historically, social workers and other concerned people first focused their attention on finding homes for these children, who were often orphans; their value to adopters in days past was as workers. Today, children play a different role in our lives and most people seek babies. Few people buy an adult cat or dog; they buy a kitten or puppy. The same is true in adoption—most people want an infant and few choose an older child. Older children are considered hard to place and also are special-needs children because they are not in as much demand as infants.

What constitutes "older" children is not always clear. It used to be infants over six months old were considered older children. Then children over three were the new breaking point. Now, older children are usually those over six or even eight years of age.

Everything we learn about child development says the personality is formed in the very early years.[42] The impact parents make on the lives of children is most significant before the age of five. Some child psychologists would say our most significant impact is made by the age of *three*. Psychologists recognize the need for bonding between parent and child to begin as early as possible in order for the child to achieve maximum emotional development; some maintain that a person who has never been able to feel love as a child will have great difficulty forming loving relationships later in life. While the younger the child, the less likely the problems, any child over the age of six months has some special issues that need to be addressed by adopting parents.[43] A relatively new phenomenon has been the placing of children who are toddlers by mothers who have tried to succeed as single mothers and, failing that, then placed their children for adoption at an early age.[44] While these children are seldom considered special-needs children because of the ease of their placements, they do have these same special issues of bonding that need to be addressed. So while the emphasis in this section is on the older child, the needs of even younger children should also be recognized.

The reasons children are older at the time of placement vary. A few become adoptable late in childhood because of the deaths of their only existing relatives. Other children are taken to agencies, usually by social workers, because of dysfunctions in their families. Since the Adoption Assistance and Child Welfare Act was passed in 1980, efforts must be made to reunify a family before adoption is considered; this often delays relinquishment of the child. In most states, once the child has been formally relinquished, the process still takes an extended period of time to reach adoption—far longer than it takes to reunite the parent and child.[45] Many of these children have been in several foster homes during their stay in the system. Finally, some children are older because problems have previously prevented their adoption, such as emotional disturbances, medical conditions, or being part of a sibling placement.

Both efforts toward reunification of families and the increased number of drug-exposed infants and young children have caused a tremendous surge in numbers of children in foster care in the last decade. This increased case load has caused adoption within the system to become even slower. It is estimated that as many as half a million children are currently waiting for families to adopt them;[46] these children become older, and thus more special-needs, every day. Ninety thousand children have been in the foster care system for three or more years.[47]

The amount of trauma the child receives because of the delay in adoption depends on his or her life history. It is possible to adopt an eight-year-old who has been in only one home; the primary problem here is dealing with separation from the one known family, as this child may have experienced great stability and love. On the other hand, a four-year-old may have had seven or eight homes. She may have lived with a parent, then relatives, then another parent, then multiple foster homes. Age alone will not tell you the extent of the rejection the child has experienced; ideally, the case history will. Be sure to learn as many details of the child's life history as possible from the agency.

Meredith and Jim were older and had already raised two children; they felt they had much to offer another child or two. When they approached a support group for couples wanting to adopt, they learned that older children are not as available in independent adoption as they were through public agencies. However, they took the recommendation of the group and went to a counselor doing independent adoptions. Their chance came relatively soon.

They met Emily, who was raising her son, David, by herself. He was out of control and she knew things were getting worse. Since David was already six, she had to do something soon. Emily liked Meredith and Jim right away. She felt they had experience raising children and she liked the fact that Jim had his own business and could spend lots of time with David. But she wanted one more thing: She wanted to be able to see David at least once a month as he grew up. She felt he would not feel as much rejection if she continued to have some contact with him. She was prepared not to interfere with Meredith and Jim's style of raising children, but she wanted to maintain the contact.

To Meredith and Jim, this sounded reasonable and actually very loving. They agreed. All three of them decided to put the agreement they had made together in writing. They wanted it clear to everyone.

David is now twelve years old and doing well. He looks forward to his visits with Emily, but his life is with Meredith and Jim, and that is where he feels he belongs. At first the visits were difficult. The day before the visit, the day of the visit, and the day after, David was difficult. He acted out with his adoptive parents, his siblings, and with Emily. Over time, the problems decreased. He now seems to understand that he can't choose where he lives—that part is up to the adults in the situation. Since it isn't his problem or decision, he can feel free to enjoy his time in both places.

Jim and Meredith are secure in their role as David's parents. They do not need to have Emily out of the picture. They discuss problems openly with her, and she with them. They have established a healthy relationship that is in everyone's best interests.

Placements of older children are usually handled very slowly in order to ensure their success. The child is usually involved in approving the prospective parents; this is why older-child adoptions are frequently said to be more like marriages than regular adoptions. Those adoptions that work do so because the adoptive parents want them to, and the older child makes a conscious decision to accept his or her new situation. Integrating the child with children already in the home is also crucial. You may have several meetings with the child, and you may take her home for a temporary visit before the actual placement occurs. Perhaps the most important reason why these adoptions work at all, despite all the potential problems that can complicate them, is this very involvement of the older child, who decides when she really wants to be adopted. Know that adopting an older child presents the highest risk of failure.[48]

When you adopt an older child, you are adopting a child who has a past. In order for the adoption to be successful, you cannot pretend that the past does not exist. Rather, it is of utmost importance that you help the child become comfortable, not just with who he is now, but also with who he was before you adopted him.

One issue from the child's past is his name. When you adopt a baby, you can give him a name, and seldom is this questioned. Never is the last name questioned. It is different with an older child. He comes with a specific name, first and last. To now ask him to give up one of those, his last name, is a major event. It, like many other times in older children adoptions, is a milestone when the child accepts his new last name. Some of these children may decide to keep their former last name as a middle name. Where possible, parents need to go along with this.

It has become common to use photo albums or "life books" from previous homes to help the child integrate his life. This simple concept is now also being used by couples involved in new baby adoptions. Scrapbooks prepared by the birth mother can be given to the adopting couple, who share them with the child as he or she grows. If the child has been in foster care for a period of time, foster parents may be helpful in filling out these books for the child. Looking at such albums can be healthy for all of the people involved in the adoption process.[49]

A new variation on the scrapbook idea has the potential adoptive parents prepare a photo album of their lives for the older child they are considering adopting. In this way, the child learns about her potential family in a controlled and cautious way. The pictures can show the child the parents who are interested in her, any other existing family members, the house, the kinds of things this family likes to do, pets, the room the child would be in, and anything else that will help the child learn about this potential family. The child finds out quite a bit about the family in a very child-friendly medium—pictures.

In adopting older children, especially in independent adoptions, there may be a need for continuing contact with significant relatives of the child, besides the birth mother. Gerald was seven when his mother, Yolanda, decided that the demands of raising this energetic, impulsive, and at times rebellious young boy were overwhelming. She saw his leadership potential being used in destructive ways and felt that without a radical change, he would become a street-gang leader rather than a student government leader. She decided he needed a chance for a structured, supervised life in a more stable family. She decided to place him for adoption.

Her decision to place this child shattered her mother, who had spent considerable time with him in his earliest years, but Yolanda was sure of what she was doing and proceeded without the blessing of her mother. Nonetheless, she decided she would need to find a home where she could learn how Gerald was doing and felt that desire precluded agency involvement. She also learned that if she went through an agency, they would place him in foster care first and would not guarantee how long that placement would last.

She decided to find on her own a couple who would take her son, and she did. She felt they were just what she was looking for, and they were excited about Gerald. Gerald checked out his new home and his brothers and sisters, and he thought it would be a good place for him. The change was made and the adoption papers were filed.

When Gerald's grandmother found out that the boy had new parents, she made contact with them. She wanted to maintain communication with her oldest grandson, but she showed her obvious unhappiness with the situation by continuing to refer to him by his previous surname. The adopting mother wrote to her to clarify their willingness to keep contact with her as long as she could accept the fact that Gerald had a new home, new parents, and a new last name. This was not easy for Gerald's grandmother, but she was slowly won over as she saw the positive progress her grandson had begun to make. Gerald still maintains contact with his grandmother and with his birth mother, whom he now refers to by her first name.

Gerald came with a history and with existing relatives. Adoption could not change that, nor should the attempt have been made to weed out people who might help to make the transition smoother for him. The adoption worked out, and everyone is satisfied.

One of the ways to learn about adopting older children is, of course, to talk with others who have done so. You'll have to talk with them for a period of time, because often people just quickly tell you all the good things and fail to mention the difficulties you should know of. Your agency worker can give you names of people or groups who work as support systems to people interested in older children.

You should read books on adopting the older child[50] and provide your child with books designed for him to understand adoption. These books don't have to reproduce your situation exactly, and they don't have to have happy endings—they do need to stimulate discussion and thought. There is a large selection of children's books about adoptions of older children (see Appendix G). One source of help for parents is *A Child's Journey Through Placement,* a book dealing with the issues of attachment, child development, separation and loss, and how to minimize the effects moving has on the child.[51]

It is becoming common for agencies to hold postadoption group sessions for parents who adopt older children. These kinds of support systems help parents deal intellectually with problems instead of just acting out of fear or some other emotion. If you adopt an older child independently, find your sources of support in your community, either through independent adoption support groups or through counselors who are familiar with adoption issues. Help is there if you seek it.

Some agencies are attempting what are called cooperative adoptions with older children, which have been used successfully in independent arrangements. These adoptions recognize the existing bond between the birth parent and the child; the legal placement takes place without ending the relationship between the child and the birth parent. In the past, some birth parents were not ready to relinquish their rights, so their children remained in foster care; this new system keeps time spent in foster care to a minimum. Cooperative adoption also benefits the child who is ready to be adopted but reluctant to lose contact with birth parents even though the relationship may have been difficult.[52]

As should be clear by now, adoption of older children, as with other special-needs children, is sometimes more complex than it appears on the surface. It is very different from adopting an infant. These children may have emotional or other problems; perhaps they have been in adoptive placements that did not work out. It may be difficult to completely piece together the history of an older child placed; as a result, his current behavior or responses can at times be difficult to understand. Yet understanding is the critical ingredient in making these (or any) adoptions work. People who anticipate the stages of adjustment that the older child experiences in an adoptive home can prepare to handle them effectively. Adopting an older child is not for everyone, but those who overcome the challenges are delighted, and many adoptions of older children are great successes.

Sibling Groups

Starting with more than one child looks good on television and in the movies. It is even a romantic concept; we think how cute twins or triplets are. Few people really want to start families this way. Yet this is just what occurs in sibling adoptions. Adopting siblings may have some disadvantages: the children may come from a difficult background; they may engage in a divide-and-conquer syndrome to gain control over the new family; and an instant large family comes with extra demands.[53] Yet some people welcome the opportunity to adopt more than one child because of the cost savings, because of the mutual support siblings offer each other, and the family enrichment of having more than one child at a time.

Sibling adoptions can be hard to arrange, not only because of the number of children involved but also because of the ages of the children, who can become quite "old" as they wait for a family. In all hard-to-place adoptions, the time lag works to the disadvantage of the children; the longer they are not adopted, the more unadoptable they become. (See the section on older children in this chapter.)

Every possible effort should be made, and usually is made, to keep siblings together. When children have been together for years, they frequently become the only stable factor in each other's lives. Siblings, as any parent can attest, usually cling together when other factors are working against them. When united, brothers and sisters can present a strong defense. This response is activated when siblings are being placed for adoption; it keeps them calm while waiting and gives them an added sense of security in their new home. To lose biological parents through rejection, or foster parents through multiple moves, is bad enough, but to then lose the brother or sister who has been a source of strength and stability can be an overwhelming hardship.

In the case of siblings, as in the case of all special-needs children, families willing to adopt these children have significantly increased since fewer infants have been available for adoption. For some people, adopting siblings can be an especially good solution to childlessness. Dorothy and Lew had three children biologically; then a relative who was having problems with a teenage son sent him to live with them. They thought they did a good job with their new addition and decided to adopt a child. They went to a private adoption agency knowing they wanted to adopt more than one child; they didn't feel it would be fair to an adoptee to be the only child in the family not biologically related to the parents. They didn't know that they would be offered a chance to adopt siblings, or that it would come so quickly.

Their caseworker called them shortly after their home study was completed. She had a brother and a sister who were six and four. Dorothy and Lew thought they sounded great. Nothing they heard deterred them; they even thought it was OK when they heard that the children had a difficult background and that their adopters needed to meet the birth mother—the agency they were working with dealt only in open adoptions.

The process went quickly. It took place in a state where adoption moves very rapidly, even though this particular process needed to be slowed down a little for the sake of the children. The birth mother arrived at Dorothy and Lew's house with the children and was ready to leave them the next day. Within the week, the boy and girl were there to stay. Everything looked great.

But Dorothy and Lew soon found that they didn't totally understand some things that were happening in their home. They realized these two children, Ellie and Austin, were quite manipulative. The two of them made decisions together and presented a formidable front to Dorothy and Lew. The couple learned that Ellie and Austin had been on their own in many ways while their mother was gone. They now had to give these children a chance to be children and not little adults. They consulted regularly with their caseworker about how to handle situations, and the caseworker was encouraging.

Once Lew and Dorothy realized what they needed to do, there was a very brief honeymoon period where everything was wonderful, then a long period where everything seemed to go wrong. Things have now begun to settle down after two years. Dorothy, Lew, and the two new children needed help but so did their biological children. Adopting is truly a family affair. It took help from the caseworker, from Lew and Dorothy's close friends, from the school counselor, and from a support group, plus books about adoption for the parents and the kids, and a lot of time talking with Dorothy's mom—but things are OK now.

Cynthia notes: *My husband and I adopted three children, ages twelve, thirteen, and fourteen. Adopting three children has been like no other experience we have ever had. These children, a sibling group, had been in foster care for eight years. The actual process of adopting these children was extended over an unreasonably long period of time and filled with bureaucratic delays. While the books, even this one, discuss the need for close communication and exchange of information, in reality the delays had little to do with having time to establish a bond with the children or with learning about their backgrounds or ours—the delays were primarily due to slowness on the part of the adoption system.*

The impact of the delays was felt especially after the children were placed. Every day has been such an important time for these children and for us—learning, trying, and testing. Every day we lost with our new children was a day we lost forever.

It is difficult to find many people who have adopted more than one child at a time; this is less common than most other types of special-needs adoptions. Few parent groups act as support systems to adopters of siblings; these parents must read, learn, and forge ahead on their own.[54] Certainly children's books about adopted siblings groups are helpful for parents and children alike.[55] However, the problems they confront can multiply those faced by the parents who adopt a single child.

Summary

One of the major changes in adoption concerns special-needs children. The definition of *special needs* changes quickly, based on demands for adoptees. Generally, a special-needs child is at high risk or already physically, mentally, or emotionally disabled; older than most adoptees; of a race different from that of the adoptive parents; or part of a sibling group.

Special-needs children have a great deal in common, partly because the specific groups of special-needs children overlap and merge. The demands on the families who adopt these children, while different in many ways, are common in many others. Another common thread is the happiness these children bring to the families who share their lives. The agencies and others wondered about the motives of people who would seek children who were not like "ordinary" children. As a result, many times special-needs children were not even offered for adoption. Even more problematic were sibling groups, which were seldom suggested, because the agency *knew* people didn't want them. Today, siblings are adoptable as a unit, and other special-needs children are finding permanent homes. What used to be "normal" adoption situations have become less common, and people wanting to adopt are rather receptive.

Yet sometimes the placement of these special children does not work, just as sometimes children and their biological parents fit badly. There is no question that more "disruptions," as failed adoptions are called in the adoption field, occur in special-needs placements than in "normal" adoptions. The amazing thing is that the great majority work. Adoptions of special-needs children work—even though everything seems to be working against them. Agency social workers say the reason they work so well is effective screening of parents. Maybe. But then again, maybe the success rate exists despite all the ways we interfere with and hinder the placement of these children. Perhaps our belief that these children are hard to place actually makes them even harder to place; our view that these are the last-chosen children may cause us to suggest them only as a last resort.

So many of the demands, problems, and joys these special-needs children share come about because they are children first and "special" second. They have been grouped under "special needs" so that we can discuss them conveniently, but in reality their specialness is not primary in their lives. On a personal basis, this label is of little value: You deal with Johnny or Suzie or Tim, who are specific children with unique sets of needs, desires, hopes, and dreams. So while you cannot separate the children from the "special needs" they have, their category is not who they are. They are much more. They are really unique individuals, just like anyone else you might meet. Ultimately, no one has such a handle on life that in some way he or she could not be labeled a "special-needs person."

3

LOOKING FOR—AND FINDING—A CHILD:

Reaching Out for Success

CHAPTER 9

Planning Your Search:
A Practical Guide

YOU SAY YOU WANT A CHILD. You think you might prefer not to go through an agency. Now ask yourself, How much time, effort, and creativity are you willing to put into finding your child?

It's one thing to engage an adoption agency and wait for them to give you a child; it's a whole different matter to go out and find one yourself. How far are you willing to go? Are you uncomfortable with the concept of hunting for a baby? If so, why?

Many people have never considered *finding* a baby. It's difficult to put yourself on the line, to stretch yourself and your creativity in order to get what you really want. (You might compare this process to hunting for the job that's perfect for you, rather than going to an employment agency.) New approaches may take some testing before they fit well into your life. Look back on ideas you considered wild a few years ago and see how familiarity has changed your attitude toward them. In the same way, consider some of these child-finding approaches, discuss them with others, become familiar with them, and *then* see how they feel to you.

The only way for you to evaluate this method in your own case is to study its advantages and risks. The first thing to know is that searching for a baby takes time, lots of time. The more time you spend, the greater the likelihood of your success. The more people you inform, the more people there will be who know of your desire to find a baby and who will be able to help you. You may be lucky and learn about an adoptable child after a contact or two. Or you may have to talk to dozens of people before you get even a trace of a lead. Patience is a critical ingredient in any search.

Knowledge is also important in your search. You need to know what you are doing. You need to understand why you should approach this group or that person. You need to know who gets pregnant and why, in order to understand where you are most likely to find a baby. You should read this book from cover to cover and find out all you can in other ways.

As you begin, resolve to develop your creativity. We are all creative in a pinch. You need to develop that creative approach because, right now, you are in a pinch. You can think of all sorts of innovative approaches to finding a baby.

An open mind is essential in searching for a baby. The more open you can be, the greater your chances of success. You need to be frank with lots of people about your feelings and about your childlessness. You should be prepared to work with the biological parents of your future child. You need to be receptive to suggested leads and to where these leads might take you.

Above all, in a baby search you must be bold. Believing that there is a child out there for you, you must be willing to venture forth to find him or her. Timidity could leave you childless. The people who will find a child are those who will go boldly after one.

All these qualities are within each of us. You may not see yourself as creative and bold, but try it—maybe you really are, or maybe you could be. The desire to have a baby is very powerful. The strength of this desire may cause you to discover characteristics which you may not believe you have.

So give it a try. What's the worst thing that can happen? It is simply that you may end up without a baby, and that's where you are right now.

Plan for Success

Before you begin your baby search, you have to plan on being successful. If you don't believe the potential for finding a child is very great, you won't put your heart into the search. And you should—there are several reasons why a child is out there for you now.

American society runs in cycles. Just as in the world of fashion, fads and cycles exist in family size, sexual behavior, contraceptive practice, unwanted pregnancy, and number of babies available for adoption. Over the years the pendulum swings back and forth.

In recent years the number of unmarried pregnancies has been somewhat level, but there has been increased pressure from taxpayers to cut back on programs that help pregnant women, as well as poor mothers. While we do not advocate these program cuts, it is likely that women who previously got help with raising their children are now being forced to consider other alternatives, such as adoption. This is good news for you.

We're also seeing less social tolerance for young single moms, and the increased negative publicity given to abortion as a solution to unwanted pregnancy is arguing positively for adoption as an alternative. The number of abortions has leveled off in recent years and may be entering a downward trend. A trend toward fewer abortions does not necessarily mean fewer pregnancies; it could mean that more women are keeping their babies or placing them for adoption. There's room for growth in the number of adoptions in that this is not a well-known or common choice for women who become accidentally pregnant (see Chapter 3). If you can reach women in these circumstances, you reach an entirely new group.

Nineteen-year-old Lisa represents this untapped source of biological mothers. She is a bright young woman who knows about contraceptives but used to find them "inconvenient" to use. She was making plans for her second abortion and had not considered adoption. She reasoned very clearly, though incorrectly, that there were already too many unwanted children in the world and she wouldn't want to contribute another. She was not at all aware of the current lack of adoptable babies. Lisa had the abortion because that is all she considered. Think how differently she might have felt if she had met a couple, you, at the time she was deciding what to do. What if she discovered that this was not a child who would be unwanted? Would she have chosen differently?

Women who abandon children are probably thinking in the same terms. It is difficult to imagine a woman leaving her child in a Dumpster if she knew how many people are waiting to adopt. How can a woman have such a poor understanding of what is happening? How can people wishing to adopt reach her and women like her? Finding a way to do so may get you a baby.

If these trends continue, and if potential adopters reach out to birth mothers, we may see an upswing in the number of adoptable babies. But even if the numbers remain stagnant, you should not be discouraged. You are not looking for large numbers of children. You are looking for one child.

Remember that statistics can be misleading. Adoption agency statistics indicate huge numbers of people waiting to adopt, but someone serious about adopting may have consulted with every agency in town and appear on every list. Many people are being counted two, three, or four times—we really don't know how many people are trying to adopt. Similarly, every doctor and attorney you approach has a list of people who would like a baby, but again these lists overlap and re-count people many times. We personally know of dozens of people waiting right now for a baby, but if we had a baby available for adoption tomorrow, many of them might no longer be looking for one. Some would have moved, some would have recently obtained a child, some would not want this particular child because they would not like his background, some would want only a girl and this a boy, and some would simply be scared off when actually confronted with a specific child. Therefore, the list is much shorter than it seems.

Young people's feelings about open adoption are changing, making this an excellent area in which to search. Today, many women would not consider placing a child with a monolithic and impersonal institution like a traditional adoption agency. Most birth mothers now want to be actively involved in the placement of their children. To give a baby up to an agency would not be comfortable for them, but to give a baby up to "real people" is worth considering. You can find these women.

Another reason we strongly believe babies are available is that we have seen couples we've worked with achieve phenomenal success:

Everyone seems to find a child. We have never seen a couple who has searched vigorously fail to find one. At times, when a birth mother comes to us and we go through our files of people seeking children, we are amazed how many of the couples have already found a child to adopt.

All these reasons support the theory that babies are there—you just need to find them. You will be successful.

Preparing Your Search

You believe you are capable of trying to search for a baby; you have looked within yourself and believe you have the creativity, the openness, the boldness, and the patience to find your own baby. You also believe there is a distinct possibility you can find one. But every search needs a plan. Where does one begin a baby search?

MENTAL PREPARATION

You need to be sure you (and your partner, if you have one) are mentally and emotionally prepared for what is coming. You need to reflect on how you would like to guide a potential adoption to make it work well for everyone involved. You also need to reflect on how you will react if the process falters or fails.

In any adoption, each of the required steps needs to be carefully and realistically considered. In an agency adoption, you will be guided through the steps. In an independent adoption, you need to be in charge. The payoff for this careful consideration is a successful adoption, with some other significant additions to your life, such as increased communication with your spouse, heightened self-understanding, expansion of your limits, the knowledge that you can take control of your life in meaningful ways, and an emotional experience that will forever change your life.

To be fully prepared, you need to explore in detail specific issues about adoption. Each partner must have the chance, even the responsibility, to delve into some very personal values. Each partner needs to talk about his or her feelings. These discussions—personal, deep, and often very emotional—can result in a healthier, happier, and more intimate relationship for the partners. Since adoption can be a difficult process, it's nice that it can have positive benefits for the couple.

You each need to share how you would ideally "program" the adoption process. Then you need to understand and communicate how much you are willing to compromise your ideals. Your partner needs to be open to listening to how you feel so you both can discuss which points need compromise. Some areas are easier to give in on than others; the compromises should stretch you, not break you. It's all right to realize there are matters on which you won't compromise and to talk about how painful a compromise would be for you. Perhaps just talking about the pain will lessen it and allow you to go further than you ever imagined.

Some areas will be quickly dealt with, and others may take hours of discussion. Some topics to explore are

- Why are we adopting?
- How difficult will it be for us to raise a child born to someone else? Should we have tried artificial insemination or other means of becoming pregnant?
- Which of us wants a baby most? (One partner almost always wants to have a baby more than the other one.) How will that affect our adoption?
- How much time and effort are we willing to put into this process? Which of us will be doing most of the work? How can we be supportive of each other?
- How much can we afford to spend on this adoption? Is this realistic, given how much we spent on infertility or on our new car this year?
- Exactly what costs should we pay? What other costs would we be willing to pay? Does our attorney agree? What is legal in our state?
- How much would we really like to know the birth mother? Would we rather not know about her?
- Are we willing to meet the birth mother? Where would we meet her?
- What if she is only a few months along? Should we meet her before the baby is born? Should we have her come to meet us or should we go to her?

- Who will be better at relating to the birth mother (you or your partner)?
- How frequently would we be comfortable having contact with her before and after the adoption?
- Would we be willing to have a pre-adoption agreement about later contact?
- Could we accept her staying with us during the pregnancy? What problems would that pose for us and our relationship? Where else could we have her stay while she is pregnant? Would we want her to come home with us after the baby is born? Can we bond as easily with the baby if she is here? Will she feel that we took the baby and ran if we have her stay elsewhere?
- What will we ask her about herself? What will we ask her about the father of the baby?
- What if someone approaches us about a child of a race different from ours? How do we ask about race or ethnicity if we are talking on the telephone?
- How can we find out about the birth mother's use of drugs or alcohol?
- Can or should we ask the birth mother to be tested for AIDS?
- How important are the birth mother's and birth father's intelligence? How can we measure that?
- Would we be upset if the birth mother was a smoker? Will she be upset when she learns that we smoke?
- How will we answer questions that she may ask about religion?
- What if she needs counseling?
- If she is young, are we willing to meet other family members?
- What if the contact comes from her mother, not from her?
- What if the baby has a problem? What if the baby has a major birth defect of some kind?
- What if we get more than one reply from birth mothers?
- How would we handle it if the birth mother changed her mind after her delivery? What about after a couple of weeks, or after five or six months?
- What are we going to tell our child about his or her birth parents? How open are we willing to be?

- What should we tell our friends and family about the birth mother? What questions will we answer? What questions will we not answer?
- What if someone calls tomorrow? Are we ready?

These questions won't cover every situation that may occur, but discussing them is a good start on communicating with your spouse and preparing to search. If you are considering adopting as a single parent, it is also worthwhile to clarify your views on these issues before you hear of a lead. Try finding someone you can talk with, because sometimes it helps to verbalize how you feel—your feelings become more concrete. For couples, remember that listening is half the process. Don't be panicked with your partner's response to any of the questions you choose to explore; the process is just that—an exploratory *process*. You will discover your views changing and softening, and somewhere at the end you will be closer to what is true for you *and* your partner. In that way, the call you receive will not be as likely to catch you mentally and emotionally unprepared.

Sometimes adoption situations come up quickly. Will you be emotionally ready to take the next step, to let a child into your life? While you should never rush if you are not prepared to move ahead, you also want to be sure not to pass up situations because of your inability to decide.

Dru describes one such situation: *The call I received from a birth mother one Friday night set even me back. I asked her how far along she was and she said her water had just broken. Even so, she still hadn't begun to have regular contractions, so we spoke about what she wanted for the racially mixed child she was carrying. We also discussed her delay in seeking help and the reasons behind it. She said she knew what she was doing and she wanted someone to pick up the baby before she left the hospital. That didn't give us much time. I called three couples about this situation. All they needed to do was give me an answer and make arrangements to fly to Texas to get the baby. The first couple said they would have to think about it and get back to me. The second couple had relatives in town for the weekend and said they could get back to me on Monday. The third couple said they were ready. It wasn't difficult to decide who was going to get this baby.*

One facilitator says she's always surprised at the number of people who say they are ready for a baby but are slow returning her phone calls once one is offered. People who want a baby mean it when they say they are ready. If you leave town, let someone know how you can be reached; if you receive phone calls, return them; and if you want a baby, *be ready.*

Readiness for adoption is important. If you need to take some time, be sure to tell the people with whom you are working that you want to move slowly. If you move quickly, you may find a baby a lot sooner than you had anticipated.

SETTING PRIORITIES AND LIMITS

Everyone has limits on what he or she will do or accept. Before you begin to search for a baby randomly, it is essential that you understand your own limits. If you definitely don't want a child from a Mexican background, don't approach Mexican people with your plight. If you would find it extremely uncomfortable to have a birth mother live with you while pregnant with the child you want to adopt, make certain this doesn't occur. If you would have difficulty meeting the biological parents, know this so that it does not become an issue; you can use an intermediary. If you know you have limited funds to adopt, begin your search but also start to save some money. (You need *some* financial resources to adopt most children.) Each limitation you have or that you put on yourself also restricts the options open to you, but recognized limits are important in making the situation comfortable for you.

The limit that Melinda and Joe had was time. They were both busy people who were very involved with work, charities, and their families. They knew they wanted a baby and felt that once the baby arrived, they could make time; but making time to *find* a baby didn't make sense to them. They went to a private adoption agency that encouraged them to do some things on their own, such as sending out résumés and making contacts with people who might know of leads. They didn't want to do that. They decided they would go to a high-powered attorney who was well known for helping couples with adoption, especially those couples who could afford his $4,000 retainer. They filled out his papers and had one interview with him, but then the process stopped. They didn't hear any more. (Unfortunately, after you pay anyone a retainer, there may be less incentive to help than there was before, when the person was trying to have you buy the services he offered.) After talking to some other couples who had adopted, they decided to contact a woman who advertised for babies across the country. She asked for a $4,800 retainer but said she would find a lead for them. She did. That is all she did to earn the retainer, but they did find a baby. Then they hired someone else to help them through the adoption process. While their time limitation didn't prevent Melinda and Joe from ultimately finding a baby, it did significantly hinder their search, and their adoption became very expensive.

Another area of limitation is in the amount of contact you are willing to have with the birth parents. Some people feel comfortable having knowledge about the biological parents but want no contact. Other people feel that it is extremely desirable to meet the biological parents.

One of the primary advantages of having more interaction is that you grow to know them. One mother of two adopted children, one an independent adoption and the other an agency adoption, discussed what this contact has meant to her. She said she knows more specific details about her first child, a son adopted through the adoption agency; she knows all sorts of medical and historical information about his family. But she knows far more about the daughter who was adopted independently because she met the birth parents. This adoptive mother says, "I can tell my first child facts about his parents, but for my second child, I can really tell her about her parents, because I know them as people and I can pass on feelings about them to her. I wish I could give this same advantage to my son." The disadvantages some people see in pre-adoption contact include discomfort and unwillingness to share their child with other parents.

Some people limit their baby search to areas and methods where they can be sure of no legal difficulties. Others are more willing to take legal risks. Carly and Jake, for example, did not feel threatened by the possibility of legal difficulties when they had a chance to adopt. Each in a second marriage, they were at the older limits of the age group that the adoption agencies were willing to accept. In addition, Carly had a strong desire to continue working. The couple knew they had little chance with a traditional agency long before they were given their rejection. They went to a private agency and were discouraged with the length of the wait that they encountered.

They were naturally disillusioned, because they sincerely felt they would be good parents. But they were undeterred in their search. They sought help, advice, ideas, and directions from anyone who might possibly help them. One of their contacts heard about a twenty-three-year-old pregnant woman who wanted to place her baby for adoption privately. Carly and Jake decided to approach her, even though she might change her mind and they learned the child's father was considering fighting for custody in court. Carly and Jake decided that they had to take some major risks if they were to achieve their desired goal. They knew that if the birth mother kept the child they would lose any financial support they gave to her during the pregnancy; but at the very least they would have done a good deed by helping this woman with her prenatal and birth expenses.

Carly and Jake's open, flexible manner was of prime importance to the biological mother, who strongly disliked secrecy and red tape. She occasionally tested their support by making additional demands, but they were unwavering in their resolve to help her in every legal way possible. The limit they imposed on getting a child was that it had to be legal; they would not waver on this issue. They were willing to face the father of the child in court and to take the risk that he might even win.

Although Carly and Jake had met with the birth mother on several occasions, they chose to have most of their contact through an intermediary. Through their meetings and from conversations with the intermediary, they learned many positive things about the way the birth mother cared about the child she was carrying. They felt they would be able to discuss the birth mother with their adopted child positively because she had loved and planned for her child, even though she could not keep her.

Their concerns about the father never materialized. He dropped out of her life after his threats about trying to win the child in court didn't elicit the response from the birth mother that he had wanted. Offers by Carly and Jake to meet him were refused. He signed a statement that he knew of the pregnancy but that he was not the father and dropped out of the picture entirely. When their baby girl was born, Carly and Jake had no legal issues to be resolved.

You may have limits on the medical history of the child and birth mother you are offered. Are you willing to accept a special-needs child? What degree of need are you willing to accept? Most of us know we can significantly improve the health, and maybe even the mental state, of our child if we can control certain prenatal factors. Nutrition is one essential ingredient in the health of an unborn child. If you could choose for the mother of your child, certainly you would want her to eat properly during her pregnancy. If, however, you have to choose between a child whose mother ate poorly during her pregnancy and not having a child, which will you choose? If you have to choose between a child whose mother did not receive any prenatal care and not having a child, which will you choose? If you must choose between a child whose mother was under great stress during her pregnancy and not having a child, which will you choose?

A limitation some couples set is possible drug use by the biological mother. They become alarmed over how drugs might affect their newly adopted child. If you want a child whose mother has never experimented with drugs, you might find yourself very limited in today's culture. You may decide to accept a child whose mother has occasionally smoked marijuana. You might have more doubts about mothers who are addicted to hard drugs like heroin. You probably would know about heavy addiction before the child was born; in fact, the greater the contact between you and the biological parents, the more likely you are to know this kind of personal information. You are certainly in as good a position to find out this information as any social worker with an adoption agency, and you are even more motivated to do so.

We believe prospective adoptive parents should seek information about drug, alcohol, and tobacco use, all of which may be harmful to the child. And you need to be sure that you know of resources for clarifying the kind of risks you are taking medically; how this behavior affects an unborn child is not a clear-cut issue. We don't know what your limits are, but you need to know what they are. You may also find that they change with time and disappointment. Will you eliminate a child from consideration if you discover that the mother uses marijuana regularly? Will you refuse a child if the mother smokes a pack of cigarettes a day while she is pregnant? Two packs a day?

Intellectual limitations are another factor. If you feel it is extremely important to adopt a child who is likely to be bright, how can you go about searching for that kind of child? As with all limitations in what you can accept, this also limits the potential for finding a child. On the other hand, if you feel strongly about intelligence, you should limit where you search for a child. Maybe you should seek a child from a woman in college; in any case, make it clear to those you contact that this is an important criterion to you. This doesn't assure you that the child will be bright—but neither does having your own biological child. This merely increases the chances of your child being bright.

Perhaps there are other areas in which you feel you should set limits. While you are exploring your own feelings, remember too that there has to be a limit *to* your limits—just as it is unrealistic to place no restrictions on your adoption, it is crippling to accept too many. Your control over your choices will be limited. Compromise is essential.

WHEN LIMITS CHANGE

As you go through your search, you may find yourself reevaluating your limits. You should compromise only as far as you are comfortable; but keep in mind that strict limitations, no matter how reasonable and well placed, are limitations on finding a child.

Lianna and Carlos believed that what was meant to be would be. That was how they approached adopting. With their first child, this was fine; a neighbor told them about a child who would be born in a month, and soon they found themselves the lucky parents of the new baby. No big search, no significant cost, no hassles. That was the same kind of situation they expected when they set out to adopt a second child. They went to a public adoption agency and found that even on a sliding scale, the cost would be more than they had spent with their first adoption, so they did not continue there. They went to a private agency that charged less than the public one and seemed to have more children available.

Children were offered to them, but the couple's limits delayed an actual adoption. They passed up one situation because they would have to pay for some clothes for the birth mother and fly to another state to get the child. They felt they shouldn't incur any expenses like this since their adoption budget was limited. They passed up a second situation because the birth mother wanted to have letters once a year. They hadn't done this for their first adoption and they were hesitant to do it now. Since then they haven't been offered any other situations. Their expectation of duplicating their first adoption is unlikely to be satisfied—their previous luck has allowed them to place too many limits on their search.

Mary Lou and Greg's case is different. They were delighted when they heard from a physician about a young girl who just had a baby and would be willing to give it to them. They tried to keep calm by talking about their "maybe baby" in case the situation fell through—they did not want their other adopted child to be too disappointed if the plans did not work out. They entered the situation very confident of their ability to handle an independent adoption. The biological mother wanted to nurse the child for a couple of weeks before she gave it to them. This was nice for the baby, but it caused fear for Mary Lou and Greg, who worried that the bonding might make the birth mother change her mind. Then she became ill and asked them to come early to get the baby. Naturally, Mary Lou and Greg were more than willing.

They drove 150 miles in a state of joy. But as the end of the journey approached, the pending meeting with the biological mother began to concern them. What if she didn't like them? What if she changed her mind? What would they talk about? The biological mother had something they wanted, a baby, so she was in a position to call the shots. They decided they would just have to take whatever came.

After meeting the biological mother and their "maybe baby," they wanted to grab the baby and run. Instead, they handled the situation with what appeared to be relative ease. When they heard that the mother had named their baby boy, they said nothing, because that could be dealt with later. When the biological mother offered them numerous items for their new son, they graciously accepted them, even though they wanted nothing but the child—everything else seemed to make their son more hers. They handled each unanticipated event smoothly, much more calmly than they thought they could. They did not anticipate a visit from the maternal grandparents the second week they had their son at home, but they weathered that potential crisis also.

They found the limits that they had set were helpful in many ways, but many issues they were forced to confront were unexpected. They had tried to remain distant until they were certain the baby would be theirs—but their excitement and anxiety came through as they drove to meet the birth mother. They originally had wanted a newborn, but the extra time the mother requested didn't seem unreasonable to them— scary yes, but not unreasonable. They had only planned on meeting the birth parents and on her territory when they originally discussed adoption. But when the birth grandparents wanted to visit in their home, it almost seemed appropriate to them. Fortunately they were open to the changes that came with the situation.

Later, as Mary Lou and Greg reflected on their son's adoption, they said that some aspects made it better than their previous agency adoption. The secrecy was gone. Everyone felt good about everyone else. The biological mother knew what kind of a home Mary Lou and Greg had, knew the town her child would be raised in, knew about the sister her child now had, and could feel comforted in her knowledge. The "weaning" process seemed healthier for her than immediately having to give up the baby would. The magnitude of the emotional response from the grandparents seemed lessened by their chance to meet the people who would be raising their first grandchild. The couple's willingness to extend their limits rewarded them in ways they did not expect.

People ask Mary Lou and Greg how they will feel if the young woman stops their son someday after school and tells him she is his birth mother. They answer that they are secure in their relationship with their son; he will be curious, but meeting her will not be a big issue because he already knows about her and he knows his "real" mom and dad are the ones who adopted him. They don't feel they own him; they just have had a fantastic opportunity of raising him. They feel very fortunate. And they are.

PRESENTING YOURSELF: YOUR ADOPTION RÉSUMÉ

Now you know what you are looking for and how far you will go to get it. The next step is to make yourself attractive as a potential parent.

Prepare something to leave with each of the contacts you make: an information sheet about you.

Résumés have proved effective in employment searches; there is every reason to believe they are helpful in a search for a baby. A résumé or personal information sheet not only shows the people who are evaluating you how serious you are, but it also keeps reminding the evaluators of who you are. The same logic applies if you want a baby. You want the people to remember who you are and to have some way to contact you if they hear of any potential children. Your contacts might also choose to pass your résumé along to others, which of course will enlarge your number of contacts. Leaving documents like these with many people obviously destroys your chances of remaining anonymous, but it vastly increases your chances of finding a child.

Since the résumé is such a critical part of the process, several examples of what we believe to be effective are included in Appendix D. Your résumé is most effective if it accurately reflects who you are. Remember, this résumé is like a brief picture of you, so individualize your letter and make it "you." You should work on it until you are very pleased.

First list your name, address, and phone number. You should indicate your willingness to receive collect calls. (You see how vulnerable you are becoming.) Be prepared for some calls you may not like. You can leave the number of an intermediary or install a separate phone line. Some adoption agencies will even act on your behalf. Attorneys, adoption facilitators, and counselors do this on a regular basis. Remember that if you list a third party's name, that person should be acting on your behalf. Make sure this is clear so that he or she does not take your leads and use them for anyone else. You also want to be sure that person will represent you the way you want to be represented.

Sally and Jacob did not prepare their information sheet and third-party resource as well as they should have. They met a facilitator and liked her well enough. She wasn't exciting, but it sounded as if she could help and they really didn't know anyone else who did this kind of work, so they hired her. She helped them with their résumé and spoke with them about places to send it. They spent a lot of money on pictures, printing, and especially postage, but they felt they were doing the right thing. They had been told that the market was becoming saturated with these kinds of résumés, but they didn't know what else to do. Three weeks after their résumé went out, they heard from a woman in Vermont. At least that is what the facilitator told them. The facilitator said this woman sounded eager about placing her child, but as the worker began to ask questions about drugs and alcohol the woman became hesitant. Then when the facilitator was trying to make certain that this wasn't a scam, the woman became offended and hung up. That was the last they would hear from that birth mother. In the course of a ten-minute call, the facilitator had gone too far and too fast with the woman. Sometimes you don't get all the information you need on a first phone call. In fact, the goal of the first phone call should be to keep the contact going. The facilitator didn't understand that, so Sally and Jacob lost their first contact.

Ideally, your résumé will include a picture of you, but make sure the picture truly represents you. A formal picture represents a formal person. A serious picture represents a serious person. Choose your picture carefully, keeping in mind how you want people to remember you, as well as how you would best come across to the pregnant woman considering placing her child for adoption. Some people create collages that represent more of their lives than one picture does. Others assemble notebooks with pictures interspersed with text. You can have color photocopies made to reduce the cost of multiple prints of photographs.

Your résumé should include something about your interests, as well as more obvious information. What do you do for a living? How much education have you had? What was your major in school? Do you own your home? Do you ski? Is traveling important in your life? Do you play the piano? Do you like camping? Do you have a cat, dog, or horse? Where did you grow up? You won't want to mention everything we have listed, just the items that would portray you most advantageously. Again, you should understand the population group of the birth mother whom you are trying to convince to place a child with you; it is usually made up of young people.

Tailor your information sheet to specific readers. If you have relatives in Minnesota, make certain you mention them when you send your résumé to Minnesota. When you send your résumé to Virginia, don't forget that you went to school in Virginia or that you were stationed there in the service. When you send your résumé to Boston, mention the fact that you are in the process of restoring an old Victorian home. You are trying to find the many ways the birth mother can identify with you and feel comfortable with you.

Try to tug lightly at the birth mother's heartstrings. You want to consider her emotional side and convince her that she would be doing a service for you or even for the world by giving her child to you. Report on how long you have been searching for a child, how important this is to you, and why you can't become pregnant. Don't be maudlin, but don't be too aloof. People open their hearts to other down-to-earth people.

Once you have a résumé, where do you send it? Now it is important to be aware of the economic issues involved in adoption. In areas that have significant economic problems, a person is more likely to consider adoption. When a birth mother has small means with which to support a family, she will look to protect her child by finding someone who can take care of him or her financially. Most adoptions would probably not occur if the birth mother were offered enough money to raise her child adequately. In some families hard hit by economics, having someone else to feed constitutes too great a burden. As you search, be aware of the economic issues of different regions of the country. If you learn that the unemployment rate in a given area is the lowest it has ever been, that could mean you are not as likely to get a lead there as in another area that is experiencing high unemployment.

One well-known adoption attorney would disagree with this conclusion. He suggests to his clients that a pregnancy in a family that is fairly well off is looked on as a greater disaster than one in a family that's used to poverty. He maintains that young people planning on going to school will look at adoption more readily than families that anticipate early pregnancies. Of course, neither of the groups should be overlooked. If you succeed in finding a baby one way, obviously that way is the right way for you.

Once your information sheet has gone out, some people will ask that you send additional information, so be prepared to respond in lengthier form to someone who wants to know more about you. One example of the kind of letter that the birth mother might ask for is in Appendix E. These more detailed letters should be friendly and go more deeply into your life than your original résumé.

There are many other people out there sending résumés to make contacts. You might figure out a way to make yours different than the rest by using an alternative to a regular résumé. The Timmonses wanted to do something a little different, and they wanted to have more opportunities to send the material over a large geographical area. They decided to send out flyers. They were able to produce these for about the same cost as a regular letter. They addressed them primarily to people they had met when Don was in the service—as a result of his military experience, they had contacts throughout the world. They found a baby in another country.

Another couple, Millie and Tim, had been Amway salespeople for eight years, and they felt they could use the same approach to adoption. They had cards printed up saying how much they wanted a baby; they included their phone number and the message that they were willing to help someone who could also help them. They made ten thousand cards. Then they had a party and asked for help from the large gathering of friends and acquaintances who came. The people who sent out the cards for them put a code number on them and were told that if their card resulted in a baby to adopt, Millie and Tim had a surprise bonus for them. These cards and fliers may not have told as much about the couples as a résumé would have, but they were a good way to get the word out to a lot of people. Their neighbor down the street won the bonus. Her sister-in-law's friend at work had a daughter, Jana, who was sixteen and pregnant. Her sister-in-law told her friend about the card she received; together they called Millie and Tim to find out more about them for Jana. After several conversations and an exchange of letters and pictures, Jana decided to place her baby with them for adoption.

The cards weren't enough, but they started the process that ended in a happy adoption. The neighbor down the street received a beautiful gold locket with a heart on it. Engraved on the back were the words "Thank you for our daughter."

Summary

Most people who want children would not first elect to go out and find their own child. Your first choice would probably be to simply become pregnant. Your second choice might be to go to an adoption agency and have them give you a child. But if neither of these choices is open to you, you need to find another option, and that is to find your own child to adopt. It may be your last resort, but there are some extremely positive benefits for you in adopting this way.

What a fantastic story to tell your child as he or she grows up! You can share with her how far you went to fulfill your tremendous desire for a child. You can share with him how much you gained from meeting and learning from others and from finding him.

Obviously there are also risks involved in seeking a baby in this way. You run the same risks anyone has who is involved in an independent adoption: contacting people who are upset with your method of adopting or people trying to make money from your plight, not finding a child, a birth mother changing her mind. You have to evaluate these risks versus the potential gains.

Not everyone should try this method. We don't know whether you should. We do believe that searching for your own child is a method seriously worth considering; it may be the only way you will get a child. But if you search, search with a positive attitude and a respect for the birth parents you hope to meet. Be optimistic as you seek assistance with this process, because most helpers are indeed there to help. And believe you will be successful—you will be!

Once you understand your options, know your limits, and have your résumé, flyer, or cards in hand, you are ready to begin making contacts. Emphasis so far has been on the fact that someone out there has something you want. Remember, though, that you, too, have something important: You have love and a home to offer a child.

CHAPTER 10

The Search:
Casting a Wide Net

NOW YOUR REAL WORK BEGINS. You are about to meet many new people in a way you are unlikely to have met anyone before. You are about to boldly ask a lot of people to help you with your problem. Of course, in order to ask for help, you need to be willing to let others know you have a problem. For some people this is a difficult step. One attorney who is very successful in helping couples locate children suggests that couples send out four thousand letters. While we have never met anyone who has sent out that many, it is worthwhile to realize the magnitude of the work that is there for you. Your search may be difficult, but it can also be fun if you keep a positive attitude.

You are about to understand the term *networking*. This is one of the essential steps in marketing yourself. You need to think of all the people you know, ask for their help, and see if they know anyone else who can help you. In the meantime, you will even begin to contact people you don't know. You are networking to try to find a baby; you are casting a wide net, hoping to pull in one fish.

Networking is especially important. Your most likely opportunities for finding a baby will be from personal contacts. While sending out résumés to large groups is still worthwhile, you need to remember that thousands of others are doing the same thing. So focus your search on people you know or people you think might be able to help you. Think about sending your résumés to the state you grew up in if it is a bit more rural than where you live now. Think about making contacts in the area where you went to college or where you were stationed when you were in the military. If you are into computers, think about sending the résumé to towns where that is a valued skill.

While these methods may not seem particularly personal, they are a way of personalizing your search. They can be more effective than merely sending out thousands of résumés across the country.

Pete and Eillie had a great way of personalizing their search. They asked their fifteen best friends over for a résumé party. They asked each person to send out twenty letters to people they knew describing Pete and Eillie's search for a baby. Each envelope would enclose an information sheet about Pete and Eillie and a personal message from the person sending it. This method worked for Pete and Eillie; one friend found them a baby.

Everybody you meet is a potential contact for a baby. Everywhere you go, you need to figure out a way to bring your search into your conversation. Every time you talk to someone, you should leave your résumé with them; just because they don't have an immediate suggestion for you doesn't mean they won't have one in a week or two. And everyone with whom you talk is a source of other contacts. (This is really networking.) Ask people for suggestions of others to contact.

As you search, you are becoming an educator about adoption. Few people understand the difficulties of adoption except those who are directly involved. The education you provide might result in the lead that gets you a baby. For example, Carlene went to a wedding shower for the daughter of a friend from church. She didn't know the friend really well, but it seemed like a nice thing to do. At the shower, she met Mrs. Turner, who seemed quite pleasant. The conversation turned to Carlene's daughter, who was searching for a baby to adopt. Most of the room listened attentively as Carlene spoke with Mrs. Turner about the many ways that her daughter was pursuing adoption. (The stories are really very interesting to most people.) Some people commented. "Why didn't they just go to an agency and get a baby?" Carlene educated the twenty-four people at the party about adoption—not necessarily to get a lead for her daughter, but just because it came up. Five weeks later, someone called Carlene about a friend who was pregnant. This caller had heard about Carlene through a friend who had gone to the party. Carlene took the woman's phone number, and that did the job. Carlene's daughter and husband are now awaiting the arrival of the baby that came about through Carlene. Carlene feels this is a very special grandchild to her because she was so instrumental in providing her daughter with the contact.

While any random contact might possibly result in the lead you need, there are some specific places where you are most likely to find a baby. The places we suggest below are where you may have contact with young people, pregnant women, women "in trouble," and women with financial problems. These are where you are most likely to find a woman who will consider your proposal to adopt her child. They are not presented in any special order; rather, you should put them in the order that seems appropriate to you, taking into account your priorities and limits. Remember, the more contacts you make, the better chance you have of finding the one you need.

Free Clinics

One of the best available sources for potentially adoptable children is free clinics. Free clinics deliver health care in a way that appeals to groups of people who might not use private physicians. They are used especially by the young or poor—likely candidates to consider placing a child for adoption.

The term *free clinic* indicates a specific philosophy of health care; not all of the groups we put into this category are called this. Included in this large group would be Planned Parenthood (see Appendix F). There are also local groups with names such as Pregnancy Center, Birth Control Institute, Pregnancy Options, Birthright, and other women's clinics and feminist clinics. Each town has a different list of groups that provide contraceptive information, pregnancy testing and counseling, vasectomies, venereal disease testing, pelvic exams, Pap smears, alternative lifestyle counseling, general health care services, and counseling to young people, minority groups, and poor people.

You can find the names of these groups in your town by checking several sources. Young people know the names; such a clinic may be their source for birth control pills. Check local newspapers' personals sections—frequently you will find ads for free pregnancy tests or birth control information. A third source is any newspaper aimed toward young people. College or counterculture papers frequently have advertisements or articles about these groups.

Both groups that support abortions and those against abortions are worthwhile to contact. Both are working with women who are pregnant and that is the group you are trying to reach.

All free clinic groups are similar in that they are usually staffed by volunteers, especially for the information and counseling services they provide. Because of the volunteer aspect, they have a significant staff turnover rate and numerous part-timers.

A lot of information is shared from one group to another, which helps increase the similarities among clinics in an area. In some regions, interagency council meetings are held to share what they are doing.

Nonetheless, few of these groups understand the difficulties encountered by the couple wishing to adopt a child. Volunteer workers have a tendency to view offering a child for adoption as a bleak alternative to an unwanted pregnancy—a much more difficult and time-consuming path for a woman to follow than having an abortion. As a result, the volunteers seldom mention adoption to the woman who says she wants an abortion. Sadly, we have talked with many volunteers from various groups who provide pregnancy counseling but who never even thought about adoption as an alternative to an unwanted pregnancy. Yet they are providing "pregnancy counseling" regularly for thousands of women with unwanted pregnancies. This is the situation you need to change.

It will help your search if you get the supervisors in these groups to learn about adoption and about you. But to really make the potential contacts, you need to talk with the workers dealing with the pregnant women. You need to talk personally to as many in each agency as possible. Tell them about your problem. Inform them about the benefits of adoption. As they meet you, they will get personally acquainted with someone who desperately wants a baby. Then the next time they give an unhappily pregnant woman her test results, they can discuss with her this wonderful couple they met the other day who has been searching everywhere for a baby to adopt.

As you finish talking with each worker, leave several of your résumés, cards, or flyers with him or her. (People hate to take the last one of anything.) The worker can help spread the word. Many of these volunteers are young people themselves, so they become "double contacts." Your sheet may be given out to the next pregnant woman they counsel, or it might be taken home to a roommate.

Of all of the untapped sources of finding a baby, groups like the free clinics provide the greatest potential for success. This is especially true if you are the kind of person who would appeal to young people or if your story is especially inspiring. Check out the local groups in your area and spend some time there.

Physicians

Doctors, especially obstetricians and gynecologists, have historically been good sources of potentially adoptable babies. This has significantly changed in recent years, as physicians have come under attack through lawsuits over mishandled adoptions. Since insurance companies may not defend physicians who practice outside their realm of expertise, some doctors are deciding that they are not the right people to be arranging adoptions. Nonetheless, some physicians still help people seeking babies.

The fact that there are fewer babies available through physicians should not eliminate them as sources in your search for a baby. Again, you are looking for only one baby. Any potential source is worth exploring. You just don't want to put all of your eggs in one basket, so let physicians be one contact in a long list.

The best way to approach a physician is through personal contact. Certainly if you know any doctors, tell them your story. Ask them to talk to their colleagues, and ask your friends to mention your adoption desires to their physicians. Basically, any way to make the contact personal increases its effectiveness for you. You probably can't meet every single physician in your city yourself, but speak personally with as many as possible and just write to others. Go as far as you can.

If you live in a large metropolitan area in a progressive state, physicians may not be a very helpful source because many people there are probably looking for infants. However, physicians in more rural areas may not have had many inquiries. Remember, attitudes toward unplanned pregnancies and single mothers differ between rural areas of sparsely populated states and more metropolitan areas.

While a physician might pass along several potential adopters' names to a pregnant woman, in the current climate they are unlikely to give her just one name. This actually works in your favor, because your name might be one of those passed on. You are not asking a physician to give you the names of pregnant women; you are merely asking him or her to pass on your résumé, card, or flyer. In some cases there will be regulations about this that may preclude him or her from even passing these along. But just in case, be sure to have an extra copy or two.

Other Medical Personnel

Other people involved in providing medical care are probably even better sources of help than physicians. If your sister is a nurse in a hospital, you have a dynamite contact. As surprising as it sounds, sometimes a pregnant woman goes into the hospital with no plan about what to do with her baby. The nurse may be the first to know about her plan to place the child for adoption.

Clinic workers you know are another source. Even clinic workers you don't know are a source. Obviously it helps if they know and like you before you begin that process, but any contact might result in a lead.

Even the clerk who is screening recipients for state aid can help you. She may come across someone seeking a place for a child. Again, it helps if you know the clerk, but don't stop talking to people just because you don't know them.

Attorneys

Attorneys fall into two categories. General attorneys used to know about adoptable babies; today they are no longer a good source of babies. With the decreased supply of babies for adoption, they have found themselves much less involved in adoption placements. However, from time to time, an attorney may still have a child for whom the biological parents say they want an attorney to find a home. Sometimes the contacts may come from the parents of someone seeking a home for a child. Adoption attorneys are in a slightly different position. They may be a source of babies, but you cannot assume they are. Some adoption attorneys help you with the legal aspects of adoption but do not find babies for you. Other adoption attorneys may have sources of babies available for potential adopting couples. So don't depend on attorneys to find you a baby, but don't ignore them; they still can be a source if you are lucky.

Try to find the names of attorneys who work a lot with the groups with whom you are trying to make contact. Attorneys giving seminars on college campuses, attorneys serving in free clinics, attorneys who work with poorer people—these are the attorneys most likely to hear about a child who might be available.

The personal approach in making contacts with attorneys is usually the best. Be in touch with every attorney you know; try to make personal contacts with as many others as possible. You should be certain to contact any attorneys who specialize in adoption. As independent adoptions have become widespread, more attorneys have begun to develop this as a specialty. While adoption attorneys are a good source, each of these attorneys already has a long list of people waiting to adopt.

When you ask for help from attorneys who specialize in adoption it probably means hiring them to represent you and paying their retainer.

That may or may not result in a baby directly from them. If you are planning to use an attorney for this purpose, certainly ask how many babies he hears about in a given period of time. Also ask the attorney about the number of people on his waiting list and how long the people waiting the longest have been there. Find out if he plans to arrange adoptions for the people who have been waiting the longest or if he chooses potential adopters another way. Some attorneys will insist that you pay a retainer prior to discussing any potential baby, and others will discuss potential adoptions and only expect a retainer if you decide to pursue a specific lead. There are many answers you need before you retain an attorney.

(Besides being a potential source of contacts about babies to adopt, attorneys are always involved in adoption; when the adoptive parents go to court to finalize the adoption, they are represented by an attorney. The involvement at that level has nothing to do with contacting an attorney to find a child.)

As with any of the contacts mentioned, the more the better. Your information sheet, mailed to many of your local attorneys, may be what it takes to find the baby you want.

Adoptive Parents

While it might not seem that adoptive parents would be a source of adoptable babies, they certainly can be. In fact, they may be one of the *best* sources of help. People involved with adoption seem to remain involved; those who have gone through the agony of infertility studies and shared the excitement of getting a child through adoption seem to be eager to help others in the same situation.

Virtually all major metropolitan areas have support groups for parents of adopted children. These groups usually meet regularly. You can get names of such organizations from your local adoption agencies. At times these groups are specialized, perhaps geared toward adopters of children from a specific country, parents of special-needs children, or parents of children from mixed-racial backgrounds.

Any of these groups will offer a lot of understanding—they know the desire to have a child. They will be able to tell you of contacts they have found helpful. They also have an exceptionally large, informal network.

Be sure to leave your résumé with strategic members of the group. Ask if you can check back with the group from time to time. The memberships change so each meeting may be attended by different people. At times the groups will have speakers on topics pertaining to adoption; these speakers are also potential contacts for you.

Infertility Groups

Most infertility groups are a good source for children to adopt; they are also a good source of information on adoption in general and where to go for help. From their personal experiences with infertility, people in these groups are more sensitive to your plight than many other people you will contact.

You can locate infertility groups in your area in several ways. Sometimes adoption agencies will know of them. RESOLVE (see Appendix F) is a national organization with local chapters throughout the United States. If you write to them, they will give you names of the group in your area. Large metropolitan centers are likely to have other groups, like the Infertility Association of San Diego or the Fertility Association of Philadelphia. You can even contact your local medical association and get the names of doctors who specialize in infertility, then ask those doctors or your own doctor if any groups of people experiencing infertility meet in your area.

Not everyone in an infertility group is in competition with you to adopt a baby. Some people who experience infertility will choose to attempt to correct the problem or remain childless. They do not necessarily consider adoption. The primary reason for contacting an infertility group is to enlarge your contacts, but you might also enjoy the camaraderie and support you get from the group. The more people who know of your desire, the greater your chances of finding a baby.

Leave your résumé with some, if not all, of the group members. Don't hesitate to go again—let them know how important this is to you.

Mindy and her husband were looking for a baby to adopt. They had gone through every test and tried each corrective procedure she thought could be dreamed up, and still they were not conceiving. She really had given up on having a biological child but cried when her period arrived each month, so she knew she still needed some help with this issue. She contacted her local RESOLVE group and went to a series of meetings. While she was there, she met others like herself who continued to struggle with infertility but who were also pursuing adoption. She met Judith at the second meeting she attended. They hit it off right away and maintained contact even after they no longer attended meetings together. Mindy was delighted when Judith and her husband adopted a baby from a private agency. In fact, Mindy was ready to try the same agency because of Judith's success. But Judith called before Mindy could get an appointment; Judith had heard about a baby who might be available for adoption and wanted to know whether Mindy and her husband were interested. Mindy jumped at the chance. Mindy and Judith continue to see each other, and so do their children, who are eight months apart.

Ministers, Priests, and Rabbis

An unhappily pregnant woman occasionally consults ministers, priests, rabbis, or other religious advisers to help her decide what to do about her situation. They can occasionally help you also. These contacts may be most helpful if you have a strong religious background yourself, but consider trying them no matter what your beliefs. Your chances may be less if you are not a member of a certain faith, but not necessarily.

If you and your spouse are Catholic, religious affiliation is especially important to emphasize in your résumé. You have a special appeal to Catholics who oppose abortion, and there are many pregnant women to whom you can appeal who want their children raised in a Catholic home.

Don't rule out other religious affiliations as possible sources. In one area of the South, a higher percentage of Baptist birth mothers relinquish children for adoption than women of any other religion.[1]

High Schools

Most young women who become pregnant and carry their baby to term keep their babies. However, this doesn't mean that you should rule out young women in your search. Since pregnancy is not unusual in high school today, this is a source worth considering; it is even worth your time to contact junior high schools.

The schools may or may not be aware of students who are pregnant. The place to start to make contacts in the schools is not at the top. Don't contact the superintendent or the principal to ask permission to do something that they would rather not know about. Contact individuals, not institutions. Maybe someone can give you the name of the next teacher you should talk with or maybe they know a minister or doctor to call. Remember, this is a personal matter between you and another individual. No one needs to approve or disapprove of your conversation. If the school finds out what you are doing, they may tell you to stop. Fine, stop—but hopefully by this point you will have contacted several people.

One teacher Cynthia encountered while on a publicity tour for an earlier adoption book was enraged at her suggestion that people contact schools; she said she would never help a couple; it would interfere with her responsibility to the student and the parents at the school. We have no difficulty with people who view the situation in this manner. But don't be discouraged by them. They are simply not the people you need to be contacting.

Schools are under considerably greater restraint than free clinics in dealing with matters such as pregnancy. Certain staff members, those who relate well with young people, are most likely to know if a student is pregnant. What you need to find out is which teachers or other school personnel the young people in the school confide in. One way to find out is by asking some of the students who the best teachers and counselors are. The people they tell you about are excellent contacts. How openly pregnancy and other personal matters are handled greatly depends on the individual staff member. One school counselor said he would never let a pregnant girl leave his office until she had called her parents and told them of her predicament. He probably did not confront this problem often, because pregnant girls would learn this and never come to him.

Besides the people the students talk to when they are in trouble, other staff members are sometimes in a position, by nature of their specific assignments, to know of pregnant girls. Physical education teachers are frequently the first to realize a young girl is pregnant; make contact with the physical education department in as many schools as you can. The school nurse knows about most students who get sick, including morning sickness. This is another source found at most high schools.

Yet another source worth checking is the high school pregnant minors program in your area. These are special programs (usually held at only one school in each district) designed to keep the pregnant girl attending school rather than dropping out. The teachers in these kinds of programs are usually selected for their ability to work with these young women. The school, recognizing that young pregnant women are very prone to dropping out, tries very hard to find teachers who relate well with youngsters in trouble. These are certainly teachers worth talking to. They do vary as much as any other kind of teacher; you may find some who are unwilling to take your résumé or even talk with you. Don't let that discourage you from contacting another. Young women who have elected to abort their pregnancies will not be in these programs, and most of those in the programs are planning to keep their babies. But occasionally, a pregnant girl may be planning to place her child for adoption, or if she plans to keep the baby, she may change her mind.

At times teachers invite couples in to speak with their classes about trying to find a child to adopt. They are usually careful to balance these presentations with talks by young women who keep their children. The talks are given to help all the pregnant women in the class consider fully their alternatives. Some will change their minds as they continue with a pregnancy. Perhaps hearing about someone who wants a baby will do it; maybe it will happen when they hear about the problems of raising a child while still in high school. The fact that an important teacher knows about you, or that a young pregnant woman heard you talk in her class, might result in you getting a child. You are trying to be in the right place at the right time.

Jadeen and Peter approached a friend who taught a class for pregnant minors. This friend told them that virtually all of her students kept their babies and she wasn't sure if it would be worth their time to come, but they were welcome to try. Both of them went to talk to the class. It certainly helped that they were fairly young and very good looking. Peter's job with a large computer company seemed very stable and Jadeen's job with a clothing distributor appealed to young people. The fact that Jadeen planned on quitting her job to stay home with the baby was a positive. They didn't ask if anyone in the class would consider them as a home for their unborn child; they merely talked about adoption. They talked about their desire for a child and the large number of people looking for babies to adopt. They talked about their infertility and the difficulties they had getting pregnant and laughed with the students as the contrast in their situations became evident. It was a friendly, free discussion.

Two months later, the mother of one of the girls in the class called Jadeen and Peter and asked if they could come over to talk with her and her daughter, Christy. They began their conversation nervously but soon became more animated. They discussed openness and what kind of an adoption was possible when people knew each other's identities. Jadeen and Peter explained how they were comfortable with that if Christy could be. After a meeting that covered a great number of subjects related to adoption but a lot more about their personal lives and goals, Christy said she wanted them to have her baby.

She imposed some conditions. She wanted them to meet Ian, her boyfriend and the father of the baby. They were delighted to. She also wanted pictures once a year, to be agreed to in writing before the baby was born; that stipulation was also easy for the couple. She discussed the fact that she would get a lot of flak from the other girls in the class for her decision, but she was sure this made more sense for her life than trying to raise a baby when she was only seventeen.

Jadeen's teacher friend was surprised at what had occurred. She was a bit uncomfortable at having become an intermediary, but the more she thought about it, the more she realized that she had inadvertently assumed all the girls in her class knew about adoption and she didn't need to talk about it with them. This situation caused her to change her mind, and thereafter, she regularly allowed students to see résumés, cards, or whatever materials couples sent to her. Not surprisingly, she received a great many from others whom Jadeen and Peter knew.

A source similar to pregnant minors' programs is the continuation or alternative high schools that many school districts have. These are schools with students who are not doing well in the regular institution; usually each district has one continuation school. The staff is also selected to work with students who have problems and who, without special treatment, are likely to quit school. These teachers and other staff members are good people to contact. Since the classes are very small and frequently run on a one-to-one basis, teachers usually know the students very well. They not only know how the students are doing academically, but they also know a lot about the students' personal lives and often about pregnancies. Students are likely to seek out teachers they know on a personal basis to discuss their problems and seek advice.

Tell each of your contacts in all the schools not only about yourself, but also about the whole adoption picture. They need to know about adoption if they are to talk knowledgeably about pregnancy alternatives with students. You are helping them to understand adoption through a personal perspective.

With each of your personal contacts at school, leave copies of whatever you have designed to put your name out in public. They need something to remember you by. It is not enough for them to remember your story—that's easy. If they have a potential child for you, you want them to have your name and phone number or some way to contact you. Remember to ask everyone to *keep* your résumé. A note on the sheet would help, like "Please keep this résumé or pass it on to someone else."

Colleges

Working with the staffs of higher education institutions is slightly easier than working with high school staffs. These people are no longer dealing with minors and are less restricted by parents and fear.

Work in the same way as you would with the high schools. Find the staff members who talk to students on a personal level. Being over eighteen does not preclude students from seeking help from their teachers. Colleges also have counseling staffs. If a pregnant woman doesn't know where to go, she may seek help from them.

One possibility in colleges is the health services center. A high school usually has one nurse, who is limited to providing a place for the sick student to rest, but at the college level, some of the health services are extensive—some administer pregnancy testing and counseling. Of course, these are valuable people to contact.

Tell each of your contacts your story, enlist their help, get new names for further contacts, and leave your résumé. By now you are getting this down to a science. None of the individual contacts takes a long time to make, but making all of them can be very time consuming. Don't give up—all you are looking for is *one* contact to succeed.

Young People

While contacting school employees is a good way to find out about young pregnant women, so is contacting school-age people directly. Young people tend to be very open; subjects that adults may hesitate to talk about may be casually discussed between young people who barely know each other. Young people can also be very open with adults.

Talk to any young people you know. Ask them if they know about anyone who is pregnant. Tell them about your problems finding a child to adopt. Enlist their help. Young people are all around you; besides the ones you know well, extend yourself and talk to those you're merely acquainted with. Talk to the teens or the twenty-somethings who live on your street. Think which of your relatives have children who fall into the right age category. Talk to your friends' teenage baby-sitters.

Then go to specific places where young people are likely to be. Go to some of the concerts that appeal to young people and try to talk with the ones who sit next to you. Go to the movies and be friendly with those around you. When you eat, go to the restaurants frequented by adolescents or young adults. The ice-skating rink, the billiard center, the video arcade, the youth-oriented dress shop, the coffee house, and the used clothing shop are all potential sources of contacts.

Again, be sure to leave your personal information sheet with every-body. If they don't know anyone who is pregnant now, ask them to keep it in case they hear of someone later.

Those most likely to succeed in this approach are people who can readily talk with the young. If you feel this is impossible for you, try to find someone who would be willing to make some of the contacts for you. That isn't quite as effective as doing it yourself, but it is far more ef-fective than not doing it at all.

Over a million young women between the ages of fifteen and nine-teen get pregnant each year; over half of these young women give birth.[2] You are trying to get your information and your story to one of these women at the right time so she will consider adoption as a solu-tion to her unwanted pregnancy. One of these million babies is all you are trying to find.

Friends, Neighbors,
Acquaintances, and Everyone Else

While you are making the specific contacts previously discussed, you should also be checking with your friends, relatives, and acquaintances. You are trying to make contacts with parents, their friends, or friends of a pregnant woman. This means that contacts with lots of people have the possibility of paying off. Talk to everyone. Here you are probably aiming at the parents of pregnant girls more than the girl herself. Many times the mother of a pregnant girl is very involved with her daughter and her pregnancy decision.

Finding that a daughter is six-months pregnant would be startling to most parents. At that point, the parents may tell their pregnant daughter they will not raise her child for her. If she had been counting on this arrangement, she will have to consider other alternatives. Hearing about you at the right time might work out to everyone's advantage: You may be just the right solution for someone's pregnancy problems.

Your neighbors are contacts. They have relatives and friends with whom they will talk about your situation; they will spread the word. People you meet at the coffee shop or at the bus stop are contacts. The clerk at the maternity shop where you are shopping with your pregnant friend is a contact. Your grocery clerk and the person bagging your groceries should all hear about your efforts. The lady with the little girl who sits next to you on the airplane—tell her how cute her daughter is and how much you are hoping to find a child. If nothing else, you will find people fascinated to hear how you are going about trying to find a baby, and they will also learn about the current state of adoption. Ideally contacts will also lead you to a child.

Choosing Specific Regions

It makes more sense to mail résumés to some areas of the country than others, depending on your background. If you are Protestant or not religious, it makes less sense to send résumés to an area that is predominately Catholic. If you are part Italian, it might be a good idea to blanket an area that has a high number of Italian people. If you are Mormon, obviously you will saturate Utah. If you are from a military background, you might want to send résumés to areas where bases are located. Even if you aren't from the military, these can be good places because of the great number of young people.

In Southwestern communities bordering Mexico, there is a large Mexican American population that may know of available babies. For people wanting to adopt children with a Mexican background, this can be an excellent source. The fact that most Mexican Americans are likely to be Catholics who disapprove of abortion also makes this group a likely place for anyone to hunt for a child. Mexican American women may know of people who have chosen not to abort but who are financially unable to raise a child.

If your sister is well known as a volunteer in a little town in the Midwest, be sure to make that connection and send out your résumés. Don't forget to send to towns where you have heard that they have a high number of women who place babies for adoption, or even just a high number of pregnancies. When you read in the paper of prolonged strikes or unemployment in some area, you should get out your résumés; if someone is unemployed and has a pregnant daughter, they will find it a lot harder to assimilate another mouth to feed. Be aware of states that have very low aid for single moms; if welfare benefits are not adequate for raising a child, a pregnant woman may consider other alternatives. Recent changes in welfare reform mandating a five-year limit to aid will also cause some women to consider adoption who otherwise might not.

These geography-based strategies for sending résumés are based on the economics of raising a child. Perhaps in a more sophisticated or caring time in our history we will provide assistance for these women to keep their children. But the importance of having the means to raise a child now is a reality. Being a single mother under the best of circumstances is difficult. As less help is being provided through good jobs or through state or federal aid for unemployed mothers, women are apt to consider alternatives to raising a child.

Friends or strangers, it doesn't matter; you need to spread the word about your search. Leave your personal information sheets and your positive contact with as many people as possible. Any contact has the possibility of being the one you need. (Some of the contacts you don't need can go to someone else who is seeking a baby to adopt. Your educating people will result in the word about adoption being spread a great deal farther than you may realize.)

Perhaps it is clearer now why it is important to start with a knowledge of your own capabilities, limits, and priorities before you begin your search. Knowing where you are on a search gives you the basis to know whom to approach and how to approach them—it is your framework for looking everywhere.

Other Ways of Marketing Your Search

Marketing is what you are doing: You are marketing yourself. Some people will be critical of you as you seek effective ways to put yourself forward. But remember, *marketing* is not a dirty word. It is a creative response to a problem you have—trying to find a baby. There are many ways to do this. Personal contact is one way. Less personal advertising— through newspapers or on the Internet, in national magazines or on billboards—is another.

ADVERTISING ANYWHERE AND EVERYWHERE

When you are trying to contact as many people as possible, one way is to advertise. You want to tell people what you want. If you need customers for your business, one way to get them is to advertise. If you need money for your new venture, you might advertise. If you want a new partner to come into business with you, you might find one by advertising. If you want a wife or a date, you might find one by advertising. And if you want a baby, you might find one by advertising.

Advertising for a baby seemed like a radical approach ten years ago, but it is certainly common today. In fact, some agencies have begun to advertise because they have seen the success of individuals who have used this way of finding a baby. Attorneys also advertise their services to try to locate pregnant women. We know of some business-minded adoption helpers that spend $10,000 a month on advertising to try to locate birth mothers for their clients.

It is always important to check with an attorney about the laws of the state you are considering advertising in before you place advertisements. It is currently illegal to advertise for a child in eleven states (see Appendix A).[3] Each state that permits it has specific laws about how this kind of advertising may be done. Be aware that the laws pertaining to advertising for children are not always clear. Currently it is legal to advertise in most states, but some states have specific provisions as to who can do it; some only allow adoption agencies to place ads. Your attorney should check out the current laws and their interpretation in your state and in any others in which you are planning on placing an ad. Some states will allow written or typed advertisements that are personally placed (that is, say, on a bulletin board) as long as they are not in printed form; others have no objections to any sort of advertising as long as you do not become involved in "buying" a child.

You can also contact the State Adoption Specialist (check local listing for the social service office that has someone in this position) in each state and ask specific questions such as:

- Is adoption advertising permitted?
- What kind of advertising can you do? Newspaper announcements? Billboards? Handwritten notices? Printed notices?
- Who is allowed to place an adoption ad? Adoptive parents? Adoptive parents with an approved home study? Attorneys? Licensed agencies? Facilitators?
- If the state doesn't permit advertising, what does that mean? Only that residents of the state are not permitted to advertise? Can nonresidents advertise? Can nonresidents who are attorneys, agencies, or facilitators advertise?

As you can see, you need to ask very precise questions, as it is not clear exactly how the state laws will be interpreted.

There are many forms of advertising you might use; all of them will publicize a brief statement (a mini résumé) of your need. You can type a card and put it on the bulletin board at a supermarket or Laundromat; they will let you keep it there for a specific length of time. (We know a couple who found a baby through just such an ad at their Laundromat.) You can take out an ad in the local newspaper or in a specialty advertising supplement that is mailed to every house in a certain area. You can have flyers printed and distribute them to sources you think might lead you to a child. You can advertise in magazines with national distribution. You can print business cards and keep them in your purse or wallet to give out; this gives people you don't know well a way to get in touch with you if they have any ideas for you. You can even hire someone to do your advertising for you.

Sarah and Josh decided to try a magazine with national distribution. They first discovered that it was very expensive. But they reasoned that they already spent sixty thousand dollars on their efforts to conceive a child, so it made sense to them to spend money in finding a baby. They knew their search would be expensive, but expected it to be a lot more fruitful than other methods. They advertised for six months and during that time had three leads. One potential birth mother was interested but not very far along; they were unable to sustain contact with her and she placed her child with a relative. Their second lead sounded like a scam: The woman had read that couples were willing to pay a lot of money and asked Sarah and Josh to send money before they had a chance to know her and meet her. They decided not to do it. That was probably a wise decision.

Their third response was the winner. They liked the thirty-five-year-old woman, Adele, who was a single mom already and didn't feel she could raise the child she was carrying. They talked on the phone several times in the next few weeks and then decided to meet. Josh and Sarah flew to her state, since her two children were in school and she didn't have anyone to take care of them if she left town. They all liked each other and decided to move ahead, agreeing that they needed help arranging the adoption. Josh called around and found a private agency that did what they termed designated adoptions, which are adoptions for which a specific birth mother has been found. (Some agencies call these identified adoptions; they are another form of independent adoption.) This sounded perfect. Then they found out that, since they were from out of state, they needed to complete a home study with an agency approved by their own state. They went home to make the arrangements. Their independent adoption was now becoming an agency adoption.

They maintained contact with Adele during the last two months of her pregnancy. They checked in with her after every prenatal visit. They paid the doctor directly for her prenatal care and helped her make arrangements with the hospital for the delivery of the baby. Adele contacted the birth father, who was eager to have her place the child for adoption. He went to the agency and signed relinquishment papers. Sarah and Josh were greatly relieved when this step was finished, even though they knew he could change his mind once the baby was born.

Sarah went to be with Adele for the last few weeks of the pregnancy, to help her with the children. Josh was to fly down when Adele went into labor. The children knew about the arrangements and seemed comfortable with the idea; Adele had always been honest with them and was unwilling to be any different on this important part of her life.

The six-pound, four-ounce baby girl was born in April. Josh didn't arrive in time to be part of the delivery, but Sarah was Adele's coach and friend throughout the process. She was very mindful of the importance of her relationship with Adele and didn't want Adele to feel she was going to be ignored once the baby had arrived. The couple made sure Adele was in a good frame of mind before they left with their new baby. Since all of the interstate laws had been complied with, Sarah and Josh came home with their week-old baby and a wonderful story to tell her as she grew. Sarah and Josh feel that the magazine's fee was the best money they ever spent.

One couple in Texas paid for a billboard in their hope of finding a baby. Not only did everyone along the highway see the ad, but it made the national news.

Two couples in one part of California elected to advertise for a child. Their methods were different and so were their results. Pat and Ray already had two adopted children and were told by the public adoption agencies that they would not get approval to adopt another child. They were both very open to contact with the biological parents. Pat was a school counselor with lots of experience talking with young people, and she felt she would be at ease interviewing potential birth mothers. So they decided to advertise. They chose the local university as a place to put their ad, reasoning that they'd have a good chance of finding a child from bright parents. The university newspaper unhesitatingly accepted their ad. The couple placed their ad after a long vacation period, when they felt young women were likely to be pregnant. Their ad ran for only one week and they heard nothing. In the meantime, one of their other contacts paid off. They canceled their ad and never found out whether it would have gotten them a child. They still believe it eventually would have been successful.

Another couple, Heidi and Jess, had a different response. They were turned down by not only the public adoption agency but also the only private adoption agency in their city. Having been told they had not been married long enough to apply, they felt they had to take more drastic action. They also had circumstances they felt could appeal to young people, so they placed the following ad:

PARALYZED VETERAN AND HIS WIFE REALLY WANT TO ADOPT A BABY. WOULD YOU CONSIDER HELPING US? CALL HEIDI OR JOE. [PHONE NUMBER]

They chose an advertising supplement sent to all homes in a given area. Within the week they received a call about a baby from Mexico, and within three months they had legally adopted a newborn baby boy.

Right after they received their call about the Mexican baby, they received a second call. This call came from one of the supervisors who had turned them down at the public agency. She called to tell them that advertising for a child was illegal and to ask why they didn't apply for a child through legal channels by contacting an adoption agency. Heidi told her of their experience with her agency. The supervisor told them that even if they had been rejected, they could not legally run printed ads for a child and must stop. Heidi told her they would. Their ad, however, had still gotten them their son.

Advertising today is not as big an issue as in times past. If you look in your local newspaper in the personals column you are likely to find one or two ads on any given day. Trying to sort out which states and which newspapers in which areas you should place your ad is not a simple process, but it is one that may have a big payoff.

Advertising is simply a way to get people who want a child together with people who have a child they don't want or can't keep. Some people feel comfortable advertising for a child and others don't. Should you advertise? You should do what you feel is right for you. There is no single effective way to advertise for a baby; the whole concept is relatively new, so you must set up your own plan. As in many areas of adoption, you must be confident in yourself and your goal as you attempt this procedure, because some people will be critical of your method.

THE INTERNET

A new source, and potentially one of the most wide-reaching, is the Internet. We are just now beginning to see the potential value of the Internet in adoption; web sites for people seeking babies are beginning to appear, and what this holds for the future is exciting. Potential adopters can harvest information at a number of web sites, or they can create their own web pages and show the world their résumés.

It will probably be a while before the Internet is used by many people as a way to find babies. At this point, it is most valuable as a source of information; the difficult part is sorting out what is on the Internet and who put it there. This can be a very time-consuming process. You can find a wealth of information, but be prepared to sort through it.

Some of the first couples to use the Internet had hoped to find that this source of birth mothers would be less likely to involve adoption scams. They have not found this to be true. One needs to take the same precautions using the Internet as any other resource you use to try to make contact with a birth mother.

If you know how to design your own web page, the cost is not an issue. If you have to hire someone, the costs can get rather high. But it probably is no more expensive than any other kind of advertising that you might try, and it gets your message and information sheet out there. So far, few adoptions have resulted from Net-working, but the method has a lot of potential.

You can also check out the Internet Adoption Registry (see Appendix F).[4] This site holds a registry for waiting adoptive families; each listing contains a letter and a photo. You don't even have to be on the Internet to become part of this group.

The impact of the Internet is also being felt in international adoptions. A recent article discusses ways to lower the cost of international adoption by using the Internet.[5] The description of the services would indicate the costs would decrease because papers could be sent to the foreign country, and pictures could be exchanged using the Internet, thereby significantly reducing the costs. As in many applications of the Internet it is too early to evaluate its potential usefulness.

MARKETING SPECIALISTS

Some people say they don't know enough about marketing to do it on their own, and they need help. There is help available. Some facilitators will help you with your résumé, while others may actually set up advertising campaigns for you. Other marketing specialists make a living sending out mailings for couples. One group, California Marketing (see Appendix F), will design a letter and provides complete printing and mailing services. They mail to OB-GYNs, family planning centers, and abortion alternative organizations in regions that you may select. Other groups throughout the United States are beginning to recognize the need to assist couples in their adoption search. For couples who believe in marketing but who don't have the time to do it, these sources might be worth checking into.

While we don't think you should turn the adoption process completely over to others, don't hesitate to check into the sources of help for areas in which you don't think you do well. If you aren't good at marketing, hire someone.

THE BUSINESS OF SEARCHING

Some people will be put off by the callousness of the suggestions we have made. They would say this sounds just like a business. It is. We wish it weren't, but it is. Currently there are more people like you who want babies than there are people who want to place babies. You are in a competitive market and you need to be able to compete.

None of this means that you should present yourself as anyone who you are not. Throughout this book, we have emphasized the importance of being honest. However, if you don't have a chance to talk with a birth mother or birth father, your honesty won't help you. Marketing yourself will give you this chance and help you find a baby. Marketing just opens the door to show who you are.

Waiting: A How-To

Waiting for a baby isn't easy. Just ask any mother who has to endure being pregnant for nine months. So you should be prepared to wait, too.

Most leads will turn up nothing. But you are looking for only one baby, so don't give up—stay patient. And be aware that it's easier to wait when you feel you are actively working on a problem and doing the most you can. You are not waiting for a call from an adoption agency that may or may not come; you are an active participant in deciding your fate.

Much can be done during this period of waiting. Not everyone is so sure of themselves that they are ready to go out and decorate the baby's room, but there are some other ways that you can begin to prepare for a baby.[6]

While you search, also arrange for a home study or other steps in the process. Take classes on adoption; learn about the process so you will be a better adoptive parent. Take a class on parenting or a class on newborn CPR. Begin to look at the children's department in your store instead of avoiding it as you may have in the past. Check into your insurance benefits for adoption; you may learn something new about how you should handle specific details. Learn about the plight of the unhappily pregnant woman. Increase your sensitivity to her issues and perhaps your issues will take on a different perspective. At the same time, you will become better at dealing with the birth mother whom you will eventually meet. If you aren't sure what age child you might receive, read about child development instead of just new babies. Look for support groups; they will help you, and you will be surrounded by the success of others. Keep reminding yourself that far more successes are involved in adoptions than failures. It's just that the failures make more dramatic stories.

Invest in your relationship with your partner during this waiting time. The better the relationship you have with your spouse before the baby arrives, the better it will be for everyone in your family. Many times, infertility puts great stress on a relationship. Now that you are ready to try something other than working on producing a baby biologically, perhaps you can spend some additional time putting back into your relationship some of the romance that might have been lost in pursuing pregnancy. This is an investment in the future.

It is easy to say, "I have already waited long enough," but infertility issues are separate from adoption issues. Treatment for infertility is something you may have decided to pursue before you began to look at adoption. When you begin to actively pursue adoption, don't assume that your wait for a child was part of your months or years of pursuing infertility.

Consider yourself pregnant. One of the advantages pregnant women have is a period of time to bond with their unborn child. A time to really prepare emotionally for having a baby. By beginning to prepare for the arrival of your baby, you are beginning the process of bonding. If you pull yourself too far away from the potential of success because you fear failure, you may find yourself unprepared for the child who *is* waiting for you somewhere.

Summary

You may have to look long and far to find a child, or you may find one with your first contact. Whatever happens, you have to be ready to make those contacts, with anyone and everyone. Be creative and thorough in your outreach—talk to everyone you think might know of a child, whether that person is a friend, a doctor, someone connected with a school . . . or anyone else. Pass out handfuls of your résumés. And consider advertising for a child, a way of contacting hundreds of people at once.

Along the way you may find people who say you can't do this or that. Maybe you can't; it may be illegal. If that is the case, stop. But think carefully about your limits. If you fear all the things you can't or shouldn't do, you will find your options limited. Don't let others set your limits. You may avoid all possible criticism—but you may miss your chance to find a baby.

Make yourself proud of your search for a baby. Remember that you are the one who will ultimately have the reward of having a baby to raise and to love. That is worth a lot.

CHAPTER 11

Are You Really Ready?

SO NOW YOU HAVE DONE everything you need to do to find a baby on your own. Your résumé is widely distributed, you're advertising on the Internet, you have an attorney who agrees with your philosophy, you know how independent adoption works, and you are waiting for the call from someone saying she has a baby for you. But you may still have a few things to do if you want to be totally prepared for what can now happen at any time.

Some people say that they are always ready for a call from anyone who says they have a baby for them. This is not always true.

Cecilia and Henry were really excited when they got a call from a birth mother responding to their letter to a gynecologist in the Midwest. As they had sought a baby to adopt, they had felt they were in complete agreement on every issue. But after the call, they found that Cecilia's degree of willingness to have contact with the birth mother was not at all the same as Henry's. Henry wanted the birth mother to have adequate counseling and financial assistance, but he wanted minimal contact with her. Cecilia wanted to be involved in every way possible. She wanted to take the birth mother to the doctor, attend natural childbirth classes with her, shop for clothes with her, have her stay with them until the delivery, and be at the delivery. Henry and Cecilia had talked about adoption, but in general phrases—"for the good of all concerned," "want it to be a healthy adoption," "OK to be open," "contact is fine." It all sounded great, but they didn't actually communicate fully with each other. When the birth mother called, Cecilia and Henry still had something to discuss. They really weren't ready.

Most of the comments in this chapter are for potential adopting parents who are trying to find a child on their own. You are the one who is guiding this process; in an agency adoption, you would be guided by a social worker. But sometimes, you can be caught unprepared for the questions a social worker may ask you even in an agency adoption. So prepare yourself now for whatever questions may arise in your adoption process (see Chapter 9).

Meeting the Birth Mother

BEING YOURSELF, BEING HONEST

Having counseled many people who plan to adopt, we think the best advice we can give you before you have contact with a birth mother is to be yourself. Honesty is, as always, important. If you have presented yourself in your résumé as someone you are not, it is likely to come out.

Next in importance, be ready. If you are not mentally or emotionally prepared, the birth mother will sense your indecisiveness and perhaps think you are not interested in or ready for her baby. If you and your spouse do not hold the same views on what is about to occur, your discord will probably show. Get in touch with who you are and resolve any uncertainties about how you are willing to proceed with this adoption.

Ideally, through the reading you have done, you have an appreciation of the birth mother's plight. Certainly you need some understanding of your role in this process. While keeping in mind both sides of the adoption picture, continue to be your most honest self as you make contact with the woman you hope will give you a child to raise.

Cynthia explains: *Maria and Jim taught me a lot about being oneself. Maria was happy but anxious about meeting the birth mother. She debated what to say, what to wear, and what to ask to make everything go well. She called me before the interview to get advice on her wardrobe. I told her to choose whatever she would feel comfortable wearing to a meeting with a seventeen-year-old pregnant girl and her mother. She finally said that she thought she would wear her "job interview" dress, which I said sounded fine. She asked if she could bring pictures of their house, their relatives, and their cats. I said fine, whatever she thought best. In my mind, pictures of family are OK—but the cats? I thought I wouldn't do that, but if she wanted to, it would probably be all right.*

Maria and Jim arrived on time. Maria was uptight. Jim was more laid back. We all sat down to talk, the five of us. As Jayme, the birth mother, asked several questions about Jim and Maria, the tension decreased. We discovered that Jim's occupation was similar to what the birth father was studying, and everyone laughed together about the coincidence. Then Maria brought out her pictures to show Jayme and her mother. When Jayme got to the pictures of the cats, she was thrilled. She also loved cats. Everyone felt more at ease. Then Jayme threw out a question that was a bombshell. She asked Maria and Jim how they would feel if the baby was born with a defect. Maria and Jim were really shocked, but they knew what the right answer was supposed to be. Then Maria told Jayme, "In all honesty, I have to tell you this is likely to be our only child. It would be really hard for us to have our only child defective, so I'm not sure what I would say." After her answer, it wasn't long before the meeting came to an end.

Maria and Jim left knowing their answer had not been what Jayme wanted to hear. When I spoke alone with Jayme and her mother, they talked positively about Maria and Jim and seemed to love their warmth and openness. Then I asked Jayme about Maria's reply to the question about a possible defect because I knew this was one of Jayme's prime areas of concern. Jayme said she actually liked the answer because it seemed genuine and honest. She felt Maria and Jim would make great parents for her baby.

Jayme told them herself that she wanted them to have her baby and that she wanted them to be there for the baby's birth. She also indicated to them that, after the baby was born, she did not want to remain in contact. She knew her baby would be in good hands. Pictures of cats and total honesty helped Maria and Jim to get their son.

Being true to yourself and being prepared for the big moment are the best ways to make sure that your first contact is positive and meaningful. Both of these are things only you can do to be ready.

GUIDELINES FOR THE FIRST CONTACT

Prospective parents who have sent out a résumé frequently ask what they should do when a birth mother calls or a meeting is arranged. While we believe you should always be yourself, there are some general guidelines to help you understand what to do and what not to do.

In your initial conversation be sure to . . .

Be open and listen carefully. You want to hear the birth mother because she will give you information you need to have.

Be prepared to carry the conversation. While you may be nervous, the birth mother is probably at least as nervous as you. If she is terribly shy, you may have to do most of the talking to keep the situation from becoming awkward. If you are not a good talker, see if someone else can be with you for your first contact.

Ask questions that encourage her to talk. As a general rule, you want to ask questions that give you a chance to hear who she is. For instance, you might say, "Can you tell us a bit about yourself?" or "What are you looking for in the people who adopt your baby?" Of course, there are going to be other, more specific questions you want to ask, but if the conversation sounds like a third-degree interrogation, you won't seem very caring.

Be reasonable about what you try to cover. If this encounter is a good one, you will have plenty of opportunities to talk again. If you try to cover too much, you may sound as though you have a long list of questions and aren't interested in letting the conversation flow.

Be willing to leave loose ends. If the birth mother asks a question and you aren't certain how to answer, it is fine to say, "I'll have to think about that," or "Let me talk that over with my husband and get back to you." If she isn't certain about meeting you or how any kind of meeting might work for her, leave that open also. The primary goal of the first contact is to learn something about each other and to like each other enough that she will want to talk to you again.

Talk about the next step before ending the conversation. The next step in a relationship is determined by what has happened so far. If the birth mother seems unsure where to go next, give her time; perhaps just acknowledge her hesitation or suggest some counseling and see if meeting again might help her to decide how to proceed. If she seems absolutely certain she wants to move ahead, you can talk about meeting a second time to arrange the details or have her contact your attorney. Know what details need to be discussed at that second meeting.

When you have your initial conversation, be cautious about . . .

Thinking you have your final adoption lead. This is a beginning step. After one encounter, you are still far from being involved in an adoption. If you look at this as the beginning of a process, you won't feel bad if the situation falls through.

Telling everyone you have found a baby to adopt. Proceed cautiously. See how this lead plays out. It may be worth talking about and may not be. If you tell everyone you have a situation and then it falls through, then you have to tell everyone it didn't work out. If you tell others you have a lead, they may stop exploring potential contacts for you; you may pass up another lead that might work out better than this one. Sometimes it is easier to go slowly.

Agreeing to anything. This is still just one potential lead. If the birth mother initially wants more than you are comfortable with, let it go. While we would never want you to be cavalier about any contacts, because no one ever knows where the next one might come from, it is important that you agree only to the things with which you can be comfortable. If you don't agree with everything she wants, this doesn't mean that you're turning her down. As she gets to know you and you to know her, what each of you is willing to do may very well change.

Sending money. Always be very cautious about sending money to a potential birth mother after merely talking with her on the telephone. If one asks you to send her money at the end of the first call, that is a red flag. (We talk more about this in Chapter 13.)

No one can give you a script for this first contact with the birth mother. We will probably heighten your anxiety by saying that this may be the most important interview you will ever have, but do be prepared for it. Find out who she is and how she might fit into your life. Be patient, warm, and open, and try to listen rather than talk too much. She is in charge whether she knows it or not, and you need to know what she wants, needs, and requires of you if she is going to choose you to be the parents of her child. Then it is up to you to see if her needs fit with yours.

Getting to Know Each Other Better

You will not decide all the issues or answer all your questions (or the birth mother's questions) in the initial contact. You need to make a plan about how you will proceed.

You need to set up a meeting plan. You need to figure out, with the birth mother's help, how this might best be done. Some people who have been using an intermediary or a mediator may want to have that person with them for the next step; you can meet in the intermediary's office. Perhaps you'd rather meet in a restaurant or at your home. If the birth mother is far away, you all should decide whether it makes more sense for you to go to her territory or for you to have her come to your home.

From now on, you will be playing the situation by ear still using your common sense. Depending on how far along the birth mother is, you may have to move very quickly. If she is just barely pregnant, you have plenty of time and you can take it a bit slowly. If she sounds committed to you as parents for her baby, then you may need to check with an attorney about how to proceed. This is where listening and your knowledge about adoption really begin to make a difference. If you know where you are going, you can chart your course with confidence If you don't know where you are going next, hire one of the helpers discussed in Chapter 6.

Making Adoption Arrangements Together

After the birth mother has agreed to place her child with you, the process isn't finished. You have to continue to *keep* the adoption working. The next step toward a successful arrangement is to set up the details. Again, the birth mother is the leader to a great extent, in that she will let you know what she needs. However, when you decide how you will respond to her needs, you are in charge. Don't let her dictate something that is impossible for you to accept, but do be willing to compromise.

How you approach one area of adoption may affect your plans in other areas. The situation facing the Phillipses is a good example. They had sufficient funds to embark on an independent adoption but not enough for an expensive one. For them to help a birth mother with living expenses, they would have had to find a birth mother who either had significant medical insurance or was eligible for state assistance. When they found Alicia, they were delighted. Alicia's mother was in the military service, and all of Alicia's medical fees and most of her counseling expenses would be paid for by insurance. As a result, they were able to help pay for Alicia's living expenses and maternity clothes. They were also able to pay for a dieting program after the baby was born, to help Alicia lose the significant weight she was gaining during the pregnancy.

The Settlemeyers had a similar situation. They knew that their birth mother, Melinda, was going to have her baby by cesarean, which they would pay for. Since the costs of a cesarean birth are significantly higher than those of a vaginal delivery, the Settlemeyers felt that they would be less able to help Melinda with other expenses. This was clear to Melinda from the very beginning. Because she liked the Settlemeyers and felt they would provide a perfect home for her baby, she agreed to live with a good friend of theirs who lived close by them until the baby was born; this would help keep down costs for the Settlemeyers. They still felt counseling was critical, and they let the therapist who would work with Melinda know ahead of time about their limited funds. It was decided that she would have four sessions with this therapist before the baby was born, then one in the hospital and three after the baby was placed for adoption. That was all agreeable to Melinda, who felt that the counseling would be very helpful. Melinda and the Settlemeyers all knew that to make the adoption work best, they would have to bend to accommodate each other.

These examples illustrate how the factors to consider in adoptions are not always as separate as they seem. Medical attention and therapy are linked to finances, for example. You may not be able to finalize your plans before getting to know a specific birth mother and her needs. In most cases you consider the entire process to determine what you are going to do about each detail.

So many of the parts of adoption have aspects that need to be worked out between the people involved. It is not clear-cut what should be done, who should do it, and even if it should be done. By this time, you are probably getting used to this ambiguity. Uncertainty and ambiguity surrounded you first as you went through your infertility studies, and then again as you attempted to find a birth mother. Now you have a birth mother in mind, and ambiguous feelings are still there. They will continue until the adoption is legally completed. But they *do* end.

MEDICAL CARE

You need to know first how much prenatal care the birth mother has had. Many women have not seen a physician, so finding appropriate care is your first priority. Offer to help your birth mother select a physician. This is an important arrangement. Some physicians are more supportive of birth mothers than others, so helping her may be very important. If you will be taking her to see the physician, then you might have a strong view about whom she should select. Some birth mothers have already started prenatal care and want to continue with their physician.

LIVING ARRANGEMENTS

Some birth mothers remain in their own homes until the delivery. If your birth mother lives in another state or is trying to keep her pregnancy secret, she may want to move before she begins to show. How you handle this is based very much on the amount of contact you choose to have with each other.

Some adoptive couples have the birth mother live with them. This can be a satisfactory arrangement, but it is one you want to think about very carefully. What happens after the baby is born? Do you take the birth mother home with you after the birth for her to recuperate? What about her and the baby being together for that length of time? On the other hand, if she is very young, she may need to be in a home situation with people who are committed to her, and that may be you.

When adopting parents have a birth mother live with a friend, they most often pay for the cost of food and transportation. If you choose this arrangement, it is essential that you spend time with the birth mother, even if she is living with your friend.

Still other adoptive parents provide an apartment for her, especially if she has been on her own for a period of time. After the baby is born, she may still need some assistance from you or from someone else until she has recuperated from the birth.

A birth mother can live in a maternity home, but if this arrangement is made, be sure that there is no pressure on her to keep the baby. While a given maternity home might not advocate keeping babies, if most of the women living there are doing so, a birth mother may meet with considerable peer pressure.

When you have your birth mother live somewhere other than by herself, it is a delicate issue. Whomever she lives with are representatives of you. If she doesn't like your friends, she may feel less positive about you. Obviously, the living arrangements cannot be decided ahead of time. But think about the various alternatives before you know of your specific birth mother's needs.

FINANCIAL ARRANGEMENTS

The financial arrangements you make will be based on the individual situation you encounter. Some birth mothers are very specific about what expenses they expect to be paid by the adoptive parents. Those expenses may include medical costs, dental care, living costs, counseling, clothes, food, rent, and car payments while the birth mother is unable to work. All of these can be legally covered in most states. Other birth mothers ask for little and incur very few birth expenses. A birth mother may be qualified to go on welfare to cover medical costs; she may make do with very few clothes and live with friends or relatives during the pregnancy. Sometimes it is appropriate to have the expenses paid through your attorney, but at other times the birth mother may resent dealing with an intermediary. Listen to her and you will know what would be most comfortable for her.

Once again, the expenses should be discussed ahead of time between you and your partner. You need to have thought them through, even though you won't know what the birth mother expects until you speak with her about these details.

LEGAL ASSISTANCE

If you have not already hired an attorney, do so when you have been selected by a birth mother. This part of the legal arrangements in most adoptions is not complex, and most attorneys can do the legal work involved. If you are not sure what you are doing, choose an attorney who specializes in adoption; she will probably give you more assistance than other attorneys.

Your attorney does not have to be involved in the specific arrangements other than on an advice-giving basis, but it is important to have someone ready to file the petition to adopt as soon as the baby is born. In many cases, the hospital will ask for a letter of intent from the attorney of the adopting parents, to be certain that someone will pay the bill. The attorney will need the names, addresses, and birth dates for each of the parties involved, information about the birth mother and birth father, data on the adopting couple's marriage and any previous marriages, the birth mother's marital history, the name of the hospital, the name of the child as it should appear on the birth certificate, the date of birth, and the name of the attending physician. In order to expedite the proceedings, you will want the attorney to have as much of this as possible before the birth mother even enters the hospital.

If your birth mother has not received legal assistance, make sure you obtain some for her. Every birth mother should have an attorney of her own. Hire an attorney for an hour or two to provide her with the legal advice she is entitled to have before she enters this process. The birth mother who knows her rights is less likely to change her mind, because she knows what the process entails. It is possible that the adoption can be challenged if she does not have her own separate representation.

COUNSELING

Counseling is an extremely important part of healthy independent adoptions. Of all the areas most frequently criticized in independent arrangements, the lack of counseling is most often mentioned. The birth mother should be able to find someone with whom she can speak about her hesitations and concerns. Counseling is probably your greatest insurance policy that she will really know what she wants to do with her baby.

It is important that the counseling be with someone who is knowledgeable about adoption (especially independent adoption) and is aware of the normal reactions a woman is likely to experience going through an adoption. Without knowledge of independent adoption, a counselor may be shocked at the way you are going about your adoption, in much the same way the general public can be. You may need to educate a therapist before you send the birth mother for counseling. Find someone the birth mother can talk easily with; this also minimizes the dependence that she may develop on you.

HOSPITAL ARRANGEMENTS

The birth mother's stay in the hospital also needs to be planned. Handle as many of the details as you can beforehand. Many of the details, of course, may be unknown until she checks in. While it helps to find out as much as possible about the hospital policy prior to the birth, you need to be prepared to do whatever is necessary if something comes up once the birth mother is there.

You may decide not to discuss the hospital with her until she is close to the delivery date. As you get to know her, you will have a better idea of how appropriate it will be for you to be involved when she is in the hospital. More and more adoptive parents are involved in the actual birth of their adopted children, as adoptions become more and more open.

Hospitals frequently treat women differently if they have had no prenatal care. Perhaps that's because the hospital is aware that many of these mothers are more likely to have other problems, both medical and emotional. If you come into the picture at the last minute, you will need to be prepared to act on the birth mother's behalf if she has not had prenatal care.

It is very helpful for the birth mother and the adoptive parents to take a hospital tour together and introduce themselves to the social worker and administrator on the maternity ward. When the hospital staff sees that a plan has been well thought out, they may react more positively to the birth mother. Whenever possible, have your attorney and counselor, if there is one, send a letter to the hospital ahead of time, further indicating that the birth plan has been discussed.

After the baby is born, the birth mother will be asked to fill out a birth certificate. She may use the first and middle names you have picked out, or she may use those she chooses. If you have spent enough time with her, you may know ahead of time what she will do. It is helpful to know exactly what name she gives the baby on the birth certificate, since your attorney will ask for this information.

A pediatrician will need to examine the baby in the hospital. One decision confronted by half of adopting parents is the issue of circumcision. You need to be cautious about this, because the birth mother must still consent to any medical procedure. Don't neglect to involve her. Sometimes the birth mother will not want to have any contact with the baby while in the hospital, so here again, accommodate her wishes to help make the process as easy as possible for her.

If you are to be there for any of the baby's feedings or are to spend time with the baby while in the hospital, you need to make certain the hospital staff is aware of this. Many times the hospital staff needs to be educated about adoption alternatives, and your way of conducting this adoption may be new for them.

Arrangements for taking the baby home from the hospital also need to be made. Most hospitals will have the birth mother sign a release giving the hospital permission to let the adoptive parents take the baby home. This release also allows you to be responsible for the medical care of the baby. It is the only legal document you have proving your right to leave with the baby.

Some hospitals will release the baby to you as soon as the child's condition is stable. Others will release the child only after the birth mother is ready to leave. Some hospitals will not release the baby until legal documents of guardianship or relinquishment have been received.

The financial arrangements also vary with each hospital. Some hospitals, caught in financial crunches, expect the adopting couple to pay for the hospital expense even if the birth mother is on state aid. This often is not legally required, but you need to be careful at this point. In some cases, the birth mother may need to take the baby out of the hospital herself in order to prevent the birth expenses being charged to the adopting couple.

Working with hospitals has become more complex in many ways. In some hospitals, couples have had difficulties with social workers on staff who try to interfere in the adoption decisions of the birth mother. Not all of the hospital staff will necessarily support a birth mother's decision to place her child for adoption, and they have a very critical role in working with the vulnerable and impressionable new mother.[1] Try to educate them as early as possible.

Dru explains: *I found this part out the hard way when one of the nurses came to talk with Holly right after she gave birth. She planned to place the baby for adoption, but the nurse invited Holly to come to her home with the baby until she had a plan. The nurse ignored the fact that Holly already had a plan, explaining to her that she, too, was a single mother, and even though it was difficult, Holly could raise this baby. This was very confusing for Holly. She told me that she felt the nurse was so disapproving of her adoption plans that she felt maybe she was doing the wrong thing.*

Holly decided to take the baby to a hotel, where she stayed for two days before calling me to have the adoptive couple come pick up the baby. I believe the reason she decided to move ahead with the adoption was that the adoptive parents were so supportive of her during the hospital stay and her time of confusion after leaving. They communicated to her in a very supportive and nonconfrontational way that they were concerned about her and that she needed to feel committed to the adoption for it to work. Their support, lack of pressure, patience, and genuine concern paid off.

AFTER THE HOSPITAL

After the baby is born and everyone is ready to go home, it is important to have made plans about where the birth mother is to go. It is in your best interests for the birth mother to be with people who care about her at this time. If she has to travel some distance to get home, help her with the arrangements.

Some adoptive parents bring her home with them. Others feel this is a time for them to bond with the baby and it should be spent alone with their new child. The important thing is not to let the birth mother feel that she is being abandoned now that she has delivered the baby. If she feels as though you don't care about her during this period, she will question your caring all along. She will already be feeling lonely now that the baby is gone; she will have even more difficulty if you abandon her emotionally. Make certain you have all made the arrangements and she is comfortable with them. Don't let this become a problem.

Once she is situated, call her frequently to make certain she is all right. If she has been in counseling, it will be important for her to continue now. If she is confused, upset, or in any way unsure, make sure she can talk with a counselor who understands adoption. Counseling can still be useful at this point in the process.

Continuing Contact

How much contact you will continue to have with the birth mother is as individual as each of the other areas we have considered. It will greatly depend on the amount of caring and trust that has developed between you. Until you go to court, she can call the shots to some extent; but you should not let a sense of coercion determine the contact— rather, think of the best interests of all involved.

Some birth mothers will want to have no contact after the child is placed with you. Others will want letters from "time to time." Make sure you agree on what "time to time" means. For some it means once a month and for others once a year. Other birth mothers may want to have some contact and meetings over the years. There is no one way to handle this request. Once the birth mother resumes her life after the adoption, she may desire less or no contact, no matter how she felt before the baby was born. Find a solution that is acceptable to all of you, and that might be renegotiated over time. Many birth parents and adoptive parents formalize these arrangements in pre-adoption contact agreements which are discussed later in this chapter.

Signing the Relinquishment

The social service department in your state usually obtains the consent from the birth mother in an independent adoption. You need to know ahead of time how this department operates so that signing the relinquishment can be handled easily. If the birth mother is returning to another state, you need to determine how this will be handled for her. Some states make the procedure very easy; others make this step an agonizing process. Know ahead of time how your state operates. You might also discover ways to simplify this process.

THE BIRTH FATHER'S INVOLVEMENT

Some birth mothers will have the birth father involved in selecting the adoptive parents. Other birth mothers feel punitive toward their partner and do not want him to know of a pregnancy or adoption. Other birth mothers may still be working out their relationships with the birth father and these men may be involved in part or all of the process.

The birth mother needs to decide for herself how she will handle this situation. You may feel strongly that you want to meet the birth father in order to decide if you want this baby. That's fine, but she may also feel strongly that she doesn't want him involved in anything other than signing papers or denying paternity. You need to decide whether you are willing to jeopardize this adoption over a disagreement on this point. Listen to what she is saying, as it will determine whether or not you adopt this child.

The birth mother is also the one to decide if she will list the birth father on the birth certificate. It is important that she understand the legal implications of whether or not she lists him, but this remains her decision. If there is any question about how this matter is to be handled, provide her with her own attorney, so she can make a good decision that will not cause the adoption to be held up in court.

PRE-ADOPTION CONTACT AGREEMENTS

More and more adoptions involve a pre-adoption agreement that specifies how much and what kind of contact will occur after the adoption has been finalized. It is usually the birth mother who wants such a contract, but these agreements can benefit everyone. The time to decide if there will be an agreement as part of the adoption is before the baby is born. Never enter into an agreement without being sure you are willing to abide by it. This is true whether it becomes part of the legal process or is informally decided between you and the birth mother. Honesty should be the basis of all adoptions.

Not all states give legal status to these contact agreements, and much legal debate on a state-by-state basis will take place before their validity is clearly established.[2] But that isn't the biggest issue. Working out an agreement can help you sort out your expectations for the relationship between the birth family and your family; the agreement will spell these out in a specific way. A pre-adoption contact agreement can help both the birth family and the adoptive family avoid future misunderstandings.

Mindy found this out the hard way. Mindy really liked Gina and Tom, the couple she picked for her baby. She had considered keeping the baby she was carrying, but she realized she would be unable to care for the baby and complete school. The lack of support from her parents made it clear that the baby would have a better life with a stable couple who had greater financial resources. She went through an intermediary and found Gina and Tom; she thought they were ideal.

And they were ideal—at the beginning. They helped her in every way possible. They made her a part of their family, they went with her to the doctor's appointments, and they were both there at the delivery and even for a month or two after. Mindy had talked with them about wanting pictures and letters "regularly" after the baby was placed, but the parameters had never been clearly defined.

After she signed the relinquishment papers and the adoption was finalized, she called them about the pictures she hadn't been receiving; they said they would mail some to her. Two months later a few pictures arrived. Three months later, the same thing happened. Mindy spoke with them about their agreement, and the couple responded that they didn't have very many pictures, but they would send some when they got new ones. Again, the wait began. After another contact, this time through the intermediary, Gina said that she felt it was time for Mindy to get beyond the birth and let their new family lead their lives. Even the intermediary was shocked at Gina's callousness and reminded Gina of the agreement. Gina said she believed "regularly" meant every few years. Unfortunately, "regularly" meant every few months to Mindy. This should have been clarified ahead of time, and probably with this couple it should have been part of a legally binding agreement prior to the adoption.

While contact agreements are most likely to benefit the birth mother, they can also benefit the adopting couple. They can keep both parties on track and serve as a written reminder of what otherwise can frequently be distorted over time.

Don't pull away from an adoption merely because a birth mother wants a legal agreement about future contacts. Try to understand it from her perspective. She will trust you to do what you have said you will do. After she puts her child in your hands, her expectations and trust need to last for a lifetime. Your trust in her and what she says she will do only needs to last until you have the baby and go to court.

If you are unwilling to sign an agreement that the birth mother wants, you may need to decline a specific adoption. Obviously, you ought to try to compromise if at all possible. But if she won't bend or you don't feel you can agree to what she wants, don't. It's OK. Even if you learn that these kinds of pre-adoption contact agreements can't be enforced in your state, you should never enter into one with the idea that you won't abide by the terms. That kind of behavior negatively impacts everyone involved in adoption. It is better to pass on an adoption than to make an agreement that you won't fulfill. Adoption is a lifelong commitment.

Handling Touchy Issues

Some subjects are difficult to broach when you first meet a birth mother. These include the possibility of AIDS, drugs or alcohol, mental illness, and questions of race. Some of these issues might be better handled by someone other than the adopting parents. If you decide to address these subjects with the birth parents directly, it is important to do so with sensitivity and honesty and, most important, to be educated about the issues.

HIV AND AIDS

Most adoptive parents today have some concerns about AIDS. Actually, most parents have some concerns about AIDS. So how do you handle this issue with the pregnant woman who is considering giving you her baby?

AIDS is confusing and frightening to most people. HIV (Human Immunodeficiency Virus) is the cause of AIDS. A person can test positive for HIV for an extended period of time before developing any symptoms which would be defined as AIDS. This disease is baffling, especially in pregnant women.

Asking a birth mother to be screened for HIV isn't always easy. Since we now know that it is in the birth mother's best interests to find out if she tests positive for HIV, it is prudent to suggest she have this screening. But in some areas of the country, the possibility of HIV will simply be overlooked. One attorney was very unhappy when we even suggested to a birth mother that she have an HIV test. He indicated that if she tested positive, we would be responsible for her emotional response to finding out that she has a fatal disease.

Walt and Jessica found out about HIV and AIDS the difficult way. They were an older couple who wanted to build a family. Jessica had two children from a previous marriage and since Walt had had a vasectomy years before, they planned to adopt.

They went to a private adoption agency that was willing to help couples who were in their forties. They wanted a baby, but they also wanted a close-to-perfect baby. And they actually found what appeared to be an ideal situation. The agency they went to was involved with open adoptions and they had a chance to meet Adelaide.

Adelaide was beautiful. She had not had an easy life, but she was obviously bright. Money issues were very important to her. She liked the fact that this couple could help financially with her pregnancy and that her child would be raised in a financially secure family.

The pregnancy went well and the delivery was relatively easy, as was emotionally separating from the baby. Adelaide's relationship with Walt and Jessica was very open and, they believed, very honest. So she was shocked when they called her two months after the birth of a son and told her they were returning him to her. They said angrily, "The baby tested positive for AIDS."

Walt and Jessica had been told by their physician that the baby tested positive for HIV, which to them meant that their perfect son had AIDS and would die an early death. Walt and Jessica were very upset, but they were also very angry. They were angry at Adelaide, who had not told them about her sexual history and had not been tested for HIV. Walt and Jessica were also angry with the agency who had arranged the adoption. (The agency policy was to let the adopting parents decide what testing would be suggested to birth mothers.) Adelaide had been tested for drugs, but no one had even thought of HIV. Walt and Jessica called the agency and told them to come get the baby; this was not something they could handle. Talking with the social worker about the issues and their need to find out more information before they decided what to do did little good; they returned the child to the agency shortly after calling Adelaide.

Meanwhile, Adelaide was equally devastated. She did not know she was HIV positive until she heard it from Walt and Jessica. She had a lot of information to process very quickly as the agency asked what she wanted to do. They indicated they could find another home for the baby, but it was up to her. She knew little about AIDS but found out a great deal more by calling the local AIDS hotline. In fact, she learned more about AIDS and her baby from three phone calls than Walt and Jessica knew before they decided to return the child.

Adelaide decided to keep her baby. After the little boy was returned, she began using the drug AZT and trying very hard to keep herself healthy. The physician at the public health department had her bring the baby back when he was eighteen months old; he no longer tested positive for HIV.

AIDS has been with us for well over a decade now, yet we continue to learn more about it every day; there is much we don't know. But for anyone considering adoption, it is important to understand what information is available so you can make informed rather than impetuous decisions (see also Chapter 8).

DRUGS AND ALCOHOL

The problem of alcohol or drug use during pregnancy is more common than HIV, yet it receives far less attention. If you are going to approach a birth mother about her use of drugs and alcohol, be cautious. If there is a counselor or social worker assisting you on your adoption, it might be better to have this person ask some of these sensitive and personal questions. Another alternative is to suggest that all of the parties agree to be tested. That way the birth mother doesn't feel discriminated against, and testing can be reassuring for everyone, since she may want to be sure of your drug and alcohol use, too. You also need to be clear what difference such use would make to you; is it worth pushing this issue? If you are going ahead anyhow, why jeopardize the adoption? On the other hand, if you have a chance to know the birth mother for a period of time, you may have less reason to make these inquiries.

Susan and Ed had been trying to adopt a baby for about a year. A couple of situations fell through for them, but they remained positive about adopting a child. When they heard about a birth mother in Oregon who wanted to place her unborn child for adoption, they were very excited. But when she began calling them at odd hours of the night stating that she needed money for this or that, they began to worry about her and the adoption. They questioned her in a gentle manner and learned she was using cocaine and had been throughout the pregnancy. She said she hadn't told them because she felt they would change their mind about adopting her baby.

Susan, who had most of the contact with this birth mother, expressed her concern and encouraged the woman to go into treatment but said she and Ed were committed to the adoption. They researched the implications of prenatal exposure to cocaine from every source they could think of, and decided they could handle the situation. Two months later their son was born and he tested positive at birth for cocaine. But three years later Ed and Susan say they have an incredibly healthy son and they were glad they took the risk.

MENTAL HEALTH

Few adopting parents check into the emotional background of the birth mother before deciding on adopting. Yet we know that mental health has a strong genetic component. You may want to find out if she or anyone in her family has a history of depression, suicide, or mental hospitalizations before moving ahead. This can be a touchy issue, so you need to evaluate if it is really worth pursuing. Would something you learned about her history make you choose not to adopt? If you feel the birth mother is stable, you may not ask any other questions.

In the time when agencies did more of the adoptions, this area was touched upon by social workers who interviewed birth mothers. In independent adoptions, it may be an issue that you want the facilitator or a counselor to explore.

RACE

Determining the racial background of the birth mother is relatively easy. Deciding where you are on racial issues is not always as simple. Since being open to racial differences frequently enables a couple to find a child faster, it is important to give the matter considerable thought (see Chapter 8).

If in the course of your conversation with a birth mother you find out the parents have some Native American blood, it is important that you investigate how this will impact a potential adoption. Until recently, *any* amount of Native American blood in the child's background meant that adopting that child required permission from the tribe. This is changing somewhat right now, as degrees of Native American ethnicity are being reevaluated; cultural and social ties with the tribe may now become a part of the decision process on whether a child is defined as a Native American. This area of adoption remains in flux. But it is important to realize that Native American issues can significantly complicate an adoption. Some tribes are supportive of adoption outside of the tribe, but others are known to block adoptions of any children with any amount of Native American in their heritage.[3]

Issues related to African American adoptions are also unclear. We have seen African American couples turn down birth mothers who are darker than they. We have seen Hispanic couples turn down birth mothers who have more Indian in their ancestry than they want. We have seen birth mothers turn down African American couples because they wanted their African American child to be raised in a Caucasian home that they felt would give more advantages to their child.

Racial issues are confusing for many of us. You can find out some information about race, but it is not always clear what it means. You need to be as clear as possible for yourself where you are on these issues before you receive a call about a baby.

Putting It All Together

An overview of what happens in adoptions is always helpful. By reading how other families put all of the pieces together, you'll see how the various factors in an adoption mesh with each other and you can imagine yourself in a situation before you actually answer the phone and need to set up arrangements of your own.

The need for adaptability was evident in the Ritters' adoption. They heard from an attorney about Penny, who was seven-and-a-half-months pregnant. She had read their résumé, liked it, and wanted to meet them.

Penny met the Ritters in the attorney's office, and arrangements were made for the couple to adopt her baby. The cost of this adoption initially seemed low because Penny had applied for welfare, and she was living with her sister, who was helping her until the baby arrived. But Penny had been experiencing problems, including a traumatic breakup with her boyfriend, being kicked out of her home when her parents discovered she was pregnant, being uprooted from high school in her senior year, and moving to a new state to have a baby. Everyone agreed that since there had been so many recent changes in Penny's life, there was a need for some counseling. The Ritters agreed to pay for those costs. They also agreed that some of the counseling should involve vocational help, since Penny was due to graduate from high school but had no idea what to do after that.

Penny's sister called the Ritters after Penny went to her assigned physician. Penny did not like him and was very upset. Now the Ritters were upset. They knew it was important for Penny to feel comfortable with her physician, and they felt the health and well-being of their child were at stake. Since they had a very friendly and comfortable relationship with their own doctor, they decided to have Penny go to him rather than to have the child on welfare. They made the expensive change, and Penny was pleased.

Penny also liked her counselor. This woman knew a great deal about adoption and was able to discuss what was ahead for Penny. During the course of the sessions, the problem Penny was having with her weight was frequently discussed. After working with the counselor on how to deal directly with the Ritters, Penny decided to ask the Ritters to help her go to a diet center after the baby was born, to help her regain her shape. It wasn't easy for Penny to do this, since she did not want to ever feel she was selling her baby. The Ritters felt that this was a reasonable expense that they might have incurred if they had given birth to the baby themselves, and they were willing to pay for it. Their attorney agreed.

Penny wanted her sister and the Ritters with her for the delivery. They all went to the Lamaze classes together. It was a real family affair. Penny also included them in visits to the doctor, and at times Mrs. Ritter went with her to help buy maternity clothes. The relationship was extremely adaptable, based on whatever came up. The Ritters felt a trust in Penny and she in them.

The delivery went well. Penny referred to the baby boy as the Ritters' from the moment he was delivered. The experience amazed the staff at the hospital, who learned a great deal about how healthy open independent adoptions can be.

Penny originally decided not to see the baby after she went home from the hospital. Then, three weeks after the baby was born, she asked to see him. She had spoken with the Ritters several times on the phone already, so her request worried them. As they discussed this, they decided there was no reason to believe that Penny had changed her mind. Nothing she had said would indicate any change from before. In some ways, it seemed she wanted to get some closure on the adoption before she returned to her home state. Maybe, the Ritters thought, she wanted them to see how much weight she had lost since the baby arrived. The meeting was arranged for two weeks later so that it would coincide with the end of her semester, just before she was to return to her home state.

They met in a neutral place where all could be at ease. But tension was evident, until Penny reassured the Ritters that even though the baby was darling, she was glad he was with them and that she wasn't a single mother. They were able to talk with her about their fears, and she told them there was nothing to worry about; she was very pleased with how well the baby seemed to be doing. It amazed Penny how different he looked. It was almost as though she really didn't feel he was her baby anymore. The meeting proved to be very helpful for Penny. She was able to return home feeling good about what she had done and good about where her son was.

Another example illustrates the complexity of some of the situations a couple can get into. The direction in which your adoption may proceed may be difficult to determine when you begin. Be prepared for the unexpected. Your adaptability will be important.

Matt and Glenda heard about several potential leads before they learned about Kim. Since none of their previous leads had worked out, they were ready to be much more accommodating on the first contact with her. They were concerned about being older and felt that they didn't have a lot of time to waste.

An adoption counselor called them to say that she knew of a nine-month-old baby girl who might be available for adoption. Were they interested? "Absolutely" was their unhesitating reply. That was the kind of answer that was needed in this situation because things were going to happen rather quickly. The counselor told them she was going to set up an interview with them and the birth mother, Kim, and her sister. The family element was rather important since Kim was severely hearing impaired.

The adoption counselor called them back shortly to say that a meeting was planned for the next day at 11:00 A.M. Although that wasn't the best time for Matt and Glenda, they made it possible. By then the counselor knew a little bit more about the potential adoption. The birth mother, who had lost her hearing because of German measles, was twenty-three, unmarried, and in need of reimbursement for expenses she had incurred for this child, about $3,500 in all. The baby girl, Marissa, seemed to be normal and so far showed no evidence of deafness. The father of the child, who lived with Kim, was also deaf; the cause of his deafness was unclear. With that little bit of information and with great anticipation, Matt and Glenda spent a sleepless night.

There were many unknowns. How would they communicate with Kim? Would they be chosen? Would this child be deaf? If she were, would they proceed with the adoption? How would it be to have a child who was already nine months old? Why was Kim placing her for adoption now? Would she change her mind? Would the birth father agree?

How had she calculated the $3,500? When would that be paid to her? When could they get the baby if Kim would let them have her? They had a favorite name for a baby girl—would they have to keep "Marissa" if they wanted to use their own chosen name? With these and many other questions, it was difficult to do anything except think about a baby that might be theirs.

They were to meet at Kim's sister house. The counselor would be there. They were nervous, anxious, excited, and scared. The counselor told them that the living conditions at Kim's sister's house were marginal and they should be prepared for a rather upset household. She thought Kim's brother-in-law seemed to be an extremely angry man who wanted very much to be in charge of the adoption proceedings. Glenda and Matt needed to win over not only Kim but also her sister and her brother-in-law.

The situation at the house was not ideal. Marissa was not clean and was in dirty clothes, but she was very cute. Kim was a very pretty young woman who seemed quite bright. The brother-in-law tried to dominate the discussion. The counselor kept trying to keep things centered on Kim and the couple; that helped a great deal. Many questions were asked and information was exchanged. Glenda and Matt explained that Matt owned his own computer business in a nearby town. He had majored in business administration in college, and they were doing very well financially. They owned their own home and had ample room for a baby. They explained that Matt had been married before and had two sons; Glenda and Matt had been married for six years. They brought a picture album showing their home and their relatives, and Kim really seemed to like being able to see some of their lifestyle. They indicated their willingness to discuss the $3,500 with Kim and to try to work out an agreement with her.

Kim did quite well lip-reading, so she understood much of what was said. At times her sister would help by repeating what had been said and also using sign language. Kim's sister offered Glenda and Matt coffee, which they took but really didn't want, given the lack of hygiene in the house; this certainly wasn't the time to be fussy.

Time wore on but no one wanted anything left out. As the discussion continued, the counselor felt Kim was ready to give them the baby. The counselor asked to speak with Matt and Glenda for a few minutes outside. She told them that if they wanted Marissa, they should strongly indicate it. Glenda said she felt funny taking the baby from her mother and just didn't know how to do it. She said she really wanted Marissa but was somewhat overwhelmed that it was happening so quickly. Matt, though, was willing to act swiftly and ask if Kim would let them have the baby now.

Inside the house, the counselor asked if Matt and Glenda were the kind of couple Kim was looking for, and Kim strongly indicated that they were. She said she wanted her baby to go to college and to live in a regular house. She liked it that Glenda would be staying at home with Marissa. Kim said she couldn't be a good mother because many times she couldn't even tell when Marissa was crying. Her sister indicated that Kim had learned few domestic skills from their own mother and that she was totally unprepared for motherhood. Though their mother wanted to raise Marissa, too, Kim and her sister had both decided this baby should be placed for adoption. They both seemed sure that it was better for the baby to be with a couple rather than with the grandmother.

Talk then began to focus on switching Marissa to Glenda and Matt. The counselor had brought a release for Kim to sign so that Matt and Glenda could have Marissa receive medical care if she needed it; Kim readily signed. Quickly the car was loaded with Marissa's clothes, food, and car seat. Phone numbers and hugs were exchanged, reassurances were given about Marissa's care, and expressions of gratitude for this marvelous child were genuinely and generously made. Kim walked them to the car and kissed Marissa. The counselor encouraged Glenda and Matt to leave and told them she would talk with Kim, her sister, and her brother-in-law for a few more minutes. They left with their new baby daughter, twenty-four hours after hearing about her.

They stopped at a local store and bought her some new clothes and some wash towels. After cleaning her up, they took her to meet her new relatives, who were rather amazed. Cautionary words and admonitions were expressed by those who couldn't understand why anyone would get involved in something like this. However, Marissa was a charmer. Concerns faded as they watched her smile. By now Marissa was already known to everyone as Marissa, so the issue of what to name her became decided. (When things finally calmed down, they gave Marissa their favorite name as a middle name, but she is still known as Marissa.)

That evening they spoke with the counselor on the phone. They had been shocked by Kim's brother-in-law and the home environment, but they'd been very impressed with Kim and Marissa. They spoke about the difficulties of having a nine-month-old baby as opposed to a newborn. The counselor encouraged them to spend time alone with Marissa and get to know her better before they tried to share her with others again. They needed to become bonded with Marissa and make her their own. They needed to become a family.

The following week, the counselor met with Kim and Marissa's father, Tim. Kim's dislike for her brother-in-law was evident as she told the counselor she wanted no more involvement from him or her sister in the adoption; she still felt it was best that her mother not know about her placing Marissa.

Kim admitted that she was unprepared for having a baby and that she was relieved to have placed the baby with Matt and Glenda. She sent many things with the counselor to give to Matt and Glenda: Marissa's baby book, medical records, a favorite toy, some additional clothes, and a note for Marissa when she was older.

Tim's parents, who were obviously very involved with this young couple, arrived during the meeting. Kim's inability to handle money had always been a problem, so they advised that the expense money be paid in monthly installments. They discussed the problems Kim had with Marissa and how the landlord had once called the police because Kim did not respond to the baby's crying.

The counselor arranged two more appointments with Kim, just to make sure she remained comfortable with the adoption. Matt and Glenda also had several appointments with the counselor; they knew that adjusting can be a problem when a new child already has a strong personality and is quite mobile. Adjusting to an adoption that happens very quickly also creates problems; Matt and Glenda's adoption of

Marissa had certainly gone quickly, and they were willing to get the help they needed to make certain everything went smoothly and positively.

Matt and Glenda's attorney filed the adoption papers for the routine adoption this seemed to be. The attorney was not happy with the financial arrangements but felt they would be acceptable.

Everything seemed fine until eight weeks later, when the counselor got a call from an angry Mrs. Broderick, Kim's mother. She wanted some answers and Kim had suggested her mother call the counselor.

Glenda and Matt were worried about the effect the grandmother might have on Marissa's adoption. While everyone understood that Mrs. Broderick didn't have the legal power to stop the adoption, she did have enough influence over Kim to cause her to stop it. Without this ever being said, everyone knew that was the issue.

The counselor met with Mrs. Broderick and Kim the following Wednesday. Mrs. Broderick was unwilling to go to the counselor's office for the meeting, or for any communication to occur between Kim and the counselor using a special telephone device for hearing-impaired people. She was extremely angry with and distrustful of the counselor; she was determined to be in charge of how this meeting would be handled.

Kim and the counselor went over the details about Marissa's placement. The question Mrs. Broderick continued to ask was why hadn't she been consulted. The role of Kim's brother-in-law seemed to take on greater complexity as the animosity between him and Mrs. Broderick became apparent.

Mrs. Broderick asked many questions about Glenda and Matt. Kim explained who they were and why she felt good about placing Marissa with them. The fact that they were a "good Christian family" helped Mrs. Broderick feel more comfortable with Kim's choice. A note the counselor had asked Glenda and Matt to write to Mrs. Broderick also helped. The more Mrs. Broderick talked with the counselor, the more it became clear that she, too, felt Kim was not a competent mother. Her biggest concern was losing contact with Marissa. The counselor spoke with her about the possibility of maintaining some contact with the adopting couple. That seemed attractive to Mrs. Broderick and significantly changed the direction of the meeting.

The two-and-a-half-hour meeting ended on a positive note. Mrs. Broderick wanted to meet with Kim, Glenda, Matt, and the counselor. She also wanted Marissa at the meeting, but the counselor felt that would be inappropriate because it might prevent the group from being able to concentrate on the issues that needed to be resolved. It was important that the counselor had taken a strong stand against some of Mrs. Broderick's demands. Not everything could be on her terms, and that needed to be demonstrated. Perhaps the counselor's show of strength, coupled with compassion for each person in this adoption, explained why the meeting was successful.

The counselor informed Matt and Glenda. They were willing to meet with Mrs. Broderick; they actually had little choice. They hadn't planned on having to sell themselves to Grandma as well as to Kim, her sister, and her brother-in-law, but if that was what was necessary, they were willing to do it. The possibility of maintaining some ongoing contact between them and Mrs. Broderick was discussed. Glenda and Matt both indicated they could handle that, as long as the meetings wouldn't be weekly and there was no question of their parental rights.

If the one-night wait to meet Kim and Marissa had seemed long, the two-night wait to meet Mrs. Broderick was agony. In the two months they'd had Marissa, they had become extremely attached to her. She was a very loving child and responded quickly and warmly toward them. They decided how far they would be willing to go to try to make this adoption work. Any differences between them were solved by long talks together. Each knew they would be able to handle some contact and it might even have some advantages. However, they knew at some point they would be unwilling to compromise their entire life in order to make the adoption work. They understood their limits before they went to the meeting. That was critical.

Glenda knew from speaking with the counselor that the primary burden for having the contact and making things go smoothly with Mrs. Broderick would be hers. They talked together about how Matt could help by being supportive of any stress this might put on her.

The meeting began with considerable anxiety, as one might imagine. After lengthy discussions, Glenda and Matt had decided to present themselves just as they were: Whatever happened, happened. They brought pictures of their families and their home, letters of reference, and a friendly, apparently relaxed manner to the meeting. All of these paid off. Mrs. Broderick liked them. She was satisfied with the way Matt and Glenda answered her questions about being able to maintain contact with Marissa. It helped that another meeting was planned, at which she could see Marissa.

While this meeting was most difficult, unforeseen hurdles remained. The first time Mrs. Broderick visited Glenda and Matt at their home was not easy. Nor was the first time Kim came to visit them. Birthday cards signed "Love, Grandma" weren't easy to explain to Glenda's mother, who was also Grandma. But Glenda and Matt were open; they shared their thoughts and concerns, loved each other, and were committed to making this work. They also strongly believed that what they were doing would ultimately be in everyone's best interest, so it was worthwhile to solve the problems now.

After they had Marissa for four months, Mrs. Broderick approached the counselor and said she wanted to talk about the strain she felt her contact generated with Glenda. She couldn't understand why Glenda wasn't comfortable with her referring to Kim as Mother Number 1 and Glenda as Mother Number 2. There was clearly a need to have a meeting between Glenda and Mrs. Broderick with the counselor present.

During that meeting, Glenda beautifully described her feelings about wanting to be a mother for so long. She went through her infertility history and the joy she felt when Kim handed her Marissa. She explained she couldn't be Mother Number 2—she had to be Mother Number 1. Mrs. Broderick could be Grandma Broderick and everyone could handle that, because we are all used to more than one grandmother in a family. But Mother Number 2 just would not do. Mrs. Broderick seemed to understand when it was discussed in this manner. She, too, had something to gain by solving this problem: She wanted to be able to have healthy contacts with Matt and Glenda, and they needed to be honest with her if these contacts were to continue. Everyone agreed on the new labels: Kim would be Kim; Glenda would be Mommy. Glenda assured Mrs. Broderick that contacts could continue and that she appreciated Mrs. Broderick's understanding of how important the mother issue was for her.

Communication had been effective. The compromises had been made. The meeting was a success, and the problem solved.

Summary

Adoption is like a puzzle—you figure out one part at a time. But before you begin, you want to try to view the whole picture. You need to be prepared philosophically before you begin the process, and you want to be sure that you and your partner are going in the same direction. While that direction may take many turns, you need to take those turns together.

Be ready for the exciting moment. Talking together prepares you for the time when someone will call to tell you they might know of a baby for you. Anything this important needs thorough planning, discussion, and understanding. So although you don't know quite what you will do at every step along the way, you need to look at the many questions you may be confronted with as you begin your adoption.

When that phone call comes, the adoption process will enter another phase: concrete planning. You have not yet arrived, but you are now ready to make the necessary arrangements, set up meetings, figure out financial and living arrangements, plan for counseling, and prepare for the delivery and transfer of your baby. This is a working stage, and preparation is crucial if the arrangements are to go well for everyone involved. If you are involved in an interstate adoption, be sure to thoroughly read the section on interstate agreements in Chapter 6.

During the entire process, considerable flexibility and adaptability are required to make adoption a success. This is the way adoption works. You don't really know how all of the details fit together until you are actually into the process. You can make many plans, but nothing will take the place of being responsive to the needs of everyone involved. You can't see the complexity by looking at each individual item that must be dealt with; the drama of adoption is in how it unfolds. It is important to be prepared.

CHAPTER 12

We Have the Baby,
But . . .

FINALLY, YOU HOLD YOUR CHILD in your arms. You take him home. The adoption is complete—or is it? This one moment, packed with so much expectation and anticipation, is difficult to comprehend once you actually reach it. What you have wanted for years is right here with you, and yet you may now find yourself pulling back, concerned about the reality of the moment and worried about your reaction to the arrival of what you hope is *your* child. All the previous plans, appointments, discussions, contacts, paperwork, and meetings have all been moving toward this one goal—finding a child. At last you have one. Now what? The truth is, the time can frequently be more disappointing and scary than exhilarating and fulfilling.

There are several reasons why you can have a sense of letdown after you actually receive your child. Actually, this is a common response even after giving birth, but it is probably even more common in adoptions. If you are still worried about the potential legal issues, you'll have to deal with, you may pull back. If you have become attached to the birth mother, you may worry about her and her response to this birth. If there are other birth relatives, such as a birth grandparent or a birth aunt, who are in the picture, even they can be a source of concern. If you have not had the opportunity to meet the birth father, the potential of his returning to claim the baby is also something that causes you to pull back. All of these anxieties can cause you to slow your emotional commitment to this baby you have wanted so much. Before we discuss the birth family and what is happening with them, it is important to look at what is happening with you and your new baby.

Keeping a Distance

Some people who begin adoption temper their excitement for fear they won't get a baby. They want to cushion any potential disappointment. These people are often the same ones who try to keep a distance even after they have the baby at home. They don't want to commit themselves to love until they are sure they will be able to keep the baby. Keeping a distance may actually cause some people to be turned down by birth parents who want someone who shows excitement.

Besides the increased risk of not being chosen if you take this more reserved stance, it also sets you up to have problems once you have your new child. And what you miss is significant. People who learn to pull back out of fear miss the wonderful excitement of these first days with their new child. Their worries prevent them from bonding with their child but also keep the child from bonding with them. Children, who sense you pulling back, don't reach out to you, either. Letting go allows you to love your child, to experience the fun of this new little person, and to enjoy the special minutes together that these first days and months bring.

No one can say your concerns are unfounded, because obviously there are some valid worries about adopting a new baby. But on the other hand, what will you save by trying to pull back and wait until the process is legally completed? That may take several days or several months, and you and your baby need this personal time together right now; this is the time to remember that most adoptions work just fine. Few birth mothers ask for their baby back. Few birth fathers come to claim their baby. Most adoptions, especially at this stage, continue flawlessly.

Of course, you need to keep the process in perspective: The most important person you need to concentrate on right now is your baby. It isn't as if you can forget about the other people involved or ignore their feelings; birth parents may be having a very difficult time, especially in the weeks right after the baby is born. Being supportive of someone else doesn't hurt your ability to bond with your baby. Fear and trepidation hurt that ability.

No matter how much you might like to ward off the potential loss you might feel if your new baby is reclaimed by the birth mother, you won't succeed. If something goes wrong, you are going to feel very bad for a time. So since you can't prevent that hurt that might occur in a rare instance where a birth mother asks for the baby to be returned, you may as well let your guard down, enjoy this exciting experience, and bond with your baby.

Bonding

But what is bonding all about—how does one go about bonding with a baby? You began bonding even before your baby arrived. When you first began this process and believed you would be a mother or a father, that was the first step of bonding. In some ways, bonding before the arrival of your child was somewhat difficult. You may have had to work a bit to help yourself become psychologically ready for the baby. As you began imagining your life with your new baby or child, as you heard the words of encouragement from your partner, and as you started treating each other as parents, you were taking steps in bonding. And as the birth of your baby approached, by going out to buy clothes, nursery furniture, or even birth announcements, you were preparing yourself to become a parent and *bond*.

While there are differences between adopting and birthing, there are many similarities. When you give birth, there are no guarantees about exactly when the baby will arrive; the closest thing to a guarantee in adoption is your sense that adoptions work and you will find a baby. Your belief in your ability to *make* this happen is what enables you to believe in the reality that you will have a baby. Let yourself enjoy the privilege of becoming ready for your new baby. Believe and get ready. It will help both you and your baby. And even if you try to hold yourself back, you won't be able to do it totally, so let the time of "your pregnancy" be one you can enjoy.

In adopting a newborn, one of the difficult times is at the hospital. We read about the importance of the baby's first hours for bonding. While it can be special to have early times with your baby, bonding is still possible without those hours. You'll simply do it later.

The baby's hospital stay is a time of transition in adoption—transition for everyone. The newborn probably has the biggest transition, from being carried inside the birth mother to living outside her. The birth mother also has to make adjustments from being pregnant to not being pregnant. Then she goes from being a pregnant mother to being a birth mother—someone who had a baby and now is placing it for adoption. She has the most control over what happens in the hospital and how much time you will spend with the new baby. So some of your early bonding depends on your relationship with the birth mother and her wishes.

The hospital is also a time of transition for you, the adoptive parents. The reality of adoption is here and now. You are right there with the baby that is probably going to be yours, but isn't totally yet. You went from not being a parent yesterday to being one today. You feel a little like a mother or a father, though you aren't totally. While you might love to go off and just spend time alone with the baby, you know that the birth mother is still in charge.

Even with a birth mother's ability to control what happens while she is in the hospital, you may be able to spend considerable time with the baby during the hospital stay. Perhaps you were at the delivery; this is not uncommon today in many open adoptions. Some new adoptive fathers even cut the umbilical cord, and depending upon your relationship with the birth mother, you may even be the first one to hold the baby.

Whatever time you spend with the baby in the hospital is more concrete bonding than you've had up to this time. You know the sex of the baby, can contemplate names, and are involved with feeding and changing diapers—each of these brings you closer to the baby.

Perhaps your first meeting with your baby will occur after the birth, in the birth mother's room or the hospital nursery. Before you go to the hospital, you and your birth mother should already have discussed what is expected so that you're confident of what you can or can't do. If you can feel sure enough of the birth mother's feelings so that you can pick up the baby confidently and happily, it will be an important step in the bonding process. One factor that has been studied in bonding is the importance to the mother of the father's response to the new baby.[1] You both have an important role in your first meeting with your new baby.

You need to meet and touch your child as soon as possible and hopefully spend considerable time with him or her. Ideally, you will be in a setting that supports you spending relaxed time with the baby. Obviously, if you can't spend time with the baby at the hospital, you'll have to do it at home. The important thing is that whatever your situation permits, you get time with your new little one.

In many ways, bonding is about establishing relationship. It happens as you have a chance to hold and talk to your baby. It continues with every contact. Bonding is becoming familiar with your baby, both consciously and subconsciously—seeing how he is different from any other child. It happens as you become a mother or a father to him and as others see you in this parental role. The child becomes yours in your eyes and everyone else's.

Bonding is a learned process—it doesn't usually happen immediately. In fact, at times the process can be quite slow. But as the process unfolds, you will grow surer of what is happening. It won't be unusual if you have many concerns and questions as you and your family anxiously wait for the adoption to be finalized:

- Can I be excited about having a new baby?
- Will the change or transfer of this baby really take place?
- What will I do if the birth mother changes her mind?
- Will the agency (facilitator, counselor) be there if I have a problem?
- Should I hold the baby in front of the birth mother if I see her?
- Can I, as the new parent, do a good job of mothering this little one?
- How can I take care of the needs of the birth family and still have time to spend with my baby?

- Is this all there is? Why don't I feel more? Is there something wrong with me?
- What is the next step?

It may help to remember that the birth mother will probably share many of the same concerns and has some additional questions:

- Can I be excited about having a new baby?
- Will the couple think this is a wonderful gift?
- Can I really go through with this adoption?
- Am I a bad person or a bad mother for giving up this baby for adoption?
- Will the agency (facilitator, counselor) be there if I have a problem?
- Should I hold the baby in front of the new mom?
- Now that they have the baby, will they ignore me?
- Will the adopting couple do what they said they would?
- What is the next step?

And, likely:

- Is that all there is? Why don't I feel more? Is there something wrong with me?

With so much emotion packed into this time, each of the participants can easily feel overwhelmed by the process and not know what should happen next or exactly what to do. Much of what happens at the hospital is focused on how to make the transition work in a positive way until you take the baby home. Many of the details will be worked out on the basis of what makes sense at the moment. The bonding that you do with your new baby will get tucked away in between the rest of this process. While it may seem that this child will never truly be yours, things will get better. You will have the opportunity to be the mom and the dad in the near future.

But when you take him home, whether he is two days old or seven years old, you'll become familiar with his toes and ears, his special sounds, his eating schedule, his sleeping schedule. You'll become an expert on your child—a parent.

The day you take your child home is special, a time for the family to savor—alone. One of the things we frequently recommend to new adoptive parents is not to invite the new grandparents or other relatives or friends over for a few days after your new baby arrives home.[2] This may seem selfish, but it isn't—you need this time. If you absolutely can't figure out a way to delay visitors, at least limit the visits for a few days. Although your mother probably knows more about babies than you do, right now, you are the one who needs to become an expert. You have already had someone else be the person who gave birth to your baby; now you don't need someone who tells you how to respond. As the new mom or new dad, you need to figure this out for yourself.

The first days at home, most new parents grope and stumble while they try to figure things out—especially with the first baby. It is a time of discovering and experimenting. Each challenge can be as simple as learning how to hold and feed your baby comfortably. No matter how meaningful or correct someone else's advice is, right now you need to begin thinking of yourself as the mother or father of this new baby. You need to be the one who feeds him, holds him, dresses him, listens for him, touches him, talks to him, tells him how great he is, changes him, worries about him, and learns to *know* him. You need to know his body, his moods, his cry, his babble, and his sleeping patterns.

Play with your baby—this sounds so simple, but it is a great way to bond. Laugh at his funny faces and his unexpected responses from the very earliest days of his life. This is what parenting—what bonding—is all about. Bonding is learning to love your baby and laying the foundation for your baby to love you. Bonding is connecting. Bonding is knowing. Bonding is enjoying.

And bonding doesn't just occur in the beginning of an adoption; it takes place throughout life. It occurs when you see her take her first steps, go to kindergarten, play T-ball, get a haircut, do her homework, enter the science fair, have a phone call from the little boy down the block, do well (or even poorly) on assignments, help with the yard work, offer opinions about clothes, come home later than you want, marry, and start a family. Investing in each stage of her development keeps the bond strong. There is never a time when bonding is finished.

But what if you don't have this feeling of love or connectedness with your baby? Don't worry. Try not to be upset if your new addition is not as comfortable with you as you would like. And even more important, be accepting of yourself if you are not ecstatic about this new child right away. Lots of people fall in love with their new baby gradually. "Bonding is a process not an event that you missed because you weren't there at the baby's birth," says Susan Freivalds of Adoptive Families of America.[3]

Penelope Leach writes about bonding in her book, *Your Baby & Child: From Birth to Age Five:*

> During these first days, don't torment yourself if you do not feel anything for the baby that you can recognize as love. When parents first meet a baby, seconds after birth, recognition can reverberate between them so that all the waiting and the wanting culminate not just in *a* baby but in *this* baby, who seems to come out of the mother's womb and into her arms and heart in a single move. People call this "bonding" and it has been so idealized in recent years that parents to whom it does not happen sometimes fear a basic lack in their relationship with their babies from the very beginning. . . . It is absurd to think that your relationship with your baby might falter or fail because no lightning bolt bonded you together on the delivery table. Love will come but it may take time.[4]

Although she is referring to biological parents, not adoptive parents, bonding, whether sooner or later, can happen for every parent.

BONDING WITH AN OLDER CHILD

The most important way to help an older child—or any child—is to provide a loving and supportive home. He needs to feel physically and emotionally safe and his needs must be met if he is to grow and develop his special qualities. If you provide a good home and encourage him to learn about himself, you'll have a good relationship with him.

In addition to meeting his basic needs, there are some special things to do. You will certainly want to become an expert on these.[5] In many ways, encouraging bonding with an older child is even more important and challenging than with a newborn; with a baby, all your behavior is related to establishing the bond—you are not trying to make up for lost months or years. With an older child (in this case, "older" means any child who is not a newborn), it is sometimes helpful to try to reconstruct some of the ways early bonds are formed. Bonding forms the basis of a child's trust.

Find out as much about his earlier life as possible to make the transition easier for him. What does he eat? (This isn't the time to change his formula or to try to introduce new foods.) Did he sleep in a room by himself or with others? What kind of soap and shampoo did he use? Did he sleep in the dark or with the shades open? Does he awaken quickly or slowly? What kind of games does he like? Have men been a part of his life? What is his favorite book, or what TV shows does he watch? No information is unimportant. Try to keep as much continuity in the initial months as possible to ease his transition.

In adoptions from other countries, too, the need to have as much information as possible is clear. One child who came from a home in Asia had difficulties adjusting at first to her new boisterous family. After seeing this eight-month-old child startle each time they became rather loud, her new family realized that their behavior was a problem. They quieted down to help her adjust, and they saw a rapid change with her.

Parents who adopt older children have a unique issue in seeking to establish a strong attachment with their newly adopted children—the other family. While at times you may wish the other family didn't exist because now the child is yours, this is neither in your child's best interest nor in yours. The new relationship your child establishes with you is not meant to replace the old relationship he had with another family; both relationships should stand side by side.[6] Just because the child may have had difficulties in previous relationships, it doesn't mean you ignore those relationships.

The child needs to have a chance to let go of the previous relationship by grieving. He needs to be able to grieve, even for a family that wasn't good for him or may have done physical or emotional harm to him. Your acceptance of the "other family," whether it is a birth family or a foster family, allows him to begin to trust you. If he can talk with you about that family, you are letting him know that he doesn't need to be afraid of the feelings he has and that you will be there to help.

In an older child adoption, the importance of bonding sometimes is forgotten if everything goes well when the child arrives. These early months, filled with the honeymoon response that new parents frequently have with older children, can be so blissful that adopting parents believe everything will be fine forever. But once this stage is past, a phase of testing begins; then the value of a strong connection with your new child becomes more evident.

With an older child, you will have to find ways to establish a physical bond. There are many ways to have physical contact, such as washing her hair, rubbing lotion on her back, or playing games that involve touching. Try touching her when you speak to her. If she is not comfortable with a lot of physical contact, you may just need to sit close to begin with and work up to putting your hand on her shoulder or taking her hand. When she misbehaves, try holding her tightly, both to stop the behavior and to make the contact. When you speak with her, try having her look at you so that eye contact can help make the connection. Older children have a lot to say, so listening to her is also a significant part of establishing the connection.

Older children will require much more from you to make the connection because many times they have not established a trusting relationship with previous parents. Having multiple parents makes it difficult to trust any single one. So you need to help your child understand and believe you are there for her and will continue to be in the future. But just because you say that doesn't mean she will believe it; trusting takes time. There is no one way to establish trust, but books can be a valuable asset in pointing out alternative ways to approach older adopted children.[7] Patience is another key ingredient.

One of the ways you establish trust is to do what you say you will do with her. If you say you will be home at 5:00 P.M., be there. If you tell her you will pick her up after school, be sure to arrive on time. If you tell her she shouldn't do something, make sure she doesn't do it. Be consistent, be reliable, and be there for her; then the trust and bond will begin to be established.

The difficulty of developing a post-adoption attachment with your older child at times makes the new adopting parents feel guilty.[8] Parents can wonder what they did wrong when frequently the biggest issue is time or something else over which they have little control. If problems occur, seek help with a therapist who is sensitive to adoption and bonding issues. Sometimes a few sessions are enough to help the family get into a better place and allow healing to occur. Certainly if your family is into the silent treatment or primarily yelling, you need to get outside help; this behavior can be destructive to bonding.

There are certain times when a child is most likely to form attachments with others. Once the child has been involved in intense situations (evoking anger, fear, etc.) and the emotion lessens (relaxation), she'll be particularly open to becoming attached or bonded. At the end of temper tantrums, for example, the child relaxes and her barriers to forming attachments are briefly lowered.[9] Emotional times followed by close times can allow the child to attach to the parent.

Another part of helping the child become attached to you and also for you to increase your attachment to the child is by letting the world know of your relationship as a family. Something as simple as introducing him or her as your son or your daughter forms a strong attachment. Let the child see that he is part of your family by involving him in everyday family activities. If the other children have chores, make sure he has chores. If the other children have special days that are celebrated, make sure your new child has a part in these family rituals. Look around for ways to have rituals in your family that include each of the family members. These are fun, but they are also excellent ways to say to each child, "you belong here."

A Parent for Life

You are now the parent of a child. The books to read are about how to parent, not necessarily about how to parent an adopted child. The advice you want (when you ask for any) should be about doing the best job you can to raise your child—not to raise your *adopted* child.

Like bonding, parenting has to be learned. Probably most of parenting is rooted in a vague remembrance of how we were raised, without any clue as to what to do in the early months; few of us receive parenting instructions, even if they would be helpful. We may have directions on how to give the baby a bath or how to do CPR on a baby, but the everyday tasks are figured out as we go along. We may have access to some wonderful books on parenting that will help us greatly, but expertise is something you get with hands-on learning.

The nice thing about learning to parent is that our children are very tolerant of our errors. They love us if we love them. They want to please us. They admire us. They also give us many opportunities to make mistakes and then make up for them. We don't have to be perfect parents. We just need to be parents who try to do a good job. And the more we know and try to do a good job, the better job we will do.

Parenting is the most important job you will ever have. No other relationship will affect a person as much as you will impact your child's life. She may come with a certain genetic background and makeup that you can do very little about. But how you raise her and respond to her will make a difference in the way her genetic history will be used; your parenting will be a part of her forever.

Debates on what counts most, genes or environment, will never end. We know more today of ways our genes affect our physical and mental health, our intelligence, and our attitudes. But does this make your role as mom or dad any less important? Absolutely not. Research also shows that your parenting role determines how much of your child's potential genetic makeup he will use. We know the importance of the first year of the child's life in influencing his potential intellectual growth. We know how the number of words he hears will determine his language skills. We know the stimulation he receives will determine the capacity of his brain. We know his curiosity, self-esteem, independence, empathy, and even his love of reading are determined by what parents do in the early years of a child's life. This baby is a joint project; he comes with potential that needs to be nurtured or it will be lost. His foundation is there from what his birth parents gave him, and now it is up to you.

THE SUPERPARENT TRAP

Having some guilt about not being able to produce a child biologically sometimes carries over into parenting. The parents decide, consciously or unconsciously, that they will be "superparents." It is as if they will make up for their "deficiency" by being the best.

The biggest problem with being a superparent is that it can't be sustained. You can do it for a while, but you can't keep it up. You can try to be the one whose baby is always clean, whose house is always picked up, and whose dinner is always on the table on time. But when something happens to upset this perfection, it can be devastating to the superparent. The baby gets diaper rash—it may make you feel neglectful. The guest arrives when the house isn't clean—it may make you feel you are a failure. Dinner is late or not very good—it may make you feel you have let your partner down. All the while you are being a superparent, it won't make up for not having a biological child. It doesn't make you look better than you really are. And besides, you certainly can't fool yourself.

Let the kind of parent you try to be reflect who you really are. You don't have to prove yourself to be a good parent and you certainly don't have to be a superparent.

Post-Adoption Blues

Some adoptive parents actually go through a period of post-adoption blues. Sometimes it is because of guilt about the sadness of the birth family. At times, you may be worried about the acceptance of your child by the rest of the family or worried about insensitive comments others have made or might make. Some parents are overwhelmed with the new responsibilities of parenting and may experience sleep deprivation or feel ignored by their partner. Others have a resurgence of infertility issues and experience temporary sadness that this child is not connected to them genetically.[10] At times their depression might be work related; perhaps they need to go back to work rather quickly because of a lack of parental leave.

Some of the feelings of sadness stem from the emotional investment you made in the adoption process. It is easy to feel almost let down now that the goal that you have been working for over the years has come to fruition. It is like being in training for the Olympics; there has to be a letdown after the gold medal.

Your sadness, post-adoption blues, or depression is just as real as the postpartum depression you might have after giving birth. It is a time to take care of yourself. Be sure to leave some time for yourself, even though there is a new baby around. Eat well—you need to keep up your energy even though you haven't given birth; you are a parent with a great responsibility. Ask a neighbor to come over for a few minutes, just to give yourself a chance to relax, take a bath, make a phone call, or take a nap. Find a support group. It feels good to get out from time to time, even with a new baby.

Invest in your marriage; no one should feel cast aside. Help each other have a significant role in raising this child from the very beginning of his life. When you are both working toward the same goal, whether in adopting or in parenting, the process can be easier.

What about the Birth Family?

Many would ask why have a section about the birth family in a book that tells people how to find a baby to adopt? You may even be tempted to skip this section, feeling as though it isn't a part of adoption you want to think about. But the birth family is a major part of your adjustment period. We have found that a sensitive response to them is critical in making the adjustment successful. You need to be able to understand what is going on in the birth family.

You are well aware of the emotional toll of adoption for you—now attempt to understand the emotional toll of adoption for the birth family. While you have been going through this process, people have been eager to help you. This same response may not have been given to the birth family. The secrecy with which you may have approached your infertility is probably the closest connection you have to the private grief that the birth family is about to experience.

In Chapter 2 we discussed the underlying feelings of hostility that sometimes come up because the birth parents can do something the adoptive parents can't do—give birth to the child. At the same time, the adoptive parents can do something the birth parents can't do—raise the child. Most adopting parents would be delighted to be pregnant, and most birth parents wish they were not pregnant. But these two come together with a shared goal—to do what is right for the child. The birth family is not on one side while the adoptive family is on the other. No one should be an enemy before the birth of the child, nor after the placement.

Competition for the baby can occur right after the birth. The birth mother may be hesitant about letting go of the child, and the adoptive parents may be too eager to take the child and run. The birth mother may want the hospital time to last while the adoptive parents can hardly wait to leave. Giving birth may leave the biological mother exhausted and sad; meanwhile the adoptive couple may be in the throes of exhilaration. It is easy with these kinds of conflicting feelings to run into problems for lack of sensitivity to the other person's issues. This is a time that you need to be keenly aware of the needs of your birth mother and the rest of the birth family.

While you are very eager to have the baby to yourself, the birth family may be involved with saying good-bye. This may include a birth mother, birth father, birth grandparents, and birth aunts and uncles. You should be aware of their need to seek some closure before the baby leaves the hospital. Remember that while you will have many years with the child, this may be their only opportunity to spend time with him or her.

At the hospital one adopting mother became exasperated with the birth mother and declared it was time to quit paying so much attention to her. The baby was here and it was time for the birth mother to get on with her life. That is quite a lot to ask from someone who has just given birth and is now about to give up her child for adoption. Be sensitive to the needs of the person who is giving you the greatest gift of your life. As she grows, your new child will ask you to tell the story of the hospital time over and over again. Make it a story you can be proud of as you talk about the birth mother and the others from the birth family who were involved in the process.

Sensitivity will be needed when you deal not only with the birth mother but also with the rest of the birth family at the hospital. We cannot stress too strongly that other members of the birth family are affected by this process. You need to be aware of everyone's response. Unfortunately, at the same time as you are trying to begin the connections with your new child, another family is trying to figure out ways to sever connections. Ambivalent feelings about the birth family, which so often exist in adoptive parents, certainly may come up in you at the time the child is born. Right after birth you are especially connected. For one thing, you are connected legally; you have the child who legally belongs to the birth mother and birth father until the relinquishment is obtained. But the far stronger connection should be an emotional one that recognizes the pain the birth family is experiencing.

Jane and Sully were excited about adopting the baby who was born to Erica, whom they had known for six weeks. Erica was very committed to them and they knew it. When she met them, she wasn't planning on telling her mother about the pregnancy or the adoption, but as the time grew closer, she decided she would. Erica's mother showed up at the hospital and was very upset with Erica and with the couple who was planning on "taking" her first grandson. For two days in the hospital, Erica's mother was very hostile toward Jane and Sully. When they saw that she had a lot of influence over what Erica was going to do, they realized they needed to win over Erica's mother. They spent time with her, talked with her, told her of their dreams, spoke of their positive feelings about Erica, introduced her to their parents, who came to visit the baby, and became friends. Without this investment of sensitivity, they might very well have lost this adoption. Erica's mother was an unexpected major factor in this adoption drama, and Jane and Sully were fortunately sensitive to what was happening.

Throughout this book, we have emphasized the lifelong issues of adopting. The place of the birth family in your life is one of those issues. Since these people are going to be in your family for life, you need to understand the role of the birth family now that you have been given a baby.

THE BIRTH MOTHER

The strongest alliance with the birth family has probably been established with the birth mother. If you have been having contact with her, it means that you are involved to some degree in an open adoption; she probably picked you to be the parents of her child.

One of the greatest aspects of openness in adoption is your ability to remain a supporting and caring person toward your birth mother during the pregnancy, at the birth, and even after she has placed a baby with you. When you have established a significant contact with her, it probably won't be easy to turn away from her in her time of need. You need to anticipate this feeling before the baby is born. Plan how you can be supportive of her and still satisfy your need to be with your new baby and your partner.

Many adoptive parents fear the connection the birth mother makes with the baby while she is in the hospital. If she has become attached, you may worry that she won't be able to go ahead with her adoption plan. While this is always a possibility, in many ways this connectedness that she is establishing with the baby will help her as she learns to let go. Birth mothers begin to bond with the baby during the pregnancy, so it isn't something you can avoid completely. Many professionals say that the grieving process the birth mother goes through will be easier if she has physical contact with baby during the hospital stay.[11] It isn't unusual for a birth mother to want mementos from the birth of her baby.

While you obviously have a vested interest in her feeling good about this adoption, you should also have her interests in mind when you attempt to help her through the difficult weeks ahead. You have been involved in her life perhaps for months while you waited for her to deliver the baby. Maybe you even went with her to doctor's appointments or were at the delivery. To some degree, you will be connected with her throughout your life, but the relationship you have while she is physically recuperating is based upon more immediate concerns: This woman, the mother of your child, has just given birth. Where does she go from here? Have you talked with her about her future? Have you discussed how she will feel when she gives the child to you? Can she call and see how the baby is doing? Will you call her and see how she is doing? Even if you have not agreed to have ongoing contact with her after the baby's birth, make sure she is OK following this physically demanding and emotionally laden time. Make sure she has the support she needs.

You may not have to be the support person, but if there is no other, then help her or find someone else who can, perhaps through the agency or through the facilitator you worked with. Help her find a counselor if she needs to talk the adoption over with a professional. Make sure the counselor understands adoption and grief issues so the service will really meet her needs. You wouldn't want to be doing this on your own if you were in her shoes—treat her as you would like to be treated. And know that no matter how much help you provide for her, the one thing she needs from you most is understanding.

The Burkes liked Patty, the birth mother of their newborn daughter, Samantha. They had met Patty three months before the birth; she wasn't at all similar to them, but she had so many wonderful traits that they just liked who she was. She was outgoing, laughed a lot, swore a lot, enjoyed life, and knew she was not ready to be a mother. She picked them because she had not grown up in a stable home and she wanted that for her daughter. She was going to school and supporting herself, but her life was far from settled when she found herself pregnant. She was working as a prostitute—but the Burkes didn't even have problems with that fact. While it was certainly far from their idea of a good life, they also learned a lot about life from her. They spent time with Patty in the hospital, talked with her about what she wanted Samantha to know about her, and discussed the future. Patty knew she wanted to get her life in a better place because she wanted her daughter to meet her some-day, and she wanted Samantha to be proud of her when she did.

The talks about the future were helpful to all of them, but especially to Patty, who needed to focus on the future as much as possible. Throughout the pregnancy she had kept a diary for her unborn daughter. She wanted the child to understand why she had placed her for adoption. The Burkes and Patty talked about when they would share this with Samantha. They all agreed that they would not meet during Samantha's growing years, but they would write to each other and keep up on the changes in their lives. They all cried because of sadness at the change that was going to occur in their relationship; they felt they had really come to know one another. The Burkes paid for several sessions of counseling for Patty before the baby was born, but Patty told them she most wanted counseling after the birth; they agreed to pay for two sessions a month for six months. The Burkes feel Patty will always be a part of their life, not just because of their connection through Samantha but because of the impact she herself has had on their lives. They are proud to have her be a part of their life.

With this kind of positive feeling, the Burkes will be able to share with their new baby daughter much about her birth mother. That is far different from how the Elliotts handled their hospital experience.

Josh and Emily Elliott had gone through years of fertility treatment without success. They met Christie, a checker at a Safeway in a neighboring city, through an adoption attorney the month before she was due to deliver. They paid her regular expenses but were not eager to have a close personal relationship with her. No one had mentioned counseling for Christie to them, nor had anyone suggested they might profit from some counseling for themselves. When they arrived at the hospital, Christie had just delivered a baby girl. Josh and Emily were delighted when they saw the perfect baby Christie was giving them. They stopped by to visit with her briefly, but they found Christie on the verge of tears and were uncomfortable. They wanted to make it better for her, but didn't know how. They couldn't express the gratitude they felt, and many important thank-yous went unsaid.

Even though Christie had to stay a couple of extra days at the hospital because of an infection, they asked to take the baby right away. Christie realized that the time she was in the hospital was the only time she would have with her baby, so she wanted him to stay until she left. Josh and Emily felt she should let go, but they couldn't really do anything about it.

Christie and the Elliotts have agreed to keep in contact with pictures and a letter once a year. But their relationship is far different from that between Patty and the Burkes. While you can't always choose how you will feel about the birth mother, the advantage of having a close and caring relationship is clear; when the Burkes tell their daughter about her birth mother it will be in a very different way than when the Elliotts speak to their daughter. Because this relationship lasts so long—a lifetime—invest in it while you have a chance, so you'll make the absolute most of it.

We have seen beautiful relationships develop between adoptive parents and birth mothers. Birth mothers involved in open adoptions have a very different response than those who place their children with an agency and don't know what is going to happen. Birth mothers who relinquished years ago are impressed with today's opportunities for birth mothers to know about the child they place for adoption.[12]

A BIRTH MOTHER FOR LIFE

Many birth mothers find that leaving the hospital empty-handed is one of the most difficult things they will ever do. To experience both the miracle of birth and the loss of a child at once makes the hospital stay a momentous period for the birth mother, one filled with sorrow, guilt, relief, sadness, happiness, and pain.

The loss of a child through adoption has much in common with the loss of a loved one through death. In the past, birth mothers were told that their sorrow and pain would fade away with time. (Many people even used to believe that birth mothers didn't go through grief—after all, no one had died.) We now know that this doesn't really happen. The intensity of the experience lessens over time, just as the intensity of the grief you feel when someone you love dies lessens. Birth mothers may learn to live with their feelings, and they should surround themselves with people who are sources of support and strength for them, but placing a child for adoption is not something that fades away. Even women who are sure they have done the right thing still have difficulty. This is not an experience one gets over—but it is something that can be healed.

Just as the birth mother went through certain stages when she found out she was pregnant—shock, denial, acceptance, and decision making—she now has to go through the stages of grieving. While each birth mother will grieve at her own pace and in her own way, there are certain feelings that appear to be experienced by most.

For some birth mothers, the emotional response is immediate. They may even fear that they are losing their minds because of the intensity of their feelings, which can cause strong physical reactions. The sense of loss and emptiness may include crying, irritability, numbness, anger at themselves or everyone else, anxiety, depression, and/or physical problems such as headaches, loss of or increase in appetite, sleep problems, aches, or dizziness.

Other birth mothers will be able to set aside the experience for months or for years and then have feelings triggered perhaps by another loss, a death, or a significant change in their life. Learning to mask feeling may cause the woman to be less involved in the joy and pain of life. But the price of trying to hide the pain will be high when her feelings finally come out.

It helps when the birth mother feels that the decision to place the child for adoption was truly hers.[13] When she can acknowledge that this was her own doing she will be ready to begin the healing process. Some birth mothers feel that having made the decision gives them no right to grieve, but that is not true. Each birth mother needs to grieve, and one stage is recognizing her own role and not blaming the situation on anyone else.

There is a public aspect to many kinds of grieving. But for the birth mother grieving for the child she placed for adoption, this kind of communal support is frequently lacking. There are no established rituals to aid her in her grief. There is no funeral. People don't bring gifts or send flowers or letters of condolence. In fact, many people don't even know what has occurred.

Some efforts are being made to help solve this problem. One of the ways to address this is for the birth mother to write a letter to the baby she has placed with you.[14] Others encourage birth mothers to keep journals of their experience that can be given to the child.[15] These are at least an effort to acknowledge the loss a little more publicly.

A further effort is made by certain people who decide to make a ceremony out of changing the baby from one family to another.[16] In one family, Nell, the baby's grandmother, and the birth mother, Jan, wanted to announce that the adoption was taking place. They specifically asked that the adopting parents, the birth father, his parents, and Jan's siblings all attend a ceremony in the hospital. Each member of the birth family gave something special to the baby; each gift contained a note with a wish for what the new baby's life would hold. They each read their notes out loud and gave them to the adoptive couple, and then Jan gave them the best gift of all, their new son. Everyone was very touched by the ceremony, including the hospital staff, who paid careful attention to it.

This sense of public acknowledgment is probably why birth mothers become so attached to presents that are given to them after the birth by the adoptive parents. Adopting parents need to be aware of the impact of these little ways of saying publicly, "Thank you for this wonderful gift." Presents, no matter how small, can have enormous meaning to the birth mother. Flowers are special and let her know there is a reason for joy.

Another suggestion being advocated by some is to celebrate a Birth Mother's Day.[17] With ten million birth mothers in our society and another ten million birth fathers, a Birth Parents' Day might be successful and also help take some of the stigma away from the people who have long been hidden in adoption.

For the rest of their lives, birth mothers will be forced to deal with uncertainty. They will be in crowds and see children that are the age of their child; they'll be overwhelmed with feelings. Baby showers, TV shows, songs, or other people's children can temporarily throw the birth mother off balance. These feelings can come with no warning and may cause great sadness. Dreams and fantasies about the child are likely to be a part of her life, as they are with other losses. When the birth mother learns to adjust to these sudden emotions, she can begin rebuilding her life and her feelings about herself.

In her book, *Saying Goodbye to a Baby: Volume I, The Birthmother's Guide to Loss and Grief in Adoption*, Patricia Roles discusses factors that can block, delay, or prolong mourning:

- Lack of knowledge of the loss by society, family, friends, and professionals
- Lack of expression of intense feelings
- Not having a mental image of the baby as a result of lack of information or not having seen the baby
- Preoccupation with the fantasy of reunion in such a way as to avoid dealing with the loss
- Belief that having a choice takes away the right to grieve

- Self-deprecation and self-blame
- Pressure from others to decide on adoption, which makes it difficult to take responsibility for making a decision
- Lack of support
- Numbing through alcohol or drug abuse
- Maintaining secrecy and not acknowledging the loss to yourself or others[18]

We are great believers in the help that books can provide in practicing roles and understanding what other people are experiencing. Books written from the perspective of the birth mother may present some problems; many currently discuss the dissatisfaction of birth mothers who have been involved in closed, traditional adoptions and whose adoptions occurred in a society exceptionally disapproving of a single woman's pregnancy.

On the other hand, any kind of material from the birth mother's perspective is also refreshing and useful. It is only in recent years that writings by birth mothers have begun to appear, but while there are more of these books than ever before, they may be unlike the adoption with which you are involved. Some will say no children should ever be relinquished, and others will advocate a healthier kind of adoption than we have had in the past. From each there is much to be learned.[19]

As you learn about adoption and its impact on the birth mother and the birth family, you will learn to respect them in a new way. This respect is crucial for you and for your child.

POTENTIAL DIFFICULTIES WITH BIRTH MOTHERS

Just as there are problem adoptive parents, there are problem birth mothers. You should be aware of a few possible difficulties that you can encounter with a birth mother. Fortunately, the problems come up with only a small percentage of birth mothers. That is reassuring as long as it isn't your birth mother.

Before the birth mother has signed relinquishment papers, she is definitely in charge. She can change her mind, say she needs extra time to decide, or ask for more involvement with the child during the growing years than was previously agreed. Even though she has this power, you should never agree to anything you are not comfortable with. If you get involved in illegal acts such as paying for expenses that are not allowed, the adoption can be set aside for fraud. No matter how far along you are in this process, keep it legal. The child is hers legally for now, and you have few rights. Assuming she tells the truth and fraud is not committed, once you go to court you are the legal parent of your child.

Once the birth mother has signed relinquishment papers and the adoption is final, problems with her are rare. The biggest fear that adoptive parents seem to have about the birth mother is that she will show up and tell the child that she is his mother. As more and more adoptive children find out who their birth mothers actually are, that will pose less of a threat. But even if the child does know her identity all along, what will happen if this actually occurs? Probably nothing. Your child will likely just come home and tell you and ask you some questions.

The next greatest fear, and one that is far more serious, is that the birth mother will take your child. But kidnapping by birth mothers is incredibly rare, and the same laws apply to kidnapping by relatives that apply to kidnapping by anyone.

Probably adoptive parents should most fear that the birth mother may become unstable and cause problems in their home. This problem can occur, but again, it's rare. Most birth mothers are stable and want normal homes for their children; the last thing they would want to do is disrupt a child's home. But just as you can marry someone who turns out to be unstable or you can have a sister or father who is that way, it is also possible to have a birth mother whose actions create problems for you. No one can tell you how to handle this kind of problem until it happens. The most reassuring thing we can say is that this does not happen frequently.

THE BIRTH FATHER

Adoptees seldom have many questions about their birth fathers. This may be because the others involved in the adoption see the birth father's role as minor, so the adoptee has few thoughts of him.[20] It may also be that so few adoptive parents know about the birth father that they have less information to share with the child. With records being open in the future to give adult adoptees information on *birth parents*, it is time we recognize the role of the both parents in this process.

Until recently birth fathers were generally ignored in adoptions. But legal rulings in recent years have held that the father of a child who is about to be placed for adoption has the right to be considered as the best home for the child. Rulings about a father's right to be informed about adoption hit the headlines when two adoptions were stopped and the children returned to their birth fathers. Birth fathers are no longer ignored. While these well-publicized cases put fear into adoptive parents across the country, they overshadow the many birth fathers who have needs in adoption but who do not go to court to obtain custody of their children.

It is difficult to say whether birth fathers are by choice uninvolved in adoption or if the process excludes them from participation. Certainly they can complicate the process, and agencies and attorneys working with the birth mothers believe the process is complicated enough without involving birth fathers. In many cases, the birth mother's view of the father as irresponsible and exploitive causes others to ignore him. Some agencies actually reinforce this view by not asking the birth father to get involved in planning for the baby. Other agencies and attorneys allow only token involvement when they ask for his signature on the relinquishment papers. And in many cases, the role of the birth father is deliberately eliminated by birth mothers who provide false or no information about his identity.

We know that the role of the birth father is far less studied than that of the birth mother.[21] But what research has been done indicates that birth fathers want to be involved and not excluded.[22] Unfortunately, the role of the birth father in adoption is currently viewed as exclusively legal, not emotional. But we know that birth fathers have some of the same emotional problems that may confront birth mothers. We also know a birth father can have a significant impact on the decision of the birth mother.[23] Some birth fathers seek reunions with their biological children, as birth mothers do—it is a mistake to assume that a birth father is unconcerned about the child being placed for adoption.

There are as many different kinds of responses to pregnancy for a birth father as there may be for a birth mother. Since he represents half of the genetic pool of the child you want to adopt, it is to your distinct advantage to meet him or to get as much information about him as possible. While this information may not affect whether you will proceed with an adoption, it does affect what you can share with your child.

POTENTIAL DIFFICULTIES WITH BIRTH FATHERS

Many of the problems birth fathers create in adoptions can be solved fairly easily. They are similar to those a birth mother can cause: not signing relinquishment papers, snatching the child, or being unstable. Seldom is the birth father's role considered as threatening to the adoption as that of the birth mother, but there is no question that fathers do have rights to their children.

The biggest problem you might face is the lack of clarity about birth fathers' legal rights. Great diversity of laws govern unwed biological fathers' rights among the states.[24] Some states give the father thirty days after the birth of the child to object to an adoption; after that, consent is implied. Other states go the opposite direction to ensure that the father's rights are considered and he may be given over a year. Even within individual states, confusion exists.[25] And while courts seek to clarify decisions by examining one after another, it is confusing for those who wish to do the right thing but also want to move ahead with an adoption.[26] One of the values of the recent highly publicized cases will probably be an increased effort to clarify birth fathers' rights; however, until we can get consistency within each state, it is highly unlikely we will achieve consistency from one state to another.

Some of the rulings say adoptions should take into consideration the "best interests of the child," and others imply the rights of the father are greater than the rights of the child. Some of the rulings say that once the birth father knows the birth mother is pregnant, he must immediately or very soon begin to participate in emotionally and financially supporting the birth mother if he wants to maintain his parental rights. Others say that if the father is *prevented* from providing support for the birth mother, his rights have been violated; this would include fathers who have not been told of the pregnancy. The courts need time to try to sort out the rights of the birth father, but it is clear that he is no longer viewed as merely a sperm donor.

In most adoptions, the birth father's identity is determined by who the birth mother says is the father of the child. If you are involved in an adoption in which the birth father is considered unknown, you have a problem. You cannot be sure if the birth mother is telling you the truth or if she really doesn't know who he is. If he finds out about the child, he may want to come forward and demand his rights to the child. If that happens in a timely fashion, he is likely to gain custody of the child.

On the other hand, even if she names a birth father you are not necessarily problem free. You can't be positive that she is naming the *real* birth father; if the real one comes forward, he may still have rights.

Some birth mothers refuse to name the birth father, as we have said earlier, you need to decide what you will do in this case. You are not any more vulnerable in this situation than you are if she doesn't tell the truth about his identity; many men do not know of the existence of a child they have fathered—some children have been placed for adoption, some aborted, and others raised by mothers who never told the fathers of their pregnancies.

When the parental rights of the father need to be terminated and he is not able to be located, the court can legally do it. The first step is publishing a legal notice in newspapers that the father might be expected to read, giving him a chance to object to the adoption before it goes to court. Most fathers located will sign relinquishment papers and not object to the proceedings.

If the birth mother is not sure which of several men the father is, you could have legal problems. You can have DNA testing done when the baby is born and learn for sure who the father is or is not. Blood samples can be taken at any local laboratory and sent to a testing center for comparison. For less than five hundred dollars, groups such as DNA Diagnostic Center or Genetica DNA Laboratories (see Appendix F) will do diagnostic testing on the birth mother, the child, and one potential birth father. For each additional person tested it costs approximately two hundred dollars.[27] The results come in about two weeks. The test can exclude with 100 percent accuracy and can be 99 percent firm on who is the father. Obviously the people involved need to consent to being tested.

You may also have difficulties if the birth mother was married at the time the baby was conceived. In these cases, you may need to obtain the consent not only of the man you believe to be the father (the "putative" father), but also of her husband, who is the "legal" father. Sometimes obtaining consent from each of these men causes problems. And, to complicate matters, there may be more than one putative father.

So does the birth father pose problems to couples who are considering adopting? Yes. Should these problems cause someone to reconsider adoption or perhaps to go toward an international adoption? Probably not. Despite the more frequent complications in obtaining his signature on relinquishment papers, most adoptions have only minor problems with the father's consent or involvement in the process. There are over fifty thousand adoptions a year in the United States and only a handful of them wind up in the courts.[28] It is also important to remember that all of these rulings and subsequent laws help society sort out its view of the father's role in the life of a child.

THE BIRTH GRANDPARENTS

Birth grandparents have become a greater issue in recent years. Their importance in making the decision to place a child for adoption is readily acknowledged, especially in situations involving teenagers. But as adoptions become more open, the role of birth grandparents is likely to change.

In many cases, the child placed for adoption is the first grandchild. In many ways, the grandparents' place in adoption has been somewhat like that of the birth father; it was felt that if we ignored them, they'd disappear. And yet a grandparent may have very strong feelings about the child who is being placed.

The grandparents' role in the birth parents' decision is very important. They must be honest about what they will or will not do to raise the child, and many times their firmness will make the decision for the birth parents. But they should be cautious not to make the decision *for* the pregnant woman because that will hinder her ability to heal after the adoption. Finally, birth grandparents need to let out their own feelings and even to have counseling when they need it.[29]

Many birth grandparents have a role in the child's life now that adoptions have become more open. It is not unusual today for them to request pictures of the child, and some birth grandparents even regularly send gifts on special occasions. Not all birth grandparents have this opportunity and some have gone to court to fight for visitation rights.[30] We hope it will not take the courts long to solve these issues.

Where the birth grandparents will fit in your own particular adoption is difficult to say. The problems may be there, just as with birth mothers and birth fathers. But there are also some distinct advantages in the contacts you might have. One children's book about an adoption involving grandparent contact, *Becky's Special Family*, discusses a child sending a letter to her birth grandmother;[31] more books will undoubtedly come along that depict open adoptions involving extended birth family members.

THE BIRTH SIBLINGS

While a significant number of birth mothers do not go on to have other children, most do. Most people acknowledge the possibility of your child having birth siblings only if the siblings already exist. They forget that a child's siblings from his birth family are actually his closest biological relatives. In closed adoptions, you may never learn if there are siblings. As a result, if your child searches when he is older, he may have to adjust not only to meeting a birth mother or a birth father, but also to the fact that he has birth siblings.

Whether you know your child has birth siblings or not, you should assume he does. Somewhere down the line, as your child asks questions about his birth family, make sure that this issue comes up; help him consider siblings as a possibility even though he may not have thought of it himself. In that way, he will be better prepared.

Phil and Lydia had been very open with their daughter, Stacy, about her adoption. While they had no contact with the birth family after the adoption, they all agreed on one person the couple could contact if

Stacy wanted to meet her birth mother. As Stacy grew up, and as she gained the maturity to understand, more and more information was divulged to her. It was clear to Stacy that if she wanted to meet her birth mother when she became a teenager, she could.

When Stacy was seventeen, she decided she wanted to know more about her biological background. Phil and Lydia got in touch with their contact, who set up a meeting with Stacy, her parents, and the birth mother. Stacy was shocked to discover that in the next town she had three younger birth brothers close to her age. She had been ready to have a birth mother and maybe even other parts of a birth family, but she was not ready for three brothers. While she eventually got over the shock and met the rest of the family, it was apparent this could have been handled better if the possibility of siblings had been discussed earlier.

Respecting the Privacy of Both Families

It is unlikely that both families are equally comfortable with openness, but everyone needs to be considered. Sensitivity includes respect for the privacy of both adoptive and birth families.

When Suzy placed her son, Jess, with the Dions she felt she had found a perfect situation. Everyone liked each other, and they were all comfortable being rather open about the process. One of the things that brought them together was that they all liked to ski. Suzy really wanted that for her child, since it had always been an important part of her life growing up in Utah. Suzy married Jeff's father after a couple of years, moved to Sun Valley, and had a son and a daughter. Suzy spoke very openly with people about Jeff, the son she had placed for adoption. She even had his picture on the wall with the other children's. (The Dions had agreed to send pictures each year.)

When Suzy told the Dions about the pictures on the wall, they were very upset. While they were willing to be open about the adoption within the family, they didn't want anyone else to know about the situation. They were worried that someone they might know would visit

Suzy's house sometime, see the picture, and find out about the connection. While this was highly unlikely, it was a possibility.

For Meredith the situation was reversed. She was an exceptionally private person, as were her parents. Her pregnancy was a source of embarrassment to her family because Meredith was well-known, popular, and had just received a scholarship to play soccer at a prestigious university on the East Coast. Everyone in the family wanted this situation kept very quiet while she made plans to place her baby through a local attorney. She took a semester's leave of absence and had the baby quietly.

While Meredith's family was very private about the situation, the birth father's family was very free. They had no hesitation about talking about their plans. They were upset that their family had been excluded from much of the process, so they talked openly about it. As a result, many in their small town knew exactly what was happening. The situation caused considerable pain to Meredith and her family, but there was little they could do to change it. Bitterness between the two families was the end result.

The issue of privacy can come up again many years after an adoption, especially when searches are conducted (see Chapter 15). While this should be discussed as part of the process of adoptions that are being arranged now, the rights of those involved in past adoptions also need to be carefully considered. No one should barge into another's life without being considerate and respectful of his or her current life situation. Most reunions can be arranged without violating the privacy of any person involved. When conflicts arise between the needs of one person and the rights of another, a mediator or counselor should be called in to assist in the process. This does not always happen, and as a result, people can be hurt and upset.

Respect for the privacy of others involved in the adoption, as in Meredith's case, extends to not sharing details about the adoption with people who don't need to know. At times this even includes close friends. Everyone needs to remember that he or she is not the only one involved in the adoption. Even the baby you have just adopted comes with the right to choose when outsiders might learn about the intimate details of his birth history.

Remember that the only way one really figures out the areas of importance for others in the adoption process is to listen. The single most important ingredient in making adoptions successful and healthy for all of the people is listening sensitively.

The Value of Keeping in Touch

Keeping in touch has many benefits for the birth family and the adoptive family. From the point of view of the birth family, knowing the child is doing well and/or being able to see her growth can be helpful in adjusting to the adoption. The continuing growth and development of the birth parents will allow them to change with time; they won't always be young people who didn't have their lives totally together. Even if they were not teenagers when they placed the child for adoption, the many changes in their lives can be relayed to the child.

For the adoptive family, keeping up-to-date on the health history of the birth family is especially important. Staying informed eliminates searching and makes reunions possible when people want them.

Those involved in adoptions where physical contact is maintained will get the same benefits, and the adoptee will know the birth parents. While research is not yet clear on the effects of these exceptionally open relationships, there is no reason to believe they are vastly different from other kinds of families in which more than two parents are involved.

Let adoption stay in your mind for the years to come. Read not just the factual manuals about adoption but also the more philosophical approaches found in books such as *Perspectives on a Grafted Tree,* which contains poems related to adoption written by people from each part of adoption: adoptees, birth parents, adoptive families, and adoption professional; also consider *An Adoptee's Dreams: Poems and Stories.*[32] Poetry has such a gentle approach to saying powerful things. *The Oldest Mommy in the Park* also has some messages for many adoptive parents.[33] Another book, *Adoption Wisdom: A Guide to the Issues and Feelings of Adoption* has comments from each part of the triad on feelings related to secrecy, rejection, infertility, healing, and therapy.[34] *Meditations for Adoptive Parents* has some very peaceful selections covering adoption issues with a more religious approach.[35] And read the children's books written for both you and your child. Their simplicity helps keep the beauty of adoption in perspective.

Continue to learn and update what you know. Adoption changes, and your adoption will involve both the rules and beliefs you began with and new ones that will emerge as your child grows. Adoption and the birth family are part of your life forever.

Summary

Finding a baby to adopt can be stressful. And when the moment finally arrives to hold your child, you are confronted with even more stress, having to take care of the needs of others involved in the adoption. It is easy to wonder when this will stop. Taking care of some of the needs of others will lessen, but being sensitive to all involved in the adoption process is a lifelong issue for you just as it is for them.

It is important during this time to be mindful of the importance of bonding with your new baby. You may not be able to begin as soon as you would like, but when you have the opportunity, remember that this is one of your most important tasks—and a wonderful one. Your baby has a major transition to make; he has to learn how you smell, how you pick him up, what you sound like, and how to become comfortable in his new environment and with his new parents. These issues are important whether he is a newborn or seven years old. Each child bonds at his own rate, and the same is also true for you.

All the time you are involved in this part of adoption, you remain involved in the issues of the birth family. The time immediately following the birth of the baby is not easy for the birth mother and may be difficult for other birth relatives as well. It is important for you to be aware of their need for support and care from you. Don't ignore them as you attempt to concentrate on the baby—there will be time for you and the baby soon enough.

In all of your efforts to find a baby, you should have attempted to learn how to deal with the birth family. Now you need to understand the emotional cost of adoption for them. Without this understanding, you will fail to meet their needs and you may create problems in your adoption. This is a time for understanding and sensitivity to each person.

You have the baby now, but there is so much more. With the birth of a baby, a baby placed with you for adoption, comes a beautiful time filled with love, pain, intensity, emptiness, bonding, loss, transitions, fear, longing, understanding, need, and sharing. There is so much going on that you need to be prepared for the enormity of this experience. It will be a time you will recount to your child many times in the coming years; make it an experience you will want to tell and retell with pride and joy.

CHAPTER 13

Anticipating, Confronting, and Solving Problems

ADOPTION, LIKE MOST EVERYTHING in life, does not come with guarantees. You are not sure if you will find a child to adopt, if the birth mother will choose you, if the adoption will go through, if the child will turn out the way you had hoped, if the child will want to find his or her birth parents, or if the child will love you the way you want to be loved. The unknowns are abundant; but looking directly at them can help you avoid some of the pitfalls that can cause problems.

Problems arise in adoption sometimes inadvertently, sometimes purposefully. Sometimes it is the birth mother who causes the problem; sometimes it is the adopting parents. It may even be just bad timing, slight changes in luck, a grandmother's intervention, the birth mother disliking your friend, or other small details over which you may have no control. But many times you will have the ability to control the course of the adoption by your behavior. Most adoptions can be saved. Compromise alone might solve a problem. Other problems will remain unsolved, and you will have to accept that fact.

Problems, compromise, solutions, and *acceptance* may sound negative. Yet many of these can be handled if we approach adoption openly, honestly, carefully, and knowledgeably. This chapter is meant to provide a realistic opportunity for you to see how you can avoid mistakes others have made.

Risks in Perspective

After having worked in adoption for years, we are extremely reassured about how small the risks are in adoption. When you think about the phenomenal complexity of changing a child's parents and pleasing everyone with the results, it is amazing that adoption works.

The risks change depending on the kind of adoption in which you are involved. In the 1970s measured failure rates for adopting young, nonhandicapped Caucasian children were estimated to be 1.9 percent. Today if you are adopting through an agency an older special-needs child with a history of previous placements, the failure rate can be over 50 percent. With these kinds of numbers, you need to be careful to assess which group a researcher is talking about when she discusses disruptions. Overall disruption or failed adoption rates today are now between 10 and 13 percent.[1]

Most of the stories you hear about "failed adoptions" are about adoptions that never took place because even before the child was placed, someone changed her mind, usually the birth mother. Some people who entered into an agreement one day with a birth mother who changed her mind the next day would say this is a failed adoption. Other people would only call it failed if a child were placed with them for a period of time and then, before the legal relinquishment was irrevocable, the birth mother changed her mind. These are two very different definitions of "failed" adoptions.

Adoptions arranged independently or with the help of an attorney or someone who is not aware of the psychological issues involved have some significant risks. Assuming that one of these adoptions has been arranged and the birth mother has made an arrangement with the adopting parents, the risks of the adoption encountering problems are probably about 25 percent. These situations hit some bumps that cause concern and fear but are usually really no big problem and are quickly resolved by just looking around for ways to make things better for everyone. A smaller group of adoptions get into some kind of significant trouble, and probably half of these problem cases are resolvable and could have been prevented by each party listening more carefully, being more responsive, and not becoming easily alarmed. In a small remaining group, probably about 5 percent, the adoptions need some outside intervention such as therapeutic assistance to aid in communication and assess ways of solving specific problems. A very small percent of troubled adoptions are probably unsalvageable. These are the adoptions that do not succeed; the birth mother or the adopting parents change their minds and the adoption fails. These statistics should be reassuring, especially since most adoptions occur with people who know little about the adopting process.

In the past if the birth mother changed her mind before a placement in an agency adoption, when identities were not exchanged and openness was not part of the process, it would not even be considered to have failed. So when you talk about failed adoptions or adoption disruptions you need to fully define exactly what criteria you are using:

- What was the loss for the people involved (emotional, time, money)?
- Who caused the failure?
- Was an actual placement of a child made before the adoption disrupted?
- How long had the process been going on?
- Was the child a special-needs child?
- How old was the child at the time of placement?
- Was the child placed in a single-parent home?
- Had the child been in a previous placement?
- Was the child placed in a home with people who had been his foster parents?
- How open an adoption was it?
- Was it an independent adoption?
- Was an agency involved?
- Was psychological help given (counseling, etc.)?

The amazing thing about adoptions that get into trouble is that in most cases the clues—the warning signs—were there from the beginning. Seldom do adoptions fail without warning. However, the picture becomes confusing when you realize that many adoptions with warning signs do *not* fail.

No one can tell whether or not you should take the risks of adoption. It may be helpful for you to get someone else to look at your situation with you to see how you can minimize the risks, even if you decide to pursue a risky opportunity. Consult an attorney who does a lot of work in adoptions; speak with a counselor or a therapist who works in adoptions and who understands the psychological issues involved. The advice of someone who knows nothing about adoptions is not helpful. In fact, such a person is likely to tell you most situations are too risky because he doesn't know enough to understand that all adoptions require a risk.

It is important to realize that if an adoption fails, all is not lost. Pain and grief will be there because you've lost something very important. You may even need to get some help to put that loss in perspective and to make certain that it doesn't interfere with your next attempt to adopt. But after you get through that, just as with your infertility, you pick up the pieces and start out again. If you are willing to risk yourself again, you will almost surely find a baby. When you have experienced failure in either arranging an adoption or in actually having a child placed with you for adoption, people will go out of their way to try to help you. It's almost as if you go to the top of the lists.

The Risks of Agency versus Independent Adoption

Some risks may be higher in independent adoptions than in agency arrangements. But for some people, these risks are worthwhile because more people seem to be finding babies independently. Some agencies are now giving support for people in independent adoptions or are providing services very similar to what people seek when adopting on their own. So comparing independent and agency adoptions is impossible unless you do it one agency at a time. It might help to remind yourself that the most difficult to place children with the greatest potential for adoption disruptions are handled by agencies.[2]

Certainly the fact that trained people work in agencies should be an asset as you seek to put an adoption together. In fact, this may be the strongest reason for anyone to consider using an agency rather than adopting independently. Being certain of this training should reassure people who are adopting.

Agencies always conduct home studies prior to placing a child. This should decrease the risks of disrupted adoptions and make agency adoptions more successful in every way. The adopting parents, birth parents, and ultimately the adoptees should be more satisfied with the adoption in an agency than with independent adoptions. That has not been found to be the case.

In an agency adoption, you should assume there is some screening of birth mothers and prospective parents. This should offer some protection from a birth mother not telling the truth; you would expect that trained people would be able to pick up on some things that you might miss—but they don't always.

In agency adoptions, the relinquishment by the birth mother is usually obtained before the child is placed in your home. This will not be true for agencies where there is more openness and placements are made directly from the birth parent to the adoptive parents. When relinquishments are obtained prior to receiving the child, this decreases the chance that the birth mother will change her mind; it also delays early placement of an infant into the adoptive home.

Since adoption agencies investigate backgrounds very thoroughly prior to placing a child, they have an opportunity to match the child's background or potential to that of the adoptive parents. In an independent adoption, your opportunity to have the best child selected for you is not possible. If you hear of a child available through independent adoption, that is likely to be the child you will get. There is little selection or matching.

Identities may be exchanged in some agency adoptions today, but certainly identities will be exchanged in independent adoptions. If the birth mother seeks to regain her child, it is much easier for her if she knows who has the child.

In an agency adoption, most legal work is handled by the agency and you won't necessarily be aware of it. In an independent adoption, an attorney you select will handle your legal work. It is more important for you to have a knowledgeable, competent attorney if you are adopting independently than if you are adopting through an agency.

The potential risk of having an adoption declared null and void is higher in independent adoption than in an agency adoption. Yet this risk is still very slight if the necessary legal procedures are followed. The primary reason this occurs is if the consent-to-adopt forms are not properly signed by the birth parents. Hire a qualified attorney and you should not have to worry.

You should be able to assume that the information an agency has received about potential problems that might affect your child will be told to you. But this has not always been the case. Previously, information was withheld to "protect" the child.[3] For the last twenty years adoption agencies have been told that there should be full disclosure.

Cynthia notes: *As we adopted our first two children from an agency before this law went into effect, I was shocked to learn that we were not likely to have received full disclosure of all the information available about them. Certainly as parents we should have learned whatever was known about our children in order to help them in the best way possible. If learning about problems would have discouraged us from the adoptions, we should have been allowed to decide for ourselves how we would handle that information.*

While laws now mandate full disclosure, even in recent years it has not always taken place. As a result it is not unusual to see such "wrongful" agency adoption cases made much of in the media.[4] The negative publicity generated by such cases will undoubtedly help to put a stop to less than full disclosure. In an independent adoption, you can be fairly sure that you know as much as anyone knows; sometimes you will learn things you don't want to know, just as someone adopting through an agency may learn. In both cases, you make the best possible decision for yourself based on the information you have.

Does this mean the risks in adoption are too great for you to take a chance? Definitely not! We'll say it again: Most adoptions, agency and independent, are successful and proceed without a problem. As the varieties of adoptions increase, there will continue to be difficulty in generalizing about the risks of each kind of adoption. It is more important to understand what factors create higher risk so you can determine the level of risk you can be comfortable with.

What If the Birth Mother Changes Her Mind?

The biggest single risk in independent adoption is that the birth mother will change her mind and ask for her child to be returned. The birth mother who changes her mind in an independent adoption may request the return of the child if she has not signed the relinquishment papers. A similar risk exists with the agencies, but it would be the adoption agency that asks for the return of the child. In an agency adoption, the birth mother's relinquishment of the child is done fairly early, and then the child "belongs" to the agency. In order for a birth mother to regain custody, she must go through the agency.

Sometimes if the birth mother changes her mind after significant bonding between the child and the adoptive family has occurred, and that bonding can be demonstrated in court, an adoption will continue even without the signed relinquishment. If the birth mother has signed the papers, it is more difficult, but still possible, for her to regain custody. Even if she has trouble regaining custody, the amount of identifying data she has about you could cause you great concern. *A birth mother's request for the return of the baby doesn't necessarily mean that she wants the baby back, nor does it mean she will get the baby back.*

While no time is a good time for you to have her change her mind, your alternatives for handling her change of heart depend on when the birth mother makes her request. Obviously the easiest time to have her change her mind, and the time you have the fewest alternatives, is before you actually take the baby home and begin to bond. The longer you have the child, the more difficult it will be to have the birth mother change her mind. However, the longer you have the baby, the less likely she is to change her mind, and the less likely it is she'll be able to get him or her back. Yet it isn't enough to prolong the time you have the child by physically preventing the birth mother from reuniting with the child, even if this is done legally. Baby Jessica is a notorious case in point; since the birth parents asked for the child back early in the process, the mere fact that the DeBoers managed to retain custody for two years did not solve the problem. The DeBoers decided to keep the child and fight even while the birth parents had the legal right to request that the child be returned. (The birth mother did not give the proper identity of the birth father and therefore his rights were denied.[5]) But without a change in the law, the DeBoers had little chance of winning despite the fact that most of the public was on their side.[6] The loss of their prolonged court battle may make significant changes in future adoptions, but it was a high price for those directly involved.

The greatest risk that a birth mother will change her mind comes in at the earliest stages in the adoption process; other key moments are at turning points in the process:

- She is most likely to change her mind after she really begins to show her pregnancy and can feel the movement of the fetus; the baby she is carrying becomes more a reality to her.
- A change of heart can also occur around the time of delivery; the pain and the joy of birth may cause the birth mother to bond with the child so that she is unwilling to proceed with the adoption.
- Doubts may also creep up in the first month after the child's birth; the birth mother may be overwhelmed by loneliness and she may reconsider the adoption.
- She may change her mind if the birth father comes back into the picture and influences her, or if another relative such as a grandmother agrees to help; the birth mother may suddenly feel that she has different options than when she decided to place her child.
- Problems may arise at the time the relinquishment papers are signed; the finalization of the process, legalized and made irreversible, may cause her to reconsider.

Most adoptive couples understand that the birth mother can change her mind any time before the adoption becomes final. No matter when she does, the pain for the adoptive parents may be as strong as when someone loses a baby after giving birth.

Birth mothers or birth fathers who change their minds at the time of the delivery are perhaps rarer in independent adoptions than in agency arrangements. Knowing the adoptive parents seems to decrease the possibility of the birth mother's changing her mind while she is in the hospital. The increased vulnerability of women at the time of birth probably also keeps some birth mothers from changing their minds. Usually, when couples have established a meaningful relationship with the birth mother, their emotional support at this time is so essential to her that she is unlikely to change her mind. Adoptive parents, however, are very fearful at this time; they have anticipated this moment so much that they sometimes imagine the birth mother is more likely to change her mind than is actually the case.

In many situations that involve agencies, the adopting parents may not know if the birth mother is wavering. Though they will not experience this anxiety, they are also missing out on this wonderful period of excitement and closeness with both the birth mother and with the unborn child.

The first few weeks after the baby is born are crucial. Now, for the first time, the birth mother may realize she is alone and the child may become more important in her mind, even though they are separated. Now perhaps she finds she is unable to get through this period; she may ask the adoptive couple to return the baby to her. At this point, the adoptive couple is on weak ground for saying no; they cannot argue that their bonding has been so significant that there would be harm to the child. Legally they would have great difficulty preventing her from taking the baby back. Their position at this point is difficult: They wonder what has changed in the birth mother's life that she now feels she can take the baby back and raise it. What happened to all her feelings about wanting this child to be raised in a two-parent home or with financial security or with a nonworking mother? All of these questions should be discussed openly with her, and they can be, if the proper kind of relationship has developed. You should anticipate this period by getting her to discuss her feelings with a counselor or social worker before she goes into the hospital. Ultimately, if she continues to want her baby, she probably will be able to get him back.

Irene and Phil were confronted with this problem. Three weeks after Paige presented them with a darling baby boy, she called to say she couldn't go through with the adoption. They were shattered. They'd had complete confidence in her. But they knew their options were limited. However, they did ask her to speak with a counselor about this before she made her final decision, and Paige agreed.

The counselor spoke first with Irene and Phil to try to learn exactly where they stood on the issues. Of course, they were extremely upset. They also said that if Paige were going to change her mind, they wanted to know now so that they would not have to go through this a second time. They wanted to keep the baby, but they did not want to live in fear for the next six months because Paige really wasn't sure of what she was doing. They were able to express their anger at Paige for letting them down, but they also felt she needed to do what she felt was right for her.

The counselor then spoke with Paige. Paige was adamant: She wanted the baby back. Her mother had recently reentered the picture and would now be available to care for the baby while Paige worked. Before, Paige had no one to care for the child and her only option had been to go on state aid. The counselor explained that no one was trying to prevent her from taking the baby back, but that Irene and Phil had the right to know why she had changed her mind and to know that the baby would be all right since, at this point, they too had an investment in this baby. After all, they had been involved with Paige and the baby for the last four months, and caring goes both ways. Paige felt that was reasonable, so she was willing to discuss her changed feelings.

No one was trying to change the birth mother's decision; the counselor merely wanted to make sure she had thoroughly weighed the issues involved in taking the baby back and in raising him. The counselor also wanted to make sure that Paige was not just reacting to the normal feelings of loss that accompany the birth of a child being placed for adoption; in that case, she might only need reassurance that these feelings would pass with time. Irene and Phil insisted that they would return the baby only to Paige herself, not an intermediary. They said that the baby came from Paige and that they would now give the baby back only to her. Despite the pain she felt because she liked Irene and Phil, Paige made the arrangements to pick up the baby from them. It was difficult for everyone, but the actual exchange process created an air of reality and finality.

Irene and Phil could have done nothing to prevent this situation.

They had done all the right things and the adoption hadn't worked. Sometimes that happens. The miracle in this example was that Irene and Phil heard the very next day of another woman who wanted them to adopt her child.

In the very early stages, counseling with the birth mother may save a faltering adoption. However, if the birth mother is certain she wants the baby back after she has considered all of the possibilities, the adoptive couple has little alternative but to return the baby.

Remember, when a birth mother asks for the baby back, it is still possible she will change her mind. Often she is still undecided after reclaiming the baby. She may have to experiment with keeping the child before she realizes she may not be able to handle it. But her indecision may be resolved if the adoptive parents get angry and terminate their relationship with her. If you have not lashed out at her, she might still like you and consider you her best alternative if she can't handle the situation. This might not feel good to you, but it might be the way the child is returned to you. It's worth trying; many times it works.

Linda and Tom were very upset when they heard that their birth mother, Janice, wanted her baby back. They tried to persuade her to change her mind, but nothing seemed to make a difference. They had her speak with a counselor, who determined that it was a change in Janice's circumstances that caused her to want the baby back and not unhappiness with anything they had done. She liked Linda and Tom and felt sorry that she was disappointing them. She just had to try to see if she could keep her baby.

Linda and Tom, working with the counselor, decided the best and, in fact, the only choice they had was to give the baby back. They decided they would do it calmly and without anger while trying to convey to Janice that they really wanted the baby. They spoke with Janice about how much the baby had meant to them and wished her the best. They were in no way punitive.

Two months went by before the counselor heard from Janice again. She wasn't succeeding as a parent. Now she wanted Linda and Tom to have the baby. Would the counselor see if they would take the baby back? She said this time she was sure.

Tom and Linda were obviously shocked. Yes, they wanted the baby, but it wasn't an easy decision to make. Their fears that she'd change her mind again and put them through another loss were serious. But this was the only way they were going to have the baby that they felt was theirs. They met with Janice and were reassured by her; now it was her turn to wish them the best as she left and never saw them again.

Undoubtedly, this passing back and forth was not in the child's best interests. But it probably had no greater detrimental effects than being in a foster home waiting to be placed for adoption.

Even if this tolerant method fails, you can console yourself with knowing you've made your best attempt to make the situation work. Then it is time to move on. If a basis of good, healthy communication has been established between you and your partner, you can help each other pull together after a difficult event like this.

While it seems like the end of the world at this point, it isn't. If you have been successful in finding a child once, there is no reason to believe you won't find one again. It is important to heal the wounds, determine what caused the problem, understand your part in the process, and then move ahead. Don't overreact to what has occurred by saying you will never meet another birth mother or that you will never deal with a birth mother who wants to see the baby in the hospital. The reason she changed her mind may be totally unrelated to seeing the baby. Assess what happened and react intelligently. Overreacting causes you to cut off potential avenues of adoption for no real reason except that you have been hurt and are unable to control your anger.

It is rare for a birth mother to reconsider and ask for the return of the child. But long delays in having her sign the relinquishment may allow problems to develop that otherwise might not have occurred. In some states the waiting period is two days. Unfortunately, some states delay this process for many months, sometimes over six months. The most difficult time to have the birth mother ask for the child to be returned is after the child has been with you for several months.

Sheila and Nick had not heard from the birth mother of their son, Michael, in over four months. It was a real shock to hear from the attorney who had arranged the adoption that she was unhappy with them and did not want to proceed. The attorney was equally upset, since he had been involved in the process all along and was certain that nothing could upset the adoption. He had monitored each contact, arranged all meetings, resisted the birth mother's desire to visit the family, and made sure that all calls came through him.

Sheila and Nick were terribly confused, because they felt they had done everything that the birth mother wanted. They decided to try to convince her to leave the child with them. They asked if a therapist who specialized in adoption would speak with her and try to understand the problem. They felt it might help if the birth mother talked with a woman who understood adoption. The therapist spoke with the young woman, and then with her and the attorney together. The birth mother was hesitant at first, but she opened up to the therapist as they shared stories about birth, adoption, and raising adopted children. The birth mother was upset because the adopting couple had had so little to do with her after they received the baby. In fact, she was insulted that they had never invited her to their home. As the therapist listened to her views, it became apparent that the attorney had done just the opposite of what this birth mother had needed. The attorney had become a screening agent, but the birth mother wanted more contact.

The couple were amazed at the birth mother's concerns. They'd had no idea that she wanted to have more contact, and they were not opposed to it as long as she was willing to sign the relinquishment papers. They set up a meeting for the next week at their home.

Then another issue developed; the birth mother did not like the name they had given the child. The birth mother was not Catholic and she didn't like her son having a "Catholic-sounding" name. Again, Nick and Sheila were surprised, since she had said nothing when she first learned what they were going to name him. They decided that adding another name that appealed more to the birth mother was the solution; it would make the adoption easier for her and was a small compromise to make. The birth mother felt much better after another meeting with the adopting couple, and she signed the relinquishment papers then.

Sheila and Nick have no hesitation about meeting her in the future. No one wants these meetings to become monthly occurrences; they are meant simply to help both sides keep in touch and let them know that the others care.

This couple found a way to communicate and compromise with the birth mother to save the adoption. Many times, such intervention may discover the roots of the problem and enable a solution to be found. Those are the happy situations. Other adoptive couples may have to go even further.

Sheila and Nick's case clearly illustrates the importance of who represents you. Whether their job is sending your letters, doing your legal work, or serving as your facilitator or counselor, make sure they do this the way you want it done. In Nick and Sheila's case, the attorney may have been qualified to handle the legal aspects, but he did not have the sensitivity this adoption required.[7] Adoption is still more of a psychological issue than a legal issue.

Another milestone in the adoption process occurs when the adoptive couple has had the child long enough to let bonding occur and there is psychological evidence to prove that it has. Separation can be detrimental to a child if it interrupts bonding at a crucial stage, particularly after the child is about five months old. The court may also consider the child legally abandoned if no contact has occurred between the child and the birth mother or birth father for six months.

Signing or not signing the relinquishment, while usually of critical importance, is not always the deciding factor. Bonding and abandonment are crucial legal issues after you have had the child for more than five or six months.

Fran and Gerald found out about the legal grounds that can support adoptive parents. Gerald was a surgeon who had heard from a colleague about a child soon to be available for adoption. He and his wife, Fran, made the necessary contacts and arranged with the pregnant woman to receive her child two days after he was born. After the birth, they had no contact with the birth mother for six and a half months. When she was finally asked to sign the relinquishment papers, she and the father of the child had resumed their relationship and they wanted the child.

Gerald and Fran were stunned. They'd felt the adoption was secure, and now they didn't know what to do. The agency said they had no choice but to comply with the wishes of the birth mother, since she had not signed the relinquishment papers. Gerald and Fran refused; they decided instead to dispute the birth mother's request. They hired psychological experts who testified that the amount of bonding that had occurred would present significant problems to the child if he were now taken from the only home he had known. The attorney presented the case that, because of no contact with the birth mother for this length of time, the child had been legally abandoned.

The birth parents appeared in court to fight. The judge took time to point out the complexities of taking away the rights of birth parents but admonished them for the several times they had neglected to preserve these rights; she ruled against the birth parents.

Andrea and Arturo had tried for years to become pregnant. After they decided to adopt a child, the answer to their dreams came when Jody saw their ad on a bulletin board at the Laundromat. She made contact with Andrea and Arturo and in the coming months they spent many hours talking as Jody prepared to have the baby. She genuinely loved the couple and they loved her. They were open with her, supportive when her boyfriend caused problems, helped her move, and were always willing to talk. They were wonderful to her and she felt good about giving them a beautiful baby girl. She continued to have contact with them until she moved to another part of the state. Then the phone calls became less frequent.

Nine months passed before any contact came from a social worker. (To us and to others concerned about issues related to bonding, nine months seems like an unreasonably long period of time before a home is evaluated for a placement that has already occurred. If social workers are concerned about protecting the child, a timely visit is essential.) And once the visit occurred, the social worker concluded that Andrea and Arturo were unacceptable. The social worker found that Arturo could be extremely opinionated, and Arturo openly disliked her intrusive questions. The worker objected to several things they were doing with the baby, even though she was healthy, happy, and thriving. She ultimately submitted a negative report on the pending adoption. She asked another social worker to speak with Jody about this negative report.

Jody didn't know what to think when she read the negative things the social worker had written. She couldn't understand why the adoption department was saying these people she liked so well were not good parents. She felt intimidated by the professionals; she thought they should know what they were doing. She felt guilty wondering if she had made a mistake placing her child with Andrea and Arturo.

Fortunately, Andrea and Arturo were not easily intimidated. They contacted Jody and explained how they felt about what was going on. They brought in a psychologist to counsel Jody and to give her another opinion on the quality of their parenting. When the psychologist met with Jody, her confusion became obvious: She liked Andrea and Arturo, but she also wanted to be a good mother by choosing good adoptive parents for her daughter. The important deciding factor for Jody was the relationship that she had already established with Andrea and Arturo. Jody, after careful deliberation, decided to trust her own judgment of Andrea and Arturo. She signed the relinquishment papers.

Whether the social worker felt Andrea and Arturo were adequate parents or not, after nine months and a positive relationship between the birth mother and the adoptive parents, the only reasonable grounds for interrupting this adoption would have been potential harm to the child. Nowhere was there any evidence that the child was being harmed in any way. The adoption department was overruled and the adoption was finalized. To this day, Jody maintains regular contact with Andrea and Arturo and their daughter.

While there are no guarantees in adoption, there are certainly ways to minimize the risks. Persuasion, compromise, and flexibility may change a birth mother's mind if she is considering asking for a child back. If that fails, legal remedies may save the adoption. How far you have to proceed in an arrangement that is in jeopardy is an individual matter based on the facts and merits of your case. Remember, most adoptions go very smoothly; your chances for an uncomplicated adoption are excellent.

What If the Adoptive Parents Are the Problem?

In some cases, the adopting parents do something that causes the adoption to fail. Some would argue that this happens because the couple didn't really want to adopt. There is also the possibility that in their zeal to adopt couples can overlook ways they may sabotage the procedure. No one sets out to make the adoption fail. There are no bad guys and good guys, but there are failures and disappointments. Studying what adoptive couples might have done to make an adoption fail may prevent you from creating your own failure.

One young couple, Ken and Colleen, worked with a birth mother and a birth father for three months. They sent them money every month, since the birth mother was unable to work; nonetheless, they had several concerns about the situation, since it was apparent that the birth mother really wanted to get married, even though the birth father did not. When Ken and Colleen heard about another baby who had just been born, they decided they would take her. They told the first birth parents they were no longer interested in their baby. These birth parents were very upset with Ken and Colleen for pulling out, and they needed to find someone else to take the baby they were willing to place for adoption.

While this makes the couple sound callous, place yourself in their position. They had a chance for an adoption that sounded very secure to them; the first situation they were in was very unsure. They felt they could not turn down a good adoption for one that might or might not work out and about which they had considerable doubts. They told the first birth parents their reasons for choosing the second situation and let them know of an adoption counselor who would help them find another couple to adopt the expected child.

The adoption counselor introduced the young couple to Tom and Patty Gills. Tom and Patty were a very quiet, serious couple. They had a strong desire to adopt and had been interviewed by several potential birth mothers but had never been chosen. Since they were an older couple, they knew that they had to move quickly and that they had fewer choices in adoption. The young birth couple chose the Gills to adopt their baby. The Gills knew that another couple had decided not to continue in this adoption because of the risks, but they decided they wanted to pursue it anyhow. Tom and Patty were responsive to each of the demands of the birth parents. They did everything they could to make the situation positive. They supported this young couple for three months, but the birth mother decided to keep her baby just before she went into the hospital and right after she received a support check from the Gills.

When the birth parents backed out of the adoption, it really didn't come as any great surprise to anyone. The counselor had consistently expressed concern about the birth mother during the process. But even knowing ahead of time that these birth parents might change their minds, Tom and Patty had decided they would take the risk. Yet Patty was particularly distraught when the counselor told her that the couple had decided to marry and keep the baby. No comfort was enough to make the pain go away. The fact that she and Tom had known of the risks did not prevent the pain.

The counselor felt especially sorry for this couple, and as soon as another birth mother, Jane, came to her, she introduced them. The initial meeting was strained because the pain from the previous situation still lingered with both Patty and Tom. Even though it had been five months since their disappointment, they remained guarded. Jane chose them, but only after waiting a long period of time; she felt they were very reserved, but she liked them better than anyone else she had met.

In fact, Jane didn't completely decide to go ahead with the adoption until the day she went into the hospital. When Patty and Tom heard at the last minute that they could have Jane's baby, they had mixed feelings. All the pain of their first encounter came back. They needed to know for sure that Jane would not change her mind. They came to the hospital prepared to make certain.

They were very quiet when they came in to see the baby, who was with Jane and her sister. There were gifts that Jane had purchased for the baby, and there were tears from Jane and her sister. Tom told Jane very firmly that she should be sure not to change her mind. He could have said that in a kind and loving way, but he didn't; he said it in an unmistakably lecturing tone. Jane said nothing, as was her way of dealing with problems, but what Tom had said bothered her immensely. As she saw them walk away from the hospital with the baby, she thought of nothing except this lecture. She felt she had given them the greatest gift she could give them; instead of being forever grateful, Tom had chosen to give her a lecture.

All the way home from the hospital, she was obsessed with what had occurred. Five hours later she couldn't take it; she went to their home and demanded the baby back. Patty and Tom were shocked. They decided they had no choice but to do as she said. They reasoned incorrectly that she had never really intended to give them the baby or that her mother had forced her to take the baby back. They were angry, and their anger made them blind to how they had ruined this adoption. They saw no fault on their side.

The sad part of this story is that Jane felt so traumatized that she was unable to approach adoption again. She kept the baby. Even though she knew it would have been better to place the baby for adoption with a nice family, she didn't have the strength to go through the process again. In many respects, adoption had failed her.

But no one should blame Patty and Tom. They had been wounded before, and they were doing the best they could at this time. Adoption had failed them, too.

Sometimes adopting couples feel they have succeeded as soon as they have made contact with a birth mother. That is certainly not the case. In order for an adoption to succeed, the adopting parents has to continue to treat the birth mother with respect and dignity. At times this may conflict with their impulses. It is very difficult for some couples to understand how a birth mother could place her child for adoption. The unconscious anger of adoptive parents toward the birth mother seems to exist to some extent in all adoptions. This may surface in how they treat the birth mother.

The Mercers wrote to gynecologists throughout the South looking for a woman who might be interested in giving them a baby. Within a month they received a call from a woman who had gotten their letter from the receptionist at her physician's office after her pregnancy had been confirmed. The birth mother, Kirsten, felt they were the answer to her problems, since she knew she could neither marry her boyfriend nor have an abortion. Being a single mother in Tennessee was more than she felt she was able to handle, so she had responded.

The Mercers brought Kirsten out to live with them in California when her pregnancy became noticeable. For the first week, things seemed not great, but OK. By the end of the second week, this bright, perceptive young woman could see major problems developing in her relationship with the couple. They seemed to resent her being there; she felt she was there only to deliver a baby and get out. At first she tried to make the situation work because of the obligation she felt toward them. But as she grew more concerned with the situation, she decided that if she felt this way now, she would never feel comfortable allowing her child to be raised by them.

Kirsten set out to find another couple. That, of course, wasn't difficult, and within a week she found the Rasmussens. After several lengthy phone calls, the new couple agreed to meet her and see if they liked each other. They immediately felt a rapport. They made Kirsten feel important and were concerned about her wishes as well as about the baby she was carrying. She called the Mercers' attorney and explained to him why she would not give them her baby. He was supportive. He told her she would live with this decision her entire life and she needed to choose carefully. The Rasmussens repaid the Mercers for the expense of bringing Kirsten to California, and Kirsten left with the new couple that afternoon. (In most situations where a birth mother changes her mind, there is no effort made to repay the money that has been paid to her. Legally, some states designate money given to a birth mother for her expenses as a gift.)

The Mercers were furious. They wanted to find Kirsten and make her live up to her "obligation"; in fact, as their attorney pointed out to them, she had no obligation. They didn't find her. The Mercers learned that the way they treated Kirsten caused them to lose a baby that could have been theirs. They had forgotten the birth mother and were only concerned about the child she would produce for them.

Phyllis and Rob learned a different lesson about the benefits of treating a birth mother with respect and concern. They had lost their only child in an accident two years before, and adoption was their only way to have more children. Carolyn was a beautiful, intelligent woman and a devout Catholic who would not consider abortion. She had already raised a family when she found herself single and pregnant. For her to have another child at thirty-eight, after already raising four children, seemed out of the question. She was pleased when she met Phyllis and Rob; they seemed ideal, especially because they acted eager to adopt the racially mixed child she was carrying. They were warm and open with her. Carolyn felt very close to them, and arrangements were made for them to adopt her baby. As the weeks went by, emotional support was freely given and a bond grew between them. They grew exceptionally fond of each other.

As the birth drew closer, however, Carolyn began to have second thoughts about placing the baby for adoption. She shared her growing hesitation with Phyllis and Rob, and they encouraged her to do whatever she felt best. Finally she told them she couldn't go through with it; she could not give the baby up. Although she had changed her mind, rather than being angry and unforgiving, they continued to offer her their care and help. They took her to the hospital when the baby was delivered, visited her after the baby was born, and maintained contact.

Six months later, Carolyn, who was serving as a volunteer at a Catholic pregnancy counseling agency, heard about a single pregnant woman who needed a place to stay. Remembering her own time of need, Carolyn took this woman in and helped her when she had nowhere to go. When Carolyn realized the woman was seeking a couple to adopt her baby, she told her about Phyllis and Rob. They all met, and the birth mother could not help but like them after the glowing remarks that Carolyn had made about them. Phyllis and Rob adopted the baby that Carolyn helped them find. Although Carolyn didn't give Phyllis and Rob her baby, their genuine care for her and continued friendship and respect helped them get another.

We discussed a few failing adoptions that were saved by counseling when the birth mother changed her mind. Failure can also occur when the adopting parents are the ones who are changing their minds.

Shauna was about as close to an ideal birth mother as a couple could find. She was bright, beautiful, healthy, college educated, and absolutely sure she was doing the right thing. Her family physician told her about a couple who wanted to adopt; she met them, liked them very much, and arranged to give them her baby. Everyone wanted things to go well, and the plans moved ahead smoothly. The couple agreed to pay for weekly counseling sessions until the birth of the baby and for four sessions afterward.

Shauna entered labor early. That in itself didn't cause any significant problem, but something else did. The baby was born with a severe birth defect: there was a serious problem with his right foot and he had an odd-shaped head. Specialists were called in and the adopting couple waited for answers. When none came, the couple decided this was more than they had bargained for and decided, after considerable soul-searching, not to continue with the adoption.

Shauna was angry and hurt by the rejection. Her counselor assured her that another couple could be found who would want her baby. When that same day she met Lillie and Frank, who were eager to have her baby, she saw the kind of love she felt the little boy needed. Shauna decided to give him to them.

With this quick and happy resolution, Shauna's angry feelings about the first couple decreased. She had been very angry and puzzled about her judgment in selecting the first couple, but now she could accept their decision—even though its effects were felt by all who worked with the baby that day. Nurses argued among themselves as to what they would have done under the same circumstances; some were appalled when the second couple came in and were willing to take this baby without a full diagnosis available. A physician, after examining the baby and presenting the unknowns to the first couple, advised them to make a quick decision and never look back. Shauna knew that several other couples who really wanted a baby had been asked if they wanted this one and decided they did not.

What was the right thing to do? Right or wrong is not clear in situations like these. No one can predict medical problems in an adoption, and unanticipated problems make for difficult decisions. Some problems can be minor and others can be major; they may be no different than what you might have with a biological child of your own. While you can begin an adoption saying you don't want to have a special-needs child, what do you do when the child you are planning to adopt has medical problems? People who adopt are in a unique position to say "Yes, I will take this baby" or "No, I will not take that one." This is a luxury less readily available to biological parents.

Other last-minute issues can also cause problems. Catherine and Juan Lopez were excited about putting an adoption together. They felt their Mexican background was an asset as they searched for a birth mother whose child would be all or partly Mexican; Juan was very proud of his heritage, and it was important for him to have a child with a similar background. Deciding to search in towns with predominantly Mexican American populations, they had a résumé printed in Spanish as well as English and sent it to all of the Spanish surname physicians along the U.S.–Mexico border. Ironically, they found Maria through their next-door neighbor, whose housekeeper knew her.

Already the mother of a three-year-old boy, Maria was having great difficulties financially when Catherine and Juan approached her. She knew how difficult it was just taking care of one son; she was unable to give him the things she felt he needed. Impressed that Juan was successful in his own business and that he felt such a connection to his heritage, Maria decided to give them her baby. Maria liked Catherine and Juan and knew they would be good parents for her baby.

The Lopezes provided a home for Maria and her son with Juan's aunt. This gave Maria an environment where Spanish was spoken and added to her comfort. They also paid her expenses, medical bills, and a little extra. She told them she planned to save some money in order to get herself a good start after the baby was born. Everyone seemed pleased with the arrangement.

Three weeks before the baby was due, Maria asked for an additional ten thousand dollars. Catherine was angry, Juan furious. They felt they had provided well for her and Juan said Maria was attempting to extort money from them. Maria explained that a friend had suggested that since they had so much more than she, they might be willing to give her extra, but she was sorry it made Juan angry. He still felt betrayed and told her to leave. Now Maria didn't know what to do.

Even in Juan's anger, he took the time to call their adoption counselor. He wanted the therapist to find another couple to take the baby.

The counselor tried to discuss resolutions to the situation, but Juan said it was impossible. He indicated they would be leaving town temporarily and wanted Maria out of his aunt's house before they returned. The counselor agreed to help.

After the counselor spoke with Maria, she felt the request for more money had been made out of Maria's ignorance in listening to a misguided friend's suggestion. Convinced that Maria really wanted Catherine and Juan to have the baby, the counselor decided to intervene with Catherine.

It was apparent that Catherine did not want this adoption to fail. The counselor described her evaluation of the situation and how she thought they really ought to reconsider. Perhaps now that Maria knew the limits of their willingness to help, the problem could be solved. The counselor also felt that if they didn't take the baby, Maria would not even place the child, feeling that she should be punished for asking for the money. Catherine asked the counselor to speak again with Juan. After conveying some of the same thoughts to Juan, the counselor asked that all three talk together before making a final decision, even though the level of trust was certainly damaged.

Juan said he would reconsider as long as Maria agreed to certain parameters. These included the length of time she would continue to stay with his aunt; specific guidelines about when she would be given money for living expenses, and how much; her continued counseling; her returning to Mexico as soon as possible after the birth of the child; and a limit to the amount of contact she would have with his family. There was no question—Juan was not going to let his family get hurt a second time.

Maria readily agreed to the guidelines Juan had set forth. She felt extremely sorry for damaging her good relationship with Juan and Catherine. She and the counselor agreed the relationship could be improved in the two months that remained to her in the United States. Maria just needed to show Juan and Catherine that she could be trusted.

The relationship did improve. Perhaps it didn't get back to where it had been, but before Maria left, she felt that Juan and Catherine liked her again. They helped her to get some new clothes and gave her money to fly home to Mexico after she signed the relinquishment papers. They continue to send gifts to her and her son. The birth of their beautiful daughter had helped heal some of the hurt, and the signing of the relinquishment papers had helped reestablish a feeling of trust. That adoption was repaired.

As in this case, money issues frequently cause problems in agreements between birth parents and adoptive parents. Probably one of the causes of these disagreements is exactly the kind of situation in which Maria found herself. Television shows highlight people who pay exorbitant fees to find a child. As some birth mothers go on TV telling of getting large sums for having babies, other birth mothers begin to believe they can ask for anything. These high prices may be true in isolated cases, but they aren't part of the kind of adoptions that we have seen; we know of no one getting huge amounts of money for having a baby. Some women may be receiving more financial help than they have at other times in their lives, but they are not becoming wealthy producing babies.

Some couples change their minds for reasons that might seem unimportant to others. Perhaps they are just looking for an excuse to stop an adoption. Ryan and Celine, for example, came to an adoption facilitator for help finding a baby. They would accept only a Caucasian infant with no problems.

Celine met the facilitator, and reluctantly Ryan went to a second appointment and discussed how he felt about adoption. The facilitator did not see that they were carefully concealing a disagreement. Ryan had three children who were grown and his recent marriage to Celine had precipitated some heated discussions about starting another family. Celine was adamant that a baby was going to be in her life, one way or another. Ryan, who was very generous in most areas of his life, had relented and said she could do what she wanted.

In a relatively short period of time, the facilitator heard of what looked like an ideal situation. She immediately thought about Ryan and Celine, who fit the description of what the birth mother had in mind. Amy, the birth mother, was adamant that she would not name the birth father. He was a family friend and she felt it would cause major problems if his identity were known. She was willing to tell the couple many things about him, but she vowed she would lie about his name to any-one who asked her. For her family, she had made up a simple story about a one-night stand: The man's name was Evan, she never heard from him again, and he was from out of town. Since the facilitator knew Amy would not reveal the man's true identity, she told this to Celine. They discussed this decision and the fact that millions of men probably do not know of children they may have fathered, and they agreed that it wasn't up to Ryan and Celine to solve Amy's issue. Celine knew that if he found out about the baby, he would have grounds for contesting the adoption, but this was not enough to discourage her. She was eager for the facilitator to move ahead. The counselor arranged a meeting be-tween them, and a match was rather easily made.

When Ryan and Celine went to their attorney, the attorney ex-plained to them, as had the facilitator to Celine, that there was a signif-icant risk in the adoption because the father's rights were being denied. Ryan was more impressed hearing this from someone with a legal back-ground than when Celine had told him about her conversation with the facilitator. He said he wanted out. He'd probably wanted out before, but now he had a good reason. He angrily called the facilitator and told her he would report her to the state for unethical practice, and that he would not pay for time she had spent on this adoption. The facilitator calmly told him that he should not pursue any adoption that caused him to be uncomfortable. The process was terminated. Amy felt upset, but she was ready to move on. The next couple benefited from Ryan's decision, and now they have a beautiful six-year-old boy.

How can a couple be sure of the information they receive from a birth mother? They can't. Amy had been very up-front about her deci-sion not to name the birth father. Not all birth mothers will be so hon-est in their dealings.

Certainly the case of Baby Richard clearly demonstrates that if the birth mother does not tell the truth, an adoption can be set aside. In this celebrated case, Baby Richard was returned to the birth father and birth mother. The birth mother, at the time she placed the child, lied to the couple about the identity of the father. She told the birth father that the child had died. When the birth mother and birth father reconciled, she told him the truth about the adoption. He sought to regain custody of the child known as Baby Richard. Because the father's rights had been denied and because he came forward as soon as he learned about the adoption, he was awarded custody. Most birth mothers will tell the truth about birth fathers or will say they don't know who he is. You cannot make someone reveal the identity of the birth father any more than the state can. The possibility that a birth mother may not be telling the truth is a risk you take.

Most couples are far more concerned about other areas where the birth mother may not be telling the truth. Drug and alcohol use, for example, is of far greater concern to most adopting parents than the identity of the birth father. The better you know a birth mother, the more likely you are to be able to judge whether she is telling the truth.

Adoption agreements are fragile contracts between people. Birth parents have their desires, and so do adopting parents. Adoption is a process that touches all of us in many ways, not just in those ways we think are related to adoption. Our strengths and weaknesses, our biases and hurts, our sense of vulnerability and judgment, our past and future—all become part of the adoption. What we receive tends to be what we can handle in life.

What If the Child Is the Problem?

If adoption is complex for birth parents and adoptive parents, imagine how the adopted child must feel. At times the process of adoption is too great for the child to handle and his behavior precipitates problems that may cause the adoption to fail.

We know that adopted children are referred for psychological treatment two to five times more frequently than their nonadopted peers.[8] Various studies have found the frequency of ADHD (Attention Deficit Hyperactivity Disorder) to be two to ten times higher among adoptees than among the nonadopted.[9] Perhaps these statistics reflect adoptive parents' willingness to seek help for psychological problems, or perhaps they show that adopted children genetically come from biological parents who tend to be impulsive or that adopted children are daydreamers, a characteristic of children with ADHD. But these problems, while significant, are usually manageable for most adoptive parents.

When you take the problems that children classified as "normal" can have, and add these to the potential problems experienced by older adoptees or those who have had many different homes, you see that sometimes the enormity of a child's problems may create major difficulties in an adoptive home. Painful and disruptive testing occurs in adoptions where previous attachments have been broken.[10] In fact, estimates on disruption rates for adoptions of children who are older increase as the child's age increases.[11]

Lou and Travis were older when they decided to adopt. They had a good life, but they felt it was one that they would like to share with children. They were very excited about the prospect of having a family when they read in the paper about a sibling group. The fact that these were older children was very appealing to them since both Lou and Travis had wanted to continue working. The fact that the article discussed the "sleep problems" that eight-year-old Elle was having and the "difficulties staying on task" that ten-year-old Austin was having didn't bother them. They felt the children's problems were normal.

They contacted the adoption agency and learned they would have to attend some classes on adopting special-needs children. That was fine as long as they would be considered for these two children. They went through the series of classes as quickly as they could complete them. They then proceeded to focus their attention on adopting Elle and Austin. They heard about the details and the several homes the children had been in and their sympathy went out to them. Certainly they understood these children would have problems, who wouldn't? However, they felt the main problem would be to help these children learn to trust them, since the children had been in foster care for four years.

There was more to it than they had bargained for. Right from the beginning, they realized that the sleep problems were different than they imagined. Elle was up most of the night, every night. She was fearful of the dark, and having a light on only helped briefly. The description of Austin having difficulties staying on task was certainly accurate.

He didn't complete most things he began. He couldn't stay still for an entire story despite his age. His troubles in school were there right from the beginning. While he was not diagnosed as having a disorder, it certainly seemed like a problem to Lou and Travis.

They were overwhelmed. It was a full-time job for each of them just to keep up with these two children. They tried many ways to remedy the problems. They sought help from their doctor, who suggested medication for both Austin and Elle. They were concerned that was too radical. The agency tried to encourage them by saying that the responses were normal for these children and to give it longer to see if things could work out.

Lou became more tired as the weeks went on. Travis was angry a lot of the time. Their marriage began to suffer in ways it never had before. After four months they decided they were not doing anyone a favor by continuing. They were concerned about their relationship and felt they were making no headway with either of the children. They told the agency they did not want to continue with the adoption.

Could this adoption have been saved? We aren't sure. It isn't easy with special-needs children. Trying to have potential adopting parents who want so much to be good parents fully understand the difficulties they may encounter as they take in older children is not an easy task. If you say too much that is negative, you discourage people from adopting or they may anticipate problems that might not occur. Certainly agencies want parents to be realistic because with each disruption everyone suffers. There is no easy answer for these difficult situations.

When you adopt a newborn child, the thought of this child being anything but perfect is difficult to imagine. (This was true of Shauna's adoption described in the previous section.) In truth, most adoptions run rather smoothly until the child enters school. Then problems related to the child's adoption may begin to emerge. Most children handle these problems relatively well and so do their parents, and life goes on. But for some children, even those adopted very early, these problems pose significant challenges.

Maggie was the delight of her parents, Tom and Marge. They had waited a long time for her arrival and felt she was the addition to their family they were looking for. They already had a son, Tim, who was three.

From the earliest days, Maggie was precocious. She talked very early and learned to read before kindergarten. She was curious about everything and her curiosity never diminished. She posed no problem until high school, and then everything broke apart.

She knew very early in life that she had been adopted and that her birth mother was Hispanic. Tom and Marge had always been honest with her about these issues, but now they were confronted with some additional ones. Maggie looked very Hispanic, and people called her names alluding to her background. After a high school assignment on making a family tree, Maggie became upset. She wanted to know more about her background. Tom and Marge had told her all they knew about the adoption and had nothing more to add. Maggie searched the house looking for information. She was openly hostile toward her parents and even her brother. She began to hang around with peers who were constantly in trouble, and her grades began to plunge.

Tom and Marge took her for counseling, but the progress was incredibly slow. She was uncooperative and belligerent. After multiple sessions and when they were about ready to give up, Maggie began to respond to the counselor. It became clear to the counselor that Maggie had some strong identity issues related to her adoption and to her heritage. They began to work on these issues. After an extended period of time, the counselor spoke with Tom and Marge about the possibility of finding Maggie's birth mother. Tom and Marge really weren't sure they could find her, but they did know the approximate area of Mexico where she was from and were willing to try. They told Maggie about their willingness in a family session, and she was pleased.

They wrote to officials in Mexico to try to find out ways to contact this remote area. They were finally able to locate someone in a village who knew Maggie's birth mother but didn't know her whereabouts any longer. Tom and Marge agreed to take Maggie to this area so that at least she could have some idea about her background.

They planned to drive there over spring break. Maggie talked a lot about the trip in the weeks before the time to go, and the more she talked, the better her behavior became; she was like her old self and was getting along better at home and at school. As plans progressed, Maggie became less and less interested in talking about going. Finally, Tom and Marge asked her if she still wanted to go. She hesitated and told them she really didn't think that she was ready to go. They told her it was totally up to her. She decided to wait but kept the door open to go at another time.

For Maggie, her parents' willingness to try to solve the problems she was dealing with made the most difference. Sometimes, being open to solving problems solves them. This doesn't mean Maggie will never have any more identity issues with being adopted or with her Hispanic background, but for now she is doing better.

Adoptive parents may have unrealistic expectations for their adopted children. It is critical for everyone to recognize that the adopted child will be less like the adoptive parents than a child who would have been born to them—but even children born to you are not necessarily like you. Being realistic about your expectations for your adopted children is essential for success. An interesting factor in the success of special-needs adoptions has been that adoptive parents from lower-income families or families of modest education are the most successful with children who have problems; their expectations are more realistic and they are able to be more accepting of the child who has problems than are affluent or well-educated couples.

When a child develops significant problems, the cost can be high for the parents, the child, and the family. Yet most parents who weather this storm would say that they would do it again, even with the most difficult children. The important point to remember is simply that adopted children may have some additional problems and you need to be prepared to deal with them. Most of them are surmountable, but some very few may be so severe that an adoption will disrupt. Even children can create failures in adoption.

What If the System Is at Fault?

Problems aren't always caused by individuals; sometimes it is a problem with the system that makes an adoption fail.[12] Like the people involved, at times the system may be right and at other times it may be wrong.

Jadene was raising two-year-old Kaelin as a single mother. She had divorced when Kaelin was three months old. The father had absolutely no contact and paid no child support; she didn't even know where he was. The last two years had been a struggle. Jadene was unable to earn enough to pay baby-sitters and come out with enough on which to live. She had reluctantly filed for state aid, but she was very unhappy with it and with how her life was moving. She was bright, pretty, ambitious, and wanted to get ahead. After debating and debating, she decided that she wasn't being fair to herself or to her daughter, Kaelin, so she decided to do something about it. She contacted an adoption agency and said she wanted to place her child for adoption. That decision was difficult; she didn't know the process would be even more difficult.

Jadene spent considerable time going through the résumés of people wanting to adopt. Her agency encouraged openness in adoptions, and she would be the one to pick the parents. She finally decided on Carl and Jo Hanks, who seemed perfect. She spoke with them on the phone, and together they agreed to move forward. The agency had her contact an attorney in her state and the process began.

When it was time for Jadene to fill out certain papers, it came out that Kaelin's father was part Native American. Still no one was upset. It just meant the tribe would have to be contacted and permission had to be obtained to place the child for adoption. Actually, Jo was also part Native American; she and Kaelin were each one-thirty-second Native American. Jadene was confident: The Native American parent in her situation had abandoned her and Kaelin. Why should anyone from his distant tribe have anything to say about her plans?

A letter was sent to the tribe requesting permission for the adoption. Two weeks later, a response came, saying that the tribe would not allow the adoption to take place; it wanted the child placed among its members. The attorney said nothing could be done about this. The adoption could not proceed. They could look into other ways of getting Kaelin into Jo and Carl's home, such as foster placement, or even guardianship, but none of those ideas appealed to either Jadene or Jo and Carl.

Everyone was upset, because they all felt stuck—nothing could be done. Jadene kept Kaelin. She knew there was no way she would allow her to be raised on a reservation with possible connections to the birth father who had abandoned them. She is coping with her life, but it is not going the way she had hoped; the question is whether this is the way it should have turned out or not.

Certain laws place restrictions on adoption. Those placing children and those wanting children are forced to deal with the laws that exist. No one doubts birth fathers have rights, but the extent of these rights is confusing and presently being litigated across the country. This confusion places a high risk on some adoptions.

The laws of some states, moreover, say that independent adoption is not allowed. So what happens if a couple in a state that prohibits this kind of adoption hears about a child in another state and wants to give a home to that child? The couple has several choices. They can forgo the adoption, they can try to turn the adoption into an agency arrangement originating in their state, or they can adopt in a third state if it does not require residency to adopt. Most couples who really want a specific child will look into ways to circumvent the law.

As when adult adoptees want their records opened, people are very resourceful when it comes to discovering ways to do what they want to do. It is always important to look at our laws to see if they are protecting people or making people figure out ways to circumvent them. Laws need scrutiny just as adoptions do.

Frauds and Scams

Most professional people involved in adoptions today would say there are more frauds and scams than in years past—in many ways, several of the situations we've already described would fit the definition of a scam. Frequently it is difficult to evaluate whether you are involved in a scam or are simply in a difficult situation.

What's amazing is that there aren't more scams. Most couples are so eager to find a child that they can become easy victims to people trying to get money from them. Many couples unknowingly send financial help to people they haven't met and know nothing about in the hopes of finding a baby. Don't be one of them.

Many times a couple does need advice or an intermediary to regulate the amount of financial help given to a birth mother; once you begin to pay for extra things, it is easy to begin to feel blackmailed, but you are not necessarily victims of fraud.

The Palmers are a good example. They are both physicians, very giving people. They really wanted a baby and were open to many situations. They met Shayna through an intermediary and hired an attorney to handle the legal aspects of their adoption.

Shayna was beautiful and impulsive, as they realized in retrospect. She liked the Palmers and agreed to have them parent her baby. They were excited and readily agreed to pay her living expenses. They were happy to provide even more; one day she called and said she needed a new bed, and as the Palmers wanted the mother of their child to have a comfortable place to sleep, they sent her an extra $600. Two weeks later, she needed some kitchen furniture and pots and pans. Certainly the Palmers wanted her to have those things also, so they sent her an additional $400. Then their intermediary told them they needed to stop doing this and stick with the original financial agreement. They agreed.

The following month, Shayna needed an extra $300 for her telephone bill. It had run especially high because it was just installed, and she had a lot of calls to make in order to keep up her story to her six-year-old son, who didn't know she was going to have another baby in three months. Without checking with their intermediary or their attorney, the Palmers sent the money. When he found out about it, the attorney spoke with the Palmers; they said it was difficult to say no because they didn't want Shayna to be unhappy with them and maybe change her mind. They didn't mind too much helping her in this way. The attorney reminded them of the state law regarding adoption expenses and told them all future money paid to Shayna needed to go through him.

Shayna visited them in their home by the beach the following month. She loved the setting and moaned about the drabness of her own apartment. While she was there, she also complained about her teeth, and the Palmers took her to the dentist. The dentist said she needed some work and the cost would be $1,100. The Palmers felt this was essential and agreed to let her go ahead and have the work done. She also complained about her clothes and they bought her several outfits, to the tune of $350. Finances were clearly out of hand.

Now the demands were coming more frequently, and the Palmers saw that they had created a problem. But since Shayna was due in only one more month, they felt compelled to hang on. Their attorney and their intermediary constantly reminded them about not paying more expenses under any circumstances. Even though the Palmers were feeling taken advantage of, they didn't know how to stop, even with the advice from those working with them. When Shayna contacted the intermediary, he would take a firm stand and said no to some of her demands; Shayna backed down on some of them, but then she would call the couple directly and get the money.

When she asked for $2,000 for a car, they said no. Shayna hinted she had to have this. They told her they'd asked the attorney and he'd said definitely no. She then began to complain about one thing or another. Three weeks before she was due to deliver, she wasn't answering her phone when they called. The Palmers left messages but she didn't return their calls. They continued to call after the due date had passed, and still no word from her. A month after she was due, they finally got hold of her; she said she had found a couple "who were supportive of her and who would give her baby the kind of home she wanted for her child." The Palmers were stunned.

Was this a scam? Did she have *no* intention of placing the baby with the Palmers from the outset? Probably, but it isn't clear. The Palmers' willingness to participate may have made what began as just greed turn into a scam. They learned some important lessons and dealt very differently with their next adoption. Let's hope that the next people Shayna contacted (if there really was a next couple) were clearer with her about the expenses they would pay.

Some adoption scams are evident. One birth mother had five couples supporting her when she went into the hospital to deliver a baby. The sad part is that even when the couples and their attorneys learned of each other, nothing was ever done about prosecuting the birth mother. The need for legal action to be taken in such cases is clear:

When we send strong messages to people who perpetrate scams, those scams will decrease.

No one can be certain that a given situation is not a scam. The deeper into a situation you get, the more difficult it will be to say "enough is enough." Yet that is just what you need to do if things are getting out of hand. If you give in to unrealistic or illegal demands from a birth parent, you make yourself vulnerable to further demands. When you start out, hire an attorney whom you trust, and then do what you should do legally. If that is not enough and there is no justification for doing more when your birth mother insists on it, you may simply have to decide that this is an adoption in which you shouldn't be involved.

Anticipating and Avoiding Problems

So, knowing about some of the problems involved in adoption, how can adoptive parents anticipate and avoid them? There is no way that anyone can tell you how to totally avoid possible problems or scams. But you can take some precautionary measures to decrease your risk:

- Learn and understand about all aspects of adoption, especially legal aspects in your state.
- Be clear on what you will do and what you won't do in an adoption.
- Talk to your partner; keep a balance of views on what is happening.
- If you aren't sure what you are doing or whether you should move ahead, seek help from people working in adoption who have skill at screening clients.
- Make sure that the people who represent you (attorney, psychologist, counselor, social worker, etc.) view adoption the same way you do, so they will really act on your behalf.
- If you feel the birth mother is unstable, move slowly.
- If the adoption discussions with a birth mother focus primarily on money, be very, very cautious.
- Listen carefully to what the birth family is telling you; find out how everyone feels about this adoption: the birth father, the grandmother, the aunts and uncles.

- If you have questions or concerns about what you know about the birth family, find out the answers before you move ahead.
- Treat the birth family with respect and dignity; you hope they will treat you the same way, but that is their issue.
- Never send money to anyone after one initial phone call.
- Don't rely on an attorney to handle the psychological side of your adoption; conversely, don't allow a psychologist, counselor, therapist, or facilitator to handle the legal side.
- Don't become desperate; this can drive you to take chances you shouldn't take.
- Remember that even if an adoption falls through, there is another one out there for you.

Within this framework, there are some additional questions that will help you decide whether to move ahead. These are not issues that should stop an adoption, but you will want to examine them, because they can create problems:

- Can you respect who the birth mother is and accept the ways she is different from you?
- Does your birth mother have some supportive people around her during the pregnancy? Will they be there after the pregnancy? If she doesn't have someone, should you obtain counseling to help her through this process and for a period of time after she has placed the child with you?
- If the birth mother already has a child, is it important to her to have a child of the opposite sex? Would it cause her to change her mind?
- Do her other children know of this pregnancy? How does she intend to handle the issue of adoption with the rest of her family?
- Does she come from a culture in which adoption is rare? Will that make a difference in this adoption?

Adoption is a sensitive issue for everyone involved. There are many reasons why adopting parents might decide not to move ahead on an adoption; the same is true for birth mothers and birth fathers. Some of these reasons are major and others are minor; you may not even know what kinds of things are interfering in your adoption's success:

- Paula and Joe turned down an adoption because the birth mother told them they would need to send her $1,000 right away or her landlord would evict her from her apartment.
- Mary Lou turned down the Myers because they were not religious enough for her.
- Sherrie rejected the Pedersons because she was uncomfortable with their religious background; they were *too* religious for her.
- The Nickersons said no to an adoption because the birth family wanted money to move 2,000 miles to a nicer area.
- After fifteen calls during which the birth mother sounded desperate, the McMillans decided that she was too unstable for them to handle and said no to her.
- The adoption agency took back a child who had been in the Kettels' home because they were having marital problems; the agency felt the child should be in a more stable home.
- Jan was unhappy with her adopting couple, the Millses, because they couldn't tell her how they were going to talk to their adopted child about adoption.
- The Peabodys decided to pull out of an adoption because on three separate occasions the birth mother said she didn't think she could handle placing the child for adoption.
- Nancy and Grant liked Audrey and Bruce Reynolds, and at first decided they wanted them to raise their baby. When they found out that Bruce drank more than they were comfortable with, they selected another couple.
- Frank and Erica decided they weren't interested in Melanie's baby because Melanie wanted to be involved in holidays with their family while the child grew up.
- Dana liked Rob and Jackie until she had a chance to see that Rob really had a temper. She was glad she had picked a couple whom she could meet and spend time with before she placed the baby, or she would never have known this. She pulled out of the adoption and found another couple.
- The Martells said no to one situation because the birth mother had a history of depression in her family and her brother had committed suicide.

- Renee picked Terry and Dean to raise her child very soon after she became pregnant. When she realized how bossy Dean was and that he was growing to dislike her, she changed her mind and kept the baby.

When you hear the story of an adoption that falls through—and you will certainly hear at least one—don't become too alarmed. Most adoptions that fail do so for good reasons. It may actually be that as many fail because of the adopting parents as because of the birth parents. Hold your judgment, and before you question the institution of adoption, remember that in reality most of us will never hear the entire story.

If you find yourself in one situation after another that fails, it will be important for you to consider what you may be doing wrong. Are you the reason things aren't working out? Is it possible that you don't really want to adopt a child? Do you make bad choices for lack of information, and might you need some help from others who view this differently than you do? This doesn't mean that you are to blame—it means you need to look at what is happening.

Some adoptions are not meant to be. Try to make yours work, but if it doesn't, move on. The lessons you learn from one adoption may teach you something about the next, even if you didn't do anything wrong.

Summary

There are risks in any adoption. But considering the positive outcome of most adoptions, the risks are not unreasonable. This is not a time to pretend problems are not possible. Your greatest protection is knowledge. In order to minimize and avoid the risks, understand them; considering potential problems allows you to have a dress rehearsal for your own contemplated adoption.

Your role in the adoption process is critical. Do not view yourself as a passive participant in this process. You are not. Just as you can take control of your life and find a baby to adopt, you can also facilitate the success or failure of your adoption. You are also responsible for the kind of people you hire to help you in this process. If you want them to represent you, be sure you hire people who share your views and who will represent you to the birth family accurately. While finding a birth mother is important, how you deal with her once you have found her is equally important. Pay careful attention to the role you play.

The primary risk facing adoptive parents is that the birth mother may change her mind and ask for the child to be returned. This risk can be diminished by knowing your alternatives, listening carefully to what is being said, and being careful when arranging the adoption. The time at which an adoption begins to fail will likely determine the degree of trauma you will experience; certainly it is more difficult to have a birth mother change her mind after you have the baby than before the baby is born.

Fully knowing your options minimizes your risks and increases your potential opportunities at every stage of adoption. Be knowledgeable, willing to compromise, open to new solutions, and mindful of your own participation in the process; then the chances are overwhelmingly in your favor for experiencing a healthy, happy adoption.

4

ADOPTION FOR LIFE:
A Lifelong Commitment for Everyone

CHAPTER 14

Talking with Your Child about Adoption

IN NO OTHER TIME in the history of adoption has it been so clear that at some point your child will have access to his or her birth records. Even though today few states have opened their adoption records, it is inevitable that they will; and with all the information available on how to search, most people who want to find their birth parents or a birth child will succeed. Your child will want to know about his or her adoption at some point. What will you say to her?

Long before your child considers a search or reunion with his or her birth parents, your honest approach to the adoption becomes important. Actually, honesty should have been a part of your adoption since the beginning stages. Talking with your child in an honest way should be merely an extension of how you have approached adoption all along.

When Do You Start? How?

Don't wait for your child to bring up adoption, and don't assume he has no questions about his adoption if he doesn't bring them up. *Just because your child doesn't mention adoption it doesn't mean he is not interested.*[1] You are in charge of helping your child become comfortable with himself, so *you* bring it up. None of this means you talk about adoption every day. Adoption is a part of your life—it isn't your whole life.

The issues of adoption will be with your child throughout his life. They never go away—they merely ebb and flow. If talking about adoption is not a regular part of growing up, the child is hindered in dealing with the issues he is supposed to handle.[2] Parents who are reluctant to bring up adoption with the child at an early age may be making adoption a bigger problem for their child than it need be.

There are enough negatives a child has to deal with about adoption without her parents adding new ones. If your child feels you believe adoption is a secret, she'll think that means there is something to hide. Help your child be proud of her adoption. Face it squarely so she can, too. If your child can't talk to you about her adoption, think of the many other areas of life she will be forced to avoid discussing with you.

Even the most difficult parts of adoption can be discussed at the right time with your child. It is important to be matter-of-fact and not make judgments, though. Even when sharing negative information you can still point out the positives that came out of the situation. Not all information about adoption needs to be rosy for your child to grow up healthy.[3] Adoptees can handle the negatives as part of life;[4] in fact, your being forthright now will help your child with the realities of searching if and when that time comes.

Talking about adoption is far more than telling the story of your child's adoption. Too frequently we fail to deal with the emotional side of adoption as we focus on what happens as opposed to how it feels.[5] Even though some of the feelings connected with adoption may be painful, they still need to be expressed. Having a chance to talk about sadness allows the child to explore and correct inappropriate ideas. The biggest confusion for children of all ages is that in some way they are responsible for being adopted—they were unlovable and therefore "given away." Talking together allows parents to help the child understand that the birth parents made a choice and the child is not the responsible party.

Before you attempt to shield your child from hurt and to change his misperceptions of the adoption responsibility, you need to first allow his feelings to be expressed. We can be too ready to make the hurt go away by trying to move on to the next subject or pretending that the hurt is no big deal. No matter what his age, the child needs a chance to talk about what he is feeling. If you don't let him talk about it, you may be "solving a problem" that doesn't involve what he is really concerned about. And if you are too quick to correct your child's incorrect ideas, he will not have a chance to talk about them or even fully understand what they are. Listen first, and then slowly help with the healing that needs to occur. Grieving requires that the child first be able to safely explore the issue.

Discussing the adoption begins the first day your new child enters your life, and it continues throughout his or her growing years. Some fundamental ingredients should be found in all of your discussions about adoption:

- *Understand your own views on adoption and on being an adoptive parent.* If you have hesitations about having adopted your child, they will show through to him. If you feel that adoption is an inferior way to have a family, it will show to your family. If you resent your spouse because you had to adopt in order to create a family, it will show to your spouse. Learn to accept your infertility, your adoption, your partner, and yourself.
- *Always tell the truth.* That doesn't mean you have to tell your child the entire story of his adoption, including every little detail, when he is four years old. It does mean you tailor the story to his level of understanding, but still always tell the truth.
- *Every conversation should have more listening than telling.* The only way you know what your child is curious about and the only way you know what she is hearing is by listening.
- *Never talk about adoption when you are angry with your child.* You may regret things said in anger.
- *Remember you are responsible for what you are saying.* In twenty or thirty years the words you use, the tone of your voice, and the honesty of your communication will be remembered by your adult child. When she meets her birth mother, the stories you have told will be validated or rejected. You want to be able to hold your head up high and be proud of how you have presented adoption to your child.
- *Be aware that a history comes with your child.* He has another family. No matter how strongly you wish that this child had been born to

you, he wasn't. That doesn't make you any less a parent, or your parenting any less important. Part of your child's history is a profound loss, a loss of his biological parent(s). Denying your child's history by ignoring or avoiding the subject will make him feel that you can't acknowledge or understand that loss. Instead, you should share information about your child's "other family" freely and openly, making sure you always consider whether those facts are developmentally appropriate for his age level. Sharing your child's history shows him that you respect his interest/curiosity and feelings of loss—and that you respect him. This will also set a pattern that will facilitate better communication in all sorts of areas.

- *Acknowledge that adoption has some grief, loss, and sadness about it for each person.* If you can express your feelings about adoption to your child, even when they aren't positive, you give your child permission to also express some of his feelings, both positive and negative, that he might not otherwise share.

- *Keep in mind that what you tell others about your child and her adoption, you are telling your child.* Telling others about the adoption is optional. Talk with your family about what should be told to strangers, relatives, and friends. Rehearse what you feel is appropriate because you will be asked questions that will shock and amaze you. Your response will be more satisfying for you if you have had time to think out how to respond to these kinds of questions. What you tell others about your child's adoption is also part of what you are telling your child. She hears the conversations, she takes in your responses; these conversations with strangers are another way you communicate about adoption with your child.

- *Plan on talking about adoption throughout your child's life.* The topic of adoption cannot be handled in a one-shot discussion. When you begin to discuss adoption early in life, it is easy to build on the earlier conversations when more difficult ones come up later. You will be prepared. It is a lot like talking about sex—if you begin with a little child, you work your way up to the more difficult conversations gradually.

- *Remember you are a family by adoption, but most important, you are a family.* Your skills as a parent are vastly more important than your skills as an adoptive parent.

Books are a great help in planning discussions about adoption. They help people to talk about adoption generally, not always from a personal focus. They suggest aspects of adoption that might not otherwise be voiced by either parent or by a child who is reluctant to talk about the subject. Sometimes the distance between your own adoption and the situation in a book makes hearing about adoption easier.

One of the very positive changes in adoption in recent years has been the publication of a surprisingly large number of books on the subject for every age level; this gives a tremendous variety of choices for parents. You can go to any bookstore and find a few books on adoption, then to the local library to find some more. Several publishers deal specifically with adoption issues: Tapestry Books and Adoptive Families of America (see Appendix F) have catalogs of books about adoption, infertility, and special-needs families. Perspectives Press (see Appendix F) publishes works related to adoption and infertility. Even books that are aimed beyond a child's specific age level can sometimes be used if you just tell the story in your own words.

The books you read with your child don't have to address your specific situation. You can tell your child his adoption was a little different from the one in the story. Some good books to use with your child at different ages, and for yourself, are listed in Appendix G. Remember that there is great overlap in the age categories and appeal. The books that may be for children are also wonderful ways for you to become comfortable with adoption from the perspective of an adoptee. Read as much as you can, and become an informed parent.

While books are wonderful vehicles for conversations, they aren't meant to take the place of the everyday opportunities to talk about adoption. When someone the family knows is planning on adopting a baby, make sure your child knows about this coming event. When a TV program offers an adoption story or you hear some reference to adoption in a conversation, make sure you comment on it. Stories in the newspaper are more opportunities to discuss adoption. People commenting on the appearance of your family—"Aren't they beautiful!"—gives you a chance to discuss similarities and differences with your child.

Adoption is a wonderful way to have a family. It has far more positives than negatives, and adopting parents can do much to minimize the negatives. Before you adopt, make a conscious decision to be receptive to talking with your child and always to be honest about his adoption. You will be an absolutely essential asset to him as he tries to understand the meaning of adoption in his life.

Your Child in the Early Years

The first years of a child's life are the foundation for becoming a healthy person. Characteristics such as the ability to trust are established in the child's first year of life. Other characteristics such as curiosity, communication skills, respect for authority, and self-control develop in the child's early years.

Even if you are there at the birth of your adopted child, or if you receive the child when he is only a few days old, your child will have to make a life transition. All infants make a transition after birth, but the adopted child has an additional adjustment: He has to adjust to having you as a parent, just as you make an adjustment to being a parent to him. And if the newborn has to make an adjustment, imagine the changes for a child who is months or years into his life before he comes into your home. These first years of your child's life will build the basis of a secure attachment so that he can develop a strong sense of trust.

As your child becomes a toddler, new issues begin to emerge and be articulated. While she seems very young to begin talking about adoption, she isn't. You are laying the foundation for her adoption story. By the time she is three, she should be familiar with the word *adoption*. That doesn't mean she will fully understand the concept, but she will recognize it.

Kendra and Max wanted to be very open with their adopted son, Dalan. They always acknowledged to him that he was adopted. Around the age of three, they began to worry; Dalan told everyone he met that he was adopted. It was one of the first things he talked about, even with total strangers. Kendra and Max were worried that they shouldn't have been talking about adoption with him this early. They were ready to take him for counseling when the references to being adopted stopped. It no longer seemed important to Dalan.

Your child's interest in adoption will ebb and flow, even when he doesn't totally understand the concept. Dalan was becoming familiar with the word, and like many other words that were new to him, he was experimenting with it. When Dalan was about six months older, his favorite story became his adoption story. But that, too, only lasted for a little while.

With a little one, you have unique chances to talk about adoption. When you are watching *Sesame Street* with him, remind him about the book you read called *Susan and Gordon Adopt a Baby*;[6] when you see Mr. Rogers, you might remind her about the book Fred Rogers wrote called *Let's Talk About It: Adoption*.[7] Keep the remarks brief, and certainly don't make them every time. Don't worry that your child doesn't seem to understand a great deal about adoption right away; the concept will begin to take hold a bit more next year. Remember adoption is just one part of who you are as a family.

From three to five years of age the child begins to develop an interest in birth and reproduction. Now he will love to hear the story of his adoption; you need to be prepared to tell it again and again. This is the kind of story a child of this age can relate to, since it is concrete and has lots of details. It is a story he understands, and it is about him. Those two ingredients are important in your communication with your child.

It was during this stage that Patty started telling her daughter her adoption story. She and three-year-old Sandra had developed a routine of reading a book or telling a made-up story every night at bedtime, so Patty was careful to emphasize that this story was true. She explained that when Sandra was born, her birth mother was a young lady who was still in school and living at home with her family. Sandra's birth was a wonderful time for her young mother but even though she loved Sandra very much, taking care of a baby was such an important job that she wasn't able to do it yet. Patty explained that Sandra's birth mother decided that the best thing she could do would be to let older married people who were ready to take care of a baby adopt Sandra. She explained that Sandra's birth mother loved her so much that she was very careful to find the very best place she could for her daughter.

Patty told Sandra that when they met her birth mother they "had to answer lots of questions about how we would take care of you, about our house, about your Gramma and Grandpa—and all about what living with us would be like." Patty told Sandra that the day they met her at the hospital for the first time, they fell in love with this beautiful baby girl, and they knew right away that they "were meant to be together as a family."

Patty always finished the story by saying how "happy-sad" Sandra's birth mother was when they took Sandra home—sad because she loved Sandra so much and was going to miss her, but also happy because she knew Sandra would be well taken care of and have a good life.

Patty reported that when she told this bedtime story, Sandra's questions were ones she already knew the answers to: "Then what happened?" "What happened at the hospital?" "What questions did she ask you?" Just like reading a favorite storybook, Sandra was anticipating what happened next and liked knowing the story by heart. At this age, such repetition fosters comfort and familiarity with the adoption story.

Sandra isn't unusual. Children love the details. Include what you were doing when you received the phone call, how far you drove, how excited you were, what the baby was wearing when you picked him up, how you gave him his name, how you felt when you held him, what it was like to give him his first bottle, and as many other little details that a child would like to hear—after all this is his own story, the story of the beginning of his life.

When a child is around the age of four or five, she begins to grasp concepts about the differences. This may be the time she starts to ask questions if her race is different from yours or from her friends'. It doesn't take racial differences to make children feel different from their parents; if you have blond hair and she has dark hair, she will take note. Children even in these very early years see that their adoptive family is different from others. Sometimes merely talking about the many ways people are different helps put adoption in perspective. Some children will avoid the subject of adoption at this age. While yours may recognize differences, that doesn't mean she likes them. She may not want to hear stories about adoption; if that is the case, it is a good time to just talk about differences rather than about adoption.

Children generally ask a lot of questions at this stage, though, so don't be surprised if many are about adoption. A questioning period like this offers wonderful opportunities to talk about anything; you won't get another chance like this until adolescence; and by then the questions a child asks may be directed more to her friends than to you. So take advantage of this special time.

Be sure that some part of your adoption discussions relates to her birth family. Talking about the birth family in a meaningful way will help her feel you accept this part of her. When she asks about her birth mother (which is not unusual), respond openly about that woman's role in her life. Be sure to let her know of the birth mother's concerns for her well-being when she was relinquished. The most common thing children of this age and through adolescence want to know is what their birth mother looks like; make sure you can answer this first question.[8] It isn't that you need to say a great deal about his birth family, but this discussion lays the foundation for your child's feelings about her birth mother and about relinquishment. If you hear of someone who places a child for adoption, talk about how she must be feeling.

When your little boy has a chance to see a new baby, talk with him about how everyone loves a baby and wants the baby to be protected and to have a family who will love him. You are helping him see that he, too, was and is lovable. When he feels loved, you are beginning the foundation of having a healthy identity; for an adopted child, healthy identity requires incorporating two families into his concept of who he is.[9]

It isn't until your child enters kindergarten that the idea she has another set of parents will be clear in her mind. Most professionals say that a child won't fully understand the concept of adoption until she is around the age of seven; even then, this process won't become suddenly clear. She is still at the sorting and gathering stage with the information. The early school years for her will be a time to try to understand more about her birth family. She may ask many questions about the birth mother and about her own role in the adoption process:

- What does my birth mother look like?
- Do I look like her?
- Do I have brothers or sisters?
- Why did she give me away?
- Didn't she love me?
- What was wrong with me that she didn't want me?
- What did I do that made her want to give me away?

- How did you find me to adopt?
- Is adoption for always?
- If my birth mother gave me away, will you do the same thing?
- Can my birth mother have me back?
- Why can't I see and meet her?
- Does she miss me?

As your child truly begins to understand that there are many different kinds of families, she will also begin to question her bonds with you, her sense of belonging. This can be a scary time for a child, so the importance of your love and support cannot be overestimated. While love is always important, there are certain developmental times when your child needs special attention. This is one of those times.

Don't be surprised if your child becomes confused with these ideas. He will misunderstand some parts of what you tell him and he will ask you questions that you have answered before. As he progresses, make sure you are not telling him merely the facts of his adoption. Tell him also about how you felt during the process. Tell him about your sadness when you found out you couldn't have a baby, if that is the case. Then tell him of the joy when you found his birth mother or when the adoption agency approved your application. Don't worry that he will think he was second choice; tell him your only sadness was for not having a baby, and he made the sadness go away.

Your Child in the Middle Years

Some of the issues that preoccupy a child in the preadolescent and early teenage years are the same as those in the earlier years. All that you told your child in the early years will now be repeated and reinforced with new details. At this age it becomes less important to deal with the facts of adoption than to deal with the feelings involved. Be sure to include lots of opportunities for your child to express her emotions. This is also the age when your child may begin to focus on more threatening issues.

Your child will begin to question the fairness of conceiving a child and then placing him for adoption; what, he may ask, is the right thing to do? We hope you will have presented the birth mother in a compassionate light; now your child might become her champion. "Why didn't someone help her to keep me . . . It wasn't fair that this happened to her and to me." In many ways the questions he will raise about fairness are valid, so sometimes they become a bit more difficult to answer. It is still worthwhile to talk about questions like these that have no clear answers. We all deal with the unfairness of life from time to time. How could you explain poverty or the death of a child in terms of fairness? Adoption is another such subject.

It is usually at this age that the child asks about the birth father. Maybe this question arises because of the child's emerging interest in his or her own sexuality. It helps if you know something about the birth father; if you don't, you can speculate along with your son or daughter. You can say you think the birth father was a bright person, because the birth mother was so smart and she would have been involved only with smart people. You can talk about his appearance by telling what you know about the birth mother's appearance and making guesses what it would have taken for your child to turn out the way he did. Even talking about how sad it is that your child doesn't know what his birth father looks like is a way to help him or her deal with the sense of loss and the rest of the emotional side of adoption. In many ways what you say isn't as important as your willingness to talk about these issues and to share struggles with him.

It is common for the first talk of reunions or searches for the birth parent to take place in the preadolescent years. While this is not when most reunions occur, it is a time that your child wants to know where you are on this issue. She can gauge your feelings by bringing it up and watching your reaction; she is most likely to bring up the subject after hearing about reunions or reading a book about adoptee searches.

As your child grows through adolescence, all of the issues of adoption become focused. Now he is seeking to form an identity. When he was little he wanted to know "Where did I come from?" As an adolescent he wants to know "Who am I?" He has been building to this stage his entire life, but now he truly questions who he is.

While adolescence is naturally a time of separation from parents in many ways, the adopted child may also seek a greater connection to something beyond himself by looking into his biological background.

Many adolescents who experience the natural separation from their parents believe they feel disconnected from their parents because they are adopted. This may cause adolescents to focus more on adoption than in the past and to want to find out about their birth parents. This desire stems from the need for a connection with something.

The adolescent feels isolated—from everyone. Even though adolescents spend considerable time with peers, at times these relationships are rather lonely; the teenager feels others live life better than he does. He is always trying so hard for the acceptance of others that he may have difficulty seeing the many ways he is accepted. Even then, he wonders if they would accept him if they *really* knew him. For the adopted child, his fantasies about the way his family could have been if he hadn't been adopted makes him feel that these normal issues may be more related to his adoption than to his stage of life. In his craving for independence, he is unlikely to take his concerns and worries to his parents, which isolates him further.

The feeling of isolation may be especially strong for children who look entirely different from their adoptive parents. Racial issues begin to emerge more strongly as the child of a race different from that of his adoptive parents may be forced to deal with the prejudices of society in a more complex and hurtful way.

Certainly the developmental changes that are occurring to the adolescent sexually pose some issues for adopting parents. Some adolescent adoptees identify with their birth mother who became pregnant early in life; an adolescent may imagine what her birth mother's life must have been like when she is the same age as when her birth mother gave birth to her. The concern of the adoptive parents may be that their child imitate the behavior of the birth mother and become pregnant, especially if the child is being at all difficult. Open and frank discussions at this time of your child's emerging sexuality are the best way to handle these issues.

It is not unusual to find adoptive parents having issues related to their infertility resurface as they watch their child's emerging sexuality. The pregnancy they wanted so much is now the pregnancy they are trying to prevent in their own daughter's life. Discussions of this kind of topic are easy to initiate if you look about you for stories of teen pregnancies or infertility statistics. Being open about issues related to your own infertility might open up discussion as it did for one young man and his father.

Stanley, an adoptive father of sixteen-year-old Ben, revealed to his son that he had suffered serious bouts of depression shortly after Ben's adoption as an infant. He told Ben that a counselor helped him understand that one of the issues he was struggling with was about his wife's infertility and the idea that he would never have a biological child. Stanley explained to his son that he had never told him about it because, at the same time, he considered Ben's adoption to be the most wonderful experience that had ever happened to him. He didn't want Ben to think the experience had been negative in any way. Stanley found that this conversation opened up freer communication between Ben and him than ever before and that there was a more adult level of trust between them.

Adolescence is not an easy period of time, whether a person is adopted or not. Issues related to loss need to be dealt with again and again. Certainly during this time of the child's life, parents need to help him deal emotionally with the loss he feels from his birth mother's apparent rejection and how it must impact his life. The adoptee's struggles with adoption are more apparent in adolescence than in earlier ages. The issue of loss lies beneath all the struggles.

Your Child in the Adult Years

Establishing careers, making a family, and creating a home dominate the early adult years. Issues of loss may remain significant, though, especially if those issues were not dealt with adequately earlier. As the young adult continues to explore adoption's implications in her own life, she might pursue searching more vigorously. Certainly having children of her own might cause her to think more about her own genetic history. Examining her own role as a parent can make her wonder more about parents who gave birth to her. It isn't surprising that most birth parent searches occur when the adoptee is in his or her thirties.

The young adult needs to have opportunities to discuss her sense of loss with others. The intimacy of adult relationships sometimes gives adult adoptees the chance to explore loss with a new partner in a meaningful way. The nesting and family-building aspects of this early adult period are in some ways a healing process for his not having been part of a genetically connected family.

These early adult years also give the adult adoptee a chance to broaden his sense of identity as he develops his independence and maturity. While many of the commitments and decisions he makes during his twenties may be questioned as he enters his thirties, this period is one of rapid change and deep thinking.

As an adult, the adoptee feels more in control of his life than ever before, yet his genetics remain beyond his control. Research now increasingly shows the profound impact of genetics in a large number of diseases, so the adult may have a heightened interest in his heredity. For the adoptee who lacks information about his biological background, every article on the importance of heredity in illness is a reminder of an important piece of information he lacks.

Marna was twenty-nine before she began to recognize that she had a medical problem. It wasn't anything serious or life threatening but it kept coming back. Kidney infection after kidney infection caused her doctor to question her genetic background. She didn't have the answers. But Marna decided she had a right to those answers, and although she had never had a burning desire to know about her birth parents, she now had that desire to learn about her medical background.

She first approached her parents. They were supportive of her desire to learn more and gave her as much information as they remembered from the discussion they had with the social worker about her background so many years ago. She went to the agency that had placed her for adoption. They knew of no genetic problems; her birth mother had been seventeen and her birth father eighteen. They were, not surprisingly, in good health. The agency had no information on their whereabouts and had not communicated with them since the relinquishment was signed twenty-eight years ago.

She joined a group that helped people locate birth parents. She learned techniques of searching that she vowed to try. The important part of this story is not that she found her birth parents, which she did, but rather the reason for the search; it didn't come from an identity problem but a medical problem. It isn't unusual for the medical problems that may have a genetic basis to begin to emerge at this time in an adult adoptee's life.

This missing part of his medical history takes on added significance as the young adult becomes more mature and can no longer hide behind beliefs in immortality. Recognizing the potential end of life forces him to realize that time precipitates loss. That realization has profound implications as he recognizes the importance of searching soon if he is to have any chance of reconnecting with birth relatives. This desire to search can be further underscored by the potential loss of either adoptive parent. The genetic link with birth parents may never seem more important than it is now.

A Developmental Overview of Adoption

Adoption and child rearing are developmental processes. Understanding adoption from a developmental perspective allows you, the adoptive parent, to lay the foundation for the productive and healthy development of your child.

Raising an adoptee isn't exactly the same as raising a biological child; it has some unique issues that need to be taken into account. The chart that follows will help you keep in mind the adoption issues and be aware of their developmental appropriateness.

Talk to your child throughout his life about adoption; entire books are available to help you.

YOUR GROWING CHILD:
A DEVELOPMENTAL PERSPECTIVE ON ADOPTION
Typical Developmental Characteristics and Adoption Perspectives

---

The First Twelve Months
Time spent with the child is important to establish the bond between parent and child. She is experiencing the world on a physical level, primarily through the senses. Touch, sight, smell,

taste, and sound all are definers of the child's reality. This is also a time when the adopted child is changing her primary caregivers from one set of parents to another. She is adjusting to a new set of experiential responses to the new adults in her life. **Adoption Perspective:** Bring new people into the child's life slowly, having as few caretakers as possible initially. Adoptive parents should not have people around who make them feel less parental than they might already be feeling. "Experts" have a way of making the new parents feel incompetent. Time spent with the child now is critical to the bonding process for both the child and the parents. Whether the adoption has been finalized or not, this is a time to love your child totally.

One Year

This is when the child begins to use words and to name pictures. He has also developed enough memory to remember parents. He can separate and still return to the parents. This is one essential step in the development of security. A child who has felt loved and secure during this first year has learned the basis for trusting others. A child at this age responds best with only a few directions and fewer choices.

Adoption Perspective: This is an important time to use the word *adopted* and familiarize each of the adoptive participants with the word; it is not a good time to emphasize the child's adoption. Books about adoption can be useful because they aren't personal but still use the right words. Try to have a minimal number of caretakers involved in this still unsure stage of developing security. Become comfortable with both his closeness and his independence as he begins to experiment with being briefly away from you.

Two Years

The two-year-old child can now use a few phrases and understand simple directions. This stage is characterized by the phrase "It's mine." The child enjoys playing with others; however, it is usually a side-by-side kind of solitary play. She has mixed feelings about her emerging independence, which is evident in her no's and even in her expressions of anger. If she has been firmly attached to her mother, she can begin to separate with greater ease. Fears may begin to emerge at this age.

Adoption Perspective: This is a perfect time to emphasize "our family" and "You're our child." A child who looks different from her parents will begin to draw attention from strangers. Parents now begin to see their child as different from themselves, which may cause her concern. Acceptance of the difference is important for the child to feel the adoption is not something bad. If other siblings arrive, they may present opportunities for talking about adoption.

Three Years

Now the prominent impulses are of delightful creativity. The child is usually happy and friendly. He will begin to have a desire to please others and to enjoy praise. (Almost all ages enjoy praise.) Cooperative attitudes are taking shape but with a clearly self-centered base. The child now knows his or her own sex and age. Imaginary companions can surface at this stage. Your child will love to be read to or hear stories. Children of this age have endless questions.

Adoption Perspective: The child's interest in birth gives some opportunities to talk about adoption and difference. Books are again ideal—about adoptions, differences, and where babies come from. Be sure to explain that all children are born and some are adopted. Your child will ask many questions, and adoption takes on a different dimension for adopting parents. Seeing pregnant women may elicit questions about his own birth or about his birth mother; this helps begin important discussions.

Four Years

The "why" questions surface, and the child may become dogmatic as well as self-assertive and argumentative. At this age she is both active and curious. Her muscles and mind know no bounds. She loves to tell experiences and to sing songs. She is beginning to understand sex differences and still loves imaginative play, which leads to fabrication, lies, and rationalizations. At this age, she is prone to unreasonable fears of the dark, dogs, death, and even loss of parents.

Adoption Perspectives: Now that the child is relating more to her peers, adoption attitudes from the outside world begin to influence her. Preschool activities related to the family must be arranged to fit the adoptive family. Personalizing the concept of adoption becomes important during this time: Adoption songs on tape or books that tell about birth and adoption are fun and educational for her. To help deal with her fears, be reassuring about the permanency in her adoption.

Five Years

This is a quieter time of life; the child is not as restless and can concentrate. He likes to please and can be a "little angel." He imitates grown-ups and enjoys close contact with parents. The child expresses great fondness for the primary caregiver but also has room in his affections for secondary caregivers and may obey them more. There's time to sort out who is in family and where he fits.

Adoption Perspective: The child enjoys playing house, and parents may even hear him use the term *adoption*. The idea of family members not looking like each other is likely to be more significant as differences are recognized. This may not be the best time to talk much about birth parents because the child is struggling to understand where he fits. Parents can become threatened when they see their child responding to others.

Six Years

The sixth year is a highly emotional time in the child's life. Active, noisy, and boisterous play are usual for a child of six. She can be very explosive and tensions often overflow. She wants her way and has difficulty losing to her peers. When instructed to cooperate with the family activities, it is not at all unusual for this child to dawdle. She is very sensitive to the actions and attitudes of the primary caregivers. (This is true even when it doesn't appear that way.)

Adoption Perspective: Stories are exceptionally important at this point in the child's development; they offer a way of releasing some emotion the child is experiencing. Use stories showing different families so that adoption is not overemphasized. Stories of stepfamilies or single parents and stories presenting normal emotional problems of children are appropriate. The child now begins to understand the concept of adoption. If the birth mother is involved in her life, the child may become aware she is a significant person.

Seven Years

The average child of seven is slow-moving and easily distracted. He forgets easily and is not prompt to respond to directions from most people. This child is serious and thoughtful. It is a time of easy embarrassment and tears during any kind of criticism. His emotional response is less aggressive and resistant; he is likely even to leave a situation when he is angry.

Adoption Perspective: Most children of this age have the intellectual ability to begin to truly understand the concept of adoption. Parents may find themselves retelling the stories they thought their child already knew about adoption. Acknowledging differences in the family will help him see adoption is OK. This is the period when the child may be teased about his adoption. Cruel comments about "Your mother didn't want you and gave you away" are not unusual. For the first time, the issue of loss becomes a major part of his life. This is the stage when he needs to understand that adoption is not the underlying cause of his sensitivity.

Eight Years

Curiosity, as well as humor, predominate at this age. Impatience with herself is typical of the eight-year-old child. She will often express affection with strong verbal or physical action. She now has "best friends" and frequently "enemies." She can be grateful, is learning to have some perspective in life, and easily talks about adoption. She now understands the family unit and the roles each member plays.

Adoption Perspective: This child appreciates unusual and humorous family situations. Yet it is also easy for her to become punitive toward parents and their vulnerabilities, including infertility and adoption. Although she can be warm and loving at this stage, she can also lash out toward others and in anger say things like "You are not my real mother." Even when adoption is not an obvious issue, it probably is internally because she wants to be the same as her peers.

Nine Years

Quick emotional shifts characterize the child of this age. While he enjoys both compliments and humor, he can be very critical of adult commands. Peer opinion begins to become important, and therefore he enjoys teams and clubs. The criticism of peers can be especially difficult for him. He often needs detailed directions and numerous reminders. He is becoming self-conscious about exposing his body.

Adoption Perspective: This child may attribute his desire for and perceived lack of acceptance to being adopted and needs to understand that seeking acceptance is part of growing up. Books that help him view what is happening as normal will be important to use, because he feels different and doesn't want to be. It is important for parents to accept his feelings without being defensive. Be available to talk, but don't overdo it.

Ten to Twelve Years

The time between ten and twelve is often tempestuous, marked by quick mood swings and changes in appearance and voice. Hormones are beginning to change the child physically, mentally, and emotionally. Relationships with peers continue to be important to her and at times can cause parents to seem unimportant. Crushes, especially for young girls, can precipitate tumultuous times. Her emerging sexuality can cause concern for everyone. This is the beginning of new attitudes about herself. **Adoption Perspective:** Bodily changes frequently cause the adopted child to become extremely sensitive to her own adoption. Beginning of menstruation makes the young adopted woman recognize her probable closeness in age to the woman who gave birth to her; her emerging sexual maturity may generate interest in searching. (Interest doesn't mean she is ready to search.) Communication needs to be open and supportive now. Cultural and racial issues also begin to emerge strongly at this age. The child may want greater control now of who learns of her adoption.

Adolescence

The individual is now looking for his own sense of identity. This search frequently causes him to identify with a variety of people and groups. He responds with strong likes and dislikes. Mentally he is now able to deal with the highest level of abstractions and questions like "What is nothing?" Interest in heredity and origins becomes strong, and the teenager often experiments with roles. Sexual identification with the birth parents can be an issue. Few parents will say this is an easy time.

Adoption Perspective: The adopted child may find great frustration during this period because some of his identity base is hidden. He is likely to search files and drawers for information about his birth, seldom with his parents' knowledge. Maintaining communication is important even when that is not the child's goal. Even when he pushes you away, that is not what he wants. He needs to depend on you being there. It is important for him to feel your support even while he tests your love and commitment to him.

Young Adulthood

The childbearing years are characterized by instinctive drive toward procreation. These drives vary in intensity for men and women. This is also a time of strong identification with sex roles, personal histories, and society's expectations. The nesting instinct may be stronger at the earlier part of this period for women than it is for men, creating some conflict.

Adoption Perspective: If the adoptee is going to search for birth parents, it is frequently in this period. It is as if the personal desire to reproduce creates the need to understand more about her origins. This may also be the reason that more adopted women search than do adopted men. Parents should not be stumbling blocks to their children's need for information about their origins.

Adulthood

The time for reflecting has arrived, due to accomplishment and lessened sexual intensity. Completion of the procreative years allows a focusing of attention toward the enjoyment of another generation. Achieving a sense of mastery over what life has brought and an acceptance of what has been missed are elements of this period. This is often a time of strong ideological commitment.

Adoption Perspective: The adult adoptee perhaps has difficulty looking at life in a generational sense. Contentment in life is based more on what has been learned and achieved than on what has been handed down. At this age, searches by adoptees are most common through personal efforts, not openness in records. The loss of adoptive parents can give some "permission" to search. To make up for links with the past, adoptees often build a family link with their own children, thus creating a family identity.

Summary

Adopting isn't easy, and neither is raising an adopted child. Both of them require a combination of love and knowledge.

Throughout your child's life, the importance of talking is easy to see. Use helpful resources both to learn about adoption and learn how to talk with your child. Some books will offer you suggestions on ways to open up communication, and others, when shared with your child, will be the vehicle for beginning discussions.[10] Take advantage of the resources open to you in your community on classes about talking about adoption or developmental issues related to adoption. Call any local adoption agency and ask if they provide classes. Read stories about adoptions because we are always finding out more information on adoption. We said early in this book that you would become an expert; it is clear now how accurate that is.

Understanding the lifelong issues of adoption is important even before you begin your search for your child. When you realize the implications of honesty both as your child grows and when he is an adult, you can make the process a good one. Keep in mind the importance of your responses to and support for your child's questions at different life stages. Understand the need to have an overall healthy and developmental perspective of adoption.

Adoptive parents, like all parents, need to understand a few things about child development—what you can realistically expect from your child at any given age. As an adoptive parent, you need to understand about both child development and what happens emotionally to a child who is adopted. You have a few special things to know about, but what you need to do is not complex. Here is a philosophical approach to raising your adopted child:

- Love your child.
- Learn about your child.
- Talk to him and be honest with him.
- Accept your child in his uniqueness.
- Understand that you cannot be all things to your child. You cannot be the birth parent.
- Recognize the loss your child has experienced; it is a major event in his life.
- Be supportive of your child as she tries to understand her life in the context of your love but also in the context of her birthright.
- Support your child in the struggles that adoption entails whether struggling with being different, seeking himself, or developing his independence.
- Enjoy being a parent. You have a wonderful opportunity to impact someone's life in a positive and healthy way.
- Use your heart and your head, and you can't go wrong.

CHAPTER 15

Open Birth Records, Searches, and Reunions

SECRETS ARE POWERFUL. They can produce curiosity, guilt, anger, rumor, and panic. They can demean and shame people. They can haunt and obsess. The impact of secrets can be jolting and far-reaching.

Despite the tremendous power—mostly negative—that secrets hold, no other institution is riddled with as much secrecy as adoption. Even today, secrecy too frequently permeates the adoption scene: when adoptive parents learn of their infertility or the birth mother discovers her unwanted pregnancy, when words are chosen to describe in non-identifying ways the "other" parents, when the child is surreptitiously transferred from one home to another, when the adoption records are sealed, and when entrenched adoption agencies reject change.

Why, in today's society, does this secrecy surround adoption? Who are we supposed to be trying to protect? Is it healthy for the people involved in an adoption to feel they have this much to hide? Are the reasons for the secrecy as valid today as they were a generation ago? What's wrong with being open about adoption?

The primary aspect of secrecy in adoption currently coming under attack is the right of the adult adoptee to learn about his history and birth family. An adult adoptee can obtain this information if his birth records are unsealed or if he can find it out for himself through a search. Opening records is a legal matter; finding out information about the birth family is a matter of perseverance. Adoptees search because records are not open; reunions will take place no matter what policies are made about sealed records.

Current Laws on Adoptees' Birth Records

Adoptees, adoptive parents, and birth parents are watching a slow change in laws relating to sealed adoption records. Many adoptees and birth parents are actively working to change the laws while moving ahead independently to obtain the information they want. Adopting parents are influencing these changes as they increasingly participate in open adoptions that make the laws less necessary. But legislators respond slowly to the changes that are happening in adoption.

So what is the sealed record? When a record is sealed, it means that at the time of an adoption, your file and that of the adoptee is no longer available to be viewed by anyone other than someone approved by the court. Your file would include:

- The original birth certificate
- The petition to adopt
- The final adoption decree
- The adoptive parents' home study
- Reports from the agency or lawyer such as intake with birth parents, birth parent medical history, or birth parent biographical information
- The signed relinquishment from the birth parent(s)

These documents are usually kept in the county courthouse in the city where the adoptive parents resided at the time of the adoption.

Then how does one go about having these records unsealed? The laws allowing adoptees access to their original birth certificates vary from state to state and certainly from country to country. Someone wishing to have the record unsealed petitions the court. Even in the most restrictive states, sealed adoption files are opened via court order. You are most likely to have records opened if there is an extenuating circumstance such as a medical condition that causes you to want access to this information.

Even if birth records are opened, exactly what information will be disclosed and how it will be disclosed to the adoptee is not universal or clear. Some states say the adoptee must be eighteen, some twenty-one. Some refer the adoptee to a review board if she doesn't like the decision to keep her record closed, and others will give out background information on the birth family but not their identities. Some states say there must be an intermediary involved and others say the intermediary must be an adoption agency. Adoptees resent the haggling about records that they believe rightfully belong to them; it is no wonder that those seeking reunions often look for other ways to obtain information about the people they seek.

In order to know what is happening in each specific state, you need to check with that state at the time you want to have access to the records. The Internet is probably the best up-to-date source of information on state laws respecting access to adoption records. Twenty-seven states have mutual consent registries that provide a nonintrusive way for adult adoptees and birth parents to waive the right to privacy if they want to be found; these registries help facilitate the process of reunions. They operate by having both parties register their desire to be found. When a match occurs, then the information is given to each party.

Other ways people search are through known names and relatives other than the adoptive parents, former addresses, dates and places of birth, and other details that they have learned. Almost anything can be a clue that leads to finding someone.[1] Support groups of people searching and businesses specializing in searches have grown across the country, providing help to those who have decided to seek information or who want to have reunions.

Secrecy in the History of Adoption

When adoption procedures were first instituted, the needs of the child were considered far less important than they are today. Adoptive parents were the primary clients. At times, the orphanage or birth parent's motivation was more to provide help to the adoptive parents than to find a home for an unwanted child, and these early adoptions were conducted on a rather informal basis.

The procedures and motivations for adoption changed as children became slightly more valued. Bloodlines were considered less important, at least intellectually, in the United States, where it was believed that anyone could be successful if he or she tried; children became more important than who they were related to. In the early 1930s, formal adoption emerged; it was a Caucasian institution founded to place white infants in white families. Concurrently, the field of social welfare developed. Adoption became a formal process, handled by the formal institution called the adoption agency. Emphasis was on screening children to find the right child for a couple. The child was still not the central ingredient; the adopting parents were.

As adoptive parents formalized this process legally, they also sought privacy to build their future around the new family that they wanted to be "normal." In order to maintain their privacy, birth records were officially sealed. In other words, no one could find out who the birth parents of an adopted child were without going through the courts.

The next change in the adoption scene was the development of the "best interests of the child" concept. This new emphasis, which originated in family law generally and in custody issues in particular, came about as infertility began to increase and as babies, especially Caucasian ones, were more in demand. So now the focus became what would be best for the child; this is a relatively new concept in adoption.

The biggest change in recent years has been the large numbers of open adoptions. Contact is made between birth parents and adoptive parents directly, and this shift changes the emphasis of adoption considerably. The process no longer means an agency is taking care of someone and making decisions for everyone; it involves the birth parent, usually the birth mother, making a choice for her child. This has produced further changes in the practice of adoption agencies, in who adopts, who decides who adopts, and what information is passed on to the new parents.

Clamor for Less Secrecy

Until fairly recently, no one seemed upset or even vocal about the fact that birth records were sealed. Adoptees seldom searched and reunions were rare. This complacency about birth information should be no surprise. First of all, even though there are at least five million adoptees in the United States, they have long constituted a small, quiet minority. This minority has been fragmented into still smaller categories, such as Caucasian adoptees, African American adoptees, older adoptees, and adoptees from foreign countries.

In the past it was difficult to get these diverse segments to identify strongly enough with each other to make their impact felt, but that is changing. Adoptees who previously acted alone are now seeing others obtain their birth information by being strong, organized, and vocal, as well as going outside the system. The effectiveness of militancy in causing changes to our society has been demonstrated: Diverse groups that unify and shout find an audience. Adult adoptees now see that the openness in adoption has not caused problems but has solved them.[2] People are writing about reunions with intensely positive feelings and in increasing numbers. Support groups are being formed by the hundreds around the country to help those wishing to search. Even studies on the impact of opening birth records and of reunions are documenting positive outcomes.

Since birth records were not sealed until around the 1940s, the demand to open these records has been fairly recent. Many of the adoptees affected by sealed records are only now reaching an age where they want to know more of their background. Another factor influencing the demands to unseal the birth records of adoptees has been the recent emphasis on genealogical and historical heritage. In the 1970s, Alex Haley's book *Roots* and the subsequent TV miniseries strongly emphasized people's heritage and links with the past.[3] Everyone is part of a long chain of history that needs to be understood if each is to understand him or herself. For the adult adoptee, one part of this chain of identity is missing. Imagine how your child feels when his high school assignment is to draw his family tree. Think of how you would feel if your friends talked of studying their family history and you couldn't join in. We encourage adopting parents to understand their new child comes with a history and another family and to help the child recognize how his identity ties to that family as well as to yours. Certainly basic information ought to be available to anyone who is adopted.

Recent advances in medicine point out the tremendous importance of the genetic background in the transmission of tendencies for certain illnesses. That's why the first form you fill out at the doctor's office asks about your family's medical history. Adoptees often can't fill out that form. The adoption process, supposedly designed to protect the adoptee, fails to let them have access to this information; it's no wonder more and more adoptees want records unsealed—it may even save their lives.

The cry of discrimination has also emphasized the need to open birth records. The banner of antidiscrimination has rallied people to specific causes, and availability of adoption information is one. Discrimination in its many forms is viewed negatively in our society, but there is no doubt that in adoption, discrimination is rampant. We discriminate against the adult who wants his adoption records. We also discriminate against potential adopting parents because of their physical appearance, their education, their medical background, their income, and even their age and how many children they have. We discriminate against birth parents in how they are treated by some social workers in adoption agencies and in some of the care they receive at the hospital. Certainly birth fathers have felt the impact of discrimination as their rights have historically been ignored. And if we are upset about discrimination in other parts of our society—that based on race, gender, and so on—why should we put up with it any longer in adoption?

The clamor for change is not voiced by all people involved in adoption. In fact, the clamor has come primarily from one group. Perhaps the new concept that adoption should be in the best interests of the child has made adoptees feel they have a central place in adoption and they sense the power this gives them. Now they want to exercise their power. They seek to have the laws changed. They want their birth records opened.

The Emotional Issues of Opening Sealed Birth Records, Conducting Searches, and Arranging Reunions

Adoption itself, as we have discussed, is riddled with emotion. The opening of the sealed record seems to be symbolic of the entire emotional package. The pain for each of the participants is real, yet none of the antagonists seem to understand the other's suffering. So the pain seems shared but different—separate but equal—to all the people involved in adoption.

Each of the participants must deal with the stigma of shame and guilt often attached to adoption and embodied in the issues of opening records, conducting searches, and holding reunions. The adoptive couple must once again confront their feelings of failure for not conceiving. Adoption brings this pain home for them as they recognize that their children are not children born to them. Our society believes that adoption is a secondary means of achieving parenthood, and so do most adoptive parents; if they had not failed to conceive in the first place, they would not be experiencing this problem. They might feel guilty and ashamed that they are not "real" parents.

The adoptee must deal with the likely stigma he feels from his past. The specter of illegitimacy is not as great today as in previous years, but it still exists. Is there any adolescent adoptee who does not wince at the word *bastard*? Or *illegitimate*? If the birth record is opened, the adoptee is no longer shielded from knowledge of potential inherited weaknesses, yet the stigma of the unknown may seem worse to the adoptee than the reality of the known, no matter how bad. The shame of rejection is never fully erased for the adoptee, even with the continual reassurance of having been "chosen" by the adoptive family. The adoptee also feels guilt for having been rejected. The difficulty of gaining information on birth background reinforces that adopted children, like adoptive parents, are different from other people. It isn't as if the adult adoptee cannot have records unsealed—he can. Actually the cost is not even terribly expensive. The fact that he has to ask permission to know his own past is the issue.

When the entire foundation of adoption is being scrutinized, the stigma of guilt and shame falls also and perhaps most heavily on the birth parents. The birth mother especially is forced to look again at a moment of great pain in her life. Her problem may be compounded by how she has incorporated thoughts of the relinquished child into her new life. A secret, this child, may cause her feelings of guilt and shame to be exacerbated. Her unresolved feelings about having "given away her child" may, with renewed attention, cause her guilt to reemerge with great intensity. Her longing for that child may be pervasive.

Birth fathers, while perhaps not as intricately involved in feelings of guilt over relinquished parenthood, nevertheless deal with their own special sense of guilt. While many of these men may not know of their children's birth, a far greater number probably do. Their sense of themselves as responsible men is affected by remembering this child they felt unable to provide for and to raise. Their guilt is compounded if they ignored their role during the decision making in the unplanned, unprepared for, or unwanted pregnancy. Guilt is not something that goes away with time or changed circumstances. Birth fathers may also long for children relinquished years before.

Guilt and shame are also a burden for many adoption agencies. Some past beliefs and policies no longer seem valid; some workers reviewing their historical roles in convincing pregnant women what was best are now not quite so sure they did the right thing. If the secrets of the past are unlocked, the former policies of the adoption agencies may not look quite so humanitarian under careful scrutiny. The adoption agencies will be asked to account for their roles in past practices in which they no longer believe and may even regret.

Along with all this guilt and shame, fear emerges. Adult adoptees are often afraid they won't like what they learn about themselves, or they may fear a second rejection from the birth parent. Birth parents usually fear their relinquished child will blame them for what they have done. Adoptive parents fear the loss of their child to another set of parents. Adoption agencies fear criticism for what they have done and for what they have tried to do.

The fear, stigma, and defensiveness that come with each of the participants affect the way they seek to solve the sealed record problem. Few listen; most try only to prove their own viewpoints. Conflicting studies, seldom conclusive, are quoted to support the side each person chooses to defend. Everyone shifts the blame to someone else. Communication becomes nonexistent. The wheels of compromise and understanding grind to a halt.

A Suggested Approach

So what is the answer to the problems posed by the recent move to open sealed records or give information to adult adoptees to help them find their birth families? How can we overcome the objections each side presents? Where will we find a meeting ground for compromise? How do adoptive parents need to approach this issue so they can lay a healthy foundation for their child's early years?

As authors, each of us has approached this chapter from a highly personal perspective. It is so easy to take a stand that will support our roles as an adoptive mother and adopted daughter. Yet personal stakes are too frequently the motivation for all of us who are so close to the issues under debate. It is time to stop taking defensive stands and approach the problem differently.

As we read and speak with the people on all sides of the issue and with each other, we are struck by several things:

- Each person we speak with or read about really believes what he or she is saying about opening the sealed adoption record is right.
- We essentially believe what each person tells us—they convince us of the rightness of their stand.
- If everyone is right, then this must be an individual issue.
- Individual issues must be handled individually, even in adoption.

The only way to solve the problem of the conflicting views must be to have a philosophical stand on the issue; Cynthia's stand is based on being an adoptive mother, a biological mother, a wife, a daughter, a psychologist, a teacher, an adoption facilitator, and an adoption agency director. Dru's stand is based on being a biological mother, an adoptee, a wife, a counselor, a young adult, and an adoption agency worker. Together we represent almost all elements of adoption, except the birth father and the birth mother and the traditional adoption agency, yet we have surprisingly similar views. Some issues are more important to one of us than to the other, but both of us agree on most.

We believe in the individual adult's ability to decide for himself or herself. To tell others what is best for them is to imply that they are not competent to run their own lives; deciding on the direction another person's life must take is arrogant and pompous. We can help people see other ways of approaching an issue, but we cannot make decisions concerning anyone's life but our own.

This is a time to try to understand the views of others, not to find fault with their views. Assessing blame is futile and divisive; we don't have to establish what's right or wrong in order to find direction. On personal issues, right is a personal matter.

The most critical ingredient in solving problems is open communication. If two opponents try to communicate only their own views, this is not communication. Talking isn't the key—*listening is.* You already know where you are on this issue; now *really* seek to hear where other people are. Try to figure out what possible reasons they have for their position rather than looking for the fallacies in their argument.

The ability to change is an essential ingredient in life, because we live in a changing world. The absolutes of yesterday are the outdated concepts of today. New situations demand new solutions. New needs demand different policies. If there is no room to change or modify our positions, there is no point in trying to communicate.

In order to evaluate the importance of any disagreement, you must evaluate the potential loss if the other side wins. If winning the battle becomes the most important goal, then the issues involved are no longer of importance; we are then arguing simply out of pride. What is the worst thing that can happen if you lose this battle? Ultimately, even if a "wrong" solution is imposed, people will survive. Adults can be as resilient as adopted children.

Different Views on Opening the Sealed Records, Searches, and Reunions

In order to better understand the issues involved in opening the birth records of an adoptee, in searching, and in reuniting, it is essential to look at some of the ways each person is or might be affected by these processes. Where do adoptees stand, and why? What do unsealing, searching, and reuniting mean to adoptive parents? What happens to the birth parents in this process? What is the role of the adoption agencies now, and what could it be? There is no way to evaluate what you think is right without trying to look at it from the perspective of each of the people involved.

ADOPTEES

When issues related to opening adoption records are discussed, it is the adoptees who are first considered. They are the ones who want information on their history. Some want only general information and others want specific facts and names, but most adoptees believe the identifying information they want should be provided after they reach adulthood.

Understanding why people search is crucial for adoptive parents. One of the major changes in recent years has been the increasing number of people who have written about reunions from a personal perspective.[4] These personal accounts are an excellent way to understand the emotional issues involved in seeking this information and in reunions. Some of these personal accounts will upset people or even make them angry. Some are better written than others. Don't rely on one book to illustrate the issues involved; understand that this is a very emotional issue for most of the people involved and is likely to be an emotional issue for you and your child at some time. Read of the people who have experienced reunions, but also read novels. Some of the literature for adolescents is especially good if a child begins rather early to ask questions about meeting a birth mother. The stories he reads don't have to be the same as his; any story will give him a chance to rehearse his feelings about why people search, what he might discover, and what it feels like to reconnect.[5]

Studies of adoptees so far are limited. We do know some general facts about those who search for additional information and reunions with their birth parents:

- Most adoptees who search are female.
- The average age of adoptee searchers is thirty-plus.
- Most reunions seem to be sought by adoptees who were told of their adoptions fairly late in life, by those who want genetic information, by those who seek missing information on who they are, and by those involved with organizations where many of the participants decide to search.
- It is easier to search when the adoptive family is supportive.
- Searches for birth parents are frequently triggered by some significant event such as the birth of a child or the death of an adoptive parent, but many times are just a matter of facilitating self-understanding or merely wanting more information. Dissatisfaction with adoptive families is not a common reason adoptees search.
- About half of the adoptees receive some kind of counseling in connection with their search, but few get it through adoption agencies.
- Most adoptees are satisfied with their reunions.
- About half the searchers develop a meaningful relationship with a birth parent.
- The adoptive family relationship is rarely permanently damaged as a result of the reunion.
- Most adoptees who search say they would do it again.[6]

Most studies have not been based on a truly random sampling of adoptee and birth parent reunions; the subjects have voluntarily come forward to be studied in response to requests. However, the findings have consistently supported the overall positive outcome of reunions.

It is not clear how many people are actively searching today; estimates range from 60,000 to 250,000. The important point is not how many are searching or will search but that searches are becoming more common. As you prepare to adopt, accept the strong possibility that a reunion will be part of the adoption process.

One reason some people adopt from other countries is to avoid issues such as the potential contact with birth parents. Since many times the adult adoptee does not want to avoid the birth parents and will in fact search, this kind of motivation should be questioned. With over 150,000 international adoptions in the last twenty years, it is no surprise that many adoptees are seeking information on their birth families in other countries.[7] The Internet and the fact that the world is becoming a global village have increased the likelihood of successful international searching. Search groups have expanded some of their registry services to include foreign search support from organizations such as the International Soundex Reunion Registry (see Appendix F) and registries for individual countries. Other adoptees will seek help through private investigators or intermediaries or merely run ads in newspapers. Since many of these reunions will take place without the adoptee understanding the culture of his country of origin, it is recommended that counseling or cultural advisers be a part of international searching.[8]

Searchers familiar with the Internet will find a worldwide Adoptees Internet Mailing List with a growing membership. Undoubtedly this is just the beginning of how we will use this source to help people searching distant places. But as of yet, these advances have not helped most people searching to find birth parents internationally; long-distance searching may be increasing, but most searchers have been unsuccessful.

There are excellent sources of help to guide an adoptee through a search. One of the most inexpensive ways to search is through registries available at low or no cost to adoptees and birth parents. Currently, twenty-seven states have mutual consent registries, allowing adoptees and birth parents to make their desire to be reunited known. International Soundex Reunion Registry, National Adoption Registry, Concerned United Birthparents, and Adoptees in Search (see Appendix F) are all organizations that offer this service. Still other groups continue to emerge to provide these services on a national basis and some on a local basis; check your Yellow Pages or local support group.

Birthparent Connection, American Adoption Congress, Adoptee's Liberty Movement Association, the Council for Equal Rights in Adoption (CERA), Adoptees in Search, and Concerned United Birthparents (see Appendix F) are all organizations concerned with opening birth records. These groups are another source of help in understanding the adoptee's point of view; why not attend some of their meetings? They usually welcome people from all sides of the adoption picture, such as birth parents and adoptive parents. Remember that each of these local groups is as individual as an adoption agency can be. Some will seem extreme in their approach; others, more moderate. The approach of each group changes as its membership changes.

Most advocates of searching and reunions would encourage adoptees to find some support as they begin their quest. The support may come from one of the groups listed, from someone who has gone through the process before, from a counselor, or even from your adoption agency. In some states there are intermediaries who also offer support.

Some argue that searchers will not like what they find. There are histories of incest, child abuse, incarceration, and mental illness. The adoptees respond that truth is better than fantasy; truth will help the adoptee know where he or she comes from, even if the reality is harsh.

It is difficult for anyone who is not adopted to fully understand what being adopted means. At times, the militancy of the searchers catches others off guard. Their anger seems so out of proportion as they feel intense frustration in their attempts to piece together their genetic medical histories or even just their social histories. Not all adoptees will experience this intense a need to search for their birth parents. For those who do search, however, the barriers they encounter seem to them to be senseless walls dividing them from themselves—they seem like roadblocks to wholeness.

ADOPTIVE PARENTS

Adoptive parents look at the current upheaval in adoption and feel their fate is once again out of their hands. Being dependent on others through their efforts to adopt a child—and possibly through an infertility struggle—was bad enough. Now they're threatened with children "taken" from them by another set of parents. Many adoptive parents are understandably but unrealistically alarmed.

As they learn more about searches, adoptive parents can become less threatened by the prospect. Knowledge, especially personal knowledge, is empowering; it seems to make searches or reunions less potentially harmful to the adoptive relationship. Through books and dialogue, adoptive parents learn how others have responded to the personal side of reunions and searches. Read the books we've suggested for adoptees; they'll help anyone involved in the process.

Many adoptive parent support groups that have helped see people through infertility and adoption quests are now fighting the opening of adoption records. The sense of isolation that comes to adoptive parents adds to their difficulties in fully exploring the search issue with others who have gone through it. With time and discussion, the isolation will lessen, as reunions and searches become more common to members of these groups. Talking about this process will help, whether it is with others who have gone through it or with a counselor who understands what searches and reunions mean to adoptive parents.[9]

No matter how hard you try, you cannot wish away the existence of another set of parents for your child. Your love for that child is a commitment to raise her, not to cut her off from anyone in her life. In fact, the child may need your love and commitment even more if she chooses to search for her birth parents. People who argue that searches bring grief or pain do not consider the potential increase in bonding with the adopted adult or adolescent if a parent can be supportive of the search efforts. Adoptive parents have already done what they sought to do— raise a child. Birth parents cannot and do not compete with what adoptive parents have done. Theirs is a different relationship with the child.

Allow your children to grow and to become whole human beings. No one can take them from you, because you do not own them. For an incredibly important part of their lives, you have been a significant person; that can never be taken away. One adoptive mother with a background in raising special children speaks poignantly of good parenting:

> *On first reflection there is something threatening to a parent about a child wanting to go off and find his or her "real parents." It feels like rejection, as if the adoptive parents were not all they should have been or did not do their job well. But when examined from the perspective of the child's needs, it is apparent that good parent-*

*ing involves encouraging or even becoming a partner in the search.
In a sense, the true function of parents is to make themselves ob-
solete; that is, to prepare their children for the time when they will
no longer be dependent on the parent.*[10]

If searching is important to your children, then help them search.
Your help and support—and maybe your permission—are what they
want and need from you. If pain is the result of their search, help them
with their pain; if joy is a part of their search, then experience this joy
with them.

Birth Parents

Birth parents are probably the primary sufferers in adoption, the ones
who may have felt the most pain and anguish. For some, pain has lingered ever since the relinquishment of the child, despite the reassurances—"You are doing the right thing" or "You will put this behind you
and build a new life." Like everyone else in an adoption, each birth parent has responded to the prospect of open birth records, searches, and
reunions in a very personal way.

Some birth parents have welcomed the opening of sealed records,
searching, and reuniting as a possible second chance to tell their story to
the child they relinquished. Others wait in dread for a phone call or
knock on the door that may bring back the past. Some birth parents
search for the children they placed for adoption, and some hide for fear
they themselves will be found, but most birth parents seem to feel positive about the potential contact they might have with the children they
placed for adoption.

As birth parents become increasingly involved in the selection of
the adoptive parents and come to meet them, many of their fears will
dissipate. The known is less of a threat than the unknown. Maintaining
some contact between the adoptive parent and the birth parent
throughout your child's growing years reduces stress at the time of a reunion. It isn't that there will be no stress, but there will be less.

The role of the birth father in reunions is more obscure than that of
the birth mother. Some reunions do take place between adoptees and

their birth fathers, but it is only in recent years that birth fathers have become organized to respond to their unique issues in adoption. Reunions between adoptees and birth fathers or other birth relatives take on an added importance if the birth mother is deceased or when there are medical circumstances that cause concern.

Organizations such as Concerned United Birthparents, Inc. (see Appendix F) help birth parents find support that will encourage them to come out of hiding. As adoption changes and more openness becomes the normal part of adoption, it is likely that birth parents will have an easier—but not necessarily easy—time.

Birth parents are frequently viewed as they were at the time they relinquished the child; the adoptive parents of the child often see them as young and mixed-up. Few people recognize that the mixed-up boy who fathers a child and takes no role in the adoption or provides no help to the birth mother may go on to become a high-powered attorney who settles million-dollar suits or the chief executive officer of an emerging company. Without continuing contact with the birth parents, we will never allow them in our minds to mature, to grow older, and to become responsible adults. In order to understand the position of birth parents in adoption, we must speak with them and listen to them. We must try to understand their place today, because viewing them from an outdated, twenty- or thirty-year-old perspective distorts who they are. If we want records opened in a kind manner, we need to understand how best to do that from the perspective of everyone involved.

ADOPTION AGENCIES

Adoption agencies approach the sealed record from a perspective different from that of the adoptee, the adoptive parent, or the birth parent. However, as with each of these other groups, they also have a personal viewpoint. The role of the agencies in searches and reunions is limited just now; however, their role in opening sealed records will be significant.

Adoption agencies and their workers feel trapped by the cries for change in opening the records. They find themselves the scapegoats for everyone's anger. At times, the criticisms are justified, and at times they are unfair. Birth mothers who look back on their time of relinquishment may feel that they were unduly influenced by the social workers who told them it was the best thing to do. They forget the confusion and desperation they felt when they came to the agency for help. Adoptive parents can also be angry with the adoption agencies that guaranteed they would be the permanent parents for their child. They frequently feel they were not given accurate and complete information on their child's background.[11] They, too, forget the gratitude they felt toward the agency as they received their greatly desired child. The adoptees, feeling like pawns in the system, vent hostility on agencies that have the information they want about who they are. They also forget the adoption agencies were acting in the way the times dictated. Times have changed rapidly, and agencies have not always changed with equal speed.

Adoption agencies have rules about how their social workers should respond to requests for birth information, but each agency has its own general framework and each worker interprets the rules of the agency somewhat differently. It is each worker who personally experiences the joy, the rejection, the hurt, or the ambivalence—the agency itself does not have these reactions. While each worker feels some obligation to support the system within which he or she works, many are actively seeking changes within the system. Other social workers are incensed with the potential opening of birth records to adoptees and are actively seeking to maintain the past system.

Some agencies believe that opening birth records will signal the end of adoption as we know it in the United States. They urge other agencies to take a stand against reunions to protect the people involved. Others are far more creative and forward-looking and are already accommodating the proposals for more openness. Some do nothing, waiting until the courts make a decision. Many are advising all the principals involved in adoption of the potential changes occurring in the law; some agencies will go no further than that. Perhaps these divergent ways of approaching the opening of sealed records are necessary so that many alternatives can be considered. One of the reasons adoption has failed to meet many people's needs is that it has been approached historically from a single, rigid standpoint. Maybe we can profit from previous mistakes and provide multiple ways to meet people's varied needs.

A Reunion Story

Reunions are like adoptions—no two are alike. In fact, the same reunion has as many stories as people involved in the reunion. One reunion we know about from many sides involved our family. It is typical and it is unique.

THE BIRTH MOTHER'S STORY

Elizabeth is Dru's birth mother. She was seventeen when she placed Dru for adoption. She was forty-four when she met Dru. Since the story began with her, let's start with her.

Elizabeth writes: *While I was pregnant, I didn't fantasize about keeping my baby and never had any doubts that adoption was the best avenue to pursue. Looking back, I'm not sure whether this decision was a sacrifice or a selfish act (being a teenage parent just was not a role I could envision). It had all happened so quickly: falling in love as only a sixteen-year-old can, having my first sexual relationship, learning that my family would move across the country to a new home during the summer before my senior year, refusing to acknowledge the physical clues until the morning of the first day of school when I nervously relayed my fears to my mom, and then experiencing the mystery and wonder of pregnancy. My mom inquired just once whether I'd want her to raise the baby, but I knew instantly that this was not a viable option for our family. After counseling with a local adoption agency, I was told that when I gave birth, the baby would be taken to its adoptive family from the hospital. I think I had steeled myself for separation all along.*

In the years between Dru's birth in 1965 and my putting my name and phone number in her adoption files in 1989, I never let myself imagine what it would be like to ever see my birth daughter. For in my mind, it would be selfish to inject myself into her adoptive family, where I could only hope she was receiving the love and support she deserved. In 1989, my perspective was shaken when a colleague, who had been adopted as a baby, described her anguish as she searched to find her birth mother. She had a wonderful relationship with her adoptive parents and was definitely not looking for a substitute but had a strong urge to unearth her biological roots. After listening to this woman, I decided to put a note in Dru's adoption file, feeling comfortable with this low-key approach, which gave Dru the option of contacting me.

Two years later when I'd almost forgotten my note, Cynthia, Dru's mother, phoned and the conversation felt as natural as if I were speaking with a next-door neighbor. Within a week, Dru and I spoke on the phone for the first time, and again the experience felt comfortable. Curious at first and rather inexperienced in the world of adoption, I asked for Cynthia's advice in approaching the entire experience. I read, read, read. I am grateful to my sister, Dorothy, who happened to live in the same area as Dru, for making the entire process easy. She agreed to meet Dru, share photo albums, and answer questions. The two liked each other immediately. I also felt very fortunate that I had never been deceitful or evasive about my first pregnancy, so I didn't have any awkward moments with my loving husband or close friends. The pieces all seemed to fit easily, and after several long phone conversations, we began to make plans to meet face-to-face.

I flew up to Seattle alone, spent the night at my sister's home, and tossed about nervously awaiting the next morning's visit with Dru and Cynthia. I think we all felt curious about and protective of each other. Although Dru and Cynthia had sent me wonderful photos documenting Dru's childhood, I was nevertheless taken aback by my birth daughter's beauty and kindness that morning. It was hard to take my eyes off of her, yet I was also acutely aware of how hard the reunion must have been for Cynthia and wanted to reassure her that I had no desire to intrude on their lives. The only painful aspect for me was that Dru had not—as I had naively imagined—gone immediately from the hospital to her new family, but had instead resided for ten weeks in foster care. That revelation stung me to my core.

I continue to be amazed at how smoothly each step toward establishing our own extended family has been. I genuinely "like" as well as "love" my birth daughter. Her entire family has been gracious and accepting, and my seven-year-old daughter adores her big sissy! Now, four years after our reunion, we're building our own shared memories, which include Dru's marriage and the birth of her two sons.

I remain cautious and hesitant at times, worried that I might be intruding, and depend upon Dru's guidance to create boundaries with which *she feels comfortable. I'll always be grateful to Cynthia and David for letting me into their lives and for being such wonderful parents to Dru.*

THE ADOPTEE'S STORY

Dru was adopted when she was two and a half months old. She was a darling baby with lots of curly hair. Cynthia and David thought they knew quite a bit about her but, in reality, knew very little. Dru was twenty-seven when she heard from the woman at the agency from which she came that there was a note from her birth mother in the file.

Dru writes: *Growing up as an adopted child, I always felt different, and during my teenage years (where we all feel different and are seeking a sense of belonging) I became more preoccupied with thoughts about my adoption. In my mid-twenties I was dealing with some medical issues and was encouraged by my physician to seek my medical records. This was just the push I needed, as it was something I had always been curious about but not courageous enough to pursue. At that time I was in graduate school and doing an internship at a search and reunion organization and facilitating a group for adoptees and birth parents. Facilitating the group was very powerful for me; it was the first time I was with a group of people where everyone was adopted and felt that everyone had similar thoughts and concerns about search and reunion. It was then that I contacted the agency that arranged my adoption and was immediately given identifying information about my birth mother. It all happened very quickly, and in hindsight, I know that it would have been helpful to have had some counseling about the reunion.*

After the reunion, I experienced a mixture of ecstasy, happiness, depression, and a feeling of being disconnected—it was very confusing. I know that reunions and post-reunion contacts do not necessarily proceed smoothly and harmoniously, but in my case I have been very fortunate to have a wonderful relationship with my birth mother and her family. And yet, it was still overwhelming.

My contact with my birth father was very different and disappointing. I spoke with him on the telephone a couple of times and he completed a medical background report and we even got as far as arranging a meeting, but he never followed through with the plan. It made me realize that we all have different levels of interest and varying capacities for giving of ourselves and I had to accept that.

The reunion itself was important, but I came to realize that the journey is just as important. The result is that I feel a strong sense of belonging on many levels, that I am able to add my biological heritage to my identity, and that I feel more in control of my life with a greater sense of being complete. Most important, I have many people who make up my "family" who I love and care deeply about and with whom I make this lifelong adoption journey.

THE ADOPTIVE MOTHER'S STORY

Cynthia was twenty-nine when Dru was born. Dru was Cynthia's second child and was very much wanted. She was the child who had questions about adoption. She was not the first child in their family to have a reunion, so the experience was familiar in some ways, yet different in others.

Cynthia writes: *Dru's desire to have additional information about her background was always something we felt was up to her. When medical problems developed, it made sense for her to seek her medical records. The first time she requested the records and was told it would cost her a large sum (for her at that time) of money, she was incensed. After all, the records were hers—why should she have to pay for them?*

The second time the records came up, she was ready to move ahead. She was not ready for what happened. After telling the social worker that she wanted copies of her medical records, the social worker hinted that there might be something else she would want. Finally Dru understood the oblique hints and asked if there was something in the record from her birth family. She was told that her birth mother had left her name and address if Dru wanted to make contact. Dru was amazed. Her amazement was nothing compared to her next response when she received a letter from the social worker saying she had sent Dru's address and phone number to her birth mother. Dru was immobilized—she truly didn't know what to do but wasn't sure she could handle this immediately. She asked me to call her birth mother, Elizabeth, and tell her she would call when she was ready. Of course, I agreed.

I really wanted to protect Dru. If she wasn't ready, I didn't want this stranger to call her and to make things difficult. I felt a contact should be at Dru's initiation only. I had no other choice but to try to call her birth mother at work. When she returned my call, she had no idea who I was. Explaining that you are the mother of her child is not easy over the phone when someone has never even heard of you. After Elizabeth got over the initial shock of my calling her, the conversation went smoothly and she readily agreed to wait for Dru to make the contact. I was impressed with how she sounded and the sensitivity she displayed.

Dru's initial hesitation was soon forgotten and she called. They began their own separate conversations and I was no longer a part of the dialogue. Intellectually, I was fine with the process, but there is no question that once again, the part I couldn't be in Dru's life was coming out. I could do nothing about it.

Our daughter Nohl had met her birth mother. I found some of the same protective things happening with Dru's reunion that I found with Nohl's. (We had helped Nohl make the contact with her birth mother, but when her birth mother wanted her to fly to San Francisco to meet her and spend the weekend, I said absolutely not! I told her that her birth mother could come to visit us, but we were not sending our seventeen-year-old daughter to a strange city to meet with someone we didn't know.) Meetings are one thing, but protection is another.

I am very good at recognizing the importance of our children's right to meet their birth parents. Actually, I think it is even a positive. But that doesn't mean I welcome the idea. I have feelings of jealousy and that maybe I will be replaced. I worry that Dru will like Elizabeth more than me. Elizabeth never had to say no to Dru or to restrict her, and I imagine that she will seem so much more understanding than I will seem to her. Elizabeth is younger than I am, and I worry that Dru will think she is pretty and I will look old.

Most of these feelings go away most of the time. Then something happens and they emerge again. When I am my usual rational self, I remind myself that Elizabeth is probably jealous of me because I was the one who had the chance to be the tooth fairy, plan the birthday parties, read the stories, watch her sleep, and see her grow. But when I have had a bad day, there is no question, I wish I were the only mother to each of my children. Most of the times, I forgive myself for these thoughts because it is OK to be ambivalent about reunions—it just isn't OK to prevent them. After all, re-unions are something that happens after the joys of watching your child grow—they are a part, not a whole. I also remind myself that I really like Dru's birth mother and I know she has added a lot to Dru's life. Why would I not want her around for Dru because I want what Dru would like—most of the time.

But Dru is the key. She is the one who makes the reunion work for Eliz-abeth and for me. We both look to her for the clues. Elizabeth and I share a great deal. Most important, we share being Dru's mother. But we also share not wanting to intrude on what Dru wants.

I have grown in my acceptance of Dru having another family as she married and asked her birth mother to attend the wedding. The sharing of my two grandsons with another grandmother is easier because time has given me a bit more understanding. But frankly, at times life seems confus-ing with birth mothers, birth fathers, birth siblings, birth grandparents, and even birth cousins. Part of the confusion is rather special and I think I like it. And sometimes I don't.

I have much to be grateful for in my life—adopting is one of those things. My children have added so much to my life. I owe much to their birth parents. The one way I can repay them is to be open with the children they gave me to love and raise. I will help each of my children who seeks additional information or reunions with his or her birth parents. I will try to help change laws, open records, advocate for less secrecy, and do all in my power to provide my children and the children of others with the informa-tion that is rightfully theirs. I owe that to them and their birth parents.

THE OTHER ADOPTION STORIES

There are other parts of this reunion story. There is the story of the re-sponse of Dru's birth father, who chose not to pursue the reunion; his part still is important. David, Cynthia's husband, has a view of re-unions, and Dru's reunion in particular, that is different from Cynthia's. There is the response from each of Dru's siblings, who are involved and watch as the picture unfolds. There are the others from both sides—the grandparents, aunts, uncles—each seeing adoption differently and each having his or her own view on reunions.

Reunions are part of adoption. We may watch how they unfold but we have no right to prevent them. We may refuse to participate but we cannot refuse to be involved. If we are part of adoption, we may have no choice but to be involved. As in all the parts of adoption, it is important to do searches and reunions in a way we can be proud of—taking into consideration the views of all the people, being honest, and being open.

Summary

The push to open adoption records continues to gain momentum, but adoptees are not waiting; the increasing number of adults who participate in adoption searches and reunions indicate that adoptees believe that having this information is their right. If the laws will not change fast enough, the adoptees and the birth parents will find a way. Even as you seek a child to adopt, you need to understand this trend.

People entering the system today recognize that open records, searches, and reunions are a part of the adoption process. Their understanding of the birth parents' view of the process and their adopted child's view of the process—as well as their own willingness to recognize that they are a family through adoption—will form a more honest basis for their relationships today and tomorrow.

Perhaps the changes brought about by opening birth records will provide the impetus to review the whole secrecy issue that has pervaded adoption in the past. As adoption sheds its dependence on secrecy, it has the potential to become a healthier process for each of the participants.

CHAPTER 16

Making Adoption Better for Everyone

NO ONE SOURCE has the final answer on ways to make adoption better for everyone and what remains to be done. There are many changes that have begun that will continue to improve the system. But the institution of adoption is adapting, responding, discarding, struggling, and changing as it should. As it continues to change, new and better approaches should be suggested and tried. With creative and positive change, adoption can be better for everyone.

Adoption can be such a wonderful solution for many people's problems. It relieves the birth mother, who knows that her child is safely being cared for and loved by someone when she is unable to provide that kind of environment. It relieves the adopting parents, who so much want to raise a child and might be unable to conceive one. It relieves society, which escapes the burden of caring for unwanted children. And it provides children with permanent homes.

We don't mean to say the adoption system does not have problems of its own—it does. But we are making headway on solving some of them. The greater openness in the entire adoption scene has been spurred on by the participants who wanted change—the birth mothers who wanted involvement in the placement of their babies, the adopting parents who wanted control over their futures, and the adoptees who wanted to know of their genetic histories. The participants are causing changes to be made, and the system is becoming healthier and more responsive to all involved.

Adoption as we know it today could change radically. New advances in curing infertility could drastically reduce the numbers of people who want to adopt children. Changes in society's attitude toward abortion could end the scarcity of babies available for adoption or create an even greater scarcity. Changes in the way our society offers financial support to single mothers and other low-income parents will affect the number of children being surrendered for adoption. The one thing of which we can be sure is that the institution of adoption will not remain the same.

In this book we have made numerous suggestions that we believe would significantly improve what is being done in adoption today. These are not the only possible solutions to the problems we see, but they are worthy of consideration if we are to make the system vibrant and responsive to all involved. Both adoption laws and adoption agencies should be adaptable to the changing needs of society. Our first two sets of recommendations are specifically directed to the state legislators and the adoption agencies, but they have strong implications for all in the adoption system.

And we have recommendations for you, the people who want to adopt a child. Our recommendations for you as potential adoptive parents are somewhat different. They are based not on a need for change, but rather on the ingredients you need to find, adopt, and raise your child in a way that is sensitive to the issues that confront adoptive families today. Following some of these recommendations can make the difference between your being successful in your search or being someone who is discouraged because you can't find a child to adopt. Being aware of ways to adopt sensitively increases your chance of success and feeling good about the process. Some of these recommendations will help make your adoption better because you will understand how to raise your adopted child in a way that's healthy for you and for the child. After all, helping you succeed in your search for a child is only part of what this book is all about. We also want you to know how to adopt in a way that recognizes the issues for you, the birth family, and your new child.

Legal and Legislative Recommendations

Some of what needs changing is the responsibility of neither the adoption agencies nor the adoptive parents; some changes involving the institution of adoption concern its legal framework. Laws, customs, and precedents now determine how adoption operates; the following recommendations are based on the belief that some of the laws in adoption need to be changed.

We have attempted to be realistic about the recommendations we are making. At times, our suggestions attempt to create an interim solution to a problem; they themselves may need to change over time. Some improvement would result if legislators accepted even just a fraction of these suggestions.

Recommendation 1:
All adoptive parents, whether waiting for independent, international, or agency placements, should be licensed before the placement.

Licensing means that adoptive parents receive a document permitting them to be parents anywhere in the United States. This document will verify that you have met the requirements necessary to adopt a child. We probably should do this for all parents, even biological ones, but that is unrealistic. It is probably also unrealistic at this time to suggest that adoptive parents should not have to go through any screening before receiving a child. Since those two alternatives are unlikely to occur, our recommendation is based on trying to streamline the process and find a more effective way to get people prepared to parent a child through adoption.

Our licensing for parenthood would be different than what currently exists. It would require that some form of preparation take place prior to placement; it would also mean that any family who is licensed would be eligible for any child who becomes available.

In order to accomplish this goal, we would have to believe that the people doing the licensing knew what they were doing. They should have training in the following areas:

- Resolving issues related to infertility
- Educating adoptive parents about the issues of raising an adopted child
- Helping potential adoptive parents prepare for a child
- Encouraging potential adoptive parents to consider all kinds of children who are available for adoption
- Helping potential adoptive parents find a child to adopt
- Helping adoptive parents bond with their new child
- Helping parents be open and honest with their children about adoption
- Helping adoptive parents be accepting of the birth family
- Providing resources to adopting parents who have some special issues in their adoption
- Helping adoptive parents be accepting of the uniqueness of adoption as a way of establishing a family

It should be clear that this is not a process of elimination. The adoption study should be an exploratory, educational, and supportive time for people who want to adopt.

The standards for receiving your parenting license should be minimal. Getting this permit should be like obtaining a driver's license—not so difficult that most people can't do it but not so easy that unfit people receive a license. If there are deficiencies in your parenting skills, remedies should be sought that will correct the problem; you should still be allowed to be licensed at a later point. Licenses should be updated periodically.

There are several reasons for this recommendation. First, we believe in some screening, though there is no evidence that being eliminated by an adoption agency stops people from adopting children. Second, adoption agencies, with all their careful techniques, show no better results than independent adoptions, where little, if any, screening takes place, and many agencies screen out competent applicants. The third reason for this recommendation is that if there were any obvious problems, prospective parents could fix them—they wouldn't just take their flaws elsewhere and adopt. The fourth reason is that if people were licensed ahead of time, any child could be placed quickly.

Licensing should be acceptable in all agencies.

Recommendation 2:

The postplacement waiting period in adoption should be reduced or eliminated entirely.

Adoptive parents go through extensive scrutiny to determine if they are qualified to be parents. If this screening is done well, the postplacement waiting period before adoptions are legalized becomes an unnecessary intrusion into an adoptive family's life. This time period does little good and great harm; it should be significantly reduced or eliminated.

If home studies prior to placement can't identify significant problems, why would additional home studies after the couple has the child be any more effective? In very few cases, a family incompatibility might be detected. But similar incompatibilities are found at times in biological families.

This unnecessary and repetitive study of the adoptive home can delay bonding between the adopted child and the adopting parents. For this period of time, the adoptive parents are merely foster parents because the agency can remove the child from the home at any time. The child and the parents need to feel a permanence in the relationship if the necessary parent-child bond is to be firmly established. This is a time for total, not partial, commitment.

Recommendation 3:

Every effort should be made to encourage more uniform laws related to international adoptions for the protection of the adopting parents, the birth parents, the adoptees, and all nations involved in the process.

Current efforts to develop more uniform laws related to international adoption should be encouraged for the protection of the rights of all of the people involved. More uniform laws would help potential adopting parents understand the process. Current abuses or believed abuses could be avoided. Uniform adoption regulations will protect the rights of each of the parties more effectively.

It is important to protect everyone involved—the adoptee, the birth parents, and the adoptive parents. It is also important to be mindful of the implications of adoption for each of the countries involved in international adoptions.

Recommendation 4:
Time limits should be placed on foster care placements and legally enforced.

Foster care is meant to be a temporary solution. Unfortunately, it can become a way for people to avoid making decisions about the child. It prevents birth parents from deciding whether to keep or relinquish a child. It prevents adoption agencies from moving ahead in placing children for adoption. It prevents potential adoptive parents from opening their homes for permanent placements of these children at the earliest possible time. It prevents the child from having a normal, loving home.

Foster care is expensive in terms of both the child's mental health and the taxpayers' money. To allow children to remain permanently in "temporary" foster care is a disservice that can be remedied by setting limits on the length of time any child can be left in this state of limbo.

Foster care serves a useful and essential approach to temporary care for families having difficulty coping with day-to-day problems. If the situation is not remedied in a brief period of time, the child still deserves to have a permanent solution.[1] Either the family should be helped to reinvolve the child in their lives or the child should be given another chance with another family.

Except in rare circumstances, every child is adoptable. There is no reason a child needs to remain in foster care for lack of an adoptive home. When agencies find no home for a specific child, it means they have not gone far enough, been open enough, or been creative enough in their approach.

Recommendation 5:
Pregnancy counseling agencies should be regulated and pregnancy counselors should be licensed to assure protection of the consumers.

In most states, counselors have to be licensed by the state to make certain that they are qualified to provide the services they advertise. Yet in the area of pregnancy counseling these same standards are not upheld; anyone is allowed to counsel a pregnant woman.

If someone or some group advertises that counseling for pregnant women is available, that person or group makes a serious commitment. Whenever such counseling is offered, the counselors should be qualified. A pregnant woman's decision about her unborn child is one of the most important she will ever make. She must believe the counselor she speaks with has the necessary qualifications and skills to help her, and she has the right to be assured that her counselor is unbiased and qualified. "Counselors" who steer women in a particular direction because of their own ideological predispositions are not counseling—they are directing.

Some agencies that offer pregnancy counseling base their financial livelihoods on which decision the woman chooses for the resolution of her pregnancy. Such kickbacks, whether for sending the woman to a certain clinic for an abortion or referring her to someone who may be involved in black market adoptions, prevent objective counseling.

Obviously, pregnancy counseling clinics are meeting a need, or they would not exist. In fact, their success should be a lesson to the usual, traditional health care systems. It is time now to improve the operation of the current pregnancy counseling groups. At the very least, these groups' headquarters should be called pregnancy information centers, not pregnancy counseling centers; then a woman would know that she received *information* about her pregnancy, not *counseling*. However, each information center should have trained and licensed counselors to help women who are trying to decide what to do. These trained counselors should fully understand the implications of each of the alternatives to an unplanned pregnancy.

The pregnancy counseling a woman receives can significantly affect her long-term medical and mental health. It is unfair for women to receive counseling that may create problems for them in years to come; they need the opportunity to make well-thought-out decisions for themselves. As in most areas of counseling, the choice must be made by the client; her manner of making the choice can be greatly aided with the help of a trained and licensed counselor.

Recommendation 6:
Adoption counselors and those providing home studies should be licensed and meet minimal standards to protect the consumer.

If we expect that the adoption process will include a time of exploration and support from those providing adoption counseling, it follows that these counselors need to have specific training. When people go to an agency or to someone advertising that they provide adoption services, a minimal level of expertise should be guaranteed through a licensing process.

As adoption is today, confusion over who provides services is rampant. The adopting parents seeking help can be easily taken in by people untrained and uninformed about the process. It is not enough to facilitate a contact between a birth mother and an adoptive couple. The process involves far more than that. Because of the long-term ramifications for each of the people in the adoption triangle, a minimal level of training should be expected of the people providing adoption counseling and assistance.

If the home study is to be a process of exploration and support, it needs to be done by someone with a thorough background in the lifelong ramifications of adoption. Home studies should not be a matter of jumping through some hoops, but an opportunity to learn about adoption as a unique way to build a family—a way to make adoption better.

Recommendation 7:
The legal process in adoption should be simplified and its costs reduced.

The legal fee for most "normal" adoption proceedings is significant. The attorney's fee includes a minimal amount of paperwork and a brief visit to court the day the adoption is legalized. In most routine adoptions, the work of the attorney can be done by a secretary or by the parties involved in the adoption; the required court appearance is a token procedure with little value. Adoption in most cases should be a routine civil procedure that requires neither an attorney nor an appearance in court.

This possibility would also reduce costs to the adoptive parents. Certainly there should be room for many kinds of adoption proceedings, just as there are many kinds of divorce proceedings. Some divorces are such that the couple is able to do the legal work without the help of an attorney; others are far more complex and require extensive legal help. Adoption is ready for a similar distinction.

Recommendation 8:
Efforts should be made within the United States to seek more uniform adoption laws, including those pertaining to the rights of the birth father.

The variety of adoption laws across the United States creates considerable confusion. The proposed Uniform Adoption Act is one attempt to sort out that confusion. Whether by this act or by some other, every effort needs to be made to impose uniformity on the current system. Some of the areas that should be addressed include the birth fathers' rights, the need to keep the best interests of the child in focus, and the need to have some definitive time after which adoptions are irrevocable.

Recommendation 9:
Legal decisions should truly be made in the best interests of the child.

The child's interests should be paramount in legal decisions related to his or her welfare. While birth parents' rights need to be carefully considered, they should not be given more weight than those of the child. Decisions should be made to protect the child and should be made in his or her best interests.

Recommendation 10:
Legal action should be taken against adoption frauds and scams.

The increased incidence of frauds and scams by people seeking to make money off vulnerable would-be adoptive parents is a source of concern. Until legal action is taken against people who perpetrate fraud and scams, these activities will continue. When perpetrators realize that legal action will be taken, they will stop.

Recommendation 11:
Laws should be changed to allow the opening of birth records for the adult adoptee.

Provisions to open all birth records of adult adoptees should be enacted. Rather than forcing the issue, the records should routinely be opened in an orderly fashion. All agencies should be encouraged to begin to prepare now for this inevitability; both birth parents and adopting parents should understand the probability that these records will be open to the adult adoptee in the future. Adoption agencies should become involved with updating past adoption cases.

State legislators' slowness to enact this kind of legislation has forced many adoptees who want access to their records to go outside of the law. These restrictive laws are no longer appropriate or effective and they should be changed.

Recommendation 12:
Many different kinds of adoption should be encouraged.

We live in a diverse society, and adoption should reflect that diversity. Open adoption is appropriate for some people; more traditional agency adoption is appropriate for others. Some people's needs will be best met in independent adoptions, others' in private agency adoptions.

Adoption monopolies must be vigorously resisted; no one system should ever gain absolute control over all adoptions. No one group, no matter how well meaning, should be allowed to dominate adoption or to set rules and regulations for everyone. To meet the problem of the lack of adoptable children by dictating that all adoptions should be agency adoptions gives all the power and control to adoption agencies, which merely creates a monopoly and provides no solution. No one group has all the answers for all the people in adoption. The law should reflect this.

Adoption Agency and Adoption Service Provider Recommendations

Although this book is intended primarily to help people find the child they want, we also need and want to communicate with the adoption agencies and others who provide services in adoption. This is a time of needed change in adoption by all sides. All providers need to carefully scrutinize their procedures, rules, and goals. The recommendations that follow are suggestions for changes needed within the adoption system. These recommendations also show adoptive applicants the obstacles that confront them.

Recommendation 1:
Adoption agencies should equally serve all the parties in adoption.

Three different groups rely on the services supplied by adoption agencies and other providers—birth parents, adopting parents, and adoptees. There is no logical reason why any one client's interests need to be served more than any other's. Agencies should be committed to meeting the needs and serving the interests of all the people involved in adoption *equally.*

This philosophical shift from serving mainly the interests of the child at the time of adoption to equally serving the interests of all the parties would create radial change. This change alone should modify and improve the approach that the adoption agencies take with birth parents and with adoptive parents. It also should change the approach the adoption agencies take with adult adoptees.

If all parties are indeed equally served, the birth mother would be treated with respect. The role of the agency with the birth mother would be to help her make the best decision possible for herself and not try to influence that decision based on a personal view of what she *should* do. No one would assume she is incapable of making a good decision for her child; no one would usurp her right to know about the people who would adopt her baby. She should be involved in the adoption process in a primary way. She should receive financial aid to live in a reasonable manner without worrying about her medical care. Counseling should be available to her throughout the process and after she has placed the child.

If all parties are indeed equally served, the adopting parents would be treated with respect. The role of the agency with the adopting couple would be to help them find a child to adopt rather than to judge their parenting skills on the basis of poorly defined criteria and personal bias.

If it is obvious that parenting skills are lacking, the agency should make every effort to help the potential parents correct the problem. But it should be remembered that most people turned down by agencies do not have glaring problems in their parenting skills; they are turned down because of vague or unjustified reasons that they will never hear about or know. If the reason people are turned away by the adoption agency cannot be clearly stated to them, then perhaps it is not a very good reason.

If all parties are indeed equally served, the adult adoptee would be treated with respect. The role of the agency with the adult adoptee would be to accept the strong wishes of the person to know more about his or her background. This respect would include making provisions for this information to be transmitted to the adult adoptee in a thoughtful and respectful manner. Certainly it should not be assumed that the person wishing information on his or her background has a problem.

When an agency says its primary client is a child, the agency becomes the person who makes the decisions for the child and no one questions that decision; no one is in a position to question that decision. Just about any decision can be made and it can be said to be in the best interest of the child; most times it is. But at times, decisions are made that are said to be in the interest of the child but may actually be more in the best interest of the agency. This phrase, *best interest of the child,* has been abused by adoption agencies.

Adoption should be a shared venture, with the agencies and their clients working toward a common goal. The agencies should commit themselves to helping each and every person who comes for help. No one should be rejected. The adoption agencies need to commit to a new mission: equality in adoption for every man, woman, and child.

Recommendation 2:
Adoption agencies should actively recruit babies for adoption.

Many changes have occurred in the kinds of adoption agencies serving our society. Some of the reasons for these changes have been the traditional agencies' failure to respond to the call for openness or to be more involved in helping potential adoptive parents find babies. The agencies that have endured are those who have attempted to incorporate the newer practices; those who have maintained secrecy and aloofness have found themselves without babies to place.

Agencies need to become advocates for adoption. This should never be done in a coercive manner, but through an educational campaign to let the public know of the great need for babies to be placed.

Adoption agencies also need to be involved in studying why women seldom consider adoption as an alternative to their unwanted pregnancy. Can we think of changes that would make adoption a more realistic and desirable alternative to these women?

More than a million women a year are obtaining abortions. Few of these women even know about or consider adoption as an alternative. Perhaps this is because much "pregnancy counseling" is being done by unlicensed counselors. Few of the groups who offer this "counseling" fully understand adoption and those who do are frequently leery of the rigidity that has been part of the system. Efforts need to be made to correct their misconceptions and show them how flexible, individually responsible, and ultimately healthy adoption can be.

Adoption agencies need to present the adoption alternative to unhappily pregnant women. Its not enough for the agencies to wait for women to show up on their doorstep between nine and five, Monday through Friday; they need to reach out when the women need the help. Stories of babies being abandoned reveal the adoption system has failed to adequately convey that there are homes waiting for babies.

Some of the marketing that is being done in independent adoptions should provide a lesson for the agencies. People who are successfully adopting independently are trying new and different ways to find and appeal to unhappily pregnant women. They are adjusting to the demands of the birth parents. Agencies need to take notice.

An attempt should be made to move out into the community to appeal to pregnant women instead of sitting back and *hoping* they will come to the established adoption agencies. Many women would elect to place their children for adoption if adoption were effectively presented. Adoption agencies need to reach out to the public more directly by hiring public relations firms that can effectively "sell" adoption through television, radio, newspapers, and magazines. Free public service advertising time should regularly be used to promote adoption as an alternative to an unwanted pregnancy. Booths should be established at local shopping centers and public events to explain adoption. These booths would not "sell" a specific agency; they would sell the concept of adoption. Schools should invite presentations by enthusiastic, young social workers telling about adoption and the large demand for babies. Newspapers are always seeking human interest stories; adoption stories are perfect. Counterculture newspapers, especially, should be approached.

Adoption agencies need to be advocates for adoption. If the agencies won't, who will be? Who is an advocate for adoption now?

Recommendation 3:
Adoption workers should make adoption more appealing and responsive to the birth mother and her needs.

A pregnant woman who is considering adoption should be able to go through her pregnancy with dignity and self-respect. If laws need to be changed to permit this, agencies should lobby legislators. Only in this way can agencies attract pregnant women.

Financial assistance would help more women place children for adoption and fewer would have abortions. If a woman is pregnant, she can obtain an abortion for a small cost. If she chooses to carry a child to term and place the child for adoption through an independent adoption, some eager couple will gladly pay her expenses. If she chooses to carry the child to term and place it for adoption with an adoption agency, she will usually have to arrange and pay for her own pregnancy expenses. She may be forced to go on welfare, borrow money from family or friends, or barely subsist. This is wrong. Agencies should change policies or even laws that prevent them from providing a woman with the financial help she needs. A pregnant woman should receive financial help with her medical and personal expenses when she plans to give up her child for adoption. Medical and living costs should be assumed by the adoptive couple in most cases. If the same couple were to adopt independently, they would usually incur these expenses for the birth mother. If they got involved in a black market adoption, they would assuredly pay far more.

In order for a pregnant woman to end up in a healthy place mentally after this experience, she needs to feel good about herself during her pregnancy. A regular financial allowance to help her with counseling and additional expenses other than medical fees is just and reasonable. This may mean making a change in the laws that govern which expenses a birth mother may be reimbursed for. Her allowance should be enough that she does not feel demeaned or punished by her decision to surrender her child.

Decisions about the adoption should be made by a birth mother with the aid of the agency social worker. She should be a participant in the decision about the family who would get her child, the amount of contact she wants to have with the adoptive parents, and the time frame for placement of the child into the new home. If she is comfortable with an immediate placement of the child into an adoptive home, that is what should be done; adoption agencies should promote this to women as an incentive for them to use an agency. Ultimately, the decisions about the pregnancy should be made by the birth mother.

Recommendation 4:
Agencies, groups, and individuals who provide adoption services should accept different kinds of adoptive parents to reflect the same qualities that occur in biological parents.

We do not prevent people from having biological children because they are different from the mainstream. We do not take children away from their genetic parents because the family does not fit into "normal" society. Adoption agencies and others who work in the adoption field should also accept human variation.

Only in the most extreme cases should adoption agencies turn people away because they do not appear to be suitable parenting candidates. With proper help and support, most people's parenting skills can improve. The focus of the adoption worker should be on improving the parenting skills of potential adopters, not on sending them elsewhere to find a baby. When these parents obtain a baby somewhere else, they will raise the child without the improvement that could have been made in their parenting skills.

Recommendation 5:
All adoption services should provide counseling to all clients both before and after the adoption.

A client—whether birth parent, adoptive parent, or adoptee—should have the freedom to explore his or her strengths and weaknesses, doubts and hesitations, fears and joys. As the current agency-dominated system is set up, this kind of exploration is impossible. Most adoption agencies are not providing counseling services to their clients. To truly counsel means to fully accept the client and be nonjudgmental. In order to be a counselor, you must believe there are choices; the person who needs to make the choices is the client, not the counselor.

When a birth mother initially debates some of these issues, she should be able to discuss them freely with a trained social worker. So should adoptive parents. Certainly adoptive parents are not free to voice their hesitations or doubts if they are trying to be among the few lucky people chosen to receive a baby. In most cases, if parents run into problems raising an adopted child, counseling services are not available through the facilitating agency. Adoptees who return for information about their adoptions are not provided these services, either.

At the very least, a pregnant woman who elects to relinquish her child to an agency should be assured that she will receive adequate counseling—counseling with no coercion of any type, in an atmosphere of respect for who she is and the struggle she faces. Anyone who disapproves of what the birth mother has done will reveal his or her disapproval and do more harm than good. The relationship between client and counselor must be based on mutual positive regard.

Certainly, an adoptive couple should be assured that they will receive counseling on how to find a child, the potential areas of difficulty they might have with adopting, and, if they are rejected, the real reasons the adoption agency is not able to help them. The adoptee having difficulty with his or her adoption should also be able to receive counseling from the original agency, even when the adopted child becomes an adult.

Unless a licensed counselor outside the agency system has specialized in adoption, few are now qualified to handle the adoption-specific issues that everyone needs to consider. People in distress over adoption issues need a chance to talk about themselves with an objective person who will help them view their situation from many sides. Adoption agencies could be an ideal place for this counseling to take place.

Recommendation 6:
Agencies, groups, and individuals who provide adoption services should also provide and encourage legal representation for their clients.

If there is a time for the birth parents to debate their decision, it is *before* the child is placed for adoption. They should enter into this process knowing what will take place, their potential emotional response, and the legal ramifications of their choice. Thus all birth parents should be encouraged to have legal representation to understand their rights and responsibilities. These services need to be provided in all kinds of adoptions.

Birth parents are, of course, entitled to have legal representation before signing adoption papers or making any binding agreement; they should understand their legal rights early in the process. This representation should not take an adversarial approach but, rather, be an opportunity to explain the legal issues of the agreement they are about to enter into.

If birth parents are represented by the same attorney who represents the adoption agency or the adopting parents, there is likely to be a conflict of interest between the clients. Separate representation should always be available.

Recommendation 7:
All agencies, groups, and individuals who provide adoption services should advocate and facilitate immediate adoptive placements with no temporary foster home care.

Nothing substitutes for a permanent adoptive home placement. This is not a negative statement about foster care; it is a statement of the importance of each day in a child's life. Foster homes are an inadequate substitute for permanent adoptive homes.

The child, adopted or not, who is being shifted from one parent or set of parents to another should have to go through as few changes as possible. In most infant placements, it would be best for the child to be placed in an adoptive home immediately after the birth mother surrenders him or her. Foster care given between the two homes may provide absolute security and certainty about the birth mother's position, but it is detrimental to the child and parents who later adopt the child.

Bonding is necessary in order for the child and parents to feel secure in their new relationship. The earlier this is done, the better. The positive benefits of early bonding far outweigh the risks that immediate placement might entail.

Some problems are possible even if this change is made. Some birth mothers may change their minds after the placement but before the legal relinquishment is made. Those will be difficult cases, and the adoptive parents need to understand the possibility. If the alternatives are properly presented, most adoptive parents will still choose this over the "security" of having a foster mother raise their child for the first month or more. While immediate placements are currently possible in some "fost-adopt" programs, these programs are limited and need to be expanded and improved. They can help make adoption satisfactory for all involved.

No matter what state laws are passed regarding foster care, everyone who provides adoption services should take an aggressive stance to prevent children from remaining in foster care for extended periods. There should be no delays for red tape, no delays because someone has a vacation, no delays unless they can be scrutinized and deemed totally necessary. A child's mental health is at stake.

The research is abundantly clear that the early months of a child's life are crucial to building trust.[2] Many other desirable characteristics such as curiosity, respect for authority, self-confidence, self-control, and the ability to get along with others are also determined in the first years of a child's life. We cannot leave a child in limbo at this critical time.

If an adoption agency does not have the right home for a specific child, other adoption providers should be informed immediately. Collaboration between agencies and others providing adoption services should develop a more cooperative attitude that would help provide homes for children. No child should have to wait for an agency to act.

Recommendation 8:

Anyone providing adoption services should be involved in recruiting adoptive minority parents and in finding homes for minority children.

All who are involved in adoption have a responsibility to reach out to minority groups and to help minority children find homes. While in some cases this may necessitate a change in the ordinary and usual practice of how individuals, groups, and agencies operate, those changes should be instituted.

When an institution such as adoption no longer is responsive to the public, it needs to change. Adoption is not currently meeting the needs of the minority community.

Recommendation 9:

All agencies, groups, and individuals who provide adoption services should promote openness and honesty in adoption.

Secrecy in adoption is not healthy, nor is it usually necessary. Hiding identities, withholding information, and keeping people separate should be purged from the system and be replaced by openness and honesty.

There is nothing to hide in adoption. The adoptive child with the absolute worst imaginable history is acceptable to someone.

Adoption agencies need to change their image to convey this openness and honesty. Visiting the typical adoption agency now is like visiting a medical clinic. The receptionist acts as a guard to all the closed doors that line long, dim corridors. The professional surroundings are foreboding at best. The setting needs to be opened, the people need to be opened, and the adoption process needs to be opened.

One means of achieving this physical openness is for adoption workers to go out more into the community, as we also suggest in recommendation 2 of this section. Take the message about adoption to the community in an open, outgoing manner. Agencies and other groups and individuals who are involved in adoptions should open small drop-in centers and talk about adoption in shopping areas. They need to have their social workers on staff at community agencies and their literature on site; both staff and literature should be carefully chosen to appeal to young women. Visits to schools can also be made outside of the ordinary adoption agency setting.

Use people who have adopted or who are adopted to openly promote adoption. Have art displays from adopted children. Certainly those who have adopted independently have found the value of making contact with others who have adopted. Encourage the sharing of information about adoption. Instead of hiding one person from another, go the opposite direction. Have open houses where people involved with adoption can tell the public how rewarding it is. Bring people together rather than separate them. Let some social life into the process.

Openness and honesty can also mean becoming actively involved in helping bring about reunions between birth parents and adult adoptees when requested. Adoption agencies have an ideal opportunity to help arrange and assist with these reunions. Reunions can be held with or without revealing identities; information can be relayed that meets some people's needs without going any further. Reunions can be made to order—service workers should let people have them in their own way.

Recommendation 10:
Adoption agencies should become information centers on adoption.

Adoption agencies should become the creative, dynamic hub of a healthy, vital adoption system. They could be the place to find out about all kinds of adoption. They could be the place to which all information on adoption is channeled. Rather than trying to choke off all other ways to adopt, adoption agencies could become centers to help all kinds of people find babies from everywhere.

The person trying to adopt a child today needs to search through huge amounts of information before beginning. The pregnant woman needs to know the right place to go for help in making her pregnancy decision. No single source of help and information is currently available to help people find their best direction; adoption agencies could be this expansive, helping source.

In addition to their usual information, adoption agencies should know which attorneys are best qualified to assist in the adoption of a child from a foreign country, which doctors are best for low-cost abortions, which parent groups provide support systems for independent adoption in a specific country, and which physicians provide the most creative help to increase fertility. Agencies that accept alternative forms of adoption and all different kinds of clients can best afford to be creative and expansive.

Recommendation 11:
All who provide adoption services should become advocates for needed change in the system.

As with all large institutions, we need to examine adoption's practices, see which ones are no longer relevant, and make changes accordingly. All agencies, groups, and individuals should be examining their everyday adoption practices and policies to see what changes are needed. New methods are being tried in independent adoptions and in newer agencies; these alternative methods have arisen from the lack of flexibility in the older adoption institutions.

Plenty of research exists on sound child development. These studies need to be combined with work done on adoptions, and results should be correlated. Studies still need to be conducted to determine clients' level of satisfaction with the system and how much they know about how to proceed after the adoption agency has done its part.

Everyone involved in adoption today has a responsibility to advocate the kinds of changes that need to be instituted. We cannot rely on someone else to lead the fight for change; each of us must become an advocate. Each of us must take a stand, negotiate with others who are on different sides of the issues, and help facilitate the changes that will make adoptions better and healthier.

Recommendations for Adoptive Parents

Many suggestions for finding a child have been given throughout this book. Underlying all the specific suggestions is a general philosophy about how to approach adoption and to conduct a successful search for a child. The following recommendations sum up that philosophy.

Recommendation 1:
Be thoroughly informed about each step you take.

Throughout this book there has been a recurring theme: Learn about every aspect of adoption before you proceed. Knowledge is a critical ingredient in achieving a successful search for a child, as it is in getting the most out of many other areas of life. You can save yourself time and frustration by knowing what you are doing before you act. The knowledge you have will enable you to ask the right questions and to give the correct answers.

Knowledge can be gained from many sources—individuals, parent groups, adoption agencies, attorneys, physicians, and books. Gather many opinions because seldom will one source inform you of all the options.

First, you need to be knowledgeable in pursuing alternative ways to have a child if you are infertile. Know the doctors to go to, read the right books, ask the important questions. Know how far you need to go for your own satisfaction.

You need to be knowledgeable when you visit an adoption agency. Learn about the agency you are going to, read about adopting through an agency, find out what agencies are looking for in adoption applicants. Know how agencies fit *you.*

You also need to be knowledgeable about independent adoption. Know its differences from agency arrangements, its similarities, its risks, and its advantages. Figure out what route sounds best to you—but don't eliminate other options. You need to know about all the kinds of children available for adoption, both in the United States and in other countries. You need to determine your limits about the kind of child you're willing to consider and see if your ideas fit with the kinds of children who currently need homes.

The knowledge with which you pursue adoption will help you assess where to go, when to stop, where to go next, and how best to proceed. Knowing yourself and the adoption system gives you the ability to most effectively attain your goal.

Recommendation 2:
Be assertive and a little bit more.

People who sit back and wait are likely to end up without a child. If you really want to find one, you need to push the issue. Be active and pursue your goal rather than passively waiting for something to happen.

At times it is necessary to take an approach that is a little bit more assertive. This does not necessarily mean being combative, but you have to do more than just take no for an answer. If an adoption agency turns you down, don't just leave; go back and ask the reasons why. After all, what do you have to lose? Find out if you can remedy your potential parenting "faults," whatever they are. What recourse is available to you to get the agency to change its position?

There are times when additional letters of reference may prove your fitness. Evaluation of your mental health by a psychologist or psychiatrist may prove to the agency that you intend to pursue adoption to the limits. Sometimes a letter from an attorney mentioning discrimination might be in order, if you feel that may be a reason for your rejection. Let the adoption agency know that you *will* find a child.

In short, take control and go after what you want. In many ways your willingness to seek your goal vigorously is the most overt sign of the strength of your desire to have a child. Fight the system if you need to; certainly fight the system if doing so might get you your baby.

Recommendation 3:
Be positive, upbeat, and polite.

Even as you assert yourself to the agency, remember the rules of adoption etiquette discussed earlier in the book (see Chapter 1). You need people to help you. While we can't guarantee that they will help if you are nice, we can guarantee they won't help if you aren't.

While we advocate that people should observe a certain etiquette, this in no way means we think you should enter the process naively. There are problems in adoption. Some people will take advantage of you if you let them. But if you approach adoption as if everyone is out to get you, it will turn the process into a dreaded experience. Besides making yourself upset, you will turn many people away from helping you. Adoption is best approached as an adventure that will lead to a much longed-for goal. Some will say they'd rather find adventures in another way; and perhaps they are right. But you probably have no choice but to embark on this process if you want to find a child. Make the best of it by having a positive, upbeat attitude.

Recommendation 4:
Be adaptable.

Adoption is a time of testing—testing your limits, your openness and flexibility, your patience and perseverance. Pursuing a child will cause you to stretch your limits in all these areas, and this requires adaptability. Be informed about and open to the many different ways to find a child. Be flexible about what kind of child you might consider adopting; think carefully before you say no to any of the suggestions that might be put before you. Is there a way for your no to possibly be a yes? Be creative in how you arrange to adopt the child you ultimately find. Basically, be adaptable to today's adoptions.

Your receptivity to different ways of looking for a child, different things to read, places to go, and people to meet significantly increases your chances of adopting a child. It is easy to sit at home and think about how it would be best to simply become pregnant or how it would be great to have the agency hand you a darling new baby. Daydreams are nice, but you have to deal realistically with the world as it is. Determine what the critical ingredients in your dreams are. See how many situations might meet your criteria and if some parts of your dreams aren't quite as critical as you imagined. Adapt your dreams to the reality of adoption today.

Recommendation 5:
Stretch your limits.

You probably have a pretty good idea what a child who would be born to you would look like. Is that the only kind of child you will take? Do you need to have a child who looks like you, or could you take a child with different coloring or with a different build or from a different race? Does the child have to *be* like you, or would you consider a child who has some problems and might not otherwise find a home? Could you work with a birth family that has a very different set of values than you have?

This is the time to consider how open you are in your adoption search. The further you can stretch your limits, the more situations will be open to you. If you can only be content with a blond, blue-eyed baby girl, you have greatly limited yourself. It means you will turn away a lot of other wonderful children.

Take your time and think this one through very carefully.

Recommendation 6:
Be ready to act quickly.

Once you begin this process, you need to be prepared to act. Opportunities may come up and you'll need to be prepared to act quickly and decisively. When people deliberate for several days about a particular situation, they are likely to find the baby has been placed with someone else. Know ahead of time what you will consider so that good opportunities do not pass you by. The time to discuss how you will respond to a particular opportunity is before it arises.

Knowing yourself and your spouse will help you be prepared. Preparation for adoption is an exciting time that allows you to learn more about yourself and your partner. Discuss together the many kinds of adoptions you have heard or read about. Rehearse what you would have done. Play "what if" and have a chance to hear where each of you are on the multitude of situations that can arise.

Recommendation 7:
Try many approaches simultaneously.

Life is short. Make the most of your time as you search for a child. Adoption should be pursued from more than one direction at a time. If you wait until you are certain that one course will not give you a child before you go on to a subsequent method, you might become too old to pursue all of the many possibilities open to you. You may even want to begin to look for a child even before you are absolutely positive that you cannot become pregnant. Pursue alternatives concurrently. Look for a child independently at the same time you are trying to adopt through the adoption agency. You will significantly increase your chances of success.

If all of a sudden you simultaneously find yourself accepted by an adoption agency, pregnant, and hearing from an attorney that he has a baby for you—that's great. There are plenty of people around who want the children you are not able to accommodate; no one will be left out. The dilemma this poses is certainly better than pursuing one alternative at a time and failing. Just knowing that you have some other possibilities and are pursuing them makes failure at any juncture easier to handle.

Recommendation 8:
Try to be comfortable with failure.

When you search for a child, all you need is one success; expect some failure before you get that one success. You may fail in your fertility attempts, you may be rejected when you apply to adopt, you may find most people unable to help you find a baby. It is important to view the search for a child as a series of failures until your one success—a baby.

One adopting couple taught us all a lesson. They struggled for years with lots of different kinds of infertility remedies and failed. They had two possible leads that fell through in the early stages of adopting. They lost an adoption just as they were about to get a baby and after they had supported the birth mother for three months. They took the failure in stride and treated the birth mother, who had changed her mind, with dignity and compassion. Six months later, that birth mother referred a pregnant woman to them, and she gave them their son.

In reality, failures may be near successes. All experiences have something to teach us. It is important that one of the lessons we learn is not to be paranoid but to move forward and begin again. Angry people do not do well in finding babies.

Recommendation 9:
Obtain both counseling and legal representation for the birth parents.

Placing a child for adoption is a major decision in a person's life. Adoptive parents need to do everything in their power to make certain that the birth parents are sure of their decision and that they have looked thoroughly at the emotional and legal sides of adoption. In many ways this is the best insurance you can have that the birth parent won't change his or her mind.

The need for counseling on an issue as important as this should be clear. You cannot be all things to the birth mother. She needs to explore some issues with other people, and therapy gives her the chance. While she should never be forced into counseling, every effort should be made in all adoptions to try to have the birth mother see a counselor, and it is important that the counseling be done by someone who is familiar with adoption issues.

The need for legal representation is equally clear. If the adoption is ever challenged and the birth parents saw your attorney or one from the adoption agency, they can certainly claim that their attorney had a conflict of interest. This will create problems with the adoption proceeding.

The time to help the birth parents decide on the right thing to do about a pregnancy is before the child is placed. Adopting parents need to encourage this full exploration for the protection of the birth parents and for their own protection.

Recommendation 10:
Treat the birth family with respect and dignity.

The birth family does not simply enter your life for a brief time—they enter it forever. They may not have direct involvement on a day-to-day basis but they will always be a part of it.

They will come up repeatedly in the questions your child asks you. They will come up in the stories you tell your child. Perhaps you will see them in the eyes of your child or in the color of her hair. Maybe your child's entire appearance will remind you of one of the birth parents. You will be involved with them further if your child chooses to search and connect with them when she is an adult. You will be involved as your child compares what you have told her about them with what she learns about them for herself. When adoption records are opened or when a reunion occurs, you will be responsible for the way you have spoken about the birth family through the years.

No one says birth parents and adoptive parents would necessarily choose each other to be best friends; that is not what respect and dignity are about. But you need to feel positively about them, because your feelings will be conveyed to your child. That doesn't mean everything you say to your child about her birth parents must be positive. But if your underlying attitude toward the birth family is one of respect, even the negative things you say will not be put-downs to them or your child.

If you don't feel positively about the birth family, this is an adoption you should reconsider. If you feel they are beneath you or less than you are, what does this say to your child about herself? If your child is to feel positive about herself, she needs to hear and feel positive things about her birth parents.

Recommendation 11:
Be honest with your child about adoption.

You can give certain gifts to your child for life. One of these is honesty. You owe your child honesty about adoption. Answer his questions; give answers to questions that aren't asked.

You may try to pretend that yours is a family like any other, but it isn't. You may avoid the issue of adoption by never telling your child about it, but that is wrong. Think how your child will feel when he ultimately learns the truth. Is the difficulty of discussing adoption worth losing your child's trust?

Talk about adoption with your child. Read about adoption. Watch TV shows that discuss it. Adoption is actually a remarkable event in each of your lives and one you should be proud of. Why hide such a wonderful event? Telling your child about his adoption will not lessen the bond you have with him. But lying will.

Recommendation 12:
Recognize that adoption is a different way to have a child and neither better nor worse than having a biological child.

Accepting the difference between an adoptive family and a biological one may seem rather insignificant. On the contrary, acceptance of this underlying difference is one of the basic reasons adoptions succeed.

Parents who accept the difference are more open to dealing with adoption issues with their children. We are well aware that adoption issues are not finished when an adoption goes to court. Many of the issues—identity formation, abandonment, trust—are lifelong issues. These are issues that can only be resolved if the foundation of the family is based upon truth and honesty.

The importance of recognizing differences between adoptive families and biological families is stressed in the work of H. David Kirk.[3] In his book *Adoptive Kinship*,[4] Kirk says adoptive parents should acknowledge the difference between being a biological child and an adopted child. In this way, the parents can put themselves into the same place the child finds himself, be empathetic, and be ready to listen to their child's questions about his background even though they might be bothered by the questions. Kirk maintains that the readiness to listen and answer the child's questions increases the child's trust with the adoptive parent and strengthens the bonds between them.

Adoptive parents need to set aside their need to be a "normal" biological family and become instead a "normal" adoptive family. They need to recognize the differences for their own sakes, but also for the sake of their children, who need to develop the bonds of trust.

Recommendation 13:
Learn from your search.

Meaningful life lessons can be learned as you seek a child—lessons about risk taking, flexibility, perseverance, openness, honesty, and assertiveness. Your journey toward adoption will probably improve your parenting ability, expand your limits, improve your communication skills, and enhance your marriage. You will undoubtedly become wiser. Your search for a child can have considerable value.

Recommendation 14:
Once you have your child, enjoy him fully for who he is as an individual. You have a special opportunity to participate in his life in a significant and special way as his parent.

Your child is now your child. Accept him for who he is. He will be like you in some ways, and in other ways he will always be a part of another person's life, too. He is not yours to keep but yours to hold. He is yours to enjoy and accept. But what you gain from this experience and what you have already gained will be yours forever.

Let the lessons you have learned from your search for this special child carry over into your concepts of parenting. Enjoy your child so that he can learn to enjoy life. Be honest with him about life and about his origins so he can learn that honesty is not only tolerable but also desirable. Teach him to pursue the things that are valuable to him, as you have done with adoption. Help him view the problems he confronts from many directions so that he sees many solutions to life's dilemmas. Encourage him to become comfortable with his failures, not so that he becomes defeated by them but so that instead he becomes resilient and ready to try new approaches. Show him the value of new ideas that open up new choices for him when he feels that other alternatives have been exhausted. Let him experience the rewards of being in charge of his life rather than being buffeted by others.

Share your learning with your child in order that he, too, may gain from your finding him.

And Finally: Making Adoption Better for Everyone

Adoption is an exciting experience. Think of it positively, and you will succeed. You can view adoption as a negative or a positive in your life. You can view infertility as a deficiency and a punishment or as an exciting opportunity to pursue a different kind of family. You can view your search for a child as an unfair task in life or as an opportunity for growth and new experiences. While feelings of rejection, deficiency, and isolation will undoubtedly be a part of your search, do all that you can to feel positive about the time of your life you are experiencing. You *can* make a positive out of a negative, and perhaps your experience in the adoption process will motivate you to change the system of adoption to one that is healthier and more vital for everyone involved.

Believe you will get a child, and you are most likely to find one. While you maintain hope, you have a chance—a good chance—of finding a child. When you become discouraged, you must talk about it, think about it, find out why you are discouraged, and then begin again. Discouragement doesn't mean defeat; rather it signals a time to approach the search in a different way.

The problem is not whether there is a child for you, but how you can get to your child. If you truly believe there is one out there for you somewhere, your goal is to be knowledgeable, creative, adaptable, and innovative in how you reach that union. Remember that your adoption involvement does not end with finding a child—that is merely a point along the way. Adoption is a lifelong commitment. Believing in yourself and what you can accomplish creates miracles—miracles like children.

APPENDIXES

APPENDIX A

States Allowing Independent Adoption and Advertising

(State laws change quickly. Check with an attorney to be sure of the current state law.)

State	Independent ● or Not ○	Advertise
Alabama	●	*no*
Alaska	●	*yes*
Arizona	●	*yes*
Arkansas	●	*yes, but only by licensed adoption agencies*
California	●	*yes, but only by licensed adoption agencies*
Colorado	○	*no*
Connecticut	○	*no*
Delaware	○	*laws not clear, but newspapers don't accept ads*
District of Columbia	●	*yes*
Florida	●	*yes, but only when placed by agency or attorney*
Georgia	●	*yes, but only by licensed adoption agencies*
Hawaii	●	*yes*
Idaho	●	*no*
Illinois	●	*yes, but only when response is directed to a licensed adoption agency or attorney*
Indiana	●	*yes*
Iowa	●	*yes*
Kansas	●	*yes, but only by licensed adoption agencies; newspapers will accept if letter from attorney accompanies ad*
Kentucky	●	*no*
Louisiana	●	*yes*

State	Independent ● or Not ○	Advertise
Maine	●	*yes, but only by licensed adoption agencies*
Maryland	●	*yes, but attorneys can't locate birth mothers*
Massachusetts	○	*yes, but only by licensed adoption agencies*
Michigan	●	*yes*
Minnesota	●	*yes*
Mississippi	●	*yes*
Missouri	●	*yes*
Montana	●	*no*
Nebraska	●	*yes*
Nevada	●	*no*
New Hampshire	●	*yes*
New Jersey	●	*yes*
New Mexico	●	*yes*
New York	●	*yes*
North Carolina	●	*yes, but only by licensed adoption agencies*
North Dakota	○	*no*
Ohio	●	*no*
Oklahoma	●	*yes*
Oregon	●	*yes*
Pennsylvania	●	*yes*
Rhode Island	●	*no*
South Carolina	●	*yes*
South Dakota	●	*yes*
Tennessee	●	*yes*
Texas	●	*yes*
Utah	●	*yes*
Vermont	●	*yes*
Virginia	●	*yes*
Washington	●	*yes, but only by adoption agencies, attorneys from Washington, or adoptive parents with an approved home study*
West Virginia	●	*yes*
Wisconsin	●	*yes*
Wyoming	●	*yes*

Appendix B

Placement Reports—Adoptive Parent Home Study and Postplacement Adoption Appraisal

---

Adoptive Parent Home Study Preplacement Report

DATE: _____ ADOPTION CASEWORKER: _____

LEGAL NAME (Last name first): _____

STREET ADDRESS: _____

CITY: _____ STATE: _____ ZIP: _____

HOME TELEPHONE: _____ WORK TELEPHONE(S): _____

DATE OF MARRIAGE: _____

DATES OF GROUP INTERVIEWS: _____

DATES OF INDIVIDUAL INTERVIEWS: _____

OTHER SOURCES OF INFORMATION (Check all provided):

References   ☐   ☐   ☐

Medical reports:

    Physician   ☐   ☐

    Self report   ☐   ☐

Copy of marriage license   ☐

Autobiography   ☐   ☐

Criminal background check   ☐   ☐

Financial statement   ☐

Birth certificates   ☐   ☐

Divorce decree (if applicable)   ☐

Adoption questionnaire ☐

Child abuse registry check ☐

Letter from employer ☐

Family Background

I. Husband

FULL NAME: _____

DATE OF BIRTH: _____ PLACE OF BIRTH: _____

HEIGHT: _____ WEIGHT: _____ COMPLEXION: _____

EYE COLOR: _____ HAIR COLOR: _____

RACE: _____ ETHNIC ORIGIN: _____

RELIGION: _____ EDUCATION: _____

GENERAL DESCRIPTION: _____

PRESENT AND PAST MARITAL STATUS: _____

CHILDREN FROM PREVIOUS MARRIAGES (list names, dates of birth, who is supporting, and places of residence): _____

SPECIAL TALENTS, HOBBIES, INTERESTS: _____

DESCRIPTION OF CHILDHOOD: _____

PERSONAL LIFE HISTORY: _____

AREAS OF PAST LIFE HUSBAND WOULD CHANGE: _____

VALUES AND GOALS FOR THE FUTURE: _____

EMPLOYMENT HISTORY: _____

FINANCIAL HISTORY (bankruptcy, other sources of income): _____

HEALTH HISTORY (include alcohol and tobacco consumption): _____

CRIMINAL, CHILD ABUSE, AND DOMESTIC VIOLENCE HISTORY: _____

LEGAL INVOLVEMENT (arrests, convictions, lawsuits, etc.): _____

HOME STUDY HISTORY (any previous home study reports): _____

II. Wife

FULL NAME: _____

DATE OF BIRTH: _____ PLACE OF BIRTH: _____

HEIGHT: _____ WEIGHT: _____ COMPLEXION: _____

EYE COLOR: _____ HAIR COLOR: _____

RACE: _____ ETHNIC ORIGIN: _____

RELIGION: _____ EDUCATION: _____

GENERAL DESCRIPTION: _____

PRESENT AND PAST MARITAL STATUS: _____

CHILDREN FROM PREVIOUS MARRIAGES (list names, dates of birth, who is supporting, and places of residence): _____

SPECIAL TALENTS, HOBBIES, INTERESTS: _____

DESCRIPTION OF CHILDHOOD: _____

PERSONAL LIFE HISTORY: _____

AREAS OF PAST LIFE WIFE WOULD CHANGE: _____

VALUES AND GOALS FOR THE FUTURE: _____

EMPLOYMENT HISTORY: _____

FINANCIAL HISTORY (bankruptcy, other sources of income): _____

HEALTH HISTORY (include alcohol and tobacco consumption): _____

CRIMINAL, CHILD ABUSE, AND DOMESTIC VIOLENCE HISTORY: _____

LEGAL INVOLVEMENT (arrests, convictions, lawsuits, etc.): _____

HOME STUDY HISTORY (any previous home study reports): _____

III. Children

NAME, DATE OF BIRTH, AND GRADE IN SCHOOL OF EACH CHILD: _____

QUALITY OF PEER RELATIONSHIPS: _____

RESPONSIBILITIES IN THE FAMILY: _____

ATTITUDES TOWARD HAVING ADDITIONAL CHILD(REN) IN THE HOME: _____

Family Life

I. Marital Relationship

DESCRIBE COURTSHIP: _____

DESCRIBE MARRIAGE: _____

DESCRIBE LIFESTYLE: _____

DESCRIBE IMPORTANT SHARED VALUES: _____

DESCRIBE DECISION MAKING PROCESS IN MARITAL RELATIONSHIP: _____

DESCRIBE RESOLUTION OF CONFLICTS IN MARITAL RELATIONSHIP: _____

DESCRIBE IMPACT OF CHANGE AND HOW COUPLE DEALS WITH CHANGE: _____

II. Parenting

DESCRIBE EXPERIENCES AND FEELINGS ABOUT CHILD REARING: _____

DESCRIBE PHILOSOPHY OF DISCIPLINE: _____

HOW HUSBAND VIEWS ROLE AS A FATHER: _____

HOW HUSBAND VIEWS ROLE OF WIFE AS A MOTHER: _____

HOW WIFE VIEWS ROLE AS A MOTHER: _____

HOW WIFE VIEWS ROLE OF HUSBAND AS A FATHER: _____

III. Extended Family

FAMILY CONSTELLATION (full names of parents and spouses' siblings, relationship to each
    spouse, dates of birth and death): _____

EXTENDED FAMILY'S INVOLVEMENT WITH APPLICANT FAMILY: _____

EXTENDED FAMILY'S EXPECTATIONS ABOUT THIS ADOPTION: _____

IV. Spiritual Background

SPIRITUAL BACKGROUND (current and past involvement, changes expected in
    future): _____

Adoption Issues

I. Background

REASONS FOR ADOPTING: _____

INFERTILITY ISSUES AND ALTERNATIVES CONSIDERED: _____

ADOPTION HISTORY (what tried to this point): _____

UNDERSTANDING OF ADOPTION (commitment to adoption, expectations for adoption,
    concerns about adopting, understanding of adoption as alternative to biological parenting,
    recognition of lifelong developmental process in adoption): _____

EXPECTATIONS OF BIRTH MOTHER AND BIRTH FATHER (criteria for
    selecting): _____

PLANS FOR DISCUSSING ADOPTION WITH CHILD (disclosing facts at what
    age): _____

PLANS FOR HANDLING CHILD'S QUESTIONS ABOUT BIRTH PARENTS AND BIRTH
    RELATIVES: _____

PLANS FOR DISCUSSING CHILD'S RACIAL, ETHNIC, AND CULTURAL
    HERITAGE: _____

PLANS FOR CHILD IN EVENT OF DEATH OR DISABILITY: _____

II. Characteristics of Child Desired

PREFERRED AGE OF CHILD: _____ ACCEPTABLE AGE RANGE: _____

SIBLING GROUPS ACCEPTABLE/WITHIN WHAT AGE RANGE: _____

PREFERRED RACIAL OR ETHNIC GROUPS: _____

   ACCEPTABLE RACIAL OR ETHNIC GROUPS: _____

INTELLECTUAL POTENTIAL PREFERENCE: _____

   INTELLECTUAL POTENTIAL ACCEPTABLE: _____

PHYSICAL OR EMOTIONAL PROBLEMS: _____

ACCEPTABLE NONCORRECTABLE CONDITIONS:

- ☐ Diabetes
- ☐ Blindness
- ☐ Down's syndrome
- ☐ Epilepsy
- ☐ Deafness
- ☐ Spina bifida
- ☐ HIV positive
- ☐ Fetal alcohol effect
- ☐ Fetal alcohol syndrome
- ☐ Learning disability
- ☐ Severe visual impairment
- ☐ Hyperactivity (diagnosed)
- ☐ Cerebral Palsy
- ☐ Severe auditory impairment
- ☐ Inability to communicate
- ☐ Drug-affected at birth
- ☐ Other_____

ACCEPTABLE BEHAVIOR PATTERNS:

- ☐ Lying
- ☐ Temper tantrums
- ☐ Stealing
- ☐ Running away
- ☐ Shoplifting
- ☐ Drug use
- ☐ Ongoing group care
- ☐ Self-mutilating behavior
- ☐ Destructive behavior
- ☐ Repeated peer conflict
- ☐ Fire setting
- ☐ Sexual acting out
- ☐ Ongoing day treatment
- ☐ Other_____

ACCEPTABLE DEVELOPMENTAL DISABILITIES:

- ☐ Help needed with feeding, dressing, or toileting
- ☐ Help needed with mobility
- ☐ Constant care and supervision needed
- ☐ Ongoing medical or psychological therapy needed
  - ☐ Daily   ☐ Weekly   ☐ Monthly
- ☐ Special education needed to develop semi-independent skills

APPROPRIATE FACILITIES AVAILABLE:

- ☐ Psychological or psychiatric
- ☐ Special education
- ☐ Child care
- ☐ Medical treatment

III. Attitude Toward Openness

WILLINGNESS TO MEET BIOLOGICAL PARENTS: _____

AMOUNT OF PREADOPTION OPENNESS ACCEPTABLE TO FAMILY:

- ☐ Open to whatever the birth mother wants on prebirth contact
- ☐ Want to meet birth mother
- ☐ Want to meet birth father
- ☐ Willing to have birth parents visit in home
- ☐ Would like to meet regularly prior to birth
- ☐ Would like to be at the hospital
- ☐ Would like to be at the birth
- ☐ Willing to have birth mother cohabitate
- ☐ Not open to any contact
- ☐ Open to limited contact
- ☐ Will not give address to birth mother
- ☐ Do not want identity divulged (names or other identifying information)
- ☐ Not sure. It would depend on the individual situation.

DESCRIBE AMOUNT OF ONGOING CONTACT WILLING TO HAVE WITH BIOLOGICAL FAMILY (including birth mother, birth father, birth grandparents, and siblings): _____

Physical Provisions

I. Housing

DESCRIPTION OF CITY AND NEIGHBORHOOD: _____

GENERAL APPEARANCE OF HOME: _____

ACCOMMODATIONS FOR ADDITIONAL CHILD(REN): _____

POTENTIAL SAFETY HAZARDS: _____

II. Community Resources

AVAILABILITY OF MEDICAL FACILITIES: _____

AVAILABILITY OF COUNSELING FACILITIES: _____

AVAILABILITY OF EDUCATIONAL FACILITIES: _____

III. Finances

PROPERTY ASSETS AND LIABILITIES: _____

INSURANCE COVERAGE FOR EACH PERSON IN HOUSEHOLD

(types and amounts): _____

HUSBAND'S EMPLOYER: _____

LENGTH OF TIME EMPLOYED HERE: _____ SALARY: $_____

WIFE'S EMPLOYER: _____

LENGTH OF TIME EMPLOYED HERE: _____ SALARY: $_____

Health

SUMMARIZE FINDINGS OF DSHS 13-01 (X) MEDICAL REPORT FOR

HUSBAND: _____

SUMMARIZE FINDINGS OF DSHS 13-01 (X) MEDICAL REPORT FOR

WIFE: _____

References and Collateral Contacts

1. NAME, DATE, AND TITLE OF REFERENCE: _____

SUMMARIZE: _____

2. NAME, DATE, AND TITLE OF REFERENCE: _____

SUMMARIZE: _____

3. NAME, DATE, AND TITLE OF REFERENCE: _____

SUMMARIZE: _____

Recommendations and Evaluation

RECOMMENDATIONS FOR CHANGE TO FAMILY: _____

EVALUATION OF FAMILY AS POTENTIAL ADOPTERS AND RECOMMENDATION FOR

PLACEMENT: _____

_____

Signature and Title   Date

Postplacement Adoption Appraisal

DATE: _____ ADOPTION CASEWORKER: _____

COUPLE NAMES (Last name first): _____

STREET ADDRESS: _____

CITY: _____ STATE: _____ ZIP: _____

TELEPHONE(S): _____

DATES OF POSTPLACEMENT INTERVIEWS: _____

PROGRESS OF CHILD: _____

OVERALL IMPRESSION OF ADJUSTMENT OF CHILD AND FAMILY: _____

INDIVIDUAL FAMILY MEMBERS' RESPONSES TO ADOPTION: _____

UNEXPECTED RESPONSES: _____

DIFFICULT AREAS: _____

NEED ASSISTANCE IN WHICH AREAS: _____

CONTACT WITH BIRTH FAMILY: _____

CHILD'S MEDICAL FORM SUMMARIZED: _____

SUMMARY OF FINDINGS: _____

_____

Signature and Title   Date

Appendix C

Preplacement Report–International Adoptive Parent Home Study

PREPLACEMENT REPORT—INTERNATIONAL
ADOPTIVE PARENT HOME STUDY

DATE: _____ ADOPTION CASEWORKER: _____

LEGAL NAME (Last name first): _____

STREET ADDRESS: _____

CITY: _____ STATE: _____ ZIP: _____

HOME TELEPHONE: _____ WORK TELEPHONE(S): _____

DATE OF MARRIAGE: _____

DATES OF GROUP INTERVIEWS: _____

DATES OF INDIVIDUAL INTERVIEWS: _____

OTHER SOURCES OF INFORMATION (Check all provided):

References	☐	☐	☐
Medical reports:			
Physician	☐	☐	
Self report	☐	☐	
Copy of marriage license	☐		
Autobiography	☐	☐	
Criminal background check	☐	☐	
Financial statement	☐		
Birth certificates	☐	☐	
Divorce decree (if applicable)	☐		
Adoption questionnaire	☐	☐	

Child abuse registry check ☐ ☐
Letter from employer ☐ ☐

Description of Applicant(s)

DATE OF MARRIAGE: _____

NAME: _____

    DATE OF BIRTH: _____ PLACE OF BIRTH: _____

    RACE: _____ ETHNIC ORIGIN: _____

    RELIGION: _____ EDUCATION: _____

    OCCUPATION: _____ SOCIAL SECURITY NUMBER: _____

NAME: _____

    DATE OF BIRTH: _____ PLACE OF BIRTH: _____

    RACE: _____ ETHNIC ORIGIN: _____

    RELIGION: _____ EDUCATION: _____

    OCCUPATION: _____ SOCIAL SECURITY NUMBER: _____

APPEARANCE AND DESCRIPTION OF APPLICANTS: _____

MOTIVATION AND READINESS FOR ADOPTION: _____

BACKGROUND, EDUCATION, WORK HISTORY, AND FUTURE GOALS OF PROSPECTIVE
    ADOPTIVE FATHER: _____

BACKGROUND, EDUCATION, WORK HISTORY, AND FUTURE GOALS OF PROSPECTIVE
    ADOPTIVE MOTHER: _____

MARRIAGE RELATIONSHIP: _____

    PRIOR MARRIAGES: _____

INTERESTS AND LIFESTYLE: _____

OTHER ADULTS LIVING IN HOME: _____

FAMILY CONSTELLATION (full names of parents and siblings, dates of birth and
    death): _____

    NAME_____ RELATIONSHIP_____ DOB_____ STATUS_____

FAITH: _____

CHILD-CARE EXPERIENCE AND PARENTING PHILOSOPHY: _____

MATERNITY PLAN: _____

FINANCIAL STATUS: _____

    GROSS ANNUAL SALARY: _____ NET WORTH: _____

    ASSETS: _____ LIABILITIES: _____

    INSURANCE COMPANY: _____ INSURANCE COVERAGE: _____

HEALTH: _____

ASSESSMENT OF PHYSICAL, MENTAL, AND EMOTIONAL CAPABILITY OF THE
PROSPECTIVE ADOPTIVE PARENTS TO PROPERLY PARENT A CHILD: _____

ASSESSMENT OF ANY POTENTIAL PROBLEM AREAS AND RECOMMENDED
RESTRICTIONS: _____

Description of Home

HOME LOCATION: _____

GENERAL APPEARANCE OF HOME: _____

ASSESSMENT OF SUITABILITY OF LIVING ACCOMMODATIONS FOR A CHILD AND
DETERMINATION WHETHER SUCH SPACE MEETS APPLICABLE STATE
REQUIREMENTS: _____

Adoption Issues

TYPE OF CHILD DESIRED

AGE RANGE: _____   PREFERRED SEX: _____

NUMBER OF CHILDREN: _____   ETHNICITY: _____

ATTITUDE TOWARD BIRTH PARENTS AND OPENNESS: _____

PLANS FOR DISCUSSING ADOPTION WITH ADOPTED CHILD: _____

PREPARATION FOR THE ADOPTION OF A CHILD OF ANOTHER RACE: _____

Additional Information

CRIMINAL, CHILD ABUSE, AND DOMESTIC VIOLENCE HISTORY: _____

HOME STUDY HISTORY: _____

REFERENCES: _____

COUNSELING GIVEN AND PLANS FOR POSTPLACEMENT COUNSELING: _____

SUMMARY AND RECOMMENDATIONS: _____

(Requires notarization of documents being submitted.)

APPENDIX D

Prospective Parent Letters

Note: The letters in Appendixes D and E are examples of "ideal" letters that prospective adoptive parents might write to a birth mother. They are composites of actual letters written by successful adoptive parents, but all identifying features, names, and details have been changed.

Dear Birth Mother,

Hi. My name is Karen Smith, and I very much want to adopt a baby. The reasons for this are many and varied. I am a single woman, but I hesitate to use the word "single" because it is inadequate to describe my lifestyle. I have a wonderful group of friends and family that includes grandparents, cousins, and a variety of children, as well as great

Picture showing Karen in the backyard of her wooded home

male role models. I know how wonderful, loving, and nurturing an adoptive family environment can be, as I have many friends who are adopted. A history of love and commitment can forge a wonderful bond, which is what family is all about.

I am currently thirty-nine and have never married but am open to the possibility one day. Commitment is something that I take very seriously and something that I am not in a rush to do. I am financially secure and have extremely stable

Ethnic designs at bottom of page

employment as an office manager for a large firm. When my baby arrives, I will take lots of time off to bond with the baby and will eventually return to work. (Even my employers are excited about the arrival of the baby.) I am so lucky to have so much support from my family and friends. They are all anxiously awaiting this event, but none as anxiously as I am.

Picture showing Karen's family and friends during the holidays

My philosophy of life is that knowledge is power; therefore, I will never keep any secrets from my child about his or her history. I will share what I know, as little or as much as that may be and as little or as much as the birth parents feel comfortable with. Should my child wish to meet or have information of a more identifying nature about his birth parents, that will be a decision he or she will be able to make when mature enough and, of course, only with the consent of the birth mother. This is the most important thing either of us will ever do, and if we both understand and respect each other's needs, the best interests of the child will be met. This, of course, is our ultimate goal.

I grew up in New Mexico, which has a racially diverse population, and my parents felt strongly that we kids should learn all we could about the many cultures around us. I recognize the beauty of diversity and how much each unique individual has to contribute and to teach me. This recognition has probably fostered my love of travel. In the past ten years, I have traveled to Central America, Mexico, the Caribbean, Europe, and Africa. My favorite thing is to stay clear of the tourist areas and explore the areas where the people live. I can say without a doubt that I believe in valuing every person for his or her uniqueness and that being "different" is something to strive for. After all, what a bland, boring, and ultimately humorless world we would live in if we were all the same!

I believe in raising children the way I was raised, with tons of love and tons of laughter. To me, life is a fun, wonderful adventure and I want my child to have the same sense of joy each day that I do. I believe in lots of positive discipline. I do not believe in spanking. I also value education and want my child to have many opportunities in life. Since I have made the decision to adopt a child, I have been reading everything I can get my hands on about adopting and parenting. I also have a wonderful resource in my sister, who has a master's degree in child development. She shares my parenting philosophy and is most excited about becoming an "aunt."

By pursuing adoption, you are committing an act of such courage, love, and generosity that I will forever be in awe of your character and kindness. Thank you for considering me as a mother for your child.

Sincerely,

Karen (XXX) XXX-XXXX (I would gladly accept your collect call.)

[Name of Counselor, Facilitator, or Adoption Counselor]
(XXX) XXX-XXXX

[Name of Attorney], Attorney (XXX) XXX-XXXX

Picture showing Karen canoeing down a
river in Mexico

Welcome to the Ellingsen family, Laurel, Dennis, and Jackson (age two). We live in a large sunny house by the beach in Southern California with our three dogs, Iz, Magik, and Norman. It's a great place to raise a family, with plenty of neighborhood friends, playgrounds, beaches, mountains, good schools, and a great zoo nearby.

The couple and their child

Being a family is what we like to do the best. Laurel and Dennis got married only two months after they met— that was six years ago. We were so crazy about each other that we eloped and told our families afterward. Since then, we've become even better friends, learning to respect each other's differences as well as appreciating the ways we are alike. Also, we come from close-knit families—both sets of parents have been married for over forty-five years. Our families live on the East Coast, but we write letters and call each other at least once a week.

After we realized we were doing a good job raising our dogs, we concentrated on a baby. As a result, our family grew in the most special way two years ago when we met our first birth mother and then adopted Jackson. We had planned and dreamed about having a child for a long time, but nothing prepared us for the joy of the wild boy with the curly hair who came into our lives. From the moment he opens his eyes in the morning and leaps on top of us with a flying hug, until "cuddle" time at night, when we all lie down together to read bedtime books, Jackson adds an unmeasurable amount of love, laughter, and learning to our lives.

Yet there is still more room in our hearts and in our house. We have been looking forward to just the right time when we can expand our family again and make Jackson an older brother. Now that Jackson is an independent toddler who wants to do everything by himself, we hope to meet another birth mother who, with our respect and sensitivity, will share a part of her life with us. We know that by adding another child to our family we will not double our happiness but increase it by a factor so big as to be yet unknown!

Now for some straight facts you might want to know:

Casual picture with family
and their dogs

Casual picture of father and child

Dennis is an engineer for a medical instrument company, but he also does other projects from home. He hopes to have his own company in the near future. When he's not working, Dennis likes to spend time outdoors—running, hiking, camping, riding his motorcycle. He also enjoys reading, painting, and woodworking. Dennis is the one who makes us laugh. When he's buying weird wind-up toys, tossing Jackson in the air, squirting us with a giant water gun, or bringing out the video camera at embarrassing times, it's hard to believe that at least for part of the day he's also a "grown-up."

Laurel is a writer/editor who stopped going to an office to work when Jackson was born. She delights in her current job of making sure Jackson's days are filled with fun activities and adventures, like finding the playgrounds with the best jungle gyms, exploring creeks, or choosing new books from the library. Laurel makes friends easily and loves to have other kids, moms, and dogs over to play. She is also active in the community—with a group trying to save a local park and with a weekly adoption play group she helped start. During quieter times, Laurel enjoys reading, movies, long walks, phone conversations with her sisters and friends, and most kinds of junk foods.

Jackson loves baseball, soccer, and basketball (not necessarily in that order). He's crazy about animals, especially horses, dogs, kittens, turtles, and monkeys. His current favorite places to go are the zoo, a nearby horse farm, a turtle pond, anywhere where there is a fish tank, and the pet store. Almost anywhere he goes, he has to stop to study the bugs, snails, or even lizards that cross his path. Running in circles on the beach with his best friend, Preston, or chasing birds and blowing bubbles with his other best friend, Jesse, puts him in ecstasy.

Casual picture of
mother and child

Now, maybe you've begun to get an idea of who

we are. We are looking forward to sharing our lives with a birth mother and her child in any way that feels right to all of us. Maybe that will be you.

Please call us, our adoption counselor, or our attorney collect.

Laurel and Dennis (XXX) XXX-XXXX

[Counselor's Name], Adoption Counselor (XXX) XXX-XXXX

[Attorney's Name], Attorney (XXX) XXX-XXXX

Casual picture of child

APPENDIX E

Letter to Birth Mother Who Requests More Information

[Date]

Dear Tracy:

When Anna and I heard through our adoption counselor that there might be a baby available for adoption, we were thrilled. We've been married for six years and have not been able to have a child. We have been through dozens of diagnostic tests and procedures, a laparotomy, and three rounds of in vitro fertilization—without success. We have been considering adoption for the past couple of years and just this past year had our adoption home study completed and began working with our adoption counselor. We have been told that it can sometimes take years to adopt, so when we heard about you, it seemed like a gift from heaven.

We know that this must be a difficult time for you. Obviously you love your baby very much, as you've chosen to give it life; we're sure you want that life to be a good one. You probably have many questions about us. We'll do our best to give you a "picture" of Anna and me—what we're like as people, what we believe in and care about. (Even though I am the one writing this letter, Anna is involved in every step.) If, after reading this letter, you think we are the kind of family you would like your baby to become a part of and you would like to meet us, we would be more than happy to meet with you.

We both want to tell you a little bit more about ourselves and let you know about our families. We have included some pictures so you can see the kind of life we lead.

Anna with her current class

Anna's family (left to right) Elizabeth (her oldest sister), Meredith (her youngest sister), Elna (her mother), and Bob (her stepfather)

Anna was born in Minneapolis, Minnesota. When she was ten her family moved to Spencerville, a small town in Pennsylvania. She graduated from the University of Pennsylvania in 1966 with a B.S. in education. She has worked as a junior high school teacher for the past seven years. She loves her work and continues to find it challenging and rewarding. Anna is planning on taking a year off once the baby arrives, and then she will probably return to work. Her schedule is

Anna's father and stepmother

great for raising children. Anna describes herself as a caring person who enjoys her life. Anna feels she had a wonderful life as a child and wants to make sure that our child has the same feeling about life. Anna's parents are divorced and have been for the past twelve years. They both have remarried and we all get along very well. All the grandparents are excited about the possibility of our adopting a child. Anna has two sisters who live nearby who are both looking forward to playing active roles in their nephew/niece's life. Both of her sisters have children who are eager for more cousins.

I was born and raised in Baltimore. I graduated from college in 1983 and have been an architect ever since. I mostly design houses. I am self-employed and have been for the past six years. I love what I do and have a very flexible schedule, with many opportunities to work out of our home. I plan on being very involved with the raising of our child. I am an only child and have a close relationship with my parents. I feel my father and mother are two of my best friends. Because I was an only

Chad and his parents

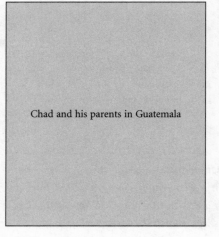

Chad and his parents in Guatemala

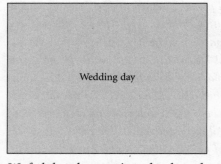

Wedding day

child, my parents took me everywhere. I had chances to spend time in many different countries as a young child and feel it really improved my life. My parents recently retired and now live in Northern California. We see them about every two months and have a great relationship with them both. They have already expressed their interest in taking their first grandchild to visit Disneyland. They were great parents and I know they will be wonderful grandparents to our child.

Anna and I met in 1985. I had just moved to Oregon and we met through a mutual friend. We dated for a year, fell in love, and were married. We continue to be in love and are both very committed to each other. The past couple of years with the infertility issues have been challenging and placed more demands on our relationship. We feel that the experience has brought us closer together, improved our communication skills, and made us realize how important having a sense of humor is. Although we both hold strong opinions that sometimes differ, we've never had any trouble resolving conflicts. We both believe in talking out our problems. I think that one of our great strengths is that we are responsive to each other. We share a strong belief that God's purpose for us, while not always clear, surely involves helping others and, in our own small way, making the world a better and more peaceful place. Raising children seems to us to be an essential part of our purpose.

Our home will be a great place to raise a family. I designed and helped build it five years ago. It has been a labor of love and we feel it is very comfortable and inviting. It has four bedrooms and a large playroom which opens up to the fenced backyard. We have two golden receivers (Honeybear and Ruby) and a cat (Sam). They are all extremely gentle and will be great with children.

We live in a wonderful neighborhood with only eight houses on our street. We

Anna and Chad sailing

Cat and dogs at home

really like our neighbors, and five of them have young children. When school gets out, our neighborhood is filled with children playing. The elementary school is two blocks from our house.

We both love to garden, walk the dogs, cook, spend time with friends and family, and go to the movies. We also love to sail on a lake that is about a half hour from our place. Actually there is even a sailing program for little kids that we have heard is lots of fun.

Most of our friends, like us, are in their thirties; many have young children. Recently, close friends of ours adopted a child from China. Being around children has intensified our own desire for a family. We are both really looking forward to becoming parents. As we have watched our friends and family members raise their children, we've seen the challenges and rewards they experience. We discuss on a regular basis our own ideas about raising children. We believe that a child needs a great deal of time with both parents—time for cuddling, storytelling, playing, and just being silly. We both are fortunate to have flexibility with our work schedules and plan on doing the majority of child care ourselves. We will try to provide a rich educational environment so that the child can find his or her love, whether it be in music, art, sports, or scholastics. We feel that a child needs discipline and order in his or her life, but in a loving and mutually respectful environment where punishment is rarely necessary. We feel that a child needs parents who are loving and consistent.

Anna and Chad with friends
July Fourth party

Anna and I don't know much about you or your needs. We would be happy to get together for dinner so that we can have an opportunity to meet and get to know each other. We'll welcome you to our home if you would like to visit us. Certainly we would be willing to assist you in any way we can, recognizing that in your last months of pregnancy it may be difficult for you to work. If you would like, we would be happy to take you to your doctor appointments and/or be with you during your labor and delivery. We would also be happy to communicate with you over the years, sending pictures and letters on the child's progress. We know that many, if not most, adopted children develop a keen interest in knowing something about their birth parents. We would not interfere with that process if it were your desire for your child to know you.

If you wish to know more about us but do not wish to meet with us, our adoption counselor has offered to meet with you on our behalf. We're sure that whatever decision you make will be the one that you believe is best for you and your baby. Whatever you decide, we wish you the best.

Sincerely,

Anna and Chad Jones

A sunny afternoon in the backyard

APPENDIX F

Organizations and Resources for Adoption

Adopt a Special Kid (AASK America)
P.O. Box 7762
Washington, DC 20013
(202) 388-3888
*Current national headquarters of AASK,
which has a registry of special-needs
children available for adoption and also
offers support for adopting parents*

Adopt a Special Kid (AASK California)
287 17th Street, #207
Oakland, CA 94612-3017
(510) 451-1748
*A nonprofit agency focusing on placement
of children with special needs*

Adopted Child newsletter
P.O. Box 9362
Moscow, ID 83843-0117
(208) 882-1794
*Four-page newsletter discussing one issue
each month for adoptive parents and
professionals*

Adoptee's Liberty Movement
   Association (ALMA)
P.O. Box 727, Radio City Station
New York, NY 10101-0727
(212) 581-1568
Nationally based adoption search resource

Adoptees in Search
P.O. Box 41016
Bethesda, MD 20824
(301) 656-8555
*Professional, nonprofit adoptee/birth
relative search and support
organization . . . provides total search and
support or passive, voluntary registry.*

Adoption Resource Exchange for Single
   Parents, Inc. (ARESP)
P.O. Box 5782
7004 Bethnal Court
Springfield, VA 22150-3061
(703) 866-5577
*A nonprofit organization staffed by
volunteers that has an exchange for
special-needs children available for
adoption by single parents*

Adoptive Families of America, Inc.
3333 Highway 100, N.
Minneapolis, MN 55422
(612) 535-4829, (800) 372-3300
http://www.adoptivefam.org/
*Supports, educates, and advocates for
adoptive families and 200 support groups
throughout the United States and world;
offers adoption information and
multicultural resources . . . helpful, well-
done magazine*

American Academy of Adoption
    Attorneys
P.O. Box 33053
Washington, DC 20033-0053
(202) 832-2222
*Referrals for adoption attorneys who
share beliefs and meet specific criteria . . .
promotes reform of adoption laws and
disseminates information on ethical
adoption practices*

American Adoption Congress (AAC)
1000 Connecticut Avenue, NW, #9
Washington, DC 20036
(202) 483-3399
*An international network of individuals
and organizations committed to truth in
adoption and to reform and protect all
involved in adoption from abuse or
exploitation*

American Association of Marriage and
    Family Therapists
1133 15th Street, NW #300
Washington, DC 20005
(202) 452-0109
*Umbrella organization for marriage and
family therapists*

American Association of Open
    Adoption Agencies (AAOAA)
1000 Hastings
Traverse City, MI 49686
(616) 947-8110
http://www.openadoption.org/
*A national association of nonprofit
adoption agencies committed to providing
open adoption services*

American Psychiatric Association
1400 K Street, NW
Washington, DC 20005-2403
(202) 682-6000
*Umbrella organization for psychiatrists in
practice*

American Psychological Association
    (APA)
1200 17th Street, NW
Washington, DC 20036-3006
(202) 955-7670
*Umbrella organization for psychologists
in practice*

Americans Adopting Orphans, Inc.
12345 Lake City Way, NE, #2001
Seattle, WA 98125-5401
(206) 524-5437
E-mail: aao@orphans.com
http://www.orphans.com
*Licensed child-placing agency but also
helps in private international adoptions*

Birthparent Connection
P.O. Box 230643
Encinitas, CA 92023-0643
(619) 753-8288
*Publishes an adoption networking
directory of search and support groups
nationwide*

Black Adoption Consortium, Inc.
5090 Central Highway, #6
Pennsauken, New Jersey 08109-4637
(609) 486-0100
Publishes African American children's
book series featuring adoptive families

California Marketing
134 Waverly Drive
Pasadena, CA 91105-2514
(818) 568-8700
Provides help to people on independent
adoptions by doing mailing to targeted
OB-GYNs, abortion alternative groups,
and family-planning centers

Child Welfare League of America, Inc.
440 First Street, NW, #310
Washington, DC 20001-2028
(202) 638-2952
http://www.cwla.org/
Provides consultation, training programs,
and conferences in areas related to child
welfare

Children Awaiting Parents (CAP Book)
700 Exchange Street
Rochester, NY 14608-2717
(716) 232-5110
http://www.adopt.org/adopt
National photolisting of hard-to-place
children available in the United States . . .
requires home study and agency
supervised postplacement

Concerned United Birthparents, Inc.
    (CUB)
2000 Walker Street
Des Moines, IA 50317-5201
(800) 822-2777, (515) 263-9558
Birth parents' group concerned with
advocacy for opening of birth records . . .
also has search registry

Council for Equal Rights in Adoption
    (CERA)
356 E. 74th Street #2
New York, NY 10021-3919
(212) 988-0110
Dedicated to the preservation and
reunification of families

Council of Three Rivers, Inc.
200 Charles Street
Pittsburgh, PA 15238-1027
(412) 782-4457
National exchange for Native Americans

DNA Diagnostic Center
205 Corporate Court
Fairfield, OH 45014
(800) 362-2368
DNA testing to establish parents
nationwide

Gay & Lesbian Parents Coalition
    International
P.O. Box 50360
Washington, DC 20091
(202) 583-8029
Publishes a newsletter and directory of
parent support groups for gay and lesbian
parents

Genetica DNA Laboratories
8740 Montgomery Road
Cincinnati, OH 45236
(800) 433-6848
DNA testing

Institute for Black Parenting
9920 La Cienega Boulevard, #806
Inglewood, CA 90301
(310) 348-1400
Local resource for parents of African
American children

International Concerns Committee for
Children
911 Cypress Drive
Boulder, CO 80303-2821
(303) 494-8333
*Offers information on adoptable
domestic and foreign children . . . puts
out Report on Foreign Adoption . . .
photolisting on international children
awaiting adoption . . . bimonthly updates
on international adoption*

International Shrine Headquarters
P.O. Box 31356
Tampa, FL 33631-3356
(813) 281-0300
*Burn and orthopedic help for children
from birth to eighteen years, free of
charge to qualifying families . . . nineteen
orthopedic hospitals and three burn
centers in the United States.*

International Soundex Reunion
Registry
P.O. Box 2312
Carson City, NV 89702-2312
(702) 882-7755
*Free mutual consent reunion registry for
adults who desire contact or reunion with
kin by birth . . . no search assistance but
does make referrals to agencies and
organizations that do provide that service*

International Waiting Children
Program at Children's Home
Society of Minnesota
2230 Como Avenue
St. Paul, MN 55108-1798
(612) 646-6393
*A local group doing international
adoptions*

Internet Adoption Registry
AOC 8640-M Guilford Road, #211
Columbia, MD 21046
E-mail: crc@clark.net
http://www.adoptiononline.com
*Provides place for prospective parents to
place letter on Internet*

Interrace *magazine*
P.O. Box 12048
Atlanta, GA 30355-2048
(404) 350-7877
*Magazines for and about "interracial"
couples, families, and "multiracial"
people distributed nationwide.* Interrace
*encourages equality and understanding.
Previously* Biracial Child *and* Child of
Color

Latin American Parents Association
(LAPA)
8646 15th Avenue
Brooklyn, NY 11228
(718) 236-8689
*National organization whose goal is to
help those seeking to adopt children from
Latin America . . . distributes
information and provides support*

MBNA America
P.O. Box 15136
Wilmington, DE 19850
(800) 262-6628
*Adoption loans . . . credit lines from
$2,500 to $25,000 at low interest rate . . .
call to ask for application*

National Adoption Center
1500 Walnut Street, #701
Philadelphia, PA 19102-3523
(215) 735-9988, (800) TO ADOPT
http://www.adopt.org/adopt
*Finds homes for children with special
needs . . . resource for prospective*

adoptive parents at all stages of the process . . . connected with National Adoption Exchange

National Adoption Exchange
1500 Walnut Street, #701
Philadelphia, PA 19102-3523
(215) 735-9988, (800) TO ADOPT
http://www.adopt.org/adopt
For adoptive parents, agencies, professionals . . . listing of children with special needs

National Adoption Information
   Clearinghouse
P.O. Box 1182
Washington, DC 20013-1182
(703) 352-3488 or (888) 251-0075
http://www.calib.com/naic
Provides information about all aspects of adoption

National Adoption Registry
1807 Hartel Avenue
Philadelphia, PA 19111-3530
(215) 728-0510
Set up to reunite those touched by adoption . . . search and reunion registry for birth families

National Association of Social Workers
750 First Street, NE, #700
Washington, DC 20002
(202) 408-8600
Umbrella organization for social workers in practice

National Center for Lesbian Rights
870 Market Street, #507
San Francisco, CA 94102-3002
(415) 392-6257
Provides adoption-related publications, information, and referrals

National Council for Single Adoptive
   Parents, Inc. (NCSAP, Inc.)
P.O. Box 15084
Chevy Chase, MD 20825
(202) 966-6367
Can help locate local groups . . . publishes handbook for single adoptive parents

National Foster Parent Association, Inc.
   (NFPA)
9 Dartmoor Drive
Crystal Lake, IL 60014
(815) 455-2527 or (800) 557-5238
Helps foster parents on any issues involving foster children

North American Council on Adoptable
   Children (NACAC)
970 Raymond Avenue, #106
St. Paul, MN 55114-1146
(612) 644-3036, Hotline (800) 470-6665
E-mail: NACAC@aol.com
http://ericps.ed.uiuc.edu/npin/reswork/
   workorgs/nacac.html
Provides significant legislative advocacy and published newsletter, Adoptalk

PACT—An Adoption Alliance
3450 Sacramento Street, #239
San Francisco, CA 94118-1914
(415) 221-6957
http://www.iwe.com/pact
Publishes quarterly magazine about adopted children of color . . . assists in adoption of children of color . . . not an agency

Perspectives Press
P.O. Box 90318
Indianapolis, IN 46290-0318
(317) 872-3055
http://www.perspectivespress.com
Publishers of books on adoption and infertility

Planned Parenthood Federation of
America, Inc.
810 Seventh Avenue
New York, NY 10019
(212) 541-7800
Family-planning organization that is
throughout the United States

RESOLVE, Inc.
1310 Broadway
Somerville, MA 02144-1731
(617) 623-0744
E-mail: resolveinc@aol.com
http://www.resolve.org/
Infertility support group, offering
information, resources, and referrals . . .
has chapters throughout the United
States . . . has information on local
chapters

Roots & Wings adoption magazine
P.O. Box 577
Hackettstown, NJ 07840
(908) 637-8828
E-mail: adoption@interactive.net
http://www.adopting.org/rw.html
Magazine for families and friends
touched by adoption

Tapestry Books
P.O. Box 359
Ringoes, NJ 08551-0359
(800) 765-2367 or (908) 806-6695
http://www.tapestrybooks.com/
Source of adoption, special-needs, and
infertility books

Three Feathers Associates, National
American Indian Adoption Service
P.O. Box 5508
Norman, OK 73070
(405) 360-2919
Adoption program for Native Americans
including national exchange for special-
needs children . . . adopting parents must
be eligible for tribal enrollment

U.S. Department of State, Bureau of
Consular Affairs
Office of Children's Issues
Room 4811, Department of State
Washington, DC 20520-4818
(202) 647-2688
http://www.travel.state.gov
Has updated adoption information for
over sixty countries . . . information on
orphan visa rules . . . will make inquiries
of the U.S. consular section abroad
regarding specific cases

Vista Del Mar Child and Family
Services
3200 Motor Avenue
Los Angeles, CA 90034-3710
(310) 836-1223
Licensed private agency in Southern
California that has been very forward
looking on openness in adoption

APPENDIX G

Children's Books on Adoption

Adoption Books for Very Young Children

Blomquist, Geraldine M., and Paul B. Blomquist. *Zachary's New Home*. New York: Magination Press, 1990. 2 to 8 years. (A confused and upset kitten is moved from one family to a foster family and then to an adoptive family . . . helps open up communication . . . well-done . . . useful for children who have had several homes)

Bloom, Suzanne. *A Family for Jamie: An Adoption Story*. New York: Clarkson W. Potter, Inc., 1991. 3 to 8 years. (A very nicely illustrated book offering a pleasant and simple introduction to adoption . . . depicts an agency worker)

Bunin, Catherine, and Bunin, Sherry. *Is That Your Sister?: A True Story of Adoption*. New York: Pantheon Books, 1992. 3 to 10 years. (Illustrates interracial adoption . . . how to handle the questions that come up from friends . . . well-done)

Caines, Jeanette. *Abby*. New York: Harper & Row, 1973. 2 to 7 years. (What might be a black baby is adopted when she is almost one year old . . . older brother isn't adopted . . . one of the few books talking about siblings and using minority-looking children to illustrate characters . . . nice picture book)

Cannon, Janell. *Stellaluna*. San Diego: Harcourt Brace & Company, 1993. (A baby bat who falls into a bird's nest is adopted by and learns from these birds before she is reunited with her mother . . . clearly illustrates importance of friendship and family)

Connelly, Maureen. *All Babies: A Coloring Book*. Edited by Joyce Sieff. Omaha, Neb.: Centering Corp., 1993. 2 to 6 years. (Unique book in coloring-book format explains adoption from birth mother's pregnancy through child's homecoming . . . simple text . . . helps explain adoption in a different way)

D'Antonio, Nancy. *Our Baby from China: An Adoption Story*. Morton Grove, Ill.: Albert

Whitman & Co., 1997. 2 to 8 years. (Simple text and photographs . . . another good beginning book on international adoption)

Davol, Marguerite W. *Black, White, Just Right.* Morton Grove, Ill.: Albert Whitman & Co., 1993. 2 to 8 years. (A wonderful picture book about a biracial child . . . shows a child with a black mother and a white father . . . describes differences between family members with an understanding that everything is just right . . . not about adoption per se, but certainly relevant)

Drescher, Joan. *Your Family My Family.* New York: Walker & Co., 1980. 3 to 8 years. (Briefly describes several kinds of families and cites some of the strengths of family life . . . interracial, adoptive, single parent, and foster families are all explored)

Fisher, Iris L. *Katie-Bo: An Adoption Story.* Bellmore, N.Y.: Modan-Adama Books, 1987. 3 to 8 years. (Discusses expecting a new sister but mom's not pregnant . . . sister is being adopted from Korea . . . explains that children enter the same family in different ways)

Fowler, Susi G. *When Joel Comes Home.* New York: Greenwillow Books, 1993. 2 to 8 years. (Chronicles the arrival of a new baby through the eyes of the youngest child but discusses the joy of adoption from the perspective of neighbors, nieces, nephews, friends, and other children . . . multicultural illustrations . . . good for almost any country)

Freudberg, Judy, and Tony Geiss, *Susan and Gordon Adopt a Baby.* New York: Random House, 1986. 2 to 7 years. (Characters from *Sesame Street,* Susan and Gordon, adopt an older child . . . Big Bird is jealous and curious . . . explains new son will be their son forever . . . one of its kind . . . worthwhile for any adoptive family)

Gordon, M., *I'd Rather Be with a Real Mom Who Loves Me.* 3 to 10 years. (Honest account of the frustrations and heartaches of a boy who lives with foster parents . . . good for a child whose life has been disrupted or sad . . . chance to have child talk about feelings with understanding and patient adult)

Herbert, Stephanie. *Being Adopted.* Washington, D.C.: Child Welfare League of America, 1991. 2 to 3 years. (A simple picture book . . . well-done)

Hicks, Randall B. *Adoption Stories for Young Children.* Sun City, Calif.: WordSlinger Press, 1995. 3 to 8 years. (Good way for younger children to learn about adoption . . . good for your child's friends, siblings, and cousins . . . discusses Ryan, who is five, and all his friends who are adopted . . . his baby-sitter, who is pregnant and not ready to be a mom, is choosing the family to adopt her child)

Jarrell, Randall. *The Animal Family.* New York: Pantheon Books, 1965. 2 to 5 years. (Good book for family where child is uncomfortable with emphasis on adoption . . . tells about different kinds of families)

Kasza, Keiko. *A Mother for Choco.* New York: G. P. Putnam's Sons, 1992. 2 to 8 years. (Adopted baby bird is looking for a mother who looks like him . . . his mom does hug, kiss, sing, and dance with him and loves him so they find she is perfect for him . . . never uses word *adopted* . . . highly recommended for even older ages)

Kates, Bobbi Jane. *We're Different, We're the Same.* New York: Random House Books for Young Readers, 1992. 2 to 6 years. (Book uses familiar *Sesame Street* Muppets and people to illustrate differences but also similarities . . . different eyes, but all eyes do the same thing . . . same for skin, feelings . . . easygoing approach makes children comfortable with differences)

Katz, Karen. *Over the Moon: An Adoption Tale.* New York: Henry Holt & Co., 1997. 2 to 8 years. (Charming book about international adoption with lots of beautiful pictures . . . good beginning book)

Keller, Holly. *Horace.* New York: Greenwillow Books, 1991. 2 to 8 years. (Horace's animal family is striped and he is spotted . . . even when he finds a spotted family, he is ready at the end of the day to go home . . . one of the better books for introducing children who look different from their parents to why color doesn't matter)

Koch, Janice. *Our Baby: A Birth and Adoption Story.* Fort Wayne, Ind.: Perspectives Press, 1986. 2 to 8 years. (Previously titled *Our Adopted Baby* . . . this edition is more up-to-date . . . discusses sperm, eggs, ovum, fetus, penis, embryo . . . facts-of-life approach, but well-done . . . responds to first questions . . . Did I grow in your tummy? . . . worthwhile addition to the field)

Koehler, Phoebe. *The Day We Met You.* New York: Bradbury Press, 1990. 1 to 5 years. (Couple tells about preparations they made to bring their baby home . . . a wonderful opportunity for telling about a child's own homecoming when it is read aloud . . . color illustrations . . . highly recommended by parents)

Kuklin, Susan. *When I See My Doctor.* New York: Bradbury Press, 1988. 3 to 6 years. (Young Asian boy goes to the doctor with his Caucasian mother)

Kurzel, K. *Pugnose Has Two Special Families.* Royal Oak, Mich.: R-Squared Press, 1997. 2 to 6 years. (Book for families involved in open adoptions . . . discusses happiness and sadness of adoption . . . more about birth family than most books)

LaCure, Jeffrey R. *Adopted Like Me.* Franklin, Mass.: Adoption Advocate Publishing Co., 1993. 2 to 9 years. (Story of a polar bear who begins to ask questions about his adoption . . . also talks about untimely pregnancy and the need to meet others who are adopted)

Lapsley, Susan. *I Am Adopted.* Scarsdale, N.Y.: Bradbury Press, 1974. 3 to 6 years. (A little boy explains what it means to be adopted . . . good, general introduction for the very young . . . questions addressed to reader invite a child to respond . . . pleasant, low-key)

London, Jonathan. *A Koala for Katie: An Adoption Story.* Morton Grove, Ill.: Albert Whitman & Co., 1993. 2 to 6 years. (Katie asks parents about her adoption . . . pretends to adopt a koala bear herself . . . helps young adopted child understand how parents love and care for adopted children)

Lowe, Darla. *Story of Adoption: Why Do I Look Different?* Minneapolis, Minn.: East-West Press, 1987. 3 to 6 years. (Three-year-old girl doesn't understand why she looks different from her parents . . . they tell her the story of how they got her from Korea . . . at the end she has new brother who looks like her . . . help for children who look different from parents)

Mandelbaum, Pili. *You Be Me, I'll Be You.* New York: Kane/Miller, 1990. 3 to 7 years. (Young girl is sad because she doesn't like the color of her face and arms and wants to be like her white father . . . they decide to switch . . . not about adoptions but great book to tell how one family handles interracial issues)

McCutcheon, John. *Happy Adoption Day*. Boston: Little, Brown & Co., 1996. 2 to 6 years. (From song . . . nice and colorful book)

Melmed, Laura Kraus. *The Rainbabies*. New York: Lothrop, Lee & Shepard Books, 1992. 3 to 8 years. (Folktale of childless couple finding tiny babies in the grass . . . because they are good, they are rewarded with a baby to love and care for . . . lots of magic and fairy-tale aspects)

Meredith, Judith. *And Now We Are a Family*. Boston: Beacon Press, 1971. 3 to 7 years. (One of the few books about adoption that talks about unwed mothers . . . says adoption means forever)

Modesitt, Jeanne. *Mama, If You Had a Wish*. New York: Green Tiger Press, 1993. 3 to 7 years. (Bunny asks his mother what she would wish and says he thinks it would be that he look different . . . mama's response is very affirming and gentle, showing love is unconditional)

Mora, Pat. *Pablo's Tree*. New York: Macmillan, 1994. 2 to 8 years. (Grandfather plants a tree in honor of his new grandson . . . he decorates it every year to celebrate Pablo's adoption day . . . good for single parents or two-parent families . . . one of few on Hispanic children)

Patterson, Eleanora. *Twice Upon-a-Time: Born and Adopted*. Brattleboro, Vt.: EP Press, 1987. 3 to 10 years. (Talks about adoption of children, babies and older, describes in simple text both the biological and social beginnings of adopted children . . . discusses how some children want to know more about adoption and others don't . . . unique, well-done picture book)

Petertyl, Mary Ebejer. *Seeds of Love: For Brothers and Sisters of International Adoption*. Grand Rapids, Mich.: Folio One Publishers, 1997. 2 to 6 years. (Well-done book that fills a need for children . . . discusses a young child whose parents will be going away to adopt from another country . . . deals with feelings of separation . . . suggests ways parents can ease anxiety . . . nice pictures)

Rondell, Florence, and Ruth Michaels. *The Family That Grew*. New York: Crown Publishers, 1951. 3 to 6 years. (Older book on adoption that still is sold . . . goes with companion volume for parents by same author)

Rosen, Michael. *Crow and Hawk: A Traditional Pueblo Indian Story*. San Diego: Harcourt Brace & Co., 1995. 3 to 8 years. (Native American story about crow laying her eggs and getting tired of waiting so she flies away only to find hawk has hatched and raised them as baby crows . . . eagle helps them decide who should be the mother . . . beautiful illustrations)

Silber, Kathleen, and Debra M. Parelskin. *My Special Family: A Children's Book about Open Adoption*. Orinda, Calif.: Open Adoption Press, 1994. 3 to 9 years. (Introduction to open adoption for child . . . has section which can be personalized and a section for guiding parents . . . one of the few books addressing this kind of adoption . . . really a baby book for open adoption)

Simon, Norma. *All Kinds of Families*. Chicago: Albert Whitman & Co., 1976. 3 to 8 years. (Not about adoption but about the similarities and differences between families [size, tastes in food, family members] . . . explains that differences make the world richer . . . does refer to adoption . . . shows diversity of families in illustrations)

——. *Why Am I Different?* Chicago: Albert Whitman & Co., 1976. 2 to 8 years. (Shows everyday situations in which children see themselves as different from others in families, preferences, aptitudes, religion, and includes part about adoption . . . emphasizes it is OK to be different)

Sly, Kathleen O'Connor. *Becky's Special Family.* Corona, Calif.: Alternative Parenting Publications, 1985. 3 to 6 years. (Very simply written book about an open adoption . . . child calls her birth mother and writes her birth grandparents . . . section for parent to fill in about their child)

Stein, Sara Bonnett. *The Adopted One: An Open Family Book for Parents and Children Together.* New York: Walker & Co., 1979. 3 to 8 years. (Both explanatory text for parents and an easily presented format for the child . . . could be used with very young child to explain adoption)

Stinson, Kathy. *Steven's Baseball Mitt: A Book about Being Adopted.* Ontario, Canada: Annick Press, 1992. 3 to 8 years. (Explores a young person's feelings and fantasies about adoption . . . good for discussions . . . Steven's search for mitt depicts his search for something missing in himself . . . some parents have mixed feelings about this book)

Swope, Julie D. *The Legend of the Bear: A Tale for Children Who Wait to Be Adopted.* York, Pa.: Jess Press, 1983. 3 to 7 years. (Story of a bear that waits a long time to be adopted . . . finds he is being given to a young Asian girl who gets off the plane when her adopting family meets her)

Taber, Barbara. *Adopting Baby Brother.* Hanover Falls, N.Y.: (n.p.), 1974. 3 to 8 years. (A nicely illustrated book on general subject of adoption for young children . . . hard to find since it is self-published)

Voake, Charlotte. *Mrs. Goose's Baby.* Boston: Joy Street Books, 1989. 3 to 6 years. (Mrs. Goose finds an egg, sits on it to keep it safe and warm, and soon has a baby of her own . . . Mrs. Goose's baby isn't just like her)

Wasson, Valentia Pavlovna. *The Chosen Baby.* Philadelphia: J. B. Lippincott, 1977. 3 to 6 years. (Older picture book, which is still available, introduces adoption . . . begins "Once upon a time" . . . current version has updated illustrations . . . still somewhat out-of-date . . . some parents really dislike this book so check it out before using)

Adoption Books for Early Elementary Age Children

Adoff, Arnold. *All the Colors of the Race.* New York: Lothrop, Lee & Shepard Books, 1982. 7 to Adolescent. (Collection of beautiful poems that help a child understand the blending of each of his parents' races . . . appropriate for child seeking to understand the unity of the world . . . worthwhile to use with mixed race children who are adopted)

Andersen, Hans Christian (retold by Lorinda Byran Cauley). *The Ugly Duckling.* New York: Harcourt Brace Jovanovich, 1979. 5 and up. (Classic story of a swan raised in a family of ducks . . . good for addressing issues of not looking like the rest of the family . . . helpful for interracial adoptions)

Angel, Ann. *Real for Sure Sister.* Fort Wayne, Ind.: Perspectives Press, 1988. 6 to 12 years.

(A look at adoption through the eyes of a nine-year-old waiting for another adoption . . . discusses international and domestic adoption of different ethnic backgrounds)

Banish, Roslyn, and J. Jordan-Wong. *A Forever Family: A Book about Adoption.* New York: HarperCollins, 1992. 5 to 12 years. (Jennifer is adopted at age seven after living with biological parents and two sets of foster parents . . . illustrated with photographs of Jennifer and her family . . . honest look at adoption from her perspective . . . upbeat)

Barris, Sara L. F., and Doryle P. Seltzer. *Together Forever: An Adoption Story Coloring Book.* Hartsdale, N.Y.: Shooting Star Press, 1992. 4 to 7 years. (Coloring book for young child with text discussing adoption . . . helps put adoption in more normal context)

Bendick, Jeanne. *What Made You You?* New York: McGraw-Hill, 1971. 6 to 10 years. (Child's-level discussion of genetics . . . unique book . . . helpful in discussions of adoption also)

Blackburn, Lynne Bennett. *Timothy Duck: The Story of the Death of a Friend.* Omaha, Neb.: Centering Corp., 1987. 4 to 8 years. (Discusses saying good-bye and letting go for children who have experienced the death of a friend or for children who are in the process of grieving for anyone)

Bond, Michael. *A Bear Called Paddington.* Boston: Houghton Mifflin, 1958. 5 and up. (Paddington is adopted from Peru . . . helpful for children to hear of this famous bear who was also adopted . . . useful in international adoptions)

Boyd, Brian. *When You Were Born in Korea: A Memory Book for Children Adopted from Korea.* St. Paul, Minn.: Yeong and Yeong, 1993. 6 to 12 years. (The growing number of international adoptions make these kinds of books important . . . describes the child's life before coming to America . . . answers many of the child's questions about coming from Korea . . . well recommended)

Brodzinsky, Anne Braff. *The Mulberry Bird: Story of an Adoption.* Indianapolis, Ind.: Perspectives Press, 1996. 4 to 10 years. (An adoption story using a mother bird to tell a birth mother's story . . . she tries to keep baby but encounters too many obstacles, so she asks for help and finds a home for the baby . . . worthwhile because of positive view of birth mother and realistic view of her plight)

Buck, Pearl S. *Welcome Child.* New York: John Day Co., 1964. 4 to 10 years. (Picture book which can be used to explain foreign or any kind of adoption to most age levels . . . problem of language not addressed and leaves big gap . . . only passages for adults in book mention adoption . . . shows adopted child becoming a citizen)

Caudill, Rebecca. *Somebody Go and Bang a Drum.* New York: E. P. Dutton & Co., 1974. 7 to 12 years. (Talks about an adopted family of ten that has an interracial mix . . . tells of family's growth)

Cole, Joanna. *How I Was Adopted: Samantha's Story.* New York: Morrow Junior Books, 1995. 4 to 8 years. (Explains how babies are born, children grow, and what makes people different and the same . . . also about love . . . at end it asks readers to tell stories of how they were adopted . . . reassuring about adoption . . . well-done . . . good introduction for parents)

Cronin, Gay Lynn. *Two Birthdays for Beth.* Indianapolis: Ind.: Perspectives Press, 1995. 4 to 8 years. (Both for single- and dual-parent families, depicts an African American mother and her adopted daughter who love the story of the daughter's arrival . . . child thinks she should have second birthday party . . . book may actually create some confusion . . . nice illustrations)

Cunningham, Julia. *Macaroon.* New York: Pantheon Books, 1962. 5 to 10 years. (A misunderstood child is adopted by a wise raccoon who teaches her the secret of contentment through a series of adventures)

Curtis, Jamie L. *Tell Me Again about the Night I was Born.* New York: HarperCollins, 1996. 4 to 8 years. (Typical infant adoption story . . . well-done book conveying the excitement of parents finding out their baby is born . . . not much about birth mother)

Dauer, Rosamond. *Bullfrog and Gertrude Go Camping.* New York: Greenwillow Books, 1980. 4 to 7 years. (Part of easy-to-read series . . . a bullfrog and mouse adopt a snake who needs a family . . . they discuss how they would be as a family . . . at first there is a slightly negative overtone because of how they treat the snake, but worthwhile)

Delaney, Richard J. *The Long Journey Home.* Fort Collins, Colo.: Journey Press, 1994. 5 to 10 years. (Book dealing more with separation from a loved one than most books . . . a book for a much-needed and seldom-covered area of adoption)

Dellinger, Annetta E. *Adopted and Loved Forever.* St. Louis, Mo.: Concordia Publishing House, 1987. 4 to 7 years. (Religious view of adoption . . . a young child discusses how parents choose their adopted children, love them, and will never leave them)

Doss, Helen. *The Really Real Family.* Boston: Little, Brown & Co., 1959. 7 to 10 years. (Tells the story of the adoption of two sisters into the Doss family . . . at last they have a "really real family")

Dower, S. *When You Were Born in China: A Memory Book for Children Adopted from China.* Saint Paul, Minn.: Yeong and Yeong, 1996. 6 and up. (A very well-done book with well-written text and photographs which explains some of whys and hows that have brought Chinese children to their new families . . . well worth using in international adoptions from China)

Dubkin, Lois. *Quiet Street.* New York: Abelard-Shuman, 1963. 4 to 7 years. (Introduces concept of adoption as wanting someone to play with . . . not a recent book and probably not one of the better ones . . . talks about a lonely girl who is adopted from a place that is called a "special family")

Eisenberg, Eleanor. *The Pretty House That Found Happiness.* Austin, Tex.: Steck-Vaughn Co., 1974. 4 to 7 years. (A picture book about a house with a man and a woman who were lonely until they adopted a child . . . it doesn't emphasize choosing a special baby and at times can be appropriate for children adopted after infancy)

Gabel, Susan. *Where the Sun Kisses the Sea.* Indianapolis, Ind.: Perspectives Press, 1989. 4 to 10 years. (Story of life in an Asian country before child is adopted . . . fantasies of children about finding permanent family . . . child is adopted and flown to the United States where he find home . . . beautifully written and illustrated)

Girard, Linda W. *Adoption Is for Always.* Niles, Ill.: Albert Whitman & Co., 1986. 4 to 10 years. (Although Cecilia reacts to having been adopted with anger and insecurity, her parents help her accept her feelings and celebrate their love for her by making her adoption day a holiday . . . factual about adoption and birth parents)

——. *We Adopted You, Benjamin Koo.* Niles, Ill.: Albert Whitman & Co., 1989. 4 to 12 years. (Nine-year-old Benjamin Koo Andrews, adopted from Korea as an infant, describes what it's like to grow up adopted from another country . . . describes problems of teasing and his anger . . . complicated story told in realistic way . . . well-done)

Gordon, Elaine R. *Mommy, Did I Grow in Your Tummy? Where Some Babies Come From.* Santa Monica, Calif.: E M Greenberg Press, Inc., 1992. 4 to 10 years. (Unique child's book discussing surrogacy, in vitro fertilization, donor insemination, and adoption . . . shows the positive results of these pregnancy options)

Gordon, Shirley. *The Boy Who Wanted a Family.* New York: Harper & Row, 1980. 5 to 8 years. (One of the few books that discusses adoption by single parents . . . discusses boy's fear his new mom will change her mind during waiting period . . . mother answers questions truthfully and openly . . . unique book)

Greenberg, Judith E., and Helen H. Carey. *Adopted.* New York: Franklin Watts, 1987. 4 to 8 years. (Because both Sarah and her new brother are adopted, Sarah's mother, father, and grandfather explain what adoption and being part of a family are about . . . black-and-white photos)

Greenfield, E. *Nathaniel Talking.* New York: Writers & Readers, 1989. 9 to 12 years. (18 poems offer an African-American child's insights into his heart and mind . . . award-winning book)

Gregg, D. *The Story of Megan.* Boulder, Colo.: Social Science Education Consortium, (n.d.). 4 to 9 years. (Story of Megan, about age five to eight years, who meets family who wants to adopt her . . . they take her to a park to get to know her . . . son involved in decision . . . worthwhile in older child adoptions)

Haywood, Carolyn. *Here's a Penny.* New York: Harcourt Brace, 1944. 6 to 10 years. (A book to be read by a young child . . . about adoption of an older child . . . out-of-date . . . discusses adopting young child . . . discusses confusion and hurt when friend makes him feel different)

Hazen, Barbara Shook. *Why Are People Different?: A Book about Prejudice.* Golden Learn About Books. New York: Golden Press, 1985. 4 to 8 years. (A book about prejudice . . . may especially be read in adoption situations)

Hess, Edith. *Peter and Susie Find a Family.* Nashville, Tenn.: Abingdon Press, 1984. 4 to 8 years. (Book discussing couple and their dog who decide to adopt a baby through an agency . . . seems like an older book)

Howard, Ellen. *Her Own Song.* New York: Atheneum, 1988. 4 to 10 years. (About turn-of-century adoption . . . Mellie is teased about adoption . . . feels kinship with Chinese laundryman . . . offers glimpse into lifestyles and historical incidents not often addressed in children's books)

Howe, James. *Pinky and Rex and the New Baby.* New York: Atheneum, 1993. 4 to 8 years. (As Rex, a girl born into her family, confronts her jealousy about parents' plan to adopt, she shuts out her best friend Pinky who has to deal with his own feelings of jealousy . . . book about friendships and ways they endure challenges)

Johnson, Doris. *Su An*. Chicago: Follett Publishing Co., 1968. 4 to 8 years. (Picture book for young children about an adopted young girl missing her Asian home)

Knight, Margy Burns. *Welcoming Babies*. Gardiner, Maine: Tilbury House Publishers, 1994. 4 and up. (Discusses the many ways babies are welcomed around the world ... shows the diversity of families but it also includes announcing adoption ... good for international adoption and other cultures)

Koch, Janice. *Our Adopted Baby—How You Came into Our World*. New York: Parkway Press, 1983. 5 to 8 years. (Book about conception and birth for adopted child ... very unusual but hard to find ... small publisher ... now published under title *Our Baby: A Birth and Adoption Story*)

Kraus, Joanna Halpert. *Tall Boy's Journey*. Minneapolis, Minn.: Carolrhoda Books, 1992. 6 to 10 years. (Story of orphaned Asian boy and his transition to becoming an adopted American boy ... help of friend makes transition better but not easy ... beautifully written ... shows how a different culture can impact a foreign child)

Kraus, Robert. *Another Mouse to Feed*. New York: Windmill/Wanderer Books, 1980. 4 to 8 years. (Family of mice all pitch in together to take in one more ... a way of discussing adoption from a broader perspective)

Kroll, Virginia. *Beginnings: How Families Come to Be*. Morton Grove, Ill.: Albert Whitman & Co., 1994. 4 to 8 years. (Picture book telling the story of six children and how they came into their families ... Korea, death, birth, foster families, adoption ... shows the many different ways to become part of a family ... nicely illustrated, happy book)

Lawrence, S. D. *We Are Family*. Washington, D.C.: Children's Bureau, 1995. 4 to 10 years. (Part of a new series designed for African American families through adoption ... greater emphasis on extended family than most books ... single parents also covered)

Lifton, Betty Jean. *Tell Me a Real Adoption Story*. New York: Alfred A. Knopf, 1993. 4 to 10 years. (Popular book emphasizes being truthful about adoption ... mom tries to tell fairy tale ... child wants to know the truth and have sense of reality about adoption ... discusses open adoption ... gives suggestions how to bring up subject ... nicely illustrated)

Livingston, Carole. *Why Was I Adopted?* Secaucus, N.J.: Lyle Stuart, 1978. 6 to Adolescent. (Cartoon illustration answering the questions many children have about their adoption ... some fairly complex issues considered ... parents should assume children have questions ... help them to understand that their feelings are normal)

McDonnell, Janet, and Sandra Ziegler. *What's So Special about Me? I'm One of a Kind*. Chicago: Children's Press, 1988. 5 to 9 years. (A girl nicknamed Anna Banana rejoices in all the ways she is special ... from the five orange freckles on her nose to the way she giggles at her brother's jokes)

Miles, Miska. *Aaron's Door*. Boston: Little, Brown & Co., 1977. 4 to 9 years. (Two siblings are adopted as older children ... girl finds new parents' love easy to accept but boy closes himself in room ... finally resolved)

Miller, Kathryn Ann. *Did My First Mother Love Me? A Story for an Adopted Child*. Buena Park, Calif.: Morning Glory Press, 1994. 4 to 8 years. (Beautifully illustrated ...

discusses letter from birth mother . . . one of better books dealing with this . . . offers suggestions of sources that help in talking to children about adoption . . . tells birth mother's hopes and dreams for her baby . . . section on talking about adoption)

Muir, Frank. *What-a-Mess*. Garden City, N.Y.: Doubleday, 1977. 5 to 8 years. (Story of a young puppy who is awkward and ugly and doesn't know what or who he is . . . doesn't identify with his beautiful mother . . . searches for himself . . . starting place to discuss identification with parents in adoption)

Pellegrini, Nina. *Families Are Different*. New York: Holiday House, 1991. 4 to 8 years. (Six-year-old girl adopted from Korea discusses the way families are different . . . she has a sister who is also adopted . . . finds her family is just like everyone else's family—different)

Portnoy, F. *One Wonderful You*. Greensboro, N.C.: Children's Home Society, 1997. 4 to 10 years. (Emphasizes creating a healthy identity when have two family legacy . . . sets groundwork for this task . . . shows how child is a blend . . . positive book for children)

Reiser, Lynne. *The Surprise Family*. New York: Greenwillow Books, 1994. 4 to 8 years. (A baby chicken accepts a young boy as her mother and later becomes a surrogate mother for some ducklings that she has hatched . . . picture book)

Rogers, Fred. *Adoption*. Let's Talk about It Series. New York: G. P. Putnam's Sons, 1994. 4 to 8 years. (Fred Rogers has an adopted sister . . . discusses how being adopted is a special kind of love story . . . importance of belonging . . . great way to begin family discussions . . . describes the many ways children feel loved)

Rosenberg, Maxine B. *Being Adopted*. New York: Lothrop, Lee & Shepard Books, 1984. 6 to 12 years. (A book designed to help children from other countries understand international adoption and multiracial families . . . three children adopted from Korea, India, and the United States . . . has bibliography and sources of help)

———. *Living in Two Worlds*. New York: Lothrop, Lee & Shepard books, 1986. 6 to 12 years. (Photoessay about special issues facing biracial children . . . discusses cultural issues and problems and prejudices that arise . . . not specifically related to adoption but for people who have biracial children, one of the few books on subject)

Sanford, Doris. *Brian Was Adopted*. In Our Neighborhood Series. Portland, Ore.: Multnomah Press, 1989. 4 to 9 years. (A boy who was adopted from Korea as an infant describes his new life in America and the love he receives from his new parents . . . discusses intercountry issues . . . religious issues stressed . . . positive about birth parents)

Schaffer, Patricia. *How Babies and Families Are Made (There IS More Than One Way!)*. Berkeley, Calif.: Tabor Sarah Books, 1988. 5 to 10 years. (Surveys ways in which children are conceived, develop, are born, and become parts of families . . . covers special situations like artificial insemination, cesarean births, adopted families, and stepchildren . . . shows different ethnic groups)

Schnitter, Jane T. *Let Me Explain: A Story about Donor Insemination*. Indianapolis, Ind.: Perspectives Press, 1995. 6 to 10 years. (Explains donor insemination . . . one of a kind . . . warm message about this kind of family building which produces a loving relationship between the father and the child)

——. *William Is My Brother.* Indianapolis, Ind.: Perspectives Press, 1991. 4 to 9 years. (Simple picture book saying one brother is adopted and one is born into the family and they are alike and they are different . . . they are both loved no matter how they joined the family)

Schwartz, Perry. *Carolyn's Story: A Book about an Adopted Girl.* Minneapolis, Minn.: Lerner Publications Co., 1996. 4 to 10 years. (Book about a young girl who was adopted from Honduras as a baby . . . covers emotions from being proud of adoption to wanting to be just like everyone else . . . reaction of others to her darker skin)

Shreve, Susan Richards. *Zoe and Columbo.* New York: Tambourine Books, 1995. 7 to 12 years. (Columbo is adopted, Zoe isn't . . . the brothers drift apart when Columbo wants to hide his adoption . . . then he works in a hospital and discovers what makes him special)

Silman, Roberta. *Somebody Else's Child.* New York: F. Warne, 1976. 7 to 10 years. (Story of a fourth grader who was adopted when he was six months old who struggles to understand adoption after a childless school bus driver he likes very much says he would never take somebody else's child)

Silverstein, Shel. *The Missing Piece.* New York: Harper & Row, 1976. 7 to Adolescent. (Story of a shape who looks for the missing piece that will make him complete . . . finds the piece but discovers he was already complete . . . good for discussion of loss of birth parents . . . covers wide range of ages)

Sobol, Harriet Langsam. *We Don't Look Like Our Mom and Dad.* New York: Coward-McCann, 1984. 6 to 12 years. (Photoessay showing Korean adopted children . . . discusses issues facing a family whose members don't look alike . . . children ask questions about their biological mother . . . talk of becoming citizens)

Sommer, Susan. *And I'm Stuck with Joseph.* Scottdale, Pa.: Herald Press, 1984. 7 to 11 years. (An eleven-year-old girl wants her parents to have a baby . . . then they adopt a three-year-old child, and it is more than she bargained for . . . written by a woman who adopted children . . . some religious emphasis . . . worthwhile in adoption of older children)

Spohn, David. *Winter Wood.* New York: Lothrop, Lee & Shepard Books, 1991. 5 to 8 years. (European father and his brown-skinned son chop wood together in the winter . . . doesn't mention adoption but shows difference in appearance of child and father)

Stein, Stephanie. *Lucy's Feet.* Indianapolis, Ind.: Perspectives Press, 1992. 4 to 10 years. (Little girl is unhappy because she didn't grow inside her mother's tummy like her brother . . . shows how she is also like other children . . . mother tells her how she did grow in her heart . . . points out anger and pain of child and mixed feelings about siblings)

Tate, Eleanora E. *Just an Overnight Guest.* New York: Dial, 1980. 6 to 12 years. (When a disruptive four-year-old moves in, the nine-year-old has problems adjusting)

Turner, Ann Warren. *Through Moon and Stars and Night Skies.* New York: Harper & Row, 1990. 2 to 7 years. (Story of an international adoption . . . describes a young boy's flight to the United States and his meeting with his new mom and dad and new dog . . . shows boy's apprehensions and fears of his new life . . . nicely illustrated)

Ward, Jeannette W. *I Have a Question, God.* Nashville, Tenn.: Broadman Press, 1981. 6 to 9 years. (Religious treatment of adoption . . . discusses a adoption of younger siblings . . . concerns over being loved)

Waybill, Marjorie Ann. *Chinese Eyes.* Scottdale, Pa.: Herald Press, 1974. 4 to 10 years. (Adopted Korean first grader is teased about the shape of her eyes . . . recognizes prejudice . . . mother's supportive help aids her in handling this problem . . . helpful for all mixed families who face prejudice in our society)

Weyn, Suzanne. *Make Room for Patty.* New York: Scholastic, 1991. 7 to 12 years. (Patty is the twelfth child adopted into a multiethnic adopted family . . . gives her perspective on her first few crazy days with her new family)

Wickstrom, Lois. *Oliver.* Wayne, Pa.: Our Child Press, 1991. 4 to 7 years. (Oliver, who is adopted, is angry with his parents . . . he imagines what his life could have been if he hadn't been adopted . . . good way to help children deal with their negative feelings or their feelings on an angry day)

Wilt, Joy. *The Nitty-Gritty of Family Life: A Children's Book about Living in a Family.* Waco, Tex.: Educational Products Division, Word, Inc., 1979. 5 to 10 years. (A book talking about family life including roles, relationships, rules, responsibilities . . . involves the child in seeing his or her place within the family . . . talks about adoption as a way of becoming a family)

Winthrop, Elizabeth. *I Think He Likes Me.* New York: Harper & Row, 1980. 4 to 8 years. (Story about new baby but doesn't discuss pregnancy . . . this could be helpful in adoption of a younger child)

Wright, Susan. *Real Sisters.* Charlottetown, PEI, Canada: Rag Weed, 1994. 4 to 10 years. (Seven-year-old is adopted but friends say her older sister is not her real sister . . . one black, one white . . . explores ways they are alike . . . concludes they are real sisters . . . can't imagine loving anyone more . . . excellent for mixed families)

Yashima, Taro. *Umbrella.* New York: Puffin Books, 1977, © 1958. 5 to 8 years. (A book, readily available, showing an Asian girl . . . not always easy to find this kind for couples who have adopted internationally or interracially . . . author of *Crow Boy*)

Zamani, Q. *The Proud Elephant.* West Sussex, England: Luzac Publishing, Ltd., 1986. 5 to 10 years. (Dual language book that tells stories that have been handed down for many generations . . . worthwhile to talk about other cultures and other languages with children who have been adopted internationally or from different cultures)

Adoption Books for Late Elementary School

Ames, Mildred. *Without Hats, Who Can Tell the Good Guys?* New York: E. P. Dutton & Co., 1976. 8 to 12 years. (Boy in foster home who resists placement, hoping his father will come back, is eventually adopted)

Bates, Betty. *Bugs in Your Ears.* New York: Holiday House, 1977. 11 to 15 years. (Thirteen-year-old has difficulty adjusting to family when mother remarries . . . stepfather wants to adopt her . . . her fantasy about her birth father has much in common with adoption fantasies)

——. *It Must've Been the Fish Sticks.* New York: Archway Pocket Books, 1982. 9 to 14 years. (Not directly related to adoption but does discuss having two mothers . . .

might be helpful for adopted child to see similarities with other children . . . worthwhile in stepparent situations as well as adoptive situations)

Bawden, Nina, and Phillida Gili. *Princess Alice.* London: A. Deutsch, 1985. 10 to Adolescent. (An adopted daughter who sometimes feels she doesn't fit in her large untidy English family reevaluates her position after a visit with her real father, an African prince)

Beatty, Patricia. *That's One Ornery Orphan.* New York: William Morrow, 1980. 10 to Adolescent. (Historical perspective on adoption . . . discusses the orphan trains and the casual placement of children for adoption . . . three unsuccessful placements of thirteen-year-old girl)

Blomquist, Geraldine M., and Paul B. Blomquist. *Coping as a Foster Child.* New York: The Rosen Publishing Group, 1992. 10 to Adolescent. (Explores good and bad choices available to foster teens . . . not many books for children that explore this)

Blume, Judy. *Starring Sally J. Freedman as Herself.* Scarsdale, N.Y.: Bradbury Press, 1977. 8 to Adolescent. (Ten-year-old Sally spends the winter of '47–'48 in Miami with her family and makes up stories, casts herself in starring roles in movies, and encounters a sinister stranger)

Buck, Pearl S. *Matthew, Mark, Luke, and John.* New York: John Day Co., 1966. 10 to 15 years. (Eleven-year-old Amerasian child abandoned in Korea who befriends three others like himself is adopted by American family . . . family helps his friends be adopted . . . deals with war-orphan issues and social issues of illegitimate mixed parentage)

Budbill, David. *Bones on Black Spruce Mountain.* New York: Dial Press, 1978. 12 to Adolescent. (Thirteen-year-old boys go camping and learn about other boy's twelve different foster homes and his inability to trust . . . recommended by *Adopted Child* newsletter . . . well-done book)

Burlingham-Brown, Barbara. *"Why Didn't She Keep Me?": Answers to the Questions Every Adopted Child Asks.* South Bend, Ind.: Langford Books, 1994. 10 to Adult. (Most common adoption questions from young people . . . firsthand narratives by birth mothers who reveal their rational, practical, and emotional reasons for placing their children for adoption)

Byars, Betsy. *The Pinballs.* New York: Harper & Row, 1977. 9 to 14 years. (The focus of this book is really on foster homes and how children may be pushed from home to home and experience severe rejection . . . a favorite author . . . good for children who have been in foster care)

Campbell, Hope. *Home to Hawaii.* New York: W. W. Norton & Co., 1977. 12 to Adolescent. (A seventeen-year-old girl runs away when she discovers she has a foster sister living in Hawaii . . . one of the earlier books on interracial adoption)

Carlson, Natalie Savage. *A Brother for the Orphelines.* New York: Harper, 1959. 9 to 14 years. (Book for children that deals with life in an orphanage from a historical perspective)

——. *The Happy Orphelines.* New York: Harper, 1957. 9 to 12 years. (First of this series . . . tells about children who don't want to be adopted because they like it in the orphanage in France . . . historical approach to adoption)

Chinnock, Frank W. *Kim: A Gift from Vietnam*. New York: World Publishers, 1969. 9 to 12 years. (A Vietnamese orphan adopted by a journalist tells of her adjustment to American life)

Christiansen, C. B. *I See the Moon*. New York: Atheneum, 1994. 10 to Adolescent. (Story of a twelve-year-old whose sister places her child for adoption . . . younger child learns about meaning of love)

Colman, Hila. *Tell Me No Lies*. New York: Crown Publishers, 1978. 11 to Adolescent. (Twelve-year-old dreams she can go to Saudi Arabia to meet her father who left her mother before she was born . . . mother has made up story . . . the girl wants to meet her father but choices made by her parents make that difficult . . . stepfather wants to adopt her)

Corcoran, Barbara. *Family Secrets*. New York: Atheneum, 1992. 12 to Adolescent. (After moving with her lively family to a small town where her father grew up, thirteen-year-old Tracy learns she is adopted . . . surprise brings her new insights into what constitutes a family . . . some other trying adventures and insights)

Doss, Helen. *The Family Nobody Wanted*. Boston: Little, Brown & Co., 1954. 8 to 11 years. (A story of an interracial family . . . shows what it was like in the 1950s)

Ellis, Sarah. *Out of the Blue*. New York: Margaret K. McElderry Books, 1995. 10 to 14 years. (A teenage girl is shocked by her mother's news that she relinquished a child for adoption twenty-four years ago . . . the girl is expected to accept this person as part of the family and it isn't easy)

Enright, Elizabeth. *Then There Were Five*. New York: Dell, 1987. 10 to 15 years. (Part of a series . . . the mother dies and the children live with the father . . . then they adopt an older boy when his uncle dies . . . older book)

Falke, Joe. *Everything You Need to Know about Living in a Foster Home*. New York: The Rosen Publishing Group, 1995. 8 to Adolescent. (Explains different kinds of foster homes and their role . . . examines feeling and problems about foster care and how to handle them . . . makes children feel important and that people do care while they are waiting to return to their first family)

Field, Rachel. *Calico Bush*. New York: Macmillan, 1966. 10 to Adolescent. (Historical perspective on adoption . . . when her grandmother dies, an eleven-year-old French girl must set out for the New World and live in bondage)

Gabel, Susan. *Filling in the Blanks: A Guided Look at Growing Up Adopted*. Fort Wayne, Ind.: Perspectives Press, 1988. 8 to Adolescent. (A fill-in-the-blank book about the many aspects of growing up adopted . . . gives child an opportunity to explore some adoption issues independently and at his or her own pace . . . very unique)

Gravelle, Karen, and Susan Fisher. *Where Are My Birth Parents?: A Guide for Teenage Adoptees*. New York: Walker & Co., 1993. 10 to Adolescent. (A practical guide and source of support for teenage adoptees who decide to search for birth parents . . . also helpful for adoptive parents to understand the adolescent's need to search for his or her individual identity)

Hall, Lynn. *Mrs. Portree's Pony*. New York: C. Scribner's Sons, 1986. 11 to Adolescent. (Addie, thirteen, finds a foster home with a woman who loves her after being passed from her mother whose new husband didn't want her to a friend who didn't really want her, either)

Karvoskaia, Natacha. *Dounia.* New York: Kane/Miller, 1995. 10 to 12 years. (A lovely picture book telling in a few words the experience of a child from Africa coming to America to live with a new family . . . features a multiracial, multicultural adoption)

Kent, Deborah. *Why Me?* New York: Scholastic, 1992. 11 to Adolescent. (A young girl with promising talent is struck with disease and needs a kidney transplant . . . she is adopted . . . finds birth mother . . . lots of issues involved with identity and reunion . . . well written and highly recommended)

Klein, Norma. *What It's All About.* New York: Dial Press, 1975. 10 to Adolescent. (Book not specifically designed to deal with adoption but it is an issue here . . . about eleven-year-old growing up and sorting out feelings about her parents . . . adoption of her sister from Vietnam is not easy for her)

Krementz, Jill. *How It Feels to Be Adopted.* New York: Alfred A. Knopf, 1982. 10 to Adolescent. (Interviews with adopted children and adoptive families about their experiences and feelings concerning adoption . . . worth reading by adoptive parents to gain more understanding from adoptee's perspective . . . highly recommended by parents)

Lifton, Betty Jean. *I'm Still Me.* New York: Alfred A. Knopf, 1981. 12 to Adolescent. (History assignment is used by a fifteen-year-old girl to look into her roots . . . insights into feelings of adolescent adoptees toward their fantasized birth parents)

Lindbergh, Anne. *Nobody's Orphan.* San Diego: Harcourt Brace Jovanovich, 1983. 8 to Adolescent. (Young girl is the only green-eyed member of a brown-eyed family . . . she is convinced she is adopted but thinks she wouldn't mind it so much if her parents would only let her have a dog)

Lindgren, Astrid. *Pippi Longstocking.* New York: Viking, 1950. 9 to Adolescent. (Classic tale about Pippi Longstocking, an orphan)

Magorian, Michelle. *Good Night, Mr. Tom.* New York: Harper & Row, 1981. 9 to Adolescent. (Children evacuated from London during WWII are taken in by a near-recluse who forms a mutually healing relationship with an eight-year-old . . . happy ending to dramatic book with touching story of love)

Martin, Ann M. *Yours Turly, Shirley.* New York: Holiday House, 1988. 9 to 12 years. (Dyslexic Shirley learns to accept her limitations and strengths, to accept and love her newly adopted Vietnamese sister who is academically brighter than she, and learns a lot about what it means to be a family)

McDonald, Joyce. *Mail-Order Kid.* New York: G. P. Putnam's Sons, 1988. 9 to 12 years. (When a teenage boy's parents decide to adopt a six-year-old Korean boy, his life is turned upside down . . . no longer an only child . . . orders a mail-order companion and begins to see problems of adjusting to a new home for his brother)

McHugh, Elisabet. *Karen's Sister.* New York: Greenwillow Books, 1983. 10 to Adolescent. (Sequel to *Raising a Mother Isn't Easy* . . . mother adopts a second Korean child . . . finds a husband with three children of his own)

———. *Raising a Mother Isn't Easy.* New York: Greenwillow Books, 1983. 10 to Adolescent. (Through faulty communication, woman's Korean daughter is unprepared for arrival of second adopted child . . . humorous presentation . . . well-done)

Milgram, Mary. *Brothers Are All the Same.* New York: E. P. Dutton & Co., 1978. 10 to Adolescent. (Upbeat story conveying positive feelings about adopting a child who is older . . . illustrations show the child adopted is black and being adopted by a white family . . . also includes a reference to an adoption from another country)

Mills, Claudia. *Boardwalk with Hotel.* New York: Macmillan, 1985. 9 to Adolescent. (Fifth grader Jessica discovers that her parents adopted her because they mistakenly believed they couldn't have children . . . then came two siblings . . . she wonders if her parents love her less than her siblings . . . rivalry and competitiveness)

Milowitz, Gloria D. *Unwed Mothers.* New York: Tempo Books, 1977. 12 to Adolescent. (Fifteen-year-old debates whether to keep her baby . . . vividly illustrates the problems she encounters . . . she eventually gives child up to worker from agency . . . almost too pat, but still helpful)

Montgomery, L. M. *Anne of Green Gables.* New York: Alfred A. Knopf, 1995. 10 to Adolescent. (Classic story of an older girl adopted by a woman and her brother)

Murphy, Francis. *Ready-Made Family.* New York: Scholastic, 1972. 9 to 12 years. (Three older siblings placed in new home . . . discusses their adjustments and their feelings . . . talks about foster care . . . reaction of neighborhood and school covered)

Myers, Walter Dean. *Me, Mop, and the Moondance Kid.* New York: Delacorte Press, 1988. 10 to Adolescent. (Adopted from an institution, eleven-year-old T. J. and his younger brother, Moondance, remain involved with their friend Mop's attempts to become adopted . . . humor and quick, natural dialogue)

Okimoto, Jean Davies. *Molly by Any Other Name.* New York: Scholastic, 1990. 11 to Adolescent. (A teenage Asian girl who has been adopted by non-Asian parents decides to find out who her biological parents are)

Paterson, Katherine. *The Great Gilly Hopkins.* New York: Thomas Y. Crowell Co., 1978. 9 to Adolescent. (Eleven-year-old Gilly Hopkins fantasizes about birth mother to the detriment of her life . . . about foster home situation, but related to adoption especially of children who have been in foster care . . . very well-written book)

Perl, Lila. *Annabelle Starr, E. S. P.* New York: Clarion Books, 1983. 10 to Adolescent. (Mystery whose main character happens to have an adopted brother . . . she is convinced a mysterious roomer is her brother's birth mother . . . brother fears the roomer is there to take him away)

Powledge, Fred. *So You're Adopted.* New York: Charles Scribner's Sons, 1982. 10 to Adolescent. (Explains that being adopted is not unusual by using historical perspective . . . discusses questions adoptees are likely to have about adoption . . . written by adoptee for adolescent adoptees)

Read, Elfreida. *Brothers by Choice.* New York: Farrar, Straus & Giroux, 1974. 10 to Adolescent. (A young boy persuades his adopted brother that he is not a family outsider after the adopted boy runs away because he feels he has disappointed his father by not going to college . . . highly recommended by parents)

Sachs, Marilyn. *What My Sister Remembered.* New York: Dutton Children's Books, 1992. 10 to Adolescent. (While visiting her younger sister, Beth confronts painful memories of the sudden death of her parents and the subsequent adoption of her sisters by different families . . . doesn't like sister being mean and rude . . . well-done)

Scott, Elaine. *Adoption.* New York: Franklin Watts, 1980. 9 to Adolescent. (Discusses various aspects of adoption as well as facts about genes and heredity)

Stahl, Hilda. Elizabeth Gail Series. Wheaton, Ill.: Tyndale House. 10 to Adolescent.

(Mystery series featuring adopted teenager, Libby . . . Libby solves various mysteries . . . religious emphasis)

Taylor, Theodore. *Tuck Triumphant.* New York: Doubleday, 1991. 11 to 15 years. (Adoption issue dealt with by well-known author . . . a family discovers that the Korean boy they adopted is deaf . . . well-done story told from perspective of a fourteen-year-old boy)

Voigt, Cynthia. *Dicey's Song.* New York: Atheneum, 1982. 10 to Adolescent. (Sequel to *Homecoming* about four abandoned children who find a home)

———. *Homecoming.* New York: Atheneum, 1981. 10 to Adolescent. (Part of series including *Dicey's Song* about four abandoned children)

Welch, Sheila Kelly. *Don't Call Me Marda.* Wayne, Pa.: Our Child Press, 1990. 10 to Adolescent. (Marsha is upset when her parents decide to adopt a mentally retarded child . . . discusses long and sometimes painful adjustment to new sibling . . . happy ending)

Windsor, Patricia. *Mad Martin.* New York: Harper & Row, 1976. 9 to 12 years. (Story about a foster child . . . good also for older adoptions . . . talks about separation, isolation, belonging)

Wright, Betty Ren. *The Scariest Night.* New York: Holiday House, 1991. 8 to 12 years. (Erin finds herself upset and jealous as her family takes her brother to Milwaukee to perfect his genius at a special piano school . . . she turns to a medium for help)

York, Carol Beach. *The Ten O'Clock Club.* New York: Franklin Watts, 1970. 8 to 11 years. (A book about twenty-eight little girls who live at the Good Day Orphanage . . . one of them decides to start a club and finds herself rejected)

Adoption Books for Adolescents

Arthur, Ruth M. *Requiem for a Princess.* New York: Atheneum, 1967. (Teenage girl discovers she was adopted and finds it a difficult and upsetting interruption in her life . . . imagines she is the proud and lonely adopted daughter of an English nobleman to help her accept her situation)

Bawden, Nina. *The Outside Child.* New York: Lothrop, Lee & Shepard, 1989. (Jane tries to learn more about her half-brother and -sister after discovering that her seafaring father remarried)

Bowe-Butman, Sonia. *Teen Pregnancy.* Minneapolis, Minn.: Lerner Publications, 1987. (Discusses social, physical, and economic problems of teenage pregnancy and parenthood . . . talks about methods of contraception . . . has case studies)

Cleaver, Vera, and Bill Cleaver. *Trial Valley.* Philadelphia: J. B. Lippincott, 1977. (A sixteen-year-old girl, orphaned and penniless, tries to keep her brothers and sisters together)

Clewes, Dorothy. *Adopted Daughter.* New York: Coward-McCann, 1968. (Seventeen-year-old Cathy is happy until her adoptive mother dies . . . questions origins . . . finds older sister is her birth mother . . . presents hidden side of adoption . . . discusses end of adolescence and beginning of adulthood)

Cohen, Shari. *Coping with Being Adopted.* New York: The Rosen Publishing Group, Inc., 1988. (Discusses feelings and questions a typical adopted adolescent might have . . . excellent book helping children with feelings they may be reluctant to share)

Derby, Pat. *Visiting Miss Pierce.* New York: Farrar, Straus & Giroux, 1986. (Fourteen-year-old visits old woman in nursing home and while encouraging her to delve into her past he finds the project affects him as an adopted child and he confronts his feelings of rejection by his birth parents)

Doherty, Berlie. *The Snake-Stone.* New York: Orchard Books, 1996. (James who is fifteen searches for his birth mother and discovers who his real parents are and where his real home is)

First, Julia. *I, Rebekah, Take You, the Lawrences.* New York: Franklin Watts, 1981. (A twelve-year-old girl adopted after living in various foster homes and an orphanage feels her place in the family is threatened when her family decides to adopt again . . . a fairly simplistic approach to some complex issues related to adoption)

Fry, Annette R. *The Orphan Trains.* New York: New Discovery Books, 1994. (Explains how the orphan trains operated and introduces adults who were "orphan train" children . . . tells how some of these children have attempted to unravel the mystery of their past and locate long-lost relatives . . . well researched)

Gibson, Eva. *Michelle.* Minneapolis, Minn.: Bethany House Publishers, 1984. (Sixteen-year-old foster child seeks to solve a mystery involving a swimming accident, a locked bedroom, and a tense reunion with her mother . . . a religious emphasis)

Holland, Isabelle. *The House in the Woods.* Boston: Little, Brown & Co., 1991. (Bridget, oldest of four children is the only adoptee in family . . . since her mother's death she feels she doesn't fit in the family . . . with her brother, a mute, she discovers an old, run-down house and she feels drawn to it as if it holds a clue to her identity)

Hulse, Jerry. *Jody.* New York: McGraw-Hill, 1976. (Search for birth parents by an adult adoptee)

Jones, Rebecca C. *The Believers.* New York: Arcade, 1989. (Adoptive mother rarely spends time with child . . . child drawn to a fundamentalist sect . . . finds a substitute mother in Aunt Evelyn . . . fast-paced, absorbing . . . well-written and still hopeful novel)

Koh, Frances M. *Adopted from Asia: How It Feels to Grow Up in America.* Minneapolis, Minn.: East-West Press, 1993. (Eleven teenagers and young adults talk about being adopted from Korea and growing up in the United States . . . discusses issues during adolescence . . . appropriate for teens as well as adults)

Leach, Christopher. *Kate's Story.* New York: Four Winds Press, 1972 © 1968. (Sixteen-year-old girl gets into trouble with police after she discovers she is adopted . . . her father dies and her mother remarries)

Lifton, Betty Jean. *Twice Born: Memoirs of an Adopted Daughter.* New York: McGraw-Hill, 1975. (Mature adolescents who want to understand pros and cons of searching may be ready for this autobiographical account of an adoptee seeking her birth mother . . . finding her birth mother was not the panacea she hoped . . . thought-provoking)

Lopez, Charlotte. *Lost in the System.* New York: Simon & Schuster, 1996. (Story of Miss Teen USA who grew up in foster care system . . . adopted when she was seventeen . . . useful for older children who are adopted to sort out foster care background . . . an indictment of the foster care system)

Lowry, Lois. *Find a Stranger, Say Goodbye.* Boston: Houghton Mifflin, 1978. (A good book for teenagers interested in reunions or in knowing more about birth parents . . . adoptive parents are supportive of girl's search . . . she finds her birth mother but feels more connected with adoptive family)

Maguire, Gregory. *Missing Sisters.* New York: Margaret K. McElderry Books, 1994. (Orphan with a physical handicap and difficult personality learns she has a twin sister nearby . . . set in 1968)

Nerlove, Evelyn. *Who Is David? The Story of an Adopted Adolescent and His Friends.* New York: Child Welfare League of America, 1985. (First novel by the Child Welfare League deals with adolescent adoptees who are viewed through the eyes of David and his family . . . discusses unique problems different adolescents face)

Neufeld, John. *Edgar Allan.* New York: S. G. Phillips, 1968. (Outstanding book about a failed adoption between a white family and a black child . . . what went wrong . . . essential reading for family considering interracial adoption . . . people either really like this book or dislike it)

Nickman, Steven. *The Adoption Experience.* New York: Julian Messner, 1985. (Seven fictional stories, each followed by comments on searching . . . discusses older children from foster homes, transracial adoptions, and adoptions from other cultures)

Oppenheimer, Joan L. *Which Mother Is Mine?* New York: Bantam Books, 1980. (Teenager in foster care since age five is confronted with conflict when his mother reenters his life and he is forced to make choices . . . shows conflicting emotions about two sets of parents)

Putterman, Ron. *To Find My Son.* New York: Avon, 1981. (A single man becomes involved with a boy while working in a home for neglected children . . . faces problems when he wants to adopt as a single father)

Richards, Arlene. *What to Do If You or Someone You Know Is under Eighteen and Pregnant.* New York: Lothrop, Lee & Shepard, 1983. (Advice and information for the pregnant teenager on sex, birth control, pregnancy, childbirth, abortion, adoption, marriage, and babies)

Rosenberg, Maxine B. *Growing Up Adopted.* New York: Bradbury Press, 1989. (Fourteen adoptees of various ages describe their experiences and feelings about being adopted and their relationship with their adoptive parents and, in some cases, their birth parents . . . honest approach)

Roth, Arthur J. *The Secret Lover of Elmtree.* New York: Four Winds Press, 1976. (Adopted boy must face a number of decisions about his future after he meets his birth father)

Witt, Reni L., and Jeannine Masterson Michael. *Mom, I'm Pregnant.* New York: Stein & Day, Publishers, 1982. (A well-done book designed both for adolescents and their parents explaining the alternatives to an unwanted pregnancy)

Wurmfeld, Hope. *Baby Blues.* New York: Viking, 1992. (Annie and Jimmy decide to place the child Annie is carrying for adoption . . . glimpse into what it might be like for teenagers, too young, immature, and with strikes against them, to face the birth of a child . . . helpful for adopted adolescents)

NOTES

CHAPTER 1: Adoption Works

1. G. Skelton, "Governor Wants a Father in the House," *Los Angeles Times,* January 8, 1996.
2. F. Bruni, "For Gay Couples. Ruling to Cheer on Adoption," *New York Times,* November 5, 1995; D. H. McIntyre, "Gay Parents and Child Custody: A Struggle under the Legal System," *Mediation Quarterly* 12 (1994): 135–48.
3. A. R. Hunt, "The Republicans Seize the High Ground on Transracial Adoption," *The Wall Street Journal,* March 9, 1995; R. L. Jackson, "U.S. Stresses No Race Bias in Adoptions," *Los Angeles Times,* April 25, 1995.
4. *Positive Adoption Attitudes in the Media* (Newsletter)
5. J. T. McQuiston, "A Novel Insanity Defense for Joel Rifkin," *New York Times,* July 26, 1994.
6. K. S. Stolley, "Statistics on Adoption in the United States," *The Future of Children* 3 (Spring 1993): 26–42.
7. J. Austin, ed., *Adoption: The Inside Story* (London: Barn Owl Books, 1985); E. Bartholet, *Family Bonds: Adoption and the Politics of Parenting* (Boston: Houghton Mifflin Company, 1993); P. L. Benson, A. L. Sharma, and E. C. Roehlkepartain, *Growing Up Adopted: A Portrait of Adolescents and Their Families* (Minneapolis, Minn.: Search Insight, 1994); D. M. Brodzinsky and M. D. Schechter, eds., *The Psychology of Adoption* (New York: Oxford University Press, 1990); T. DeAngeles, "Adoptees, New Families Fare Well, Studies Show," *APA Monitor* (January 1995): 36; A. Goetting and M. G. Goetting, "Adoptive Parents to Children with Severe Developmental Disabilities: A Profile," *Children & Youth Services Review* 15 (1993): 489–506; V. K. Groze, *Successful Adoption Families* (Westport, Conn.: Praeger, 1996); J. LaCure, *Remembering: Reflections of Growing Up Adopted* (Franklin, Mass.: Adoption Advocate Pub-

lishing, 1995); J. A. Rosenthal, V. Groze, and H. Curiel, "Race, Social Class, and Special Needs Adoption," *Social Work* 35 (1990): 532–39; W. Thorkelson, "Study: Most Adoptive Families OK," *The Lutheran* (August 1994): 34; S. Waldman and L. Caplan, "The Politics of Adoption," *Newsweek,* March 21, 1994.

8. B. Tremitiere, "Genetics and Adoption: The Part You Never Met," *Roots & Wings* (April/May/June 1996): 8–9.
9. D. M. Brodzinsky, "Long-term Outcomes in Adoption," *The Future of Children* 3 (Spring 1993): 153–66; R. J. Cadoret, W. R. Yates, E. Troughton, and G. Woodworth, "Adoption Study Demonstrating Two Genetic Pathways to Drug Abuse," *Archives of General Psychiatry* 52 (January 1995): 42–52; D. M. Ferguson, M. Lynskey, and L. J. Horwood, "The Adolescent Outcomes of Adoption: A 16-Year Longitudinal Study," *Journal of Child Psychology & Psychiatry & Allied Disciplines* 36 (1995): 597–615; S. A. Frankel, "Pathogenic Factors in the Experience of Early and Late Adopted Children," *Psychoanalytic Study of the Child* 46 (1991): 91–108; S. Kotsopoulos et al., "A Psychiatric Follow-Up Study of Adoptees," *Canadian Journal of Psychiatry* 38 (August 1993): 391–96; E. L. Lipman et al., "Psychiatric Disorders in Adopted Children: A Profile from the Ontario Child Health Study," *Canadian Journal of Psychiatry* 37 (November 1992): 627–33; S. Scarr, R. A. Weinberg, and I. D. Waldman, "IQ Correlations in Transracial Adoptive Families," *Intelligence* 17 (October/December 1993): 541–55; D. A. Mason and P. J. Frick, "The Heritability of Antisocial Behavior: A Meta-Analysis of Twin and Adoption Studies," *Journal of Psychopathology & Behavioral Assessment* 16 (December 1994): 301–23; P. J. Tienari and L. C. Wynn, "Adoption Studies of Schizophrenia," *Annals of Medicine* 26 (August 1994): 233–37; L. Willerman, J. C. Loehlin, and J. M. Horn, "An Adoption and a Cross-Fostering Study of the Minnesota Multiphasic Personality Inventory (MMPI) Psychopathic Deviate Scale," *Behavior Genetics* 22 (September 1992): 515–29.
10. R. Diamond, "Secrecy vs. Privacy," *Adoptive Families* (September/October 1995): 9–11; L. R. Melina, ed., "Differentiating between Secrecy, Privacy, and Openness in Adoption," *Adopted Child* 12 (May 1993).

CHAPTER 2: Before You Begin

1. M. Berry, "Risks and Benefits of Open Adoption," *The Future of Children* 3 (Spring 1993): 125–38; M. B. Style, "Issues in Practice: It's Not the Contact, but the Reasons for the Contact," *National Adoption Reports* (September 1995): 5.
2. L. Caplan, *An Open Adoption* (Boston: Houghton Mifflin, 1990); P. M. Dorner, *How to Open an Adoption* (Royal Oak, Mich.: R-Squared Press, 1997); J. L. Gritter, *Adoption without Fear* (San Antonio, Tex.: Corona Publishing Co., 1989); J. L. Gritter, *The Spirit of Open Adoption* (Washington, D.C.: Child Welfare League, 1997); S. Kaplan and M. J. Rillera, *Cooperative Adoption: A Handbook,* 2nd ed. (Westminister, Calif.: Triadoption Library, 1991); J. W. Lindsay, *Open Adoption: A Caring Option* (Buena Park, Calif.: Morning Glory Press, 1987); L. R. Melina and S. K. Roszia, *The Open Adoption Experience* (New York: HarperCollins, 1993); C. V. N. Peck, *Adoption Today: Options and Outcomes* (Great Meadows, N.J.: Roots and Wings, 1997); B. M. Rappaport, *The Open Adoption Book: A Guide to Adoption without Tears* (New York:

Macmillan, 1992); M. Ryburn, *Open Adoption: Research, Theory, and Practice* (Aldershot, Hants, England: Avebury, 1994); K. Silber and P. M. Dorner, *Children of Open Adoption* (San Antonio, Tex.: Corona Publishing Co., 1990).

3. D. Howells and K. W. Pritchard, *The Story of David: How We Created a Family through Open Adoption* (New York: Bantam, 1997); K. Kurzel, *Pugnose Has Two Special Families* (Royal Oak, Mich.: R-Squared Press, 1997); K. Silber and D. M. Parelskin, *My Special Family: A Children's Book about Open Adoption* (Orinda, Calif.: Open Adoption Press, 1994); K. O. Sly, *Becky's Special Family* (Corona, Calif.: Alternative Parenting Publications, 1985).

4. B. Romanchik, *A Birthmother's Book of Memories* (Royal Oak, Mich.: R-Squared Press, 1994).

5. A. Baran and R. Pannor, "Perspectives on Open Adoption," *The Future of Children* 3 (Spring 1993): 119–24.

6. L. Burgess, *The Art of Adoption* (Washington, D.C.: Acropolis Books, 1976).

7. M. Berry, "Adoptive Parents' Perceptions of, and Comfort with, Open Adoption," *Child Welfare* 72 (May/June 1993): 231–53; M. Berry, "Risks and Benefits of Open Adoption," *The Future of Children* 3 (Spring 1993): 125–38; M. Berry, "The Effects of Open Adoption on Biological and Adoptive Parents and the Children: The Arguments and the Evidence," *Child Welfare* 70 (November/December 1991): 637–51.

8. M. Beek, "The Reality of Face-to-Face Contact after Adoption," *Adoption & Fostering* 18 (Summer 1994): 39–45; M. Berry, "Risks and Benefits of Open Adoption," *The Future of Children* 3 (Spring 1993): 125–38; H. D. Grotevant et al., "Adoptive Family System Dynamics: Variations by Level of Openness in the Adoption," *Family Process* 33 (June 1994): 125–46; D. H. Siegel, "Open Adoption of Infants: Adoptive Parents' Perceptions of Advantages and Disadvantages," *Social Work* 38 (January 1993): 15–23.

9. J. Etter, "Levels of Cooperation and Satisfaction in 56 Open Adoptions," *Child Welfare* 72 (May/June 1993): 257–67; H. E. Gross, "Open Adoption: A Research-Based Literature Review and New Data," *Child Welfare* 72 (May/June 1993): 269–84; D. H. Siegel, "Open Adoption of Infants: Adoptive Parents' Perceptions of Advantages and Disadvantages," *Social Work* 38 (January 1993): 15–23.

CHAPTER 3: An Underlying Issue

1. P. I. Johnston, *Adopting after Infertility* (Indianapolis, Ind.: Perspectives Press, 1993); P. I. Johnston, *Taking Charge of Infertility* (Indianapolis, Ind.: Perspectives Press, 1994); V. K. Miller, *Meditations for Adoptive Parents* (Scottdale, Pa.: Herald Press, 1992); N. V. Oberto and L. Oberto, *Men Have Hormones, Too! One Man's Humorous Story of Infertility, Pregnancy, and Other Surprises* (Decatur, Ill.: Polestar Press, 1995); L. P. Salzer, *Surviving Infertility* (New York: HarperPerennial, 1991); B. Shulgold and L. Sipiora, *Dear Barbara, Dear Lynne* (Reading, Mass.: Addison-Wesley, 1992).

2. M. S. Rosenthal, *The Fertility Sourcebook* (Los Angeles, Calif.: Lowell House, 1995).

3. S. Begley, "The Baby," *Newsweek,* September 4, 1995.

4. L. Steinberg, "No Baby on Board," *Seattle Post–Intelligencer,* May 1, 1995.

5. L. Lafayette, *Why Don't You Have Kids? Living a Full Life without Parenthood* (New York: Kensington Books, 1995).

6. R. R. Franklin and D. K. Brockman, *In Pursuit of Fertility: A Fertility Expert Tells You How to Get Pregnant,* 2nd ed. (New York: Holt, 1995); H. A. Goldfarb, *Overcoming Infertility: 12 Couples Share Their Success Stories* (New York: J. Wiley, 1995); D. Raab, *Getting Pregnant and Staying Pregnant: Overcoming Infertility and Managing Your High-Risk Pregnancy* (Alameda, Calif.: Hunter House, 1991); T. Weschler, *Taking Charge of Your Fertility: The Definitive Guide to Natural Birth Control and Pregnancy Achievement* (New York: HarperCollins, 1995).

7. S. Begley, "The Baby," *Newsweek,* September 4, 1995.

8. G. Cowley, "The Future of Birth," *Newsweek,* September 4, 1995.

9. E. Noble, *Having Your Baby by Donor Insemination* (Boston: Houghton Mifflin, 1987); M. S. Rosenthal, *The Fertility Sourcebook* (Los Angeles, Calif.: Lowell House, 1995); C. Saban, *Miracle Child: Genetic Mother, Surrogate Womb* (Fair Hills, N.J.: New Horizon Press, 1993); L. L. Schwartz, *Alternatives to Infertility: Is Surrogacy the Answer* (New York: Brunner/Mazel, 1991); S. J. Silber, *How to Get Pregnant with the New Technology* (New York: Warner Books, 1991); S. L. Tan, H. S. Jacobs, and M. M. Seibel, *Infertility: Your Questions Answered,* updated ed. (Secaucus, N.J.: Carol Publishing Group, 1997).

10. K. Bradstreet, *Overcoming Infertility Naturally: The Relationship between Nutrition, Emotions, and Reproduction* (Pleasant Grove, Utah: Woodland Publishing, 1993); B. Kass-Annese and H. Danzer, *The Fertility Awareness Handbook* (Claremont, Calif.: Hunter House, 1992); A. P. Zoldbrod, *Getting around the Boulder in the Road: Using Imagery to Cope with Fertility Problems* (Lexington, Mass.: Center for Reproductive Problems, 1990).

11. B. Azar, "Foster Care Has Bleak History," *APA Monitor* (November 1995): 8.

12. J. A. Rosenthal, "Outcomes of Adoption of Children with Special Needs," *The Future of Children* 3 (Spring 1993): 77–88.

13. J. Carter and M. Carter, *Sweet Grapes: How to Stop Being Infertile and Start Living Again* (Indianapolis, Ind.: Perspectives Press, 1989); S. L. Cooper and E. S. Glazer, *Beyond Infertility: The New Paths to Parenthood* (New York: Free Press, 1994); P. I. Johnston, *Taking Charge of Infertility* (Indianapolis, Ind.: Perspectives Press, 1994); S. Powell, *When You Can't Have a Child* (Australia: Allen & Unwin, 1993); L. P. Salzer, *Surviving Infertility* (New York: HarperPerennial, 1991).

14. C. Leynes, "Keep or Adopt: A Study of Factors Influencing Pregnant Adolescents' Plans for Their Babies," *Child Psychiatry and Human Development* 11 (1980): 105–12; C. Martin, "Psychological Problems of Abortion for the Unwed Teenage Girl," *Genetic Psychology Monographs* 88 (1973): 23–110; R. H. Rosen, T. Benson, and J. M. Stack, "Help or Hindrance: Parental Impact on Pregnant Teenagers' Resolution Decisions," *Family Relations* 31 (1982): 271–80.

CHAPTER 4: Special Parents with Special Needs

1. J. J. Curto, *How to Become a Single Parent: A Guide for Single People Considering Adoption or Natural Parenthood Alone* (Englewood Cliffs, N.J.: Prentice Hall, Inc., 1983).

2. S. Alexander, *In Praise of Single Parents: Mothers and Fathers Embracing the Challenge* (Boston: Houghton Mifflin, 1994); J. Mattes, *Single Mothers by Choice: A Guidebook*

for Single Women Who Are Considering or Have Chosen Motherhood (New York: Times Books, Random House, 1994); H. Marindin, ed., *The Handbook for Single Adoptive Parents* (Chevy Chase, Md.: Committee for Single Adoptive Parents, 1997).

3. G. M. Drake, ed., *Directory for Adoptive Parents over 40* (North Carolina: Sylvia A. Waiters, 1993).

4. J. P. Blank, *19 Steps up the Mountain: The Story of the DeBolt Family* (Philadelphia, Pa.: J. B. Lippincott, 1976).

5. M. Ward, "Large Adoptive Families: A Special Resource," *Social Casework* 59 (1978): 411–18.

6. B. Azar, "Foster Care Has Bleak History," *APA Monitor* (November 1995): 8.

7. R. Barth, "Adoption Research: Building Blocks for the Next Decade," *Child Welfare* 73 (September/October 1994): 625–38; S. A. Holmes, "The Tie That Binds: The Constitutional Right of Children to Maintain Relationships with Parent-Like Individuals," *Maryland Law Review* 53 (1994): 358–411.

8. W. Meezan and J. F. Shireman, *Care and Commitment: Foster Parent Adoption Decisions* (Albany, N.Y.: State University of New York Press, 1985).

9. J. Goldstein, A. Freud, and A. J. Solnit, *Beyond the Best Interests of the Child* (New York: Free Press, 1973).

10. "Tough Law in Oregon Separates Children from Flawed Parents," *Seattle Times,* September 15, 1997.

11. J. K. McKenzie, "Adoption of Children with Special Needs," *The Future of Children* 3 (Spring 1993): 62–76; J. Rosenthal, "Outcomes of Adoption of Children with Special Needs," *The Future of Children,* 3 (Spring 1993): 77–88.

12. F. Cavaliere, "Society Appears More Open to Gay Parenting," *APA Monitor* (July 1995): 51; "Lesbian Couples Raise Psychologically Healthy Children," *Philadelphia Inquirer,* May 4, 1994.

13. "Gay Adoption Case Raises Questions about Parents', Children's Rights," *Adopted Child* 13 (April 1994).

14. F. Cavaliere, "Society Appears More Open to Gay Parenting," *APA Monitor* (July 1995): 51; "Gay Adoption Case Raises Questions about Parents', Children's Rights," *Adopted Child* 13 (April 1994).

15. F. Bruni, "For Gay Couples, Ruling to Cheer on Adoption," *New York Times,* November 5, 1995; J. Dao, "New York's Highest Court Rules Unmarried Couples Can Adopt," *New York Times,* November 3, 1995.

16. "Gay Adoption Case Raises Questions about Parents', Children's Rights," *Adopted Child* 13 (April 1994); D. H. McIntyre, "Gay Parents and Child Custody: A Struggle under the Legal System," *Mediation Quarterly* 12 (1994): 135–48; S. C. McMillan, "Neither Gays nor Singles Should Adopt," *Los Angeles Times,* April 2, 1995.

17. "Gay Adoption Case Raises Questions about Parents', Children's Rights," *Adopted Child* 13 (April 1994)

18. S. Arms, *Adoption: A Handful of Hope* (Berkeley, Calif.: Celestial Arts, 1990); F. Bozett and M. B. Sussman, eds., *Homosexuality and Family Relations* (New York: Haworth Press, 1990); P. Burke, *Family Values: Two Moms and Their Son* (New York: Random House, 1993); J. Dahl and N. Hardesty, eds., *River of Promise: Two Women's*

Story of Love & Adoption (Philadelphia: LuraMedia, 1989); A. Martin, *The Lesbian and Gay Parenting Handbook: Creating and Raising Our Families* (New York: Harper-Collins, 1993); K. Morgen, *Getting Simon: Two Gay Doctors' Journey to Fatherhood* (New York: Bramble Books, 1995).

19. K. B. Morgen, *Getting Simon: Two Gay Doctors' Journey to Fatherhood* (New York: Bramble Books, 1995).

20. "Lesbian Couples Raise Psychologically Healthy Children," *Philadelphia Inquirer,* May 4, 1994.

21. "Kids Get Homes with Gays," *Lesbian Tide* 9 (1980).

22. E. Mehren, "Lesbian Mothers: Two New Studies Shatter Stereotypes," *Los Angeles Times,* June 1, 1983.

CHAPTER 5: Agencies in Transition

1. E. Bartholet, *Family Bonds: Adoption and the Politics of Parenting* (Boston: Houghton Mifflin, 1993); A. Bussier, "Eligibility Criteria," *Adoptive Families* (September/October 1995): 37–38.

2. J. O'Riordan, "Choosing an Agency," *Adoptive Families* (November/December 1995): 34–35.

3. K. J. Daly and M. P. Sobol, "Public and Private Adoption: A Comparison of Service and Accessibility," *Family Relations* 43 (January 1994): 86–93.

4. J. Palmer, "Hey, Fatso!" *Barron's,* July 1, 1996.

5. "Parents Who Smoke Need Not Apply," *Technology Review* 96 (1993): 80.

CHAPTER 6: Different Ways for Different People

1. C. Alexander-Roberts, *The Legal Adoption Guide* (Dallas, Tex.: Taylor Publishing, 1997).

2. S. Arms, *To Love and Let Go* (New York: Alfred A. Knopf, 1983); M. B. Jones, *Birth-mothers: Women Who Have Relinquished Babies for Adoption Tell Their Stories* (Chicago: Chicago Review Press, 1993); C. Schaefer, *The Other Mother: A Woman's Love for the Child She Gave Up for Adoption* (New York: Soho Press, 1991); K. Silber and P. Speedlin, *Dear Birthmother, Thank You for Our Baby* (San Antonio, Tex.: Corona Publishing Co., 1983).

3. S. Waldman and L. Caplan, "The Politics of Adoption," *Newsweek,* March 21, 1994.

4. L. McTaggart, *The Baby Brokers: The Marketing of White Babies in America* (New York: Dial Press, 1980).

5. R. S. Lasnik, *A Parent's Guide to Adoption* (New York: Sterling, 1979).

CHAPTER 7: A Distant Resource

1. H. Altstein, *Intercountry Adoption: A Multinational Perspective* (New York: Praeger, 1991); C. Bagley, *International and Transracial Adoption: A Mental Health Perspective* (Aldershot, Hants, England: Avebury, 1993); J. S. Cohen and A. Westhues, "A Comparison of Self-Esteem, School Achievement, and Friends between Intercountry Adoptees and Their Siblings," *Early Child Development and Care* 106 (1995): 205–24; W. Fiegelman and A. R. Silverman, *Chosen Children* (New York: Praeger,

1983); R. A. C. Hoksbergen, ed., *Adoption in Worldwide Perspective* (Berwyn, Ill.: Swets North America, 1986); F. Koh, *Oriental Children in American Homes: How Do They Adjust*, rev. ed. (Minneapolis, Minn.: East-West Press, 1988); R. J. Simon and H. Altstein, *Intercountry Adoption* (New York: Praeger, 1991); B. Tizard, "Intercountry Adoption: A Review of the Evidence," *Journal of Child Psychology and Psychiatry* 32 (1991): 743–56.

2. E. H. Brooke, "Adoption Saga of Rio's Streets," *New York Times*, December 29, 1994; D. Scanlan, "Stolen Children?" *Maclean's*, April 18, 1994.

3. E. Barthlolet, "International Adoption: Current Status and Future Prospects," *The Future of Children* 3 (Spring 1993): 89–103; C. Bogert et al., "Bringing Back Baby," *Newsweek*, November 21, 1994.

4. H. Mark, "Foreign Couples Adopting American Babies," *Seattle Times*, August 17, 1997.

5. M. M. Mason, "Global Trends in Adoption," *Adoptive Families* (March/April 1996): 8–11; T. Watanabe, "Earthquake Upsets Traditional Attitudes on Adoption," *Los Angeles Times*, February 28, 1995.

6. Department of State, "International Adoption and Child Abduction, Sources of Orphans Immigrating to United States," Internet.

7. S. D. Driedger, "Bringing Home Baby," *Maclean's*, August 21, 1995.

8. E. Bartholet, "International Adoption: Current Status and Future Prospects," *The Future of Children* 3 (Spring 1993): 89–103.

9. "Hague Treaty Hopes to Solve Problems in Intercountry Adoptions," *Adopted Child* 12 (August 1993).

10. B. B. Bascom and C. A. McKelvey, *The Complete Guide to Foreign Adoptions: What to Expect and How to Prepare for Your New Child* (New York: Pocket Books, 1997); E. D. Hibbs, ed., *Adoption: International Perspectives* (Madison, Conn.: International Universities Press, 1991); R. A. C. Hoksbergen, *Adoption in Worldwide Perspective* (Berwyn, Ill.: Swets North America, 1986); M. Humphrey and H. Humphrey, eds., *Inter-Country Adoption: Practical Experiences* (London: Travistock/Routledge, 1993); R. Miller and M. Miller, *Home Is Where the Heart Wants to Be* (Minneapolis, Minn.: LN Press, 1993); J. Nelson-Erichsen and H. R. Erichsen, *How to Adopt Internationally* (Fort Worth: Tex.: Mesa House, 1997); E. Paul, *Adoption Choices: A Guidebook to National and International Adoption Resources* (Detroit: Visible Ink Press, 1991); O. R. Sweet and P. Bryan, *Adopt International: Everything You Need to Know to Adopt a Child from Abroad* (New York: Farrar, Straus & Giroux, 1996); S. T. Viguers, *With Child: One Couple's Journey to Their Adopted Children* (San Diego: Harcourt Brace Jovanovich, 1986); E. L. Walker, *Loving Journeys: Guide to Adoption* (Petersborough, N.H.: Loving Journeys, 1992); J. Wine, *The Canadian Adoption Guide: A Family at Last* (Ontario, Canada: McGraw-Hill Ryerson, 1995); E. Wirth and J. Worden, *How to Adopt a Child from Another Country* (Nashville, Tenn.: Abingdon Press, 1993).

11. S. Marcovich et al., "Romanian Adoption: Parents' Dreams, Nightmares, and Realities," *Child Welfare* 74 (September/October 1995): 993–1017.

12. S. Marcovitch et al., "Romanian Adoption: Parents' Dreams, Nightmares, and Realities," *Child Welfare* 74 (September/October 1995): 993–1017; S. J. Morrison, "The

Development of Children Adopted from Romanian Orphanages," *Merrill-Palmer Quarterly* 41 (October 1995): 411–30.

13. "Differences in Language and Culture Complicate but Do Not Preclude International Searches," *Adopted Child* 16 (March 1997); L. Smith, "Adoptees Search the World for Their Roots," *Los Angeles Times,* June 17, 1996.

14. "Advice Given on Starting a Successful Culture Camp for Adoptees," *Adopted Child* 14 (March 1995); J. S. Bond, "Instilling Cultural Pride," *Adoptive Families* (November/December 1995): 60–61; J. McFarlane, "Building Self-Esteem in Children and Teenagers of Color," *OURS* (May/June 1992): 28–33; J. Ramos, "Ethnic Images: A Primer for Adoptive Parents," *OURS* (May/June 1990): 18.

15. "Ethnic Identity Includes Ancestry, but Is Shaped by Experience," *Adopted Child* 15 (September 1996).

16. J. S. Phinney, "When We Talk about American Ethnic Groups What Do We Mean?" *American Psychologist* 51 (September 1966): 918–27.

17. A. A. Joshi, "Cross-Cultural Encounters: Lessons to Learn From . . . ," *Biracial Child* 6, 20.

18. D. Hopson and D. Hopson, *Different and Wonderful: Raising Black Children in a Race-Conscious Society* (New York: Prentice Hall, 1990); D. Hopson and D. Hopson, *Raising the Rainbow Generation: Teaching Your Children to be Successful in a Multicultural Society* (New York: Simon & Schuster, 1993).

19. M. E. Petertyl, *Seeds of Love: For Brothers and Sisters of International Adoptions* (Grand Rapids, Mich.: Folio 1 Publications, 1997).

CHAPTER 8: An Option Worth Considering

1. J. Finnegan, *Shattered Dreams—Lonely Choices: Birthparents of Babies with Disabilities Talk about Adoption* (Westport, Conn.: Bergin & Garvey, 1993).

2. J. K. McKenzie, "Adoption of Children with Special Needs," *The Future of Children* 3 (Spring 1993): 62–76.

3. W. Hamm, T. Morton, and L. M. Flynn, *Self-Awareness, Self-Selection and Success: A Parent Preparation Guidebook for Special Needs Adoptions* (Washington, D.C.: North American Council on Adoptable Children, 1985).

4. L. A. Babb and R. Laws, *Adopting and Advocating for the Special Needs Child: A Guide for Parents and Professionals* (Westport, Conn.: Bergin & Garvey, 1997); G. C. Keck and R. M. Kupecky, *Adopting the Hurt Child: Hope for Families with Special-Needs Kids* (Colorado Springs, Colo.: Piñon Press, 1995); J. E. Kloeppel and D. A. Kloeppel, *Forever Parents: Adopting Older Children* (Union City, Ga.: Adele Enterprises, 1995); C. H. Lindsay, *Nothing Good Ever Happens to Me: An Adoption Love Story* (Washington, D.C.: Child Welfare League of America, 1996).

5. R. J. Delaney, *The Healing Power of the Family* (Fort Collins, Colo.: Journey Press, 1995); G. C. Keck and R. M. Kupecky, *Adopting the Hurt Child: Hope for Families with Special-Needs Kids* (Colorado Springs, Colo.: Piñon Press, 1995).

6. W. Hamm, T. Morton, and L. M. Flynn, *Self-Awareness, Self-Selection and Success: A Parent Preparation Guidebook for Special Needs Adoptions* (Washington, D.C.: North American Council on Adoptable Children, 1985).

7. R. Laws, "Between the Lines," *Adoptive Families* (September/October 1995): 34–35.

8. R. J. Delaney, *The Healing Power of the Family* (Fort Collins, Colo.: Journey Press, 1995).

9. A. Bullock, E. Grimes, and J. McNamara, *Bruised before Birth: Parenting Children Exposed to Prenatal Substance Abuse* (Greensboro, N.C.: Family Resources, 1995); D. D. Davis, *Reaching Out to Children with FAS/FAE* (West Nyack, N.Y.: Center for Applied Research in Education, 1994); M. Dorris, *The Broken Cord* (New York: Harper & Row, 1989); "Prenatal Drug Exposure Affects School-Age Child's Behavior," *Adopted Child* 15 (January 1996).

10. R. P. Barth, "Revisiting the Issues: Adoption of Drug-Exposed Children," *The Future of Children* 3 (Spring 1993): 168; B. Zuckerman, "Drug-Exposed Infants: Understanding the Medical Risks," *The Future of Children* 1 (Spring 1991): 26–35.

11. "Prenatal Drug Exposure Affects School-Age Child's Behavior," *Adopted Child* 15 (January 1996).

12. T. Paulson, "Alcohol's Damage—From Fetus to Adult," *Seattle Post–Intelligencer*, September 5, 1996.

13. "Some Infants Shake Off HIV Virus," *Peninsula Daily News*, January 26, 1996.

14. Telephone Conversation with Northwest AIDS Foundation Epidemiology Department, April 30, 1996; I. Fisher, "HIV Test for Newborns Moves Ahead," *Seattle Post–Intelligencer*, May 1, 1996.

15. L. Glidden, *Formed Families: Adoption of Children with Handicaps* (New York: Haworth Press, 1990).

16. J. P. Blank, *19 Steps up the Mountain: The Story of the DeBolt Family* (Philadelphia: J. B. Lippincott, 1976).

17. T. O'Hanlon, *Accessing Federal Adoption Subsidies after Legalization* (Washington, D.C.: Child Welfare League of America, 1995).

18. J. A. Rosenthal and V. K. Groze, "A Longitudinal Study of Special-Needs Adoptive Families," *Child Welfare* 73 (November/December 1994): 689–706.

19. D. Keyes, *Flowers for Algernon* (New York: Harcourt Brace & World, 1966).

20. B. D. Ingersoll and S. Goldstein, *Attention Deficit Disorder and Learning Disabilities: Realities, Myths, and Controversial Treatments* (New York: Doubleday, 1993).

21. "Prenatal Drug Exposure Affects School-Age Child's Behavior," *Adopted Child* 15 (January 1996): 3.

22. C. Alexander-Roberts, *The ADHD Parenting Handbook* (Dallas, Tex.: Taylor Publishing, 1994); T. Armstrong, *The Myth of the A.D.D. Child* (New York: E. P. Dutton & Co., 1995); R. E. Duke, *How to Help Your Learning-Challenged Child Be a Winner* (Far Hills, N.J.: New Horizon Press, 1993); G. Fisher and R. Cummings, *When Your Child Has LD (Learning Difficulties): A Survival Guide for Parents* (Minneapolis, Minn.: Free Spirit Publishing, Inc. 1995); M. Fowler, *Maybe You Know My Kid* (New York: Carol Publishing Group, 1993); E. Hallowell and J. J. Ratey, *Answers to Distractions* (New York: Pantheon Books, 1994); R. Kajander, *Living with ADHD* (Minneapolis, Minn.: Park Nicollet Medical Foundation, 1995); K. Nosek, *The Dyslexic Scholar* (Dallas, Tex.: Taylor Publishing, 1995); S. Smith, *No Easy Answers: The Learning Disabled Child at Home and at School* (New York: Bantam Books, 1995);

C. G. Tuttle and P. Paquette, *Parenting a Child with a Learning Disability* (Los Angeles, Calif.: Lowell House, 1993).

23. M. K. Rudman, "Children's Literature: An Issues Approach," *Teaching Guide* (1995): 512.

24. J. A. Rosenthal, "Outcomes of Adoption of Children with Special Needs," *The Future of Children* 3 (Spring 1993): 77–88.

25. J. Peterson, *The Invisible Road: Parental Insight to Attachment Disorders* (Pueblo, Colo.: Loving Homes, 1995).

26. R. J. Delaney and F. R. Kustal, *Troubled Transplants: Unconventional Strategies for Helping Disturbed Foster and Adoptive Children* (Portland, Maine: University of Southern Maine, 1993); G. C. Keck and R. M. Kupecky, *Adopting the Hurt Child: Hope for Families with Special-Needs Kids* (Colorado Spring, Colo.: Piñon Books, 1995); K. Magid and C. A. McKelvey, *High Risk: Children without a Conscience* (New York: Bantam Books, 1988); J. McNamara, *Sexually Reactive Children in Adoption and Foster Care* (Greensboro, N.C.: Family Resources, 1994); D. H. Minshew and C. Hooper, *The Adoptive Family as a Healing Resource for the Sexually Abused Child: A Trained Manual* (Washington, D.C.: Child Welfare League of America, 1990); E. Randolph, *Children Who Shock and Surprise* (Yuba City, Calif.: RFR Publications, 1994); M. G. Welch, *Holding Time* (New York: Simon & Schuster, 1988).

27. J. McNamara and B. McNamara, *Adoption and the Sexually Abused Child* (Portland, Maine: Human Services Development Institute, University of Southern Maine, 1990).

28. E. E. Werner, "Children of the Garden Island," *Scientific American* (April 1989): 106–11.

29. E. E. Werner, "Children of the Garden Island," *Scientific American* (April 1989): 111.

30. J. C. Lythcott-Haims, "Where Do Mixed Babies Belong?" *Harvard Civil Rights–Civil Liberties Law Review* 29 (Summer 1994): 531–58.

31. D. Fanshel, *Far from the Reservations: The Transracial Adoption of American Indian Children* (Metuchen, N.J.: Scarecrow Press, 1972); M. Mannes, "Factors and Events Leading to the Passage of the Indian Child Welfare Act," *Child Welfare* 74 (January/February 1995): 264–82; L. Matheson, "The Politics of the Indian Child Welfare Act," *Social Work* 41 (March 1996): 232–35.

32. C. F. Hairston and V. G. Williams, "Black Adoptive Parents: How They View Agency Adoption Practices," *Social Casework: The Journal of Contemporary Social Work* (November 1989): 534–39; M. Jones, "Adoption Agencies: Can They Service African-Americans?" *Crisis* 99, no. 8 (November/December 1992): 26–28.

33. S. D. Molock, "Adoption Barriers for African-American Families," *Adoptive Families* (March/April 1995): 14–16.

34. S. D. Molock, "Adoption Barriers for African-American Families," *Adoptive Families* (March/April 1995): 14–16; A. S. Tyson, "Removing Race from Adoption," *Christian Science Monitor,* May 7, 1996.

35. E. Bartholet, *Family Bonds: Adoption and the Politics of Parenting* (Boston: Houghton Mifflin, 1993); A. Harnack, ed., *Adoption: Opposing Viewpoints* (San Diego, Calif.: Greenhaven Press, 1995); R. K. Fitten, "Transracial Adoption: Searching for a Middle

Ground," *Seattle Times,* October 23, 1995; A. R. Silverman, "Outcomes of Transracial Adoption," *The Future of Children* 3 (Spring 1993): 104–18; A. S. Tyson, "Removing Race from Adoption," *Christian Science Monitor,* May 7, 1996.

36. A. R. Silverman, "Outcomes of Transracial Adoption," *The Future of Children* 3 (Spring 1993): 104–18; A. S. Tyson, "Removing Race from Adoption," *Christian Science Monitor,* May 7, 1996.

37. N. Rommelman, "'A Big Guiding Light': The Institute of Black Parenting Offers Classes and Advice for Families Involved in Interracial Adoptions," *Los Angeles Times,* June 9, 1996.

38. C. Bagley, "Transracial Adoption in Britain: A Follow-Up Study, with Policy Considerations," *Child Welfare* 72 (May/June 1993): 285–99; P. Hayes, "Transracial Adoption: Politics and Ideology," *Child Welfare* 72 (May/June 1993): 301–10; J. A. Rosenthal, V. Groze, and H. Curiel, "Race, Social Class, and Special Needs Adoption," *Social Work* 35 (1990): 532–39; C. Pohl and K. Harris, *Transracial Adoption* (New York: Franklin Watts, 1992); A. R. Silverman, "Outcomes of Transracial Adoption," *The Future of Children* 3 (Spring 1993): 104–18; "Are Transracial Adoptions Bad for Black Children?" *CQ Researcher* 3 (November 26, 1993): 1049.

39. C. Bagley, *International and Transracial Adoption: A Mental Health Perspective* (Aldershot, Hants, England: Avebury, 1993); R. Barn, *Black Children in the Public Care System* (London: B. T. Batsford in Association with British Agencies for Adoption and Fostering, 1993); J. D. Bates, *Gift Children: A Story of Race, Family, and Adoption in a Divided America* (New York: Ticknor & Fields, 1993); I. Gaber and J. Aldridge, eds., *In the Best Interest of the Child's Culture: Identity & Transracial Adoption* (London: Free Association Books, 1995); C. Pohl and K. Harris, *Transracial Adoption* (New York: Franklin Watts, 1992); R. J. Simon and H. Altstein, *Adoption, Race, and Identity: From Infancy through Adolescence* (New York: Praeger, 1992); R. J. Simon and H. Altstein, *Transracial Adoptees and Their Families* (New York: Praeger, 1987).

40. L. Derman-Sparks and the A.B.C. Task Force, *Anti-Bias Curriculum: Tools for Empowering Young Children* (Washington, D.C.: National Association for the Education of Young Children, 1989).

41. J. Neufeld, *Edgar Allan* (New York: S. G. Phillips, 1968).

42. Heart Start Task Force Staff. *Heart Start: The Emotional Foundation of School Readiness* (Arlington, Va.: National Center for Clinical Infant Programs, 1992).

43. D. A. Hughes, *Facilitating Development Attachment: The Road to Emotional Recovery and Behavioral Change in Foster and Adopted Children* (Northvale, N.J.: Jason Aronson, 1997).

44. M. Best-Hopkins, *Toddler Adoption: The Weaver's Craft* (Indianapolis, Ind.: Perspectives Press, 1997).

45. J. K. McKenzie, "Adoption of Children with Special Needs," *The Future of Children* 3 (Spring 1993): 62–76.

46. B. Azar, "Foster Care Has Bleak History," *APA Monitor* (November 1995): 8; J. K. McKenzie, "Adoption of Children with Special Needs," *The Future of Children* 3 (Spring 1993): 66.

47. B. Chapman, "Adoption Option Too Often Neglected in State Foster Care Mess," *Seattle Post–Intelligencer,* April 4, 1997.

48. J. A. Rosenthal, "Outcomes of Adoption of Children with Special Needs," *The Future of Children* 3 (Spring 1993): 79.

49. K. Fernandez, *My Journal* (San Jose, Calif.: Lifeworks, 1995); B. Romanchik, *A Birthmother's Book of Memories* (Royal Oak, Mich.: R-Squared Press, 1994); K. Silber and D. M. Parelskin, *My Special Family: A Children's Book about Open Adoption* (Orinda, Calif.: Open Adoption Press, 1994).

50. V. Fahlberg, *A Child's Journey through Placement* (Indianapolis, Ind.: Perspectives Press, 1991); D. A. Hughes, *Facilitating Developmental Attachment: The Road to Emotional Recovery and Behavioral Changes in Foster and Adopted Children* (Northvale, N.J.: Jason Aronson, 1997); C. Jewett Jaratt, *Adopting the Older Child* (Harvard, Mass.: Harvard Common Press, 1978); C. Jewett Jaratt, *Helping Children Cope with Separation and Loss*, rev. ed. (Harvard, Mass.: Harvard Common Press, 1994); J. E. Kloeppel and D. A. Kloeppel, *Forever Parents: Adopting Older Children* (Union City, Ga.: Adele Enterprises, 1995).

51. V. I. Fahlberg, *A Child's Journey through Placement* (Indianapolis, Ind.: Perspectives Press, 1991).

52. J. Kenny, B. Pryor, and D. Watson-Duvall, "Cooperative Adoption: One Solution to Foster Care Drift," *Adoptalk* (Winter 1995): 6.

53. L. N. Tauer, "Multiple Challenges, Multiple Rewards," *Adoptive Families* (March/April 1996): 14–16.

54. R. Helgesen, "More Can Be Better: Adopting Five at One Time," *Adoptive Families* (March/April 1996): 30–32; D. W. Le Pere, *Large Sibling Groups: Adoption Experiences* (Washington, D.C.: Child Welfare League of America, 1986); P. Wedge and G. Mantle, *Sibling Groups and Social Work* (Aldershot, Hants, England: Avebury, 1991).

55. L. K. Melmed, *The Rainbabies* (New York: Lothrop, Lee & Shepard, 1992); M. Miles, *Aaron's Door* (Boston: Little, Brown & Co., 1977); F. Murphy, *Ready-Made Family* (New York: Scholastic, 1972); M. Rosen, *Crow and Hawk: A Traditional Pueblo Indian Story* (San Diego: Harcourt Brace & Co., 1995); C. Voigt, *Dicey's Song* (New York: Atheneum, 1982).

CHAPTER 10: The Search: Casting a Wide Net

1. Center for Disease Control and Prevention, "National Teen Pregnancy Trend," March 9, 1995.

2. R. Hicks, *Adopting in America: How to Adopt within One Year* (Sun City, Calif.: WordSlinger Press, 1995).

3. "Internet Adoption Registry," *Adoptive Families* (March/April 1996): 6.

4. "Orphans in Brazil Can Be Adopted Via the Internet," *Seattle Post–Intelligencer,* July 25, 1996.

5. P. I. Johnston, *Launching a Baby's Adoption: Practical Strategies for Parents and Professionals* (Indianapolis, Ind.: Perspectives Press, 1997).

CHAPTER 11: Are You Really Ready?

1. J. Lindsay and C. Monserrat, *Adoption Awareness: A Guide for Teachers, Counselors, Nurses, and Caring Others* (Buena Park, Calif.: Morning Glory Press, 1989).

2. J. H. Hollinger, "Adoption Law," *The Future of Children* 3 (Spring 1993): 42–61.

3. R. B. Hicks, *Adopting in America: How to Adopt within One Year* (Sun City, Calif.: WordSlinger Press, 1995).

Chapter 12: We Have the Baby, But...

1. D. W. Smith and L. N. Sherwen, *Mothers and Their Adopted Children: The Bonding Process* (New York: Tiresias Press, 1983).

2. P. Holmes, *Supporting an Adoption* (Wayne, Pa.: Our Child Press, 1986).

3. L. Jordon, "Becoming an Adoptive Family," *Parents,* August 1995.

4. P. Leach, *Your Baby & Child: From Birth to Age Five,* 2nd ed. (New York: Alfred A. Knopf, 1994): 28.

5. T. B. Brazelton, *On Becoming a Family: The Growth of Attachment* (New York: Dell Publishing, 1981); J. Bowlby, *Attachment and Loss* (New York: Basic Books, 1980); V. I. Fahlberg, *A Child's Journey through Placement* (Indianapolis, Ind.: Perspectives Press, 1991).

6. J. Bowlby, *Attachment and Loss* (New York: Basic Books, 1980).

7. D. Brodzinsky and M. Schechter, eds., *The Psychology of Adoption* (New York: Oxford University Press, 1990); V. Fahlberg, *A Child's Journey through Placement* (Indianapolis, Ind.: Perspectives Press, 1991); J. E. Schooler, *The Whole Life Adoption Book* (Colorado Springs, Colo.: Piñon Press, 1993); D. W. Smith and L. N. Sherwen, *Mothers and Their Adopted Children: The Bonding Process* (New York: Tiresias Press, 1983); H. van Gulden, and L. Bartels-Rabb, *Real Parents, Real Children: Parenting the Adopted Child* (New York: Crossroads Publishing, 1993); "Variety of Attachment Disorders Need Variety of Treatment Options," *Adopted Child* 13 (May 1994).

8. A. McCabe, "The Post's Adoption Therapist Helpline," *The Post* (Winter 1996).

9. V. Fahlberg, *A Child's Journey through Placement* (Indianapolis, Ind.: Perspectives Press, 1991).

10. P. I. Johnston, "Baby Blues," *Adoptive Families* (September/October 1995).

11. P. Roles, *Saying Goodbye to a Baby: Vol 1—The Birthparent's Guide to Loss and Grief in Adoption* (Washington, D.C.: Child Welfare League of America, 1989).

12. M. B. Jones, *Birthmothers: Women Who Have Relinquished Babies for Adoption Tell Their Stories* (Chicago: Chicago Review Press, 1993).

13. K. M. Becker and C. K. Heckert, *To Keera with Love: Abortion, Adoption, or Keeping the Baby, the Story of One Teen's Choice* (Kansas City, Miss.: Sheed & Ward, 1987).

14. K. Silber and P. Speedlin, *Dear Birthmother: Thank You for Our Baby* (San Antonio, Tex.: Corona Publishing Co., 1983).

15. B. Romanchik, *A Birthmother's Book of Memories* (Royal Oak, Mich.: R-Squared Press, 1994.)

16. J. W. Lindsay, *Parents, Pregnant Teens, and the Adoption Option* (Buena Park, Calif.: Morning Glory Press, 1989).

17. L. Lynch, "Birthmother's Day," *Adoptive Families* (May/June 1995): 54–55; M. J. Marsh, *Planning a Birthmother's Day Celebration* (Royal Oak, Mich.: R-Squared Press, 1996).

18. P. Roles, *Saying Goodbye to a Baby: Vol 1—The Birthparent's Guide to Loss and Grief in Adoption* (Washington, D.C.: Child Welfare League of America, 1989): 27–28.

19. S. Arms, *Adoption: A Handful of Hope* (Berkeley, Calif.: Celestial Arts, 1990); K. M. Becker and C. K. Heckert, *To Keera with Love* (Kansas City, Miss.: Sheed & Ward, 1987); P. Collins, *Letter to Louise* (New York: HarperCollins, 1992); M. Connelly, *Given in Love: For Mothers Releasing a Child for Adoption*, ed. J. Johnson (Omaha, Neb.: Centering Corporation, 1989); CUB, *The Birthparent's Perspective on Adoption* (Des Moines, Iowa: CUB, Inc., 1987); R. Harsin, *Wanted—First Child: A Birth Mother's Story* (Santa Barbara, Calif.: Fithian Press, 1991); M. B. Jones, *Birthmothers: Women Who Have Relinquished Babies for Adoption Tell Their Stories* (Chicago: Chicago Review Press, 1993); L. Jurgens, *Turn from the Heart* (Lower Lake, Calif.: Asian Publishing, 1992); J. W. Lindsay, *Pregnant Too Soon: Adoption Is an Option* (Buena Park, Calif.: Morning Glory Press, 1988); R. Mander, *The Care of the Mother: Grieving a Baby Relinquished for Adoption* (Aldershot, Hants, England: Avebury, 1995); S. K. Musser, *What Kind of Love Is This!* (Oaklyn, N.J.: Jan Publications, 1982); A. Perkins and R. Townsend, eds., *Bitter Fruit: Women's Experiences of Unplanned Pregnancy, Abortion, and Adoption* (Alameda, Calif.: Hunter House, 1992); P. Roles, *Saying Goodbye to a Baby*, 2 vols. (Washington, D.C.: Child Welfare League of America, 1989); E. B. Rosenberg, *The Adoption Life Cycle: The Children and Their Families through the Years* (New York: Free Press, 1992); K. Ryan, *From We to Just Me* (Manitoba, Canada: Freedom to Be Me Seminars, 1990); C. Schaefer, *The Other Mother* (New York: Soho Press, 1991); J. L. Waldron, *Giving Away Simone: A Memoir* (New York: Times Books, 1995).
20. P. Sachdev. "The Birth Father: A Neglected Element in the Adoption Equation," *Families in Society: The Journal of Contemporary Human Services* (March 1991): 131–39.
21. G. L. Grief and C. Bailey, "Where Are the Fathers in Social Work Literature," *Families in Society* 71 (1990): 88–92.
22. E. Y. Deykin, P. Patti, and J. Ryan, "Fathers of Adopted Children: A Study of the Impact of Child Surrender on Birth Fathers," *American Journal of Orthopsychiatry* 58 (1988): 240–48; M. M. Mason, *Out of the Shadows: Birthfathers' Stories* (Edina, Minn.: O. J. Howard Publishing, 1995); R. Pannor, F. Massarik, and B. Evans, *The Unmarried Father* (New York: Springer Publishing Co., 1971); M. A. Redmond, "Attitudes of Adolescent Males toward Adolescent Pregnancy and Fatherhood," *Family Relations* 34 (1985): 337–42; B. E. Robinson, "Teenage Pregnancy from the Father's Perspective," *American Journal of Orthopsychiatry* 58 (1988): 46–51; R. W. Severson, *Dear Birthfather* (Dallas, Tex.: House of Tomorrow, n.d.); O. E. Westney, O. J. Cole, and T. L. Munford, "Adolescent Unwed Prospective Fathers: Readiness for Fatherhood and Behaviors toward the Mother and the Expected Infant," *Adolescence* 21 (1986): 901–11.
23. R. J. Dworkin, "Parenting or Placing: Decision Making by Pregnant Teens," *Youth and Society* 25 (September 1993): 75–92.
24. A. Gray, "Birthfathers and Legal Risks: Good News for Adoptive Parents," *Adoptive Families* (March/April 1996): 18–20; M. L. Shanley, "Unwed Fathers' Rights, Adoption, and Sex Equality: Gender Neutrality and the Perpetuation of Patriarchy," *Columbia Law Review* 95 (January 1995): 60–103.

25. T. Eckert, "State Justices Take the Role of Solomon in the Baby Richard Saga: The Case Shows the Tensions between the Law and the Impulses of Humanity," *Illinois Issues* 21 (March 1995); B. Egelro, "Supreme Court Limits Father's Rights," *Orange County Register*, August 1, 1995; "Florida Blazes New Path in Adoption Challenges," *Peninsula Daily News*, July 23, 1995; B. A. Gershon, "Throwing Out the Baby with the Bathwater: Adoption of Kelsey S. Raises the Rights of Unwed Fathers above the Best Interest of the Child," *Loyola of Los Angeles Law Review* 28 (January 1995): 741–57; H. J. Gitlin, "'Baby Richard' Law Poses Many Questions for Adoption Attorneys," *Chicago Daily Law Bulletin* 141 (June 19, 1995): 6; J. H. Hollinger, "A Failed System Is Tearing Kids Apart," *National Law Journal* 15 (August 9, 1993): 17; D. G. Savage, "Unmarried Father Loses Custody Bid in High Court," *Los Angeles Times*, December 7, 1988; M. L. Shanley, "Unwed Fathers' Rights, Adoption, and Sex Equality: Gender Neutrality and the Perpetuation of Patriarchy," *Columbia Law Review* 95 (January 1995): 60–103.

26. R. DeBoer, *Losing Jessica* (New York: Doubleday, 1994).

27. DNA Diagnostic Center and Genetica DNA Laboratories per telephone conversation.

28. J. Wilkens, "Whose Child Is This? Courts Make New Demands of Birth Fathers," *San Diego Union–Tribune*, August 12, 1995.

29. J. W. Lindsay, *Parents, Pregnant Teens, and the Adoption Option* (Buena Park, Calif.: Morning Glory Press, 1989).

30. P. A. Hintz, "Grandparents' Visitation Rights Following Adoption: Expanding Traditional Boundaries in Wisconsin," *Wisconsin Law Review* 2 (1994): 483–510.

31. K. O. Sly, *Becky's Special Family* (Corona, Calif.: Alternative Parenting Publications, 1985).

32. P. I. Johnston, ed., *Perspectives on a Grafted Tree* (Fort Wayne, Ind.: Perspectives Press, 1983); P. C. Partridge, *An Adoptee's Dreams: Poems and Stories* (Baltimore, Md.: Gateway Press, 1995).

33. B. Grancell-Frank, *The Oldest Mommy in the Park* (Birmingham, Ala.: Colonial Press, 1993).

34. M. Russell, *Adoption Wisdom: A Guide to the Issues and Feelings of Adoption* (Santa Monica, Calif.: Broken Branch Productions, 1996).

35. V. K. Miller, *Meditations for Adoptive Parents* (Scottdale, Pa.: Herald Press, 1992).

CHAPTER 13: Anticipating, Confronting, and Solving Problems

1. R. P. Barth and M. Berry, *Adoption and Disruption: Rates, Risks, and Responses* (New York: A. de Gruyter, 1988); T. Festinger, *Necessary Risks: A Study of Adoption and Disrupted Adoptive Placements* (Washington, D.C.: Child Welfare League of America, 1986); K. S. Stolley, "Statistics on Adoption in the United States," *The Future of Children* 3 (Spring 1993): 26–42.

2. J. A. Rosenthal, "Outcomes of Adoption of Children with Special Needs," *The Future of Children* 3 (Spring 1993): 77–88.

3. E. W. Carp, "Adoption and Disclosure of Family Information: A Historical Perspective," *Child Welfare* 74 (January/February 1995): 217–39.

4. J. Hadley, "Parents Sue over Adoption," *Seattle Post–Intelligencer,* February 23, 1995; J. Hellwege, "More Courts Allow Adoptive Parents, Children to Sue for 'Wrongful Adoptions,'" *Trial* 31 (June 1995): 12; K. Johnson, "Family Sues over Adoption," *USA Today,* March 8, 1990; S. Kopels, "Wrongful Adoption: Litigation and Liability," *Family in Society: The Journal of Contemporary Human Services* (January 1995): 20–28; D. Postman, "Sins of Silence," *Seattle Times,* January 14, 1996; T. Weidlich, "N. Y. Case Signals Trend on 'Wrongful Adoption' Tort: Laws Requiring Disclosure of Background Spark Suits," *National Law Journal* 17 (February 6, 1995): 13.

5. T. Lewin, "The Strain on the Bonds of Adoption," *New York Times,* August 8, 1993.

6. J. H. Hollinger, "A Failed System Is Tearing Kids Apart," *National Law Journal* 15 (August 9, 1993): 17.

7. L. Gubernick, "How Much Is That Baby in the Window?" *Forbes,* October 14, 1991.

8. D. M. Brodzinsky, "Long-Term Outcomes in Adoption," *The Future of Children* 3 (Spring 1993): 153–66.

9. K. D. Fishman, "Problem Adoptions," *Atlantic Monthly,* September 1992.

10. J. Goldstein, A. Freud, and A. J. Solnit, *Beyond the Best Interests of the Child* (New York: Free Press, 1973).

11. J. A. Rosenthal, "Outcomes of Adoption of Children with Special Needs," *The Future of Children* 3 (Spring 1993): 77–88.

12. S. L. Nickman and R. G. Lewis, "Adoptive Families and Professionals: When the Experts Make Things Worse," *Journal of American Academy of Child & Adolescent Psychiatry* 33 (June 1994): 753–55.

CHAPTER 14: Talking with Your Child about Adoption

1. "Children's Reluctance to Discuss Adoption May Hide Real Interest," *Adopted Child* 10 (August 1991).

2. J. C. MacIntyre, "Resolved: Children Should Be Told of Their Adoption before They Ask: Affirmative," *Journal of the American Academy of Child & Adolescent Psychiatry* 29 (September 1990): 828–29.

3. B. Lockhart, "Talking about Difficult Adoption Information," *OURS* (March/April 1994).

4. A. D. Sorosky, A. Baran, and R. Pannor, *The Adoption Triangle: The Effects of the Sealed Record on Adoptees, Birth Parents, and Adoptive Parents* (San Antonio, Tex.: Corona Publishing Co., 1989).

5. H. van Gulden and L. M. Bartels-Rabb, "Parenting Is Parenting—Or Is It?" *Adoptive Families* (November/December 1995): 8–12.

6. J. Freudberg and T. Geiss, *Susan and Gordon Adopt a Baby* (New York: Random House, 1986).

7. F. Rogers, *Adoption,* Let's Talk about It Series (New York: G. P. Putnam's Sons, 1994).

8. J. Harper, "What Does She Look Like? What Children Want to Know about Their Birthparents," *Adoption & Fostering* 17 (1993): 27–29.

9. F. Portnoy, *One Wonderful You* (Greensboro, N.C.: Children's Home Society, 1997).

10. L. Bothun, *Dialogues about Adoption: Conversations between Parents and Their Children* (Chevy Chase, Md.: Swan Publications, 1994); D. M. Brodzinsky, M. D. Schechter, and

R. M. Henig, *Being Adopted: The Lifelong Search for Self* (New York: Doubleday, 1992); P. M. Dorner, *Talking to Your Child about Adoption* (Santa Cruz, Calif.: Schaefer Publishing, 1991); R. B. Hicks, *Adoption Stories for Young Children* (Sun City, Calif.: Word-Slinger Press, 1995); M. Komar, *Communicating with the Adopted Child* (New York: Walker & Co., 1991); L. R. Melina, *Raising Adopted Children: A Manual for Adoptive Parents* (New York: Harper & Row, 1986); F. Rohr, *How Parents Tell Their Children They Are Adopted* (New York: New York State Adoptive Parents Committee, Inc., 1988); J. Schaffer and C. Lindstrom, *How to Raise an Adopted Child: A Guide to Help Your Child Flourish from Infancy through Adolescence* (New York: A Plume Book, 1991); S. E. Siegel, *Parenting Your Adopted Child: A Complete and Loving Guide* (New York: Prentice Hall, 1989); K. Silber and P. M. Dorner, *Children of Open Adoption and Their Families* (San Antonio, Tex.: Corona Publishing Co., 1990); M. Watkins, and S. Fisher, *Talking with Young Children about Adoption* (New Haven, Conn.: Yale University Press, 1993).

CHAPTER 15: Open Birth Records, Searches, and Reunions

1. V. L. Klunder, *Lifeline: The Action Guide to Adoption Search* (Cape Coral, Fla.: Caradium, 1991); M. J. Rillera, *The Adoption Searchbook: Techniques for Tracing People,* 2nd ed. (Huntington Beach, Calif.: Triadoption Library, 1988); J. E. Schooler, *Searching for a Past: The Adopted Adult's Unique Process of Finding Identity* (Colorado Spring, Colo.: Piñon Press, 1995); J. Strauss, *Birthright: The Guide to Search and Reunion for Adoptees, Birthparents, and Adoptive Parents* (New York: Penguin Press, 1994); J. Strauss, *The Great Adoptee Search Book* (Worcester, Mass.: Castle Rock, 1990).
2. S. Musser, *To Prison With Love: The True Story of Sandy Musser's Indecent Indictment and America's Adoption Travesty* (Cape Coral, Fla.: Adoption Awareness Press, 1995).
3. A. Haley, *Roots* (Garden City, N.Y.: Doubleday, 1976).
4. E. Blau, *Stories of Adoption: Loss and Reunion* (Portland, Ore.: New Sage Press, 1993); P. Collins, *Letter to Louise* (New York: HarperCollins, 1992); A. E. Dean, *Letters to My Birthmother: An Adoptee's Diary of Her Search for Her Identity* (New York: Pharos Books, 1991); F. Fisher, *The Search for Anna Fisher* (New York: Arthur Fields Books, 1973); R. Harsin, *Wanted—First Child: A Birth Mother's Story* (Santa Barbara, Calif.: Fithian Press, 1991); A. M. Homes, *In a Country of Mothers* (New York: Alfred A. Knopf, 1993); M. B. Jones, *Birthmothers: Women Who Have Relinquished Babies for Adoption Tell Their Stories* (Chicago: Chicago Review Press, 1993); L. Jurgens, *Turn from the Heart* (Lower Lake, Calif.: Asian Publishing, 1992); R. H. Kittson, *Orphan Voyage* (New York: Vantage Press, 1968); B. J. Lifton, *Lost and Found: The Adoption Experience* (New York: Dial Press, 1979); B. J. Lifton, *Twice Born: Memoirs of an Adopted Daughter* (New York: McGraw-Hill, 1975); K. R. March, *The Stranger Who Bore Me: Interactions of Adoptees and Birth Mothers* (Toronto: University of Toronto Press, 1995); K. Maxtone-Graham, *An Adopted Woman: Her Search, Her Discoveries. A True Story* (New York: Râemi Books, 1983); D. McMillon, *Mixed Blessing: The Dramatic True Story of a Woman's Search for Her Real Mother* (New York: St. Martin's Press, 1985); J. M. Paton, *The Adopted Break Silence* (Philadelphia, Pa.: Life History Study Center, 1954); C. Schaefer, *The Other Mother* (New York:

Soho Press, 1991); D. D. Smith, *A Limb of Your Tree: The Story of an Adopted Twin's Search for Her Roots* (Smithtown, N.Y.: Exposition, 1978); J. L. Waldron, *Giving Away Simone: A Memoir* (New York: Times Books, 1995).

5. N. Bawden, *The Outside Child* (New York: Lothrop, Lee & Shepard Books, 1989); N. Bawden and P. Gili, *Princess Alice* (London: A Deutsch, 1985); K. Gravelle and S. Fisher, *Where Are My Birth Parents?* (New York: Walker & Co., 1993); J. Hulse, *Jody* (New York: McGraw-Hill, 1976); B. J. Lifton, *I'm Still Me* (New York: Alfred A. Knopf, 1981); L. Lowry, *Find a Stranger, Say Goodbye* (Boston: Houghton Mifflin, 1978); J. D. Okimoto, *Molly by Any Other Name* (New York: Scholastic 1990); J. L. Oppenheimer, *Which Mother Is Mine?* (New York: Bantam Books, 1980).

6. D. M. Brodzinsky, M. D. Schechter, and R. M. Henig, *Being Adopted: The Lifelong Search for Self* (New York: Doubleday, 1992); C. L. Demuth, *Courageous Blessings: Adoptive Parents and the Search* (Garland, Tex.: Aries Center, 1993); J. DuPrau, *Adoption: The Facts, Feelings, and Issues of a Double Heritage* (Englewood Cliffs, N.J.: Julian Messner, 1990); J. S. Gediman and L. P. Brown, *Birth Bond: Reunions between Birthparents and Adoptees* (Far Hills, N.J.: New Horizon Press, 1989); B. J. Lifton, *Journey of the Adopted Self: A Quest for Wholeness* (New York: Basic Books, 1994); M. McColm, *Adoption Reunions: A Book for Adoptees, Birth Parents, and Adoptive Families* (Ontario, Canada: Second Story Press, 1993); P. Sachdev, "Adoption Reunion and After: A Study of the Search Process and Experience of Adoptees," *Child Welfare* (January/February 1992): 53–68; A. D. Sorosky, A. Baran, and R. Pannor, *The Adoption Triangle: The Effects of the Sealed Record on Adoptees, Birth Parents, and Adoptive Parents* (San Antonio, Tex.: Corona Publishing Co., 1989); L. H. Stiffler, *Synchronicity and Reunion: The Genetic Connection of Adoptees and Birthparents* (Hobe Sound, Fla.: FEA Publication, 1992); J. P. Triseliotis, *In Search of Origins: The Experiences of Adopted People* (Boston: Beacon Press, 1975); N. N. Verrier, *The Primal Wound: Understanding the Adopted Child* (Baltimore, Md.: Gateway Press, 1993).

7. L. Smith, "Adoptees Search the World for Their Roots," *Los Angeles Times,* June 17, 1996.

8. "Differences in Language and Culture Complicate But Do Not Preclude International Searches," *Adopted Child* 16 (March 1997).

9. "Adoptive Parents Need Support When Son or Daughter Searches," *Adopted Child* 13 (February 1994); C. L. Demuth, *Courageous Blessing: Adoptive Parents and the Search* (Garland, Tex.: Aries Center, 1993); P. R. Silverman, L. Campbell, and P. Patti, "Reunions between Adoptees and Birth Parents: The Adoptive Parents' View," *Social Work* 39 (1994): 542–49.

10. L. Flynn, "A Parent's Perspective," *Public Welfare* 37 (1979): 28–33.

11. K. Johnson, "Family Sues over Adoption," *USA Today,* March 8, 1990; S. Kopels, "Wrongful Adoption: Litigation and Liability," *Families in Society—The Journal of Contemporary Human Services* (January 1995): 20–28; "Lawsuit over Girl's Background," *Seattle Post–Intelligencer,* October 17, 1995; D. Postman, "Sins of Silence," *Seattle Times,* January 14, 1996; T. Weidlich, "N.Y. Case Signals Trend on 'Wrongful Adoption' Tort: Laws Requiring Disclosure of Background Spark Suits," *National Law Journal* 17 (February 6, 1995): 13.

CHAPTER 16: Making Adoption Better for Everyone

1. J. Goldstein, A. Freud, and A. J. Solnit, "On Continuity, a Child's Sense of Time, and the Limits of Both Law and Prediction," *Beyond the Best Interest of the Child* (New York: Free Press, 1973).

2. S. Begley, "How to Build a Baby's Brain," *Newsweek,* Special Issue (Spring/Summer 1997); Heart Start Task Force Staff, *Heart Start: The Emotional Foundations of School Readiness* (Arlington, Va.: National Center for Clinical Infant Programs, 1992).

3. H. David Kirk, *Exploring Adoptive Family Life: The Collected Adoption Papers of H. David Kirk,* ed. B. J. Tansey (Port Angeles, Wash.: Ben-Simon Publications, 1988); H. David Kirk, *Shared Fate: A Theory of Adoption and Mental Health* (New York: Free Press of Glencoe, 1964).

4. H. David Kirk, *Adoptive Kinship: A Modern Institution in Need of Reform* (Brentwood Bay, B.C.: Ben-Simon Publications, 1985): 157–58.

BIBLIOGRAPHY

Adamec, C. A. *There Are Babies to Adopt: A Resource Guide for Prospective Parents*. Rev. ed. New York: Kensington Books, 1996, © 1987.

Adamec, C. A., and W. Pierce. *The Encyclopedia of Adoption*. New York: Facts on File, 1991.

Adcock, G. B. *Intercountry Adoptions: Where Do They Go from Here: An Overview*. Edited by Sandra Adcock. Dearborn, Mich.: Bouldin-Haigh-Irwin, 1979.

"Adopting Native American Children." *CQ Researcher* 3 (1993): 1047.

"Adoption Experience May Cultivate Traits, Life Directions, in Adoptees." *Adopted Child* 14 (September 1995): 1–4.

"Adoptive Parents Grieve When Birth Parents Change Mind." *Adopted Child* 12 (October 1993): 1–4.

"Adoptive Parents Need Support When Son or Daughter Searches." *Adopted Child* 13 (February 1994): 1–4.

"Advice Given on Starting a Successful Culture Camp for Adoptees." *Adopted Child* 14 (March 1995): 1–4.

Aigner, H. *Faint Trails: An Introduction to the Fundamentals of Adult Adoptee–Birth Parent Reunification Searches*. Greenbrae, Calif.: Paradigm Press, 1980.

Aitken, G. "Changing Adoption Policy and Practice to Deal with Children in Limbo." *Child Welfare* 74 (1995): 679–93.

Alexander, S. *In Praise of Single Parents*. Boston: Houghton Mifflin, 1994.

Alexander-Roberts, C. *The ADHD Parenting Handbook*. Dallas, Tex.: Taylor Publishing, 1994.

———. *The Essential Adoption Handbook*. Dallas, Tex.: Taylor Publishing, 1993.

———. *The Legal Adoption Guide*. Dallas, Tex.: Taylor Publishing, 1996.

Altstein, H. *Intercountry Adoption: A Multinational Perspective*. New York: Praeger, 1991.

Altstein, H., et al. "Clinical Observations of Adult Intercountry Adoptees and Their Adoptive Children." *Child Welfare* 73 (May/June 1994): 261–69.

Alty, A. "Transracial Adoption." *Sojourner: The Women's Forum* (April 1993): 1.

Andersen, R. *Second Choice: Growing Up Adopted.* Chesterfield, Miss.: Badger Hill Press, 1993.

Anderson, C. J. *Thoughts for Birth Parents Newly Considering Search.* Des Moines, Iowa: CUB, Inc., 1987.

Anderson, D. C. *Children of Special Value: Interracial Adoption in America.* New York: St. Martin's Press, 1971.

Anderson, G. R. *Children and AIDS: The Challenge for Child Welfare.* Washington, D.C.: Child Welfare League of America, 1986.

Andrews, L. B. *Between Strangers: Surrogate Mothers, Expectant Fathers, and Brave New Babies.* New York: Harper & Row, 1989.

Apelquist, F. "Babies for Sale." *Interrace Magazine* 34:10.

"Are Trans-Racial Adoptions Bad for Black Children?" *CQ Researcher* 3 (November 26, 1993): 1049.

Arms, S. *Adoption: A Handful of Hope.* Berkeley, Calif.: Celestial Arts, 1990.

———. *To Love and Let Go.* New York: Alfred A. Knopf, 1983.

Armstrong, T. *The Myth of the A.D.D. Child.* New York: E. P. Dutton & Co., 1995.

Askin, J., and B. Oskam. *Search: A Handbook for Adoptees and Birthparents.* New York: Harper & Row, 1982.

Austad, C. C., and T. L. Simmons. "Symptoms of Adopted Children Presenting to a Large Mental Health Clinic." *Child Psychiatry and Human Development* 9 (1978): 20–27.

Austin, J., ed. *Adoption: The Inside Story.* London: Barn Owl Books, 1985.

Austin, L. T. *Babies for Sale: The Tennessee Children's Home Adoption Scandal.* Westport, Conn.: Praeger, 1993.

Azar, B. "Foster Care Has Bleak History." *APA Monitor* (November 1995): 8.

———. "Foster Children Get a Taste of Stability." *APA Monitor* (November 1995): 8.

Babb, L. A. "Adoption in Cyberspace." *Adoptive Families* (January/February 1996): 26–27.

Babb, L. A, and R. Laws. *Adopting and Advocating for the Special Needs Child: A Guide for Parents and Professionals.* Westport, Conn.: Bergin & Garvey, 1997.

Backrach, C. A. "Adoption Plans, Adopted Children, and Adoptive Mothers." *Journal of Marriage and the Family* 48 (1986): 243–53.

Bagley, C. *International and Transracial Adoption: A Mental Health Perspective.* Aldershot, Hants, England: Avebury, 1993.

———. "Transracial Adoption in Britain: A Follow-Up Study, with Policy Considerations." *Child Welfare* 72 (May/June 1993): 285–99.

Baird, P. A., and B. McGillivray. "Children of Incest." *Journal of Pediatrics* 5 (November 1982): 854–57.

Baldwin, P. *The 125 Most Asked Questions about Adoption (and the Answers).* New York: William Morrow, 1993.

Baran, A., and R. Pannor. "Perspectives on Open Adoption." *The Future of Children* 3 (Spring 1993): 119–24.

Barcus, N. B. *The Family Takes a Child.* Valley Forge, Pa.: Judson Press, 1983.

Barn, R. *Black Children in the Public Care System.* London: B. T. Batsford, in association with British Agencies for Adoption and Fostering, 1993.

Barth, R. P. "Adoption Research: Building Blocks for the Next Decade." *Child Welfare* 73 (September/October 1994): 625–38.

——. "Revisiting the Issues: Adoption of Drug-Exposed Children." *The Future of Children* 3 (Spring 1993): 167–75.

——. "Timing Is Everything: An Analysis of the Time to Adoption and Legalization." *Social Work Research* 18 (September 1994): 39–48.

Barth, R. P., and M. Berry. *Adoption and Disruption*. New York: A. de Gruyter, 1988.

Bartholet, E. *Family Bonds: Adoption and the Politics of Parenting*. Boston: Houghton Mifflin, 1993.

——. "International Adoption: Current Status and Future Prospects." *The Future of Children* 3 (Spring 1993): 89–103.

Bascom, B., and C. A. McKelvey. *The Complete Guide to Foreign Adoption: What to Expect and How to Prepare for Your New Child*. New York: Pocket Books, 1997.

Bates, J. D. *Gift Children: A Story of Race, Family, and Adoption in a Divided America*. New York: Ticknor & Fields, 1993.

Bean, P. *Adoption: Essays in Social Policy, Law, and Sociology*. London: Tavistock, 1984.

Beauvais-Godwin, L., and R. Godwin. *The Independent Adoption Manual*. Lakewood, N.J.: Advocate Press, 1993.

Becker, K. M., and C. K. Heckert. *To Keera with Love: Abortion, Adoption, or Keeping the Baby, the Story of One Teen's Choice*. Kansas City, Miss.: Sheed & Ward, 1987.

Beek, M. "The Reality of Face-to-Face Contact after Adoption." *Adoption & Fostering* 18 (Summer 1994): 39–45.

Begley, S. "The Baby." *Newsweek*, September 4, 1995.

——. "How to Build a Baby's Brain." *Newsweek* (Spring/Summer 1997).

Belbas, N. F. "Staying in Touch: Empathy in Open Adoptions." *Smith College School for Social Work* (1986).

Bennett, K. E. "Advocating for Adoption Equity in the Workplace: Adoption Benefits." *Adoptive Families* (September/October 1995): 15–17.

Benson, P. L., A. R. Sharma, and E. C. Roehlkepartain. *Growing Up Adopted: A Portrait of Adolescents and Their Families*. Minneapolis, Minn.: Search Insight, 1994.

Berke, J. "Deaf Adoption News Service." *Adoptive Families* (July/August 1995): 14–16.

Berman, C. *We Take This Child: A Candid Look at Modern Adoption*. Garden City, N.Y.: Doubleday, 1974.

Berman, L. C., and R. K. Bufferd. "Family Treatment to Address Loss in Adoptive Families." *Social Casework* 67 (1986): 3–11.

Berry, M. "Adoptive Parents' Perceptions of, and Comfort with, Open Adoption." *Child Welfare* 72 (May/June 1993): 231–53.

——. "The Effects of Open Adoption on Biological and Adoptive Parents and the Children." *Child Welfare* 70 (November/December 1991): 637–51.

——. "The Practice of Open Adoption: Findings from a Study of 1,396 Adoptive Families." *Children & Youth Services Review* 13 (1991): 379–95.

——. "Preparing and Supporting Special Needs Adoptive Families: A Review of the Literature." *Child & Adolescent Social Work* 7 (1990): 403–18.

——. "Risks and Benefits of Open Adoption." *The Future of Children* 3 (Spring 1993): 125–38.

Bilitski, D. "Termination of Parental Rights." *University of Louisville, Journal of Family Law* 32 (Summer 1994): 744–49.

Billimoria, H. M. *Child Adoption: A Study of Indian Experience.* Bombay: Himalaya Publishing House, 1984.

Blacher, J., ed. *When There's No Place Like Home: Options for Children Living Apart from Their National Families.* Baltimore, Md.: P. H. Brookes Publishing, 1994.

"Black Identity Serves to Protect Ego, Give Purpose, & Bridge Cultures." *Adopted Child* 14 (January 1995): 1–4.

Blank, J. P. *19 Steps up the Mountain: The Story of the DeBolt Family.* Philadelphia: J. B. Lippincott, 1976.

Blanton, T. L., and J. Deschner. "Biological Mothers' Grief: The Postadoptive Experience in Open Versus Confidential Adoption." *Child Welfare* 69 (1990): 525–35.

Blau, E. *Stories of Adoption: Loss and Reunion.* Portland, Ore.: New Sage Press, 1993.

Bogert, C., et al. "Bringing Back Baby." *Newsweek,* November 21, 1994.

Bond, J. S. "Instilling Cultural Pride." *Adoptive Families* (November/December 1995): 60–61.

Borgman, R. "The Consequences of Open and Closed Adoption for Older Children." *Child Welfare* 41 (April 1982): 217–26.

Bothun, L. *Dialogues about Adoption.* Chevy Chase, Md.: Swan Publications, 1994.

——. *When Friends Ask about Adoption.* Chevy Chase, Md.: Swan Publications, 1987.

Bourguignon, J., and K. W. Watson. *Making Placement That Work: Guidelines for Assessing and Selecting Families for the Special Needs Child.* Evanston, Ill.: NBI Press, 1990.

Bowlby, J. *Attachment and Loss.* New York: Basic Books, 1980.

——. *Separation: Anxiety and Anger.* New York: Basic Books, 1973.

Bozett, F. W., and M. B. Sussman, eds. *Homosexuality and Family Relations.* New York: Haworth Press, 1990.

Bradstreet, K. *Overcoming Infertility Naturally: The Relationship between Nutrition, Emotions, and Reproduction.* Pleasant Grove, Utah: Woodland Publishing, 1993.

Brazelton, T. B. *On Becoming a Family.* New York: Dell Publishing, 1981.

Brink, S., A. R. Wright, and R. J. Newman. "Higher Adoption Hurdle." *US News & World Report* 117 (July 21, 1994): 97.

Brodzinsky, D. M. "Adjustment to Adoption: A Psychosocial Perspective." *Clinical Psychology Review* 7 (1987): 25–47.

——. "Long-term Outcomes in Adoption." *The Future of Children* 3 (Spring 1993): 153–66.

Brodzinsky, D. M., M. D. Schechter, and R. M. Henig. *Being Adopted: The Lifelong Search for Self.* New York: Doubleday, 1992.

Brodzinsky, D., and M. D. Schechter, eds. *The Psychology of Adoption.* New York: Oxford University Press, 1990.

Brooke, E. H. "Adoption Saga of Rio's Streets." *New York Times,* December 29, 1994.

Brooks, L. M. *Adventuring in Adoption.* Chapel Hill, N.C.: University of North Carolina Press, 1939.

Bruni, F. "For Gay Couples, Ruling to Cheer on Adoption." *New York Times,* November 5, 1995.

Bibliography / 559

Bullock, A., E. Grimes, and J. McNamara. *Bruised before Birth: Parenting Children Exposed to Prenatal Substance Abuse.* Greensboro, N.C.: Family Resources, 1995.

Burgess, L. C. *The Art of Adoption.* Washington, D.C.: Acropolis Books, 1976.

Burke, P. *Family Values: Two Moms and Their Sons.* New York: Random House, 1993.

Bussier, A. "Eligibility Criteria." *Adoptive Families* (September/October 1995): 37–38.

Cadoret, R. J., et al. "Adoption Study Demonstrating Two Genetic Pathways to Drug Abuse." *Archives of General Psychiatry* 52 (January 1995): 42–52.

Campbell, L. H., P. R. Silverman, and P. B. Patti. "Reunions between Adoptees and Birth Parents: The Adoptees' Experience." *Social Work* 36 (July 1991): 329–35.

Campion, M. J. *Who's Fit to Be a Parent?* London: Routledge, 1995.

Canape, C. *Adoption: Parenthood without Pregnancy.* New York: H. Holt, 1986.

Caplan, L. *An Open Adoption.* Boston: Houghton Mifflin, 1990.

Carney, A. *No More Here and There: Adopting the Older Child.* Chapel Hill, N.C.: University of North Carolina Press, 1976.

Carp, E. W. "Adoption and Disclosure of Family Information: A Historical Perspective." *Child Welfare* 74 (January/February 1995): 217–39.

Carter, J. W., and M. P. Carter. *Sweet Grapes: How to Stop Being Infertile and Start Living Again.* Indianapolis, Ind.: Perspectives Press, 1989.

Casey, H. M. "Where Should We Draw the Color Line on Adoption?" *Seattle Post–Intelligencer,* April 14, 1995.

Cavaliere, F. "Society Appears More Open to Gay Parenting." *APA Monitor* (July 1995): 51.

Center for Disease Control and Prevention. "National Teen Pregnancy Trend." March 9, 1995.

Chapman, B. "Adoption Options Too Often Neglected in State Foster Care Mess." *Seattle Post–Intelligencer,* April 4, 1997.

"Children's Reluctance to Discuss Adoption May Hide Real Interest." *Adopted Child* 10 (August 1991): 1–4.

Chira, S. "Adoption Is Getting Some Harder Looks." *New York Times,* April 25, 1993.

Cimons, M. "Adoption Secrecy Gives Way to a New Openness." *Los Angeles Times,* September 3, 1996.

Clayton, L., and J. Morrison. *Coping with a Learning Disability.* Edited by Ruth Rosen. New York: Rosen Publishing Group, Inc., 1995.

Cleland, N. "Mother and Child Reunion." *Parents* 69 (July 1994): 116.

Clinton, H. R. "A Crying Need to Reform." *Examiner* (1995).

Cohen, J. S., and A. Westhues. *Well-Functioning Families for Adoptive and Foster Children: A Handbook for Child Welfare Workers.* Toronto: University of Toronto Press, 1990.

———. "A Comparison of Self-Esteem, School Achievement, and Friends between Intercountry Adoptees and Their Siblings." *Early Child Development and Care* 106 (1995): 205–24.

Coleman, L., et al. *Working with Older Adoptees: A Sourcebook of Innovative Models.* Portland, Maine: University of Southern Maine, 1988.

Collins, P. *Letter to Louise: A Loving Memoir to the Daughter I Gave Up for Adoption Twenty-Five Years Ago.* New York: HarperCollins, 1992.

Connelly, L. M. "Blood Thicker than Law in Massachusetts." *New England Law Review* 28 (Winter 1993): 515–42.

Connelly, M. *Given in Love: For Mothers Releasing a Child for Adoption.* Edited by J. Johnson. Omaha, Neb.: Centering Corp., 1989.

Cook. J. F. "A History of Placing-Out: The Orphan Trains." *Child Welfare* 74 (January/February 1995): 181–87.

Cooper, S. L., and E. S. Glazer. *Beyond Infertility.* New York: Free Press, 1994.

Corlindres, F., and C. Morales. "Guatemala: Babies for Sale." *World Press Review* 41 (1994): 45.

"Court Decides for Adoptive Parents." *Los Angeles Daily Journal,* July 24, 1995.

"Court Hears Unwed Dad's Rights Plea." *San Diego Union,* November 25, 1988.

Cowley, G. "The Future of Birth." *Newsweek,* September 4, 1995.

Crain, C., and J. Duffy. *How to Adopt a Child.* Nashville, Tenn.: Thomas Nelson, Inc., 1994.

Concerned United Birthparents (CUB). *The Birthparent's Perspective on Adoption.* Des Moines, Iowa: CUB, Inc., 1987.

——. *Thoughts to Consider for Newly Searching Adoptees.* Des Moines, Iowa: CUB, Inc., 1987.

——. *Why Won't My Birthmother Meet Me?* Des Moines, Iowa: CUB, Inc., 1987.

Conroy, M. F. *A World of Love.* New York: Kensington Publishers, 1997.

Cummings, R., and G. Fisher. *The School Survival Guide for Kids with LD (Learning Differences).* Minneapolis, Minn.: Free Spirit Publishing, Inc., 1991.

——. *The Survival Guide for Teenagers with LD (Learning Differences).* Edited by P. Espeland. Minneapolis, Minn.: Free Spirit Publishing, Inc., 1993.

Curran-Downey, M. "Number of Abandoned Babies Rises." *San Diego Union,* November 27, 1988.

Curto, J. *How to Become a Single Parent.* Englewood Cliffs, N.J.: Prentice-Hall, Inc., 1983.

Cushman, L. F. "Placing an Infant for Adoption: The Experiences of Young Birthmothers." *Social Work* 38 (May 1993): 264–72.

Custer, M. "Adoption as an Option for Unmarried Pregnant Teens." *Adolescence* 28 (Winter 1993): 891–902.

Dahl, J. *River of Promise: Two Women's Story of Love & Adoption.* Edited by N. Hardesty. Philadelphia: LuraMedia, 1989.

Daly, K. J., and M. P. Sobol. "Public and Private Adoption: A Comparison of Service and Accessibility." *Family Relations* 43 (January 1994): 88–93.

Dao, J. "New York's Highest Court Rules Unmarried Couples Can Adopt." *New York Times,* November 3, 1995.

Davis, D. *Reaching Out to Children with FAS/FAE.* West Nyack, N.Y.: Center for Applied Research in Education, 1994.

Dean, A. E. *Letters to My Birthmother.* New York: Pharos Books, 1991.

DeAngelis, T. "Adoptees, New Families Fare Well, Studies Show." *APA Monitor* (January 1995): 36.

DeBoer, R. *Losing Jessica.* New York: Doubleday, 1994.

Delaney, R. J. *The Healing Power of the Family.* Fort Collins, Colo.: Journey Press, 1995.

Delaney, R. J., and F. R. Kunstal. *Troubled Transplants: Unconventional Strategies for Helping Disturbed Foster and Adopted Children.* Portland, Maine: University of Southern Maine, 1993.

de Leon, F. M., and S. Macdonald. "Name Power." *Seattle Times,* June 28, 1992.

Demuth, C. L. *Courageous Blessing: Adoptive Parents and the Search.* Garland, Tex.: Aries Center, 1993.

Department of State. *International Adoption and Child Abduction.* "Source of Orphans Immigrating to United States." Internet.

Derman-Sparks, L., and the A.B.C. Task Force. *Anti-Bias Curriculum: Tools for Empowering Your Children.* Washington, D.C.: National Association for the Education of Young Children, 1989.

DeWoody, M. *Adoption and Disclosure: A Review of the Law.* Washington, D.C.: Child Welfare League of America, 1994.

Deykin, E. Y., P. Patti, and J. Ryan. "Fathers of Adopted Children: A Study of the Impact of Child Surrender on Birth Fathers." *American Journal of Orthopsychiatry* 58 (1988): 240–48.

Diamond, R. "Secrecy vs. Privacy." *Adoptive Families* (September/October 1995): 9–11.

"Differences in Language and Culture Complicate But Do Not Preclude International Searches." *Adopted Child* 16 (March 1997).

Donnelly, D. R. *A Guide to Adoption.* Arcadia, Calif.: Focus on the Family, 1987.

Dorner, P. *How to Open an Adoption.* Royal Oak, Mich.: R-Squared Press, 1997.

———. *Talking to Your Child about Adoption.* Santa Cruz, Calif.: Schaefer Publishing, 1991.

Dorris, M. *The Broken Cord: A Family's Ongoing Struggle with Fetal Alcohol Syndrome.* New York: Harper & Row, 1989.

Drake, G. M., ed. *Directory for Adoptive Parents over 40.* North Carolina: Sylvia A. Waiters, 1993.

Driedger, S. D. "Bringing Home Baby." *Maclean's,* August 21, 1995.

Duke, R. E. *How to Help Your Learning-Challenged Child Be a Winner.* Far Hills, N.J.: New Horizon Press, 1993.

DuPrau, J. *Adoption: The Facts, Feelings, and Issues of a Double Heritage.* Englewood Cliffs, N.J.: Julian Messner, 1990.

Dusky, L. *Birthmark.* New York: M. Evans, 1979.

Dworkin, R. J. "Parenting or Placing: Decision Making by Pregnant Teens." *Youth and Society* 25 (September 1993): 75–92.

Eckert, T. "State Justices Take the Role of Solomon in the Baby Richard Saga." *Illinois Issues* 21 (March 1995).

Efron, S. "Russia Suspends Adoption by Foreigners." *Los Angeles Times,* November 19, 1994.

Egelro, B. "Supreme Court Limits Father's Rights." *Orange County Register,* August 1, 1995.

Ehrlich, H. ed. *A Time to Search: The Moving and Dramatic Stories of Adoptees in Search of Their Natural Parents.* New York: Paddington Press, Ltd., 1977.

Elgart, A., and C. Berman. *The Golden Cradle: How the Adoption Establishment Works— and How to Make It Work for You.* Secaucus, N.J.: Carol Publishing Group, 1991.

Emery, L. J. "The Case for Agency Adoption." *The Future of Children* 3 (Spring 1993): 139–45.

"Entrustment Ceremonies Provide Benefits to Birth Families and Adoptive Families." *Adopted Child* 16 (April 1997): 1–4.

Erbaugh, S. E. "Adapting to Adoption." *Adoptive Families* (September/October 1995): 22–24.

"Establishing Control, Overcoming Fear Are Keys to Semi-Open Adoption." *Adopted Child* 15 (May 1996): 1–4.

"Ethnic Identity Includes Ancestry, but Is Shaped by Experience." *Adopted Child* 15 (September 1996): 1–4.

Etter, J. "Levels of Cooperation and Satisfaction in 56 Open Adoptions." *Child Welfare* 72 (May/June 1993): 257–67.

"Even Well Adjusted Parents Can Be Uneasy Disclosing Adoption." *Adopted Child* 10 (January 1991): 1–4.

Ewy, D., and R. Ewy. *Teen Pregnancy.* Boulder, Colo.: Pruett Publishing Company, 1984.

Fahlberg, V. *A Child's Journey through Placement.* Indianapolis, Ind.: Perspectives Press, 1991.

Fales, M. J. *Post-Legal Adoption Services Today.* New York: Child Welfare League of America, 1986.

Fanshel, D. *Far from the Reservation: The Transracial Adoption of American Indian Children.* Metuchen, N.J.: Scarecrow Press, 1972.

———. *On the Road to Permanency: An Expanded Data Base for Service to Children in Foster Care.* New York: Columbia University School of Social Work, Child Welfare League of America, 1982.

Feigelman, W., and A. R. Silverman. *Chosen Children: New Patterns of Adoptive Relationships.* New York: Praeger, 1983.

Ferguson, D. M., M. Lynskey, and L. J. Horwood. "The Adolescent Outcomes of Adoption: A 16-Year Longitudinal Study." *Journal of Child Psychology & Psychiatry & Allied Disciplines* 36 (1995): 597–615.

Fernandez, K. *My Journal.* San Jose, Calif.: Lifeworks, 1995.

"Fertility Clinics." *Consumer Reports,* February 1996.

Festinger, T. *Necessary Risk: A Study of Adoptions and Disrupted Adoptive Placements.* Washington, D.C.: Child Welfare League of America, 1986.

Finch, S. J. *Data Collection in Adoption and Foster Care.* Washington, D.C.: Child Welfare League of America, 1991.

Finnegan, J. *Shattered Dreams—Lonely Choices: Birthparents of Babies with Disabilities Talk about Adoption.* Westport, Conn.: Bergin & Garvey, 1993.

Fisher, F. *The Search for Anna Fisher.* New York: Arthur Fields Books, 1973.

Fisher, G., and R. Cummings. *When Your Child Has LD (Learning Differences).* Edited by P. Espeland. Minneapolis, Minn.: Free Spirit Publishing, Inc., 1995.

Fisher, I. "Adoptions Can Be Compelled, Appeals Court Rules." *New York Times,* June 15, 1994.

Fisher, I. "HIV Test for Newborns Moves Ahead." *Seattle Post–Intelligencer,* May 1, 1996.

Fishman, K. D. "Problem Adoptions." *Atlantic Monthly,* September 1992.

Fitten, R. K. "Agencies' Policies on Race Differ." *Seattle Times,* October 22, 1995.

———. "Mixing Color and Family: Can We Successfully Integrate Issues of Race and Culture with Issues of Child Rearing?" *Seattle Times,* October 22, 1995.

——. "Transracial Adoption: Searching for a Middle Ground." *Seattle Times,* October 23, 1995.

Flango, V. E., and C. R. Flango. "How Many Children Were Adopted in 1992." *Child Welfare* 74 (September/October 1995): 1018–32.

"Florida Blazes New Path in Adoption Challenges." *Peninsula Daily News,* July 23, 1995.

Flynn, L. "A Parent's Perspective." *Public Welfare* 37 (1979): 28–33.

"Foreign Adoption Made Easier; Clinton Expected to Sign." *Congressional Quarterly Weekly Report* 53 (November 4, 1995): 3385.

"Foster Kids Need Good Parents, Period." *Los Angeles Times,* May 7, 1995.

"Foster Parents Fight for Inter-Racial Adoptions." *CQ Researcher* 3 (1993): 1038.

Fowler, M. *Maybe You Know My Kid: A Parent's Guide to Identifying, Understanding, and Helping Your Child with Attention-Deficit Hyperactivity Disorder.* Rev. ed. New York: Carol Publishing Group, 1993.

Frankel, S. A. "Pathogenic Factors in the Experience of Early and Late Adopted Children." *Psychoanalytic Study of the Child* 46 (1991): 91–108.

Franklin, R. R., and D. K. Brockman. *In Pursuit of Fertility: A Fertility Expert Tells You How to Get Pregnant,* 2nd ed. New York: Holt, 1995.

Fullerton, C. S., W. Goodrich, and L. B. Berman. "Adoption Predicts Psychiatric Treatment Resistances in Hospitalized Adolescents." *Journal of American Academy of Child & Adolescent Psychiatry* 25 (1986): 542–51.

Gaber, I., and J. Aldridge, eds. *In the Best Interest of the Child's Culture: Identity & Transracial Adoption.* London: Free Association Press, 1995.

Galvin, M. R. *Otto Learns about His Medicine: A Story about Medication for Children with ADHD.* Rev. ed. New York: Magination Press, 1995.

"Gay Adoption Case Raises Questions about Parents', Children's Rights." *Adopted Child* 13 (April 1994): 1–4.

Gediman, J. S., and L. P. Brown. *Birth Bond: Reunions between Birthparents and Adoptees.* Rev. ed. Far Hills, N.J.: New Horizon Press, 1996.

Gehret, J. *The Don't-Give-Up Kid and Learning Differences: Learning Differences.* Rev. ed. Fairport, N.Y.: Verbal Images Press, 1996.

——. *Eagle Eyes: A Child's Guide to Paying Attention,* 2nd ed. Fairport, N.Y.: Verbal Images Press, 1991.

George, K. *The Adoption Option: A Practical Handbook for Prospective Adoptive Parents.* Springfield, Ill.: Charles C. Thomas, 1990.

Gerlach, K. "Stress in Children Bibliography, 1992." *Bibliography,* 1992.

Gershenson, C. P. "1983 Trend of Children in Foster Care." *Child Welfare Research Notes* 11 (1995).

Gershon, B. A. "Throwing Out the Baby with the Bathwater: Adoption of Kelsey S. Raises the Rights of Unwed Fathers above the Best Interests of the Child." *Loyola of Los Angeles Law Review* 28 (January 1995): 741–57.

Giang, K. M. "The Tale of Two Adoption Laws." *Children's Advocate* (May/June 1995): 6.

Gidron, A. "Bartered Babies?" *World Press Review* 41 (1994): 27.

Gill, O., and B. Jackson. *Adoption and Race.* New York: St. Martin's Press, 1983.

Gillespie, P. *Of Many Colors: Portraits of Multiracial Families.* Photographs by G. Kaeser. Amherst, Mass.: University of Massachusetts Press, 1997.

Gilman, L. *The Adoption Resource Book,* 3rd ed. New York: HarperPerrenial, 1992.

Gitlin, H. J. "'Baby Richard' Law Poses Many Questions for Adoption Attorneys." *Chicago Daily Law Bulletin* 141 (June 19, 1995): 6.

Glazer, E. S. *The Long Awaited Stork: A Guide to Parenting after Infertility.* Lexington, Mass.: Lexington Books, 1990.

Glidden, L. M. *Formed Families: Adoption of Children with Handicaps.* New York: Haworth Press, 1990.

——. *Parents for Children, Children for Parents: The Adoption Alternative.* Washington, D.C.: American Association on Mental Retardation, 1989.

——. "The Wanted Ones: Families Adopting Children with Mental Retardation." *Journal of Children in Contemporary Society* 21 (1990): 177–205.

Goetting, A., and M. G. Goetting. "Adoptive Parents to Children with Severe Developmental Disabilities: A Profile." *Children & Youth Services Review* 15 (1993): 489–506.

Gold, M. *And Hannah Wept: Infertility, Adoption, and the Jewish Couple.* Philadelphia: Jewish Publication Society, 1988.

Goldfarb, H. A. *Overcoming Infertility: 12 Couples Share Their Success Stories.* New York: J. Wiley, 1995.

Goldstein, J., A. Freud, and A. J. Solnit. *Before the Best Interests of the Child.* New York: Free Press, 1979.

——. *Beyond the Best Interests of the Child.* New York: Free Press, 1973.

Gordon, M. *Jumpin' Johnny, Get Back to Work! A Child's Guide to ADHD/Hyperactivity.* De Witt, N.Y.: GSI Publications, 1991.

Grancell-Frank, B. *The Oldest Mommy in the Park.* Birmingham, Ala.: Colonial Press, 1993.

Gray, A. "Birthfathers and Legal Risks: Good News for Adoptive Parents?" *Adoptive Families* (March/April 1996): 18–20.

Green, T. *A Man and His Mother: An Adopted Son's Search.* New York: HarperCollins, 1997.

Grief, G. L., and C. Bailey. "Where Are the Fathers in Social Work Literature?" *Families in Society* 71 (1990): 88–92.

Griffith, K. C., ed. *The Right to Know Who You Are.* Ottawa, Canada: Katherine W. Kimbell, 1991.

Gritter, J. L. *Adoption without Fear.* San Antonio, Tex.: Corona Publishing Co., 1989.

——. *The Spirit of Open Adoption.* Washington, D.C.: The Child Welfare League of America, 1997.

Gross, H. E. "Open Adoption." *Child Welfare* 72 (May/June 1993): 269–84.

Grotevant, H. D., et al. "Adoptive Family System Dynamics." *Family Process* 33 (June 1994): 125–46.

Groze, V. K. "Adoption, Attachment, and Self-Concept." *Child & Adolescent Social Work* 9 (April 1992): 169–91.

——. *Successful Adoption Families: A Longitudinal Study of Special Needs Adoption.* Westport, Conn.: Praeger, 1996.

Gubernick, L. "How Much Is That Baby in the Window?" *Forbes,* October 14, 1991.

Hadley, J. "Parents Sue over Adoptions." *Seattle Post–Intelligencer,* February 23, 1995.

"Hague Treaty Hopes to Solve Problems in Intercountry Adoptions." *Adopted Child* 12 (August 1993): 1–4.

Hairston, C. F., and V. G. Williams. "Black Adoptive Parents: How They View Agency Adoption Practices." *Social Casework: The Journal of Contemporary Social Work* (November 1989): 534–39.

Haley, A. *Roots.* Garden City, N.Y.: Doubleday, 1976.

Hallenbeck, C. A. *Our Child: Preparation for Parenting in Adoption—Instructor's Guide.* Wayne, Pa.: Our Child Press, 1984.

Hallowell, E., and J. J. Ratey. *Answers to Distraction.* New York: Pantheon Books, 1994.

Hamilton, V. *Many Thousand Gone: African Americans from Slavery to Freedom.* New York: Alfred A. Knopf, 1993.

Hamm, W., T. Morton, and L. M. Flynn. *Self-Awareness, Self-Selection and Success: A Parent Preparation Guidebook for Special Needs Adoptions.* Washington, D.C.: North American Council on Adoptable Children, 1985.

Harkness, C. *The Infertility Book.* Berkeley, Calif.: Celestial Arts, 1992.

Harnack, A., ed., *Adoption: Opposing Viewpoints.* San Diego, Calif.: Greenhaven Press, 1995.

Harper, J. "Counseling Issues in Intercountry Adoption Disruptions." *Adoption & Fostering* 18 (Summer 1994): 20–26.

———. "What Does She Look Like? What Children Want to Know about Their Birth Parents." *Adoption & Fostering* 17 (Summer 1993): 27–29.

Harry A. Waisman Center on Mental Retardation and Human Development. *Family History: An Aid to Better Health of Adoptive Children.* Washington, D.C.: National Center for Education in Maternal and Child Health, 1984.

Harsin, R. *Wanted—First Child: A Birth Mother's Story.* Santa Barbara, Calif.: Fithian Press, 1991.

Hartman, A. "Every Clinical Social Worker Is in Post-Adoption Practice." *Journal of Independent Social Work* 5 (1991): 149–63.

Hayes, P. "Transracial Adoption." *Child Welfare* 72 (May/June 1993): 301–10.

Hazen, B. S. *Why Are People Different?: A Book about Prejudice.* Racine, Wis.: Western Publishing Company, Inc., 1985.

Heart Start Task Force Staff. *Heart Start: The Emotional Foundation of School Readiness.* Arlington, Va.: National Center for Clinical Infant Programs, 1992.

Helgesen, R. "More Can Be Better: Adopting Five at One Time." *Adoptive Families* (March/April 1996): 30–32.

Hellwege, J. "More Courts Allow Adoptive Parents, Children to Sue for 'Wrongful Adoptions,'" *Trial* 31 (June 1995): 12.

Hibbs, E. D., ed. *Adoption: International Perspectives.* Madison, Conn.: International Universities Press, 1991.

Hicks, R. B. *Adopting in America: How to Adopt within One Year.* Rev. ed. Sun City, Calif.: WordSlinger Press, 1995.

Hintz, P. A. "Grandparents' Visitation Rights Following Adoption: Expanding Traditional Boundaries in Wisconsin." *Wisconsin Law Review* 2 (1994): 483–510.

Hodges, J., and B. Tizard. "IQ and Behavioral Adjustment of Ex-Institutionalized Adolescents." *Journal of Child Psychology and Psychiatry* 30 (1989): 53–75.

Hoksbergen, R. A. C., ed. *Adoption in Worldwide Perspective: A Review of Programs, Policies, and Legislation in 14 Countries.* Berwyn, Ill.: Swets North American, 1986.

Holden, N. L. "Adoption and Eating Disorders: A High-Risk Group?" *British Journal of Psychiatry* 158 (1991): 829–33.

Hollinger, J. H. "Adoption Law." *The Future of Children* 3 (Spring 1993): 43–61.

——. "A Failed System Is Tearing Kids Apart." *National Law Journal* 15 (August 9, 1993): 17.

Holmes, P. *Concepts in Adoption*. Gig Harbor, Wash.: Richlynn Publications, 1984.

——. *Supporting an Adoption*. Wayne, Pa.: Our Child Press, 1986.

Holmes, S. A. "The Tie That Binds: The Constitutional Right of Children to Maintain Relationship with Parent-Like Individuals." *Maryland Law Review* 53 (1994): 358–411.

Holtan, B., and L. Strassberger, eds. *They Became Part of Us: The Experiences of Families Adopting Children Everywhere*. Maple Grove, Minn.: Mini-World Publications, 1985.

Homes, A. M. *In a Country of Mothers*. New York: Alfred A. Knopf, 1993.

Hopkins-Best, M. *Toddler Adoption*. Indianapolis, Ind.: Perspectives Press, 1997.

Hopson, D., and D. Hopson. *Different and Wonderful: Raising Black Children in A Race-Conscious Society*. New York: Prentice Hall, 1990.

——. *Raising the Rainbow Generation: Teaching Your Children to be Successful in a Multicultural Society*. New York: Simon & Schuster, 1993.

Howells, D., and K. W. Pritchard. *The Story of David: How We Created a Family Through Open Adoption*. New York: Delacorte Press, 1997.

Hughes, D. A. *Facilitating Developmental Attachment: The Road to Emotional Recovery and Behavioral Change in Foster and Adopted Children*. Northvale, N.J.: Jason Aronson, 1997.

Humphrey, M. *Empty Cradles*. New York: Doubleday, 1994.

Humphrey, M., and H. Humphrey, eds. *Inter-Country Adoption: Practical Experiences*. London: Tavistock/Routledge, 1993.

Hunt, A. R. "The Republicans Seize the High Ground on Transracial Adoption." *Wall Street Journal*, March 9, 1995.

"If You're Thinking of Adopting." *Consumer Reports*, February 1996.

Ingersoll, B. D., and S. Goldstein. *Attention Deficit Disorder and Learning Disabilities: Realities, Myths, and Controversial Treatments*. New York: Doubleday, 1993.

Inglis, K. *Living Mistakes: Mothers Who Consented to Adoption*. Boston: G. Allen & Unwin, 1984.

"Institutionalized Children Have Problems, Show Progress after Adoption." *Adopted Child* 14 (November 1995): 1–4.

"Internet Adoption Registry." *Adoptive Families* (March/April 1996): 6.

Jackson, M. "Aspiring Adoptive Parents Face Greed, Competition, Exploitation." *Los Angeles Times*, April 23, 1995.

Jackson, R. L. "U.S. Stresses No Race Bias in Adoptions." *Los Angeles Times*, April 25, 1995.

Jaffee, E. D., ed. *Intercountry Adoptions*. Boston: M. Nijhoff Publishers, 1995.

Jarratt, C. J. *Adopting the Older Child*. Harvard, Mass.: Harvard Common Press, 1978.

——. *Helping Children Cope with Separation and Loss*. Rev. ed. Harvard, Mass.: Harvard Common Press, 1994.

Johnson, J. L., F. T. McAndrew, and P. B. Harris. "Sociology and the Naming of Adopted and Natural Children." *Ethology and Sociobiology* 12 (September 1991): 365–75.

Johnson, K. "Family Sues over Adoption." *USA Today,* March 8, 1990.

Johnson, S., "Foreign Couples Adopting Babies," *Seattle Times,* August 27, 1997.

Johnston, P. I. *Adopting after Infertility.* Indianapolis, Ind.: Perspectives Press, 1993.

———. *An Adoptor's Advocate.* Fort Wayne, Ind.: Perspectives Press, 1984.

———. "Baby Blues." *Adoptive Families,* September/October 1995.

———. *Launching a Baby's Adoption: Practical Strategies for Parents and Professionals.* Indianapolis, Ind.: Perspectives Press, 1997.

———. *Taking Charge of Infertility.* Indianapolis, Ind.: Perspectives Press, 1994.

Johnston, P. I., ed. *Perspectives on a Grafted Tree: Thoughts for Those Touched by Adoption.* Fort Wayne, Ind.: Perspectives Press, 1983.

Jones, C. "Debate on Race and Adoptions Is Being Reborn." *New York Times,* October 24, 1993.

Jones, M. "Adoption Agencies: Can They Service African-Americans?" *Crisis* 99, no. 8 (November/December 1992): 26–28.

Jones, M. B. *Birthmothers: Women Who Have Relinquished Babies for Adoption Tell Their Stories.* Chicago: Chicago Review Press, 1993.

Jordon, L. "Becoming an Adoptive Family." *Parents,* August 1995.

Joshi, A. A. "Cross-Cultural Encounters: Lessons to Learn From . . ." *Biracial Child* Issue 6, 20.

Jurgens, L. *Turn from the Heart.* Lower Lake, Calif.: Asian Publishing, 1992.

Kadushin, A. *Adopting Older Children.* New York: Columbia University Press, 1970.

Kajander, R. *Living with ADHD.* Minneapolis, Minn.: Park Nicollet Medical Foundation, 1995.

Kaplan, S., and C. Land. *Winning at Adoption.* Studio City, Calif.: Family Network, 1995.

Kaplan, S., and M. J. Rillera. *Cooperative Adoption: A Handbook.* 2nd ed. Westminster, Calif.: Triadoption Library, 1991.

Kass, C. "Failed Adoption: Dream Turns to Nightmare When Baby Is Reclaimed." *Richmond Times–Dispatch,* July 29, 1990.

Kass-Annese, B., and H. Danzer. *The Fertility Awareness Handbook.* Claremont, Calif.: Hunter House, 1992.

Katz, M. M. *Understanding and Helping Adopted and Foster Children.* Brighton, Mich.: Psychotherapy Center for Adoptive Families, n.d.

Keck, G. C., and R. M. Kupecky. *Adopting the Hurt Child: Hope for Families with Special-Needs Kids.* Colorado Springs, Colo.: Piñon Press, 1995.

Kendler, K. S., A. M. Gruenberg, and D. K. Kinney. "Independent Diagnoses of Adoptees and Relatives as Defined by DSM-III in the Provincial and National Samples of the Danish Adoption Study of Schizophrenia." *Archives of General Psychiatry* 51 (June 1994): 456–68.

Kenny, J., B. Pryor, and D. Watson-Duval. "Cooperative Adoption: One Solution to Foster Care Drift." *Adoptalk* (Winter 1995): 6.

Keyes, D. *Flowers for Algernon.* New York: Harcourt, Brace & World, 1966.

"Kids Get Homes with Gays." *Lesbian Tide* 9 (1980).

Kindersley, B., and A. Kindersley. *Children Just Like Me.* New York: Dorling Kindersley, 1995.

Kingsolver, B. *Pigs in Heaven.* New York: HarperCollins, 1993.

Kirk, H. D. *Adoptive Kinship.* Brentwood Bay, B.C.: Ben-Simon Publications, 1985.

———. *Exploring Adoptive Family Life: The Collected Adoption Papers of H. David Kirk.* Edited by B. J. Tansey. Port Angeles, Wash.: Ben-Simon Publications, 1988.

———. *Looking Back, Looking Forward: An Adoptive Father's Sociological Testament.* Indianapolis, Ind.: Perspectives Press, 1995.

———. *Shared Fate: A Theory and Method of Adoptive Relationships.* Rev. ed. Port Angeles, Wash.: Ben-Simon Publications, 1984.

———. *Shared Fate: A Theory of Adoption and Mental Health.* New York: Free Press of Glencoe, 1964.

Kittson, R. H. *Orphan Voyage.* New York: Vantage Press, 1968.

Klaus, M., and J. Kennell. *Parent-Infant Bonding,* 2nd ed. St. Louis, Mo.: C. V. Mosby, 1982.

Kleinfeld, J, and S. Wescott, eds. *Fantastic Antone Succeeds: Experiences in Educating Children with Fetal Alcohol Syndrome.* Fairbanks, Alaska: University of Alaska Press, 1993.

Kloeppel, J. E., and D. A. Kloeppel. *Forever Parents: Adopting Older Children.* Union City, Ga.: Adele Enterprises, 1995.

Klunder, V. L. *Lifeline: The Action Guide to Adoption Search.* Cape Coral, Fla.: Caradium, 1991.

Knoll, J., and M. Murphy. *International Adoption.* Chicago: Chicago Review Press, 1994.

Koh, F. *Oriental Children in American Homes: How Do They Adjust.* Rev. ed. Minneapolis, Minn.: East-West Press, 1988.

Komar, M. *Communicating with the Adopted Child.* New York: Walker & Co., 1991.

Kopels, S. "Wrongful Adoption: Litigation and Liability." *Families in Society: The Journal of Contemporary Human Services* (January 1995): 20–28.

Korn, K. "The Struggle for the Child: Preserving the Family in Adoption Disputes between Biological Parents and Third Parties." *North Carolina Law Review* 72 (1994): 1279–1331.

Kotsopoulos, S., et al. "A Psychiatric Follow-Up Study of Adoptees." *Canadian Journal of Psychiatry* 38 (August 1993): 391–96.

Kulp, J. *Families at Risk: A Guide to Understand and Protect Children and Care Givers Involved in Out-of-Home or Adoptive Care.* Minneapolis, Minn.: Better Endings New Beginnings, 1993.

LaCure, J. R. *Remembering: Reflections of Growing Up Adopted.* Franklin, Mass.: Adoption Advocate Publishing Company, 1995.

Lafayette, L. *Why Don't You Have Kids?* New York: Kensington Books, 1995.

Lahti, I. "An Adopted Child in Adolescence: A Psychiatric Study of Adopted Adolescents and Their Families." *Psychiatria Fennica* 24 (1993): 67–74.

Lancaster, K. *Keys to Adopting a Child.* Hauppauge, N.Y.: Barron's, 1994.

Landers, S. "Knowledge of Heritage Important to Adoptees." *APA Monitor* (December 1988): 30.

Lasnik, R. S. *A Parent's Guide to Adoption.* New York: Sterling, 1979.

Laws, R. "Between the Lines." *Adoptive Families* (September/October 1995): 34–35.

"Lawsuit over Girls' Background." *Seattle Post–Intelligencer,* October 17, 1995.

Leach, P. *Your Baby & Child: From Birth to Age Five.* 2nd ed. New York: Knopf, 1994.

Leavitt, D. K. *Counseling Clients in Independent Adoptions: Program material, October–November, 1980.* Berkeley, Calif.: California Continuing Education of the Bar, 1980.

Lee, F. R. "Anxious Vigils for Chinese Babies." *New York Times,* January 18, 1996.

Le Pere, D. W. *Large Sibling Groups: Adoption Experiences.* Washington, D.C.: Child Welfare League of America, 1986.

"Lesbian Couples Raise Psychologically Healthy Children." *Philadelphia Inquirer,* May 4, 1994.

Levyshiff, R., I. Goldshmidt, and D. Hareven. "Transition to Parenthood in Adoptive Families." *Developmental Psychology* 27 (January 1991): 131–40.

Lewin, T. "The Strain on the Bonds of Adoption." *New York Times,* August 8, 1993.

Leynes, C. "Keep or Adopt: A Study of Factors Influencing Pregnant Adolescents' Plans for Their Babies." *Child Psychiatry and Human Development* 11 (1980): 105–12.

Lifton, B. J. *Journey of the Adopted Self.* New York: Basic Books, 1994.

———. *Lost and Found: The Adoption Experience.* New York: Dial Press, 1979.

Lindsay, C. H. *Nothing Good Ever Happens to Me: An Adoption Love Story.* Washington, D.C.: Child Welfare League of America, 1996.

Lindsay, J. W. *Open Adoption.* Buena Park, Calif.: Morning Glory Press, 1987.

———. *Parents, Pregnant Teens, and the Adoption Option: Help for Families.* Buena Park, Calif.: Morning Glory Press, 1989.

———. *Pregnant Too Soon.* Buena Park, Calif.: Morning Glory Press, 1988.

Lindsay, J. W., and C. P. Monserrat. *Adoption Awareness: A Guide for Teachers, Counselors, Nurses, and Caring Others.* Buena Park, Calif.: Morning Glory Press, 1989.

Lindsay, S., and K. A. Howze. "It Takes a Whole Village to Raise a Child." *Public Welfare* (Winter 1996): 4–20.

Lipman, E. L., et al. "Psychiatric Disorders in Adopted Children." *Canadian Journal of Psychiatry* 37 (November 1992): 627–33.

Liptak, K. *Adoption Controversies.* New York: Franklin Watts, 1993.

Lockhart, B. "Talking about Difficult Adoption Information." *OURS* (March/April 1994).

Lundy, M. *Baby Farm: A Novel.* Secaucus, N.J.: Lyle Stuart, 1987.

Lynch, L. "Birthmother's Day." *Adoptive Families* (May/June 1995): 54–55.

Lythcott-Haims, J. C. "Where Do Mixed Babies Belong? Racial Classification in America and Its Implications for Transracial Adoption." *Harvard Civil Rights–Civil Liberties Law Review* 29 (Summer 1994): 531–58.

MacIntyre, J. C. "Resolved: Children Should Be Told of Their Adoption before They Ask: Affirmative." *Journal of American Academy of Child & Adolescent Psychiatry* 29 (September 1990): 828–29.

Magid, K, and C. A. McKelvey. *High Risk: Children without a Conscience.* New York: Bantam Books, 1988.

Mamanus, S. *Adoption: A Viable Alternative.* Ramsey, N.Y.: Paulist Press, 1984.

Mander, R. *The Care of the Mother: Grieving a Baby Relinquished for Adoption.* Aldershot, Hants, England: Avebury, 1995.

Mannes, M. "Factors and Events Leading to the Passage of the Indian Child Welfare Act." *Child Welfare* 74 (January/February 1995): 264–82.

Manooja, D. C. *Adoption Law & Practice.* New Delhi: Deep & Deep Publications, 1993.

"The Many Shades of Transracial & Transnational Adoptions." *New York Times,* July 15, 1994.

March, K. R. *The Stranger Who Bore Me: Interactions of Adoptees and Birth Mothers.* Toronto: University of Toronto Press, 1995.

Marcovitch, S., et al. "Romanian Adoption: Parents' Dreams, Nightmares, and Realities." *Child Welfare* 74 (September/October 1995): 993–1017.

Marindin, H., ed. *The Handbook for Single Adoptive Parents.* 6th ed. Chevy Chase, Md.: National Council for Single Adoptive Parents, 1997.

Mark, H. "Foreign Couples Adopting American Babies." *Seattle Times,* August 17, 1997.

Markman, J. D. "Jury Rules for Unwed Father in Landmark Adoption." *Los Angeles Times,* December 5, 1995.

Marsh, M. J. *Planning a Birthmother's Day Celebration.* Royal Oak, Mich.: R-Squared Press, 1996.

Martin, A. *The Lesbian and Gay Parenting Handbook.* New York: HarperCollins, 1993.

Martin, A. "Birth Pangs: Rapid Rise in Multiple Births." *Seattle Post–Intelligencer,* February 13, 1996.

Martin, C. D. *Beating the Adoption Game.* Rev. ed. San Diego: Harcourt Brace Jovanovich, 1988.

——. "Psychological Problems of Abortion for the Unwed Teenage Girl." *Genetic Psychology Monographs* 88 (1973): 23–110.

Mason, D. A., and P. J. Frick. "The Heritability of Antisocial Behavior: A Meta-Analysis of Twin and Adoption Studies." *Journal of Psychopathology & Behavioral Assessment* 16 (December 1994): 301–23.

Mason, M. M. "Global Trends in Adoption." *Adoptive Families* (March/April 1996): 8–11.

——. *Out of the Shadows: Birthfathers' Stories.* Edina, Minn.: O. J. Howard Publishing, 1995.

Matheson, L. "The Politics of the Indian Child Welfare Act." *Social Work* 41 (March 1996): 232–35.

Mattes, J. *Single Mothers by Choice.* New York: Times Books, 1994.

Maxtone-Graham, K. *An Adopted Woman: Her Search: Her Discoveries. A True Story.* New York: Râemi Books, 1983.

Maza, P. L. "Adoption Trends: 1944–1975." *Child Welfare Research Notes* 9 (1993).

McCabe, A. "The *Post*'s Adoption Therapist Helpline." *The Post* (Winter 1996).

McColm, M. *Adoption Reunions: A Book for Adoptees, Birth Parents, and Adoptive Families.* Ontario, Canada: Second Story Press, 1993.

McDermott, M. T. "The Case for Independent Adoption." *The Future of Children* 3 (Spring 1993): 146–52.

McFarlane, J. "Building Self-Esteem in Children and Teenagers of Color." *OURS* (May/June 1992): 28–33.

McIntyre, D. H. "Gay Parents and Child Custody." *Mediation Quarterly* 12 (1994): 135–48.

McKelvery, C. A., and J. E. Stevens. *Adoption Crisis: The Truth behind Adoption and Foster Care.* Golden, Colo.: Fulcrum Publications, 1994.

McKenzie, J. K. "Adoption of Children with Special Needs." *The Future of Children* 3 (Spring 1993): 62–76.

McMillan, S. C. "Neither Gays Nor Singles Should Adopt." *Los Angeles Times,* April 2, 1995.

McMillon, D. *Mixed Blessing: The Dramatic True Story of a Woman's Search for Her Real Mother.* New York: St. Martin's Press, 1985.

McNamara, J. *Sexually Reactive Children in Adoption and Foster Care.* Greensboro, N.C.: Family Resources, 1994.

McNamara, J, and B. H. McNamara, eds. *Adoption and the Sexually Abused Child.* Portland, Maine: Human Services Development Institute, University of Southern Maine, 1990.

McNichols, T. "The Battle over Making Babies." *USA Weekend,* March 22–24, 1996.

McQuiston, J. T. "A Novel Insanity Defense for Joel Rifkin." *New York Times,* July 26, 1994.

McTaggart, L. *The Baby Brokers: The Marketing of White Babies in America.* New York: Dial Press, 1980.

Meckler, L. "Adoption Rates Vary among States." *Seattle Times,* August 8, 1997.

Meezan, W., and J. F. Shireman. *Care and Commitment: Foster Parent Adoption Decisions.* Albany: State University of New York Press, 1985.

Mehren, E. "Lesbian Mothers: Two New Studies Shatter Stereotypes." *Los Angeles Times,* June 1, 1983.

Melina, L. R. *Adoption: An Annotated Bibliography and Guide.* New York: Garland, 1987.

——. *Making Sense of Adoption: A Parent's Guide.* New York: Perennial Libraries, 1989.

——. *Raising Adopted Children.* New York: Harper & Row, 1986.

Melina, L. R., ed. "Differentiating between Secrecy, Privacy, and Openness in Adoption." *Adopted Child* 12 (May 1993): 1–4.

Melina, L. R., and S. K. Roszia. *The Open Adoption Experience.* New York: HarperCollins, 1993.

Michelman, S. B., and M. Schneider. *The Private Adoption Handbook.* New York: Villard Books, 1988.

Michelsen, D. "Finding Your Adoption Attorney." *Conceive* (September/October 1989): 11.

"Middle Childhood May Be Time to Contact Birth Parents." *Adopted Child* 9 (December 1990): 1–4.

Miller, M., and N. Ward, *With Eyes Wide Open: A Workbook for Parents Adopting International Children Over Age One,* Minnesota, Children's Home Society, 1996.

Miller, R., and M. Miller. *Home Is Where the Heart Wants to Be.* Minneapolis, Minn.: LN Press, 1993.

Miller, V. K. *Meditations for Adoptive Parents.* Scottdale, Pa.: Herald Press, 1992.

Mills, C. *Boardwalk with Hotel.* New York: Macmillan, 1985.

Minshew, D. H., and C. Hooper. *The Adoptive Family as a Healing Resource for the Sexually Abused Child.* Washington, D.C.: Child Welfare League of America, 1990.

Mitchell, A. "Clinton Backs Adoption Tax Credit in GOP 'Contract.'" *Seattle Post–Intelligencer,* May 7, 1996.

Modell, J. S. *Kinship with Strangers: Adoption and Interpretations of Kinship in American Culture.* Berkeley, Calif.: University of California Press, 1994.

Molock, S. D. "Adoption Barriers for African-American Families." *Adoptive Families* (March/April 1995): 14–16.

Moran, R. A. "Stages of Emotion: An Adult Adoptee's Postreunion Perspective." *Child Welfare* 73 (May/June 1994): 249–60.

Morgen, K. B. *Getting Simon: Two Gay Doctors' Journey to Fatherhood.* New York: Bramble Books, 1995.

Morrison, S. J. "The Development of Children Adopted from Romanian Orphanages." *Merrill-Palmer Quarterly* 41 (October 1995): 411–30.

Mosiman, D. "Gay Dads Raise a 'Lucky Child.'" *Peninsula Daily News,* May 23, 1995.

Musser, S. *To Prison with Love: The True Story of Sandy Musser's Indecent Indictment and America's Adoption Travesty.* Edited by T. Pesahice. Cape Coral, Fla.: Adoption Awareness Press, 1995.

"National Adoption Foundation Offers Loans, Grants for Adopting Parents." *Adoptive Families* (July/August 1995): 6.

Nelson, K. A. *On the Frontier of Adoption: A Study of Special-Needs Adoptive Families.* New York: Research Center, Child Welfare League of America, 1985.

Nelson-Erichsen, J., and H. R. Erichsen. *Butterflies in the Wind: Spanish/Indian Children with White Parents.* The Woodlands, Tex.: Los Niños International Adoption Center, 1992.

———. *How to Adopt Internationally.* Rev. ed. Fort Worth, Tex.: Mesa House, 1997.

"New Evidence in an Adoption Case." *Alberta Report/Western Report* 20 (1993): 43.

Nickman, S. L., and R. G. Lewis. "Adoptive Families and Professionals: When the Experts Make Things Worse." *Journal of American Academy of Child & Adolescent Psychiatry* 33 (June 1994): 753–55.

Noble, E. *Having Your Baby by Donor Insemination.* Boston: Houghton Mifflin, 1987.

Nosek, K. *The Dyslexic Scholar: Helping Your Child Succeed in the School System.* Dallas, Tex.: Taylor Publishing, 1995.

O'Hanlon, T. *Accessing Federal Adoption Subsidies after Legalization.* Washington, D.C.: Child Welfare League of America, 1995.

———. *Adoption Subsidy: A Guide for Adoptive Parents.* Washington, D.C.: Child Welfare League of America, 1995.

O'Riordan, J. "Choosing an Agency." *Adoptive Families* (November/December 1995): 34–35.

Oberto, N. V., and L. Oberto. *Men Have Hormones, Too! One Man's Humorous Story of Infertility, Pregnancy, and Other Surprises.* Decatur, Ill.: Polestar Press, 1995.

"The Orphanage." *Newsweek,* December 2, 1994.

"Orphans in Brazil Can Be Adopted Via the Internet." *Seattle Post–Intelligencer,* July 25, 1996.

Palmer, J. "Hey, Fatso!" *Barron's,* July 1, 1996.

Pannor, R., F. Massarik, and B. Evans. *The Unmarried Father: New Approaches for Helping Unmarried Young Parents.* New York: Springer Publishing Co., 1971.

"Parents of Romanian Children Face Adoption, International Issues." *Adopted Child* 12 (April 1993): 1–4.

"Parents Who Smoke Need Not Apply." *Technology Review* 96 (1993): 80.

Pardeck, J. T. "Literature and Adoptive Children with Disabilities, 1993." *Early Child Development and Care* 91 (1993): 33–39.

Partridge, P. C. *An Adoptee's Dreams: Poems and Stories.* Baltimore, Md.: Gateway Press, 1995.

Partridge, S., H. Hornby, and T. McDonald. *Learning from Adoption Disruption: Insights for Practice.* Portland, Maine: Human Services Development Institute, Center for Research and Advanced Study, University of Southern Maine, 1986.

Paton, J. M. *The Adopted Break Silence.* Philadelphia, Pa.: Life History Study Center, 1954.

Paul, E. *Adoption Choices: A Guidebook to National and International Adoption Resources.* Detroit: Visible Ink Press, 1991.

Paul, E., ed. *The Adoption Directory.* New York: Gale Research, 1995.

Paulson, T. "Alcohol's Damage—From Fetus to Adult." *Seattle Post–Intelligencer,* September 5, 1996.

Peck, C., *Adoption Today.* Great Meadows, N.J.: Roots & Wings, 1997.

Perez-Pena, R. "Report Finds the Limbo of Foster Care Is Growing Larger." *New York Times,* December 22, 1994.

Perkins, A., and R. Townsend, eds. *Bitter Fruit: Women's Experiences of Unplanned Pregnancy, Abortion, and Adoption.* Alameda, Calif.: Hunter House, 1992.

Perlman, E. "The Failure of the Adoption Machine." *Governing* 7 (July 1994): 32–36.

Peterson, D. S. *Breastfeeding the Adopted Baby.* San Antonio, Tex.: Corona Publishing Co., 1995.

Peterson, J. *The Invisible Road: Parental Insight to Attachment Disorders.* Pueblo, Colo.: Loving Homes, 1995.

Peterson, J. *Tapestry: Exploring the World of Trans-Racial Adoption.* U.S.A.: J. Peterson, 1995.

Petertyl, M. E. *International Adoption Travel Journal.* Grand Rapids, Mich.: Folio One Publishing, 1997.

Piersma, H. L. "Adopted Children and Inpatient Psychiatric Treatment: A Retrospective Study." *Psychiatric Hospital* 18 (1987): 153–58.

Phinney, J. S. "When We Talk about American Ethnic Groups What Do We Mean?" *American Psychologist* 51 (September 1966): 918–27.

Pohl, C., and K. Harris. *Transracial Adoption.* New York: Franklin Watts, 1992.

Portello, J. Y. "The Mother-Infant Attachment Process in Adoptive Families." *Canadian Journal of Counseling* 27 (July 1993): 177–90.

Posner, J., and J. Guilianelli. *The Adoption Resource Guide: A National Directory of Licensed Agencies.* Washington, D.C.: Child Welfare League of America, 1990.

Postman, D. "Sins of Silence." *Seattle Times,* January 14, 1996.

Powell, S. *When You Can't Have a Child: Personal Stories of Living through Infertility and Childlessness.* Australia: Allen & Unwin, 1993.

Prager, D. "The Court That Cut that Baby in Half." *Los Angeles Times,* May 16, 1995.

"Prenatal Drug Exposure Affects School-Age Child's Behavior." *Adopted Child* 15 (January 1996): 1–4.

Pressman, S. "The Baby Brokers: Bending the Rules of Adoption Law." *California Lawyer* (July 1991): 29.

Quinn, P. O., and J. M. Stern. *Putting on the Brakes: Young People's Guide to Understanding Attention Deficit Hyperactivity Disorder (ADHD).* New York: Magination Press, 1991.

Raab, D. *Getting Pregnant and Staying Pregnant: Overcoming Infertility and Managing Your High-Risk Pregnancy.* Alameda, Calif.: Hunter House, 1991.

Rainey, J. "Custody Case Tests Indian Law." *Los Angeles Times,* June 7, 1995.

———. "Solution on Twins' Future Eludes Judges." *Los Angeles Times,* October 19, 1995.

Ramos, J. "Ethnic Images: A Primer for Adoptive Parents." *OURS* (May/June 1990): 18.

Randolph, E. *Children Who Shock and Surprise.* Rev. ed. Yuba City, Calif.: RFR Publications, 1997.

Rappaport, B. M. *The Open Adoption Book.* New York: Macmillan, 1992.

Rasmussen, S. A. "The Hospital Experience of Adoptive Parents Participating in Open Infant Adoption." Master's thesis, University of Washington, 1993.

Razzi, E. "Considering the Options: Infertility and Adoption Books." *Library Journal* 119 (1994).

Redmond, M. A. "Attitudes of Adolescent Males toward Adolescent Pregnancy and Fatherhood." *Family Relations* 34 (1985): 337–42.

Register, C. *Are Those Kids Yours?* New York: Free Press, 1991.

Reitz, M., and K. W. Watson. *Adoption and the Family System: Strategies for Treatment.* New York: Guilford Press, 1992.

Reynolds, N. T. *Adopting Your Child.* North Vancouver, B.C.: Self-Counsel Press, 1993.

Richardson, L. "Adoptions That Lack Papers, Not Purpose." *New York Times,* November 25, 1993.

Rillera, M. J. *Adoption Encounter: Hurt, Transition, Healing.* Westminster, Calif.: Pure, Inc., 1991.

———. *The Adoption Searchbook: Techniques for Tracing People.* 2nd ed. Huntington Beach, Calif.: Triadoption Library, 1988.

Robinson, B. E. "Teenage Pregnancy from the Father's Perspective." *American Journal of Orthopsychiatry* 58 (1988): 46–51.

Rohr, F. *How Parents Tell Their Children They Are Adopted.* New York: New York State Adoptive Parents Committee, Inc., 1988.

Roles, P. *Saying Goodbye to a Baby, Volume I—The Birthparents' Guide to Loss and Grief in Adoption.* Washington, D.C.: Child Welfare League of America, 1989.

———. *Saying Goodbye to a Baby, Volume II—A Counselor's Guide to Birthparent Loss and Grief in Adoption.* Washington, D.C.: Child Welfare League of America, 1989.

Romanchik, B. *A Birthmother's Book of Memories.* Royal Oak, Mich.: R-Square Press, 1994.

Rommelmann, N. "'A Big Guiding Light': The Institute of Black Parenting Offers Classes and Advice for Families Involved in Interracial Adoptions," *Los Angeles Times,* June 9, 1996.

Rompf, E. L. "Open Adoption: What does the 'Average Person' Think?" *Child Welfare* 72 (May/June 1993): 219–30.

Rosen, R. H., T. Benson, and J. M. Stack. "Help or Hindrance: Parental Impact on Pregnant Teenagers' Resolution Decisions." *Family Relations* 31 (1982): 271–80.

Rosenberg, E. B. *The Adoption Life Cycle: The Children and Their Families through the Years.* New York: Free Press, 1992.

———. "Birthparent Romances and Identity Formation in Adopted Children." *American Journal of Orthopsychiatry* 61 (1991): 70–77.

Rosenthal, J. A. "Outcomes of Adoption of Children with Special Needs." *The Future of Children* 3 (Spring 1993): 77–88.

Rosenthal, J. A., and V. K. Groze. *Special-Needs Adoption: A Study of Intact Families.* New York: Praeger, 1992.

——. "A Longitudinal Study of Special-Needs Adoptive Families." *Child Welfare* 73 (November/December 1994): 689–706.

Rosenthal, J. A., V. K. Groze, and H. Curiel. "Race, Social Class, and Special Needs Adoptions." *Social Work* 35 (1990): 532–39.

Rosenthal, M. S. *The Fertility Sourcebook.* Los Angeles, Calif.: Lowell House, 1995.

Rudman, M. K. "Children's Literature: An Issues Approach." *Teaching Guide* (1995): 512.

Rushton, A. "New Parents for Older Children: Support Services During Eight Years of Placement." *Adoption & Fostering* 17 (Winter 1993): 39–45.

Russell, M. *Adoption Wisdom: A Guide to the Issues and Feelings of Adoption.* Santa Monica, Calif.: Broken Branch Productions, 1996.

Ruston, A., J. Treseder, and D. Quinton. "An Eight-Year Prospective Study of Older Boys Placed in Permanent Substitute Families: A Research Note." *Journal of Child Psychology & Psychiatry & Applied Disciplines* 36 (1995): 687–95.

Ryan, K. *From We to Just Me.* Manitoba, Canada: Freedom to Be Me Seminars, 1990.

Ryburn, M. *Open Adoption.* Aldershot, Hants, England: Avebury, 1994.

Saban, C. *Miracle Child: Genetic Mother, Surrogate Womb.* Fair Hills, N.J.: New Horizon Press, 1993.

Sachdev. P. "Achieving Openness in Adoption: Some Critical Issues in Policy Formulation." *American Journal of Orthopsychiatry* 61 (1991): 241–49.

——. "Adoption Reunion and After: A Study of the Search Process and Experience of Adoptees." *Child Welfare* 71 (January/February 1992): 53–68.

——. "The Birth Father: A Neglected Element in the Adoption Equation." *Families in Society: The Journal of Contemporary Human Services* (March 1991): 131–39.

——. *Unlocking the Adoption Files.* Lexington, Mass.: Lexington Books, 1989.

Saidman, S. O. "10 Adoption Lessons." *Adoptive Families* (November/December 1995): 30–31.

Salzer, L. P. *Surviving Infertility.* New York: HarperPerennial, 1991.

Sanders, P. "The Eleven Myths of Searching." *AdoptNet* (September/October 1992): 24–25.

Sandmaier, M. *When Love Is Not Enough: How Mental Health Professionals Can Help Special-Needs Adoptive Families.* Washington, D.C.: Child Welfare League of America, 1988.

Sandness, G. L. *Beginnings: True Experiences in Adoption.* Maple Grove, Minn.: Mini-World Publications, 1980.

——. *Brimming Over.* Minneapolis, Minn.: Mini-World Publications, 1978.

——. *Commitment: The Reality of Adoption.* Maple Grove, Minn.: Mini-World Publications, 1984.

Sanford, D. *Don't Look at Me: A Child's Book about Feeling Different.* Portland, Ore.: Multnomah Press, 1986.

Savage, D. G. "Unmarried Father Loses Custody Bid in High Court." *Los Angeles Times,* December 7, 1988.

Scanlan, D. "Stolen Children?" *Maclean's*, April 18, 1994.

Scarr, S., R. A. Weinberg, and I. D. Waldman. "IQ Correlations in Transracial Adoptive Families." *Intelligence* 17 (October/December 1993): 541–55.

Schaefer, C. *The Other Mother: A Woman's Love for the Child She Gave Up for Adoption.* New York: Soho Press, 1991.

Schaffer, J., and C. Lindstrom. *How to Raise an Adopted Child: A Guide to Help Your Child Flourish from Infancy through Adolescence.* New York: A Plume Book, 1991.

Schooler, J. E. *Searching for a Past: The Adopted Adult's Unique Process of Finding Identity.* Colorado Springs, Colo.: Piñon Press, 1995.

——. *The Whole Life Adoption Book.* Colorado Springs, Colo.: Piñon Press, 1993.

Schulman, I., and R. E. Behrman. "Adoption: Overview and Major Recommendations." *The Future of Children* 3 (Spring 1993): 4–16.

Schwartz, L. L. *Alternatives to Infertility: Is Surrogacy the Answer?* New York: Brunner/ Mazel, 1991.

Schwarz, T. *To Love a Child.* Far Hills, N.J.: Horizon Press, 1996.

Severson, R. W. *Adoption: Charms and Rituals for Healing.* Dallas, Tex.: House of Tomorrow, 1991.

——. *Dear Birthfather.* Dallas, Tex.: House of Tomorrow, n.d.

Shanley, M. L. "Unwed Fathers' Rights, Adoption, and Sex Equality." *Columbia Law Review* 95 (January 1995): 60–103.

Sharkey, P. B. "Being Adopted: Books to Help Children Understand." *Emergency Librarian* 20 (May/June 1993): 28–31.

Sherman, A. *Everything You Need to Know About Placing Your Baby for Adoption.* New York: The Rosen Publishing Group, 1997.

Shoop, J. G. "Unwed Fathers Can Block Adoptions." *Trial* 28 (May 1992): 14.

Shulgold, B., and L. Sipiora. *Dear Barbara, Dear Lynne: The True Story of Two Women in Search of Motherhood.* Reading, Mass.: Addison-Wesley, 1992.

Siegel, D. H. "Open Adoption of Infants: Adoptive Parents' Perceptions of Advantages and Disadvantages." *Social Work* 38 (January 1993): 15–23.

Siegel, S. E. *Parenting Your Adopted Child: A Complete and Loving Guide.* New York: Prentice Hall, 1989.

Sifferman, K. A. *Adoption: A Legal Guide for Birth and Adoptive Parents.* Hawthorne, N.J.: Career Press, 1994.

Silber, K., and D. M. Dorner. *Children of Open Adoption and Their Families.* San Antonio, Tex.: Corona Publishing Co., 1990.

Silber, K., and P. Speedlin. *Dear Birthmother, Thank You for Our Baby.* San Antonio, Tex.: Corona Publishing Co., 1983.

Silber, S. J. *How to Get Pregnant with the New Technology.* New York: Warner Books, 1991.

Silver, L. B. *The Misunderstood Child: A Guide for Parents of Children with Learning Disabilities.* Blue Ridge Summit, Pa.: TAB Books, 1992.

Silverman, A. R. "Outcomes of Transracial Adoption." *The Future of Children* 3 (Spring 1993): 104–18.

Silverman, P. R., L. Campbell, and P. Patti. "Reunions between Adoptees and Birth Parents: The Adoptive Parents' View." *Social Work* 39 (1994): 542–49.

Simon, R. J., and H. Altstein. *Adoption, Race, and Identity.* New York: Praeger, 1992.

——. *Intercountry Adoption: A Multinational Perspective.* New York: Praeger, 1991.

——. *Transracial Adoptees and Their Families.* New York: Praeger, 1987.

Skelton, G. "Governor Wants a Father in the House." *Los Angeles Times,* January 8, 1996.

Sloan, G. A. *Postponing Parenthood.* New York: Insight Books, 1993.

Smith, D. D. *A Limb of Your Tree: The Story of an Adopted Twin's Search for Her Roots.* Smithtown, N.Y.: Exposition, 1978.

Smith, D. W., and D. M. Brodzinsky. "Stress and Coping in Adopted Children: A Developmental Study." *Journal of Clinical Child Psychology* 23 (1994): 81–99.

Smith, D. W., and L. N. Sherwen. *Mothers and Their Adopted Children: The Bonding Process.* New York: Tiresias Press, 1983.

Smith, J., and F. Miroff. *You're Our Child: A Social/Psychology Approach to Adoption.* Washington, D.C.: University Press of America, 1981.

Smith, L. "Adoptees Search the World for Their Roots." *Los Angeles Times,* June 17, 1996.

Smith, S. L. *No Easy Answers: The Learning Disabled Child at Home and at School.* New York: Bantam Books, 1995.

Smith, R., ed. "Your Child." *Newsweek.* Special Edition (Spring/Summer 1997).

Smith-Pliner, D., and D. H. Siegel. "The Second Time Around: Adopting a Second Child Involves Special Issues." *Adoptive Families* (March/April 1996): 21–23.

Smolowe, J. "Saving the Orphans." *Time,* January 22, 1996.

Solnit, A. J., B. F. Nordhaus, and R. Lord. *When Home Is No Haven: Child Placement Issues.* New Haven, Conn.: Yale University Press, 1992.

"Some Infants Shake Off HIV Virus." *Peninsula Daily News,* January 26, 1996.

Sorosky, A. D., A. Baran, and R. Pannor. *The Adoption Triangle: The Effects of the Sealed Record on Adoptees, Birth Parents, and Adoptive Parents.* San Antonio, Tex.: Corona Publishing Co., 1989.

Steinberg, L. "No Baby on Board." *Seattle Post–Intelligencer,* May 1, 1995.

Stephenson, M. *My Child Is a Mother.* San Antonio, Tex.: Corona Publishing Co., 1991.

Stiffler, L. H. "Adoptees and Birthparents Connected by Design: Surprising Synchronicities in Histories of Union/Loss/Reunion." *Pre- & Peri-Natal Psychology* 7 (Summer 1993): 267–86.

——. *Synchronicity and Reunions: The Genetic Connection of Adoptees and Birthparents.* Hobe Sound, Fla.: FEA Publication, 1992.

Stolley, K. S. "Statistics on Adoption in the United States." *The Future of Children* 3 (Spring 1993): 26–42.

Stone, S. *The Naughty Mouse.* West Sussex, England: Luzac Publishers, Ltd., 1986.

"The Stork Delivers Good Tax News for People Planning to Adopt." *Los Angeles Times,* March 9, 1997.

"The Strange Tale of Baby Richard." *Los Angeles Times,* May 3, 1995.

Strassberger, L. *Our Children from Latin America.* New York: Tiresias Press, 1992.

Strauss, J. A. S. *Birthright: The Guide to Search and Reunion for Adoptees, Birthparents, and Adoptive Parents.* New York: Penguin Press, 1994.

——. *The Great Adoptee Search Book.* Worcester, Mass.: Castle Rock, 1990.

"Study Sheds Light on Outcome for Adolescent, Adult Adoptees." *Adopted Child* 14 (August 1995): 1–4.

Style, M. B. "Issues in Practice." *National Adoption Reports* (September 1995): 5.

Sullivan, A., "Special Needs Adoption in the U.S.: Lessons from Experience." *Children's Voice* (Winter 1996): 20–21.

Sullivan, M. R. *Adopt the Baby You Want*. New York: Simon & Schuster, 1990.

Sweet, O. R., and P. Bryan. *Adopt International: Everything You Need to Know to Adopt a Child from Abroad*. New York: Farrar, Straus & Giroux, 1996.

Takas, M., and E. Warner. *To Love a Child: A Complete Guide to Adoption, Foster Parenting, and Other Ways to Share Your Life with Children*. Reading, Mass.: Addison-Wesley, 1992.

Tan, S. L., H. S. Jacobs, and M. M. Seibel. *Infertility: Your Questions Answered*. Updated ed. Secaucus, N.J.: Carol Publishing Group, 1997.

Tauer, L. N. "Multiple Challenges, Multiple Rewards." *Adoptive Families* (March/April 1996): 14–16.

Terry, D. "Storm Rages in Chicago over Revoked Adoption." *New York Times*, July 15, 1994.

Thoburn, J. *Child Placement: Principals and Practice*. 2nd ed. Aldershot, Hants, England: Avebury, 1994.

Thorkelson, W. "Study: Most Adoptive Families OK." *The Lutheran* (August 1994): 34.

Tienari, P. J., and L. C. Wynn. "Adoption Studies of Schizophrenia." *Annals of Medicine* 26 (August 1994): 233–37.

Tizard, B. "Intercountry Adoption: A Review of the Evidence." *Journal of Child Psychology and Psychiatry* 32 (1991): 743–56.

"Too Many Parents." *Economist* 33 (November 12, 1994): 35.

Toth, J. *Orphans of the Living: Stories of America's Children in Foster Care*. New York: Simon & Schuster, 1997.

"Tough Law in Oregon Separates Children from Flawed Parents." *Seattle Times*, September 15, 1997.

"Transracial Adoptees Can Develop Racial Identity, Coping Strategies." *Adopted Child* 13 (January 1994): 1–4.

Tremitier, B. "Genetics and Adoption." *Roots & Wings* (April/May/June 1996): 8–9.

Triseliotis, J. P. *In Search of Origins: The Experiences of Adopted People*. Boston: Beacon Press, 1975, © 1973.

Triseliotis, J., and C. Sellick. *Foster Care: Theory and Practice*. B. T. Batsford, 1995.

Turpenny, P. "Genes, Identity, and Adoption." *Adoption & Fostering* 19 (Spring 1995): 24–33.

Tuttle, C. G., and P. Paquette. *Parenting a Child with a Learning Disability: A Practical, Empathetic Guide*. Los Angeles, Calif.: Lowell House, 1993.

Tyler, P. E. "China Accused of Letting Orphans Die by Thousands." *Seattle Post–Intelligencer,* January 6, 1996.

Tyson, A. S. "Removing Race from Adoption." *Christian Science Monitor,* May 7, 1996.

Valenti, L. L. *The Fifteen Most Asked Questions about Adoption*. Scottdale, Pa.: Herald Press, 1985.

van Gulden, H., and L. M. Bartels-Rabb. "Parenting Is Parenting—Or Is It?" *Adoptive Families* (November/December 1995): 8–12.

——. *Real Parents, Real Children: Parenting the Adopted Child.* New York: Crossroads Publishing, 1993.

"Variety of Attachment Disorders Need Variety of Treatment Options." *Adopted Child* 13 (May 1994): 1–4.

Vasilakis, N. "Booklist: Picture Books." *Horn Book Magazine* 70 (1994).

Verhulst, F. C., M. Althaus, and B. Versluis-den Bieman. "Damaging Backgrounds: Later Adjustment of International Adoptees." *Journal of American Academy of Child & Adolescent Psychiatry* 31 (1992): 518–24.

Verrier, N. N. *The Primal Wound: Understanding the Adopted Child.* Baltimore, Md.: Gateway Press, 1993.

Vick, C. "Where Kids Get Stuck in the System." *Adoptive Families* (November/December 1995): 14.

Viguers, S. T. *With Child: One Couple's Journey to Their Adopted Children.* San Diego: Harcourt Brace Jovanovich, 1986.

Voss, I. N. "In the Best Interest: The Adoption of F. H., an Indian Child." *BYU Journal of Public Law* 8 (Spring 1994): 151–71.

Waddoups, J. "Open Adoption, Human Capital Formation, and Uncertainty." *Journal of Family & Economic Issues* 15 (Spring 1994): 5–21.

Wadia-Ells, S., ed. *The Adoption Reader: Birth Mothers, Adoptive Mothers, and Adopted Daughters Tell Their Stories.* Seattle, Wash.: Seal Press, 1995.

Waldman, S., and L. Caplan. "The Politics of Adoption." *Newsweek,* March 21, 1994.

Waldron, J. L. *Giving Away Simone: A Memoir.* New York: Times Books, 1995.

Walker, E. L. *Loving Journeys Guide to Adoption.* Peterborough, N.H.: Loving Journeys, 1992.

Wallmark, L. S. *Adopting: The Tapestry Guide.* Ringoes, N.J.: Tapestry Books, 1996.

——. *Infertility: The Tapestry Guide.* Ringoes, N.J.: Tapestry Books, 1997.

Ward, M. "Large Adoptive Families." *Social Casework* 59 (1978): 411–18.

Warren, S. B. "Lower Threshold for Referral for Psychiatric Treatment for Adopted Adolescents." *Journal of American Academy of Child & Adolescent Psychiatry* 31 (1992): 512–27.

Watanabe, T. "Earthquake Upsets Traditional Attitudes on Adoption." *Los Angeles Times,* February 28, 1995.

Watkins, M., and S. Fisher. *Talking with Young Children about Adoption.* New Haven, Conn.: Yale University Press, 1993.

Wedge, P., and G. Mantle. *Sibling Groups and Social Work: A Study of Children Referred for Permanent Substitute Family Placement.* Aldershot, Hants, England: Avebury, 1991.

Weidlich, T. "Contested Adoption Pushes the Hot Button: Relatives of a Black Child Contest His Adoption by His Foster Mother, a White Lesbian." *National Law Journal* 17 (May 29, 1995): 10.

——. "N.Y. Case Signals Trend on 'Wrongful Adoption' Tort: Laws Requiring Disclosure of Background Spark Suits." *National Law Journal* 17 (February 6, 1995): 13.

Welch, M. G. *Holding Time: How to Eliminate Conflict, Temper Tantrums, and Sibling Rivalry and Raise Happy, Loving, Successful Children.* New York: Simon & Schuster, 1988.

Werner, E. E. "Children of the Garden Island." *Scientific American,* April 1989, 106–11.

Weschler, T. *Taking Charge of Your Fertility.* New York: HarperCollins, 1995.

Westney, O. E., O. J. Cole, and T. L. Munford. "Adolescent Unwed Prospective Fathers: Readiness for Fatherhood and Behaviors toward the Mother and the Expected Infant." *Adolescence* 21 (1986): 901–11.

Wilkens, J. "Whose Child Is This? Courts Make New Demands of Birth Fathers." *San Diego Union–Tribune,* August 12, 1995.

Wilkinson, H. S. P. *Birth Is More Than Once: The Inner World of Adopted Korean Children.* Bloomfield Hills, Mich.: Sunrise Ventures, 1985.

Willerman, L., J. C. Loehlin, and J. M. Horn. "An Adoption and a Cross-Fostering Study of the Minnesota Multiphasic Personality Inventory (MMPI) Psychopathic Deviate Scale." *Behavior Genetics* 22 (September 1992): 515–29.

Wine, J. *The Canadian Adoption Guide.* Ontario, Canada: McGraw-Hill Ryerson, 1995.

Winkler, R. C. *Clinical Practice in Adoption.* New York: Pergamon, 1988.

Wirth, E. M., and J. Worden. *How to Adopt a Child from Another Country.* Nashville, Tenn.: Abingdon Press, 1993.

Wolff, J. *Secret Thoughts of an Adoptive Mother.* Kansas City, Miss.: Andrews and McNeel, 1997.

Zibart, R. "Adopting a New World View." *USA Weekend,* February 9–11, 1996.

Zimmerman, M. *Should I Keep My Baby?* Minneapolis, Minn.: Bethany House, 1983.

Zoldbrod, A. P. *Getting around the Boulder in the Road: Using Imagery to Cope with Fertility Problems.* Lexington, Mass.: Center for Reproductive Problems, 1990.

Zuckerman, B. "Drug-Exposed Infants." *The Future of Children* 1 (Spring 1991): 26–35.

INDEX